CW00665614

THE POLITICS
— OF —
WAR

DAVID DAY

HarperCollins*Publishers*

HarperCollins*Publishers*

First published in Australia in 2003
by HarperCollins*Publishers* Pty Limited
ABN 36 009 913 517
A member of HarperCollins*Publishers* (Australia) Pty Limited Group
www.harpercollins.com.au

Copyright © David Day 2003

The right of David Day to be identified as the moral rights author
of this work has been asserted by him in accordance with the
Copyright Amendment (Moral Rights) Act 2000 (Cth).

This book is copyright.
Apart from any fair dealing for the purposes of private study, research,
criticism or review, as permitted under the Copyright Act, no part may
be reproduced by any process without written permission.
Inquiries should be addressed to the publishers.

HarperCollins*Publishers*
25 Ryde Road, Pymble, Sydney NSW 2073, Australia
31 View Road, Glenfield, Auckland 10, New Zealand
77–85 Fulham Palace Road, London W6 8JB, United Kingdom
Hazelton Lanes, 55 Avenue Road, Suite 2900, Toronto, Ontario M5R 3L2
and 1995 Markham Road, Scarborough, Ontario M1B 5M8, Canada
10 East 53rd Street, New York NY 10022, USA

National Library of Australia Cataloguing-in-Publication data:

Day, David, 1949– .
   [Reluctant nation]
   The politics of war: Australia at war 1939–45,
   from Churchill to Macarthur.
   Bibliography.
   Includes index.
   ISBN 0 7322 7333 1.
   1. World War, 1939–1945 – Australia. 2. World War, 1939–1945 – Diplomatic history.
   3. World War, 1939–1945 – Campaigns – Pacific Ocean. 4. Australia – Military relations –
   Great Britain. 5. Great Britain – Military relations – Australia.
   I. Day, David, 1949– Great betrayal. II. Title.
940.540994

Front cover photo: AWM 139812
Back cover photo: AWM 072431
Cover, maps and internal design by Christa Edmonds, HarperCollins Design Studio
Typeset in 10 on 15.5 Sabon by HarperCollins Design Studio
Printed and bound in Australia by Griffin Press on 70gsm Bulky Book Ivory

6 5 4 3 2 1   03 04 05 06

To Alan and Judy Day

CONTENTS

PREFACE

This book has been more than twenty years in the making. It began life in 1981 as a PhD thesis that was intended to examine Australia's foreign and defence policy from the beginning of the Second World War until the signing of the ANZUS agreement in 1951. As with many theses, it was progressively scaled back to a more manageable size until it eventually examined the crisis in Anglo–Australian relations caused by the loss of Singapore. This was published by Angus & Robertson in 1988 as *The Great Betrayal: Britain, Australia and the Onset of the Pacific War 1939–42.*

Although it inevitably caused some controversy, the book enjoyed critical acclaim and some popular success in Australia and Britain, as well as in the United States where it was published later by W. W. Norton & Co. A subsequent study examined Anglo–Australian relations from the Battle of Midway in June 1942 until the coming of peace to the Pacific in August 1945. It charted the ways in which Australia pursued independent initiatives in its foreign and defence policy, only to end the war by re-embracing the British option. This was published by Oxford University Press in 1992 as *Reluctant Nation: Australia and the Allied Defeat of Japan 1942–45.*

Although *The Great Betrayal* was republished by Oxford University Press at that time, both books have now been out of print for several years. Rather than simply reprint them in their separate and original forms, I decided to rewrite them completely. New material that has since come to light has been added and the judgments that I made in the 1980s have been reassessed. Both books were then combined in a single study spanning the entire war. At a time when Australia's relations with the outside world have returned to the forefront of political debate, and when Australia's reliance on a powerful protector is being questioned anew, the history of its experience during the Second World War has particular and continuing relevance.

Over the years of researching and writing this book, I have incurred many debts of gratitude to people and organisations. For their friendship or their insights or their practical assistance, or for all three, I would like to thank Correlli Barnett, Geoffrey Bolton, Judith Brett, Carl Bridge, David and Sheila Fieldhouse, Alex Gray, Warren Kimball, David Lowe, John McCarthy, Nan McNab, the late Tom Millar, David Reynolds, Peter Rose, Norman Rowe, Richard Walsh, Jill Wayment, and Claude and Irene Wischik. There are many more who will have to make do with a general thank you that is no less sincere.

This book would also not have been possible without the resources of many archives in Britain and Australia and the helpfulness and efficiency of their staff. In Britain, I would particularly like to acknowledge the British Library, the Cambridge University Library, the Churchill College Archives Centre, the House of Lords Record Office, the Imperial War Museum, the India Office Library, the Liddell Hart Centre for Military Archives at King's College London, the London School of Economics, the National Maritime Museum, the Public Record Office, the Reading University Library and the Scottish Record Office. In Australia, my work was assisted by the Australian War Memorial, the John Curtin Prime Ministerial Library, the Flinders University Library, the National Archives of Australia, the National Library of Australia and the University of Melbourne Archives.

Over the years of this book's gestation, various bodies have generously provided support for its research and writing. In Britain, the Nuffield Foundation, the Smuts and Holland Rose Funds at Cambridge, together with Churchill and Clare Colleges, provided funding or other assistance during the initial research period. More recently, this book was written while I was a senior research fellow funded by the Australian Research Council, the assistance of which is most gratefully acknowledged. Despite continuing funding cutbacks, my colleagues in the History Program at La Trobe University provided friendly and stimulating company during the completion of this work. For permission to quote from the various private papers and published works, I would like to thank the many copyright holders who gave their permission and to apologise to those who were inadvertently missed or proved impossible to contact.

Lastly, I have been fortunate in having a supportive publisher in HarperCollins, where Shona Martyn, Helen Littleton and Jesse Fink have guided this book through the press, while Neil Thomas has been, as always, an efficient and consummate editor. On a more personal note, my wife Silvia and children, Michael, Emily and Kelly, have sustained me with their love and companionship over the years that this book has taken to prepare. Indeed, Emily and Kelly, who were born during the early years of the research, have recently assisted with typing the manuscript. The responsibility for what follows, though, is mine alone.

David Day
Aberdeen, Scotland, July 2002

ABBREVIATIONS

AIF	Australian Imperial Force
AMF	Australian Military Force
ANIB	Australian News and Information Bureau
ANZAC	Australian and New Zealand Army Corps
AWC	Advisory War Council
BBC	British Broadcasting Corporation
BCOF	British Commonwealth Occupation Force
BL	British Library, London
BPF	British Pacific Fleet
CAS	Chief of the Air Staff
CC	Churchill College Archives Centre, Cambridge
CGS	Chief of the General Staff
CUL	Cambridge University Library
DAFP	*Documents on Australian Foreign Policy 1937–49*
EATS	Empire Air Training Scheme
FUL	Flinders University Library, Adelaide
HLRO	House of Lords Record Office
HMG	His Majesty's Government
HMSO	Her Majesty's Stationery Office
IOL	India Office Library

IWM	Imperial War Museum
KC	Liddell Hart Centre for Military Archives, King's College, London
LSE	London School of Economics
NAA	National Archives of Australia
NEI	Netherlands East Indies
NLA	National Library of Australia
NMM	National Maritime Museum, Greenwich
PRO	Public Record Office, London
RAAF	Royal Australian Air Force
RAF	Royal Air Force
RAN	Royal Australian Navy
RN	Royal Navy
RUL	Reading University Library
SEAC	South East Asia Command
SWPA	South West Pacific Area
UAP	United Australia Party
UMA	University of Melbourne Archives
USAAF	United States Army Air Force
USCOS	United States Chief(s) of Staff
VE Day	8 May 1945, official end of hostilities in Europe
VLR	very long range (aircraft)

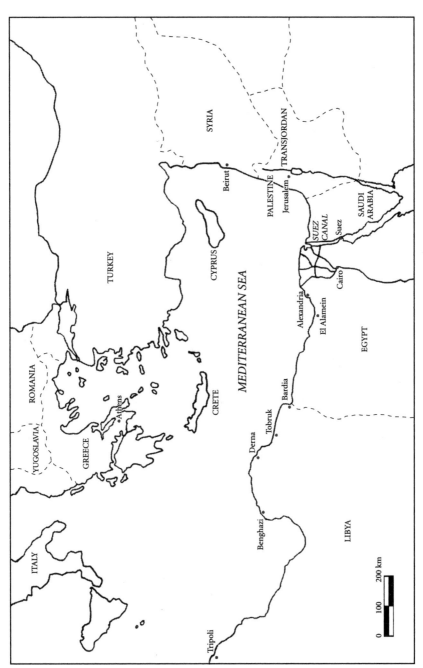

THE EASTERN MEDITERRANEAN

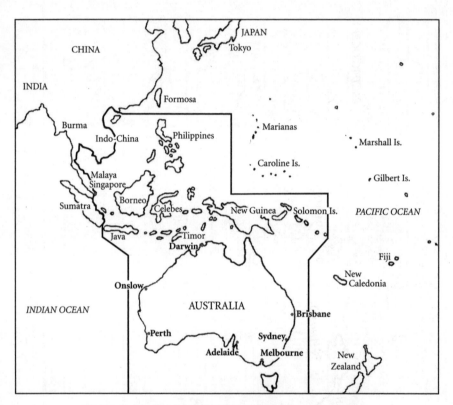

GENERAL MACARTHUR'S SOUTH WEST PACIFIC AREA

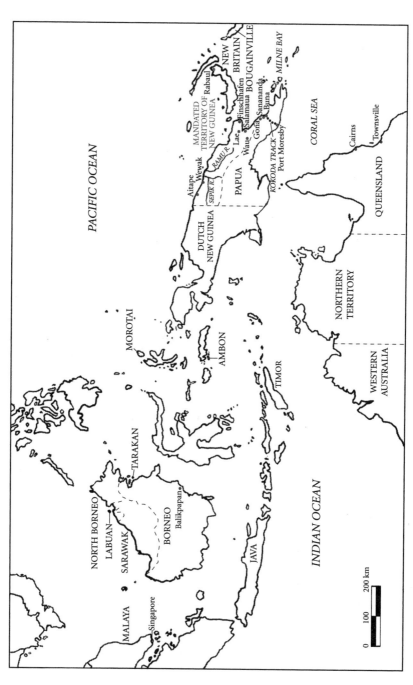

AUSTRALIAN BATTLEFIELDS IN THE PACIFIC WAR

ONE

'not quite as clear as I should like to be'

In December 1941, the forces of the Japanese emperor suddenly struck at British, Dutch and American colonies throughout the Pacific as Tokyo sought to replace the old imperial order in Asia with a new order of its own. The powerful navies of Britain and the United States were left floundering as Japanese warships laid down a daring and humiliating challenge to London and Washington. As one of Britain's former colonies, and now a dominion, Australia lay practically defenceless in the path of the Japanese onslaught. With its best forces fighting alongside Britain in the war against Germany and Italy, the Australian government looked to London for the urgent assistance that had long been promised in such circumstances. It was not forthcoming. At the most critical time in Australia's modern history, Britain's priorities lay elsewhere as it concentrated its resources on the European war rather than fulfil its imperial defence guarantees in the Far East.

This alarming situation had been a long time developing. Ever since the First World War, it had been acknowledged that the Pacific Ocean would probably provide the arena for the next world conflict. The rising power and territorial ambitions of Japan had been apparent since the late nineteenth century but they

1

were brought into particularly sharp focus by Japan's startling defeat of the Russian navy at Tsushima in May 1905. The Anglo–Japanese alliance of 1902 was an effective admission of Japan's new position in the Pacific and, equally, an admission of Britain's relative decline. Britain was conceding that it could no longer assert the power of its navy without an ally to support it. That alliance proved valuable during the First World War when the Japanese navy guarded the Pacific on Britain's behalf, even helping to escort the first Australian expeditionary force in 1914 as it headed off to Egypt. The price for Japan's policing was a swathe of former German islands across the Pacific, which Japan was given at the Versailles peace conference of 1919 and which it subsequently occupied and secretly fortified.

There were hopes that this postwar period would see an end to the devastation of war and to the ruinous arms races that were believed to be partly responsible for creating conditions conducive to war. The race to build ever-bigger battleships was particularly blamed for starting the First World War. At the end of that war, the warships and submarines of the German navy were destroyed or otherwise disbanded while a disarmament conference in Washington in 1922 set limits to the size of the rival navies of Britain, the United States, France, Italy and Japan. As part of Britain's agreement to reduce the size of its navy, Australia's most powerful warship, the battle cruiser *Australia*, was stripped of its guns and towed out of Sydney Heads to be sunk in the depths of the Pacific. Under this naval treaty, Britain essentially conceded that its fleet no longer had the power to confront a combination of the next two most powerful navies. This had potentially grave implications for Australia if Britain was ever faced with fighting Germany and Japan at the same time, with Japan's naval superiority in the western Pacific now being formally acknowledged.

There would have been limited security implications for Australia had Britain continued its alliance with Japan, but it chose instead to ally itself with the United States. To guard against the possibility of a hostile Japan, Britain announced that it would construct a naval base at Singapore. From an Australian vantage point, Singapore seemed well placed to project British naval power throughout the Pacific and to deter, or if necessary intercept, any hostile naval move towards Australia from the direction of Japan. However, from the vantage point of British politicians and defence planners, Singapore lay at the limit of British power. Rather than being used as a base from which to project British power across the Pacific, Singapore was athwart the gateway to the Indian Ocean with its rich panoply of British possessions, including the richest prize of all: India. It was as a barrier to the possible ambitions of the Japanese and American empires that Singapore was attractive to Britain. In particular, the presence of a naval base at Singapore bottled up the Japanese in the Pacific Ocean. So long as Singapore was in British hands, Britain's Indian Ocean empire was secure. Australia's security was another matter.

In 1919, Britain's former naval chief, Lord Jellicoe, had submitted a report on Australia's defences which had warned that the dominion could not depend upon a British fleet being sent to meet a threat in the Pacific if there was a concurrent conflict in Europe. Since Australia could not provide for such an eventuality by building a sufficiently powerful fleet of its own, Jellicoe recommended instead that a Far Eastern fleet be jointly financed by Britain, Australia and New Zealand and that it be permanently based at Singapore. In the context of the postwar disarmament atmosphere and budgetary restrictions, Jellicoe's proposal was quietly shelved. While the idea of a powerful Far Eastern fleet was rejected, the idea of building a naval base at Singapore was accepted, although its ability to provide protection for Australia was called into question even before it was built. As early as 1921, a British admiral had queried how its position so far from the Australian east coast could adequately secure the dominion's defence.[1]

It would take nearly twenty years for the base, with its expensive graving dock for the repair of battleships, to be completed. During the years that it was being planned and constructed, the value of the Singapore base and the capacity of Britain to send a fleet to the Far East during a war in two hemispheres were repeatedly questioned. Each time, British officials answered these queries with varying degrees of assurance. At the 1923 imperial conference in London, the first lord of the Admiralty, Leo Amery, provided one such assurance to the Australian prime minister, Stanley Melbourne Bruce. It caused Bruce to observe that, while he was 'not quite as clear as I should like to be as to how the protection of Singapore is to be assured, I am clear on this point, that apparently it can be done'.[2]

Similar exchanges were repeated many times in the years leading up to Singapore's fall. Britain revealed a readiness to give an assurance when none was warranted, while Australia accepted each assurance without much close scrutiny or questioning. Instead of disputing the efficacy of the Singapore base for Australia's defence, Australian governments were more concerned during the interwar years with ensuring that a British fleet would be there when required. Britain never failed to assure the dominion that it could rely on the arrival of the fleet to repel attacks. No one seems to have asked why Britain was so confident of dispatching a fleet in war when it had never proved possible to do so in peace.

Although various British officials occasionally conceded that Britain would have problems in fulfilling its guarantee, there was no retreat from the unequivocal promise to ensure Australian security by a naval fleet operating out of Singapore. As Michael Howard has noted, Britain's commitment in the 1930s to the defence of Australia was 'absolute'. Howard claimed that, in the minds of its military advisers, the 'need to defend Britain's Eastern Empire bulked at least as large as the need to redress the balance of force in Europe, and at times, one is tempted to believe, very much larger'.[3] However, experience would reveal that Britain distinguished between its dominions of Australia and New Zealand and the other territories of its eastern empire, with different priorities being accorded to each. This was something that Australian leaders were loath to acknowledge and which British leaders were equally loath to concede.

Britain had good reasons for assuring Australia about its capacity to fulfil its defence guarantee. Any refusal to provide Australia with an assurance of protection would call into question British power worldwide and make plain the shrinking power of the British navy. The empire had been held together by a belief in the navy's ability to patrol and control the world's oceans, even though Britain's declining strength relative to other naval powers should have increasingly called that belief into question. If those doubts about Britain's naval power were allowed to surface, it would inevitably weaken the bonds of empire and possibly cause its dissolution. As the most distant and most threatened of the self-governing dominions, Australia and New Zealand would have found it difficult to give continued allegiance to an empire that was plainly not ruling the waves.

So British political and military leaders repeatedly kept that knowledge from their dominion counterparts. Even after declaring war in Europe, with all the naval commitments that involved, Britain would still assure the Australian government of its continuing responsibility for the dominion's defence.[4] Yet earlier in 1939, Britain had felt so insecure in Europe that it had asked the United States to transfer a fleet to the Pacific in order to allay rising Australian concern about its security.[5] For Britain, it was a game of poker in which the stakes were the empire itself and where its bluff could only be called by Japan declaring war concurrently with Germany. If that occurred, the Singapore base would be revealed for what it was: a means of securing Australia's allegiance to an imperial system that had been declining for decades and an economical means of giving an appearance of continued British strength to potential enemies.

Britain could console itself with the thought that its assurances to Australia would never be tested. And even if Japan did declare war while Britain was occupied in Europe, the situation would not be one of total gloom. After all, both France and Holland had important possessions in the Pacific and substantial naval forces with which to protect them. Together with Britain they constituted a potentially powerful foe for an expansionist Japan. British optimism was also fuelled by the apparent lack of military prowess shown by Japan in its ongoing war against China. British ignorance of the Japanese military build-up combined dangerously with a sense of Anglo–Saxon superiority to produce a feeling that Japan could easily be defeated in any war with Britain. In addition, Russia was a continuing check on Japanese expansion, making it unsound for Japan to commit itself to distant adventures. Then there were the American forces in the Philippines and the might of the United States fleet at Pearl Harbor, lying as it did on the flank of any southerly thrust by Japan. Lastly, there was a feeling in London that even if everything else failed, Australia simply was too big and too far from Japan for it to be worth the effort to invade. In the event, this would prove to be Australia's most useful defence.

For Australia's part, there were important political reasons for not examining Britain's defence capability too closely. If it was to admit that British defence arrangements in the Pacific were inadequate, the responsibility would shift onto the Australian taxpayer and require a greater diversion of resources into defence. At a time of economic depression, Australia was extremely reluctant to accept an additional burden on the public purse. Far better to trust the succession of British statements than open a veritable Pandora's box by calling the entire Far Eastern strategy into question. As Paul Hasluck has shown, Australia's defence expenditure during the 1930s was woefully inadequate. In 1927–28, defence spending represented just 1.04 per cent of national income. Over the next decade it shrank to 0.61 per cent in 1932–33 and had only risen to 1.09 per cent by 1936–37. This was much less than Britain was spending on a per capita basis, although it was more than the other British dominions were spending.[6] Yet Australia needed to spend much more than the other dominions because of its greater size and distance from Britain. It was also much more likely than the other dominions to be in the front line of any future war. Even with its increased defence spending from the mid-1930s, the Australian rearmament program was less than the figures suggested, with much of the money being spent on making good the deterioration caused by a lack of maintenance in the preceding years. Although finance was approved for capital spending, much of it remained unspent. Of nearly £25 million voted in 1937 for a three-year program of capital spending, little more than a third was spent by July 1939. As Hasluck noted, it was 'a tiny proportion of the nation's resources' when 'the dangers were so great and so immediate'.[7]

The effect of this parsimony was seen dramatically in September 1939 when Australia entered the war with a defence force hardly worthy of the name. The permanent army was a skeleton force of several thousand with little modern equipment. There were no operational tanks or other major units of the mechanised equipment that would prove so decisive in Europe. The voluntary militia was 80 000 strong but its members only spent twelve days training in military camp each year. Despite the increasing risk of war, the conservative Australian government had resisted proposals to raise a proper standing army. In any event, it would have been a force mainly of riflemen equipped for combat in the style of the First World War. The only modern aircraft in the air force were seven recently delivered Wirraways. In reality, these American-designed planes were trainers, although they had been sold to the dominion as multi-purpose, two-seater fighters. When put to the test against the Japanese in 1942, they would be found seriously deficient in that role. As for the navy, it had no battleships or aircraft carriers, while three of its six cruisers were more than ten years old and its five destroyers dated from the First World War. According to the dogma of imperial defence, the role of these ships was to protect against cruiser raids on imperial shipping routes and to provide a useful supplement to the strength of the Royal Navy. Security against an invasion of Australia relied as it had always done on Britain's promise to reciprocate Australian cooperation in a European conflict with the timely dispatch of a fleet to the Far East to ensure that Singapore would not fall.

As federal treasurer, Richard Casey was in charge of financing the increased defence spending prior to the war. He was a strong proponent of rearmament, mainly because he felt that Australia was not doing enough to share the burden of imperial defence. In January 1938, Casey claimed that the defence department was the only one that could 'write its own ticket'; that any money it wanted it would get. Later that year, following the Munich agreement by which Britain and France acceded to German demands over Czechoslovakia, Casey wrote of his apprehension regarding the international situation and of the need for Australians to 'pawn our shirts to try to ensure our security'. As he noted, Britain had 'already decided on the shirt pawning business' and Australia had to 'take our cue from her and do the same — for the obvious reason that our security and our future go up and down with hers'.[8] After the war, though, Casey admitted that his campaign to boost rearmament had been almost totally unsuccessful. Looking back at the statistics, he was unable to provide 'any arguments to support the belief that the Lyons Government went out, horse, foot and artillery, to improve and increase Australia's defensive equipment'.[9]

Apart from the issue of cost, a critical examination by Australia of Britain's defence capability would have called into question a central tenet of Australian political life: that Australia owed allegiance to Britain because it in turn guaranteed Australian 'independence'. A large part of the continued Australian confidence in British power was based on a firm but unspoken conviction that Australia bulked as large in British minds as Britain bulked in Australian minds. If Britain was the mother country to most Australians, the implicit corollary in most antipodean minds was that the Pacific dominions were regarded as sturdy sons by most Britons. Countless cartoons of the period portrayed just such a relationship. Viewing international relationships in these idealistic, familial terms inevitably led to the conviction that the mother country would protect its 'children'. It was inconceivable that Britain could have extra-imperial interests, such as those in the Middle East, that would outrank in priority its responsibility for Australia and, within the empire, that Britain would probably feel more protective of India than it did of Australia. It is probably true to say that Australia saw *itself* as the jewel in the British crown.

In the rush to rearm in the late 1930s Australia was also hamstrung by the requirement to purchase only British equipment. As John McCarthy revealed, Britain worked hard to bar American products and expertise from the Australian market. Australia's defence position was seriously compromised by this requirement since British factories often were unable to supply Australian orders and in some cases the material supplied was second-rate. Only when Australia became so vulnerable through inaction, the threat from Japan so palpable, and the government so obviously culpable, did Prime Minister Lyons move to explore alternative sources of supply. But when a proposal for an aircraft factory with American participation was mooted, Lyons was faced with protracted and strenuous objections from Britain, which was fearful of losing its dominance of the Australian vehicle market.[10] As a result, the outbreak of war in 1939 found Australia with an air force totally inadequate and unsuitable for modern combat.

As a self-governing federation of former colonies for three decades, and given the great distance between London and Canberra, Australia might have been expected to adopt a more independent defence and foreign policy and be less attached to its former colonial 'master'. However, it was not as 'master' but as 'mother' that Britain was regarded by Australia. And it was Australia's distance from Britain and its proximity to Asia that ensured the tenacity of Australia's hold on the bonds of empire. From our distant postwar vantage point, it is easy to miss this essential fact about interwar Australian society: that there was an underdeveloped sense of Australian nationality caused by the country's incorporation within a wider and very powerful empire. Most Australians were probably far from clear whether their primary allegiance lay with Australia or Britain. Moreover, they would have denied any conflict between the two, believing that it was perfectly possible to be both British and Australian in the same way as modern-day Queenslanders or Victorians have both state and national allegiances. They saw Australians as being part of a wider British 'nation'. This sense of dual allegiance was fostered by the continuing importance of British-born Australians as a proportion of the Australian population. Even though the great majority of Australians were native-born by the 1930s, many were born to British-born parents.

Reporting the results of the 1933 census, the official statistician classified Australians by nationality or allegiance, with the overwhelming proportion of the population being classified as 'British'. He noted that Australians were 'fundamentally British in race and nationality' and had the 'essential characteristics of their British ancestors, with perhaps some accentuation of the desire for freedom from restraint'.[11] The idea that Britain was 'home' was a long time dying in the harsh climate of the distant dominion. While the declining number of British-born Australians could still be counted upon to provide a solid counterweight to the gradual development of Australian nationalism, they were ably assisted by the many other Australians whose allegiance to Britain and the empire remained undimmed by time, distance or immediate ancestry. The epitome of this was Australia's longest serving prime minister, Robert Menzies, the son of native-born Australians who nevertheless developed such an abiding attachment to Britain and its institutions that it provided the core of his existence throughout his long political career.

The sense of racial identification was fundamental to the continuing Australian attachment to Britain. The so-called 'White Australia' policy underlay Australia's federation, with the Immigration Restriction Act being the first piece of legislation enacted by the new parliament in 1901. Nearly four decades on, the White Australia policy continued to receive unquestioned and vigorous support from all Australian political parties. It effectively excluded non-white immigrants from Australia, retaining the sparsely populated continent as a white-dominated country within the surrounding and more heavily populated Asian region. The British connection allowed Australians to surmount this sea of coloured faces that they found so threatening and to reach out for the reassuring hand of the country from which they had originally sprung. At the same time, this comforting British hand ensured that the immigration barrier erected by the White Australia policy could stay firmly in place.

In theory, the constitutional framework of the British empire by 1931 allowed for the almost complete independence of the dominions. Under the Statute of Westminster of that year, dominion laws could no longer be rejected on the basis that they conflicted with those of Britain. Dominions were empowered to legislate with extraterritorial effect and were given full legislative power to deal with matters of dominion concern. In effect, their status as independent countries was officially acknowledged. However, along with New Zealand and Newfoundland, Australia declined to adopt the enabling legislation, preferring to remain in a state of formal dependence. The Labor prime minister, James Scullin, who had earlier fought for the appointment of an Australian-born governor-general, described the Statute of Westminster as being of 'little importance' and refused to introduce it.[12] By not adopting the statute, Australia denied itself certain practical benefits, particularly in the areas of shipping and trade. Even the arch-imperialist Robert Menzies acknowledged the statute's value. However, it faced strong opposition from MPs worried that it might 'give some support to the idea of separatism from Great Britain'.[13]

They were similarly dismayed by any suggestion of Australia developing its own foreign policy. Indeed, in the area of foreign policy, there was probably less dissension between Australia and Britain than between the various parts of the British government. Yet there was sufficient precedent provided by Canada and South Africa for Australia to develop an independent foreign service capable of developing an Australian view of the world and of projecting an Australian view onto the world. Australia mostly chose not to exercise that right until its precarious wartime position made it unavoidable. Until then, apart from several trade commissioners, its overseas representatives were limited to the high commissioner in London, the former prime minister S. M. Bruce, and, from 1937, a counsellor at the British embassy in Washington. Bruce also represented Australia at the League of Nations in Geneva. Elsewhere, Britain represented Australian interests and pursued policies that were meant to be both British and Australian. As the Australian government declared in 1940, its foreign policy would 'be so woven into the pattern of British foreign policy that it can be said that we make our contribution, exercise our influence but do not duplicate, or contrast with British policy'.[14]

The Australian government was supplied by the British Dominions Office with most of the information on which its foreign policy was determined. The Australian representatives in London and Washington were similarly reliant on British sources for the bulk of their intelligence. This was buttressed by Britain's control of communications to Australia, with the news of world events being channelled from London through British wire and radio services to receptive Australian audiences. Even the officials in Australia's external affairs department were forced to rely on the BBC news service to keep abreast of overseas developments. This virtual monopoly on information ensured that Australia looked at the world through British eyes, thereby hampering the development of an independent perception of national interests and helping to ensure a continuation of the dominion's dependence.[15] Consequently, Australia was able to exert little influence on British policy makers or do much to determine the direction of British foreign policy.[16] This was shown when Britain unilaterally reversed imperial foreign policy in March 1939, abandoning the agreed policy of appeasement and commencing on a course that would lead to war with Germany.[17]

Successive Australian governments seemed largely content with their position vis-à-vis Britain. They exhibited an almost total lack of interest in foreign affairs, with the only notable initiative during the 1930s being a suggestion by Prime Minister Lyons for a Pacific pact linking Britain, the United States and Japan. However, such a pact was never a viable option in the context of the 1930s and it was quietly abandoned by Lyons in the face of British opposition. As John McCarthy observed in his landmark study of

Australian involvement in imperial defence during the interwar years, the dominion 'did not possess an independent defence and foreign policy and the low politico-military status this fact implied was largely accepted without question by the Australian government'.[18]

Although in hindsight the approach of war seems to have dominated the 1930s, economic problems also loomed large. The decade was marked by Australian attempts to obtain guaranteed access to the British market for their primary products and by British attempts to retain and increase its share of the Australian market in manufactured goods. For some British politicians, the empire was seen as a means of halting their nation's postwar economic decline and of insulating itself from the effects of the depression. In this scheme of things, the empire was to operate as a self-sufficient organism, with the dominions and colonies being in a symbiotic economic relationship to the mother country.[19] Britain would exchange industrial goods for cheap primary products from the empire. This required the dominions to remain underdeveloped, concentrating on their role as suppliers of food and raw materials. Although there was no British master plan for the economic subordination of the empire, British officials tended to regard such a theory as an ideal and their policies usually had the practical effect of encouraging subordination.

The Ottawa economic conference of 1932 marked the high point for the concept of a self-contained empire. The conference of British and dominion representatives established a series of trade agreements that gave preferential access to the markets of each member country. For its part, Australia agreed to give British manufacturers access to the dominion market, although it did so by raising tariffs on non-British imports rather than lowering tariffs on British goods. This left Britain only partly satisfied while at the same time it antagonised a host of foreign competitors, who retaliated against Australian exports. As such, the system of imperial preference had the effect of building fences between Australia and non-British countries where there should have been bridges. Australia's blinkered view of the world seemed to make it incapable of foreseeing the repercussions that were likely to flow from such policies. And the offence was compounded in 1936 when a so-called trade diversion policy replaced the import of Japanese textiles and American automobile parts with British goods. At one stroke, Australia managed to offend its most likely enemy in the Pacific while at the same time causing similar offence to its most likely ally.

The great size of the British market helped to foster a state of dependence by the dominions upon Britain. In the context of the 1930s, with closed trading blocs and high tariff barriers, the dominions saw little alternative to selling the bulk of their produce to Britain. This greatly reduced their bargaining power, especially as Britain often had access to non-imperial, and often cheaper, sources of food and raw materials. Even in 1938, six years after imperial preference schemes were introduced on a large scale, Britain was drawing on non-imperial sources for 61 per cent of its imports. In addition, imports were decreasing as a proportion of British national expenditure, making them less important to the British economy as a whole.[20] For the dominions, though, the British market continued to be vital for many of their primary products. Moreover, British-manufactured goods were almost guaranteed their place in the Australian market,[21] while British money dominated the capital market and British firms enjoyed a far stronger hold on the Australian economy than any foreign competitor.[22]

Australia's desire to placate British economic demands and maintain the ethos of empire, with its explicit promise of protection against attack, produced a policy with fundamental flaws. By offending non-British trading nations, Australia cut itself off from countries that could have assisted its economic recovery. It was increasingly apparent that the empire alone was insufficient to absorb Australia's surplus produce, yet the tariff system established at Ottawa acted as a barrier blocking the necessary expansion of trade with non-British nations. Dependence on British manufacturers also hampered the growth of Australian secondary industries and thereby limited the ability of the government to reduce the army of unemployed. Without a diverse and modern industrial base, the timely development of defence production would prove difficult when war came. Indeed, the constant exhortation for Australians to 'buy British' during the interwar decades was a factor in causing the poor Australian defence position in 1939.

It was Britain that led the way out of this economic morass when it concluded a trade agreement with the United States in 1938, effectively signalling the end of efforts to devise a purely imperial solution to its economic ills. Despite having a large part of the world's population and area under its influence or control, Britain was acknowledging that it could not create a self-sufficient economic unit along the lines proposed by its more enthusiastic imperial boosters. America's economic power and potential as a market, as well as its military might, could no longer be denied. While Britain's economic rapprochement with the United States began the collapse of the imperial economic order, it would soon be followed by the collapse of the imperial military order. In both cases, Australia was overtaken by events over which it had little control.

With the twin issues of economic and military security dominating Anglo–Australian relations during the 1930s, Britain held itself out as providing the answer to both these problems. And Australia was all too ready to believe in a British solution, with possible alternative options being severely circumscribed by Australia's membership of the British empire. Such was the extent of its dependence on Britain that Australia slipped into a position of increasing peril in the Pacific. Despite clear indications that Australia could no longer rely on imperial defence, the dominion could not make the imaginative leap necessary to surmount the century and a half of colonialism and to recognise the peril that surrounded it. Time and the fall of events would soon test the strength of Australia's colonial mentality and the worth of the British defence assurance.

NOTES

1 John McCarthy, *Australia and Imperial Defence 1918–39*, Brisbane, 1976, pp. 8–9, 46; See also J. Neidpath, *The Singapore Naval Base and the Defence of Britain's Eastern Empire, 1919–1941*, Oxford, 1981, and B. Primrose, 'Australia's Naval Policy 1919–1942: A Case Study in Empire Relations', PhD thesis, Australian National University, Canberra, 1974.
2 McCarthy, *Australia and Imperial Defence 1918–39*, p. 47.
3 Michael Howard, *The Continental Commitment*, London, 1972, p. 100.
4 ibid., p. 146.
5 Cordell Hull, *The Memoirs of Cordell Hull*, Vol. 1, London, 1948, p. 630.
6 In 1927–28, Australian spending on defence was £1 5s 5d per head, Canada 5s 7d, New Zealand 14s 1d, South Africa 11s 4d (whites only), and Britain £2 12s 2d. Paul Hasluck, *The Government and the People 1939–41*, Canberra, 1952, Chap. 2.
7 Hasluck, *The Government and the People 1939–41*, Chap. 2.
8 ibid., p. 104; Letter, Casey to Keith Officer, 5 December 1938, Officer Papers, MS 2629, 1/631, NLA; See also Note for Cabinet speech prior to 1937 Imperial Conference by Sir Samuel Hoare, Templewood Papers, IX:2, CUL.
9 Letter, Casey to Earle Page, 19 July 1957, Page Papers, MS 1633, Folder 1773, NLA.

[10] McCarthy, *Australia and Imperial Defence 1918–39*, Chap. 5.

[11] The 1933 census revealed a rise in the proportion of native-born Australians in the population to 86.3 per cent (up from 84.5 per cent in 1921). Those born in the British Isles represented 10.7 per cent of the population (down from 12.4 per cent in 1921). If those born in Britain are added to those Australians whose parents were born in Britain, the total would become much greater, although no such breakdown was provided in the figures. *Official Year Book of the Commonwealth of Australia: No. 32, 1939*, Canberra, 1940.

[12] Scullin was politically embattled at the time and his rejection of the statute was recognition that the Australian electorate, unlike that of South Africa or Canada, would not reward political leaders who pressed too hard for Australia's independence from Britain. John Robertson, *J. H. Scullin*, Perth, 1974, p. 276.

[13] N. Mansergh (ed.), *Documents and Speeches on British Commonwealth Affairs 1931–1952*, Vol. 1, London, 1953, p. 21.

[14] W. J. Hudson et al (eds), *Documents on Australian Foreign Policy*, Vol. 4, Canberra, 1980, p. 117.

[15] P. G. Edwards (ed.), *Australia Through American Eyes 1935–1945*, Brisbane, 1979, p. 54.

[16] See Australian Institute of International Affairs, *Australia and the Pacific*, Princeton, 1944, pp. 6–7; E. M. Andrews, *Isolationism and Appeasement in Australia*, Canberra, 1970, p. 211; R. F. Holland, *Britain and the Commonwealth Alliance 1918–1939*, London, 1981, p. 167.

[17] N. Mansergh, *The Commonwealth Experience*, London, 1969, pp. 282–3. Bruce later recalled the difficulties he had faced as high commissioner in learning of British policies as they were being formulated and before they moved beyond the reach of dominion pressure, complaining that it was only after policies were 'almost unalterable that one can find out anything'. N. Mansergh (ed.), *Documents and Speeches on British Commonwealth Affairs 1931–1952*, Vol. 1, p. 599.

[18] McCarthy, *Australia and Imperial Defence 1918–39*, p. 148.

[19] For an influential example of this view from a prominent Tory politician, see Leo Amery, *The Forward View*, London, 1935.

[20] Ian Drummond, *British Economic Policy and the Empire*, London, 1972, p. 21.

[21] In September 1936, the US consul in Sydney reported slight inroads by American goods despite 'a large Ottawa preference, despite additional advantages in primage taxes ... and despite an inherent predilection to "buy British"'. P. G. Edwards (ed.), *Australia Through American Eyes 1935–1945*, pp. 41–2.

[22] While there was some scope for bargaining by Australia, and there was an acknowledgment by Britain of the dominion's retaliatory power, it was not a power that could be easily or lightly used. J. O. N. Perkins, 'Changing Economic Relations', in A. F. Madden and W. H. Morris-Jones (eds), *Australia and Britain*, London, 1980, pp. 180–6; Drummond, *British Economic Policy and the Empire*, p. 231.

TWO

'press them strongly to do more'

On 1 September 1939 German troops began the invasion of neighbouring Poland, triggering ultimatums from Britain and France that would set in motion the second European war of the twentieth century. When the crackling voice of the British prime minister, Neville Chamberlain, was heard in distant Australia solemnly announcing on the BBC world service the outbreak of hostilities with Germany, Australia once more lined up behind the 'mother country'. This apparent unanimity of view between Australia and Britain concealed a widening divergence of interest between these two imperial partners at opposite ends of the world. Rather than drawing them closer together, the war would pitch Britain and Australia into a competitive struggle for the survival of their respective nations.

Australia was unique among the self-governing dominions of the British empire in being precariously placed beyond the effective limit of British sea power while at the same time being in the front line facing the likely prospect of Japanese military and economic expansion. The outbreak of war therefore raised the question of how far Australia should go in supporting Britain against Germany, where the military threat to Australia was limited, while a possibly imminent and very direct threat loomed large in the Pacific.

There was no question in the mind of the Australian prime minister, Robert Menzies, that when Britain was at war so too was Australia. As soon as he had heard Chamberlain's declaration of war on the radio, Menzies made his own sombre announcement of Australia's involvement. There was no triumphant flag-flying or the grandiose protestations of imperial loyalty that Australian leaders had used at the beginning of the First World War. The ravages of that war had removed any illusions Australians might have entertained about the nature of modern warfare. With the trenches of the First World War in mind, Menzies declared that it was his 'melancholy duty' to announce Australia's involvement as a simple consequence of Britain's involvement in events over which Australia had no control. After relating at some length for his radio audience the history of the dispute between Germany and its neighbours, Menzies beseeched 'God in His mercy and compassion' to deliver the world 'from this agony'.[1]

Unlike Canada or South Africa, where the declaration of war was left to the respective parliaments to deliberate upon, Menzies was sufficiently confident to embroil Australia in the war as soon as he learnt of the British declaration. The British viceroy of India similarly plunged his charge into the distant struggle without reference to his subjects. According to Menzies, 'where Great Britain stands there stand the people of the entire British world'.[2] When he was criticised for abandoning any semblance of Australian independence, he pointed to the popular sentiment for war, that the British people needed quick assurances of support and that the King's declaration of war automatically created a state of war between Australia and Germany. This last justification was the one that most determined Menzies' action. His legalistic background, combined with his sense of empire, could not conceive of the possibility of the King being at war in Britain but not in Australia.[3] As it happened, the King remained monarch of neutral Ireland throughout the war and was not at war in South Africa and Canada until the parliaments of those dominions had met and decided to throw in their lot with Britain's.

While Australia's involvement in the war might not, in Menzies' view, have been a matter for debate, the extent of its contribution to the far-off conflict was yet to be decided. Unlike the First World War, when the Anglo–Japanese alliance had allowed Australia to commit its forces to Europe without concern for its own defence position, the situation in 1939 was very different. There was no alliance to keep the Japanese at bay. There was instead the very real prospect that the Japanese, already at war with China, would seize the opportunity presented by the European war to advance their imperial pretensions in the Pacific. For twenty years, British and Australian strategists had raised precisely this prospect, of Britain's preoccupation in Europe allowing unimpeded Japanese expansion in the Pacific. Although its involvement in a European war might expose Australia to the threat of a Japanese invasion, and while it was relatively unprepared to defend itself against such an invasion, there was never any doubt that Australia would be a co-belligerent with Britain. The whole thrust of imperial defence arrangements between the wars demanded an Australian response in defence of Britain on the understanding that the imperial connection would, if necessary, operate in the other direction and see British forces defending Australia.

For Australians, most of whom saw themselves as being part of the British people, the link with Britain was indissoluble and of paramount importance. There was an implicit faith in Britain and the empire and an almost blind trust in Britain's benevolence towards Australia. Part racial and cultural identification, part military and economic dependence, the imperial idea reached an almost metaphysical plane, vying with the Anglican religion as the cloak of respectability for Australian conservatism. Menzies, with his *Boys' Own* outlook on the world, recalled his formative years when 'the maps of the world were patterned with great areas of red' and 'of all the ancient landmarks that might be moved the British empire seemed to be the most unlikely'.[4] Menzies was far from alone in his views, with allegiance to Britain ingrained deep in the Australian psyche. As one contemporary observer noted, 'Australia took it for granted, as part of the natural order of things, that Britain would maintain her general security.' Even Labor leader John Curtin argued that 'no part of the British Commonwealth is more steadfast in its devotion to the British way of life and British institutions than Australia'.[5]

Although Australia gave the appearance of unquestioning allegiance to Britain by lining up immediately at its side in the conflict with Germany, it did have differences of outlook caused by its very different position in the world and the parlous state of its defences. Thus, while donning the British colours, Australia continued with its prewar commitment to policies of appeasement. Up until the very outbreak of war, Menzies had urged an attitude of compromise upon the British government.[6] And when war was declared, Australian ministers were as anxious as most of their British counterparts to limit its extent and, if possible, to find ways to bring it to an early end. Nobody wanted the expected repetition of the slaughter of the First World War and there was a fear in Canberra that an Australian commitment to Europe would leave it vulnerable to a Japanese attack.

The Labor Party had urged during the 1930s that an Australian defence policy should have as its first priority the local defence of Australia, which would be provided by shifting the defence effort away from the navy and more towards the army and air force. The party argued that a strong air force that could be moved quickly to any point on the coastline and which would be supported by a large militia could prevent an invasion force gaining a foothold on Australian shores. Menzies and his conservative colleagues argued instead for a continuing commitment to the concept of imperial defence, which relied heavily on the power of the Royal Navy in the confident belief that it would either deter a potential invasion force from striking out for Australian shores or intercept and sink such a force before it was able to reach Australian shores. The Labor Party concept of local defence may have ensured Australia's defence but would have limited any Australian contribution to the wider imperial effort. The conservative concept did the opposite, skimping on measures for local defence while making generous contributions to the imperial effort in the belief that the empire would be there when needed.

In the twelve months prior to the outbreak of war, the conservative United Australia Party government under Joe Lyons, and later under Menzies, did begin to hedge its bets by increasing its spending on local defence. But it was too late to make up for two decades of relative indifference. Partly because of the consequent poor defences of Australia, and partly because of his embattled political position as the leader of a minority government relying upon the support of the Country Party, Menzies was cautious about committing Australian forces overseas until the uncertainty about Japan's intentions could be clarified. On 5 September, just two days after the outbreak of war, he advised the Australian high commissioner in London and former prime minister, S. M. Bruce, that the question of an expeditionary force along the lines of the previous war would not be decided until the 'position of Japan has been cleared up'. Although Menzies confided that he could envisage the possibility of Australian forces being used to reinforce Singapore 'or putting garrisons into places in [the] Middle East', he felt unable to even consider the question at an official level since 'any suggestion at present of sending troops out of Australia would be widely condemned'.[7]

The Australian military historian David Horner has suggested that Menzies was greatly troubled by the potential threat from Japan and that this made him averse to the concept of an expeditionary force. But, as Horner also shows, Menzies was equally troubled by the political threat that confronted him as a prime minister of just six months' standing presiding over a minority government that was being hard-pressed by both the Labor and Country parties.[8] As he explained his predicament to Bruce on 27 October, he was being criticised by sections of the press while the Country Party was conducting a 'specially poisonous public campaign'. Menzies anticipated a serious challenge in parliament in mid-November, just at the time his cabinet would be deciding on the dispatch of an expeditionary force.[9] So he held back from committing it.

The Labor Party was opposed to the dispatch of an expeditionary force so long as there was uncertainty about the intentions of Japan. For its part, the Country Party was concerned about the possible losses for primary producers caused by the war, the shortage of labour during the forthcoming harvest and the war-induced shortage of shipping for exports of primary produce. As well, among his cabinet colleagues there were men more inclined than Menzies to accord the local defence of Australia a high priority, though not to place it above the security of the empire as a whole. The Labor Party and Menzies' sceptical colleagues would have to be appeased by British assurances about Japan while the Country Party would require more basic British undertakings regarding the purchase of Australian primary produce. So, although Menzies' personal inclination was to provide an expeditionary force, first he would have to disarm his critics. Meanwhile, he would continue with preparing the groundwork for such a commitment.

In the absence of a permanent Australian army, there was no way that an expeditionary force could be sent immediately on the outbreak of war. Despite the clear signs of an impending war in the late 1930s, and the massive rearmament effort in Britain, the Australian government of Joe Lyons had resisted calls for a standing army, preferring to maintain its skeleton force of permanent personnel backed by a large, part-time militia. As a result, before an expeditionary force could be dispatched, it would first have to be enlisted, equipped and at least partly trained. Eleven days after the outbreak of war, the Australian cabinet tentatively decided to raise one division of troops for 'general war purposes' and to call up the militia for a period of more intensive training.[10] When Menzies announced this decision, he tried to satisfy both sides of the debate, claiming that, while the 'prime necessity' was to defend Australia, it 'might be used to garrison some Pacific islands, to co-operate with New Zealand, or to relieve British troops in Singapore and at other points round the Indian Ocean, or it might be practicable to send some forces to Europe'. On the one hand, he promised not to 'diminish the security of Australia', while on the other, he reminded Australians of their obligation to maintain the 'security of the Empire as a whole'.[11]

Despite this decision, there was still no explicit mention of the division forming the first echelon of a second Australian Imperial Force (AIF). Instead, it was called a 'special' force. Menzies was trying to appease those clamouring for the immediate raising and dispatch of an expeditionary force while at the same time assuaging those who wanted Australia's local defences to be secured before any forces were sent overseas. In fact, by raising the special division, Menzies was preparing an expeditionary force while paying lip-service to his local defence critics. As the military board had advised, the training and equipping of the division could only be undertaken at the expense of the militia and to the short-term cost of home defence. It was with reluctance that the board agreed to the government's plan and only on condition that the first priority remain that of training the militia for its home defence role.[12]

Although the military board advice was soundly based, it was not calculated to capture the popular imagination which was keen to see the dispatch of a second AIF. Nor would it satisfy those critics who compared Menzies' measured war effort with the patriotic rush of 1914, when there was little threat to Australia. It was with such critics in mind that the government pressed ahead with the raising of a full-time infantry division even though it could not be equipped adequately for action within Australia. In his announcement of the force, Menzies claimed that Australia was further advanced in its mobilisation than in the previous war and dismissed any suggestion that he had 'an easy-going attitude' to defence. The division, he said, 'completely disproves the ill-founded and damaging suggestion that Australia is hanging back; that her Government is not alive to its responsibilities; that the spirit of 1914 is lacking'.[13]

While Menzies was moving cautiously towards the formation of an expeditionary force, the announcement of the infantry division did not satisfy those critics calling urgently for the creation of a second AIF. Within days of Menzies' announcement, the Melbourne *Argus* berated the government for incompetence in not responding to the popular mood which, the paper asserted, wanted immediate action. On 20 October, the *Argus* returned to the attack, urging the government to abandon its 'obstinate adherence to the discredited theory that the Militia is still the first line of defence' and to make the formation of a second AIF its top priority. It wanted the militia returned to part-time training on a level sufficient to 'meet the fading emergency of an invasion of Australia' while allowing 'normal peace-time industry' to be 'as little disturbed as possible'.[14]

While Menzies tried to satisfy all his domestic critics, harsh words were being uttered in London at Australia's niggardly effort. Winston Churchill had been brought into Chamberlain's government as first lord of the Admiralty, a position he had occupied during the First World War when Australian troops had been used in his questionable strategy to capture Turkey's Gallipoli peninsula. Churchill now wanted Australian troops to 'be in France by the Spring' but was disturbed to find that 'Australia appeared to be forming only one division, and even that was remaining at home for the present'. He thought Britain should 'press them strongly to do more'.[15] Churchill's complaint was not shared generally by his colleagues, who were much less eager to rush into the total war that Churchill was keen to fight. He remained a strident but relatively lonely voice in a British cabinet room still dominated by the so-called 'men of Munich'.

In order to clarify British needs, and to satisfy Australian concerns about the position in the Pacific, Menzies dispatched to London his minister for supply and development, Richard Casey, for a meeting between dominion ministers and British officials. In preparation for Casey's arrival, the British chiefs of staff prepared a report on the strategic situation, which suggested that dominion troops, with the exception of those from Canada, would be employed best in the Middle East. However, this suggestion was struck out by the war cabinet for fear that it might not be acceptable to the dominions.[16] At least in Australia's case, this fear was unfounded.

Very quickly after his arrival, Casey let it be known that Australia was keen to dispatch its forces overseas but wanted an assurance from the British government about the likely threat from Japan. After an informal discussion with several cabinet ministers, Casey agreed to put the British arguments to the Australian government in order to 'pave the way' for the official British assurance. As the new dominions secretary, Anthony Eden, explained to Prime Minister Chamberlain, 'if we can give Casey a measure of comfort in respect of Japan's political attitude, combined with an indication of our willingness and ability to send capital ships to Singapore, should the need arise, the Commonwealth Government will then at once decide that the division which they are now training can proceed overseas'.[17] Eden made it quite clear that Britain was in the possibly invidious position of deciding whether to provide a verbal assurance about something that could not definitely be known in order to secure Australian assistance for the British war effort.

If the position was invidious, the British war cabinet did not seem to notice it. Only the foreign secretary, Lord Halifax, cautioned his colleagues to wait for opinions from the British ambassadors in Washington and Tokyo before giving Australia and New Zealand a 'strong lead to send troops overseas'. Churchill's reaction is interesting to note in view of his later elevation to the prime ministership. He dismissed Halifax's objections out of hand, claiming that the most Australia had to fear from Japan was a 'tip-and-run raid, to repel which land forces were not required'.[18] Despite Churchill's optimistic assessment, Casey spent more than a month in London seeking what Britain was unable to provide: a guarantee that Australian security would not be imperilled by the dispatch of its troops.

Initially, it seemed like plain sailing. Casey expressed a willingness to send the partly trained troops and suggested the Middle East as the best destination for them. They could complete their training there, be supplied with British equipment and release British garrison troops for use in France. Casey informed his colleagues in Australia that Britain regarded any danger from Japan as being 'remote', confided that both Canada and India had already agreed to the dispatch of their troops and argued that it was important to counter German propaganda, which claimed that cooperation from the dominions was 'half-hearted'.[19]

British ministers were heartened by the readiness of Casey to fall in with British needs. As one member of the war cabinet confided to a friend, the dominions 'seem to be playing up well. They have sent over a good lot of representatives and, as far as I can judge, there are no difficult questions between us.'[20] After crossing the English Channel to visit the Anglo–French defensive positions in France, Eden reported that the dominion ministers had been 'very forthcoming as to the extent of the forces which they hoped to make available'.[21] Casey, who had been a staff officer in France during the First World War, may have been forthcoming but he was also shocked at the inadequate preparations being made to meet a German attack. He returned to London concerned to obtain definite assurances about the Far East and determined that Australian troops should not go to France.

Casey wanted an assurance not just about Japan's military intentions, but also about Britain's reaction to a war in the Pacific. Specifically, in what circumstances would a British fleet be dispatched to the Far East? This was the question that a succession of Australian ministers had asked of their British counterparts during the interwar period and to which they had signally failed to receive a satisfactory reply. Casey was to fare no better. As first lord of the Admiralty, it fell to Churchill to set Casey's mind at rest. Churchill was both dismissive of Japanese naval capability and keen to obtain a commitment of troops from Australia. He also was convinced that a serious Japanese threat to Australia was an extremely remote possibility. These considerations combined to make him remarkably ready to provide the kind of assurance that could fob off the querulous Australians once again. Churchill gave the assurance, believing that it would never be put to the test. It would be the first of many such assurances by Churchill, the value of which could only be known in the event of a Japanese invasion.

NOTES

[1] Broadcast message by Menzies, 3 September 1939, in R. G. Neale (ed.), *Documents on Australian Foreign Policy* (hereafter *DAFP*), Vol. 2, Australian Government Publishing Service, Canberra, 1976, pp. 221–6.

[2] ibid., p. 226.

[3] Robert Menzies, *Afternoon Light*, London, 1967, p. 16.

[4] ibid., p. 187.

[5] Australian Institute of International Affairs, *Australia and the Pacific*, Princeton, 1944, pp. 6 and 16.

[6] See Cable, Menzies to Chamberlain, 1 September 1939, *DAFP*, Vol. 2, Doc. 174.

[7] Cable, Menzies to Bruce, 5 September 1939, *DAFP*, Vol. 2, Doc. 195.

[8] David Horner, *High Command*, Allen & Unwin, Sydney, 1982, pp. 28–31.

[9] Cable, Menzies to Bruce, 27 October 1939, *DAFP*, Vol. 2, Doc. 309.

[10] Cabinet Minutes, 14 September 1939, CRS A2697, Vol. 2, NAA.

[11] *Times*, London, 16 September 1939, p. 8.

[12] Report by Military Board on the Raising of a Special Force for Continuous Service either in Australia or Overseas, 13 September 1939, CRS A5954, Box 261, NAA.

[13] Transcript of a broadcast by Menzies, 15 September 1939, CRS A5954, Box 261, NAA.

[14] *Argus*, Melbourne, 20 September and 20 October 1939.

[15] War Cabinet Conclusions, 19 October 1939, CAB 65/1, W.M. 53(39), PRO.

[16] War Cabinet Conclusions, 30 October 1939, CAB 65/1, W.M. 65(39), PRO.

[17] Letter, Eden to Chamberlain, 3 November 1939, *DAFP*, Vol. 2, Doc. 325.

[18] War Cabinet Conclusions, 2 November 1939, CAB 65/2, W.M. 68(39), PRO.

[19] Cables C4 and C7, Casey to Menzies, 5 and 6 November 1939, *DAFP*, Vol. 2, Docs 327 and 332.

[20] Letter, Sir Samuel Hoare to Lord Lothian, 12 November 1939, XI:5, Templewood Papers, CUL.

[21] War Cabinet Conclusions, 18 November 1939, CAB 65/2, W.M. 87(39), PRO.

THREE

'a somewhat over-optimistic picture'

With a war in Europe that was about to erupt, combined with a possible war in the Pacific, the system of imperial defence could be put to the test that interwar planners had shrunk from confronting: a war on two fronts. How could Britain's navy cope with simultaneous threats on opposite sides of the world? For the time being, London could take comfort from Italy and Japan remaining on the sidelines while the French navy in the Mediterranean joined its formidable naval force to Britain's. But there was no telling what might happen if Britain and France had trouble withstanding a German offensive and if the Soviet Union, which had joined with Germany in carving up Poland, should join Germany in the war against the western powers. While it might have been sensible for Australia to guard against the possibility of a war with Japan, Churchill's preoccupation was simply to obtain the use of Australian forces for the European war. And he was prepared to give whatever assurance was necessary to secure them.

The British war cabinet did not share Churchill's bravado and took fright at his promise to abandon the Mediterranean if Australian security was threatened. Churchill explained to his colleagues that his commitment was not intended to be an official commitment to Australia but was merely made to assure Casey that there was 'nothing to prevent the dispatch of an Australian force to the Middle East'. Chamberlain immediately objected, pointing out that Britain had always managed to avoid such definite commitments to Australia and to escape with vague assurances. In particular, Britain had 'not been prepared to decide, in advance of the event, whether the Mediterranean should be abandoned to allow of a Fleet to go to the Far East'.[1] Britain had pre-existing commitments to France and Turkey to maintain a naval presence in the eastern Mediterranean, which would be compromised by Churchill's apparent assurance to Australia.

Churchill did not see it as a problem. He pointed out that his guarantee to Australia was hedged with sufficient provisos as to make it most unlikely to be tested. For one thing, a fleet would not be dispatched simply on the declaration of war by Japan. There would first have to be an 'invasion in force' of Australia, a situation Churchill could not envisage. His guarantee also depended on the continued neutrality of Italy allowing the Mediterranean to be largely abandoned by the Royal Navy. Of course, as a succession of interwar critics of the Singapore strategy had pointed out, it was most unlikely that the Japanese would threaten Australia unless Italy became a belligerent or some other occurrence tied the Royal Navy to the western hemisphere. If this possibility disturbed Churchill, he made no sign of it. As he confided to the war cabinet, the crucial thing was to 'reassure the Dominions, so that they would consent to the dispatch of their forces'. Make the promise and get the troops. That was the thing. His colleagues bowed to Churchill's argument — provided he made clear to the dominions that the precise British reaction to a Japanese attack would depend on the circumstances.[2]

With the agreement of his colleagues secured, Churchill met that same afternoon with Casey to relay the qualified British assurance, only to find that his confidence about Casey's malleability was a trifle misplaced. Acting on cabled instructions from Menzies,[3] Casey now wanted an assurance about the British reaction in the event of the Japanese seeking to secure the oilfields of Borneo by attacking the Netherlands East Indies (NEI) while leaving British possessions untouched. If the British refused to go to war over such an attack, it would allow the Japanese to be lodged on Australia's doorstep from where they would be able to launch lightning attacks or even mount an invasion of Australia before any adequate defence could be organised. It was therefore imperative that Australia know the British reaction before denuding itself of troops.

Though Britain could justifiably refuse to make definite commitments in terms of ships in the case of unspecified Japanese aggression, it was harder to escape with a vague assurance in the case of a Japanese attack on the NEI. Either Britain would regard it as a cause for war, or it would not. But even here Britain managed to hedge its obligations by playing the American card, claiming that it could not commit itself beforehand to a war against Japan over the NEI without knowing the attitude of the United States to such a conflict. It did not want to be in the position of fighting the Japanese single-handed in the Pacific while also being occupied with the Germans in Europe. Round and round the arguments went as Casey sought what Britain would never provide. Later, the permanent secretary of the Foreign Office, Sir Alexander Cadogan, confided in his diary that Casey was 'being tiresome, but he was more or less knocked on the head'.[4]

The British may have found Casey tiresome at times, but the Australian minister was doing what he could to fit in with British needs. In his cables to Australia there was little indication that Casey was seeking to protect Australian interests or that he had any appreciation of Australia having defence interests separate from those of Britain. His efforts were directed towards incorporating Australia into the imperial war effort and assurances were sought simply as the necessary precondition for such incorporation. Even before his discussion with Churchill, Casey had received the Foreign Office view of the Far Eastern situation and had accepted it totally. He immediately informed Menzies that it 'reads very satisfactorily from the point of view of our security in the Far East'. Perhaps more importantly, he warned that New Zealand had already sanctioned the dispatch of their expeditionary force before even receiving the Foreign Office view.[5] In attempting to satisfy his critics, Menzies was in danger of upsetting his supporters by hanging back from an imperial commitment that the New Zealanders had already approved.

The Admiralty backed up the optimism of the Foreign Office with a naval appreciation that almost totally discounted the possibility of serious Japanese aggression against Australia. As Casey confidently interpreted the message to Menzies, a Japanese invasion of Australia was not possible 'as long as there is a well-armed Australian military force and a superior British fleet in being in any part of the world'. Moreover, Casey assured Menzies that Britain would place the security of Australia above that of its interests in the Mediterranean and that a squadron of battleships 'sufficient to act as [a] major deterrent on Japanese action' would be dispatched to the Far East 'from the moment that danger to either Singapore or Australia developed in a manner which made their protection a real and practical war need'. Britain, he claimed, accepted 'full responsibility of defending Australia or Singapore from a Japanese attack on a large scale and have forces at their disposal for these essential purposes'.[6]

As a result of the Australian pressure for a more specific assurance, Churchill returned to the war cabinet to obtain his colleagues' approval of a revised memorandum, which was still couched in generalities and hedged with provisos. Unlike Casey, Bruce had tried to tie Churchill down to a specific promise to send a particular number of ships to Singapore, claiming that Britain had previously made a 'definite pledge to send 7 capital ships to Singapore in the event of Japan entering the war'. This, Churchill made clear, was 'out of the question' since it would commit Britain to basing a large part of its navy at Singapore as soon as Japan entered the war and before it had made any overtly aggressive moves in Australia's direction. As for the promise that had so alarmed Chamberlain, for Britain to abandon the Mediterranean in favour of the Far East in the event of Australia being attacked, Churchill confided to the war cabinet that he had gone no further than the assurances given to Australia at the 1937 imperial conference and that his assurance was, in fact, 'more elastic' than the one given two years previously. Unable, or unwilling, to acknowledge the real and justifiable concern for its security displayed by the Australian questioning, Churchill dismissed it simply as a 'long campaign of propaganda by the General Staff of Australia to divert money from the naval forces of the Commonwealth to the land forces'. Churchill's revised memorandum was accepted, with

Chamberlain meeting that same afternoon with Casey and Bruce to pass on its supposedly reassuring provisions.[7] Once again, Australia's concerns were fobbed off and its representatives led to believe that it remained safely under the umbrella of British naval protection.

Despite the doubtful worth of the British assurances, they were the most that Australia could obtain in the circumstances and went further than those demanded by the other dominions. But then Australia needed more reassurance than the others because it was more vulnerable than they were. Whatever their private reservations, Bruce and Casey claimed now to be satisfied, with Casey promising Chamberlain that he would cable immediately to Canberra urging Menzies that the 'wise and proper course would be for them now to authorise the dispatch to Europe of the Australian Expeditionary Force'. The following day, Eden told the British war cabinet that it could expect a quick and favourable decision from Canberra, with the troops sailing within a few weeks.[8] But Menzies was not finished yet with ensuring that his commitment of a second AIF was done with the minimum risk to his own political fortunes.

The Australian government had already instructed, before the British assurance was received, that plans be prepared for the dispatch of an expeditionary force. But it withheld any decision on whether the plans would actually be put into operation.[9] Menzies first had to ensure that the commitment reaped the maximum possible political rewards. This required, among other things, that New Zealand did not act out of step with Australia and allow it to be alleged that Menzies was slow to support the empire. To try and stay the hand of his counterpart across the Tasman while Casey was negotiating with the British, Menzies asked that New Zealand not commit its forces for several weeks, ostensibly because there was still some uncertainty regarding a possible German invasion of Holland which might in turn unleash a Japanese attack on the NEI. Menzies also revealed some annoyance at Britain being able to find the shipping for Australian troops but not for Australian exports of primary produce.[10]

It was on the question of primary produce exports that Menzies wanted to wring an important concession from Britain. On 21 November, the same day as he cabled unsuccessfully to New Zealand and as Casey continued his negotiations in London, Menzies suddenly disturbed the discussions by claiming that the situation in France, where the Germans had not yet launched any attack, did not seem 'sufficiently urgent to justify us incurring risk with our own defensive position'. In a blatant act of political horse-trading, Menzies then suggested that Australia would be willing to endure such risks by dispatching an expeditionary force provided that Britain agreed to buy Australia's coming wheat harvest which might otherwise be left to rot unsold for want of sufficient shipping. As he informed Casey, 'having regard to the shipping position, we must determine the relative priority of such things as wool and wheat, and the special Division'.[11]

Menzies' bluff worked. Just as it had in the First World War,[12] Britain agreed to purchase a huge quantity of Australian wheat that was far beyond its needs or its capacity to ship across the world. Menzies had protected himself politically, with the wheat sale satisfying the Country Party, the renewed British assurances about a fleet for Singapore helping to appease the Labor Party, and his own Anglophile supporters being delighted when Menzies finally announced on 28 November the commitment of Australian forces to Britain's war effort. As it happened, Menzies' success with the wheat sale was timed fortuitously, occurring just when Britain was under pressure from Canada, their usual principal supplier, to buy wheat above the ruling market price.[13]

It was anticipated that the special division, now named the 6th Division in numerical succession to the five divisions sent overseas during the First World War, would leave for the Middle East in January 1940 where it would complete its training and release part of the British garrison in Egypt for deployment in France. After training, the division would then be ready for service in France to meet the German offensive that was expected in the spring of 1940. Although Menzies emphasised to Casey that the weeks of basic training in Australia would allow a 'period for clarification of [the] international situation without prejudicing our strength here', this was a consideration probably of more moment to some of his colleagues than to Menzies himself. As he indicated, it was the view of *the government* and not necessarily his personal view that the extra period in Australia would be valuable.[14] While Menzies' imperial zeal made him keen to see the troops dispatched, he was also keen to avoid any allegation that he was thereby selling Australian security short, allegations that had been made after his prewar support for exporting pig-iron to Japan despite bitter union opposition. This support had caused him to be known in Labor circles as 'pig-iron Bob'.

It has been claimed that the Australian barter of men for wheat sales was evidence of Australia having 'a clear appreciation of what it considered its own vital interests to be and was quite capable of looking after them'.[15] This view is given added force by Menzies' angry reaction to news that Britain had diverted shipping to pick up the 6th Division before the Australian government had announced its decision in principle to send the men. The 'general feeling of Cabinet', Menzies informed Casey, was resentment at the British tendency to 'treat Australia as a Colony and make insufficient allowance for the fact that it is for the Government of Australia to determine whether and when Australian Forces shall go out of Australia'.[16]

This outburst by Menzies, and his successful attempt to link wheat sales with the dispatch of the division, certainly gave the appearance of Australia being able to disentangle its national interests from those of Britain or the wider empire. But the reality is not so stark. After all, Menzies continually stressed the concern of his government with the situation in the Pacific and its determination that the dispatch of the troops would be dependent on the government being satisfied that the threat from Japan could be discounted. And yet the dispatch of the troops was authorised after learning of New Zealand's decision, rather than because of any guaranteed stability in the Pacific. Though Menzies expressed his government's annoyance at the British-imposed timetable for the departure of the troops, Australia fell in with the British plans and dropped any stipulation that their departure would depend on the prevailing situation in the Pacific.

Britain would not stand or fall depending on the commitment of one Australian division. Australia, however, well might, especially as the division was the only body of even partially trained, full-time soldiers that Australia possessed. It was in Australia's national interest that its own security be assured before the dispatch of any troops from its shores. This the government failed to do, though it did exhibit a clear appreciation of its own vital political interests. Australia was treated like a colony because it often acted like one. Its troops were committed to Europe despite serious, but unspoken, reservations held by Australia's representatives in London.

After the meeting between Bruce, Casey and several British ministers on 20 November, Bruce was left with serious misgivings about the value of the British assurances regarding Australian security. They were reservations that would prove to be remarkably prescient in the fullness of time. In particular, Bruce questioned in his notes the ability of Britain's overstretched navy to 'deal with the situation in Home waters, in the Mediterranean and in the Pacific at the same time'. He also doubted the sincerity of Churchill's promise as first lord of the Admiralty to protect Australia, suspecting that his 'real' strategy was to 'win in the European theatre with a full concentration of our forces and not dissipate them by trying to deal with the situation in the Far East at the same time'.[17] Despite Bruce's misgivings about the dispatch of the Second AIF, Canberra was never advised of them. Instead, Australia committed its troops to a distant theatre of war based on an assessment of probabilities that was known by at least one of its authors to be unrealistic. As Bruce confided to a colleague, the British assessments of the Far East 'drew a somewhat over-optimistic picture' and were 'obviously framed in order to reassure Australia and make certain that the Expeditionary Force should be dispatched at an early date'.[18]

It was not only the 6th Division that Australia committed to Britain's war effort. The Royal Australian Navy (RAN) was taken over almost completely by Britain and set war tasks far from Australian shores. Though Australia now exercised more control over its navy than in 1914, it still accepted that the RAN would be ordered to commence hostilities on a signal from the Admiralty in London rather than the Navy Office in Melbourne.[19] Under Menzies, and according to the accepted strategy of imperial defence, the RAN was expected to play the main role in the protection of Australia from invasion. It would do this as an integral part of the Royal Navy (RN), of which it became a minor and largely subservient part.

Just prior to the declaration of war, Britain advised Australia that the assistance of the RAN was required in the Mediterranean. At the same time, an Australian cruiser, HMAS *Perth*, was in the process of being delivered from Britain but was intercepted en route by order of the Admiralty and detained for use in the West Indies, almost as far from Australia as it was possible to be. Britain was within its rights to do this, but it understandably caused considerable dissension within the Australian cabinet, which was only placated by an assurance from Menzies that the arrangement was 'merely a temporary one' that 'could be reviewed at a subsequent date'.[20] In fact, the cruiser was retained in the West Indies until March 1940. As for the British request for help in the Mediterranean, the Australian government was advised by its naval board, which was dominated by British officers on secondment, that it should comply with the request in order to ensure that Britain would provide its promised help in the event of Australia being threatened.[21] On the actual outbreak of war several days later, the British request was put to one side until the international situation, particularly the attitude of Japan and Italy, became clearer.

Within a week of war being declared, the British government had suggested that Australia send a cruiser and five destroyers to Singapore. This suggestion was based on the assumption that Japan would remain neutral and the naval threat to Australia would consist of occasional attacks on shipping by armed German raiders. After Australia agreed on 6 October to the dispatch of the ships, provided that they be returned if Japan entered the war, Britain requested that the five destroyers be sent instead to the Mediterranean in exchange for two British cruisers being sent to Australia. The cruisers would provide better protection against armed raiders preying upon Australian trade routes while the destroyers in the Mediterranean would release British destroyers for anti-submarine work in the Atlantic.[22]

Australian agreement to the British request was made in principle on 6 November. Eight days later, Britain asked that the ships be moved forthwith since the British ships had already been moved from the Mediterranean in anticipation of the Australian arrival. Australia was also now informed that the two British cruisers would not arrive in November as promised but, at the earliest, in February 1940. In the event, the cruisers never arrived. But the Australian government accepted the British explanation and authorised the dispatch of the destroyers. This decision was based, at least in part, on advice received from the chief of the Australian navy, Admiral Colvin, who in turn had been secretly briefed from London by his British naval colleagues.[23]

By the end of November, Australia had more or less willingly agreed to denude itself of trained men and naval ships based upon the increasingly tenuous expectation that Britain would provide assistance in the case of Australia being attacked by Japan. By the middle of December, it had made a similar agreement with regard to its air force. Before the war, the Labor Party had argued in favour of a strong air force as the most suitable and economical means by which a small population occupying a large territory could deter an invasion force. With the army and navy now committed to overseas theatres of operation, the development of the Royal Australian Air Force (RAAF) as a viable deterrent force should have been regarded as a matter of vital national interest. Instead, the government agreed to support the Empire Air Training Scheme (EATS), a scheme inspired at least partly by Bruce, which had the effect of transforming the RAAF into an organisation devoted to the recruitment and basic training of aircrew destined for operations in Europe.

Menzies announced the scheme on 11 October in terms designed to camouflage its real purpose. While acknowledging its importance for the defence of Britain, he also claimed that it provided a 'powerful deterrent to aggression against Australia'. This was nonsense and Menzies presumably realised it. But it was essential to appease those Australians who wanted the first defence priority to be, as it was in other countries, that of home defence. In a statement several months later, Menzies scaled new heights of absurdity when he justified the EATS effort with the claim that it put Australia 'well on the way to becoming a Great Air Power'. He conjured up a vision of the mostly unarmed training aircraft that were buzzing in the skies above Australian cities, together with their partly trained pilots, being 'organized at relatively short notice into an effective striking force against an aggressor' such that they would 'render the Commonwealth secure against any serious attack'.[24] Even allowing for the widely held low opinion of Japanese ability in the air, Menzies' claim was a reckless exaggeration made for political purposes and in the expectation that it would never be tested. When it was put to the test in 1942, it produced the inevitable disaster when the Australian training aircraft were pitched against the superior Japanese fighters.

The government's air defence priorities were further confirmed in February 1940 with the appointment from Britain of Air Chief Marshal Burnett to head the RAAF. As David Horner has observed, Burnett's 'main purpose was to train aircrew for the RAF and he was little interested in the home defence of Australia'.[25] With General Squires heading its army, Australia now had a triumvirate of British officers in charge of its defence.[26] More importantly, the political and diplomatic triumvirate of Casey, Bruce and Menzies ensured that the Australian government was broadly in accord with the British imperial imperatives that largely guided the actions of these officers.

Menzies' view was clear: Australia's continued 'independence' could only be achieved by its continued dependence on Britain. He claimed that a self-reliant defence policy would force Australia to 'mortgage itself for the next century'. Using an argument that still echoes with great force in Australia today, Menzies declared that Australia was only able to maintain its independent existence because it belonged to 'a family of nations, the central nation of which is still ... the most powerful and the most resolute country in the world'.[27] Menzies' failure to understand that Australia's continued survival, as with any country, rested primarily upon its own efforts was to place Australia in a position of great peril. In Britain's view, the security of the distant dominion was only one of many interests and was, as would soon be plain, far from the most important.

NOTES

[1] War Cabinet Conclusions, 20 November 1939, CAB 65/2, W.M. 89(39), PRO.
[2] ibid.
[3] Cable, Menzies to Casey, 14 November 1939, *DAFP*, Vol. 2, Doc. 361.
[4] Cadogan diary, 20 November 1939, ACAD 1/8, Cadogan papers, CC.
[5] Cable C24, Casey to Menzies, 16 November 1939, *DAFP*, Vol. 2, Doc. 368.
[6] Cable, Casey to Menzies, 17 November 1939, *DAFP*, Vol. 2, Doc. 372.
[7] War Cabinet Conclusions, 23 November 1939, CAB 65/2, W.M. 92(39), PRO.
[8] War Cabinet Conclusions, 24 November 1939, CAB 65/2, W.M. 93(39), PRO.
[9] Cabinet minute, 20 November 1939, *DAFP*, Vol. 2, Doc. 374.
[10] Cable, Menzies to Savage, 21 November 1939, *DAFP*, Vol. 2, Doc. 378.
[11] Cable, Menzies to Casey, 21 November 1939, *DAFP*, Vol. 2, Doc. 379.
[12] Joan Beaumont (ed.), *Australia's War, 1914–18*, Allen & Unwin, Sydney, 1995, pp. 97–8.
[13] R. J. Hammond, *Food*, Vol. 3, HMSO, London, 1962, pp. 522–4; J. L. Granatstein, *Canada's War: The Politics of the Mackenzie King Government 1939–1945*, Toronto, 1975, pp. 63–4; S. J. Butlin, *War Economy 1939–1942*, Canberra, 1955, pp. 86–94; Ian Hamill, 'An Expeditionary Force Mentality?: The Despatch of Australian Troops to the Middle East, 1939–1940', *Australian Outlook*, 1977, pp. 319–29.

14 Cable, Menzies to Casey, 28 November 1939, *DAFP*, Vol. 2, Doc. 392.

15 Hamill, 'An Expeditionary Force Mentality?', pp. 319–29.

16 Cable, Menzies to Casey, 1 December 1939, *DAFP*, Vol. 2, Doc. 398 (author's emphasis in italics).

17 'Joint Meeting', note by Bruce, 20 November 1939, CRS M100, 'November 1939', NAA.

18 Letter, Bruce to Officer, 12 December 1939, MS 2629, 1/879, Officer Papers, NLA.

19 G. H. Gill, *Royal Australian Navy, 1939–1942*, Australian War Memorial, Canberra, 1957, pp. 61–4.

20 Cabinet minutes, 29 August 1939, CRS A2697, Vol. 2, NAA.

21 McCarthy, *Australia and Imperial Defence*, p. 146.

22 Cable No. 191, Eden to Whiskard, 8 September 1939, *DAFP*, Vol. 2, Doc. 214; War Cabinet Minutes, 17 October 1939, CRS A2673, Vol. 1, Minute 32 and Cabinet Minutes, 31 October 1939, CRS A2697, Vol. 3, NAA.

23 Horner, *High Command*, p. 25.

24 Transcript of broadcast by Menzies, 11 October 1939, CRS A5954, Box 235, NAA; 'The Empire Air Scheme: What it Involves and How it Increases Australia's Security', press statement by Menzies, 29 February 1940, CRS A5954, Box 103, NAA.

25 Horner, *High Command*, p. 28.

26 As it happened, Squires had also fagged for Colvin at Eton. See Crace diary, 30 October 1939, 69/18/1, Crace Papers, Imperial War Museum (hereafter IWM).

27 *Herald*, Melbourne, 17 October 1939.

FOUR

'the bitterness and privations of war'

Australians welcomed in 1940 with all the gusto of peacetime. Shortages were still unknown and Menzies' prescription of 'business as usual' proved to be popular medicine for most people. In Britain it was much the same, except for the nightly blackout which darkened the normal New Year gaiety; but it was widely regarded as more nuisance than necessity. The expected bombing of London had not eventuated. Only at sea was the war carried on in earnest. In France, British and French soldiers manned the extensive fortifications of the supposedly impregnable Maginot Line while hastily extending its defences to the sea. Their enemy was that year's severe winter rather than the Germans, who still declined to attack. There was no certainty that the so-called 'phoney war' would ever be more than just that. John Colville, a young private secretary to Neville Chamberlain, looked out from Downing Street on New Year's Eve to ponder the chances of a return to 'peace or the real outbreak of war', which he put at 'fifty-fifty'.[1] Although the possibility of peace remained on the British agenda, the war machine on both sides of the Maginot Line was beginning to build up such momentum that soon it would be impossible to stop.

Across the world, Sydney Harbour became crowded with the passenger liners that normally maintained the umbilical cord between Australia and the mother country. On this occasion, though, they were there to collect part of the dominion's manhood for the second European war. Not that Australian men were loath to leave behind the lingering atmosphere of the 1930s depression and embark on the cruise of a lifetime, although for many it would prove to be their first and last. Their departure represented the dues being paid by Australia on its imperial defence insurance policy. The first payment was 6500 men of the 6th Division, the initial contingent of the Second Australian Imperial Force (AIF).

With their departure, Australia became firmly tied to the British cause against Germany. Australian ships were operating with their British counterparts in the Mediterranean; Australian aircrew were training for roles in the RAF to be played out in the cold and distant skies of the northern hemisphere; and Australian troops were taking up temporary garrison duties in the deserts of the Middle East to release British troops for service in France. With its defences depleted by their departure, the security of Australia was dependent on two assumptions: that the Pacific would remain aptly named and that, if not, Britain would be willing and able to rush to Australia's defence.

The eight and a half months of 'phoney war', from September 1939 to May 1940, provided Australia with a quiet period in which to enlist, equip and train its forces so that they might be sufficient to meet any local emergency. Despite initial fears about their intentions, the Japanese had made no immediate move southward. Their existing military commitments in China, and the uncertainty surrounding events in Europe, caused them to stay their hand. Australia made little use of this opportunity to build up its defences to cover the possibility of Britain not being able to help. Instead, in the soporific atmosphere of an Australian summer, Menzies' government seemed to succumb to the unreal nature of this war without fighting. In January, the war cabinet even had time to approve a proposal for 'someone with a thorough knowledge of Palestine ... to organise trips so that parties of men could be taken ... to some of the many interesting places that abound in that country'.[2]

Instead of boosting Australian security, Menzies ordered a re-examination of the country's war effort in early 1940 for fear that the rush of measures introduced at the beginning of the war were placing unreasonable strains on the Australian economy and unduly disrupting civilian production. To Menzies, the war was an unfortunate interruption to his vision for the industrialisation of Australia. Rather than mobilising the nation to win the war, Menzies preferred to concentrate on preparing for the postwar period which, he predicted, would 'witness a great growth in Australia's importance as an industrial and manufacturing nation'. As part of this plan, Menzies tried to establish an Australian car manufacturing industry, albeit controlled by British capital, to combat the increasing penetration of the local market by the American industry. However, it all came unstuck when details were revealed of a secret deal giving the proposed company a government-guaranteed monopoly of the market. When this was combined with suggestions of corruption, the resulting furore forced Menzies to scuttle the plan.[3]

Menzies' half-hearted approach to war measures appalled those Australians who could foresee the potential scale of the European conflict. From London, the powerful Australian businessman Sir Clive Baillieu warned his business colleagues that the 'phoney war' would soon become a 'supreme conflict with Germany'. Puzzled by the continuing importation of luxuries into Australia, Baillieu feared that domestic political factors were unduly influencing the government to delay taking action. Baillieu argued instead that it was 'good politics as well as sound patriotism' for the government to get 'public endorsement of a program of action which will enable the Government to direct the resources of Australia without limit'.[4] Such a program would also be good business for the mining and manufacturing interests that his family controlled.

Baillieu's worries were as well founded as his prediction of total war. In the financial year 1939–40, Australian expenditure on the war represented just 4.9 per cent of gross national expenditure. Though this was more than a threefold increase on the previous financial year, it was coming off a low base and remained minuscule compared to the proportion Britain spent on the war and to the proportion Australia would spend later. By 1942–43, the figure for Australia would be 36.8 per cent.[5]

Of course, Australia was not in the front line in 1940 and little fighting had yet occurred. But a more fundamental reason for the government's failure to mobilise resources for defence was Menzies' continuing faith in the possibility of a peace settlement. In 1939 he had consistently pressed Britain to accommodate German demands. Now the hiatus in the war provided him with new hopes for peace. On the one hand, Australia provided Britain with the resources of war while, on the other, it urged Britain to adopt measures that might avoid those resources ever being used. Menzies' peace moves took three forms. The first was to press for the formulation by Britain of 'peace aims' that could provide the basis for any negotiated settlement. The second approach was to resist strenuously any proposals that might extend the conflict in Europe and reduce the chances of peace. And the third was to try to prevent by whatever means the entry of Japan into the war. Menzies and Bruce became a two-man peace party as they searched for a way out of the trenches.

On 2 January 1940, Bruce sought Menzies' support for a campaign to wean the truculent French government from its plan to impose another harsh peace on a defeated Germany. Engaged as it was in its third war with Germany within seventy years, France was understandably anxious to prevent a repetition by limiting Germany's ability to wage war. Unlike the French government, Bruce visualised a postwar world in which 'Germany would play an appropriate part as a great nation' following a 'peace settlement which had faced the vital problem of disarmament, territorial adjustments, Colonies and the economic needs of all nations'.[6] According to Bruce, such a peace settlement could be achieved after Britain and France had won the war decisively. But he was not confident that such a clear victory could be achieved.[7] His proposal for a 'soft' peace was designed to weaken the German will and entice Germany to the peace table well before military means alone were able to achieve it.

Menzies was eager to support Bruce's proposed campaign but was constrained by political imperatives not to reveal his views either to his colleagues or the Australian people. Instead, he used his private correspondence with Bruce to release his frustration about the likely course of the conflict, angrily denouncing Churchill as a 'menace' and a 'publicity seeker' who 'stirs up hatreds in a world already seething with them' and who was 'lacking in judgment'. Like Bruce, Menzies foresaw a possible need for a 'new alignment of nations in which not only Great Britain and France, but Germany and Italy, combined to resist Bolshevism'. Despite the German takeover of Czechoslovakia and Poland and the outbreak of war with Britain and France, Menzies still saw Russia as a greater danger than Germany and was concerned to keep Germany strong and intact so that it could help to contain Russia. With this in mind, it was vital that 'soft' peace terms were formulated before the 'heat of battle and the bitterness and privations of war ... inevitably lead us to another Versailles'.[8]

Menzies' concerns were not shared by his cabinet. As he confided to Bruce, when he had carefully raised the issue he had found his ministers 'with one or two exceptions, quite unresponsive' and committed to what Menzies described as the 'almost pathetic belief that the dismemberment of Germany would alter the German spirit and outlook'. Though he promised Bruce that he would 'work upon their minds', Menzies was anxious about the political reaction to any attempt at diluting the Australian ardour for war.[9] His public image was already tainted by his prewar support for appeasement and his support for the supply of pig-iron for Japan, as well as by laudatory remarks about the fascists in Italy and the Nazis in Germany. He had also been taunted about his failure to enlist in the First World War, despite holding a commission in the Melbourne University Rifles and being an outspoken supporter of the war.[10]

While Menzies was constrained in pushing openly for measures that would see the Allies go soft on Germany, he was able quite openly to oppose moves that would widen the, as yet, limited war and which might cause it to achieve an unstoppable momentum. In London, it was Churchill who was most keen for British and French forces to get to grips with Germany and who, as first lord of the Admiralty, backed a proposal to mine the coastal waters of Norway so as to block the transport by sea of Swedish iron ore to Germany. The wider the war and the more intense the struggle, the greater the chances of the more belligerent Churchill being drafted to replace the man of Munich, the ailing prime minister, Neville Chamberlain. Bruce was wise to the danger and, in tandem with Menzies, led the opposition to what he called Churchill's 'ill-considered stunt'.[11] Initially, they were successful in outmanoeuvring the bellicose Churchill, with Chamberlain citing Menzies' cabled objections to the plan when throwing his own weight against it at a war cabinet meeting on 12 January. A defeated Churchill railed against the 'evident necessity to carry the Dominions with us in any direction'.[12]

Australian appeasement of Japan was the third strand of the dominion's continuing efforts to limit the war. With the country devoid of basic defence equipment and busily dispatching its trained troops overseas, it was important that Japan remain neutral. But this objective was pursued with almost leisurely detachment. The Japanese were keen to see the appointment of an Australian diplomat to Tokyo after Menzies sent Richard Casey off as Australia's first minister in Washington. Although making a decision in principle to make such an appointment, Menzies then deferred to the opinion of Bruce and the British Foreign Office and allowed the matter to lapse.[13] It was only after the disastrous fall of France in June 1940, and with the prospect of Japan consequently being drawn into the war, that Australia raised the matter again and pressed it with any degree of urgency.[14] The lack of a minister in Tokyo meant that Australia continued to rely mainly on the British embassy for advice about Japanese intentions in the Pacific, with the British being intent on telling the Australians what best suited their own war effort rather than what best suited the security of Australia.

Not that Australia always toed the British line. When London sought in February 1940 to tighten the economic embargo against Japan by restricting sales to Tokyo of Australian wool and wheat, Menzies opposed the move. As he advised Bruce, it would have a 'disastrous effect on [the] Australian wool market' while also posing 'a serious menace to friendly relations with Japan'.[15] It would also complicate his political position by upsetting the Country Party, the support of which was necessary for his continued survival. When Bruce urged the necessity of staying onside with the United States on this issue, Menzies pointed instead to his political position, confiding to Bruce that his 'difficulties on all war matters are great and growing'.[16] The appointment of Casey to Washington had caused a by-election in Casey's electorate, which had been won by the Labor candidate. This did not bode well for the federal election that Menzies was required to call within six months. To shore up his position, Menzies brought the Country Party into his cabinet, which in turn increased the pressure to resolve the impasse over wool sales. Bruce was instructed to adopt a 'stiff attitude' with British officials.[17]

With the appointment of the Country Party leader, Archie Cameron, as minister for commerce, the pressure on Menzies to resolve the wool issue became more intense. It was not only wool that concerned Cameron. At the end of March, he warned the cabinet of Britain's 'growing tendency' to emphasise its 'own particular requirements' while displaying 'indifference to the fate of Australia's other exports'. Cameron's immediate complaint was a decision by Britain to reduce its purchases of Australian dried fruit in favour of sourcing them from Turkey, with which it had recently concluded a diplomatic agreement and which it was anxious to keep out of the German camp. Despite his strident economic nationalism, Cameron did not recognise the deeper significance of the British move, which betrayed the order of its strategic priorities. For it was not only in the matter of sultana purchases that Britain was discarding its dominion, but also in the more important matter of defence equipment, with a range of modern equipment including fighter aircraft being supplied to Turkey to keep it from joining with Germany. Despite the assurances by Churchill to the contrary, the British position in the Middle East would be protected at all costs while Australia would be left to languish in an increasingly perilous Pacific.[18]

More than indifference to the fate of Australia's export industries, the dispute over the embargo against Japan revealed increasing evidence of British indifference to the fate of Australia *per se*. As Bruce had indicated, Britain was adopting a tough line with Japan at the behest of the United States. Although the British war cabinet was ambivalent about the American stand, it wanted to 'keep in step with the United States Administration', which was increasingly underwriting the British war effort.[19] Churchill was a strong supporter of the tough American action, claiming that it was 'very much to our interest that the United States should bring increasing pressure to bear on Japan, as this would not only help China but embarrass Japan, without causing any blame to rest upon us'.[20] This argument had little appeal to the Australian government, which was less cavalier about disturbing the stability of the Pacific and less interested in helping China throw off the Japanese than in keeping Japan and China bogged down in war.

These differences between Australia and Britain in their approach towards Japan would become more marked with the passage of time. But it was already apparent which ways they both were heading. Britain's dominant and ever-increasing interest was to retain American support for its war effort and even enlist it as an ally. This British interest made the mere entry of Japan into the war of lesser concern in Whitehall than the manner of its entry. What particularly concerned defence planners was the possibility of Japan attacking the Netherlands East Indies and leaving the United States on the sidelines. In such a situation, Britain might feel bound to confront the Japanese alone and thereby place itself in the untenable position of fighting without crucial American support in the Pacific. Even a Japanese attack on British positions in Malaya or Hong Kong could not be guaranteed to bring the Americans into the conflict. However, if Britain could so arrange things that the Japanese attacked both Britain and the United States, it would overcome the American public's distaste for involvement in another European war and bring the United States into the war against Germany by the 'back door' of the Pacific.

The American public were less antipathetic to the prospect of a war against Japan which, it was popularly expected, would be mainly naval and therefore not involve the huge casualties expected in a European land war. It also had racial overtones, which helped to ensure greater support. In the event, the American public would find that war with Japan would also make it a belligerent in Europe. Britain had to achieve the closer involvement of America in the Anglo–French war against Germany and did not shrink from the prospect of war with Japan if it brought America in as well. Since British planners did not have a high regard for Japanese military ability, they did not expect to have to pay too high a price in terms of lost territory for American entry. Moreover, there was an assumption that Britain would inevitably face a challenge from the Japanese and that it was better that it be faced in the context of the present war rather than after the defeat of Germany when a war-weary British public might not have the heart for a war in the Pacific. So began a more or less conscious policy by Britain to produce a situation in the Pacific where Japan and the United States would be at war. The seeds of this policy were planted in January 1940 with the tougher American attitude towards Japan. Churchill became its foremost advocate in London.

Australia was slow to sense the drift in British policy. According to the accepted imperial dogma, Australian and British foreign policies were one and the same. Australia took its lead from the British Foreign Office and was dependent upon it for information and advice. Consequently, Australia looked at the world largely through London's eyes and felt comforted by doing so. As a result, it was difficult for Australian policy makers to acknowledge that Britain might pursue interests that were not only opposed to those of Australia but which placed Australia at considerable risk. Any Australian criticism of British foreign policy in the Pacific blamed the blinkered view of the bureaucrats in the British Foreign Office who had supposedly lost sight of the wider imperial interest and whose distance from the Pacific left them, Menzies argued, without a 'practical and realistic view of the Far-Eastern position'. He urged Britain to make a 'real gesture of friendship' to Japan, arguing that 'some real assistance in the settlement of the Chinese question, accompanied by a proper recognition of Japanese trading ambitions, might very easily produce peace in the Far East'.[21]

As a Pacific country, it was also in Australia's interest that the closest links be developed with the United States. From its base at Pearl Harbor, the US Pacific fleet provided a real deterrent to Japanese expansion and, in the absence of the British fleet, could be crucial to Australia's defence. Yet Australia continued to hold America at arm's length. Australian cable communications with America continued to be routed through Canada in order to protect the business of the British empire cable system. Despite pressure from American companies, backed by the US State Department, Australia refused to allow direct wireless communication between the two countries although a radiotelephone link had been permitted. In the view of the worldly-wise John McEwen, Australia's minister for external affairs and a fruit grower from central Victoria, 'the fact that the Empire is at war makes it particularly desirable that the Empire cable system should be protected ...'.[22] One effect of this shortsighted effort to protect British commercial interests was to limit severely the amount of Australian material in American newspapers and thereby hamper the development of those close relations that Menzies claimed to want with Washington.

In the case of civil aviation, Australia resisted American attempts to establish a direct aerial route across the Pacific to Sydney despite the obvious advantages for Australian–American links. Again the Australian opposition was prompted by a desire to protect British commercial interests, with Australia refusing to allow the American route unless the United States agreed to allow a British route across the Pacific to pass through Hawaii. Although Britain had no immediate plans to develop such a route, Australia stuck to its demand, allowing the possible postwar economic benefit to Britain to outweigh its own commercial and defence interests. As a result, when the government decided in October 1939 to send an industrialist to examine the possibility of purchasing defence equipment from America, it had to dispatch him by the first available ship.[23] Not only did Australia refuse to permit an American air route, but it also refused to develop an alternative air route itself that would have avoided Hawaii and provided an additional aerial lifeline linking Australia to Britain and America.[24]

Similarly, when Richard Casey became the Australian representative to Washington in February 1940, he was assiduous in pushing the British case for greater American involvement in the war against Germany rather than seeking American help for Australia. So close did the relations become between Casey and the British ambassador, Lord Lothian, that they were likened by Lothian to the blades of a pair of scissors.[25] This was especially the case when the 'phoney war' came to a sudden end following the German invasion of Norway and Denmark on 8 April.

The German invasion was a well-executed pre-emptive strike that saw German troops seize Denmark almost overnight and land at several strategic points along the Norwegian coast. The move secured the Swedish iron ore supplies that Britain was about to threaten with its own invasion of Norway. Over the next few weeks, the British infantry forces that had already been landed in Norway, and which were devoid of protective air cover, were quickly routed and evacuated after suffering severe punishment from German aircraft. It emphasised the difficulties faced by infantry when their forces lack control of the air.[26] Now it was up to the Anglo–French forces waiting behind the defensive barrier of the Maginot Line to resist the coming German offensive.

NOTES

[1] Colville diary, 31 December 1939, in John Colville, *The Fringes of Power*, London, 1985, p. 62.

[2] War Cabinet Minutes, 18 January 1940, CRS A2673, Vol. 1, NAA.

[3] Letter, Fairbairn to Menzies, 16 January 1940, CRS A5954, Box 235; 'Motor Car Industry', statement by Menzies, 31 January 1940, CRS A5954, Box 103, NAA; Article by Menzies, *Herald*, Melbourne, 7 February 1940.

[4] Letter (copy), Sir Clive Baillieu to M. H. Baillieu, 11 March 1940, AA 1970/559, Bundle 2, High Commissioner Bruce — Miscellaneous Papers — 1939–1945, NAA.

[5] Butlin, *War Economy 1939–1942*, p. 489.

[6] Letter, Bruce to Menzies, 2 January 1940, CRS M103, 'January–June 1940', NAA.

[7] Letter, Bruce to Menzies, 6 February 1940, CRS M103, 'January–June 1940', NAA.

[8] Letter, Menzies to Bruce, 22 February 1940, CRS M103, 'January–June 1940', NAA.

[9] ibid.; War Cabinet Minutes, 5 February 1940, CRS A2673, Vol. 1, NAA.

[10] Allan Martin, *Robert Menzies: A Life*, Vol. 1, Melbourne, 1993, pp. 24–31, 274–6.

[11] Cable No. 72, Bruce to Menzies, 26 January 1940, *DAFP*, Vol. 3, Doc. 34; See also other relevant documents in this volume.

[12] Martin Gilbert, *Finest Hour*, London, 1983, pp. 130–1.

[13] See *DAFP*, Vol. 3, Docs 27, 42, 89 and 111; P. G. Edwards, *Prime Ministers and Diplomats*, Melbourne, 1983, p. 124.

[14] Australia had had a trade commissioner in Japan since 1935, with his title being changed in 1937 to government commissioner. See *DAFP*, Vol. 3, Docs 405, 418 and 441.

[15] Cable, Prime Minister's Department to Bruce, 5 February 1940, *DAFP*, Vol. 3, Doc. 41.

[16] Cable No. 127, Bruce to Menzies, 17 February 1940, CRS M100, 'February 1940', NAA; Cable, Menzies to Bruce, 21 February 1940, *DAFP*, Vol. 3, Doc. 70.

[17] Cable, Prime Minister's Department to Bruce, 9 April 1940, *DAFP*, Vol. 3, Doc. 128.

[18] Cabinet minutes, 29 March 1940, and Memorandum by Cameron, 'Economic Relations with United Kingdom Government', CRS A2697, Vol. 3, NAA.

[19] War Cabinet Conclusions, 23 January 1940, CAB 65/5, W.M. 21(40), PRO.

[20] War Cabinet Conclusions, 10 February 1940, CAB 65/5, W.M. 38(40), PRO.

[21] Letter, Menzies to Bruce, 22 February 1940, CRS M103, 'January–June 1940', NAA.

[22] Letter, McEwen to Casey, 27 May 1940, CRS A3300, Item 91, NAA.

[23] See Correspondence file concerning Trans-Pacific Air Service, CRS A461, I 314/1/4, Part 2; War Cabinet Minutes, 5 October 1939, CRS A2673, Vol. 1, NAA.

[24] War Cabinet Minutes, 4 and 29 April 1940, CRS A2673, Vol. 2, NAA.

[25] See CRS A3300, Vol. 1, NAA; R. G. Casey, *Personal Experience 1939–46*, London, 1962, p. 43.

[26] It was a lesson that the ageing Churchill was slow to learn, as many Australian troops would find to their cost in Greece and Singapore.

FIVE

'unprepared, muddled, and confused'

Even though the Norwegian fiasco was largely Churchill's design, it was Prime Minister Neville Chamberlain who had to pay the political cost for it. And it was the wily Churchill who reaped the benefit on 10 May when he assumed the prime ministership of a new coalition government. He was not the only candidate for the post. Both the foreign secretary, Lord Halifax, and a former prime minister, David Lloyd George, were each touted for the job by factions within Westminster.[1] Of the candidates, only Churchill wanted an all-out war with Germany until it was utterly defeated. This commitment to total war required the gathering together of all imperial resources for the titanic struggle in Europe. There could be no diversion to the Pacific to meet possible threats or even, as it turned out, actual ones. Also central to Churchill's strategy was the need to draw the Americans into the war in Europe, even at the price of provoking war with Japan in the Pacific.

As it happened, the war widened out suddenly and dramatically to Hitler's design rather than Churchill's. On the same day that Churchill was made prime minister, German forces crossed into Holland and Belgium, outflanking the much-vaunted, but necessarily stationary, Maginot Line before swinging around to lunge towards the heart of France. It was 'a most glorious spring day', wrote Britain's General Sir Alan Brooke in his diary, as he prepared his forces to fight 'what must become one of the greatest battles in history!'.[2] It would also be one of the shortest. Belgium had maintained its neutrality until being invaded, thereby preventing the British and French from taking up defensive positions in that country. Only after the Germans had crossed the Belgian border were the Allied armies allowed in. And then it was too late. While Churchill battled to control the fast-deteriorating situation in Europe, the unexpectedly easy German successes had ramifications for the Pacific where the Dutch colonies were now cut off from Holland like so much windblown fruit. If France also fell, it would add Indo-China and the French Pacific islands to the territories ripe for gathering by the Japanese.

Australia, hostage to its past policies, reacted to the unfolding events in Europe with much alarm; but there was still little action directed towards its own local protection. Earlier, the government had decided to produce aircraft locally as a way around the difficulty of purchasing aircraft from Britain's overtaxed factories. It would also create manufacturing skills and capacity that could be switched to civilian purposes, such as car manufacture, once the war was over. The initial plan was to manufacture 180 two-engine Beaufort aircraft, the first 90 for purchase by Britain, after which Australia would take, by late 1941 at the earliest, the second 90 for itself. The planes were designed for sea reconnaissance and bombing in line with the British opinion that the threat to Australia would be posed by occasional German cruiser raids on its shipping.

Following the German attack on Denmark and Norway, it no longer seemed wise to rely mainly on the production of the Beauforts and to anticipate only the limited scale of attack that they were designed to counter. But a proposal to purchase 49 Hudson aircraft from the United States caused serious dissension within the government amid fears that the Hudsons would make the Beauforts, when they were eventually produced, appear outdated by comparison and fit only for training purposes. The treasury remained cost-conscious despite the deteriorating war situation and proposed that Australia make do with the training aircraft supplied by

Britain under the Empire Air Training Scheme. Though Menzies was opposed to the Hudson proposal, the combined weight of the chiefs of staff forced him to give way. The powerful defence department head, Frederick Shedden, warned that 'it would be risky to take the responsibility of not adopting their decision, unless financial considerations absolutely preclude such a course'. He pointed out to Menzies that the worsening situation 'may focus local public opinion on the adequacy of our local Defence measures even more than on our Empire contribution'.[3] So the purchase of Hudsons went ahead.

So too did the commitment of Australian troops to the European theatre proceed, although there was a brief pause while the government considered the possible implications for the Pacific of Germany's westward moves. There was also the worry of the Italians possibly joining the German side and challenging the Anglo–French naval forces in the Mediterranean. On 30 April, in the expectation that this might occur, the Dominions Office had suggested that the second and third convoys of the AIF should be diverted to Britain rather than proceed on to the Middle East. For a time, Australia overruled the advice of the Dominions Office and halted one convoy at Colombo and the other at Fremantle until it had assurances about the effects on the Pacific of the latest developments in Europe. Until March 1940 the three Australian chiefs of staff had been British officers on secondment from London. After the death of General Squires in March, an Australian, Sir Brudenell White, was hauled from retirement and appointed chief of the general staff (CGS). White had served in the Boer War and the First World War, had trained at the British Army Staff College and had spent three years at the British War Office. He was 64 when appointed CGS. With White now in attendance, the chiefs recommended that the advice of the Dominions Office should be 'conformed to unreservedly'. Although the Australian war cabinet demurred at accepting this advice, it was only until it had also received advice from the British chiefs of staff, which was hardly likely to differ from that of their subordinates in the Antipodes.[4]

In the event, Italy held its hand and the Dominions Office withdrew its advice for the diversion of the convoys. Instead, Britain requested the power to divert the convoys without reference to Australia if Italy again seemed likely to enter the war and so threaten the passage of the convoys through the Red Sea. The war cabinet agreed to the British request on the understanding that it was for the safety of the convoy, but asked that any such decision be communicated to Australia for its agreement. Australia's concurrence would be largely a matter of form.[5] The episode revealed once again how the government was giving little consideration to local defence. Britain's difficulties in Norway and the possibility of Italy entering the war were precisely the sort of events likely to entice Japan into adopting a more aggressive policy. Yet this aspect of the strategic situation received little immediate consideration in Canberra.

Menzies ensured that the Anglophile advice of Bruce and the 'Australian' chiefs of staff received a good hearing in cabinet. After seven months of war, his political survival remained at the top of his personal agenda. He could not acknowledge that Australia's survival and his own could be pursued at one and the same time: that by energetically working for Australia's survival, he would be ensuring his own. On 2 May, as London grappled with the growing political and military crisis, Menzies informed Chamberlain that the possibility of his attendance at a proposed meeting in London of dominion prime ministers would depend on the political situation in Australia at the time of the conference and when the forthcoming federal election was to be held. As well, Menzies added, there was the 'necessity of continual watchfulness over [the] Australian war effort', though this too had 'political implications'.[6]

If anything should have rushed Australia to action stations in the Pacific, it was the German invasion of the Low Countries, not only because of its European implications but because of the instability it caused in the Pacific. Instead, Menzies blithely relayed to his war cabinet on 13 May the advice of his chiefs of staff that 'no military action was necessary at present in addition to that already in hand'. This bland pronouncement apparently caused consternation among some of his colleagues who rejected his advice and agreed to accelerate the war measures already approved and even to examine the possibility of increasing them. It was not a full-blooded roar of disapproval for Menzies' complacency, but it was a sign of his colleagues sensing that the contributions to imperial defence had left Australia dangerously exposed. However, this did not stop them deciding on 14 May to dispatch to Britain a large proportion of Australia's stock of small arms ammunition and to examine the 'practicability of accelerating deliveries [of other munitions] to the United Kingdom and the effect this would have on the requirements of the Australian Defence Services'.[7]

By 21 May the German tank columns had struck deep into France and the outlook was becoming increasingly gloomy for the French army and the British expeditionary force that was fighting alongside them. Churchill's mind was already turning towards the dogged defence of Britain itself.[8] While Britain anxiously counted its meagre stock of rifles, the Australian government was beginning to accelerate its own war effort, though much of it was destined for the defence of Britain. At the war cabinet on 21 May, the Australian industrialist Essington Lewis was appointed director-general of munitions supply with direct access to Menzies and given the 'greatest possible degree of freedom from ordinary rules and regulations'. Newspaper proprietor Sir Keith Murdoch was appointed director-general of information and given similarly wide-ranging powers and responsibilities. A director-general of recruiting was also appointed. As a mark of the deteriorating situation, and perhaps at last betraying official doubts about the Singapore strategy, approval was given for a dry dock to be constructed in Sydney capable of accommodating capital ships, that is battleships and aircraft carriers, although it would not be completed until after the crisis year of 1942 had passed.[9] These were dramatic responses to a critical situation, but they were also largely cosmetic, especially with regard to the vital defence of Australia.

On 22 May, Australia allowed the Admiralty to divert the two British cruisers it had been promised in 1939 and which were finally en route to Australia. It also agreed to recruit and train nearly 2000 sailors for various duties outside the Australian naval station. And approval was given for the raising of a third army division for use overseas. Although the government baulked at the recommendation of General White that it concentrate its 'further efforts on the raising of forces for service abroad rather than on provision for home defence', it noted that training for the militia, Australia's home defence force, might have to be postponed until 1941. As for the acceleration of munitions production, the war cabinet approved the expenditure of £425 000 to establish extra production capacity for ammunition and explosives while simultaneously approving the diversion to Britain of substantial quantities of mortar and other shells.[10]

Six days later, in the midst of the Dunkirk evacuation, Australia agreed to release to Britain the 49 Hudson aircraft that it had on order in the United States and to dispatch an RAAF Hudson squadron to Singapore in order to release a British squadron for use elsewhere 'in accordance with the principles of Empire Defence'. All these decisions were predicated on the assumption and the promise that they would be reciprocated by Britain if Australia experienced a similar level of threat. Although Australia was not yet making the all-out war effort that the situation now demanded, it was making real sacrifices in its own defence position to shore up the embattled British position. As the chiefs of staff indicated to the war cabinet, the measures adopted would 'naturally reduce the scale of Australian defence ultimately aimed at' although they would 'not reduce the scale that has been existing up to now'. Cold comfort indeed. But the war cabinet fell in with this advice, apparently agreeing with the chiefs on 'the vital and immediate necessity for reinforcing the United Kingdom'.[11]

The German *Blitzkrieg* into France had confirmed the worst fears of Menzies and Bruce. They had always doubted the ability of the Allies to secure victory against Germany and they now began to foresee, from their separate positions on opposite sides of the world, the unthinkable: that Britain might succumb instead to the Germans. Australia was kept ignorant of the parlous position in France. The British government refused to answer Menzies' requests for detailed information and did not inform him of the evacuation from Dunkirk until it was almost over and had been made public by the BBC. In the absence of information, Menzies relied heavily on the pessimistic opinions of Bruce and quickly and correctly assumed, to the consternation of the British war cabinet, that France was in imminent danger of collapse.[12]

This had important implications for the disposition of Australian troops, with two convoys of the AIF already arrived in the Middle East and a third on its way. In the light of the European situation, the question arose again of diverting this third convoy to Britain. The Australian war cabinet, though, was opposed to splitting the AIF between the Middle East and Britain and suggested instead that they be sent either to South Africa or India for the completion of their training before being reunited with the troops from the previous convoys and deployed in an operational theatre. Menzies did not share his colleagues' misgivings and asked Bruce to inform Britain that he would be 'strongly advising' them to accept Britain as the troops' destination.[13]

On 25 May, Bruce met with the new first lord of the Admiralty, A. V. Alexander, to explain the Australian disquiet and to satisfy his concerns about the naval preparations for a German invasion of Britain. Alexander simply brushed off Bruce's questions, providing no information about his plans other than to say that the navy would do its best and that his admirals were 'full of beans'. However plans were being made and they had possibly dire implications for Australia. On the day of Bruce's meeting with Alexander, the chiefs of staff reported to the war cabinet on the implications of a French collapse, including its effect on Singapore, a base still judged to be 'very important for economic control, particularly of rubber and tin'. They made the awful admission that a French defeat would make it 'most improbable that we could send any naval forces there, and reliance would have to be placed upon the United States to safeguard our interests'.[14] This was a view that destroyed Australia's whole understanding of imperial defence and should have immediately called into question any further Australian contributions overseas. But Bruce did not think to question Alexander on this vital aspect of the changed circumstances now facing Britain and its dominions. And Britain was slow to alert Australia to the implications for Singapore and the Pacific.

On 30 May, the dominions secretary, Lord Caldecote, assured Menzies that even the possible collapse of France and entry of Italy into the war would still leave Britain with 'every intention of maintaining the security of our vital interests in the Near East and of course in the Far East'.[15] Two weeks later, with Italy now in the war and France almost out of it, Britain finally provided Menzies with a more realistic assessment of its ability to uphold its end of the imperial defence bargain. It revealed for the first time

Britain's determination to secure its interests in the Mediterranean at the possible cost of those in the Far East. In order to 'hold Egypt', Britain intended to 'retain a Capital ship fleet based at Alexandria as long as possible' from where it would also 'exercise a restraining influence on Turkey and the Middle East'. In the event of Japan also declaring war, Britain admitted it would be 'most unlikely that we could send adequate reinforcements to the Far East' and would 'therefore have to rely on the USA to safeguard our interests there'. This gloomy prognosis was balanced by an overoptimistic forecast for British plans against Germany which suggested that a combination of naval blockade, bombing and internal revolt could bring Germany to its knees within a year.[16]

Menzies seems to have seized upon the optimism regarding Germany and brushed off the pessimism about the Pacific. On 17 June, he pledged Australia's full support for Churchill's decision to fight on and promised to follow Britain into 'whatever sacrifice victory may demand'.[17] Eleven days later, with German troops in Paris, Britain advised Menzies of the naval implications of the French collapse. It claimed that Britain had formerly been prepared to 'abandon the Eastern Mediterranean and dispatch a fleet to the Far East relying on the French Fleet in the Western Mediterranean to contain the Italian Fleet'. Now, though, Britain had to 'retain in European waters sufficient naval forces to watch both the German and Italian Fleets and we cannot do this and send a fleet to the Far East'. This should have been the introduction to a cable urging Australia to greater self-reliance in the absence of the fleet. But it was neither used as such by Britain nor read that way by Australia. Instead, London used it as an argument for Australia to denude itself still further of men and equipment, asking that Australia send a division of troops and two squadrons of aircraft to defend Malaya.[18]

In the absence of ships at Singapore, there was little sense for Australia in protecting an empty naval base. But there was much sense for Britain in denying to Japan and the Axis powers the rubber and tin resources of Malaya. With the collapse of France, British hopes for victory against Germany rested more than ever on a naval blockade stopping the flow of essential commodities. Rubber and tin were high on this list and the defence of Malayan rubber trees assumed a higher importance in British plans than the defence of the nearby naval base at Singapore that had never seen a British fleet and now probably never would.[19] But Australia remained transfixed by the vision of British ships steaming to its rescue and reacted agreeably to the British request on the assumption that its troops would be protecting the base at Singapore rather than the bowls of latex attached to the bases of countless rubber trees in the Malayan hinterland.

Both Britain and Australia were in positions that they had always sought to avoid. Britain was at war with a combination of European powers but with no European allies capable of balancing its strength at sea with a numerically strong army on land. Australia had been committed by the system of imperial defence to a distant war, and had allowed its local defence to languish, only to discover that the promised British naval protection in the Pacific was, at best, problematic. Though both countries were facing desperate times, their reactions were quite different. Under Churchill, and with its danger more immediate, Britain battened down its island fortress and prepared to withstand whatever Hitler cared to throw at it. Under Menzies, Australia certainly accelerated its lacklustre war effort but much of the benefit was still destined for Britain. This was despite increasing concern in the Australian press about the state of its local defences.

With the unthinkable prospect of Britain being invaded now looking like an imminent possibility, the Australian press was worried that Australia might soon be in Britain's position and have to face a Japanese invasion. There was little indication from the flaccidity and direction of the government's response that it fully appreciated the dreadful possibilities of the dominion's new-found predicament. On 7 June, the Sydney *Daily Telegraph* had called on Menzies to smarten up his bumbling administration and go to the United States to buy aircraft and other war supplies, warning that Australia was 'as unprepared, muddled, and confused as Britain was 18 months ago'.[20] But Menzies had already agreed to hand over to Britain the aircraft it had on order in the United States and remained more concerned with protecting Britain from the present danger of a likely German invasion than in protecting Australia from the future danger of a possible Japanese invasion. Nevertheless, with an election in the offing, the public disquiet had to be allayed.

On 12 June, Menzies called together his defence chiefs to meet with Murdoch only to find that the disquiet was more than justified. General White advised that a limited mobilisation of the militia to meet the heightened possibility of invasion would see 202 000 men being called up; but he confessed that the army could not contemplate such a figure since there was insufficient equipment with which to arm them. At the most, he could envisage equipping a home defence force of 130 000. But Australia had nowhere near that number of personnel trained for the required four months and returned to civilian employment ready to be called upon in an emergency. After nearly twelve months of war, and with much of its trained manpower dispatched overseas, White did not have even 75 000 trained men on hand in Australia, about a third of the number required for a limited mobilisation.[21]

The elderly White was still comforted by illusions about the promised British fleet, assuring Murdoch that distance from Japan was Australia's best safeguard since 'no bolt from the blue could descend upon you, and until the British Navy is defeated you cannot have anything of strength descend upon you very suddenly'. He remained committed to calling up only part of the militia at a time to minimise disturbance to the civilian population and to economise on 'equipment, accommodation and clothing, as well as meeting civil needs as far as possible'. Even when the planned 130 000 personnel had been trained, he conceded that it would only be sufficient to defend against raids rather than an invasion. If an invasion occurred, there was little that could be done since the guns and ammunition on hand would not last the defenders more than a month. As Murdoch observed, 'that is what you cannot tell the public'.[22]

Again, White took comfort from his conviction that a Japanese invasion would only be mounted after the unthinkable had occurred: if the Royal Navy was 'wiped off and Japan had complete control'. In such an eventuality, White echoed previous British advice in claiming that even the most desperate defence by Australia would not be able to withstand the Japanese for more than six months. Under further questioning from Murdoch, who had played such a crucial role in pulling the plug on the disastrous Gallipoli campaign of 1915, White conceded that his limited call-up of the militia was determined by financial considerations rather than the level of threat Australia was now likely to face. He agreed that he could 'enlarge our camps very considerably at a considerable expense. There are money limits. The amounts spent on these hutted quarters horrify me, knowing that at the end of the war they will be debris.' In addition, there was a serious shortage of instructors, caused by the drain of trained men to the Middle East, while the reserve of ammunition was seriously depleted after supplying fifty million rounds to Britain. A survey of strategic raw material stocks revealed a similarly sorry state with, in some cases, no stocks on hand at all.[23]

Although one participant at the meeting suggested that Australia could overcome the equipment shortage by mass-producing a simpler standard of equipment more commensurate with the country's industrial base and allowing for a large, lightly armed and mobile army more suited to the defence of the expansive continent, the suggestion was not taken up. Instead, and on the spur of the moment, Menzies gave his production supremo, Essington Lewis, authority to investigate the local manufacture of tanks, of which Australia presently had none, after Murdoch had mentioned that the 'public would love to know you are making tanks'. This off-hand decision led quickly to a full-scale development program that absorbed much money and manpower before being wound up in 1943 without producing one operational tank. At the same time as approving this program, Menzies rejected the idea of industrial conscription to boost munitions production, claiming that it would only cause trouble with the trade unions which were led by 'simply impossible people', many of them communists. So the public were to be dazzled with the promise of tanks while the government and its defence chiefs remained as dependent as ever on the promised ability of the Royal Navy to intercept and defeat an invasion force before it reached Australia's relatively defenceless shores.[24]

It might have been an opportune moment to begin looking also to the United States for naval protection. Although Menzies did adopt a suggestion from Bruce and Churchill to make an appeal to President Roosevelt for aircraft and pilots, it was for the defence of Britain rather than Australia. In his private message to the American president, made against the dramatic backdrop of British troops fighting a desperate rearguard action on the beaches of Dunkirk, Menzies conjured up the spectre of a total capitulation by Britain and the loss of the Royal Navy to Germany.[25] Although it has been claimed that these appeals 'represent a noteworthy stage in the development of Australian foreign policy',[26] this is hardly sustainable by the facts. After all, Menzies was acting on the advice of Bruce and with the encouragement of Churchill to enlist American support for Britain's cause in Europe. There was little attempt to replace, or even supplement, Britain with America as the guarantor of Australian security in the Pacific.

Yet that was what Australia desperately needed. Instead, it adopted an awkward ostrich-like posture, afraid to make energetic arrangements for its own defence for fear of antagonising the Japanese. Thus, when considering the position of the nickel-rich French island of New Caledonia, just 800 kilometres by bomber or battleship from Brisbane, Australia was loath to interfere with its control in the wake of France's fall. A proposal before the war cabinet on 18 June for Australia to occupy the island was dismissed for fear of the Japanese reaction and Australia's inability to hold it in the face of Japanese action. It might also provoke the Japanese to seize the Dutch East Indies. The fears of the government's military chiefs raised new doubts about the country's defence preparedness, doubts that were confirmed when it was admitted that the scale of munitions production was designed only to meet a minor attack. Menzies tried to allay the consequent alarm among his colleagues by assuring them that this was an initial objective and that the director-general of munitions had 'a mandate for the production of the greatest possible quantity in the shortest possible time'.[27] As for New Caledonia, Australia continued to pursue an ultra-cautious policy, with the external affairs department even arguing that Australia's interests would be served best by New Caledonia coming under Vichy French jurisdiction rather than invite possible Japanese intervention by encouraging a Free French administration.[28]

The suddenness of the Anglo–French collapse in Europe seriously exacerbated Australia's defence position but did not weaken Australia's attachment to imperial defence. Although there was some acceleration in defence spending, the main change to Australia's defence armoury was the adoption of an even more craven policy of appeasement towards Japan.

Canberra had always been averse to implementing Britain's blacklist of Japanese firms alleged to be diverting trade to Germany.[29] Although continuing with its ban on the export of iron ore to Japan, Menzies did allow the export of scrap iron to continue while ensuring that news of his decision was kept secret from the Australian public. The war cabinet also decided on 19 June to finally establish a legation in Tokyo 'before the international situation deteriorated further to the disadvantage of the British empire'.[30] The purpose of the legation, though, was to pursue with more vigour the Australian policy of appeasement at the expense of the hard-pressed Chinese.

On 27 June, the Australian cabinet decided that, in the absence of a general settlement in the Pacific, it was in Australia's interest for Japan to continue in its conquest of China. London was informed that Australia 'could not contemplate being at war with the Japanese' and requested that Britain 'persuade the United States to allow their Fleet to remain in the Pacific' as a deterrent to the Japanese.[31] However, any move of the United States fleet to the Atlantic was counted by Churchill as a positive move towards embroiling it in war with Germany, and therefore to be applauded.

Japan was even then testing the British resolve in Asia now that it was fighting for its life in Europe. It demanded that Britain withdraw its garrison at Shanghai and close the Hong Kong frontier and the Burma Road, both being important Chinese lifelines to the outside world. If it acceded to the Japanese, Britain would offend the Americans, who were committed to a Chinese victory. On the other hand, if Britain rejected the demands it might provoke the Japanese to attack Britain's distant outposts. In such an event, there was little likelihood of the Americans lending their active support despite their backing of China. This was made plain to the British war cabinet on 29 June when Lord Lothian advised from Washington that, with Roosevelt facing a presidential election in November, America was 'unlikely to use force in defence of British or French interests in the Far East' and would leave Britain 'to rely on their own resources'.[32] Britain's ability to resist the Japanese demands, and to postpone the reckoning for Australia, would depend on the outcome of the air battle that was even then beginning to take shape in the skies over Britain.

NOTES

1 David Day, *Menzies and Churchill at War*, Sydney, 2001, pp. 18–19.

2 Alanbrooke diary, 10 May 1940, in Danchev and Todman (eds), *War Diaries*, London, 2001, p. 59.

3 Teleprinter messages M.1663 and M.1672, Shedden to Menzies, 16 and 17 April 1940; Defence Committee Minute, 17 April 1940; Report by Treasury Finance Committee, 17 April 1940; all in CRS A5954, Box 232, NAA.

4 War Cabinet Minutes, 1 May 1940, CRS A2673, Vol. 2, NAA.

5 War Cabinet Minutes, 8 May 1940, CRS A2673, Vol. 2, NAA.

6 Cable No. 197, Menzies to Chamberlain, 2 May 1940, PREM 4/43A/11, PRO.

7 War Cabinet Minutes, 13 and 14 May 1940, CRS A2673, Vol. 2, NAA.

8 Gilbert, *Finest Hour*, p. 376.

9 War Cabinet Minutes, 21 May 1940, CRS A2673, Vol. 2, NAA.

10 War Cabinet Minutes, 22 May 1940, CRS A2673, Vol. 2, NAA.

11 War Cabinet Minutes, 28 May 1940, CRS A2673, Vol. 2, NAA.

12 War Cabinet Minutes, 16 May 1940, CRS A2673, Vol. 2, NAA.

13 War Cabinet Conclusions, 26 and 29 May, 5, 13 and 16 June 1940, CAB 65/7, W.M. (40)139, 146, 155, 165 and 168, PRO; Cable, Menzies to Bruce, 18 May 1940, *DAFP*, Vol. 3, Doc. 253.

14 Note of interview between the First Lord and Bruce, 25 May 1940, Alexander Papers, AVAR, 5/4/12(a), CC; 'British Strategy in a Certain Eventuality', Report by Chiefs of Staff, 25 May 1940, CAB 66/7, W.P. (40)168, PRO.

15 Cable, Caldecote to Commonwealth Government, 30 May 1940, *DAFP*, Vol. 3, Doc. 317.

16 Cable, Caldecote to Whiskard for Menzies, 13 June 1940, *DAFP*, Vol. 3, Doc. 376.

17 Cable, Menzies to Bruce for Churchill, 17 June 1940, *DAFP*, Vol. 3, Doc. 392.

18 Cable, Caldecote to Commonwealth Government, 28 June 1940, *DAFP*, Vol. 3, Doc. 459.

19 Report by the Chiefs of Staff, 25 June 1940, CAB 66/9, W.P. (40)222, PRO.

20 *Daily Telegraph*, Sydney, 7 June 1940.

21 'Notes of Discussion in War Cabinet Room', 12 June 1940, CRS A5954, Box 468, NAA.

22 ibid.

23 ibid.

24 ibid.; 'Production Orders for Armoured Fighting Vehicles', War Cabinet Agendum No. 150/1940, by Brigadier Street, 26 June 1940, CRS A5954, Box 262, NAA.

25 Granatstein, *Canada's War*, p. 120; War Cabinet Conclusions, 23 May 1940, CAB 65/7, W.M. (40)139, PRO; Cables, Menzies to Casey, 26 May and 14 June 1940, *DAFP*, Vol. 3, Docs 280 and 380.

26 P. G. Edwards, 'R. G. Menzies Appeals to the United States, May–June 1940', *Australian Outlook*, April 1974, p. 70.

27 War Cabinet Minute, 18 June 1940, *DAFP*, Vol. 3, Doc. 399.

28 Cable, Menzies to Governor of New Caledonia, 24 June 1940; War Cabinet Minute, 25 June 1940; Departmental Memorandum for Mr J. McEwen, *DAFP*, Vol. 3, Docs 427, 435 and 440.

29 War Cabinet Minutes, 16 May 1940, CRS A2673, Vol. 2, NAA.

30 Cabinet Minutes, 17 June 1940, CRS A2697, Vol. 4, NAA; War Cabinet Minute, 19 June 1940, *DAFP*, Vol. 3, Doc. 405.

31 Cabinet Minutes, 27 June 1940, CRS A2697, Vol. 4; Cable, Menzies to Dominions Office, 27 June 1940, AA CP 290/9, Bundle 1[16]SC, NAA.

32 'Policy in the Far East', Memorandum by Halifax, 29 June 1940, CAB 66/9, W.P. (40)234, PRO.

SIX

'playing for time'

Following the fall of France in June 1940, it was widely expected that the victorious German army would rush on to invade Britain. Only the defensive ditch of the English Channel stood between the vanquished and disorganised British army and their German opponents. Few would have backed a British victory. At the Foreign Office, Sir Alexander Cadogan confided in his diary that Britain was 'completely unprepared. We have simply got to die at our posts — a far better fate than capitulating to Hitler as these damned Frogs have done. But uncomfortable.'[1] The French High Command predicted that Britain would quickly have its neck 'wrung like a chicken's',[2] an opinion that was shared by General Brooke when he returned to Britain after the defeat of his forces in France. Following a quick tour of various army bases, he confessed in his diary on 1 July that 'the shortage of trained men and of equipment is appalling' such that he could not see 'how we can make this country safe against attack'.[3]

In Washington, President Roosevelt desperately tried to ensure that the British fleet would not fall into the hands of the Germans but be transferred instead across the Atlantic to Canada. Even Churchill, despite his public image, tentatively explored with Germany the terms that might be imposed on Britain under an armistice agreement similar to that concluded with the French. In a move to pressure the United States into the war, he encouraged Roosevelt to believe that such a deal might be struck, if not by Churchill then by a replacement prime minister.[4]

Australia also confronted the possibility of a British collapse and the consequences that would have for itself, making it a dominion without an empire. The chief justice of the High Court and a former conservative politician, Sir John Latham, suggested to Menzies on 20 June that Australia and the other British dominions should consider attaching themselves to the United States in the event of Britain being ruled by a puppet government. Though not wanting to overemphasise the possibility of such an event, Latham counselled Menzies to be 'prepared for events which may possibly take place with very little warning and which we are unable by our own efforts to prevent'. Menzies' mind may have already been turning in this direction for he thought Latham's warning was 'undoubtedly a realistic one' and promised to involve both Latham and the governor-general, Lord Gowrie, in any decision concerning a possible transfer of allegiance to Washington.[5]

The French collapse not only left Britain vulnerable to a similar fate but also left the British position in the Mediterranean dangerously exposed to the now-belligerent Italians. With its control of the Suez Canal and Gibraltar, Britain could have corked the Mediterranean and thereby contained the Italian fleet while withdrawing much of its own fleet from that confined sea for use elsewhere in the world. Although this option was urged upon Britain, it was never adopted.[6] This was partly due to concerns such a withdrawal might have on British influence in the Middle East with its important oil supplies, and also due to Churchill's fixation with creating an anti-German coalition among the countries of the Balkans and Turkey that could strike at what Churchill was wont to call 'Germany's soft underbelly'. This nursery-room notion of Germany as a vulnerable crocodile was developed by Churchill when pushing for the disastrous Gallipoli campaign of the First World War, and much effort and many lives would again be lost in unsuccessfully trying to implement this vision.[7]

The collapse of France also complicated Britain's position in the Far East where it was facing pressure from Japan to close the supply routes to China. Although the United States refused to back up its sympathy for China with armed support for Britain in resisting the Japanese, the Foreign Office urged that Britain take a tough line against the Japanese demands. This tough line, which received the initial support of the war cabinet, would be implemented despite Menzies urging Britain to be 'very careful to avoid any action which would cause Japan to become involved in the war'.[8] But the toughness was short-lived when the chiefs of staff and Churchill combined to reverse the decision for fear that the British bluff would be called by Japan going to war. As the chiefs warned the war cabinet, if Britain adopted

a policy in the Far East which may lead us to war with Japan, having at the same time informed our Dominions that we are unable to render the assistance which we promised them, it seems to us extremely unlikely that Australia and New Zealand will release any further forces for service overseas.

When the war cabinet discussed this report on 5 July, it was also pointed out that British trade in the Far East 'would be put in peril' by a war with Japan.[9] For once, it seemed that British policy and Australia's expressed interest seemed to coincide rather than collide. In fact, the differences were as deep as ever.

Although Australia was opposed to risking war with Japan, Menzies wanted to avoid war by agreeing with Japan on an overall Far Eastern settlement that would satisfy Japanese economic and territorial ambitions within certain defined limits. While the British retreat in the face of the Japanese demands would buy temporary peace in the Pacific, Australia feared that it would begin a process of retreat with no limit on the extent of Japanese economic or territorial expansion. Since this could have serious consequences for Australia, which feared that the Japanese had designs on its relatively unpopulated northern parts, the dominion made a determined effort once again to convince Britain of the need for a permanent settlement. Bruce told Foreign Office officials of his own ideas for a 'broad settlement' which involved Britain forcing China to the peace table where Japan would be given 'economic opportunity' in China, in the form of a guaranteed market for its consumer goods, while America and Britain would supply capital goods for China's reconstruction. Bruce intended that Britain also open its colonies to Japanese trade while the dominions would consider providing them with greater economic opportunities than they presently enjoyed. Bruce seems also to have intended that other European empires, now under the thumb of the Germans, cede part or all of their territories to the Japanese.[10]

The cost of Bruce's plan for a broad settlement would be borne by the Chinese, who would lose their economic independence; by the British, who would lose commercial advantages within their colonies and perhaps even some of their colonies; and by other European powers and America, who would cede part of their possessions to Japan. In contrast, Australia would be a major beneficiary from any settlement that removed the threat of war with Japan. Bruce also intended that Australia be given an increased share of the Japanese market for its iron ore and wool.[11] Menzies backed the Bruce plan while dismissing the issue of the Burma Road, one of China's main lifelines, as a 'trifle' which should not be 'allowed to stand in the way of a Japanese settlement'. Confiding to Bruce that Australia 'would not relish having to defend ourselves against even a minor attack from Japan in less than a year from now', Menzies advised that his cabinet colleagues were understandably jittery about the confessed inability of Britain to send a fleet to Singapore and this nervousness, he warned, would be heightened by any proposed settlement 'which stops short of being realistic and comprehensive'. A sign of the nervousness was seen in the cabinet's decision to defer sending the requested troops and aircraft to Malaya until it had received a further military report from the British chiefs of staff.[12]

While Australia regarded war with Japan as anathema, Churchill regarded it as such only in so far as it might detract from the war against Germany. In the context of mid-1940, with America unwilling to back Britain militarily against Japan, a Pacific war probably would have spelt doom for Britain in both the Far East and Europe. Churchill's inclination therefore was directed towards appeasing the Japanese with a view to retrieving the position once the war in Europe was over. A broad settlement was not part of Churchill's scheme as it would solidify the Japanese expansion and make it difficult to roll back. However, talks about a settlement were permissible as they bought time and kept Japan out of the war. In the event, Britain managed to provide some scraps for all the hounds snapping at its heels. It partly acceded to the Japanese demand on the Burma Road, closing it for three months over the wet season when traffic would be difficult anyway. During that period, talks would be held with Japan on a wider settlement. So Australia was consoled although, as Halifax conceded privately, Britain's main intention was to buy time rather than achieve a broad settlement. Time would see the battle of Britain decided and the threat of a German invasion of Britain recede over the northern winter.[13]

Despite the worsening situation in the Pacific, Australia continued to hold the United States at arm's length, rejecting a request in early July by Pan American Airways for landing rights in Sydney. After five years of negotiation, the airline was planning to inaugurate a trans-Pacific service to New Zealand and wanted to fly its Australia-bound passengers direct from New Caledonia to Sydney, thereby saving at least a day from a journey that otherwise took them to New Zealand to connect with a Qantas Empire Airways flight.[14] Pan American tried to ridicule the government decision by announcing that Australia-bound passengers would be off-loaded in New Caledonia and put on a yacht for their onward passage to Sydney. Still the government refused to budge, opting instead to ensure that the Qantas flight from Auckland would allow a more timely connection with the Pan American flight and thereby dissuade any passengers from using the yacht option. If this did not work, then a Qantas flight would be sent from Sydney to New Caledonia to fly any passengers opting to go direct by yacht rather than through New Zealand. When the airline then threatened Casey in Washington that it might withdraw its service to New Zealand if Australia remained obdurate, Casey dismissed it as being 'typical of this company's tactics' which were 'notably lacking in frankness and honesty'. He recommended that no landing rights in Australia be given to Pan American without prior discussion with Britain 'who may ask that you make your agreement conditional [upon] certain matters connected [with the] Atlantic service'. So Pan American's plans were thwarted and a direct air link between Australia and the United States was prevented from being established. This was despite the obvious defence advantages for such an air link and in the knowledge that the US Navy had been 'quietly slipping funds to Pan American Airways for the development of civil air bases'.[15] So Australian security again took second place to the possible commercial advantage of Britain, leaving the dominion in self-imposed semi-isolation at a most critical time in its history.

Britain also was enduring a critical time as it prepared to withstand the might of the German air force. In mid-July, Hitler ordered preparations to be organised for a possible invasion of Britain while German bombers were already making raids over British cities, though still on a small scale. It was a brief interregnum before the dogs of war were unleashed again in all their fury. Hoping for a cut-price victory against his last enemy in the west, Hitler made peace overtures, which some in Britain were prepared to entertain. With the last war in mind, Lloyd George argued that Britain would, sooner or later, have to negotiate peace with Germany and described Churchill's policy of total war as a very dubious gamble. For their part, Menzies and Bruce tried to prepare the ground for such a peace by again pressing Britain to formulate definite war aims, ostensibly to counter Hitler's peace proposals.[16] Their real objective was to establish clear negotiating positions on both sides so that the chances of a negotiated settlement could be enhanced.

Churchill was wise to their objective and dismissed any suggestion of formulating war aims more specific than his overriding one of total military victory. Bruce, though, was undeterred and promised Menzies that he would 'hammer at other members of the Government'.[17] But talk of peace was drowned out in the explosive months of August and September 1940 as the earlier, almost tentative German air raids escalated into the nightly terror of the Blitz, with death and destruction raining down upon the doughty populace. Rather than being cowed, the British people reacted with a dogged determination that Churchill was able to mould into a national will to defeat their German enemy. It was all encapsulated in his characteristic V for victory sign. This sign was less encouraging to Menzies, signifying as it did a prolonged period of peril for Australia due to the increased risk of war in the Pacific, as well as ensuring a further battering for Britain and the empire.

In the changed circumstances wrought by Britain's struggle for survival in the skies over England, together with a threatening change of government in Tokyo, Australia reassessed its former support for a broad settlement with Japan in the Pacific. Prompted by Bruce in London, Menzies set out the new Australian view, which was pessimistic about the chances for meaningful discussion with Japan until the course of the battle over Britain was clear. Menzies now urged a policy of 'playing for time in discussions for a general settlement while ... working in as close co-operation as obtainable with the U.S.A., giving way only under *force majeure* on questions which are not absolutely vital'.[18] Once the battle for Britain was won, then the notion of a general settlement could be resuscitated. By contrast, the New Zealanders rejected absolutely the idea of a settlement with Japan, arguing that an appeasement policy was 'no more likely to be successful in the Far East than it was in Europe'. Nevertheless, New Zealand was prepared to follow the British line, with Prime Minister Peter Fraser not wanting 'to add unnecessarily and perhaps uselessly to the difficulties' of the British government 'whose decision on this difficult and delicate matter we have accepted in the past and will no doubt accept in the future'.[19] So the two dominions with the most to lose accepted, albeit with misgivings, the British lead on the Far East on the assumption that Britain had their interests at heart as much as its own. But Britain was fighting for its own survival at home and the interests of the dominions were understandably far from the centre of its own concern.

While the Royal Air Force fended off the aircraft of the Luftwaffe over England, the new government in Tokyo tested the resolve of the British by arresting fourteen British citizens in Japan and Korea. At the same time, the United States increased its pressure on Tokyo by banning the export of aviation spirit to Japan in an attempt to bring the Sino–Japanese war to an end. It only increased the chances of the Japanese striking out to secure the oil reserves of the Netherlands East Indies. This possibility, and how Britain would react to it, presented defence planners with a difficult predicament as they agonised over an assessment of the Far East being prepared in late July for the Australian government, upon which the future dispatch of Australian troops would depend. Churchill argued that any Japanese move against the

NEI would force Britain to declare war since Australia and New Zealand would 'regard our acquiescence as desertion'. The chiefs of staff, though, were perplexed as to where they would find the forces to fight such a war and wished to avoid making any such pledge. They looked to the war cabinet for a political direction while reminding the cabinet that 'Australia has indicated that it is in the light of this appreciation that the decision will be taken as to whether they can spare an additional division for Malaya.'[20]

When the question came before the war cabinet on 29 July, Churchill readily agreed that a Japanese attack on the NEI would provoke Britain to declare war but then jibbed at the notion that Britain would 'resist by force'. Such resistance, if it was to be more than token, could only come at the expense of the British effort in the Mediterranean and this Churchill was not prepared to countenance. With Australian convoys waiting on the British report before they could sail, Churchill instructed the chiefs of staff to prepare a report for the Australians suggesting that Britain would resist a Japanese attack on the NEI. At the same time, though, the Dutch were to be advised that Britain's capacity to assist them would depend on the United States and that the Dutch should sound out the United States government as to what its attitude would be. Britain's attitude was summed up by Churchill's comment on 'the importance of playing for time' in the hope that within several months Britain's position 'might well be much stronger'.[21] So the chiefs were sent away to prepare yet another reassuring report for Australia that was not justified by the prevailing circumstances of the war.

When the report was duly completed, the war cabinet was requested to provide a quick decision as Australia and New Zealand were becoming 'somewhat restive' and were 'reluctant to dispatch further troops until they have received the military appreciation'. The war cabinet secretary, Sir Edward Bridges, advised that the report did not commit Britain to any particular policy if the NEI was attacked. Moreover, it downplayed any threat to Australia while emphasising the importance of Australian reinforcements for Malaya.[22] An additional report, dealing with possible assistance to the Dutch in the event of a Japanese attack on the NEI, admitted that British forces in the Far East were too weak to 'give any appreciable assistance' and argued that any idea of concentrating a fleet at

Singapore would, at present, be 'unsound'. Without active support from the United States, the chiefs considered the maximum British effort would be to 'send one battle-cruiser and one aircraft carrier to the Indian Ocean to be based at Ceylon for the purpose of protecting our vital communications and those round the Cape to the Middle East'.[23] This was an admission of British priorities that would see its reinforcements concentrated in the Indian Ocean, leaving Singapore empty of its fleet and Australia devoid of its promised naval cover. However realistic and attuned to Britain's national interest, such a report could never be revealed to Australia.

The pessimistic overtones of the reports posed a problem for the war cabinet when it met to consider them on 8 August, threatening to discourage the Australians from sending further forces overseas, particularly to Malaya. Churchill's solution was to gloss over the supposed pessimism of the chiefs with an optimistic appreciation of his own, sent by cable to Menzies, that would conceal Britain's weakness in the Far East and the greater priority that it was giving to the Mediterranean. Churchill's cable brimmed with an optimism that his chiefs clearly did not share. He told Menzies that the Japanese would not go to war unless Germany had successfully invaded Britain and that, in its yielding policy towards Japan, the British government had 'always in mind [Australia's] interests and safety'. While Churchill knew that Roosevelt would not threaten his presidential election chances by reacting militarily to a Japanese attack on the NEI, he claimed that the American fleet remained 'a grave preoccupation to the Japanese Admiralty'. To further allay the Australian concern, Churchill declared that Britain would 'of course defend Singapore which, if attacked, which is unlikely, ought to stand a long siege'. He also promised to 'base on Ceylon a battle cruiser and a fast aircraft carrier' as a 'very powerful deterrent upon hostile raiding cruisers', although without advising that this meagre commitment of vessels was meant for the protection of the Middle East reinforcement route rather than for the protection of distant Australia.[24]

As for the long-promised Singapore fleet, Churchill suggested that the strengthened British fleet in the Mediterranean could 'at any time be sent through the [Suez] Canal into the Indian Ocean or to relieve Singapore', although he admitted that this would not be done 'even if Japan declares war' but only when 'it is found to be vital to your safety'. Again, it was obvious that Churchill was making a promise that he confidently believed would never have to be implemented. As he assured Menzies, a serious Japanese invasion of Australia, which would be the trigger for sending the fleet from the Mediterranean, was 'very unlikely'. Nevertheless, in a solemn promise made with the aim of securing the dispatch of further Australian forces and in the expectation that it would never be called upon, Churchill informed Menzies that,

[if] Japan set about invading Australia or New Zealand on a large scale I have explicit authority of Cabinet to assure you that we should then cut our losses in the Mediterranean and proceed to your aid sacrificing every interest except only [the] defence position of this island on which all else depends.[25]

This rash promise, made as the battle for Britain was unfolding, had the effect that Churchill intended. For more than a year, it provided a touchstone to reassure the Australian government whenever it considered the commitment of further forces to the British cause.

NOTES

[1] Cadogan diary, 29 June 1940, in David Dilks (ed.), *The Diaries of Sir Alexander Cadogan O.M. 1938–1945*, London, 1971, p. 308.

[2] Arthur Bryant, *The Turn of the Tide*, London, 1957, p. 189.

[3] Alanbrooke diary, 1 July 1940, in Danchev and Todman (eds), *War Diaries*, p. 90.

[4] Warren Kimball, *Forged in War*, New York, 1997, pp. 54–5.

[5] Letters, Latham to Menzies, 20 June 1940, and Menzies to Latham, 22 June 1940, Latham Papers, MS 1009/1/5459, NLA.

[6] W. K. Hancock, *Smuts*, Vol. 2, Cambridge, 1968, p. 354; R. A. Callahan, *Churchill: Retreat from Empire*, Tunbridge Wells, 1984, pp. 102–03.

[7] See A. J. P. Taylor, 'The Statesman', in A. J. P. Taylor (ed.), *Churchill: Four Faces and the Man*, London, 1969, pp. 42–3.

[8] 'Policy in the Far East', Memorandum by Halifax, 29 June 1940, CAB 66/9, W.P. (40)234 and War Cabinet Conclusions, 1 July 1940, CAB 65/8, W.M. 189(40), PRO.

[9] 'Policy in the Far East', Report by the Chiefs of Staff, 4 July 1940, CAB 66/9, W.P. (40)249, PRO; War Cabinet Conclusions, 5 July 1940, CAB 65/8, W.M. 194(40), PRO.

[10] Talk with Sir Horace Seymour and Mr Ashley Clarke, 5 July 1940, CRS M100, 'July 1940'; Cable No. 520, Bruce to Menzies, 6 July 1940, CP 290/7, Bundle 2, Item 12, NAA.

[11] ibid.

[12] Cable, Menzies to Bruce, 9 July 1940, CP290/9, Bundle 1[16]SC, NAA.

[13] Letter, Halifax to Sir Samuel Hoare, 17 July 1940, Templewood Papers, XIII, 20, CUL; War Cabinet Conclusions, 10 and 11 July 1940, CAB 65/8, W.M. 199 and 200(40), PRO.

[14] War Cabinet Minutes, 11 July 1940, CRS A2673, Vol. 3, NAA; See also Letter (copy), Fairbairn to Massey-Greene, 13 July 1940, and given to Casey in Washington by W. S. Robinson, 21 August 1940, CRS A3300, Item 89, NAA.

[15] See CRS A461, I314/1/4, Part 3, NAA; Letters, Casey to Group Captain Pirie at the British Embassy, 26 April 1940, Pirie to Casey, 8 May 1940, and Cable No. 201, Casey to Minister for Air, 18 August 1940, CRS A3300, Items 87 and 89, NAA.

[16] Talk with Lloyd George, 23 July 1940, 11/1940/74, Liddell Hart Papers, KC; See also Channon diary, 24 July 1940, in R. R. James (ed.), *Chips: The Diaries of Sir Henry Channon*, London, 1967, p. 262; Letter and Memorandum, Bruce to Halifax, 21 July 1940, CRS M103, 'July–December 1940', NAA; Cable, Menzies to Bruce, 22 July 1940, *DAFP*, Vol. 4, Doc. 30.

[17] Cable, Bruce to Menzies, 26 July 1940, *DAFP*, Vol. 4, Doc. 36.

[18] Cable, Menzies to Bruce, 25 July 1940, *DAFP*, Vol. 4, Doc. 34.

[19] Cable, Fraser to Commonwealth Government, 30 July 1940, *DAFP*, Vol. 4, Doc. 42.

[20] Minute, Churchill to Ismay, 25 July 1940, quoted in Gilbert, *Finest Hour*, p. 679; 'Far Eastern Policy', Report by the Chiefs of Staff, 27 July 1940, CAB 66/10, W.P. (40)289, PRO.

[21] War Cabinet Conclusions/Confidential Annex, 29 July 1940, CAB 65/14, W.M. (40)214; War Cabinet Conclusions, 29 July 1940, CAB 65/8, W.M. (40)214, PRO; Gilbert, *Finest Hour*, p. 686.

[22] 'The Far East. Appreciation by the Chiefs of Staff', 5 August 1940, with covering note by Bridges, CAB 66/10, W.P. (40)302, PRO.

[23] 'Assistance to the Dutch in the Event of Japanese Aggression in Netherlands East Indies', Report by Chiefs of Staff, 7 August 1940, CAB 66/10, W.P. (40)308, PRO.

[24] War Cabinet Conclusions/Confidential Annex, 8 August 1940, CAB 65/14, W.M. (40)222, PRO; Cable, Caldecote to Whiskard, 11 August 1940, *DAFP*, Vol. 4, Doc. 64.

[25] ibid.

SEVEN

'the only battle that counted'

Churchill's grand promise to defend Australia, in return for more of its troops, was couched in deliberately vague terms. It did not specify at what point during a Japanese invasion Britain would rush to Australia's assistance. Churchill implied that it would be only after substantial Japanese forces had lodged on Australian soil but that would probably be too late. It would take several months to assemble and dispatch across the world a naval force sufficiently strong to confront the Japanese. Yet General White had acknowledged in June that there were only enough guns and ammunition in Australia for a month of heavy fighting. Moreover, there was little indication in Churchill's promise as to how many rescuing British ships would come steaming over the horizon in the event of an invasion. The Italian fleet would still need to be contained in the Mediterranean and the considerable British garrison in the Middle East, including important Australian forces, would still need to be protected and sustained.

In fact, Australia shared Britain's concern about the importance of the Middle East and was aware of Britain's relatively weak military position there, with Italian forces in adjacent Libya far outnumbering the British and dominion forces in Egypt. Menzies was as committed as Churchill to defending the British position in the Middle East, acknowledging that Britain's expulsion would 'give spectacular and far-reaching results, involving not only our elimination from a vital sphere but endangering our interests in Iraq, Iran and India, as well as giving encouragement to Japan for acts of further aggression'.[1] By Menzies' tortured logic, Australia was now fighting in the Middle East to preserve peace in the Pacific. In fact, the British and Australian commitment to the Middle East would see Australia placed in deadly peril in the Pacific.

So involved was Australia in defending British interests in the Middle East that Menzies and Bruce argued for even greater British forces to be sent there. With the battle of Britain still undecided, Bruce was particularly concerned after talks with disaffected political and military leaders in London that British and Australian forces in the Middle East were being placed in jeopardy as Britain concentrated its strength, particularly as regards aircraft, in repelling the Germans at home. Instead of appealing for modern fighter aircraft for Australia, of which it still had none, Bruce urged Menzies in early September to impress upon Britain 'our vital interest in [the] Middle East' and to advocate the 'maximum effort there compatible with [the] safety of [the] United Kingdom'. Menzies duly complied, calling on Churchill to make a greater effort to secure the Mediterranean and the Middle East and implying that Britain was overprotected at home.[2] Menzies did not seem to be aware that the more forces that were concentrated in the Mediterranean the less chance there was of a future British fleet being dispatched to the Far East.

With its forces committed to fighting in battlefields as distant as Britain and the Middle East, and preparing to defend Malaya and Australia itself, it is not surprising that the Australian government and its representatives had difficulty in discerning where Australian interests properly resided. So confused was its foreign policy that, for a time in August 1940, Menzies, Bruce and Casey were each pushing a different and conflicting policy towards Japan. At the war cabinet on 2 August, Menzies set out the latest Australian view as being in accord with that of Britain: avoiding war in the Pacific with a mixture of firmness on vital matters and flexibility on others until the situation in Europe was clarified by the ongoing fighting. Only then could the question of a general settlement with Japan be pursued.[3] But agreeing on what was vital and knowing when to be firm were questions fraught with difficulty.

After the Japanese arrest of fourteen British citizens, London retaliated with the tit-for-tat arrest of Japanese citizens in Britain. Though Bruce had supported this action, the government in Australia was not consulted by Britain beforehand. Menzies was alarmed at the danger of these petty provocations escalating into war, warning Britain against what he saw as the tactics of bluff and urging that it pursue a policy that was 'firm but such as will, if possible, avoid war'.[4] On the same day that Menzies was urging, through Bruce, the Australian government's revised policy regarding Japan, Bruce was pursuing activities in the opposing direction. At a private lunch with the Japanese ambassador in London, Bruce set out his plan for a general settlement in the Pacific along the lines he had previously discussed with Menzies but which Menzies now believed to be inappropriate. He also pressed his views on British cabinet ministers known to be sympathetic and encouraged British businessmen with interests in Japan to add their weight to the pressure on the British government.[5] Meanwhile, in Washington, Casey seems to have been influenced by the anti-Japanese lobby in the United States and, on his own initiative, urged Halifax to adopt a firm policy towards Japan. Though Bruce kept his activities concealed from Menzies, the Australian prime minister did learn of Casey's and quickly countermanded him, describing the proposal as calculated to provide 'maximum irritation to Japan by [the] Empire single handed'.[6] Without a guarantee of American support, Britain had to continue playing for time and Australia essentially had to follow the British lead. The dominion's ability to influence events in the Pacific independently was strictly limited and even more so when it appeared to be speaking with three discordant voices.

Australia's readiness to follow the British lead, despite the dramatically changed circumstances of the war, was shown in its delayed agreement to dispatch its forces to Malaya. As soon as it received the much-discussed British military report on the Far Eastern situation, the Australian government seized with relief, and little scrutiny of its unspoken provisos, the accompanying historic promise by Churchill to abandon the Middle East in the event of Australia being seriously invaded. Although the Australian war cabinet would have preferred to send its troops to India rather than Malaya, and to have Britain equip them with artillery and machine-guns rather than have to strip the Australian militia of such weapons, Australia again complied with British wishes.[7] Ironically, the less likely that a British fleet would materialise at Singapore, the more Australia committed personnel and equipment to the protection of the empty naval base.

As Australia made its commitment to Malaya, it retreated from its former firmness towards a possible Japanese attack on the NEI. After trying for so long to obtain a British commitment to treat such an attack as a *casus belli*, Australia now acknowledged that an automatic British commitment would produce war with Japan but would not necessarily produce the means from Britain to fight such a war. Though a Japanese occupation of the NEI would largely neutralise the Singapore naval base, and thereby leave Australia's long-time defence strategy in tatters, the government now wanted Britain 'to take a realistic view of such an act of aggression in the light of our military position at the time'.[8] So much for Australia's policy of firmness towards Japan on vital matters. If the NEI was not considered vital, it is difficult to conceive of anything short of a direct invasion of Australia being considered sufficiently vital. Perhaps even then it would have been argued that, provided Sydney and Melbourne were left inviolate, Australia could live with a partial Japanese occupation as the French were doing with a partial German occupation. Such were the straits to which Australia was reduced by its imperial commitment to the Middle East.

This commitment, together with the ongoing battle for Britain, left Australia's defence seriously imperilled, particularly in the air. And Britain ensured that it remained in that parlous state. In early July, Casey had organised a meeting in New York between representatives of Britain's dominions and an official of the British ministry of aircraft production to press, in Australia's case, for the release of aircraft engines ordered from the United States. Australia was persuaded to channel its request through the Dominions Office in London where it was filed and forgotten. On 21 August, Britain's minister for aircraft production and powerful newspaper baron Lord

Beaverbrook urged the dominions secretary, Lord Caldecote, at least to acknowledge the request. Rather candidly, Caldecote replied that the problem of 'how best to tell the Dominion Governments that we cannot give them what they want has presented some difficulty'.[9] His problem was solved by Bruce, who absolved Britain from any immediate need to respond to Australia's requirements.

Bruce had been given the task of expediting the delivery to Australia of aircraft and of the tools with which to manufacture them. Much too late, Australia was finally taking seriously its air defences and planning to build up an air force of 571 aircraft, mainly for the local defence of the continent. But there was a substantial barrier to achieving this aim in the asthmatic person of Beaverbrook whose considerable energy was directed into producing aircraft to fight the battle of Britain. As Beaverbrook informed the British war cabinet in September, the 'Battle of Britain was the only battle that counted'. Bruce tended to agree. Thus, when pressing Australia's case with Beaverbrook on 27 August, Bruce was careful to assure him of Australia's 'preparedness to fit in with the United Kingdom requirements'. Although Bruce suspected that Beaverbrook was concealing the extent of British aircraft production, with many more aircraft being produced than there were pilots to fly them, he did not press hard for Australia's requirements to be filled.[10]

Apart from his concern for the continuing battle in the skies above him, Bruce was also hamstrung in his efforts to obtain aircraft for Australia by the pressure he had been applying to have aircraft dispatched to the Middle East. As a result, rather than seeking the immediate delivery of the 571 aircraft that Australia required for the planned expansion of the RAAF, Bruce simply requested that Britain agree to a program for the delivery of the planes no matter how extended the program or how much it was hedged about with provisos related to the battle of Britain. Bruce was doing his utmost to protect British interests while appeasing Australian anxieties with a conditional British undertaking of doubtful value. As Beaverbrook acknowledged when pressing his colleagues at the beginning of September to provide such an undertaking, 'the Dominions are completely sympathetic to the urgent, over-riding considerations which prevent our meeting their aircraft requirements just now'. In fact, Bruce was prepared to allow another month for the program of deliveries to be decided, once the position in Britain was clearer, and promised British officials that he would 'try and induce Australia to allow the matter to remain in abeyance until the beginning of October'.[11] It now would take that much longer for Australia to realise that Britain did not intend to supply it with any modern aircraft.

While Whitehall continually delayed a decision on the supply of aircraft for Australia, British factories were producing more aircraft than could be used and the air ministry was busily shipping many of them abroad, mostly to the Middle East. As Beaverbrook announced triumphantly to Churchill on 2 September, the RAF strength had increased by some one thousand aircraft since mid-May, with 720 aircraft having been shipped abroad.[12]

While Bruce was allowing Britain to continue temporising over aircraft supplies for Australia, the question arose of whether to reopen the Burma Road when its three-month closure was completed. No progress had been made in Anglo–Japanese talks, since their course was determined by the outcome of the battle still raging in Britain's skies. Nevertheless, the British ambassador in Tokyo, Sir Robert Craigie, planned in early September to raise with the Japanese the notion of a general settlement. Though such a settlement had been favoured by Bruce, he was concerned that Craigie would go into the talks without a clear sense of what Britain was prepared to concede to the Japanese or of what Britain wanted in return, and without the all-important involvement of the United States.[13]

In fact, Churchill was still intent on playing for time and was neither prepared to confront the Japanese nor to agree to a general settlement that would confirm Japanese supremacy in the Pacific. As Churchill now admitted to his war cabinet, this policy of playing for time would not be abandoned even if Britain won the present battle against the Luftwaffe. Victory in the battle of Britain would not strengthen Britain's position in the Far East, which was caused by the overriding commitment to the Middle East where Churchill was building up forces for a large-scale battle against the Italians. If the Americans were staying on the sidelines, Britain would have to play for time with the Japanese until the European war was fought to a final conclusion. British policy therefore had to continue to 'go some way in offering inducements to Japan, and possibly also to go some way in using threats, but not to commit ourselves irrevocably to forcible action'.[14]

Menzies supported this policy of delay but hoped that victory in the battle of Britain would allow scope for a general settlement in the Pacific. However, when consulted by London, the Australian government was content to allow Britain to decide how best such a settlement could be achieved since Britain could 'best judge the danger of war with Japan'. Implicit in the Australian view was an assumption that British policy would have the security of Australia as a top priority. With *carte blanche* from Australia, and after the most token prior consultation with the dominions, Britain announced in early October its intention to reopen the Burma Road despite the possible risk of it provoking war with Japan.[15]

Beset by hostile forces on so many fronts, Britain was conducting a delicate and potentially dangerous balancing act with its distant interests and obligations in the Pacific. In September, the British chiefs of staff conceded that Singapore's value had shrunk in strategic terms to being just 'a potential base'. Although asserting that it would, even when empty, 'restrict Japan's naval action', the chiefs acknowledged that its main value now lay in the 'exercise of economic pressure and for the control of commodities [Malayan rubber and tin] essential to our own economic structure'. It would also provide a 'footing from which, eventually, we can retrieve the damage to our interests when stronger forces become available'. This suggested that the chiefs expected to lose territory in the Pacific before they could finish off the Germans and turn to confront the Japanese. They did not concede, however, that Australia and New Zealand were in any danger of 'full-scale invasion' unless the Japanese 'had seized Singapore and consolidated her position in the Far East'. In such an event, they repeated Churchill's pledge to abandon the Middle East and spring to Australia's assistance.[16] As usual, Australia desperately wanted to believe in the British assurance, taking it at face value and handing over personnel and equipment in exchange for a blank cheque of doubtful value that could only be banked after the bailiffs had broken down the front door.

Australia's reliance on Britain to preserve the peace with Japan was as misplaced as its reliance on the British defence guarantee. Britain certainly was anxious to avoid a single-handed war against Japan, but Churchill quickly jumped on the Foreign Office when it argued that it was not in Britain's interest 'that the United States should be involved in war in the Pacific'. Nothing could be further from the truth as far as Churchill was concerned. He was so disturbed at the effect of such an argument that he immediately instructed that Britain's ambassadors be clearly informed that 'nothing ... can compare with the importance of the British empire and the United States being co-belligerent'.[17] For Australia, there was the unsettling prospect of its security being sacrificed to the Japanese in order to satisfy the paramount British interest of drawing the Americans into war with Germany by way of a conflict in the Pacific. But the dominion remained blind to its dilemma.

NOTES

[1] Cable, Menzies to Bruce, 8 August 1940, *DAFP*, Vol. 4, Doc. 54.

[2] Cables, Bruce to Menzies, 4 September 1940, and Cable, Commonwealth Government to Caldecote, 7 September 1940, *DAFP*, Vol. 4, Docs 101 and 106; See also Doc. 136.

[3] War Cabinet Minutes, 2 August 1940, CRS A2673, Vol. 3, NAA.

[4] War Cabinet Conclusions, 1 August 1940, CAB 65/8, W.M. (40)217, PRO; Cable, Menzies to Bruce, 6 August 1940, CRS A3300, Item 9, NAA.

[5] Talk with Japanese Ambassador, 6 August 1940, CRS M100, 'August 1940'; Letter, Sempill to Bruce, 19 August 1940, AA1970/559/2, NAA.

[6] Cable No. 120, Menzies to Casey, 12 August 1940, CRS A3300, Item 9, NAA.

[7] Cable, Menzies to Caldecote, 29 August 1940, *DAFP*, Vol. 4, Doc. 84.

[8] ibid.

[9] See Letters, Beaverbrook to Caldecote, 21 August 1940, and Caldecote to Beaverbrook, 24 and 29 August 1940, BBK D/333, Beaverbrook Papers, HLRO.

[10] See PREM 3/33, PRO; War Cabinet Conclusions 27 September 1940, CAB 65/9, W.M. (40)260, PRO; Dalton diary, 27 September 1940, Dalton Papers, LSE; Talks with Sinclair and Beaverbrook, both 27 August 1940, CRS M100, 'August 1940', NAA.

[11] Talk with Beaverbrook, 28 August 1940, CRS M100, 'August 1940', NAA; Letter, Beaverbrook to Caldecote, 1 September 1940, BBK D/333, Beaverbrook Papers, HLRO; Talk with Sir Christopher Courtney, 31 August 1940, CRS M100, 'August 1940', and Talk with Air Commodore Slessor (Air Ministry) and Major Buchanan (Aircraft Production), 2 September 1940, CRS M100, 'September 1940', NAA.

[12] Minute, Beaverbrook to Churchill, 2 September 1940, BBK D/414, Beaverbrook Papers, HLRO.

[13] Cables, Bruce to Menzies, 3 and 5 September 1940, *DAFP*, Vol. 4, Docs 97 and 103; Talk with Major Morton, 6 September 1940, CRS M100, 'September 1940', NAA.

[14] War Cabinet Conclusions, 4 September 1940, CAB 65/9, W.M. (40)241, PRO.

[15] Cable, Menzies to Bruce, 10 September 1940, and Cable, Menzies to Caldecote, 17 September 1940, *DAFP*, Vol. 4, Docs 116 and 121; War Cabinet Minutes, 10 and 16 September 1940, CRS A2673, Vol. 3, NAA; War Cabinet Conclusions, 3 October 1940, CAB 65/9, W.M. (40)265, PRO.

[16] 'Future Strategy', Appreciation by the Chiefs of Staff, 4 September 1940, CAB 66/11, W.P. (40)362, PRO.

[17] War Cabinet Conclusions, 2 October 1940, CAB 65/9, W.M. 264(40); Minute, Churchill to Eden, 4 October 1940, PREM 3/476/10, PRO.

EIGHT

'a first class brawl'

By the beginning of October 1940, the battle of Britain had raged for nearly three months, with the distant throbbing of German bombers causing anti-aircraft guns to beat out their defiant tattoo across the sky while fighter planes screamed in pursuit of the intruders. On the ground, Britons hurried nightly to their shelters while Churchill and his government, huddled in their underground headquarters, made what preparations they could to meet the repeated rumours of invasion. Across the world, Australians gathered round their wireless sets to listen with trepidation to the daily short-wave news, or packed into newsreel cinemas to gaze in horror at the destruction wreaked upon British cities. Gradually, as the dark chill of the northern winter approached, the risk of a German invasion receded. While Britain would be able to rest secure, at least for a time, Australia's predicament in the Pacific was set to worsen.

As Churchill had acknowledged at the beginning of September, a British victory in the air over England would enhance the country's prestige in the Far East, and perhaps help to deter Japan, but would not change Britain's strength there. Its military commitment to the Far East would remain limited due to the greater priority given by Britain to its interests in the Middle East. And the deterrent effect on Japan was difficult to discern. During September, Japan continued its southward march with its troops moving into northern French Indo-China, ostensibly to continue its encirclement of China but coincidentally to bring its aircraft within easier reach of Singapore. As well, Japan signed the Tripartite Pact with Germany and Italy on 27 September, recognising their separate territorial ambitions and agreeing to combine against the United States if it entered the war. As Paul Hasluck wrote later, the pact 'made it more probable than ever that sooner or later, at a moment when the British Commonwealth was most distressed, Japan would strike'. Despite this, the Australian government kept to its commitment to send the 7th Division for garrison duty at Singapore[1] while Churchill took heart from a clause in the Tripartite Pact which was 'aimed plum at the United States'.[2]

Churchill was gambling with Britain's interests in the Far East in order to protect its interests in the Middle East, where he hoped 'to wage war on a great scale'.[3] But this long-term strategy was put at risk when Italian forces broke out from Libya and headed along the narrow coastal plain towards the important British naval base at Alexandria. Outnumbered five to one, the British defenders in Egypt faced the prospect of defeat while Britain faced the ignominious prospect of losing its hold on the eastern Mediterranean and perhaps of being expelled altogether from the Middle East. Australian troops and ships were committed to hold this axis of empire for Britain, with the 7th Division being diverted to the Middle East from its intended destination of Singapore. There were now some 50 000 Australian troops in that theatre and another 60 000 in AIF training camps in Australia. As well, the Australian troops diverted to Britain during the battle for France were sent on to the Middle East to form the basis of the 9th Division, so that by early 1941 three divisions of the AIF were in the Middle East.

Australia was as resolved as Britain that the Middle East must be held and the presence of its troops helped to ensure that its will did not weaken. This was despite the possible implications for its own defence. The Australian commitment to the Middle East not only depleted its reserves of men and equipment at home but reduced Britain's ability to dispatch a fleet to the Far East in the event of hostilities with Japan. The struggle in the Middle East also soaked up the aircraft, tanks, and other equipment surplus to Britain's own defence requirements but of which Australia was particularly deficient. This effectively limited the extent to which Australia could appeal for such equipment for its own defence since it would be at the expense of its troops fighting real battles in the Middle East. Even if such appeals were mounted, Churchill made clear to Menzies in early October that he would not be deflected from his overriding aim of bringing on a great battle with the Italians for control of the Mediterranean.

As a minor part of this grand strategy, and in a move to boost the fortunes of the Free French forces of General Charles de Gaulle, British forces supported the Free French in a naval attack against the Vichy-controlled west African port of Dakar. But the plan went awry when the Vichy forces, reinforced by cruisers, fought back strongly against the besieging British ships which included the Australian flagship, the cruiser *Australia*. The British had counted upon a quick victory and now, for fear of driving the Vichy government further into the arms of the Germans, sensibly withdrew from the fray. Menzies first heard of the failure of the operation when he read of it in his newspaper. Although Australia had never succeeded in throwing off its colonial mentality, being treated in a colonial manner still rankled. So the Dakar dispute produced another spat between Canberra and London.

It was ironic that Australia should become so disturbed over a matter of form rather than substance. There were good reasons for having a serious set-to with London over its refusal to fulfil Australian requirements of aircraft and the effective negation of its repeated commitment to dispatch a fleet to the Far East. But it was over a matter of appearances that Menzies was urged by Bruce to make a stand. In a strongly worded message to Churchill on 29 September, Menzies questioned the decision to attack Dakar without 'overwhelming chances of success' and berated him for not keeping the Australian government informed, which had 'frequently proved humiliating'. As a final dig, Menzies advised Churchill that the Australian government feared that the difficulties in the Middle East, where 'clear cut victory is essential', may have been underestimated.[4]

Menzies' message caused considerable annoyance in Whitehall. With the unanimous approval of his war cabinet, Churchill produced a stinging rebuttal of the Australian criticisms. Dismissing the Dakar attack as just a minor operation, Churchill chided Menzies for not extending a 'broad and generous measure of indulgence' towards Britain for the 'great exertions we have made' in the general war effort. As for the particular criticisms of the attack, he refused to accept that an operation must have an overwhelming chance of success or that the Dakar operation was 'half-hearted'. It was galling for Churchill to receive any criticism of his strategic prowess and particularly so at a time when the greatest achievement of his life, the battle of Britain, was being fought to a successful conclusion. He had outmanoeuvred those people in Britain who had been prepared to accept a compromise peace with Germany only to find a querulous Australian government undermining his authority from afar. Churchill had incurred the displeasure of some of his colleagues in reinforcing the Middle East at the expense of Britain's own defence and now Menzies was suggesting that he had not done enough. Churchill rounded on his Australian counterpart over this, supplying Menzies with details of the British reinforcements and strenuously denying that the 'Mother Country has shirked her share of perils and sacrifice'.[5]

Menzies' critical cable had been sent to Churchill in the immediate wake of the Australian federal election on 21 September when the Labor Party had come close to ousting Menzies from office. His continued tenure in the Lodge depended now on the support of two independent MPs. As one sympathetic observer noted, Menzies' position was 'extremely difficult' as he had 'made so many enemies in politics and has so few real friends'.[6] Menzies was well aware of his vulnerability but remained determined to shore up his crumbling political position and retain his hold on power.[7] This may have been responsible for his craven reaction to Churchill's angry cable.

While humiliating incidents like Dakar might have threatened Menzies' political survival, his position depended even more on a close identification with Britain and its combative prime minister. A vote for Menzies was a vote for Churchill, or so Menzies had implied during the election campaign. As such, any public breach between the two men could have devastating political results. So Menzies was as alarmed by Churchill's cable as Churchill had been angered by Menzies'. In a humiliating backdown, Menzies conceded that his cable had been 'crudely expressed' while denying 'even the faintest suggestion that you or the British Government are half-hearted in policy, spirit or achievement'. He pointed to the political problems that soon might see him removed from office and gushingly proclaimed his pride to be associated 'with the efforts of Winston Churchill and the British people'. Menzies denied suggesting that Britain had 'shirked her share of the perils or sacrifice' in the Middle East but equally defended his own government's contribution in raising naval, air and military forces for Britain's use overseas in the face of 'much public doubt caused by a real fear of what Japan may do'.[8]

The Labor Party had been fuelling such doubts by stressing the need for local defence and highlighting inadequacies in the defence preparations to date. In Britain, party political criticism had been quelled for the duration of the war by the formation under Churchill of a national government linking the Conservative, Labour and Liberal parties. One of the consequences of Australia's close election contest in September was a renewal of calls for the establishment of a national administration in Canberra.[9] But most leading figures in the Labor Party were opposed to such a course. The party was still racked by divisions, especially in New South Wales, and was barely held together by the force of John Curtin's leadership. Curtin was not sufficiently safe from attack to adopt the notion of a national government even if he accepted it as a dire national need. The election result had left the parliament so evenly divided that most Labor tacticians preferred to bide their time in the expectation that they soon would be able to form a government in their own right. As well, bitter experience had taught Labor politicians to be suspicious of supposedly 'national' administrations which were seen as a ruse by conservatives, allied with renegade Labor MPs, to keep the Labor Party out of power. During the First World War, Billy Hughes had formed such a national government after walking out of the Labor Party caucus with his supporters. In the 1930s, a similar government under another renegade Labor MP, Joe Lyons, was formed out of conservative and some Labor MPs, keeping Labor out of power for a decade.[10]

With a national government ruled out, Menzies finally agreed to a compromise suggestion by Curtin, establishing on 28 October an advisory war council of four government and four opposition members. Though this helped to stabilise the political situation for Menzies and to quell the calls for a national government, there was a price to be paid. The Labor members had to be taken into the government's confidence and made privy to decisions on defence. In the privacy of the council room, the Labor members were able to question the rationale of government defence policy and exploit the potential differences among the government ranks on the relative priority of local over imperial defence. They also had the valuable opportunity to interrogate the chiefs of staff about the government's defence effort and the state of the war in the Middle East and elsewhere.

At the first meeting of the council, held on 29 October, Curtin requested information on the 'present disposition of the ships of the R.A.N. and the possibility of disposing them for the defence of the waters to the north of Australia' as well as 'information regarding naval mines and the possibility of arranging for a battleship to be located near Singapore'. Two weeks later, Labor's deputy leader, Frank Forde, followed up Curtin's question by asking for the time it would take RAN units to return in the case of an attack against Australia. He also asked the new chief of the general staff (CGS), Lieutenant General Sturdee, whether Australia was 'in a position to defend herself today' and, if not, 'when it is expected that Australia will be in such a position'.[11] As Curtin's question regarding a battleship for Singapore indicated, the Labor Party, despite its arguing for local defence to be given greater priority, still retained considerable faith in the ability of the Singapore naval base to exercise a deterrent effect upon Japan. Britain's plight in mid-1940 would have also evoked sympathy from Labor politicians and even support for imperial defence. However, while Menzies and his military advisers were puzzling over how to answer the probing questions of their Labor interrogators, military representatives from Britain, Australia and New Zealand were attending a conference in Singapore on Far Eastern defence at which the startling deficiencies in the base's defences were exposed.

British plans had always been premised on defending just the base and on an assumption that an attack would come most likely from seaward by a Japanese fleet. It was now acknowledged that defending Singapore alone would not be sufficient and that the defence of the rubber and tin resources of Malaya was of more importance than the defence of the empty naval base. However, as the newly appointed British commander-in-chief at Singapore, Air Chief Marshal Sir Robert Brooke-Popham, known disparagingly as 'old Pop-off', advised London in late October following the conference with dominion representatives, the present defences were insufficient to prevent a Japanese takeover. While acknowledging that the 'requirements of Singapore must come a bad third to those of the British Isles and of the Middle East', he pressed for the deficiencies in his command to be made good before they were tested by a Japanese attack. He complained that his front-line air strength was 14 per cent of the level recommended by the British chiefs of staff and that there were no modern fighters or long-range bombers. He was also 'very short' of field artillery and had less than half the recommended level of anti-aircraft guns.[12]

The weaknesses now apparent at Singapore, with the much-vaunted naval base shown to be a paper fortress, did not prompt the Australian government to increase its local defences or concentrate its forces at home. Instead, the results of the Singapore conference simply reaffirmed Australia's strategic touchstone — that the defence of Australia hinged on the defence of Singapore — and increased Australia's calls for the island's defence deficiencies to be made good. For its part, Britain looked largely to Australia to fill the gaps. On the advice of his chiefs of staff, Menzies agreed to dispatch to Malaya a brigade of the still-forming 8th Division on the understanding that it would be replaced eventually by Indian troops, with the Australians being sent on to join their comrades in the Middle East.[13] It was a fateful decision that would see all of the 8th Division gradually committed to Malaya where it would prepare to meet a Japanese attack while being bereft of adequate air cover.

Australia also remained seriously deficient in air defences. Following the revelations of the Singapore conference, and Britain's success in fending off the German air force, it was more important than ever that Australia secure a supply of modern fighter and bomber aircraft for its own defence against invasion. But Britain was determined that these not be made available. Bruce had fulfilled his undertaking not to press British officials for aircraft during

September while the air ministry was supposedly preparing its planned program of deliveries to Australia. Bruce waited nine valuable weeks, rather than four, before he raised the matter again only to find that Britain still refused to provide any written undertaking as to how it proposed to supply the dominion's aircraft requirements.[14] Bruce confided that this would create a 'most deplorable impression upon the Australian Government' and pleaded with air ministry officials to be able to 'send at least a reasonable reply to Australia'. Ever-conscious of British needs, Bruce pointed out that Britain would be 'committing itself to very little if it agreed [to] a tentative programme' while saving itself from 'what looked like ... degenerating into a first class brawl'.[15] Bruce failed to realise that Britain would not draw up such a program of deliveries because it had no intention of sending operational aircraft to non-active theatres such as Australia, whatever the risk might be of hostilities with Japan.

It was a further week before Bruce reported his difficulties to Menzies. Cabling on 14 November, Bruce claimed that he had refused to accept a blank refusal from Whitehall and had demanded from the ministry of aircraft production 'reasonable information' about 'how and when it is contemplated your requirements will be met'. Failing satisfaction, Bruce proposed to approach Churchill directly as the 'present position is quite intolerable'.[16] It was nearly three months since Bruce had first raised the matter with British officials. He had not only failed to secure the delivery of even one aircraft to Australia during that time but had failed even in his limited aim of securing a tentative program of deliveries. He also had deliberately failed to keep Australia informed on the progress of his efforts for fear of causing a dispute between the two countries. Bruce's sympathy for Britain's predicament in Europe, and his concern for its commitment to the Middle East, had left him relatively blind to Australia's potential peril in the Pacific. He was able to escape censure from Australia because his apparent apathy was matched by an almost similar lack of concern in Canberra where the post-election struggle for political survival outranked national survival in the priorities of Australian leaders.

Only at the end of November, in the wake of the defence conference at Singapore, did Australia increase the pressure on Britain for the supply of aircraft that it had on order. Australia was planning a minimum strength for the RAAF of 32 squadrons operating 320 modern aircraft. Even this strength for the whole of Australia was less than that recommended by Britain for the defence of Singapore and Malaya. The problem was that Australia at the end of November had just 42 aircraft that it could class as 'modern', that is capable of being used against the Japanese, and none of these were fighter planes. Moreover, because of its reluctance to abandon its attachment to imperial defence, and to concede that the British navy would not be able to hold a hostile Japanese fleet at bay, Australia was not planning to equip more than two of its 32 squadrons with fighter aircraft since it was believed that the British navy would prevent the possibility of Japan establishing high-performance, land-based planes on airfields close enough to attack Australia. Thus, even if the RAAF had been supplied in 1940 with the aircraft it requested, it would not have been much better equipped to face the threat that eventually developed in 1942.[17]

In the absence of modern British or American aircraft, the Australian government could have done more to manufacture them locally. But Menzies and his predecessor concentrated on the manufacture of training aircraft — Tiger Moths and Wirraways — and on producing operational aircraft — Beaufort bombers — that were to be shared with Britain. Menzies' primary concern in aircraft manufacture was to develop an industry that would be of advantage to Australia's postwar industrial development rather than to solve its pressing defence predicament. Menzies also entertained similar hopes about the establishment, with British assistance, of a ship-building industry in Australia.

In the case of the aircraft industry, Menzies hoped to use it as the basis for a British-controlled automobile manufacturing industry in peacetime that would be able to quash prewar moves by the American industry to dominate the Australian market. However, for such an industry to be established, trained men, machine tools and other scarce equipment would have to come from Britain. Australia would face the same problem in extracting these as Bruce experienced in trying to extract promises of aircraft. As well, the whole scheme was predicated on the understanding that Australia would specialise in the production of certain types of aircraft for general use, with other types such as fighters being sourced from Britain.[18] And that all depended on Britain being willing and able to make up Australia's alarming deficiencies in aircraft before an invasion threatened.

NOTES

[1] Hasluck, *The Government and the People 1939–41*, pp. 229, 294.
[2] Colville diary, 27 September 1940, in Colville, *The Fringes of Power*, p. 252.
[3] ibid.
[4] Cable, Menzies to Bruce, 29 September 1940, *DAFP*, Vol. 4, Doc. 144.
[5] Cable, Churchill to Menzies, 2 October 1940, *DAFP*, Vol. 4, Doc. 152; See also War Cabinet Conclusions, 1 October 1940, CAB 65/9, W.M. 263(40), PRO; Talk with Churchill, 2 October 1940, *DAFP*, Vol. 4, Doc. 153.
[6] Letter, Sir Frederick Eggleston to R. Mackay, 8 October 1940, MS 423/1/143, Eggleston Papers, NLA.
[7] Cable, Menzies to Bruce, 4 October 1940, CRS M100, 'October 1940', NAA.
[8] Cable, Menzies to Churchill, 4 October 1940, *DAFP*, Vol. 4, Doc. 158.
[9] See *Sun, Sydney Morning Herald*, Sydney, *Advertiser*, Adelaide, 14 October 1940; *Sun, Herald*, Melbourne, *Courier-Mail, Telegraph*, Brisbane, 15 October 1940.
[10] See Hasluck, *The Government and the People 1939–41*, pp. 247–71.
[11] Advisory War Council Minutes, 29 October 1940, CRS A2682, Vol. 1, Minute 7; Letter, Forde to Shedden, 12 November 1940, CRS A5954, Box 495, NAA.
[12] Letter, Brooke-Popham to Ismay, 26 October 1940, V/1/1, Brooke-Popham Papers, KC; Christopher Thorne, *Allies of a Kind*, London, 1978, p. 55.
[13] See, Hasluck, *The Government and the People 1939–41*, pp. 294–7; Horner, *High Command*, pp. 51–2.
[14] Talk with Captain Balfour (Air Ministry), 5 November 1940, CRS M100, 'November 1940', NAA.
[15] Talk with Sir Charles Gardner, 6 November 1940, CRS M100, 'November 1940', NAA.
[16] Cable No. 1006, Bruce to Menzies, 14 November 1940, CRS M100, 'November 1940', NAA.
[17] War Cabinet Minutes, 26 November 1940, CRS A2673, Vol. 4, Minute 632, NAA.
[18] Cable No. 122, Menzies to Bruce, 9 September 1940, CRS A5954, Box 223; 'Production of Aircraft in Australia', War Cabinet Agendum No. 229/1940, by Fadden, 14 October 1940, CRS A5954, Box 223; War Cabinet Minutes, 31 October 1940, CRS A2673, Vol. 4, Minute 598; and Cables, Menzies to Bruce, 5 November 1940, and Bruce to Menzies, 28 November 1940, CRS A1608, H61/2/1, NAA.

NINE

'for the sake of our kith and kin'

Despite mounting evidence that the system of imperial defence would not provide for Australia's defence against Japan, the dominion was slow to seek alternative arrangements to secure peace in the Pacific. There were three alternatives that could have been tried, either singly or in some combination: Australia could try and appease Japan's territorial and economic ambitions short of sacrificing Australia itself; it could turn towards the United States and seek a guarantee of protection from Washington; or it could concentrate all its forces at home to try and deter the Japanese from developing their threat into reality.

The belated appointment of Sir John Latham as Australian minister in Tokyo could have been used as a means of achieving the first alternative. Under pressure from Whitehall and Bruce, Menzies had delayed making an appointment to Tokyo for more than a year, announcing it finally in August 1940 just prior to calling the federal election. Despite the concern about Britain's deteriorating relations with Japan, Latham did not present his credentials in Tokyo for another four months. Part of the delay was caused by the apparent obligation to travel by a British ship and thereby take

38 days to do what could be done in fourteen days by a Japanese ship. He was also delayed by having to await the outcome of the election so that he could consult with the incoming government and the advisory war council. His brief was to foster friendship with Japan, although on important issues he was instructed to 'temporise and gain time to allow for the development of the growing strength of our defences'. The concept of a general settlement in the Pacific was left to one side.[1]

As for Australian relations with the United States, there was a growing conviction that Australian security, in the absence of the British fleet at Singapore, hinged on the US Pacific fleet at Pearl Harbor. But this conviction still was not reflected in any rush by Australia to develop closer relations with Washington. Casey, as the Australian minister, had carved out a position of some influence in the American capital but his role remained one of acting in close consultation and coordination with the British ambassador, Lord Lothian. They talked together practically every day and often would visit the State Department or Roosevelt in tandem, as if there was no distinction between the interests they were representing.[2] In 1940, Casey tried energetically to publicise the British cause, as he sought to move the United States closer to involvement in the war against Germany, while he expended little effort in creating in the American official mind a specific sense of responsibility for Australian security rather than for the empire generally. Flying his own plane to speaking engagements, Casey cut a dashing figure and was able to speak to suspicious American audiences with a supposedly independent Australian voice in support of Britain's cause.

It was partly to support Britain's cause with an Australian voice that Casey convinced the government to establish the Australian News and Information Bureau in New York in December 1940, although Menzies justified the move to Labor members of the advisory war council by suggesting that Britain 'might be defeated in the war and a re-grouping of English-speaking countries might arise'.[3] Even Casey seemed to sense that Australia and Britain might have conflicting interests in Washington. This was true with regard to their competing demands for American aircraft and also with regard to occasional proposals that arose for the transfer of part of the US Pacific fleet to the Atlantic. Churchill usually supported these plans as providing a visible sign of American support against Germany, of deterring the German U-boat campaign in the Atlantic and of perhaps providing a naval incident between American and German forces that could propel Washington into war. Casey opposed it for fear of such a move giving the Japanese a green light for expansion in the Pacific. And it is possible that his close relationship with Lord Lothian, who shared Casey's misgivings, served Australia well when they jointly opposed the transfer of the Pacific fleet.[4] At the same time, the Australian government remained reluctant to forge any closer defence links that could imply any diminution of its links with Britain.

At the beginning of September, Casey foresaw the possibility of the United States obtaining base facilities in the south-west Pacific, including Australia, along lines recently granted to them by Churchill in the British West Indies. Although an American request for such facilities had not yet been made, Casey wanted Canberra to provide him with the 'most telling arguments that I could have up my sleeve for use on appropriate opportunities' when American interest in such facilities might be aroused. Three weeks went by without a word from Canberra. Casey repeated his request, assuring Australia that it would not commit it to any particular action but simply provide Casey with 'talking points as to broad avenues of possible cooperation in [the] South-western Pacific'. From his Washington vantage point, Casey seems to have had a clearer view of Australia's dangerously exposed position than the government in Canberra, which remained anxious about protecting British interests in the Pacific from possible American encroachments. The war cabinet advised that Casey's proposal would require a 'considered appreciation' from Britain since it involved colonies such as Fiji. There was no sense of urgency in the Australian response nor any apparent eagerness to place Australian facilities at the disposal of the United States, at least for the duration of the war. Frustrated by the Australian inaction, Casey later urged Lothian to 'seek authority to offer free joint use to [the] United States for any defence purpose of any of [the] Pacific Islands regarding which [the] United States have claimed sovereignty from Britain'.[5]

Although Casey's efforts were designed primarily to entice the United States into a closer alliance with Britain, and thereby ensure its security, there were clear benefits for Australia in having the United States extend its reach in the Pacific. Indeed, Casey made more attempts on his own initiative to develop defence ties between Australia and the United States than the Australian government ever sought to make during 1940.[6] It was not that Casey wanted the United States to permanently replace Britain as Australia's protector in the Pacific. The basis for all his dealings in Washington was that Australia was a British country. Without interfering with this rigid relationship, Casey tried to use his position as an Australian to break down American philosophical objections to the concept of colonies and to induce a reluctant Roosevelt to regard the defence of Britain's empire as an American interest.[7]

Of course, marching in step with Washington could also have its dangers for Australia. When the United States and Britain increased the economic pressure on Japan in late 1940, Australia joined in despite fears that it might push Tokyo towards war. Australia had formerly resisted public pressure to ban the export of scrap iron to Japan, both for economic reasons and for fear of causing resentment in Japan. However, in early November, it agreed to impose an embargo on the export of scrap iron and other strategic war materials in an effort to prevent Japan accumulating stockpiles with which it might wage war in the Pacific.[8] Once implemented, such an embargo would gradually deplete the existing Japanese stockpiles to the point at which Japan would be forced either to abandon its ambitions for expansion, and perhaps even sue for peace in China, or strike out while it still could. The embargo therefore might hasten the outbreak of hostilities between Britain and Japan rather than delay it.

Britain's readiness to be more provocative in its dealings with Japan was helped by the reduced likelihood of its own invasion by Germany. With the RAF still undefeated by the Luftwaffe, Hitler agreed on 17 September to postpone his invasion plans. Although there were still fears in London that a German invasion fleet might use the cover of an October fog to make its approach to England's shores, steadier heads realised that Hitler's window of opportunity had closed, at least for 1940. By 2 October, the director of naval intelligence, Admiral Godfrey, advised that the threat of invasion was steadily diminishing, a view echoed by Churchill a week later when he confided to Beaverbrook that the

'Invasion danger is easier'. Finally, on 12 October, Hitler instructed his commanders to abandon plans for an invasion until at least the spring of 1941. He now had other plans, switching the weight of his forces to the east as he prepared to support his embattled Italian ally in its war with Greece before unleashing his own onslaught against Russia. By the end of October, British intelligence had conclusive evidence that the German juggernaut had changed direction.[9]

Meanwhile, Australia was steadily drifting into a position of great peril. As a naval officer in the RN's plans division recalled, British naval opinion was convinced by late 1940 that Japan would enter the war 'as soon as she could swallow up the British Far Eastern Empire — Australia included, without undue hazard to herself'.[10] Acknowledging its weakness at sea in the Far East, Britain was planning to allocate the Pacific as a sphere of American control, assuming that America was drawn into the war, while retaining control of the Indian Ocean for itself. Australia complied with this arrangement, although making little effort to encourage closer collaboration with its possible protector in the Pacific, the United States. This was partly but not wholly due to America's reluctance to be seen publicly edging towards war during a presidential election year.[11]

Britain's policy for any Far Eastern war was established by Churchill to be one of strict defence until the war in Europe was won. In late October, Churchill supported the restoration of the British battleship construction program because, he argued, 'at the end of the war we should be faced with the formidable task of clearing up the situation in the Far East, and we should be unequal to the task if we fell behind Japan in capital ship construction'.[12] This implied a definite commitment to wrest back from Japan any gains it might make during the war. But Britain did not envisage having to make any great commitment during the war to prevent those gains becoming too extensive. According to Churchill, British policy called for a 'strict defensive in the Far East and the acceptance of its consequences'.[13] In settling on this policy, Churchill and the chiefs of staff relied on an optimistic perception of Japan's military prowess that was partly based on Japanese difficulties in the war against China and partly on racist notions of Japanese inferiority.[14]

While establishing a strictly defensive policy in the Far East, Churchill continued to maintain the fiction that Australia's security remained guaranteed by Britain. Even as he divulged to Menzies his plans to amass a 'very large army representing the whole Empire and ample sea power in the Middle East', he was careful to add that such a build-up incidentally would allow for a 'move eastward in your direction if need be'.[15] This worthless assurance made no mention of how Britain would react if there were attacks simultaneously by Germany and Italy in the Middle East and Japan in the Far East, as would happen in 1941–42. Australia preferred to accept Churchill's assurance at face value rather than possibly find it wanting and then have to adopt an expensive policy of greater defence self-reliance. After decades of dependence, and in the depths of a war when items of defence equipment were almost impossible to obtain, such a switch in defence policy would have been fraught with difficulties. Not least would have been the political difficulty of explaining to an anxious electorate that the conservative touchstone of imperial defence had ceased to exist.

While Churchill was willing to accept the territorial losses that would result from a war with Japan, he was also in late 1940 'tightening the screw' on Japan in ways that would make such a war more likely. Not all British ministers shared Churchill's insouciance. 'Rab' Butler, parliamentary under-secretary at the Foreign Office and also chairman of the war cabinet's Far Eastern committee, warned the war cabinet in mid-December that the 'cumulative effect' of Britain's economic embargo 'may be considerable' but that it lacked the 'backing of potential force'.[16] Stripped of diplomat-speak, Butler was pointing out that Britain's policy in the Pacific was a game of bluff which, if called by Japan, would be at the considerable cost of British interests in the Far East. But Churchill's eyes were on the European war which could only be won, so he believed, by the entry of the United States on the British side. Now that Roosevelt was safely re-elected, albeit on a no-war platform, the shifting design of Churchill's war policy was to have the Americans fighting again in Europe even at the expense of provoking war in the Pacific. He was particularly pleased to learn in late November that the Americans were planning, like the British, to concentrate on Germany and fight a holding war in the Pacific in the event of the United States and Japan both entering the war. This, exulted Churchill, was not only 'strategically sound' but also 'most highly adapted to our interests'.[17]

Churchill justified Britain's tightrope act in the Pacific with the argument that, if it fell, little of consequence would be lost. According to his mistaken calculation, Japan would not move in great force against Britain's Far Eastern empire, except for Hong Kong, so long as the US Pacific fleet remained intact at Pearl Harbor. Although Churchill was sanguine about the security of Australia in the scenario that he was planning to play out in the Pacific, the possible implications for the relatively defenceless dominion were dire. But Australia remained, at best, dimly aware of its predicament. It continued with its commitment to the Middle East and maintained pressure on Britain to build up its forces in that region. As for Singapore, now revealed as woefully protected, Australia's reaction was to dispatch poorly equipped troops to help defend, without adequate air cover, a naval base empty of ships.[18] Despite mounting evidence that the system of imperial defence would not work in its favour, the Australian government's commitment remained undiminished. And Menzies was anxious to ensure that the Australian people continued to share this faith and not become aware of the deficiencies at Singapore. His political survival depended upon it.

So Menzies argued for the deficiencies at Singapore, as exposed by the recent defence conference, to be rectified. Accepting the absence of a British fleet at Singapore, Menzies pressed Whitehall on 1 December for 'immediate action to remedy deficiencies [at Singapore] in Army and Air Forces both in numbers and equipment', warning that the extent of Australian cooperation in overseas theatres was dependent on the Australian public's *impression of the degree of local security that exists*. He then undercut his own argument, and reduced the pressure on Britain, by agreeing to the dispatch to Singapore of a brigade of the 8th Division. Thus Australia became depleted of yet more trained troops for the sake of maintaining the myth of Singapore in the consciousness of the public.[19] Menzies also had to allay the concern of the Labor members of the advisory war council.

When Menzies advised the council on 2 December of his cable to Whitehall, it sparked a flurry of suggestions by the Labor members as to ways in which Australian security could be enhanced. One of the more fanciful ones was to adopt a suggestion made by Australia's minister in Tokyo, Sir John Latham, for Australia to purchase modern fighter aircraft from Japan. Menzies was now urged to inquire from Tokyo as to whether Australia could obtain 'immediate delivery of fighter types of aircraft'. When he did so, he found that Japan was 'anxious to supply both service and training types' but regretted that it was unable to deliver until the end of 1941. Then it delivered with a vengeance.[20]

A more promising suggestion from the Labor members was for Britain, in the wake of naval successes against the Italians in the Mediterranean, to send three or four battleships from the Mediterranean to Singapore. Rather than cabling Churchill direct with this appeal, Menzies asked Bruce to raise the matter informally with Churchill or his naval chief and to suggest that the improved naval situation should allow either a few battleships or Churchill's earlier idea of a battleship and a fast aircraft carrier to be dispatched to Singapore. Bruce simply asked the British for a fresh naval appreciation in the light of the recent successes while on 8 January 1941 Menzies fobbed off the advisory war council with a pre-Christmas cable from Churchill, ostensibly responding to the Labor suggestion but actually replying to Menzies' cable of 1 December.[21]

In his cable, Churchill tried to allay Australian concern about the Far East and the ramshackle nature of the Singapore defences. He claimed that the danger of war with Japan was 'definitely less' than six months previously and that, even if war with Japan occurred, he was 'persuaded' that the United States would 'come in on our side, which will put the naval boot very much on the other leg, and be deliverance from many perils'. Churchill rejected any immediate possibility of dispatching the Mediterranean fleet to Singapore, counselling Australia to 'bear our Eastern anxieties patiently and doggedly', while again wheeling out the supposedly cast-iron promise that 'if Australia is seriously threatened by invasion we should not hesitate to compromise or sacrifice the Mediterranean position for the sake of our kith and kin'.[22]

On the face of it, Churchill's latest assurance suggested that Britain would abandon the Mediterranean if Australia was only 'seriously threatened' and that British battleships would be steaming towards the Pacific before a single

Japanese soldier had landed on Australian shores. As such, it seemed to go even further than previous cavalier promises by Churchill which suggested that a serious invasion of Australia must first occur before Britain would consider abandoning its position in the Mediterranean. Whatever the wording, this latest promise was identical to the others in being made with the purpose of extracting yet further Australian forces for Britain's use overseas.

Churchill's grand scheme was to amass an army in the Middle East capable of expelling the Italians from north Africa; to bring over the French colonies in north Africa, and the French fleet stationed there, to the British side; to keep the numerically strong and neutral Turkish army out of the German grasp; and to build a Balkan alliance that would allow British forces, hopefully reinforced with Turkish troops, to grapple with Germany on European soil without having to mount a difficult invasion across the English Channel against the heavily defended French coast. For all this, he needed an army in the Middle East, of which the Australians would provide an important component, and he needed a strong naval force in the Mediterranean that would otherwise have been based at Singapore. To ensure that he obtained the Australian troops, Churchill confided to Canberra that the imperial forces in the Middle East would be kept in a 'fluid condition' so that they could be switched as needs dictated between the Middle East and Singapore. Steeling the Australians to be stalwart, Churchill argued that 'great objects are at stake and risks must be run in every quarter of the globe'.[23] In fact, Australia was being asked to run great risks in its quarter of the globe in order to shore up British interests in another quarter. However, Churchill's optimistic scenario and his restated promise to abandon the Mediterranean had the effect he desired. Australia went ahead with the proposal to send a brigade of its troops to Malaya, kept to its Middle East commitment and accepted Britain's refusal to send a fleet to Singapore. Meanwhile, Menzies now had other matters on his mind.

In late November, Menzies suddenly announced his intention to visit London to discuss the defence of Singapore in the light of the alarming conclusions of the Singapore defence conference. However, such a visit had been on Menzies' private agenda almost from the beginning of the war, with the recent close election result making him more amenable to take political risks that would either shore up his position in Canberra or even lead to greater heights in London, perhaps sitting in an imperial war cabinet as Billy Hughes had done during the First World War. At just 46 years of age, Menzies had reached the peak of Australian politics only to find the view from the top disappointing. Despite his unanimous re-election to the party leadership after the election, he remained ensconced in the Lodge on sufferance from MPs who resented his arrogance and from a country unable to see a viable alternative in the still-divided Labor Party. And the baying for Menzies' blood increased with his wounding in the election. When he criticised public apathy towards the war, the Sydney *Sun* rounded on him for creating the apathy and argued that it was 'not apathy that is the trouble, but the lack of confidence in leaders who fail to lead'.[24]

Under pressure from such criticism, Menzies made a private approach to Churchill through the British high commissioner in Canberra, urging that he call a conference of dominion prime ministers in London. Menzies made this suggestion in late October before the results of the Singapore conference had been relayed to Australia.[25] Churchill, though, was not about to play Menzies' game and have a cabal of dominion prime ministers possibly curbing his control of war strategy so he simply invited Menzies to come alone. This was not what Menzies wanted but he was so intent on travelling to London that he seized upon the conclusions of the Singapore conference, informing the advisory war council on 25 November that it required him having urgent talks with Churchill. Although the council fell in with his scheme, problems in parliament in early December prevented Menzies from making firm plans for the visit.[26]

Despite the supposed urgency of his visit, it was not until 17 December that Menzies advised Bruce he was going to accept the 'outstanding invitation to visit London to discuss matters of mutual war importance'. Even so, he did not propose leaving Australia until mid-January, after taking a Christmas holiday with his family and during the parliamentary recess when he could not be ousted in his absence. En route to these urgent talks, Menzies proposed stopping off to visit Australian troops in the Middle East. He would not be landing in London until February 1941, some three months after he had informed the advisory war council of the pressing need for consultations with Churchill. Menzies had complained long and often about Britain's lack of consultation on policies affecting Australia's national interest. His visit to London would provide him with an opportunity to put the dominion's view at the highest level and in the most direct manner. There was much that needed to be said if Australian security was to be safeguarded in the Pacific. Events would reveal that Menzies was not the person to say it.

NOTES

1 Advisory War Council Minutes, 29 October 1940, CRS A2682, Vol. 1, Minute 4, NAA.

2 Letter, Casey to Norman Makin, 6 June 1946, MS 4663, Makin Papers, NLA.

3 Letter, Keith Murdoch to Casey, 9 September 1940, enclosing report by R. J. F. Boyer, head of the American section at the Department of Information, and Cable No. 52, Menzies to Casey, 28 December 1940, CRS A3300, Item 66; Advisory War Council Minutes, 25 November 1940, CRS A2682, Vol. 1, Minute 41, NAA.

4 R. G. Casey, *Personal Experience, 1939–46*, London, 1962, p. 40; Cable, Casey to Department of External Affairs, 3 October 1940, CRS A3300, Item 10, NAA.

5 Cables No. 240 and 280, Casey to External Affairs Department, 3 and 24 September 1940, CRS A3300, Item 38; War Cabinet Minutes, 24 September 1940, CRS A2673, Vol. 4, Minute 526, NAA; Cable, Casey to Menzies, 1 October 1940, *DAFP*, Vol. 4, Doc. 151.

6 See, Casey, *Personal Experience*, pp. 36–7, 50; See also for example, *DAFP*, Vol. 4, Docs 99, 151, 168, 173, 177.

7 Cable, Casey to Department of External Affairs, 24 September 1940, *DAFP*, Vol. 4, Doc. 137.

8 Draft Cabinet Submission by Department of External Affairs, 7 October 1940, and Cabinet Submission by E. J. Harrison, Minister for Trade and Customs, 1 November 1940, *DAFP*, Vol. 4, Docs 161 and 186.

9 'The Naval Memoirs of Admiral J. H. Godfrey', Vol. 5, pp. 161–2, GDFY 1/6, Godfrey Papers, CC; Minute, Churchill to Beaverbrook, 9 October 1940, BBK D/414, HLRO; Harvey diary, 24 November 1940, ADD. MS. 56397, Harvey Papers, BL; Cadogan diary, 31 December 1940, in Dilks (ed.), *The Diaries of Sir Alexander Cadogan*, p. 346; Dalton diary, 16 October 1940, Dalton Papers, LSE; F. H. Hinsley, *British Intelligence in the Second World War*, Vol. 1, HMSO, London, 1979, pp. 259–60.

10 'My Life', Memoirs of Admiral Davis, p. 203, WDVS 1/3, Davis Papers, CC.

11 See, CRS CP 290/7, Bundle 1, Items 2 and 4, NAA.

12 War Cabinet Conclusions, 25 October 1940, CAB 65/9, W.M. 277(40), PRO.

13 Minute M.333, Churchill to First Lord of the Admiralty and First Sea Lord, 22 November 1940, PREM 3/489/4, PRO.

14 See, Thorne, *Allies of a Kind*, pp. 3–7.

15 Cable (draft), Churchill to Menzies, 12 December 1940 (sent 13 December), PREM 4/43B/1, PRO.

16 Report by the Far Eastern Committee, 17 December 1940, CAB 66/14, W.P. (40)484, PRO.

17 Minute M.333, Churchill to First Lord of the Admiralty and First Sea Lord, 22 November 1940, PREM 3/489/4, PRO.

18 War Cabinet Minutes, 26 November CRS A2673, Vol. 4, Minute 632, NAA.

19 Cable No. 627, Commonwealth Government to Cranborne, 1 December 1940, *DAFP*, Vol. 4, Doc. 212 (author's emphasis in italics).

20 Advisory War Council Minutes, 2 December 1940, CRS A2682, Vol. 1, Minute 50, NAA; See also Letters, McEwen to Menzies, 14 November and 12 December 1940, CRS A5954, Box 230, NAA.

21 Cable, Menzies to Bruce, 3 December 1940, *DAFP*, Vol. 4, Doc. 214; Cable Z.408, Dominions Secretary to Menzies, 12 December 1940, CRS CP 290/7, Bundle 1, Item 3; Advisory War Council Minutes, 2, 8 and 12 January 1940, CRS A2682, Vol. 1, Minutes 48, 53 and 80, NAA.

[22] Cable, Cranborne to Commonwealth Government, 23 December 1940, *DAFP*, Vol. 4, Doc. 236.

[23] ibid.

[24] See, Day, *Menzies and Churchill at War*, Chaps 1–3; *Sun*, Sydney, 12 November 1940.

[25] The alarming results of that conference are usually put forward as providing the reason for Menzies' trip to London. Instead, it just provided him with a compelling rationale for doing something that he was already intending to do. Cable No. 377, UK High Commissioner to Dominions Office, 23 October 1940, PREM 4/43A/13, PRO. Ignoring the contrary evidence, Allan Martin presents the conventional view of Menzies' motivation. Martin, *Robert Menzies*, Vol. 1, pp. 316–7.

[26] War Cabinet Conclusions, 4 November 1940, CAB 65/10, W.M. 282(40), PRO; Advisory War Council Minutes, 25 November 1940, CRS A2682, Vol. 1, Minute 39, NAA.

TEN

'We will not let Singapore fall'

By January 1941, the war looked much brighter for Britain. Rather than greeting each day with foreboding, as Churchill had in mid-1940, he confided on 24 January that he awoke each morning 'feeling as if he had a bottle of champagne inside him and glad that another day had come'.[1] Despite the doubts of some of his colleagues, and amid the shattering convulsions of the continuing bombing onslaught, Churchill was convinced that Britain no longer faced the danger of a German invasion. Britain's strength in the air would ensure defeat for any force attempting to land on English shores. Hitler had already acknowledged as much, albeit secretly. On 10 January he finally cancelled preparations for an invasion of Britain and directed German efforts towards an attack on Russia in the coming spring.

The position in the Mediterranean also looked promising for Britain, with its naval forces having punctured the overblown confidence of the Italian navy by sinking three of its battleships with torpedo bombers. On land, the Italian thrust towards Alexandria had been halted and turned into a rout, with audacious British strikes across the desert now causing disarray among the retreating Italians. In Greece, the Italians were also hard-pressed to make any headway against the pugnacious Greeks. But there were signs that Hitler was about to lend a hand to his Italian ally and Churchill was determined, against all the conventions of military strategy, to disperse his forces, including the Australian divisions as they stood on the verge of a great triumph in Libya, so that they might be dispatched across the Mediterranean to shore up the Greeks.

Churchill could take such foolish risks because of his broader view of the war which seemed more sanguine with each passing day. Roosevelt's re-election to the American presidency the previous November had buoyed Churchill's hopes for securing American involvement upon which ultimate victory against Germany rested. Although Roosevelt still publicly resiled from the active involvement of American forces in the war, he had effectively committed the United States to a British victory, contributing 50 superannuated destroyers to Britain's war at sea and announcing on 29 December 1940 that the United States would become 'the great arsenal of democracy'. A grateful Churchill thanked Roosevelt for his 'trumpet-call', claiming that Britain could now 'march forward heartened and fortified and with the confidence ... that in the end all will be well for the English speaking peoples ... '.[2]

From now on, it would become increasingly difficult for Britain to refuse the dispatch of defence matériel because of any overwhelming threat to its own survival. Both Australia and Britain were competing now for resources to meet potential rather than actual threats. While Britain's threat from Germany lay just across the nation's narrow moat, the Japanese threat to Australia was still far distant, but coming closer and growing in intensity. Compared to Britain, Australia had much less capacity to meet its potential threat in the Pacific. The powerful battleships and aircraft carriers of Britain's navy remained in home waters or nearby; the massive force of heavy bombers and modern fighter planes remained largely based on the many British airfields that were scattered across the cornfields of the southern counties; and the artillery, tanks and infantry of the British army mostly remained rooted to the protection of its homeland. Of 36 British army divisions formed or forming, only four were overseas. One was in Iceland to pre-empt a German invasion, while three were in Egypt. Nearly two million troops of the British army, albeit at various stages of preparedness, remained in Britain's island garrison.[3]

Australia also had three divisions in the Middle East but they represented almost the whole of its trained troops. At home, the local defence forces remained at a rudimentary level of equipment and readiness. The enthusiasm of the troops could not compensate for the lack of modern equipment. Seven months after Menzies authorised the local production of tanks, the first wooden mock-up was nearing completion. Without the finished article, there was no hope of repelling a serious invasion force once it had established a foothold on Australia's shores. And there was little to prevent such a force from being landed. Naval forces in Australian waters were only sufficient to provide a small measure of protection against armed raiders stalking the trade routes of the Indian and Pacific Oceans and were incapable of intercepting and destroying an invasion fleet backed by battleships and aircraft carriers. In the air, Australia had nothing that could match the Japanese fighter planes. So, while Australia's threat was further distant than Britain's, the risks it was running were very much greater as it had no real defence against invasion. That did not prevent the first echelons of the third Australian division committed to the Middle East from arriving there in January. At the same time, Menzies prepared for a four-month trip around the world that was supposedly meant to secure Australia's defence position.

While the defence of Australia certainly figured among the reasons Menzies used to justify his visit to London, it was not his first priority. As he explained to Bruce on 3 January, he wanted to obtain a 'clear definition of where we stand in [the] Far East, and [a] reasonably long range policy [in the] Middle East' so that he could 'plan Australia's effort on [the] man-power side more soundly'. He also wanted to give the British government 'a clear picture of [the] amazing munitions potential developed and developing here, and to see how far greater joint use of it could be arranged'. There was no explicit mention in Menzies' cable of Australia's serious defence deficiencies or those of Singapore. Menzies' concern was to be assured of continued peace in the Pacific so that Australia could quietly transform itself into an imperial workshop that was, unlike Britain, safe from the nightly depredations of German bombers. But he could not plan this industrial development without having a better sense of the demands that military operations were likely to place upon Australian manpower. Such development also could not occur in the context of the war without the backing of the British government and of British industrialists, something that Menzies hoped to secure while in London.[4]

To Menzies' surprise, Bruce advised against the visit, warning that, if it was to be productive for Menzies, he would have to bring on a damaging confrontation with Churchill. While Menzies might achieve an immediate aim through such a confrontation, it was likely to prove counterproductive. Moreover, Bruce claimed that recent developments — presumably referring to Britain's success in the Middle East — had removed 'all the major issues on which you would have had to take a strong line'.[5] But Menzies, refreshed after a summer holiday at his mountain retreat at Macedon outside Melbourne and sustained by expressions of support from his businessman backers in Victoria, was set upon going.[6] Meeting with the advisory war council on 8 January, Menzies set out his reasons. Foremost was to gain a clear sense of the situation in the Far East as seen from London and to consult on the empire's attitude towards Japan, with the position at Singapore being a 'matter for frank discussion'. He also wanted to consult with British officials on issues, some of them trivial, related to the Middle East. Perhaps most important in securing the approval of the Labor members, Menzies held out the prospect of him securing in London the transfer to Australia of aircraft and ship-building productive capacity.[7]

Menzies' vision of an industrialised Australia had been pursued vigorously by governments in the wake of the 1930s depression but had little immediate application for Australia's defence. Australia was already manufacturing some rudimentary training aircraft for Britain as well as Beaufort bombers. Menzies wanted to build on these small beginnings and organise the transfer of machine tools and skilled tradesmen from bomb-battered Britain. He faced an impossible task. Not only was the British government, particularly aircraft production supremo Lord Beaverbrook, reluctant to release either men or machine tools to Australia but it was also averse to placing large orders for aircraft or ships. It was already ordering merchant ships and aircraft on a large scale from North America. Distance was Australia's downfall. It was simply cheaper, quicker and easier to purchase ships and aircraft from existing suppliers rather than establish new industries in the Antipodes. It was also better for British morale, and for its defences, to repair bomb-damaged factories rather than ship their tools to Australia.

As Menzies packed his bags for London, the British chiefs of staff imperilled Singapore even more by reducing the number of aircraft judged to be necessary for its defence. Instead of the former 582 planes, the chiefs decreed on 10 January that '336 should give [a] very fair degree of security'. Although the Far East commander, Sir Robert Brooke-Popham, observed privately that this reduced number was also meant to cover the defence of adjacent Burma, thereby reducing the effective level still further, he bowed to the inevitable, accepting that he would make do with just 336 for the year 1941. It would be worse than he thought. Although the chiefs had made the commitment to have 336 aircraft in Malaya conditional on the 'general situation and supply of aircraft', Churchill immediately countermanded it. Pointing out that he had not approved what he called these 'very large diversions of Force', Churchill claimed that his instructions to the chiefs had 'an opposite tendency'. He argued that the 'political situation in the Far East does not seem to require, and the strength of our Air Force by no means warrants, the maintenance of such large forces in the Far East at this time'.[8]

The chiefs of staff struggled to put Churchill's mind at rest while still trying to make a start on satisfying the defence needs of Singapore. They assured him that the figure of 336 planes was a 'long-term target' and there would be no 'appreciable diversion of our war effort to the Far East at the present time'. But they did want to make a start with a 'very small increase', proposing that two fighter squadrons be formed at Singapore since at present there were none there at all. Churchill even baulked at this, until the chiefs pointed out that it would mean a loss of just eight pilots from Britain with the remainder coming fresh from flying schools in Australia and New Zealand. He was satisfied further when he learnt that the aircraft would be Brewster Buffaloes from America, an outmoded type unsuited for use against the latest German or, as it proved in 1942, Japanese fighters.[9] So Menzies was defeated on Singapore even before he left Australia. His vision of transferring industrial capacity to Australia was also unattainable, with the British war cabinet making clear in early January that it was opposed to any transfer of productive resources from Britain that would 'conflict with our vital requirements in the near future' or harm future British trade.[10]

When he finally stepped aboard the Qantas Empire Airways flying boat at Sydney's Rose Bay on 24 January, Menzies was well aware of both the physical and political risks entailed in his trip across a warring world. Not only was he going against the advice of Bruce but also against the wishes of his wife, Pattie. As he acknowledged in his diary upon departure, 'for once in my life I am off upon a chancy undertaking'.[11] The visit would either restore his political fortunes in Australia or perhaps reveal fresh political pastures in London. In his four-month absence, Menzies left the genial Country Party leader and former Queensland accountant, Arthur Fadden, as acting prime minister. Fadden had only been in parliament for four years and had been party leader for less than four months after being chosen as a compromise candidate to end a deadlock between two rival factions. As Paul Hasluck observed, Fadden was 'not the cleverest, the most experienced, or the wisest man in the Country Party, but he was the best colleague and probably the staunchest character'. The British high commissioner in Canberra reported to London that Fadden was the 'arch-mixer', claiming that 'you couldn't meet a better chap in a bar. Streams of rollicking smut ... Good-natured, shrewd, likeable, has hardly any real thought of his own, means well.'[12] Fadden's limitations proved to be strengths in the circumstances of 1941, with his affability allowing a spirit of cooperation with his Labor opponents that the more arrogant Menzies had been unable to produce.

Despite receiving disturbing reports the previous year about the defence position of Singapore, the experience of seeing it for himself and of talking to the lacklustre British commanders startled Menzies out of his relatively complacent view of the supposed fortress. While previously supporting the British decision to concentrate naval forces in the Mediterranean rather than the Far East, Menzies now observed that the 'absence of naval craft must encourage the Japanese'. He was also highly critical of the calibre of the

British officers at Singapore and left the island determined to ensure in London that the 'Far Eastern problem' was 'taken seriously and urgently'. As his flying boat clawed its way into the torpid air, he asked in his diary:

Why cannot one squadron of fighters be sent out from N. Africa? Why cannot some positive commitment be entered into regarding naval reinforcement of Singapore? At this stage, misty generalizations will please and sustain the Japanese and nobody else.[13]

This was the first and last time that Menzies would reveal such a fervent concern about Far Eastern defence. As Singapore slipped into the distance behind his throbbing plane, so the problem receded in his consciousness.

Back in Australia, the Labor Party made the most of Fadden's position as acting prime minister by pushing for a greater concentration on local defence. While not expressing resentment at Britain's failure to fulfil its part of the imperial defence bargain, there was a growing realisation that Australia would be left vulnerable in the initial phase of a war with Japan. Curtin warned his colleagues on the advisory war council on 5 February that Australia had to prepare for the possibility of a partial Japanese occupation and its citizens must 'put their best efforts forward to maintain both Australian and Empire integrity'. Implicitly calling into question British assurances about likely Japanese moves, Curtin predicted with considerable prescience that Japan might make a 'bold move contrary to strategy' and called for a greater defence effort to 'ensure that all steps possible are being taken for effective defence'. But his fears were dismissed by the chief of the air staff, a British officer on secondment, who pointed to the long lines of communication that Japan would have to defend in any invasion of Australia and the vulnerability of these lines of communication to 'the British stronghold at Singapore and the possible assistance that would be rendered by the Netherlands East Indies'. He combined with the naval chief, another British officer, to quash any suggestion by Curtin, and in the face of all the damning evidence to the contrary, that Australia's commitment to imperial defence was detracting from the local defence effort. These assurances seem to have worked.[14]

NLA

Prime Minister Robert Menzies performs his 'melancholy duty', announcing that, as a consequence of Britain being at war with Germany, Australia was also at war.

AWM 000700

Three Wirraway training aircraft fly over Melbourne in 1940, part of the supposed great air armada that was meant to keep Australia secure from invasion.

AWM 001286

Menzies (*second from right*) and his wife, Pattie, join Admiral Colvin (*right*) and other naval officers on the steps of Sydney Town Hall to review a march-past by the sailors of HMAS *Perth*, in April 1940.

AWM P02018.012

The ageing and formerly discredited politician, and now British prime minister, Winston Churchill, lights up his cigar after making his defiant 'finest hour' speech on 18 June 1940.

AWM 005784

Australian soldiers at camp in the Middle East in February 1941 stand to attention for their prime minister as Menzies' cavalcade glides by.

AWM 006419

Arriving at his spiritual home in February 1941, a hatless Menzies alights from his flying boat in England to be greeted by his high commissioner, the former Australian prime minister, S.M. Bruce (*fourth from right*).

AWM 020072

A line of Italian prisoners is led off after being captured by Australian troops at Tobruk in early 1941. It was one of many defeats for the Italian army in north Africa before the arrival of German forces turned the tide.

AWM P00048

Menzies is greeted by the Canadian prime minister, Mackenzie King, in May 1941 while Australia's high commissioner, Sir William Glasgow, looks on and the influential secretary of the defence department, Frederick Shedden, hovers in the background.

AWM 074445

Troops from Australia's 6th Division step ashore on Crete in May 1941 after the failure of their expedition to Greece.

AWM 304791

Roosevelt and Churchill share a joke at the Atlantic Charter meeting in August 1941, held aboard the ill-fated British battleship *Prince of Wales* that was sunk off Singapore by the Japanese just four months later.

AWM MED0225

Six Australian-built Beaufort bombers line up at Singapore for refuelling in December 1941. Shortly after, all but one were withdrawn to Australia.

AWM 127905

Banzai! Victorious Japanese troops celebrate their capture of Singapore, the supposedly impregnable British bastion, in February 1942.

Rather than calling for the government to make a greater effort, the Labor members agreed that the problem lay with the Australian public who were ignorant of their country's 'alarming situation'. They urged that the council issue a press statement to alert the public to the gravity of the situation. At the same time, after discussing Britain's response to the Singapore defence conference, the council accepted that 'everything possible was being done to remedy the situation, having regard to the demands of theatres which are the scenes of war', namely the Middle East and Britain itself. So the Australians effectively fell in with the order of British priorities which had seen Singapore suffer for the sake of the Middle East.[15] If the Australian public was ignorant of its peril, so too was its government. It had taken risks with Australian security, dispatching its best troops overseas and forgoing the opportunity to build up its local defences, confident that the British promise to defend Australia would be made good. However, while the advisory war council was affirming its support for imperial defence, a British delegation was in Washington to conclude an Anglo–American agreement that would leave Australia largely at the mercy of the Japanese.

The staff conversations in Washington provided a reassuring sign for Churchill that the United States was moving closer to involvement in the war. The talks between British and American military officers were called to decide on a joint reaction to the possibility of a Pacific war, with both delegations confirming their pre-existing but separate decisions in such an eventuality to fight a defensive holding war against Japan while concentrating their principal effort against Germany, thereby enshrining the so-called 'Germany first' policy as the accepted Anglo–American strategy in the event of a two-front war. Churchill had been anxious that public opinion might push Roosevelt into concentrating more on the Pacific, which did not have as many negative connotations for American public opinion as involvement in another European land war. He was equally anxious to allay any American concern that, by fighting Japan, it would be fighting to defend Britain's colonial empire. In his instructions to the British delegation, Churchill made clear that the US navy would be 'in charge in the Pacific' and that the British officials were not to press their American counterparts to 'come and protect Singapore, Australia and India against the Japanese'.

Above all, he stipulated that 'nothing should stand in the way of the main principle, which was that all efforts should be directed to the defeat of Germany — the minimum force being left to hold Japan in check'.[16]

The subsequent Anglo–American agreement along these lines was a simple recognition of their national interests: that no calamity in the Pacific could compare with defeat in Europe. Only after Germany had been subdued would they turn their attention to Japan and retrieve what they had lost in the interim. Australia obviously could not be so complacent. Its national interest could not encompass the possibility of invasion by Japan and its possible 'retrieval' by Britain at some later date. The problem was that Australian leaders had no clear conception of a national interest separate from that of Britain. When the Australian naval attaché in Washington, who was an observer at the talks, cabled news of them to Canberra on 7 February, the Australian government was on notice as to the risks it must run in the Pacific. But it was not that simple. Even while determining to concentrate on Germany, and ensuring that America did likewise, Britain still professed in these talks that Australia was 'essential to our defence' and reaffirmed the necessity to retain control of Singapore.[17] How Britain was to retain Singapore and protect Australia while concentrating on Germany was not explained. The possible implications for Australia of this strategy were too terrible to contemplate. Rather than questioning it, the Australian government took solace from Britain's commitment on paper and tried not to wonder why it never seemed possible to transform this commitment into real troops, aircraft and ships in the Far East.

In mid-February, the Japanese provided a short-lived war scare when it appeared that they might be on the point of striking at British possessions in the Pacific. The scare provided Curtin with an opportunity to stir the Australian people into greater activity for their own defence, using the advisory war council to broadcast a call for the 'greatest effort of preparedness this country has ever made'. But there remained considerable complacency among the government itself, with a stronger draft of this statement by Curtin being watered down for fear of creating panic while Curtin's suggestion for a practice mobilisation to meet an invasion was refused because of 'its effect on industry'. There were panic headlines anyway when the statement was published in the press. Fadden was rebuked by his colleagues for issuing a joint statement with the Labor Party and instructed that future statements be subject to censorship. When the panic headlines were read in London, Bruce warned Canberra of British government fears that an 'over excited press' might 'increase an already high tension and even precipitate war'.[18]

Given what was to come at Pearl Harbor just ten months later, the council's call for greater Australian preparedness was well made. It was a brief storm of activity, made possible by Menzies' absence, in an otherwise calm sea of complacency. On 14 February, the day the statement appeared in the banner headlines of the morning press, the council assembled again, this time to hear the comforting words of Brooke-Popham, who had flown to Australia to reassure the dominion about the state of Singapore's defences and to extract further Australian contributions for its garrison and reinforcements for the Middle East. He told the war cabinet that Singapore was designed to withstand an attack for six months, but could probably last for nine months, and that a landward attack by way of the Malayan peninsula was unlikely because of the unsuitable terrain. When the army minister, Percy Spender, lately returned from Singapore, questioned the strength of Britain's commitment to the island's defence in view of its refusal to base a fleet there, Brooke-Popham confided that Churchill's instruction to him on his departure from London had been to 'hold Singapore until capital ships could be sent' and that Churchill had promised: 'We will not let Singapore fall.' With a flourish, Brooke-Popham then revealed Britain's commitment to Singapore of Brewster Buffalo aircraft, blithely maintaining that British pilots and aircraft in Malaya were 'considerably superior' to the Japanese who were not 'air-minded'.[19]

The commitment of the outmoded Brewster Buffaloes, which had been initially opposed by Churchill, largely quelled any lurking Australian suspicions about British intentions. The government and the advisory war council reaffirmed the Australian commitment to imperial defence, allowing a relieved Brooke-Popham to inform London that the dominion was 'definitely out to help and fully realised that the defence of the whole area from Burma to New Zealand was essentially one problem'. Despite its call for greater defence preparedness the previous day, the council now fell in with recommendations of the chiefs of staff to maintain Australia's emphasis on raising and equipping troops for overseas rather than for the local militia. In fact, on 5 February, after Spender had provided a personal account to the council of Singapore's defences, Curtin had suggested sending even more Australians there to beef up its defences. Now, in his ignorance of Churchill's thinking on the Far East, Curtin conceded that Britain was doing its utmost to strengthen Singapore and he pledged to intervene in industrial disputes threatening the production of munitions. Although the Labor members of the council proved more querulous than their conservative colleagues, Brooke-Popham advised London that he was 'very glad' that, under questioning from the Labor members, he had been 'able to rub in the fact of those 67 Brewster Buffaloes being on the way to Singapore'. He had earlier warned London of the danger of him going to Australia 'empty-handed'.[20] The commitment of the aircraft proved as decisive as the later commitment of the *Prince of Wales* and *Repulse* would be in beguiling Australians into believing that Britain accorded a high priority to the security of the dominion. Churchill also tried, for different purposes, to beguile Roosevelt into believing the same thing.

The war scare, raising the immediate prospect of a war in the Pacific, was not calculated to appeal to Churchill if it did not also involve the United States. But Roosevelt still refrained from providing Churchill with a guarantee of American support in the event of British possessions in the Pacific being attacked. Churchill now used the scare to try and move Roosevelt closer to such involvement, calling upon him on 15 February to 'inspire the Japanese with the fear of a double war' and warning that 'any threat of a major invasion of Australia or New Zealand would, of course, force us to withdraw our Fleet from the Eastern Mediterranean with disastrous military possibilities there'. Churchill held out the prospect of the Balkan countries, Turkey and the Middle East all coming under the control of the Axis powers. In such an event, German power in Europe would be practically unassailable. Although Roosevelt held back from threatening the Japanese along the lines suggested by Churchill, he was now on notice that a British war with Japan could have calamitous consequences for American strategic and economic interests. To ensure that Roosevelt got the message, Churchill repeated it five days later, pointedly warning the president that the 'naval consequences following Japanese aggression against Great Britain holds good in all circumstances'.[21]

Although Australia accepted Britain's good intentions in regard to the dominion's defence, it was anxious about the level of naval assistance that it could now count on in the event of war with Japan. The latest indication from London had been its declared intention to base a battle cruiser and an aircraft carrier in the Indian Ocean that could form the basis of a Far Eastern fleet. No indication was provided of when such a fleet would be formed or of its planned strength. Accordingly, Fadden pressed London to provide a full statement of the existing British naval force in the Indian Ocean and of 'any action proposed to augment it in [the] event of hostilities with Japan'. Fadden also asked Menzies to try to extract this information out of Whitehall.[22] As it happened, Churchill was even then planning his Greek adventure that would lead to the destruction of much of the British fleet in the Mediterranean and put paid even to paper plans for the dispatch of a fleet to the Far East.

On 12 February, Churchill sent his foreign secretary, Anthony Eden, off to Cairo with clear instructions to arrange the dispatch of 'speedy succour to Greece', arguing that it was Britain's 'duty to fight, and, if need be, suffer with Greece'.[23] While it might have been Britain's duty, it would be mostly Australian and New Zealand troops who would suffer. The concept of an expeditionary force to pre-empt the expected German invasion of Greece had important implications for Australia. Not least was the fact that Australian troops would comprise a large part of the force. Apart from concern for their safety in this risky enterprise, which Churchill privately anticipated would ultimately fail,[24] the deeper involvement of the Australians in the European struggle would make it that much more difficult for them to be extricated in the event of them being required for the defence of their homeland. There was also the distinct possibility that depleting the imperial forces in Egypt for the sake of Greece would transform the so-far successful campaign against the Italians in Libya into a defeat. The naval implications were just as serious. It would add substantially to the tasks of the

Mediterranean fleet and create a line of communication across the Mediterranean, where enemy aircraft would control the skies, that would have to be defended by British ships. The possibility of transforming the Mediterranean fleet into a force for the protection of Australia might be lost forever.

Britain's commanders in the Middle East were divided about the wisdom of the proposed Greek expedition while Australia's commander in Cairo, the hard-living General Blamey, harboured serious misgivings about it. Menzies had been warned by Bruce before he left Australia of the possibility of such an expedition and of the fundamental strategic problems that it posed.[25] It constituted a gross dereliction of duty when Menzies ignored these warnings and failed to avail himself of the military counsel on hand in the Middle East to reach a considered judgment on the expedition. Had he done so, and had Blamey and Menzies agreed on the foolhardiness of the expedition, it could have been sufficient to obstruct Eden when he arrived in Cairo to give effect to Churchill's instructions and a disaster might have been averted. Instead, Menzies played the politician, patting his troops on the back, taking movie film of their conquests and generally building up political credits.[26]

Although his biographer has sought to excuse Menzies by dumping the blame for the subsequent debacle on the British commander, Field Marshal Wavell, accusing him of deliberate deception of Blamey, Menzies and the British and Australian governments,[27] nothing can excuse the forewarned Menzies from properly assessing the proposal while he was able to consult on the spot with Blamey. But he was neither by temperament nor inclination up to the task. As his plane took him on a great arc through Lagos and Lisbon to London, Eden and the chief of the imperial general staff, General Dill, were setting down in Cairo after a nearly disastrous flight by way of Gibraltar. By the time Menzies' plane crossed the coast of England, prompting him to write fondly in his diary of the snow-covered, Devonshire fields below,[28] the die for a disaster in Greece had been cast. Eden and Dill had been charged by Churchill with organising such an expedition and this they quickly did, convincing Britain's commanders in the Middle East to agree to the diversion of their forces. It would be that much harder for Menzies to oppose it, even if he had been so inclined.

NOTES

1. Colville diary, 24 January 1941, in Colville, *The Fringes of Power*, p. 341; While Churchill was personally convinced that the danger of invasion was over, Germany maintained the appearance of preparing for an invasion, thereby deceiving British intelligence into believing that it remained the principal German preoccupation. See Hinsley, *British Intelligence in the Second World War*, Vol. 1, p. 261.

2. Warren Kimball (ed.), *Churchill and Roosevelt: The Complete Correspondence*, Vol. 1, London, 1984, pp. 119–20.

3. 'Army Scales', Directive by Churchill, 6 March 1941, CAB 66/15, W.P. (41)69, PRO.

4. Cable, Menzies to Bruce, 3 January 1941, CRS CP 290/9, Bundle 1, Folder 5, NAA; See also R. G. Menzies, *The Measure of the Years*, London, 1970, p. 45. Menzies later claimed in this volume of his memoirs that the 'whole reason' for his London visit was to 'discuss what my Government believed to be a serious menace from Japan ... and to urge the strengthening of the defences of Singapore'.

5. Cable No. 14, Bruce to Menzies, 5 January 1941, CRS M100, 'January 1941', NAA.

6. Martin, *Robert Menzies*, Vol. 1, pp. 313–14.

7. Advisory War Council Minutes, 8 and 9 January 1941, CRS A2682, Vol. 1, Minutes 79 and 82, NAA.

8. Cable No. 39, Chiefs of Staff to Brooke-Popham, 10 January 1941, with attached note, V/4/6–7, Brooke-Popham Papers, KC; Minute D15/1, Churchill to Ismay, 13 January 1941, PREM 3/156/3, PRO.

9. 'Air Reinforcements, Far East', Note by Chiefs of Staff, 24 January 1941, with Note by Churchill, 25 January 1941, and Minute, Hollis to Churchill, 27 January 1941, PREM 3/156/3, PRO.

10. Memorandum by Secretary of State for India and Minister of Supply, 6 January 1941, CAB 66/14, W.P. (41)4; War Cabinet Conclusions, 9 January 1941, CAB 65/17, W.M. 4(41), PRO.

11. Menzies diary, 24 January 1941, MS 4936, Series 13, Folder 3, Menzies Papers, NLA (hereafter listed as Menzies diary).

12. Hasluck, *The Government and the People 1939–41*, p. 266; Letter, Sir Ronald Cross to Cranborne, 20 January 1942, ADD. MS. 58240, Emrys-Evans Papers, BL.

13. Menzies diary, 29 January 1941.

14. Advisory War Council Minutes, 5 February 1941, CRS A2682, Vol. 1, Minute 119, NAA.

15. ibid., Minutes 119 and 135.

16. Defence Committee (Operations) Minutes, 17 December 1940, CAB 69/1, D.O. (40)51, PRO.

17. Cable, Burrell to Colvin, 7 February 1941, *DAFP*, Vol. 4, Doc. 278.

18. Advisory War Council Minutes, 13 February 1941, CRS A2682, Vol. 1, Minute 145; War Cabinet Minutes, 14 February 1941, CRS A2673, Vol. 5, Minute 801; Cable No. 125, Bruce to Fadden, 14 February 1941, CRS M100, 'February 1941', NAA.

19. War Cabinet Minutes, 14 February 1941, CRS A2673, Vol. 5, Minute 802, NAA. In fact, Spender had already informed his colleagues of the commitment of Brewster Buffaloes on 5 February.

20. Letters, Brooke-Popham to Ismay, 28 February 1941, and Brooke-Popham to Sir Arthur Street, Under Secretary of State for Air, 22 February 1941, V/1/7 and V/2/4, Brooke-Popham Papers, KC; Advisory War Council Minute, 5 February 1941, in John Robertson and John McCarthy (eds), *Australian War Strategy 1939–1945*, Brisbane, 1985, p. 153.

21. Kimball, *Churchill and Roosevelt*, Vol. 1, pp. 135–37.

22. Cables, Fadden to Cranborne, and Fadden to Menzies (in Cairo), 12 February 1941, *DAFP*, Vol. 4, Doc. 287.

23. Note, Churchill to Eden, 12 February 1941, PREM 3/294/2, PRO.

24. See R. Sherwood, *The White House Papers of Harry L. Hopkins*, Vol. 1, London, 1948, p. 240.

25. Cable No. 38, Bruce to Menzies, 14 January 1941, CRS M100, 'January 1941', NAA.

26. See Day, *Menzies and Churchill at War*, Chap. 3.

27. Martin, *Robert Menzies*, Vol. 1, pp. 323–25.

28. 'Came in across N. Devon. Many fields white with snow. The dark woods, the myriad hedges. What a lovely place at any time.' Menzies diary, 20 February 1941.

ELEVEN

'too many unknown factors'

After his flying boat landed in Poole harbour, Menzies and his party were driven by Bruce through bomb-ravaged London streets to their lodgings behind the sandbagged windows of the Dorchester hotel. Menzies was back in his beloved London. But what a different London it was to the imperial capital he had visited in the 1930s. And what a different agenda now confronted him as wartime prime minister. Prominent on that agenda was the need, prompted by a cable from Fadden, to discover with some certainty the British reaction to a war with Japan.

At a meeting with the British chiefs of staff and service ministers on 27 February, the now-decrepit British assurance about abandoning the Mediterranean for the sake of Australia was polished up and wheeled out for Menzies' inspection. The flaws in its design suddenly seemed obvious. After having visited the huge military establishment, much of it Australian, that was being built up in the Middle East, Menzies realised that a naval withdrawal from the Mediterranean would not be easy and could be at the cost of the Australian troops. He questioned how Britain could dispatch a fleet to the Far East when there were 'land forces which cannot be deserted'.

Though the inherent contradictions in the assurance, and its important provisos, should have suggested to Menzies that it was never intended by Churchill to be implemented, this was something that Menzies seemed unable to see. Although he could recognise the flaws in the British design, he blamed them all on muddle-headed British planners rather than on the politician who had drawn it up.[1]

The more that Menzies pressed British ministers and officials to explain precisely how they intended safely to discharge their promise to defend Australia, to secure Singapore and at the same time not abandon Australian forces in the Middle East, the more these British officials revealed their reluctance to do so. This reluctance was partly due to the practical difficulties of predicting the course of such hypothetical events. But it was also due to a desire to conceal from Australia the extent of its vulnerability, which might otherwise cause the dominion to divert its energies away from imperial defence. So successful were they in doing this, and so profound had been the effect on Menzies of his time in the Middle East and his experience of war-damaged London, that Menzies now absolved Britain of its promise to abandon the Mediterranean for the sake of the Far East. At a meeting with naval chiefs on 8 March, Menzies announced that Australia was 'no longer satisfied with the general round statement that in the event of the outbreak of hostilities with Japan ... [Britain] would, if necessary abandon the Mediterranean and come to the assistance of the Dominions with capital ships'. Conceding that Australia was in a bind, with 'very large forces on land in the Middle East', Menzies declared that 'public opinion would not stand for those forces being left improperly protected by a complete withdrawal of Naval Forces from the Mediterranean'.[2]

Australia was now in the position of having absolved Britain of its promise to provide naval protection, of having been informed by the Americans that it should expect no help from Washington,[3] and yet still it stayed loyal to notions of imperial defence. While releasing Britain from its promise to send ships to Singapore, Menzies sought instead for the British to send modern fighter planes. These would have a political as well as a military value. Thus Menzies requested that the aircraft should be Hurricanes, which had a high public profile following their successful sorties during the battle of Britain. Menzies' political survival might be enhanced if he returned with a promise in his briefcase of Hurricanes for Singapore. Certainly he could not return with a simple restatement of vague promises already given. As he informed the naval chiefs, he would 'rather take back with him the certainty that some definite help would be given to the Dominions in the case of a war with Japan, even if it were less than they had perhaps, in the past, been led to suppose'. What would not suffice, said Menzies, were 'rhetorical phrases such as "cutting our losses in the Mediterranean and proceeding to your assistance"'.[4] But, under Churchill, Britain remained rich in rhetorical phrases and poor in concrete commitments to the Far East.

Menzies' willingness to absolve Britain of its traditional undertaking reflected his personal commitment as a British–Australian to the priorities of the empire. He justified the consequent effect on Australian security by taking comfort from British assertions about Japanese military inferiority. Accepting these assertions, Menzies argued that aircraft rather than ships would provide the 'great deterrent' at Singapore. Had Menzies' call been answered, it might have tipped the balance in the subsequent unsuccessful defence of Singapore in 1942. But his call was not answered and, after a disastrous turn of events in the Middle East, Menzies would later retract it in return for a British promise to reinforce Singapore only after it had been attacked. In the event, the Hurricanes were sent to Singapore in January 1942. But there were only 51 of them and they were unassembled, sent by ship in crates. They were too little and too late to change the course of the battle.[5]

Although Menzies realised that the long-promised Far East fleet was no longer possible, if it ever had been, the Australian people were kept ignorant of their exposed circumstances. On 12 March, four days after Menzies effectively released Britain from its naval promise, Fadden reported to the Commonwealth Parliament on his talks with Brooke-Popham. Acknowledging the 'importance to Australia of the defence of Singapore', Fadden confidently proclaimed that the 'assurances we have received from the British Government ... enable me to tell you that the defence of Singapore will be an Empire defence. Australia will not be alone.' Accepting

Churchill's argument that it would be 'folly to have too many units *idly standing by* to meet the *possibility* of a threat to Singapore', Fadden nevertheless told the parliament that

in the event of Japan entering the war against us we are assured by the United Kingdom Government that an immediate redistribution of the Naval Forces would be made should the threat to our communications in the Pacific and Indian Oceans be relatively greater than that in the Atlantic.

This was not much of a promise on which to base Australia's defence but it was deemed sufficient to allow the dominion to continue its industrial transformation without the disruptive efforts entailed by a policy of defence self-reliance and total mobilisation. It was this that Fadden stressed in concluding his comforting address, noting the export orders for defence equipment that had been won by Australian manufacturers and leaving to the imagination of his audience 'the future results of the industrial and manufacturing revolution which is now taking shape in our midst'.[6]

While in London, Menzies tried to compensate for the absence of the Far East fleet by renewing his search for a lasting settlement with Japan, fearing that British policy could provoke Tokyo into war. After visiting the Foreign Office, he described the British policy towards Japan as one of 'drift' and bemoaned the 'mental condition of thinking that all was lost and making up our minds that there must be war'. However, his proposal for a settlement was rejected by British officials who pointed out that a settlement would demand territorial concessions and 'throwing over China ... a thing to which the United States would never agree'. Menzies hoped that the return of Eden, who was in Cairo coordinating policy towards Greece, would force on the Foreign Office what he saw as a less dangerous policy towards Japan.[7] In order to bring his own pressure to bear, Menzies made a powerful speech in London arguing that peace with Japan remained possible. However, he was forced to retreat when news of the speech reached Australia, provoking allegations by Labor MPs of appeasement by Menzies and expressions of dismay by his own colleagues that the speech would deflate in the public's mind the sense of urgency about the war that they had been trying during the recent war scare to encourage. Menzies was put on notice about the political risks involved in his search for peace and trod much more warily as a result.[8]

Menzies' political troubles were increased by the deteriorating position in Greece. He had agreed to Australian participation in the expedition during an after-dinner discussion with Churchill at Chequers. Without seeking advice from Blamey, and despite the continuing reservations of Bruce, Menzies asked his war cabinet also to approve the participation of its troops. He had sought an assurance from Churchill that the expedition would not be a 'forlorn hope' but then pressed on without that assurance being provided. The Australian war cabinet also had serious reservations about the expedition but fell in with Menzies without seeking the approval of, or even informing, the advisory war council until after the government's consent had reached London.[9]

When Australian reservations about the expedition were borne out by subsequent events, Menzies was bitter in his denunciation of Churchill and his control over the British war machine. On 14 April, he vented his frustration in his diary, describing the British war cabinet as 'deplorable — dumb men most of whom disagree with Winston but none of whom dare to say so ... The Chiefs of Staff are without exception Yes-men, and a politician runs the Services. Winston is a dictator ...'[10] He resolved to remain even longer in London to oversee the deteriorating situation in Greece and the Middle East. Not only was the British expedition to Greece summarily expelled by the tanks and dive-bombers of the German invaders, and evacuated off the beaches at great cost to the ships of the Royal Navy, but the weakened British forces in Libya were confronted with Germany's General Rommel and the first elements of the future Afrika Korps, which began to redress the thrashing of their Italian allies. For a time during April, it seemed that Britain might be forced into a hasty withdrawal from the entire Middle East region under the impact of the two-pronged German assault through Greece and Libya.

The situation in the Mediterranean did not help Menzies in his efforts to extricate aircraft for the Far East. On 9 April, after Menzies had been in London for seven weeks, the defence committee of the war cabinet finally approved a program of aircraft deliveries for Australia. Such a program had been first requested by Bruce nearly a year beforehand. It was like drawing teeth from a tiger, with the belated program comprising the absolute minimum number of aircraft, and mainly types that were unwanted by Britain. The air minister, Sir Archibald Sinclair, intended to offer Australia twelve Beaufighters for delivery in December 1941 although, 'if pressed', he might increase this to twenty. It would not be much of a sacrifice by Britain since they would only be delivered after 22 British squadrons had been equipped with Beaufighters and when production of the planes was running at 150 a month. The main aircraft to be supplied to Australia were Brewster Bermudas, an American aircraft that was still being developed and 'in which the Royal Air Force was not particularly interested'. And they would not arrive until mid-1942.[11]

Even so, Churchill tried to prevent this parsimonious commitment of aircraft, arguing that it was 'most unwise to fritter away aircraft to Australia, where they would not come into action against the Germans'. However, as the chief of the air staff, Sir Charles Portal, pointed out, Britain did not have the aircrew to man all the planes that it was producing. Moreover, the dispatch of aircraft to Australia would deter a possible Japanese attack, and therefore save Britain from having to send naval forces to the Pacific, while the Australians would probably agree to base some of the resulting squadrons outside of Australia. In supporting Portal, the dominions secretary, Lord Cranborne, urged that Churchill give Menzies some crumbs to take back with him as Britain would 'not be satisfying many of his other demands'. Churchill reluctantly agreed, provided that Menzies was not promised 'more than was absolutely necessary'.[12]

When Menzies and Bruce met with Sinclair and Beaverbrook the following day, the visiting Australian agreed to a delivery program that was even more extended than that to which Churchill had grudgingly agreed. He agreed to take twelve of the Beaufighters by December 1941, even though Sinclair had been prepared to concede twenty if he was pressed by Menzies. As for the rest, Beaverbrook promised to expedite delivery of 52 Hudsons from the United States, while 243 Bermudas were promised for delivery by mid-1942. But there was no guarantee that these promised deliveries would ever be made. As Sinclair told Beaverbrook prior to the meeting, he would make sure that 'these Dominions do not strip us of everything' and would make clear to Menzies that any promises were 'not firm and that delivery must be governed by the war situation'. Not that Britain was suffering from a shortage of aircraft. As Beaverbrook had informed Churchill just five days previously, Britain's total aircraft production for March 1941 was 1853, twice that of March 1940, while the production of fighter planes was three times that of the previous year. Britain was now producing 'more aircraft than the Air Ministry can use', trumpeted Beaverbrook.[13]

Menzies was kept in the dark on this, and accepted the relatively paltry provision of planes even though it would leave Australia poorly defended. He told Fadden that Britain's needs, both at home and in the Middle East, must take priority over Australia's and assured his colleagues in Canberra that Britain was 'sincerely desirous of helping us to the greatest extent possible'. The deluded Menzies was caught in a bind. As he advised Fadden, he felt unable to pressure Britain for aircraft for Australia at the same time as he was pressuring it to provide 'adequate air strength in the Middle East' to protect the embattled Australian divisions.[14] It was left to Bruce to press Australia's case with a force that Menzies was not inclined to apply. He told Beaverbrook and Sinclair that it would be 'a little difficult to convince the Government and people of Australia that the whole of the requirements of the United Kingdom must be satisfied before any of the Australian aircraft were released'. But he was not supported by Menzies, who believed, as he wrote in his diary, that Britain was 'treating us fairly'. Moreover, as Menzies assured Fadden, Britain had also given him a 'categorical assurance that should war occur in the Far East there will be an immediate review of air resources with a view to their re-disposition to meet the dangers on all fronts'.[15] This was just the sort of general assurance that he had deemed unacceptable with regard to the dispatch of the Far East fleet.

Menzies' efforts to achieve a transfer of Britain's productive capacity to Australia were also unsuccessful. If Britain shifted some of its aircraft production to Australia, argued Menzies, it would be safe from the German bombing that was devastating the factories of the Midlands. From Australia's point of view, it might also be the only way that the dominion could guarantee itself a supply of aircraft. More broadly, it would fulfil

Menzies' aim of maintaining the economic interdependence of the British empire, shutting American capital out of Australia and promoting Australia's peacetime development.[16] Although Beaverbrook and other British ministers expressed agreement in principle with Menzies' proposal, they ensured that it would be rejected by Churchill and his war cabinet.[17] For one thing, German bombing was not affecting Britain's aircraft production to the extent that it was necessary to shift some of these factories offshore, and particularly not to the other side of the world.

Neither was Menzies successful in boosting the defences of Singapore by having Britain dispatch Hurricane fighters or additional naval forces there. The chiefs of staff argued that the demands of the Middle East must take priority and that the Buffalo aircraft would 'probably prove more than a match for any Japanese aircraft'.[18] As for naval forces, no additional forces would be sent. Nor would Britain provide any precise undertaking as to the extent of naval reinforcements that would be dispatched to the Pacific in the event of Japan entering the war. Waiting until just prior to Menzies' departure from London, the defence committee was advised by the first sea lord, Admiral Pound, that there were 'too many unknown factors' to provide Menzies with a precise timetable of naval reinforcements in the event of a Pacific war. As for Britain's promise to abandon the Middle East in order to save the Far East, Pound argued that it would be 'wrong to abandon the whole of our interests in the Middle East until it became absolutely necessary to do so'. Just so, agreed Churchill, who suggested that Menzies simply be given a restatement of this promise, but with the proviso that Britain would not surrender its 'great interests in the Middle East on account of a few raids by Japanese cruisers'. Churchill clearly believed that Menzies was under pressure to obtain an unequivocal assurance from London in order to appease the 'nervous nellies' within the Labor opposition. And he was not about to provide him with one and thereby surrender what he called 'sound strategical ideas in order to satisfy the ignorance of the Australian Opposition'. Instead of providing forces for the Far East, Churchill intended to ask Australia to raise a fifth division of the AIF for Britain's use overseas.[19] It was a measure of the gulf between the British and Australian viewpoints.

Britain's refusal to provide a detailed timetable for its promised naval reinforcement of the Far East convinced Frederick Shedden, secretary of Australia's defence department and a member of Menzies' group in London, that Australia would have to concentrate on its local defence by aircraft. He advised Menzies that 'all possible efforts and resources should be directed to producing as much as we are able to do, as quickly as we can'. At the same time, he criticised the British chiefs of staff for exhibiting a 'degree of complacency which we have come to expect about the defence of the Pacific region', while conceding that Australia had for too long 'readily accepted the general assurances about the defence of this area'. Bruce agreed, advising Menzies of the political necessity of him returning to Australia with specific defence achievements and urging him, if necessary, to confront Churchill with the threat of Australia withdrawing its contribution from the British war effort unless it was given adequate assurances about its defence.[20]

For some years, the Labor Party under John Curtin, together with various army officers and public commentators, had been arguing against Australia's reliance on the Singapore strategy, which depended on Britain's ability and willingness to spring to Australia's defence in the context of a war on two fronts. Until now, Shedden had been one of the stalwart defenders of that strategy, and of Australia's commitment to imperial defence, and had been dismissive of its critics.[21] Although his experience in London had finally alerted Shedden to the basic contradiction of the Singapore strategy, he was unable to convince Menzies to recant his own long commitment to that strategy. Menzies comforted himself with the conviction, shared by Churchill, that a Japanese invasion of Australia was unlikely. Moreover, he had other more pressing concerns. He feared that the British position in the Middle East might have to be abandoned, with all that meant for the many Australian troops in that theatre and for his own tenuous political position in Australia. He could hardly press strongly for Britain to send forces to the Far East, which was still at peace, when it might mean the sacrifice of Australian and other forces in the Middle East. As he confided to General Dill, chief of the imperial general staff, he was so worried about the political implications of the possible fall of Tobruk and Greece that 'he would hardly dare go home, and that he might as well go for a trip to the North Pole'. He was also being drawn into a political intrigue that had as its eventual aim the unseating of Churchill from the British prime ministership. Incredible as it may seem at this distance, Menzies' eyes were drawn to the tantalising prospect of forging a political future in London and perhaps even being the man to replace Churchill.[22]

For these reasons, Menzies accepted Britain's refusal to give precision to its traditional guarantee to provide for Australia's security. When he attended a meeting of the defence committee on 29 April, his principal concern was British strategy in the Middle East and the need to plan for a possible evacuation. This did not endear him to Churchill, who was adamantly opposed to such a possibility even being suggested and who had, just the previous day, ordered that Egypt be held to the death. As much as anything, his political survival depended upon it. And with access to Rommel's coded wireless communications, Churchill could be quietly confident that Rommel's increasing supply difficulties would soon halt his advance into Egypt. Menzies had not been made privy to this secret information and could only foresee defeat for the troops he had so recently reviewed in the Middle East.[23]

As for the Far East, Menzies had failed during more than two months in London to achieve the urgent supplies for Singapore that had been the ostensible purpose of his mission. On 28 April, Churchill directed his chiefs of staff not to 'make any further dispositions for the defence of Malaya and Singapore, beyond those modest arrangements which are in progress ...'.[24] Menzies was left clinging to the verbal assurances of the British government, and the confident prediction by Churchill that 'if the Japanese did come in, he felt sure the United States would declare war'. Such a prospect might comfort Churchill, who was keen above everything else to repeat his experience of the First World War and draw the Americans into another European war, but it should not have provided much comfort to Menzies in view of the agreed Anglo–American strategy in such an eventuality to concentrate their resources against Germany.[25]

Menzies not only accepted the British view of the Far East but also concurred in a decision that would place Australia in even greater peril. On 30 April, just two days before Menzies' departure from London, Churchill had thrown his support behind an American proposal to transfer part of the US Pacific fleet to the Atlantic Ocean. Although it was of vital concern to Australia, Churchill had not planned to consult Menzies before confirming his support to Washington. When he learnt of the development, a furious Menzies ensured that consultation with Australia did take place but he made no effort to stop the shift of US naval forces from the Pacific. Instead, Menzies ensured that the support of his government would be given to the move, despite advice from Casey in Washington that the transfer of ships would 'leave British countries and interests in the Pacific in considerable peril'. Menzies accepted the British argument that the 'entry of the United States of America into the war transcends in importance every other present issue'. He also told his cabinet colleagues in Canberra that the evidence of increasing American belligerence would probably deter Japan, while the assistance to British naval forces in the Atlantic might allow Britain to send a fleet to the Far East.[26] Whether or not Menzies really believed these arguments, they proved disastrously wrong. Japan was not deterred and Britain's Far Eastern fleet was never formed.

On 2 May, Menzies finally left London on his journey back to Australia. Before leaving he had two important meetings. The first was with Churchill on whom Menzies tried unsuccessfully to press the case for a reorganised war cabinet over which Churchill would have less sway. The second meeting was with Beaverbrook who, despite refusing Menzies' requests for aircraft production equipment, was keen to enlist the Australian in his own campaign to limit Churchill's practically unbridled power over policy. He told Menzies that it was 'absurd' that he should go back to Australia and promptly began a relentless press campaign in his *Daily Express* newspaper calling for Menzies' return to London as an imperial representative in the British war cabinet. With Churchill's determined pursuit of total victory, and the sorry consequences of this in Greece, Menzies' outlook was bleak as he left for home. He wrote in his diary that he was 'desperately afraid of the future in Great Britain'.[27]

Churchill's outlook could not have been more different. The United States Congress had approved the Lend-Lease Bill, thereby assuring Britain of a continuing flow of war supplies from America despite British dollar reserves becoming exhausted. The shift of US warships to the Atlantic lightened the load of the Royal Navy and helped to tip the balance in the vital battle of the Atlantic on which Germany was now concentrating most of its naval power. Although the Middle East situation looked perilous, Churchill knew of Rommel's supply problems and the slender thread on which his run of victories was hanging. While Greece was a military disaster for Britain, Churchill knew that it had the effect of disrupting Germany's planned attack on Russia. The seal on Churchill's optimism came with the confirmation that Germany would soon direct its military might against Russia rather than against Britain. The threat of a cross-Channel invasion had receded, at least for 1941, and possibly forever.[28]

The stark contrast in the outlooks of Menzies and Churchill would cause a series of increasingly bitter disputes between Britain and its distant dominion. It was regrettable that Churchill felt unable to share with Menzies the secret information on which his confidence was based. Instead, Menzies returned to Australia as a determined opponent of the British leader and with a gloomy view of the European war and the prospects for Britain. Unfortunately for Australia, Menzies largely shared Churchill's optimism about the Far East and the inability of Japan to mount a serious challenge to Australian security.

This relative optimism about the Far East, together with his abiding attachment to the British empire, caused Menzies to continue holding America at arm's length. His government had rejected a proposal in March 1941 to allow a direct radiotelegraph link between Australia and the United States, preferring instead to protect the British cable monopoly from competition. Similarly, Menzies rejected renewed attempts by Pan American Airways to gain landing rights in Australia without the Americans granting reciprocal rights to British airlines. Menzies maintained his intransigent attitude despite Britain having agreed unconditionally to Pan American flying via Hong Kong to Singapore. By May 1941, the indirect air link between Australia and the United States via New Zealand was reduced to a once-weekly service, causing costly delays in vital mail deliveries and passenger traffic. As for defence industry links, Menzies was adamant that the 'lines of industrial communication' must be 'between Australia and Britain, not Australia and America'.[29]

Menzies had left for London in January 1941 with his own political security and the country's military security both vying for his attention. In his absence, his political position had worsened. Fadden proved to be a popular and energetic leader who was willing to allow his ministers greater freedom to use their initiative than Menzies had been willing to do.[30] As well, the Labor Party had been invigorated by the healing of the split within its New South Wales branch, which caused an immediate jump in its popular support. As an indirect consequence, the ambitious Labor MP and former High Court judge, Dr H. V. Evatt, was brought into the advisory war council where he curbed Curtin's more accommodating attitude towards the government. Evatt was keen to take on the responsibility of government, either under Curtin or in a national administration, perhaps with himself as leader.[31] Menzies' agreement to the Greek expedition and his failure to obtain any real improvement in Australia's defence position eroded his fragile political leadership even further. In vain, he had tried from London to draw Curtin into a national government, although his efforts were not helped by newspaper speculation that he wanted such an administration as a means of allowing his own retention in Britain.[32] With all these worries and little to show for his absence, it is not surprising that Menzies, as his aircraft laboured through threatening skies above the Tasman Sea, wrote in his diary of the 'sick feeling of repugnance and apprehension [that] grows in me as I near Australia'.[33]

After five wasted months, Menzies had failed in his stated purpose to obtain aircraft for the defence of Singapore. At the same time, he had approved the dispatch of Australian troops to Malaya where they lacked proper protection from the sea and air and would face almost certain defeat if Japan cared to attack. He had not obtained the transfer of aircraft factories from Britain and had vetoed his cabinet's attempt to explore the American alternatives. He had left London with his relations with Churchill embittered, which flowed over into the relationship between the two governments. Menzies' main achievement was a program of aircraft deliveries that provided little immediate succour for the dominion's defence. Moreover, the promised aircraft would prove to be unsuitable for use against the Japanese. While Menzies' prolonged visit abroad had enlightened the dominion about its predicament, its continuing devotion to the empire made it blind to any solutions. And time was no longer on its side.

NOTES

[1] Menzies diary, 27 February 1941; Cable, Menzies to Fadden, 1 March 1941, *DAFP*, Vol. 4, Doc. 328.

[2] Note of conversation, Menzies, Shedden and Bruce with Alexander and Phillips, 8 March 1941, AVAR 5/5/13, Alexander Papers, CC.

[3] Cable, Burrell to Colvin, 24 February 1941, *DAFP*, Vol. 4, Doc. 318.

[4] ibid.; Cable, Menzies to Fadden, 4 March 1941, and Note of Conversations at UK Admiralty, 8 March 1941, *DAFP*, Vol. 4, Docs 330 and 343; Menzies diary, 8 March 1941.

[5] Menzies diary, 8 March 1941; S. Roskill, *The War at Sea*, Vol. 2, London, 1956, p. 8; Two later deliveries of 50 and 40 Hurricanes arrived in the Far East in late January and early February as Singapore was set to fall. Most were retained for use in the NEI.

[6] Address by Fadden to joint Meeting of both Houses of Parliament, 12 March 1941, CRS A5954, Box 308, NAA (author's emphasis in italics).

[7] Record of meeting at UK Foreign Office, 26 February 1941, *DAFP*, Vol. 4, Doc. 324; See also J. Kennedy, *The Business of War*, London, 1957, p. 190; Letter, Sir Horace Seymour to his wife, 27 February 1941, SEYR 2/4, Seymour Papers, CC; Cadogan diary, 26 February 1941, in Dilks (ed.), *The Diaries of Sir Alexander Cadogan*, p. 358; Menzies diary, 26 February 1941.

[8] Advisory War Council Minutes, 28 February 1941, CRS A2682, Vol. 2, Minute 174, NAA; See also Day, *Menzies and Churchill at War*, Chaps 4–5; War Cabinet Minutes, 5 March 1941, CRS A2673, Vol. 6, Minute 894; Cable No. 98, Fadden to Menzies, 5 March 1941, CRS CP290/9, Bundle 1[11]SC; Cable No. 17, Menzies to Fadden, 6 March 1941, CRS M100, 'March 1941', NAA.

[9] Menzies diary, 23 February 1941; Cable No. 82, Fadden to Menzies, 26 February 1941, CRS CP 290/9, Bundle 1[11]SC; Advisory War Council Minutes, 28 February 1941, CRS A2682, Vol. 2, Minute 223, NAA.

[10] Menzies diary, 14 April 1941; See Cadogan diary, 7 April 1941, in Dilks (ed.), *The Diaries of Sir Alexander Cadogan*, p. 370.

[11] Defence Committee (Operations) Minutes, 9 April 1941, CAB 69/2, D.O. (41)12, PRO.

[12] ibid.

[13] Minute (copy), Beaverbrook to Churchill, 5 April 1941, BBK D416; Letters, Beaverbrook to Sinclair, and Sinclair to Beaverbrook, both 16 March 1941, BBK D/32; Letter, Beaverbrook to Sir Charles Wilson, 19 April 1941, BBK D/141, Beaverbrook Papers, HLRO.

[14] Cable M57, Menzies to Fadden, 10 April 1941, CRS A5954, Box 617, 'Prime Minister's Visit to United Kingdom 1941. Paper No. 19', NAA.

[15] Minutes of meeting at Ministry of Aircraft Production, 10 April 1941 and Cable M57, Menzies to Fadden, 10 April 1941, CRS 5954, Box 617, 'Prime Minister's Visit to United Kingdom 1941. Paper No. 19', NAA; Menzies diary, 10 April 1941.

[16] At one stage during his London visit, Menzies reacted angrily when he wrongly believed that the Australian war cabinet had undercut his efforts by agreeing to establish an American aircraft engine factory in Australia. In fact, it was just exploring the possibilities and no agreement had been reached. Day, *Menzies and Churchill at War*, p. 99.

[17] Day, *Menzies and Churchill at War*, p. 146.

[18] Draft reply by Chiefs of Staff to Memorandum by Menzies, 9 April 1941, PREM 3/156/4, PRO.

[19] Defence Committee (Operations) Minutes, 9 April 1941, CAB 69/2, D.O. (41)12, PRO.

[20] Memorandum, Shedden to Menzies, 14 April 1941, CRS A5954, Box 625, 'Prime Minister's Visit to U.K., 1941. Paper 7A'; Letter, drafted by Bruce and apparently intended for submission by Menzies to Churchill, 7 April 1941, CRS M103, '1941', NAA.

[21] David Horner, *Defence Supremo: Sir Frederick Shedden and the Making of Australian Defence Policy*, Sydney, 2000, pp. 52–3.

[22] For details of Menzies' political ambitions in London, see Day, *Menzies and Churchill at War*, Chaps 10–11.

[23] Defence Committee (Operations) Minutes, 29 April 1941, CAB 69/2, D.O. (41)20, PRO.

[24] Directive by Churchill, 28 April 1941, PREM 3/156/6; Defence Committee (Operations) Minutes, 29 April 1941, CAB 69/2, D.O. (41)20, PRO.

[25] Defence Committee (Operations) Minutes, 29 April 1941, CAB 69/2, D.O. (41)20, PRO.

[26] Defence Committee (Operations) Minutes, 30 April and 1 May 1941, CAB 69/2, D.O. (41)21 and 22, PRO; Cable, Menzies to Fadden, 2 May 1941, and Cable, Casey to Department of External Affairs, 2 May 1941, *DAFP*, Vol. 4, Docs 443 and 445.

[27] Menzies diary, 1 and 2 May 1941.

[28] For the effect of the Greek campaign on Germany's planned attack on Russia, see Cable, Churchill to Eden, 30 March 1941, ISMAY VI/1, Ismay Papers, KC; On 27 April, Britain's Joint Intelligence Committee finally conceded that an invasion of Britain was no longer Germany's immediate priority. The dominions were kept ignorant of this change in Britain's fortunes. On 31 May, Australia was advised that an 'invasion of the United Kingdom probably remains Germany's 1941 objective'. See Hinsley, *British Intelligence in the Second World War*, Vol. 1, p. 264; Cable Z196, Cranborne to Menzies, 31 May 1941, AA CP 290/7, Folder 1, Item 5, NAA.

[29] Letter, Stewart to McEwen, 25 March 1941, Cable No. 164, Fadden to Menzies, 16 March 1941, and Cable M81, Menzies to Fadden, 25 April 1941, CRS A461, I 314/1/4, Part 3; Cable No. 165, Fadden to New Zealand Government, 7 May 1941, CRS A5954, Box 343; and Letter, Menzies to Churchill, 29 March 1941, CRS A5954, Box 617, NAA.

[30] Letter, Hughes to Menzies, 21 February 1941, CRS A5954, Box 630, NAA.

[31] Letter, Evatt to Menzies, 24 May 1941, Evatt Papers, 'War — ALP Government, Formation of, 1941', FUL.

[32] Cable M72, Menzies to Curtin, and Cable, Menzies to Fadden, both 22 April 1941, CRS A5954, Box 630, NAA; *Sun*, Sydney, 23 April 1941.

[33] Prior to Menzies' landing in Sydney, his friends and supporters had warned him of the political plotters who had been scheming to cause his downfall during his absence in London. Martin, *Robert Menzies*, Vol. 1, p. 361; Menzies diary, 23 May 1941.

TWELVE

'the sky will be the limit'

On 3 May 1941, Menzies had flown out of Bristol bound for Australia by way of North America and New Zealand. With the campaign in the Mediterranean looking desperate for Britain, Menzies was deeply depressed about the possible future course of the war. As were many military and political figures in Britain. After being bundled out of Greece by the German army and the Luftwaffe, Britain was thrown onto the defensive as it fought desperately to retain its hold on the Middle East. Many of the evacuated troops from Greece were offloaded in Crete, where Churchill hoped to establish a fortress capable of stemming the German tide southwards. But Crete was set upon in its turn by the overwhelming force of the Luftwaffe, which dropped paratroops and landed gliders to capture the island's airfields. Another rushed evacuation was in prospect for the exhausted Australian, British and New Zealand troops. Across in Libya, Rommel had outflanked the weakened British forces, which had been operating at the end of extended supply lines, and sent them scurrying far back into Egypt. The run of spectacular successes that Menzies had witnessed just three months earlier had been swept away. Australia's 9th Division retreated to Tobruk where it dug in for one of the longest sieges of the war, while contingency plans were prepared in Cairo for the complete evacuation of British forces from Egypt.

During his time in London, Menzies had become disenchanted with Churchill's leadership and had been made aware of the widespread opposition among military and political figures to Churchill's control of strategy. He allowed himself to be enticed by siren calls from these figures which suggested he might topple Churchill himself. He decided that Churchill's untrammelled hold over strategy had to be broken by the combined pressure of the dominions and saw himself playing a leading part in the political changes that he believed were necessary in London. As a result, Australia was saddled with a prime minister who had become more concerned with political intrigue against Churchill than with the security of the country in his charge.[1]

During Menzies' absence, the Australian government had adopted a slightly more resolute attitude towards local defence. The political position remained precarious for the coalition cabinet and the Labor Party was applying increasing pressure on the government to accord the defence of Australia as much priority as it was giving to the defence of the British position in the Middle East. On 8 May, Curtin used his position on the advisory war council to oppose any further reinforcement of Egypt and to suggest that Britain's Mediterranean fleet be withdrawn before it became trapped there by the possible German capture of Gibraltar and Suez. Such a timely withdrawal, argued Curtin, would improve the 'prospects of a British Fleet based on Singapore, immediately relieving Australia and the empire of the danger of Japanese entry into the war'. While Curtin accepted that the defence of Britain was of 'paramount importance', he questioned whether 'this should be wholly accepted from the point of view of the requirements of Australian defence'.[2]

Curtin was in good company in pressing this suggestion. Two days beforehand, General Dill had proposed an even more drastic plan to Churchill, urging that Britain abandon the Middle East altogether and concentrate its armoured forces in England to guard against a possible invasion. Though Churchill rejected such an idea, Dill did succeed at the end of June in blocking a move by Churchill to dispatch an additional supply of tanks through the hazards of the Mediterranean to the embattled forces in Egypt. As Dill argued, Britain could not afford to 'run any more risks in home defence, where disaster would lose the war — disaster in the Middle East would not'.[3] It was a view shared by Britain's minister for economic warfare, Hugh Dalton, who wrote in his diary of being 'mentally prepared to lose Egypt, Syria and Palestine, in addition to North Africa, Spain and Portugal and also a part of the fleet while we are trying to get it out'. Such a disaster, argued Dalton, 'would lengthen the war though not alter its end'.[4] The planners at the War Office agreed, assessing the importance of the Middle East as being of the first magnitude to Britain, but not vital, while Admiral Sir Gerald Dickens at the Admiralty was similarly relaxed about the prospect of withdrawing the fleet from the Mediterranean. As he reminded Britain's naval commander in the Mediterranean, Admiral Sir Andrew Cunningham, the British had 'evacuated the Mediterranean before and we survived'. Indeed, in the long view, 'one could watch a series of withdrawals on our part in the Near and Middle East with a good deal of resignation'.[5]

Although Curtin's suggestions may have been received well in some British quarters, and certainly made sense in terms of Australia's defence interests, they received scant regard from the government members of Australia's advisory war council. The army minister, Percy Spender, warned that a British withdrawal would discourage the entry of the United States into the war, while the navy minister, Billy Hughes, dismissed the idea completely, maintaining that the Mediterranean position was not desperate and 'must be resolutely faced'. Although this caused Curtin to back down, his colleagues were even more resolute in their demands. The ambitious Dr Evatt, who was secretly scheming to join a national government with Menzies, urged that Britain be pressured to supply the military appreciation of the Middle East that Australia had requested two weeks previously and that 'no further troops should be sent abroad, as every trained and equipped man in Australia was an additional protection against Japanese intervention'. For his part, the Labor MP Norman Makin pointed to the 'tendency to commit Australia to greater obligations overseas than originally contemplated', referring in particular to the way in which the 9th Division was formed from troops originally sent overseas as reinforcements for the 6th Division.[6]

Although Curtin was consistently helpful to Menzies' minority administration, he could not ignore the strengthening of his party's fortunes that might see it forming a government before the next federal election in 1943. In February 1941, the breach in the Labor Party ranks had been healed when the breakaway branch in New South Wales reunited behind Curtin's leadership. The political gains were immediate, with the New South Wales election in May returning the Labor Party to power in that state. Later that month, a federal by-election in South Australia confirmed the trend away from the conservatives. This reminded MPs on both sides of parliament that it would only take a switch of allegiance by the two independent MPs for Menzies to be evicted from the Lodge and Curtin to be installed in his place. For the conservatives to be secure, it would be up to Menzies to provide the inspirational war leadership that could scupper Labor's campaign.

Fadden had warned Menzies that the Australian public was waiting for a decisive lead from the government for a 'fuller war effort' and that the New South Wales election result could precipitate a 'frontal attack' by the Labor Party. Though he resented the implied criticism, Menzies reassured Fadden that he was returning 'impressed with [the] gravity and urgency of our position and, so far as Australia's war effort [was] concerned, the sky will be the limit'. He promised to make public statements that would call for everything to be placed on a complete war basis.[7] Australia needed more than statements. The press were already renewing their clamour for a national government that would be able to produce an intensified war effort. And Evatt was prepared to do just that, greeting Menzies upon his arrival in Sydney with a private offer to join a national administration.[8] At the same time, some of Menzies' colleagues were actively conspiring to depose him as prime minister.[9] But they could not strike until Menzies had been given another opportunity, following his London experience, to provide the leadership that the country demanded.

One possible challenger to Menzies was Percy Spender, who had already been putting a forceful case for a greater war effort. In a secret memorandum to Fadden on 21 April, he had predicted the possibility of Australia's three divisions in the Middle East being lost to the Germans and warned of the open invitation this would provide to the Japanese to attack Australia. More importantly, he confided that, after eighteen months of war, the army remained unable to 'face an enemy powerful enough to reach these shores in any substantial force'. Stressing the 'extreme gravity of the present situation', Spender claimed that anti-tank units had been sent overseas 'without having even seen an anti-tank gun', while there was a 'stream of men for military and other national services who are still being dammed back'. While he wanted the government to organise Australian industry and manpower onto 'a full war footing', he wanted it to be 'a gradual and largely voluntary process'. It was a harsh indictment of Menzies' war leadership and an eloquent and soundly based plea for switching the emphasis of Australian defence policy from imperial to local defence.[10]

Spender's warnings were largely unheeded and his proposals unimplemented. Ironically, the parlous situation in the Middle East had the effect of concentrating Australian efforts on ensuring that the Middle East did not fall to the Germans rather than ensuring that Australia did not fall to the Japanese. In addition, Admiral Colvin had returned from another conference of defence representatives in Singapore with assurances about Australia's defence that conflicted markedly with Spender's allegations. As a result of his discussions with the British commander-in-chief at Singapore, Sir Robert Brooke-Popham, Colvin reported that the reinforcements of Malaya since the alarming report of the previous October had 'so materially strengthened their position that he was optimistic as to the ability of Singapore to hold out [against any attack by Japan], and to continue to operate as a Fleet Base'. Although Colvin's report was unjustifiably optimistic, it seemed to be what the Australian government wanted to hear and it helped to elicit an even greater Australian contribution to the defence of the empty British naval base.[11] But the conflict between imperial and local defence would not disappear.

Menzies was not the man to resolve the conflict. Speeches were his strength, with his homecoming speech before a packed and enthusiastic audience at the Sydney Town Hall on 26 May being described by the *Sydney*

Morning Herald as 'the most stirring speech of his political career'. It called on Australians to make a greater war effort and display greater unity. 'GO TO IT,' he exhorted.[12] However, when he had to translate these sentiments into action, Menzies faltered. Instead, his efforts were directed towards securing his early return to Britain where he had been led to believe a promising political future beckoned. His ambition was so clear, and his efforts to achieve it so clumsy, that the press in Britain and Australia soon filled with stories regarding his intentions.[13] They undercut his proclaimed intent to promote an all-out war effort in Australia.

When Menzies reported to the advisory war council on 28 May about the results of his London sojourn, he regaled his fellow MPs with a litany of complaints about Churchill and the workings of the British war cabinet in order to establish the rationale for another trip. He argued strongly for the inclusion of a dominion representative in the war cabinet, a post that he hoped to fill himself, although Menzies did not disclose that ambition to his colleagues.[14] Only at later meetings did Menzies begin to reveal his failure in London to achieve the hoped-for results in regard to the defence of Singapore. Meanwhile, the military situation in the Middle East continued to worsen.

There seemed to be the danger of a German attack on Syria, which raised the prospect of British empire forces in Egypt being caught in a pincer movement from the east and west. As a result, the Australian war cabinet pressed Churchill to dispatch more fighter aircraft from Britain to guard against such a possibility. The request provided Churchill with the perfect foil to deflect any Australian demands for the dispatch of fighter aircraft to Singapore or Australia. He could hardly send them everywhere. Or so he would argue. It also gave him what he took to be a green light to send Australian troops off in a pre-emptive strike into Vichy French-controlled Syria without first consulting with the Australian government.[15]

As the Middle Eastern situation deteriorated, Australia found it increasingly difficult to focus on its own defence. The 9th Division remained trapped in Tobruk where its troops had to fend off repeated assaults by Italian and German troops. At the end of May, Crete fell to German paratroops, causing thousands of British, Australian and New Zealand troops to be captured while a hasty evacuation from the island's southern coast managed to rescue many others. But only at more cost to Britain's naval forces in the Mediterranean. Since Singapore was less likely to obtain ships or aircraft for its defence, Australia agreed on 11 June to the dispatch of another infantry brigade to Malaya, making two-thirds of the 8th Division committed to that theatre.[16] Although Menzies well knew the parlous situation at Singapore, he still sent troops to defend the indefensible while encouraging the United States to switch part of its naval forces to the Atlantic. At the same time, Australia's chiefs of staff conceded that they had no joint plans to meet specific forms of attack against Australia.[17] Moreover, Australia only possessed a few of the basic weapons essential for defence against invasion.

One of those weapons was naval mines to protect the sea lanes and ports around Australia. In late April 1941, Billy Hughes had scribbled an anxious note to the acting chief of the naval staff expressing his concern that 'if it were known that we have *no* mines after *18* months of war — for Port Stephens or any other port — there would be trouble'.[18] Hughes was right to be worried. Although plans had been laid before the war to commence production of naval mines, the first order was for only 500 mines and was not completed until mid-1941. This was despite advice in September 1940 that Australia would need 4000 mines to cope with a Pacific war. The government was also advised that it could no longer rely on a British fleet being deployed at Singapore on the outbreak of a Pacific war and that it must therefore prepare itself for a defensive naval strategy. As part of that strategy, naval mines were recommended as providing 'one of the cheapest and best means of defence'. Although the government consequently increased its order by an additional 1000 mines, it was still far short of the number needed for a Pacific war. At the same time, it accepted orders to supply Britain, New Zealand and Noumea with a total of 1400 mines.[19]

In June 1941, Menzies was informed that the first minefield would be laid near Port Moresby and that Britain had placed an order for more mines. Menzies seems to have been unaware that mines were even being produced in Australia and questioned whether defensive minefields should be laid prior to the outbreak of hostilities in the Pacific. Meanwhile, Port Stephens, the gateway to the vital industrial area of Newcastle, was still without mines, as was the rest of the east and north coast of Australia. The RAN simply did not have the mines to do it. It was not until the Labor government assumed office in October 1941 that an order for an additional 2000 mines was proposed to protect the eastern seaboard.[20] The tardy provision of mines was an indication of what an 'all-in war' meant under Menzies' leadership. The government was still guided by financial stringency, while export orders were still given a higher priority than making mines for Australia's defence. Imperial defence still held sway, with the needs of Britain and the Middle East coming before those of Australia. It was in the Middle East where most Australian forces were engaged and it was in the Middle East where the Australian government felt most at risk. As for local defence, it was imperative that Australians be made to *feel* secure rather than actually *be* secure, in order for the Middle East commitment to continue.

As for Menzies, he placed his personal faith in the Japanese not entering the war. If they did so, he confidently expected that the United States would come in on the British side and prevent any serious threat to Australia. After finishing his trip across the United States in May, Menzies claimed in his diary to have been 'left in no doubt (without words) that America will not stand by and see Australia attacked'.[21] As he admitted, this was more a feeling than something for which he had hard evidence. In fact, the evidence was pointing in a different direction. America had explicitly disavowed any responsibility for Australia's naval defence and Menzies had been advised that it would be 'quite impossible' for Australia to obtain American medium tanks 'in any reasonable time'. That left Australia with just ten light tanks that were used for training an armoured division that was intended for dispatch to the Middle East. The supply of any light tanks that Australia had on order from the United States would depend on British requirements in the Middle East being satisfied.[22]

Menzies' confidence about the Japanese not entering the war had been buttressed by his experience in London where he had met with British businessmen seeking friendly relations with Japan. He even seems to have dallied with the idea of making a Munich-type trip to Tokyo.[23] On his return to Australia, Menzies continued to argue for a 'realistic approach' towards

Japan.[24] He still felt that Japan could be prevented from expanding southwards towards Australia if various countries would agree to make various territorial and trade concessions to Tokyo. This may have been due to the influence of the Japanese minister in Australia, Tatsuo Kawai, who in 1938 had published a book, *The Goal of Japanese Expansion*, which argued the case for Japanese expansion but limited such expansion to the north Pacific. Although Menzies had been berated by the Labor Party for his London speech on peace in the Pacific, Curtin now joined him in trying to reach an agreement with Japan. The Labor leader had cultivated private contacts with Kawai and, on 5 June, received the consent of the advisory war council for these contacts to continue.[25]

Despite Menzies' criticism of the Foreign Office policy toward Japan, it was the foreign secretary, Anthony Eden, who made prolonged efforts to promote the sort of joint declaration advocated by Menzies. Unlike Menzies, though, he did not envisage it as part of a general Pacific settlement. In November 1940, the exiled Dutch government had asked Britain for an assurance of military assistance in the event of a Japanese attack on the NEI. Throughout 1941, Eden urged that such an assurance should be provided.[26] In mid-May, Eden seemed to achieve his objective when the matter came before the defence committee where he argued that British support for the NEI would be inevitable whatever the United States' attitude and that it was better to make such a declaration now and possibly deter a Japanese attack. The first sea lord, Admiral Pound, was appalled by the practical implications of committing to support the Dutch without an assurance that the United States would also stand with Britain alongside the Dutch. He reminded the committee that Britain's navy in the Far East was 'very weak' and that it would be foolish to declare war automatically when 'such action might lead to a damaging attack on our trade'. He argued for Britain to 'keep an open mind and to decide at the time whether it was to our advantage to declare war or not'. In a remarkable switch of position, the committee overruled Pound and threw its support behind Eden. Churchill, who was politically vulnerable at the time because of the sorry state of the war in the Mediterranean, bowed to the wishes of his colleagues and allowed the decision to stand, at least for the time being. At the same time, he emphasised that 'there could be no redistribution of naval forces to strengthen the Far East'. Churchill had a second line of defence with the committee's instruction for Eden to consult with the dominions and obtain their agreement to the declaration as well as to inform the United States.[27]

These conditions, and the passage of time, would allow scope for the decision to be reversed. Australia helped with this by opposing any public declaration of assistance for the Dutch if it did not also involve the United States. Acting on advice from Casey in Washington, Menzies argued that any unilateral declaration by the British empire could suggest to Tokyo that there was dissension between Britain and the United States on the issue and thereby have the opposite effect on Tokyo to that intended. Menzies proposed instead that a private assurance be made to the Dutch and that the United States be invited to join in such a message. Whatever happened, declared Menzies, Australia could not allow a Japanese invasion of the NEI, so close to Australia's northern coastline, to go unanswered.[28]

The United States government, as well as the British ambassador in Tokyo, agreed with the Australian opposition to making a public declaration of support for the Dutch. For its part, Washington instructed its ambassador in Tokyo to inform the Japanese privately that the United States had an interest in Britain's Far Eastern interests not being attacked.[29] The conflicting messages caused the British government to hesitate until Washington made its position clearer. When Eden brought the matter back before the war cabinet at the end of July, he found that his previous support had withered away. Churchill's political position had strengthened in the interim, allowing him twice to have a decision on the question deferred. Churchill refused to believe that Japan had designs on Singapore and argued against any commitment to defend the NEI while being unable to dispatch an adequate fleet. He advised his war cabinet to await the stiffening of American opinion before issuing any declaration.[30] Churchill's determination to avoid a single-handed war against Japan, and his refusal to draw a line on the map below which Japan would not be allowed to go, left Menzies' desire for a Pacific settlement unsatisfied. In the absence of such a settlement, Australia proposed pre-empting a Japanese attack on the NEI by stationing Australian forces there. But its proposal was rejected by Britain for fear of provoking the Japanese.[31]

The saga of the NEI declaration was overtaken by more momentous events in Europe. On 22 June 1941, Hitler unleashed the full might of his armed forces in a massive thrust into the heart of the Soviet Union. Although rumours of such an attack had been received in London from 1940 onwards, and British intelligence had reported on the shift of German forces eastward, Britain had been slow to give them credence. Moreover, when the attack finally occurred, few in London thought that Russia could resist for more than a few months. After all, the mighty French army had collapsed very quickly under the weight of the German armour and the pounding of the Luftwaffe. Why should the Russians, who had been humiliated by the Finns in 1940 and whose army had performed poorly in the First World War, be any more resilient than the French? Had he been alive, Napoleon could have suggested a few reasons why the Germans should have hesitated before unleashing their forces across the vastness of the Russian plains.

NOTES

1. For an extended discussion of this, see Day, *Menzies and Churchill at War*.
2. Advisory War Council Minutes, 8 May 1941, CRS A2682, Vol. 2, Minute 313, NAA.
3. Sir Ronald Wingate, *Lord Ismay*, London, 1970, p. 58; Pownall diary, 30 June 1941, in Brian Bond (ed.), *Chief of Staff*, Vol. 2, London, 1974, p. 30.
4. Dalton diary, 29 April 1941, I/24/100–101, Dalton Papers, LSE; See also Letter, Smuts to Wavell, 19 May 1941, in J. Van Der Poel (ed.), *Selections from the Smuts Papers*, Vol. 4, Cambridge, 1973, p. 299; Casey, *Personal Experience*, p. 73.
5. Pownall diary, 16 June 1941, in Bond (ed.), *Chief of Staff*, Vol. 2, p. 22; Letter, Dickens to Cunningham, 20 May 1941, ADD. MS. 52569, Cunningham Papers, BL. Not all the Admiralty were so sanguine about the prospect of abandoning the Mediterranean. A member of the Plans Division recalled how his group considered the Middle East and Mediterranean vital for the 'whole backbone of our strategy'. As of course did Churchill. 'My Life', autobiography of Admiral Sir William Davis, p. 256, WDVS 1/3, Davis Papers, CC.
6. Advisory War Council Minutes, 8 May 1941, CRS A2682, Vol. 2, Minute 313, NAA.
7. Cable, Fadden to Menzies, 11 May 1941, CRS A5954, Box 630; Cable, Menzies (in Washington) to Fadden, 13 May 1941, CRS CP 290/9, [15] S.C., NAA.
8. Letter, Evatt to Menzies, 24 May 1941, Evatt Collection, 'War — ALP Government, Formation of, 1941', FUL.
9. Cameron Hazlehurst, *Menzies Observed*, Sydney, 1979, p. 230.
10. Letter, Spender to Fadden, 21 April 1941, MS 4875, Box 1, Correspondence 1939–1949, Spender Papers, NLA.
11. War Cabinet Minutes, 15 May 1941, CRS A2673, Vol. 7, Minute 1073, NAA; Letter, Brooke-Popham to Ismay, 16 May 1941, V/1/12, Brooke-Popham Papers, KC.
12. Martin, *Robert Menzies*, Vol. 1, pp. 365–8.
13. See Day, *Menzies and Churchill at War*, Chaps 13–14.
14. Advisory War Council Minutes, 28 May 1941, CRS A2682, Vol. 2, Minute 346, NAA.
15. War Cabinet Minutes, 29 May 1941, CRS A2673, Vol. 7, Minute 1111, NAA; Cables No. 2649, 347 and 363, Menzies to Churchill, 29 May, 6 and 12 June 1941, PREM 3/281/10, PRO; Hasluck, *The Government and the People*, Vol. 1, pp. 341–4; Horner, *High Command*, pp. 108–11.
16. War Cabinet Minutes, 10 and 11 June 1941, CRS A2673, Vol. 7, Minutes 1138 and 1145, NAA.

17 War Cabinet Minutes, 10 June 1941, CRS A2673, Vol. 7, Minute 1136, NAA.

18 Note by Hughes, undated, JWD 5, Durnford Papers, IWM. The note was probably written during a war cabinet meeting on 24 April 1941, when mines were discussed with Durnford in attendance as Acting Chief of the Naval Staff. See CRS A5954, Box 483, NAA.

19 See CRS A5954, Box 483, NAA.

20 ibid.

21 Menzies diary, May 1941.

22 Letter (copy), M. Dewar (head of British Tank Mission in the United States) to A. Chamberlain (British Purchasing Mission in Washington), 13 May 1941, CRS A5954, Box 619, NAA.

23 Letters, Lord Sempill to Menzies, 23 April 1941, and Menzies to Sempill, 30 April 1941, CRS A5954, Box 625, NAA; *Tatler*, London, 14 May 1941.

24 Advisory War Council Minutes, 28 May 1941, CRS A2682, Vol. 2, Minute 346, NAA.

25 Curtin's contacts with Kawai came to nothing. The question of war or peace in the Pacific would be decided in Washington and Tokyo rather than Canberra. Advisory War Council Minutes, 5 June 1941, CRS A2682, Vol. 2, Minute 356, NAA; David Day, *John Curtin: A Life*, Sydney, 1999, pp. 423–24.

26 Cooperation with the Netherlands East Indies', Memorandum by Eden, 5 February 1941, CAB 66/14, W.P. (41)24, PRO.

27 Defence Committee (Operations) Minutes, 15 May 1941, CAB 69/2, D.O. (41)30, PRO.

28 Cable, Casey to External Affairs Department, 27 May 1941, and Cable, Commonwealth Government to Cranborne, 30 May 1941, *DAFP*, Vol. 4, Docs 473 and 476.

29 See *DAFP*, Vol. 4, Docs 485, 490, 512, 517 and 521.

30 War Cabinet Conclusions/ Confidential Annex, 21 and 28 July 1941, CAB 65/23, W.M. 72 and 75(41), PRO; See also Cadogan diary, 21 July 1941, in Dilks (ed.), *The Diaries of Sir Alexander Cadogan*, p. 393.

31 Cable, Cranborne to Menzies, 14 June 1941, *DAFP*, Vol. 4, Doc. 504.

THIRTEEN

'true children of magnificent Britain'

The implications of the German attack on Russia were considerable for both Britain and Australia. In hindsight, it was the event that largely won the war for the Allies, although that was not clear at the time. The immediate effect was to relieve the pressure on Britain in the Middle East, at least for a time, while the prospect of a German invasion of Britain could be disregarded until at least the spring of 1942. Any development that enhanced British security and made ultimate victory more likely should have brought comfort to Australia. But the German onslaught against Russia had darker portents for Australia. It created a new theatre of active operations against Germany that would eat greedily away at the mountain of munitions that was being produced in Britain and the United States. It also had the potential of drawing Russian forces away from its far-flung eastern territories and thereby releasing Japanese forces in Manchuria for adventures elsewhere.

Putting his anti-Bolshevism to one side, Churchill immediately undertook to supply Stalin with the wherewithal of war. If the Russians could be kept fighting, German attention would be diverted from British forces. But it would not bring any relief for Singapore. As General Ismay later explained,

Britain faced a choice between reinforcing Russia or the Far East and decided that 'the Russians must have priority and that a grave risk must be accepted in the Far East'. After all, argued Ismay, 'the collapse of Russia would mean Hitler's hegemony in Europe, while the collapse of Singapore could be retrieved after Hitler had been dealt with'.[1] Britain's commitment to support Russia also placed an added burden on the Royal Navy which had to patrol the icy wastes of the Arctic Ocean to protect the sea route to Russia, while the naval commitment in the Mediterranean continued as usual.

As a side effect, the German attack on Russia diverted attention in London from Churchill's war leadership and defused the criticism that had been growing since the defeat and partial evacuation from Crete. Three cruisers and six destroyers had been lost in the desperate attempt to rescue the defeated troops, while eight thousand Australian casualties had been suffered in the Greek and Crete campaigns. An influential and growing group of British MPs thought that Churchill should be forced to resign over the Crete debacle, just as Neville Chamberlain had been forced to resign over the Norwegian debacle in 1940. However, there was no obvious successor to Churchill. So they stayed their hands.[2]

As the details of the defeats in Greece and Crete filtered back to Australia, considerable bitterness was aroused by the cavalier manner in which the dominion troops had been committed to the battle bereft of proper equipment and lacking the all-important element of air support. Ever since the defeat in Norway a year before, it had been a cardinal principle of modern battle that infantry could not operate effectively without control of the skies above them. Menzies joined the howl of outrage following Crete, directing a very public and political barb straight at Churchill, the architect of the Norwegian campaign who had never been called to account for it. Warning that Crete 'must be the final lesson', Menzies noted how Australian forces on Crete had 'suffered so much through the lack of proper equipment, and a full and adequate Air Force'.[3] Without urgent reinforcements of aircraft being sent to the Middle East, he feared that the experience would be repeated again.

In particular, Menzies feared for the tiny British garrison on Cyprus, where some eight hundred Australian troops comprised half the British defenders. They had been ordered to resist a German attack, although no reinforcements would be sent to help them do so. Menzies stressed to Churchill the possible political implications in Australia that could result from a vain defence and a further defeat involving Australian forces. His fears were not well received by Churchill, who saw it as revealing a lack of fortitude by Australia.[4] This feeling of Churchill's would be confirmed for him even more as the Australian government began an incessant campaign for the relief of its troops in the besieged town of Tobruk, where military disaster was expected on an even greater scale.[5]

Menzies had visited Tobruk during his tour of the Middle East and had seen how its Italian defenders had been overcome. It did not take much for him to envisage a similar outcome for the mostly Australian defenders.[6] With the Labor Party increasing the political pressure on Menzies, he feared the ramifications of another defeat. Although Curtin was not anxious to assume the prime ministership until he could claim a popular mandate for doing so, he was under pressure from Evatt to take a more forthright stand. Evatt had not resigned from the High Court bench just to sit on the opposition benches. He was keen to become part of the government, preferably the leader, either by pushing the conservatives aside or by joining with them in a national administration. Meanwhile, Menzies remained transfixed by the political future that was beckoning from Westminster which depended on him remaining as prime minister until he could make the switch. In the midst of these swirling political currents, and dragged down by the weight of imperial ties, it is not surprising that Australia's national interest only came to the surface intermittently.

For all his criticism of the debacle on Crete, it had not shaken Menzies' faith in imperial defence. It had just confirmed his disillusionment with Churchill. As for the Labor Party, the defeats of Greece and Crete further diminished its willingness to have imperial defence as the first priority of Australian forces. At an advisory war council meeting on 12 June, Curtin urged that Australia, like Britain, must have its own defence as its first priority. Not that he wanted Australian forces withdrawn from the Middle East. Rather, he feared that Britain was not giving the region sufficient priority compared with its own defence, and wanted a greater effort in the

Middle East to ensure that it could be held. Although Curtin challenged the British view of the Mediterranean as the 'pivotal point of the Empire', he agreed with Menzies that the Middle East was a 'crucial theatre' and wanted assurances that Churchill regarded it in the same way. Otherwise, argued Curtin, Australia would be 'not only imperilling our men but the Fleet, which was the key to Empire Defence'. As he had urged before, Curtin preferred to 'close the Mediterranean with some salvage rather than with none'. Although, if he could be 'assured of reasonable chances of success', Curtin 'preferred to fight in the Middle East, and would do so to the extent of taking risks in Australia'. The council agreed to cable Churchill for details of the present and prospective British aircraft and tank forces in the Middle East, while Menzies privately suggested to Churchill that he also provide a message 'expressed in your own characteristic way, indicating the significance which you attach to the defence of the Middle East'.[7] A bit of Churchillian rhetoric might yet still the concerns of the increasingly querulous Labor MPs.

Despite the realisation that modern fighter aircraft were the key to success in the Mediterranean, Australia had none of its own. Menzies had returned from London flourishing a plan to produce aircraft in Australia. Although he had not managed to obtain any guarantee of British assistance for his plan, the official report of his British tour claimed that he had received the backing of Beaverbrook and Sinclair and that 'assurances of the fullest possible co-operation from the British Government were given without hesitation'. Menzies' aim was to lay the foundation for a postwar, British-owned automobile industry in Australia rather than the urgent production of fighter aircraft. In spite of the steadily worsening defence position, 'primary importance' would be given to ensuring that the aircraft factories would be 'planned so that they could be effectively used in peace time'. Under the proposed program, Australia would make aircraft for sale to Britain's Eastern empire, principally India, rather than ones necessarily needed for its own defence. It would be two to three years before it would be in full operation.[8]

Not that Australia lacked aircraft production facilities. But they were relatively rudimentary and had been kept going by British orders for training aircraft: wood and fabric Tiger Moths and the more advanced Wirraways. Although Australia needed operational aircraft, government policy stipulated that the production facilities were not to be switched to other aircraft types when the Australian orders for training aircraft had been filled. Instead, they would be used to fill possible export orders. In June 1941, it was planned to transfer Tiger Moth facilities to the production of Beauforts in February 1942, but only after Britain had declined to order any more Tiger Moths.[9] This policy elevated efficiency and imperial integration above the need for Australian security. It was no good Britain specialising in the production of fighter aircraft, and Australia making training aircraft, if Australia could not then be guaranteed a supply of the fighter aircraft that it was not otherwise allowed to make.

Of the 270 Beaufort aircraft on order in Australia, the first batch of 90 were for Britain, the next 90 for Australia and the final 90 for Britain. To Menzies' disappointment, Whitehall intended to dispatch the planes Britain had on order to Singapore. Menzies had hoped they would be sent to the Middle East. In July, the Australian government considered a proposal for the expansion of Beaufort production and, in the more distant future, the commencement of Beaufighter and Lancaster bomber production. Again, they were based more on the prospect of export orders and for reasons of efficiency, with the Beauforts and Beaufighters having many components in common, than on deciding the best aircraft for Australia's defence. In discussing the proposals, the Lancaster was dropped for practical reasons while the remainder of the planned program was referred to London for approval. In September, Australia was informed that Britain would purchase any Beauforts that were surplus to Australian requirements but that it would not buy any Beaufighters. Accordingly, Australia abandoned its plans for Beaufighter production and expanded the production of Beauforts, most of them being destined for the RAF, despite fears that the Beaufort would be obsolete before it could be produced in any number.[10]

Menzies accepted the British view that Australia did not need any fighter planes in the immediate future, but for 'psychological' purposes it could form some squadrons that could then be used 'as reinforcements or [for] employment elsewhere in the Far East theatre'. He told his colleagues of the conditional program of aircraft deliveries that he had managed to obtain from Beaverbrook and repeated Britain's 'categorical assurance' that, in the case of a Far East war, there would be an 'immediate review of air resources'.[11] This meant different things in Whitehall than it did to Menzies and his war cabinet.

Unbeknown to Menzies, there were already problems with the delivery of the 243 Brewster aircraft that had been promised to him. Deliveries had been supposed to begin in May 1941 but were progressively put forward to the future. In June, RAAF officers left for the United States to familiarise themselves with the aircraft only to find on their arrival that the aircraft would not even have a test flight before September. Delivery of the first 50 planes was not expected before February 1942 at the earliest. Britain refused to help expedite their production, advising Australia in September to switch their order to another aircraft entirely. An RAAF report concluded that Beaverbrook had been 'apparently completely in the dark about the Brewster project and [that] the undertakings given to the Prime Minister in respect of deliveries were without justification or foundation'.[12] So much for Menzies' proclaimed success in London.

At the same time as Australia was slowly becoming aware of Menzies' failure to secure the defence of Australia or Singapore, there were increasing fears about war in the Pacific. At the beginning of July, the British Foreign Office became convinced that the 'beastly Japs', as one official referred to them, were intent on consolidating their hold on French Indo-China 'as a stepping stone to other things'.[13] In the event of such a move, Eden urged that Britain should increase its defences in Malaya, that Australian troops be sent to Dutch Timor and Ambon and that Britain renounce its trade treaty with Japan. Britain had already been progressively imposing trade restrictions against Japan while taking 'constant care and vigilance' not to 'push restrictions to the point of provoking Japan to war'.[14] While this may have been the stated aim of the restrictions, they had the effect of forcing Japan either to concede the end of its imperial ambitions or to attack the European empires in the Pacific while they were preoccupied with Germany.

Although Britain was anxious not to provoke Japan into war while leaving the United States on the sidelines, it was prepared to have Japan in the war if the United States could be brought in at the same time. As Hugh

Dalton made clear to his war cabinet colleagues, the Japanese complaints about the economic restrictions and the 'threatening attitude of the Japanese press to the Netherlands East Indies' were proof that British policy had 'begun to bear fruit'. The Japanese sabre-rattling indicated that Tokyo was being brought to the point of its fateful decision. Dalton noted with approval that the Japanese were 'finding it more and more difficult to avoid drawing on their reserves' of strategic raw materials, while throughout the world they were 'meeting with obstruction ultimately caused either by British or United States action'. He complained that Australia had not played the game and had, in some instances, 'been reluctant to restrict their exports even to normal quantities'.[15]

The war cabinet dismissed Eden's call for 'strong deterrent measures' to prevent Japanese encroachments, deciding instead that Britain simply take 'appropriate counter-action after each encroachment'. It would react to Japanese moves rather than try to prevent them. At the same time, it instructed Eden and Dalton to consider 'tightening the screw still further against Japan by means of increased economic restrictions, even in the absence of further provocation'.[16] As Christopher Thorne has observed, British policy was directed 'above all' towards an 'American entry into the war — the current, German war — and if a showdown with Japan would provide that supreme blessing in addition to its direct Asian benefits, then so much the better'.[17] This was confirmed by the war cabinet when it gathered to discuss an American threat to tighten its economic restrictions against Japan in the event of the Japanese moving into Indo-China. In deciding whether to support the Americans, even at the risk of war with Japan, Eden told his colleagues that the 'issue with Japan must be faced sooner or later and that the risk of the United States not intervening in a war between ourselves and Japan is small'. Accordingly, he urged that Britain match any American action.[18] Although their approaches to the problem diverged, Eden and Churchill were united in not shrinking from the thought of provoking war with Japan, just at the thought of being left out on a limb by the United States in the event of such a war.

This thought also dominated Menzies' mind when he urged Britain to take the toughest action against Japan, even to the extent of a 'complete economic embargo', but subject to Washington being prepared to act concurrently with Britain.[19] Menzies' suggestion was dismissed by the Foreign Office, which knew that Washington would not agree to any such open coordination of policies against Japan. As Cadogan scathingly observed, the 'stupid Dominions ... get cold feet, and don't want to freeze Japanese assets without an assurance of support from [the] U.S. They *must* know that they can't *get* this.'[20] Britain was prepared to talk tough with Tokyo, and thereby run the risk of war in the Pacific, without a prior guarantee of support from Washington. The British government knew that political considerations would preclude President Roosevelt from extending such a guarantee for fear of upsetting his largely isolationist electorate. But it was confident that Washington would act against Japan in the event of an attack on European interests in the Pacific. The following day, after Roosevelt froze Japanese assets in the United States, Britain did likewise.

While increasing its pressure on Japan, and making war more likely, Britain remained reluctant to increase its preparations for fighting such a war. When the Japanese moved into Indo-China, Brooke-Popham suggested to London that his staff in Singapore be placed on a 'full war footing' and urged that its defences be improved 'while there is yet time'.[21] He was told not to worry, since Churchill would provide him with 'three months warning of any serious explosion in the Far East'.[22] Not that Churchill would back this warning with any substantial diversion of forces to meet such a 'serious explosion'. He remained committed to the agreed Anglo–American strategy of concentrating on Germany and fighting a holding war in the Pacific. As one of Churchill's staff later recalled, he used this promise of three months' notice as a way of overcoming opposition to the continued reinforcements for Russia. When any proposals were put to him for reinforcing the Far East, he would simply repeat his promise of being able to provide three months' warning of any Pacific war. And the proposals would be put to one side.[23]

Australia's Labor opposition was becoming increasingly alarmed about the predicament in which Churchill's strategy was placing the dominion and pressured Menzies to reconsider the country's commitment to imperial defence. On 29 July, Menzies informed the advisory war council that his government's policy towards Japan was to 'move together with the United

Kingdom and the U.S.A.'. Despite having appointed Sir John Latham as Australian minister in Tokyo, Menzies admitted that little independent advice was being received from him and that relations were being 'handled by the British Ambassador and full advice was being received from him through the Dominions Office'. In the event of war, Menzies confided that Britain would not send the promised fleet to ensure Australia's security, but only a battleship and an aircraft carrier to the Indian Ocean. This was troubling news for the Labor members of the council. In Curtin's absence, his deputy, Frank Forde, complained that Australia was being 'borne along by the tide of events' and without any assurances of American support. Without American help, declared Forde, 'we could not keep an enemy out of Australia'. With the Singapore naval base being left as an 'empty garage', Forde urged Menzies to recall parliament to discuss Australia's 'very grave' position.[24]

The radical Labor MP Jack Beasley went even further, questioning Australia's continuing commitment to imperial defence and pressing for the return of Australian troops from the Middle East. As Beasley argued, in deciding on the disposition of Australian troops, the defence of Australia 'should be considered first'. But his concerns were quashed by government MPs who stressed the importance of the Middle East as the 'gateway for a German advance into Egypt and Asia' and which therefore 'had to be held'. Not only would the Australian troops not be withdrawn, but the government refused to order a full mobilisation of the militia in Australia to meet the increasing threat of invasion.[25] Publicly, Menzies again called for 'sacrifice and a great national effort', exhorting Australians to be 'true children of magnificent Britain from where we come'.[26]

If the Australian troops were to remain in the Middle East, and there were doubts about British naval dispositions in the event of war with Japan, then the possibility of such a war had to be averted by agreement with Japan. This was the thrust of the argument by Curtin when he attended the advisory war council on 6 August, agreeing with Menzies that Britain should try to reach an agreement with Tokyo that would limit its expansion in the Pacific and suggesting that the Japanese were 'still susceptible to a face-saving arrangement'. It was no good relying upon American support to save

Australia in a Pacific war, argued Curtin, since it would be outweighed by the opposition from Japan. Far better to prevent a war altogether and allow for forces to continue to be concentrated against Germany. Curtin's argument was based on the mistaken assumption that Japan's entry into the war would cause a dangerous diversion of British resources to meet the threat in the Far East. It was also based on the fear that Japanese raids on Australia, when the AIF was fighting overseas, would cause a situation that was 'politically unmanageable'. Menzies raised the idea of flying to Tokyo to seek an understanding with the Japanese, but was worried by the possibility of it being compared with Chamberlain's 1938 trip to Munich. The concern by Menzies and Curtin for reaching an agreement with Japan was not shared by their colleagues on the council, who stressed instead the importance of remaining in step with the United States.[27]

Instead of flying off to Tokyo, Menzies set out by train the following evening on the first stage of a two-and-a-half-week tour of Australia that was designed to lift his stocks with the public. Disgruntled MPs from all parties had been publicly demanding his resignation, while his attempts to return to London had come to nothing. Three days after embarking on his tour, Menzies dramatically announced in Adelaide that he was cancelling it, ostensibly because reported Japanese concentrations in Indo-China might be poised to launch an invasion of Malaya or the Netherlands East Indies. With his alarmist warnings resounding around the world, Menzies returned to Melbourne for meetings of the war cabinet and the advisory war council. He planned to emphasise the gravity of the situation in order to bludgeon his way back to London past the opposition from suspicious MPs on all sides. In London, the British war cabinet was critical of his 'alarmist' public statement and ensured that the British press did not 'exaggerate the immediate seriousness of the situation'. At the time, Churchill was in Newfoundland for his first wartime meeting with Roosevelt, which Menzies apparently feared might have negative implications for the future of the British empire. Menzies hoped to return to London and use the visit there of two other dominion prime ministers to force his way into the British war cabinet.[28]

Although Curtin was willing to agree to Menzies' return to London, his fellow Labor MPs were not so amenable. Menzies did not help matters by proposing, without first consulting the advisory war council, that Britain should guarantee the security of Siam and that Australia would regard a Japanese seizure of the strategically important Kra isthmus that connected Siam to Malaya as a *casus belli*, something that Churchill remained unwilling to do. Menzies and Curtin justified the commitment by claiming that it was in accordance with the previously expressed views of the council, a claim that was well wide of the mark.[29]

The argument in London over whether Britain should provide a guarantee to Siam provided a further insight into British thinking on the Far East and its strategy towards Japan. The question was brought before the defence committee by Anthony Eden on 7 August, while Churchill was still in Newfoundland. The committee was aware of his strong opposition to any such guarantee, except over something that was 'immediate and vital'. The Admiralty agreed with Churchill's position, again stressing the need to avoid war in the Pacific for as long as possible. The committee therefore rejected Eden's latest attempt to find some non-British territory in the Far East that Britain was willing to pledge to defend. The vice-chief of the imperial general staff, General Pownall, explained the basis of the military opposition to a Siamese guarantee, pointing out that it was 'quite certain that America would *not* go to war for Siam and the last thing in the world we want to do is to have to take on Japan without America'.[30]

The issue returned to the defence committee the following day, with Admiral Tom Phillips arguing for its members to take a 'realistic view' of Britain's ability to effect its will in the Far East. He claimed that Britain had 'readjusted' its ideas as to its vital interests and cautioned that immediate American intervention could not be relied upon. He also reminded the committee of Britain's pledge to abandon the Middle East if Australia was facing a 'mortal threat', implying that this pledge was now worthless since it had been made before Britain had 'amassed an Army of 600 000 men in that theatre, a large part of whom were Australians and New Zealanders'. In order to protect this huge army, Britain needed to retain the Mediterranean fleet rather than dispatch it to the Far East. Even with the fleet, suggested Phillips, it would be doubtful whether Britain could maintain its 'exposed communications with Egypt ... in the face of enterprising Japanese action in the Indian Ocean'.[31]

This discussion had possibly dire implications for Australian security. It raised the vital question of what value could be placed on Britain's defence assurance towards Australia in view of the ongoing 'readjustment' of thinking as to Britain's vital interests and in view of the build-up of British forces in the Middle East. As well, with the 'Germany first' strategy in place, how much assistance could Australia count upon even if the United States joined Britain in a war against Japan? These questions were never addressed properly in Australia. As prime minister, Menzies' gaze was firmly fixed on his own political advancement in London. On 19 August, he gained the support of his cabinet for his plan to seek representation for the dominions in the British war cabinet.[32] However, Churchill was aware of Menzies' ambition and, with the help of the other dominions, ensured that it could not reach fruition. Neither would the Labor Party give its blessing to another trip by Menzies to London.

On finding his path to London blocked, and with his political support in Australia withering away, Menzies finally agreed to step down as prime minister, although still hoping that he might get to London and achieve his hoped-for destiny.[33] His fall from power was a vital victory for Australia in its efforts to develop some sense of its predicament in the Pacific. But it still had a long way to go. Although his successor, Arthur Fadden, was prepared to give greater priority to local defence, it still came a poor third behind the needs of imperial defence and the competing needs of Australia's civil economy. Moreover, Menzies' fall allowed Churchill to tear up the proposal for a meeting in London of dominion prime ministers at which Far Eastern defence would have figured high on the agenda. With Australia remaining in a state of some political turmoil, and Fadden relying on the doubtful support of two independent MPs, the dominion still lacked the decisive leadership that it so desperately needed.

NOTES

[1] Letter, Ismay to General Henry C. Jackson, 18 February 1959, I/14/72, Ismay Papers, KC.
[2] See Day, *Menzies and Churchill at War*, Chap. 13.
[3] *Daily Sketch*, London, 6 June 1941.
[4] Cable, Menzies to Bruce, 8 June 1941, and Cable, Churchill to Menzies, 11 June 1941, *DAFP*, Vol. 4, Docs 493 and 497.
[5] See David Day, 'Anzacs on the Run: The View from Whitehall, 1941–2', *Journal of Imperial and Commonwealth History*, May 1986.

6   For his impressions of Tobruk during his Middle East tour, see Menzies diary, 8 and 11 April 1941.

7   Advisory War Council Minutes, 12 June 1941, CRS A2682, Vol. 2, Minute 373, NAA; Cable Gordon 2, Menzies to Churchill, 13 June 1941, PREM 3/281/10, PRO.

8   'Report by Mr John Storey, Member, Aircraft Production Commission, on his visit to England and USA with the Right Hon. R. G. Menzies Prime Minister of Australia — January 24th to June 6th 1941', CRS A5954, Box 617, NAA.

9   War Cabinet Agendum, Supplement No. 1 to Agendum No. 229/1940, by Fadden, 26 March 1941; Cable No. 3065, Clapp to Hyland, 17 June 1941 and Cable H. 491, Hyland to Clapp, 9 July 1941, CRS A5954, Box 223, NAA.

10 Notes of Proceedings of Conference called to discuss Aircraft Manufacturing Development in Australia, 14 June 1941 and War Cabinet Minute, 22 July 1941, CRS A5954, Box 223, NAA; Douglas Gillison, *Royal Australian Air Force 1939–1942*, Canberra, 1962, pp. 138–40; See also Cable Z88, Burnett to Brooke-Popham, 12 August 1941, V/4/21, Brooke-Popham Papers, KC.

11 War Cabinet Minutes, 10 June 1941, CRS A2673, Vol. 7, Minute 1139, NAA.

12 'Aircraft Requirements for RAAF: Supply Position', Report by Air Staff, 12 August 1941, CRS A5954, Box 230, NAA; 'Vultee and Brewster Bermuda Aircraft' Folder, CRS A5954, Box 232, NAA.

13 Letter, Sir Horace Seymour to his wife, 4 July 1941, SEYR 2/5, Seymour Papers, CC; Harvey diary, 6 July 1941, ADD. MS. 56398, Harvey Papers, BL.

14 'Japanese Intentions in Indo-China' and 'Nature and Extent of our Economic Restrictions Against Japan', Memoranda by Eden, 6 and 7 July 1941, CAB 66/17. W.P. (41)154 and 155, PRO.

15 'Economic Restrictions Against Japan', Memorandum by Dalton, 7 July 1941, CAB 66/17, W.P. (41)155, PRO.

16 War Cabinet Conclusions, 7 July 1941, CAB 65/19, W.M. 66(41), PRO.

17 Thorne, *Allies of a Kind*, p. 73.

18 'Japanese Plans in Indo-China', Memorandum by Eden, 20 July 1941, CAB 66/17, W.P. (41)172, PRO.

19 War Cabinet Conclusions, 21 July 1941, CAB 65/19, W.M. 72(41), PRO.

20 Cadogan diary, 24 July 1941, in Dilks (ed.), *The Diaries of Sir Alexander Cadogan*, p. 394.

21 Cable No. 111/4, Brooke-Popham to Chiefs of Staff, 26 July 1941, V/4/17, Brooke-Popham Papers, KC.

22 Letter, Air Marshal J. Babington to Brooke-Popham, 1 August 1941, V/11/1, Brooke-Popham Papers, KC.

23 Letter, Ian Jacob to Ismay, 24 January 1959, I/14/69, Ismay Papers, KC.

24 Advisory War Council Minutes, 29 July 1941, CRS A2682, Vol. 2, Minute 431, NAA.

25 ibid.

26 *Daily Herald*, London, 1 August 1941.

27 Advisory War Council Minutes, 6 August 1941, CRS A2682, Vol. 3, Minute 451, NAA.

28 War Cabinet Conclusions, 11 August 1941, CAB 65/19, W.M. 79(41), PRO; See also Day, *Menzies and Churchill at War*, Chap. 14.

29 Advisory War Council Minutes, 14 August 1941, CRS A2682, Vol. 3, Minutes 466 and 467, NAA; See also Cable, Menzies to Churchill, 12 August 1941, CAB 66/18, W.P. (41)203, PRO.

30 Defence Committee (Operations) Minutes, 7 August 1941, CAB 69/2, D.O. (41)55, PRO; See also Pownall diary, 8 August 1941, in Bond (ed.), *Chief of Staff*, Vol. 2, p. 35.

31 Defence Committee (Operations) Minutes, 8 August 1941, CAB 69/2, D.O. (41)56, PRO.

32 Cabinet Minutes, 19 August 1941, CRS A2697, Vol. 7, NAA.

33 As a deposed prime minister, Menzies presented a lesser threat to Churchill who now found it relatively simple to prevent Menzies' return to London.

FOURTEEN

'a political insurance policy'

When Fadden succeeded Menzies as prime minister the prospects for peace in the Pacific were more precarious than ever. It was becoming a question of when, not if, the Japanese would strike. Yet many Australians seemed blissfully unaware of their country's predicament and resented the measures that needed to be implemented if Australia was to be secure. They basked in the economic sunshine produced by the demands of the war economy, with many incomes boosted by overtime and able to be spent freely on the consumer goods of their choice. While government and business leaders used the war to promote the greater industrialisation of Australia, the labour movement saw it as an opportunity for workers to make good the deprivation suffered during the 1930s depression. Even Curtin, who wanted an 'unlimited war effort', also wanted his supporters to be given 'some instalments of the new social order as opportunity offers'.[1]

It was not intended that the new social order should allow the greater involvement of women in the workforce, which was stoutly resisted by the male-dominated trade unions. Despite increasing manpower problems for the armed services and the production of munitions, women were refused admission to the ranks except in their traditional roles, such as nurses, cooks and typists. But change came nonetheless. The boom in consumer spending, and the dearth of male workers, allowed women to desert domestic service in droves and find work in factories and shops.[2] Neither was it intended that the new social order should encompass non-Europeans, with the White Australia policy staying firmly in place. Despite the wartime friendship with China, restrictions on the admission of Chinese students and businessmen remained. Though the dominion agreed to allow Britain to send prisoners of war for imprisonment in Australia, it was careful to stipulate that they were all to be white. And Jewish refugees, including 300 French children, were refused admission to Australia despite eloquent pleas on their behalf.[3]

With less than eight million Australians trying to assert their claim to the continent, the country should not have been so particular about the people it admitted to its midst. Australians would need all the help they could get if their nation was to survive the looming challenge from the Japanese. Certainly, little assistance would be forthcoming from Britain, which viewed the possibility of a Pacific war in an increasingly positive light, confident that it would lead to the United States finally entering the war against Hitler. At his shipboard meeting with Roosevelt off the coast of Newfoundland in August, Churchill had been relieved to find that the American president was 'obviously determined to come in'. Churchill succeeded in stiffening an American message to Tokyo to include a warning that further Japanese encroachment in the south-west Pacific would compel the United States to 'take counter-measures, even though these might lead to war between the United States and Japan'.[4]

This support from Roosevelt would have been one of the reasons why Churchill was described by one observer as being in 'very good spirits, and far calmer after his sea trip'.[5] According to General Pownall, Roosevelt was

all for coming into the war, and as soon as possible ... but he said that he would never declare war, he wishes to provoke it. He wants to create an incident that brings war about, being no doubt sure that he will then be fully supported by the people.[6]

Churchill's new-found optimism about the Americans was shared by his ministers, who were beginning to welcome the prospect of war with Japan as probably the only means of drawing the United States back into Europe. Even the arch-imperialist, Leo Amery, Britain's secretary of state for India, thought it was 'worth making a big effort to keep [Japan] out of the war' but 'if her coming into the war brought in the United States the balance of advantage would presently be in our favour'. Although Britain 'might have to face some bad months in the Indian ocean and at Singapore', Amery now believed that the 'additional fighting power and munition power that would come in if America were really at war and not a spectator would outweigh all that in the end'.[7]

Apart from wanting the United States as an ally against Germany, there was also a growing conviction in London that the war should be used to cement a permanent Anglo–American alliance that could act as the postwar policeman of Europe. This was a vision harboured by Churchill[8] and it was shared by officials at the Foreign Office. As Anthony Eden's secretary, Oliver Harvey, confided to Eden the British would be

exhausted after the war and will refuse to police Europe alone. But if it is an Anglo–American operation, then you will get what you want, and I am sure we can manage the Americans. They are children, simple, naif, yet suspicious.[9]

Such an Anglo–American alliance would have serious implications for the future of the British empire. While the empire increased Britain's relative strength within such an alliance, it was also the aspect of Britain that Americans found most offensive. Britain's real strength in any Anglo–American alliance, as would increasingly be obvious, was its strategic position as a virtual aircraft carrier permanently anchored off the shore of western Europe.

While Australia's conservative government had been reluctant to forge closer ties with the United States if they were at the expense of Britain, it was as keen as Churchill to strengthen the ties between Britain and the United States. There was a realisation that the 1930s vision of the British empire as a self-contained trading bloc could not be sustained after the war. Officials such as Bruce recognised that Australia would face economic stagnation and the withering of its carefully cultivated secondary industries if it had to rely largely on Britain for its markets. There were still those in the British government who believed that the imperial trading system could provide Britain's economic salvation and who were prepared to fight a trade war with the United States to protect it. Bruce warned that Australia would not support Britain in any such trade war, urging instead that the British empire had to cooperate with the United States in expanding the total volume of world trade rather than fighting over the existing volume.[10]

With both the economic and strategic rationales of empire looking increasingly tenuous, the costs of Australia's attachment to Britain were fast outweighing the actual and potential benefits. Nevertheless, Australia pushed for closer Anglo–American cooperation, albeit on the firm understanding that its own future remained securely tied to that of Britain. There was certainly little consideration given to Australia forging an independent existence in the Pacific. Not that it was a propitious time to consider such matters. Instead, the Australian government continued to press Britain for assurances about its security.

Following Menzies' resignation as prime minister on 28 August, Australia went ahead with plans to send a ministerial representative to London. It would not be Menzies making the trip, and the representative would face great difficulty in having Australia's security concerns addressed. Indeed, Churchill had tried to prevent such a representative being sent at all and had only reluctantly agreed in the face of Fadden's determination to proceed with the plan. Churchill made clear that an Australian minister would not enjoy the same privileges as Menzies would have enjoyed as prime minister. And he would not be accorded a seat in the war cabinet.[11]

The rank of the Australian representative was not the only barrier to the dominion's views being heard. Australia had also undergone a drastic transformation in the affections of British political and military leaders. Menzies' bid for power in Westminster had put him at odds with Churchill, as well as with most of the war cabinet. As the chancellor of the exchequer, Sir Kingsley Wood, informed Bruce, there were a *number of people over here who could not feel very sympathetic towards him [Menzies] as he had been very outspoken in his criticisms — the specific instance he gave was that Menzies had said the Prime Minister was surrounded by 'Yes' men, and added — naturally many of us do not like a suggestion of this sort.*[12]

While the personal rivalry between Menzies and Churchill soured the relationship between their countries, the dispute over Britain's handling of the war in the Mediterranean only served to exacerbate it.

The successive defeats in Greece and Crete had led to harsh words about Britain being voiced in the Australian parliament and in the pages of the press.[13] But it was the long-running dispute over the relief of the Australian garrison in Tobruk that seriously damaged Anglo–Australian relations and practically destroyed Australia's reputation in the eyes of Britain's political and military leaders for the duration of the war.[14] Even the King was moved to remark on 'how different the Australians seemed to be to any of the other Dominions', noting how 'in Australia they were always being critical', while Lord Cranborne wrote bitterly about the 'rather hectic time' the government had been having with the 'miserable Australians'.[15]

The argument over Tobruk had originated with Menzies who had been apprehensive about the ability of the garrison to withstand a sustained German assault. In Cairo, Blamey became aware of Menzies' concern and used it to request the relief of the trapped 9th Division and the reconstitution of the scattered Australian forces in the Middle East into a single corps under his command. Seizing upon a medical report that cast doubt on the fitness of the Australians in Tobruk after months of siege, Blamey called for their relief on military grounds, confident that Menzies had political grounds for supporting him.[16] By the time Fadden took over as prime minister, one brigade of the Australians had been removed, using the small naval ships that slipped into Tobruk at night to resupply the embattled garrison. Blamey pressed for the remainder of the Australians to be removed and for them not to be replaced by other Australians. Only by doing so, argued Blamey, could the Australian government be saved from having 'another Greece and Crete experience'. This clinched the matter in Canberra.[17]

Like Menzies, Fadden was just as conscious of the political implications of the Tobruk garrison falling to the Germans. And he was similarly dependent on the support of independent MPs for his political survival. On receipt of Blamey's advice, he immediately requested that Churchill ensure the relief of the remaining Australians, phrasing his request in a way that revealed the political imperative for it. Fadden informed Churchill that the Australian parliament would be meeting in mid-September and that it was his 'desire to make a statement when the withdrawal had been completed'. In terms not calculated to endear him to Churchill, he warned that the relief of Tobruk was a 'vital national question here and should any catastrophe occur to the Tobruk garrison ... there would be grave repercussions'.[18] Whatever his private feelings about the request, Churchill agreed to comply on condition that the withdrawal would not hamper the prospective offensive being planned by the newly appointed British commander in the Middle East, General Sir Claude Auchinleck.[19]

It is likely that Churchill intended that Auchinleck should raise military objections to the withdrawal, which he promptly did. With a massive offensive being planned to push the Germans back past Tobruk, Auchinleck wanted the garrison to be kept intact and not risked by any withdrawal. He also wanted to avoid denuding his forces for the coming offensive, which he would have to do if he was to send replacements into Tobruk for the withdrawing Australians. For these reasons, Auchinleck argued that the relief of the Australian troops was not justified, suggesting that they be strengthened instead with the addition of a tank brigade. He was supported by the British minister to the Middle East, Oliver Lyttelton, who claimed that the military arguments were 'unanswerable' and that, if they were British troops, 'no Commander would consider relief'. He perceptively observed that the Australian government was 'anxious to take out a political insurance policy', but argued that the military 'premium to be paid' was 'too high'.[20]

Armed with this unequivocal military advice, Churchill informed his war cabinet that he would send Auchinleck's report to Fadden, emphasising the 'grave consequences which might ensue, not only to the Australian forces but to our future plans'. During discussion, British ministers made it clear that they understood that the Australian agitation was motivated by political imperatives. As Cranborne explained, the press had led the Australian public to believe that their troops were 'bearing the brunt of the fighting in the Middle East', while the Australian Labor Party was 'apt to argue that Australian troops should be kept for the defence of Australian soil'. Such notions were dangerous to the British cause and had to be countered.[21] In his cable to Fadden, Churchill warned him to 'weigh carefully the immense responsibility which you would assume before history by depriving Australia of the glory of holding Tobruk till victory was won'.[22]

Fadden was unimpressed. Armed with Blamey's military advice to the contrary, Fadden rejected the arguments of Auchinleck and Churchill and reiterated the Australian request. In informing Auchinleck of Fadden's intransigence, Churchill claimed to be 'grieved' by the Australian attitude, although admitting that he had 'long feared the dangerous reactions on Australian and world opinion of our seeming to fight all our battles in the Middle East only with Dominion troops'. Auchinleck was less restrained in his reaction, being infuriated by Fadden's cable and by Churchill's acceptance of it, which he interpreted as a lack of confidence in his military judgment. It was with some difficulty that Lyttelton prevented him from submitting his resignation, while at the same time urging Churchill to have the 'weak and disingenuous' Blamey relieved by the Australian government.[23]

Churchill shared the anger of Auchinleck and Lyttelton, as did most of Britain's political and military leadership. As one well-placed observer confided, 'everybody was furious'.[24] But this was carefully concealed from the Australians, who remained important pillars of the British empire in Egypt and the Far East. As Churchill argued when trying to soothe Auchinleck's anger, 'great allowances must be made for a Government with a majority of one playing politics with a bitter Opposition, part of whom at least are isolationist'. He urged Auchinleck to put aside his personal feelings since it was 'our duty at all costs to prevent an open dispute with the Australian Government' which might otherwise 'injure [the] foundations of Empire and be disastrous to our general position in the war'.[25] Churchill also instructed the British high commissioner in Canberra not to discuss Tobruk with the Australian government and, if the matter was raised, to say that he had 'no information and abstain from argument and, above all, reproaches'.[26] Although Churchill believed that Australia deserved to be reproached, it was not worth the possible risk to the British war effort. So the issue was allowed to fester below the surface of Anglo–Australian relations, infecting for some years the attitude of British policy makers towards Australia.

To reassure his own war cabinet that there was no basis to the Australian resentment, Churchill ordered the circulation to its members of the Mediterranean casualty figures, broken down by the country of origin. These were meant to disprove the allegation from Australia, as well as from German propaganda, that Britain would fight to the death of the last Australian in the Middle East. On first reading, they certainly served Churchill's purpose, showing that more than half of the casualties were British. However, if those declared missing and taken prisoner were excluded, the British proportion was reduced to less than a third. The figures were also not sufficiently detailed to distinguish the other national groups fighting on the British side in the Middle East — such as the Greeks and Poles — that would have reduced the British proportion still further.[27] But it was a sign of how seriously Churchill regarded the dispute, and the associated allegations, that he had bothered to have the figures tabulated.

The risk of recriminations with Australia was heightened by the personality of the British high commissioner, Sir Ronald Cross, who had been successively minister for economic warfare and minister for shipping until his posting to Canberra in May 1941. Despite his political experience, he was ill-suited to his new role. By August, Cranborne was complaining that Cross had 'taken to lecturing Australian Ministers as if they were small and rather dirty boys'.[28] Although Cranborne kept Cross on a short leash to prevent any gratuitous attacks on the Australian government, it would not be long before Churchill was ignoring his own admonitions and openly barking his annoyance at Canberra. All of this boded ill for the success of the proposed ministerial mission to London.

The mission almost became an issue of dispute itself when Fadden attempted unilaterally to elevate the role of the Australian envoy to membership of the British war cabinet after Churchill had agreed to

welcome the envoy with the 'utmost consideration and honour'.[29] Fadden
seized upon this as implying that Churchill would 'welcome the presence of
an Australian Minister in the War Cabinet when matters relating to higher
policy, operations or other questions which affect the Australian war effort
or the Australian forces were being considered'.[30] Churchill certainly did not
mean this, but Fadden had already announced that a minister would go to
London and he quickly followed his presumptuous cable to Churchill with
another one announcing that his Country Party colleague, Sir Earle Page,
would be the minister.[31] Although Churchill realised that the plain-speaking
Fadden was wilfully misinterpreting the sense of his deliberately obtuse
message, he was not too concerned. There would be plenty of scope for
interpreting the standing of Page's mission once he arrived in London. In the
interim, Churchill simply signalled that he would confer with Page 'freely
and fully on all matters concerning Australian interests and the common
cause'. As he confided to Cranborne, Britain had to 'treat these people, who
are politically embarrassed but are sending a splendid army into the field,
with the utmost consideration'.[32] In the event, the problem was averted when
Page let it be known that he had no expectation of occupying a war cabinet
seat.[33]

Although Menzies had first suggested the idea of sending a representative
to London on 10 August, claiming urgent reasons of Far Eastern security as
the rationale, Page waited for the federal budget to be safely passed through
parliament, and the government's future apparently secured, before leaving
for London by way of the Netherlands East Indies, Singapore, the
Philippines, the United States and Canada. It was not until 6 November,
three months after Menzies had urgently broached the matter and only one
month before the Japanese attack on Pearl Harbor, that Page appeared
before the British war cabinet to put Australia's views regarding the urgent
need for reinforcements in the Far East.[34] It was much too late.

When originally proposing the mission, Menzies had political ambition
high among his priorities. In persisting with the mission following Menzies'
fall, Fadden probably also had political rather than military considerations
in mind, with the press and parliament calling for such a representative to be
sent. As a possible rival for leadership of the Country Party, Page was an

ideal choice for the post, at least as far as Fadden was concerned. As far as securing Australia's defence, Page was an inappropriate choice since his political experience had been restricted to the treasury and commerce departments, rather than one of the defence portfolios. The army minister, Percy Spender, would have been a far better choice. But then Fadden did not seem to expect much from Page, instructing him merely to discuss the Middle Eastern and Far Eastern situations but investing him with no initiative to commit Australia to anything. Rather, he was instructed to refer anything of substance back to Canberra.[35] In London, he would become an awkward fifth wheel to Bruce's diplomatic coach.

NOTES

[1] Speech by Curtin in House of Representatives, 18 June 1941, CRS A5954, Box 308, NAA.

[2] Hasluck, *The Government and the People 1939–41*, Chaps 9–10.

[3] Advisory War Council Minutes, 6 August 1941, CRS A2682, Vol. 3, Minute 542; 'Summary of Australian Army War Effort', September 1941, p. 9, CRS A5954, Box 313; Cabinet Minutes, 24 January 1941, CRS A2697, Vol. 5, NAA. For details of Australia's response to Jewish refugees, see Paul Bartrop, *Australia and the Holocaust, 1933–45*, Melbourne, 1994.

[4] Cable, Churchill to Attlee, 11 August 1941, in Gilbert, *Finest Hour*, p. 1160.

[5] Letter, Cranborne to Emrys-Evans, 31 August 1941, ADD. MS. 58240, Emrys-Evans Papers, BL.

[6] Pownall diary, 20 August 1941, in Bond (ed.), *Chief of Staff*, Vol. 2, p. 37.

[7] Letter, Amery to Lord Hankey, 5 September 1941, HNKY 11/14, Hankey Papers, KC.

[8] Mackenzie King diary, 5 September 1941, CUL.

[9] Eden told Harvey that he would not regard Roosevelt as either 'simple or naif'. Minute, Harvey to Eden, 24 August 1941, ADD. MS. 56402, Harvey Papers, BL.

[10] See Letter, Bruce to Fadden, 25 September 1941, CRS M104, 'British Empire — America', Item 9(1); Talk with Sir John Anderson, 29 September 1941, CRS M100, 'September 1941'; Cable No. 5779, Bruce to Curtin, 4 October 1941, and Talk with Sir Kingsley Wood, 15 October 1941, CRS M100, 'October 1941'; Letter, Bruce to Sumner Welles, 14 November 1941, CRS M103, '1941', NAA.

[11] War Cabinet Conclusions, 28 August and 1 September 1941, CAB 65/19, W.M. 87 and 88(41); Cable (draft), Churchill to Fadden, 29 August 1941, PREM 4/50/4A, PRO.

[12] Talk with Sir Kingsley Wood, 15 October 1941, CRS M100, 'October 1941', NAA; See also Letter, Cranborne to Emrys-Evans, 31 August 1941, ADD. MS. 58240, Emrys-Evans Papers, BL.

[13] 'The Political Situation in the Commonwealth of Australia', Memorandum by Cranborne, 21 August 1941, CAB 66/18, W.P. (41)198, PRO.

[14] See Day, 'Anzacs on the Run: The View from Whitehall'.

[15] Mackenzie King diary, 30 August 1941, CUL; Letter, Cranborne to Emrys-Evans, 31 August 1941, ADD. MS. 58240, Emrys-Evans Papers, BL.

[16] See Day, 'Anzacs on the Run: The View from Whitehall'; Day, *Menzies and Churchill at War*, Chap. 14; For other views see David Horner, *High Command*, pp. 111–7; W.S. Churchill, *The Second World War*, Vol. 3, *passim*; Hasluck, *The Government and the People 1939–41*, Appendix 10.

[17] Letter, Blamey to Spender, 8 September 1941, CRS A5954, Box 260, NAA; Cable, Blamey to Fadden, 4 September 1941, *DAFP*, Vol. 5, Doc. 58.

[18] Cable, Fadden to Cranborne, 5 September 1941, *DAFP*, Vol. 5, Doc. 59.

19 Cable T549, Churchill to Auchinleck, 6 September 1941, PREM 3/63/2, PRO.
20 Cable, Auchinleck to Churchill, 10 September 1941, and Cable, Lyttelton to Churchill, 11 September 1941, PREM 3/63/2, PRO.
21 War Cabinet Conclusions/Confidential Annex, 11 September 1941, CAB 65/23, W.M. 92(41), PRO.
22 Cable, Churchill to Fadden, 11 September 1941, PREM 3/63/2, PRO.
23 Cable No. 590, Fadden to Churchill, (rec'd) 14 September 1941, Cable, Churchill to Fadden, 15 September 1941, Cable, Churchill to Auchinleck, 18 September 1941, Cable, Lyttelton to Churchill, 18 September 1941, PREM 3/63/2, PRO.
24 Harvey diary, 15 September, ADD. MS. 56398, Harvey Papers, BL. In the discussion of Fadden's cable by the British war cabinet, 'the view was expressed that the decision was a lamentable one'. See War Cabinet Conclusions/Confidential Annex, 16 September 1941, CAB 65/23, W.M. 93(41), PRO; See also Cazalet diary, 20 September 1941, in Robert Rhodes James (ed.), *Victor Cazalet*, London, 1976, p. 264; Letters, Cunningham to Pound and Pound to Cunningham, 18 September 1941, ADD. MS. 5261, Cunningham Papers, BL.
25 Cable No. 094, Churchill to Auchinleck, CAB 65/23, W.M. 94(41), PRO; See also Cable, Churchill to Lyttelton, 18 September 1941, 'The Prime Minister's Personal Telegrams 1941', VI/1, Ismay Papers, KC.
26 Minute M902/1, Churchill to Cranborne, 15 September 1941, PREM 3/63/2, PRO.
27 'Total Battle Casualties — Middle East', 22 September 1941, CAB 66/18, W.P. (41)225, PRO.
28 Letter, Cranborne to Emrys-Evans, 31 August 1941, ADD. MS. 58240, Emrys-Evans Papers, BL.
29 Cable, Cranborne to Fadden, 28 August 1941, *DAFP*, Vol. 5, Doc. 53.
30 Cable, Fadden to Cranborne, 5 September 1941, *DAFP*, Vol. 5, Doc. 60.
31 Cable No. 586, Fadden to Churchill, (rec'd) 6 September 1941, PREM 4/50/5, PRO.
32 Minute M873/5, Churchill to Cranborne, 6 September 1941, PREM 4/50/5, PRO.
33 Page let his intentions be known during a visit to the Canadian prime minister while en route to London. Mackenzie King then warned Churchill of Page's attitude. Cable No. 217, Mackenzie King to Churchill, 25 October 1941, PREM 4/50/5, PRO.
34 For Page's very subjective account of his mission, see Sir Earle Page, *Truant Surgeon*, Sydney, 1963.
35 Letter, Fadden to Page, 16 September 1941, CRS A5954, Box 475, NAA.

FIFTEEN

'the common Empire cause'

While Australia had been embroiled in political turmoil culminating in Menzies' resignation, its military position had continued to deteriorate. A Pacific war seemed more likely with the dawning of each day, but the means to meet such an eventuality were less likely to be provided. Yet Churchill's confidence about eventual victory in Europe was steadily increasing. So confident was he that he ignored a series of German peace feelers in September 1941, instructing that 'no contact of any kind be made' with German emissaries by British representatives overseas.[1] Churchill was committed to fighting the war to a finish in fulfilment of the historic role that he clearly believed was his destiny. Although he claimed to have no idea as to how total victory against Germany would be achieved, he conceded privately on 23 August that Britain's military position had 'vastly improved' and that he could no longer envisage the Germans mounting a successful invasion of Britain. Tobruk was still surrounded by German and Italian tanks, but Auchinleck was busily preparing for a counterattack that was hoped to reverse Britain's recent misfortunes in the Middle East. As for the Far East, Churchill predicted that 'the Japs would shout and threaten, but would not move'.[2]

If the Japanese did move, Australia was ill-prepared to defend itself. And the situation was worsening. One of the main outcomes of Churchill's meeting with Roosevelt was the decision to coordinate a vastly increased contribution of war supplies to Russia. At the end of August, Churchill offered Stalin an extra 200 Hurricane fighter aircraft on top of the 40 that had already been sent and 200 Tomahawk fighter planes that had been promised.[3] Partly as a result of this, Singapore was refused the promised reinforcement of its air strength. In mid-September, the chiefs of staff informed Brooke-Popham that their plan to accumulate a force of 336 aircraft under his command by the end of 1941 could no longer be achieved. They cited the greater priority of Russia and the Middle East, where fighting was proceeding, and production shortfalls in Britain and the United States.[4] This force already had been slashed from the recommended level to the bare minimum. Now Singapore and the defending garrison of British, Australian and Indian troops would not even have that.

Australia was probably in an even worse position than Singapore. Although the war had stimulated the development of its industrial base, it still lacked the ability to defend itself from serious attack. The navy was effectively an adjunct of the Royal Navy and much of its limited strength was scattered around the Middle East and Far East. It relied, as it had always done, on the potential power of the Royal Navy to repel any direct naval threat to Australia. The army was similarly scattered on various imperial missions overseas, with home defence relying on the presence of partly trained and ill-equipped AIF and militia forces. An armoured division was in the process of being formed, but its intended destination was the Middle East and only training tanks were provided by Britain for its use in Australia.[5]

It was no better prepared in the air. Although Menzies had claimed that the Empire Air Training Scheme provided Australia with a formidable air force, the reality could not have been more different. While 1400 aircraft were involved in the scheme in Australia, none of them were suitable as first-line combat aircraft. Instead, at considerable expense to Australia, thousands of aircrew were trained for use by the RAF in Europe and elsewhere. By September 1941, nearly 12 000 men were either in training or had been dispatched overseas under the terms of the scheme. Under a further agreement reached in January 1941, Australia was to provide eighteen squadrons by May 1942 for use overseas. This was in addition to the five squadrons already serving in distant parts. For home defence, it was planned to have 32 squadrons. By September, twenty squadrons had been formed, but seven of them were serving outside of Australia. Although there were 227 aircraft within Australia for home defence, most of them were training aircraft flying under the guise of being first-line planes. In addition, the stocks of aviation fuel were perilously low, being just one-fifth of the level deemed necessary to fight a Pacific war.[6]

As the Pacific situation deteriorated, a public campaign was launched for Australia to acquire fighter aircraft for home defence. Britain had refused to concede the possibility that such aircraft might be required by Australia, except for psychological purposes. It disparaged fears of Australia being invaded, arguing that the most Australia would have to face were cruiser raids on its trade routes. Naval ships, and perhaps Beaufort bombers and seaplanes, were the best defence against such raiders whereas fighter aircraft were used for warding off an invasion or repelling an attacking army or bomber force. If Britain conceded that Australia might need fighter aircraft, it would be acknowledging the possibility of an invasion and perhaps lead Australia thereby to concentrate on local defence rather than imperial defence.

The Australian government had accepted the British view until a pioneer Australian aviator, P. G. Taylor, launched a campaign in the *Sydney Morning Herald* for fighter aircraft to be included in the strength of the RAAF. The paper supported his call, suggesting that its readers would be surprised to learn of their absence. It argued that fighters were 'indispensable to our security' and vital if the RAAF was going to 'meet an invader at least on equal terms'. Australians had presumably been deluded until then into believing that the hundreds of training aircraft filling the skies had some operational value. The Melbourne newspapers joined in the growing chorus of outrage, while the Burns Philp company donated £10000 towards the cost of providing fighter aircraft. Unnerved by the clamour, the minister for air, John McEwen, claimed falsely that the RAAF was being expanded along such lines with 'alacrity and intensity', and even claiming that 'certain types of these aircraft are being made in Australia'.[7] Public disquiet was soothed at some cost to the truth.

Despite the government claims, Australia had not decided on its future plans for aircraft production. It had abandoned its plan to produce Beaufighter aircraft for local use, as well as for export, when the British government announced that it would not be buying any of them. Instead, Australia would buy Beaufighters produced in British factories but scheduled for delivery far into the future. When the British refusal came before a government committee on 3 October 1941, with the deposed Menzies in the chair as minister for defence coordination, the committee was assured by the chief of the air staff, Air Chief Marshal Sir Charles Burnett, that the local production of Beaufighters was 'rated lowest in Air Force priorities'. The RAAF effort was still directed primarily towards fulfilling the requirements of the Empire Air Training Scheme. Nevertheless, in view of the recent public campaign for fighter aircraft, McEwen had sufficient sense to recognise the possible political and military risks the government might incur by not producing Beaufighters. Accordingly, he suggested that Britain provide 'an assurance in general terms ... that if hostilities extend to Australia, adequate supplies of fighter aircraft will be made available'.[8] In fact, Menzies had already been given such a general assurance when in London. And similar empty assurances had been given over the years in regard to the dispatch of a British fleet. It was a mark of the bankruptcy of Australia's defence policy that it continued to clutch at such straws.

Without waiting for the British assurance, the committee rubber-stamped the production program that Britain had foisted upon it. The same day, Fadden accepted the committee's recommendations, dashing off a cable to London advising that he had ordered 'all work necessary to achieve the proposed programme be put in hand immediately'.[9] It was the day he faced a vote of no confidence in parliament and his short-lived government was forced to resign after just six weeks in power. His inordinate rush to commit Australia to the British program suggests that Fadden was anxious to prevent his Labor successors from establishing a program more suited to the defence of Australia, rather than to maximising its export earnings. As a result of this commitment, Australia remained dependent on Britain for the supply of fighter aircraft and continued to clutch at the British assurance that fighters would be sent to Australia in the event of an attack.

Australia's attention remained divided between the Middle East and its own predicament in the Pacific, with its trapped division in Tobruk and the dispute over its relief helping to concentrate anxiety in that distant theatre and divert attention from local defence. In September, American officials had predicted that Germany might soon launch as many as 750 000 troops in an assault against Britain's position in the Middle East. The threat was taken very seriously in Australia, especially when Blamey advised of the poor equipment position in Egypt. As army minister, it was Spender's responsibility to provide personnel for the AIF and for home defence. Though the defeat of Britain's garrison in the Middle East would see Australia losing most of its trained troops, Spender could see no alternative other than to keep Australia tied to imperial defence. He merely counselled Fadden to plan for possible setbacks while proceeding in the Middle East, 'as proceed we must, upon all too slender margins'.[10]

Beset with these competing priorities, the government was able to take some confidence from an unexpected quarter when Britain resuscitated the notion of sending a Far East fleet. Earlier in 1941, Churchill had informed Menzies of British plans to dispatch a battleship and an aircraft carrier to the Indian Ocean on the outbreak of war with Japan. It was the most minimal contribution and would have done little to deter or impede the Japanese. Now that the United States was adopting a higher naval profile in the Atlantic and taking on part of the responsibility for escorting convoys, the Admiralty was able to consider a plan for the gradual build-up of its naval strength in the east. The plan seems to have originated with Churchill and Eden and caused considerable dissension within the navy, mainly over whether it was strategically sound to dispatch in piecemeal fashion a fleet that was supposed to deter the formidable naval power of Japan.[11]

While the argument was still proceeding within the Admiralty, Churchill informed Fadden in late August that Britain was contemplating 'placing a force of capital ships, including first class units, in the triangle Aden–Singapore–Simonstown before the end of the year', though he was careful to stipulate that it would be 'without prejudice to our control of the Eastern Mediterranean'. Again he assured Australia that Britain will 'never let you down if real danger comes'. As Churchill made fairly clear, the previous British promise to abandon the Mediterranean for the sake of forming a Far East fleet was no longer operative. No matter. Fadden seized upon the promised fleet, even though Australia did not fall within the naval triangle described by Churchill. He confided to Churchill that the absence of a fleet at Singapore had 'aroused a feeling of uneasiness in the minds of many people here, and ... undoubtedly had an adverse effect on recruiting for service overseas'.[12] This was presumably designed to put Churchill on notice to provide the proposed ships in return for continuing Australian contributions to Britain's war effort. Fadden clearly confused this new fleet with the long-promised, but now abandoned, fleet for Singapore. Churchill had other things in mind for his ships.

The naval triangle to be covered by the proposed British force would provide protection to the Middle East and to India, which was even more important than Australia in supplying troops for Britain and which occupied the central place in Churchill's imperial cosmos. In the words of Lord Moran, Churchill 'looked with pride on the story of our Indian Empire ... His India was the land he knew as a subaltern. He could not conceive of an India without the British.'[13] The proposed ships would protect the important convoys that plied the sea lanes along the east African coast, bringing reinforcements of men and supplies for the Middle East. The apex of the naval triangle, and its most protected point, was the Red Sea and the Suez Canal. As the point most exposed to Japanese attack, Singapore would provide some protection against Japanese entry into the Indian Ocean but could do little to limit Japan's freedom of movement in the Pacific.

The composition of the proposed Eastern fleet confirmed Churchill's purpose. It was designed for escorting convoys rather than constituting a well-balanced battle fleet capable of confronting a Japanese fleet. The planned fleet would be comprised of four elderly *Royal Sovereign* class battleships, the modern battleship *Prince of Wales*, the battle cruiser *Repulse*, and the new aircraft carrier *Indomitable*.[14] Eighteen months earlier, Churchill had judged the four *Royal Sovereign* battleships and the *Repulse* to be unsuitable for use against the Japanese.[15] Even now he described the four older battleships as 'floating coffins' that could only be used for convoy work if there also were 'one or two fast heavy units' nearby to deter attacks on the convoys by individual heavy raiders.[16]

As a result of pressure from Churchill and Eden, the Admiralty reluctantly agreed to include the *Prince of Wales* in the initial group. Admiral Somerville, who later commanded the Eastern fleet, described the dispatch of the *Prince of Wales* as a 'great mistake'. He blamed Churchill and Eden for insisting on the ship's inclusion, 'though what it had to do with the latter I don't know and can't imagine'.[17] Churchill's readiness to dispatch ill-suited ships to the Indian Ocean was not foolhardiness on his part, nor was it forced upon him by necessity. It was done partly to satisfy restive allies: the United States was keen for Britain to send naval forces to the Far East, while Australia wanted some confirmation that its contributions to imperial defence would be reciprocated by Britain. Australia was easily convinced, seizing upon the proposed Eastern fleet as a measure planned for its protection and which appeared to accord with the accepted principles of imperial defence.[18]

For Churchill, the fleet had more important purposes. It would throw a protective naval mantle over the Indian Ocean, and particularly the reinforcement route to the Middle East. Any effect on the Japanese in the Pacific would be solely as a distant and doubtful deterrent. Indeed, it may have been intended by Churchill to have the opposite effect on the Japanese. Along with an American build-up in the Philippines, the widely publicised news of its dispatch would increase the military and economic pressure on Japan and force its government either to launch its long-anticipated lunge to secure the oil supplies of the Netherlands East Indies and the rubber supplies of Malaya or to tear up its plans for creating an empire in Asia. And perhaps even force Japan into a humiliating capitulation in China. On 29 August, Churchill accurately predicted that it was 'very likely' that Japan would 'negotiate with the United States for at least three months without making any further aggressive move or joining the Axis actively'.[19] By Churchill's own reckoning, the Eastern fleet would arrive at its proposed station in the Indian Ocean just at the time when he expected Japan might be provoked into war. The arrival of the ships could help to convince Japan to launch its war, and thereby serve the crucial purpose for Britain of also bringing the United States into the war. The ships also would be well placed to prevent any interference by a hostile Japan with the vital sea routes to the Middle East and India.

Australia's political leaders seemed relatively oblivious of their nation's increasing peril and had an untoward concern with protecting the civilian economy and the government's budget. As Sir Earle Page had explained to the advisory war council on 12 September, he would try to obtain strong naval and air forces for Singapore in order to release even more Australian forces from home defence and allow them to rejoin the civilian workforce. The reinforcement of Singapore, argued Page, would mitigate the 'consequent burden on the Budget and manpower that resulted in the calling up for continuous service or long periods of training of a large Home Defence army'. Despite his long-time commitment to boosting local defence, it seemed that Curtin basically agreed with the priorities of Page. He cited financial reasons for restricting to its present level Australia's contribution to the British war effort, while at the same time supporting Page's call for 'a strong force of capital ships east of Suez'. If Page was successful in achieving this, observed Curtin, Page would be in a 'better position to discuss the Australian contribution to the common Empire cause'.[20] Both men clearly continued to operate under the illusion that Britain had Australian defence as a high priority and that the dispatch of British ships to the Indian Ocean would secure it.

In later discussions with the Australian chiefs of staff, Page was informed of Britain's intention to gradually build up its naval strength in the East. Page welcomed this information, reasoning that it would prevent Australian forces in the Middle East from being isolated, while also easing Australia's manpower shortage by allowing as many as 50 000 men to be released from the army into 'essential industries and for primary production'. He was encouraged by the chiefs of staff to believe such an outcome might be possible, with the defence chiefs adopting an unrealistically optimistic view of Australia's defence position and the security of Singapore.[21]

Page was able to see for himself the situation at Singapore when he called there at the end of September for discussions with Brooke-Popham and other British officials.[22] After a meeting with Page, Brooke-Popham cabled London with the meeting's 'emphatic opinion' that 'the only real deterrent to further Japanese aggression would be a British fleet based at Singapore and in the absence of this fleet there is little doubt that Japan will be able to strike at her selected moment'. Page asked Fadden to throw his weight behind this pressure, claiming that a fleet would make Singapore so impregnable that it would not even be challenged. Although Page held out the prospect of a Far East fleet allowing for a greater Australian contribution to imperial defence, it is clear that he was primarily concerned with putting soldiers back onto the farms of his party's rural constituents, as well as into the booming factories of the towns and cities.[23] In the event, Fadden was unable to respond to Page's suggestions after Australia was plunged into a fresh political crisis.

By throwing Menzies aside just six weeks previously, Fadden had earned the enmity of one of the independent MPs crucial for his political survival. Along with the other independent MP, who had received assurances from Curtin about wheat prices for his farmer constituents, he threw his support behind the Labor Party in the hope that they could provide the strong and unifying leadership that Australia so desperately needed. Deprived of their support in parliament on 3 October, Fadden was forced to resign. So, at the most crucial period in its modern history, Australia was given its third prime minister in six weeks by the rather quixotic switch of allegiance by one MP and a pragmatic personal calculation by another. Meanwhile, the Pacific peace steadily crumbled and Page's cable lay in Canberra unconsidered for two weeks.

NOTES

[1] Dalton diary, 7 September 1941, I/25/63, Dalton Papers, LSE.

[2] King diary, in Cecil King, *With Malice Toward None*, London, 1970, p. 140.

[3] Cable, Churchill to Stalin, 29 August 1941, 'The Prime Minister's Personal Telegrams 1941', VI/I, Ismay Papers, KC.

[4] Cable No. 34, Chiefs of Staff to Brooke-Popham, 17 September 1941, V/4/33, Brooke-Popham Papers, KC.

[5] 'Summary of Australian Army War Effort, September 1941', CRS A5954, Box 313, NAA.

[6] 'Summary of Australian Air War Effort, September 1941', CRS A5954, Box 313, NAA.

[7] *Sydney Morning Herald*, 17 September 1941; *Age*, Melbourne, 18 and 24 September 1941; *Argus*, Melbourne, 18 September 1941.

8   'Programme for Future Aircraft Construction in Australia', Notes of conference in Canberra, 3 October 1941, CRS A5954, Box 223, NAA.

9   Cable No. 5834, Fadden to Bruce, 3 October 1941, CRS A5954, Box 225, NAA.

10 Letter (copy), Spender to Fadden, 30 September 1941, MS 4875, Box 1, Correspondence 1939–1949, Spender Papers, NLA.

11 For details of the dispute, see Stephen Roskill, *The War at Sea, 1939–1945*, Vol. 1, London, 1954, pp. 555–9.

12 Cable, Cranborne to Fadden, 31 August 1941, and Cable, Fadden to Churchill, 4 September 1941, *DAFP*, Vol. 5, Doc. 54 and fn. 5.

13 Moran, *Winston Churchill*, p. 31.

14 Roskill, *The War at Sea*, Vol. 1, p. 491.

15 'Comparison of British and Japanese Fleets', Note by Churchill, 12 March 1940, CAB 66/6, W.P. (40)95, PRO.

16 Churchill, *The Second World War*, Vol. 3, Appendix K.

17 Letter, Somerville to Cunningham, 5 October 1941, ADD. MS. 52563, Cunningham Papers, BL.

18 Page later wrongly claimed that it was partly due to his efforts that the battleships were dispatched. Page, *Truant Surgeon*, p. 311.

19 Minute, Churchill to Pound, 29 August 1941, in Churchill, *The Second World War*, Vol. 3, p. 524.

20 Advisory War Council Minutes, 12 September 1941, *DAFP*, Vol. 5, Doc. 65.

21 Notes of Discussion between Sir Earle Page and the Chiefs of Staff, Canberra, 17 September 1941, CRS A5954, Box 475, NAA.

22 Brooke-Popham described Page as a 'straight, kindly country gentleman' who was a 'little inclined to stress the obvious at some length and without any pause ... for interruption'. Letter, Brooke-Popham to Ismay, 10 October 1941, V/1/18, Brooke-Popham Papers, KC.

23 Cable, Page to Fadden, 1 October 1941, *DAFP*, Vol. 5, Doc. 75; Page diary, 29 September 1941, MS 1633, Folder 2345, Page Papers, NLA; Page, *Truant Surgeon*, p. 311; 'Observations by Sir Earle Page on the General Headquarters Situation in the Far East — Singapore, 29/9/41', and Letters, Page to Fadden, 1 and 2 October 1941, CRS A5954, Box 475, NAA.

SIXTEEN

'an endless, cockney monotone'

Taking over as prime minister on 7 October 1941, John Curtin had no greater political security than his two predecessors. Like them, he would have to protect his position, both within the parliament and within his own party. As Sir Ronald Cross observed, Curtin had two powerful rivals in Beasley and Evatt, each of whom was 'determined to stab the other on the steps of the throne'.[1] He also had to contend with the endemic Australian apathy towards their own defence. Although the public was anxious about invasion, their colonial mentality had left them with little sense that it was incumbent upon themselves to provide for their own protection. A century and a half of dependence upon Britain could not be shrugged off easily. This presented very real problems to Curtin's new cabinet, as they quickly discovered. After meeting in Canberra, they tried to depart for Melbourne to take charge of their separate departments, which remained headquartered in that southern city, only to find that the train was fully booked, mainly by people on their way from Sydney to Melbourne for the spring race meetings.[2]

The new government had a more formidable task than dislodging a crowd of racegoers from their carriage. It was taking control of a country that had been at war for more than two years but which still lacked the basic means for its own defence. Its naval forces were scattered from Singapore to Alexandria, while the efforts of its army and air force were predominantly directed towards providing trained men for Britain's use overseas. There were critical shortages of equipment ranging from binoculars for the army to parachutes for the air force. More seriously, there were no modern fighter aircraft, no tanks worthy of the name, and shortages of every type of gun from rifles to anti-aircraft guns and artillery.[3]

The Labor Party had been shouting from the sidelines in the defence debate. Now it had the power to put its policies into practice. It had opposed the original commitment of forces to the Middle East in 1939 and various Labor members had called during 1941 for the recall of the Australian forces. However, once in power the party fell in with Curtin's more accommodating view and continued with the policy of Fadden and Menzies. Imperial defence still largely held sway. It was simply too difficult from a political and military point of view to undo everything that had been done since 1939 and refocus the separate services on local defence. As a result, the three AIF divisions would be allowed to remain in the Middle East and be kept up to strength by regular convoys of reinforcements. Britain had actually wanted Australia to supply three more infantry divisions for the Middle East. But Fadden had refused, citing the burden of supplying the reinforcements for the existing divisions and agreeing instead, if the situation in the Far East permitted, to send the armoured portion of a division that was then being raised.[4] Fadden had also insisted, despite fresh appeals from Churchill, that the relief of the Australian troops from Tobruk be completed. Shortly after taking over from Fadden, Curtin was faced with yet another appeal to delay the relief of the Tobruk force but stuck by the decision of his predecessor.[5]

Churchill previously had blamed the Labor Party for the Australian pressure over Tobruk. Despite this, he still requested Curtin to relent and allow the Australians to remain until the coming British offensive lifted their siege. It was a sign of Churchill's frustration with the Australians that he should make this request to Curtin while believing, as he admitted to colleagues, that there was little prospect of it causing a change of mind in

Canberra. It was also a sign of his deep desire to see Auchinleck's offensive succeed, since his own political future could hang on the outcome. After prevaricating over whether to send the request, Churchill went ahead with his appeal to Curtin after learning from Cairo that it would assist Auchinleck's operation. He assured Curtin that postponing their relief would not 'expose your troops to any undue or invidious risks and would at the same time be taken very kindly as an act of comradeship in the present struggle'. There was a clear implication as to how a refusal would be regarded in London. As Churchill put it to Auchinleck, he would be 'glad for the sake of Australia and history if they would do this'. He addressed his war cabinet in a similar vein, warning that the 'effect on the prestige of the Australian troops would be very great when the full facts and the correspondence became known'.[6]

As Churchill had anticipated, Curtin remained adamant about the withdrawal. When one of the small naval ships was sunk during the evacuation with the loss of British sailors, Churchill felt added vindication for his position and immediately informed Australia of the cost of its stubborn stand. At the same time, he allowed Curtin to believe for a day or so that Australian troops had also been lost in the sinking. Still Curtin would not budge, merely repeating that all the troops should be withdrawn at the earliest date. In the event, some still remained when Auchinleck's long-delayed offensive was finally launched and the siege of Tobruk was soon after lifted. In this instance, Churchill was proved correct.[7]

Tobruk was a dispute marked by a depth of bitterness seldom experienced in previous relations between Australia and Britain. In Churchill's view, and that of many of his colleagues, the dominion's demand for the relief of the Australian portion of the garrison was shameful and unforgivable. It was made worse for Churchill by him having to keep his annoyance in check and concealed from public gaze. At the end of November, Churchill reminded Curtin that Australia's insistence on withdrawal had cost Britain 'life and ships' but that 'no one here ... outside the circles of Government has the slightest inkling of the distress which we felt'.[8] It was the most serious in a succession of *contretemps* between Australia and Britain since the beginning of the war, and Churchill and his colleagues would be slow to forget the distress that had been caused to them.

The dispute had been started and sustained by a trio of Australian prime ministers who each were motivated more by considerations of political rather than military survival. On the military side, Blamey supported the relief in order to aggregate his scattered forces into a unified corps. Where was Australia's national interest in all this? Once committed to the Middle East and to the defence of Tobruk, it was incumbent on the Australians to remain with the rest of the garrison and see the battle through to a finish. By not doing so, British antipathy towards Australia was enhanced at a time when British sympathy was required above all else. It may have been possible to justify the cost of the dispute in retrospect if the relieved 9th Division had thereby become available for Australia's defence during the anxious days of 1942. But this did not happen. The division did not leave the Middle East until January 1943. Neither was the relief of Tobruk part of an attempt by the new Labor government to wind back the Australian commitment to the Middle East. Rather, it continued on the mistaken understanding that a fleet for the Far East was being gradually assembled.

As for the promised British fleet, Curtin took up a suggestion by Bruce that a modern battleship should be included in the squadron being planned for the Indian Ocean. And Labor's war cabinet added its combined voice, impressing upon Churchill the 'importance of the proposed re-dispositions for the defence of Empire interests in the Eastern Hemisphere, for the maintenance of communications to the Middle East and for sustaining generally the war efforts of the Dominions in the Pacific and their overseas forces in particular'. Again, there was an implicit warning that Australia's commitment to the British war effort would depend on the dispatch of this squadron, including one modern battleship.[9] As if one modern battleship in the Indian Ocean could deter the formidable power of the Japanese fleet in the Pacific Ocean. Anyway, unbeknown to the Australians, Churchill already favoured the inclusion of a modern battleship but faced opposition from his admirals.

On 17 October 1941, Churchill finally reached a compromise agreement with his colleagues and defence advisers over the vexed issue of the naval squadron that was meant to constitute the first echelon of an Eastern fleet. At a meeting of the defence committee, the strenuous objections of the tired and aged Admiral Dudley Pound were overruled by Churchill and his colleagues, who instructed Pound to plan for the dispatch of one modern battleship and an aircraft carrier from the Atlantic to join the battle cruiser *Repulse* at Singapore. There would be opportunity when the ships arrived at Cape Town to reverse the decision if necessary. So Australia obtained its modern battleship for the Indian Ocean, although it is doubtful whether dominion opinion played much part in the decision finally being made.[10] Churchill tried to calm the concerns of the Admiralty by predicting that Japan would not make war on Britain and the United States, that they would not 'attack in force in Malaya' and that the main danger was from cruiser attacks on British trade — a threat best countered by a fast striking force which included a modern battleship.[11] How wrong he would prove to be on all those counts, as many service personnel would find to their cost.

The Foreign Office did not share Churchill's apparent confidence about the Japanese. Eden told his war cabinet colleagues that he expected trouble from the Japanese in about three weeks, while his assistant under-secretary, Sir Horace Seymour, sagely observed to his wife that 'the Japs move slowly, but I suppose they mean to come in ... each change of Govt. seems to make them more inclined to take the plunge, cautious as they are'.[12] Once again, Eden tried to convince the war cabinet to declare that a Japanese attack on either Siam, Russia or the Burma Road would cause Britain to go to war against Japan. But Churchill still refused to make any such commitment, while comforting his colleagues with his belief that the United States was 'nearer to a commitment than they had been in the past' and that Britain ought to regard Washington as 'having taken charge in the Far East'.[13]

Meanwhile, Australia's fears were calmed to some extent by a visit from Brooke-Popham who, in a generally optimistic report to the advisory war council on 16 October, claimed that the aircraft under his command at Singapore were superior to those of the Japanese. Although he conceded that Singapore's planned allocation of aircraft for 1941 was unlikely to be received in full, he claimed that Japan was preoccupied with launching an attack against Russia and that 'for the next three months she would not be able to undertake a large-scale attack in the south'. Curtin had heard it all before and quizzed Brooke-Popham as to why little seemed to have been sent to Singapore since Menzies first raised the problem in April. Oblivious to the strategic priorities that had caused Singapore to be relatively undefended, Curtin urged that the needs of the Far East should be 'represented strongly to the United Kingdom authorities'. Not that another cable to London would make any difference. Upset by the implied criticism, Brooke-Popham pointed out that he had 'made all representations short of resigning'. At the same time, he defended his superiors in London, claiming that they were 'not neglecting the Far East and that probably they have made a fair allocation from the resources available'. This seemed to silence Curtin, who took solace in various paltry efforts by Britain and the United States to reinforce respectively Hong Kong and the Philippines.[14]

As for boosting the defence of Australia, Curtin's government did order an extra two thousand naval mines to be added to the thousand ordered by its predecessor. This was still less than the four thousand considered necessary for a Pacific war, and it would be many months before his belated order would become available.[15] Moreover, even when deployed, such mines could only have a limited delaying action against a serious Japanese attack on Australia. Of potentially greater benefit was Curtin's reversal of the previous government's refusal to allow landing rights for American aircraft. Menzies had been anxious to protect Britain's commercial aviation interests, but Curtin offered the Americans landing rights for the duration of the war and twelve months thereafter without any preconditions about protecting British interests. Britain would be informed but not consulted by Australia.[16] The government also agreed immediately to an American government request to establish an alternative air route between Hawaii and the Philippines via Australia and to provide air bases at Rabaul, Port Moresby, Rockhampton and Darwin.[17] It would prove to be too late, with the Japanese attacking before the decisions could be implemented.

Other decisions by the incoming Curtin government suggested that Australia was still prepared to make sacrifices with respect to its own defence for the sake of the wider struggle. It agreed to send fifteen million rounds of rifle ammunition to China and four anti-aircraft guns to the Middle East.[18] The dispatch of these munitions was based on the continuing assumption that British assistance would be forthcoming in the event of a Japanese attack. Even had the Labor government been so minded, there were considerable impediments preventing the adoption of a more self-reliant defence posture. The decades of dependence on Britain had left Australia with little choice other than to continue in dutiful devotion to its protecting power. Partly due to its self-induced neglect, Australia lacked the necessary military resources to provide for its own defence. The Curtin government was taking up the ministerial reins after a decade of opposition. Despite their membership of the advisory war council, the Labor leaders had not been taken into the full confidence of the previous administrations and now were dependent on the advice of their defence advisers. As Brooke-Popham reported to Whitehall, the defence chiefs were 'all pleased with their new Ministers', who were 'fully ready to take the advice of their respective Chiefs of Staff'. Despite this, Brooke-Popham acknowledged that the Labor government was more critical of Britain and more conscious of its predicament in the Pacific. He warned London of the importance of making Australia 'feel that we, in England, look upon them as definitely part of one Empire and we must do everything we can to keep them in the Empire and not run any risk of their slipping out of it'.[19]

Apart from relying upon imperial-minded defence chiefs, Curtin's government inherited a legacy of conservative politicians occupying its diplomatic posts and giving advice to Canberra that was generally in harmony with British interests.[20] Even Page, who was still in Singapore when Curtin took over, was allowed to continue to London on the understanding that he would ditch the conservative instructions he had taken from Australia. Instead the former Country Party leader remained committed to his original aims of securing ships for Singapore and British purchases of Australian primary produce.[21] Not that he would have much success with either of those aims. At his first meeting of the British war cabinet on 30 October, Page was welcomed by Churchill and invited to address them the following week. He was not given a seat in the war cabinet, nor was he necessarily invited when matters affecting the higher direction of the war or the Pacific in particular were discussed.

Page was not present at the war cabinet's next meeting when it discussed yet another proposal by Eden for a British declaration on the Netherlands East Indies, despite it being a matter of vital significance for Australia. As

Page had indicated during a meeting with Eden, Australia was keen to send forces to the NEI to pre-empt any moves by Japan in that direction, but was hampered by the lack of any defence agreement with the Dutch.[22] Despite this Australian desire, Churchill again countered Eden's proposal, claiming that there was 'no evidence of any early intention' by Japan to attack the NEI and that Britain's policy must remain directed towards persuading the United States to cover Britain's 'weak position in that area'. Although Cranborne warned of the 'painful impression' that would be created in Australia if Britain failed to respond to an attack on the NEI, Churchill succeeded in postponing consideration of the issue while he sought to organise a public declaration from Washington.[23]

Churchill and his colleagues finally gathered to hear Page address the war cabinet on 5 November. Like Menzies before him, he spoke of the deficiencies he had found at Singapore and pressed for them to be rectified so that 'those forces would constitute an effective deterrent by December or early January at the latest'. This might then ensure that the Pacific and Indian Oceans remained peaceful for the next few months, 'so that the Empire could continue to transport the supplies necessary for our war effort'. He pointed to the alarming deficiency in air strength at Singapore, which still had nearly two hundred aircraft less than its recommended minimum level. But no one was listening. Cadogan wrote dismissively in his diary of Page being a 'non-stop talker — goes on in an endless, cockney monotone. I asked A. [Eden], who was sitting next to him, whether he couldn't find a handle or something that would switch off the talk.'[24] Churchill was similarly unsympathetic to Page's appeal, pointing to the competing demands on Britain. It was sending two hundred aircraft to Russia, it had to attain air superiority in the Middle East and it had to retain sufficient aircraft to keep Britain secure from invasion. Not that Churchill believed that Britain was in danger of invasion any longer. In fact, he felt Britain was so secure that he instructed the chiefs of staff in early October to plan for a British invasion of Norway.[25] Although this mad plan never eventuated, it revealed how Churchill could readily contemplate the added burden of invading Norway while at the same time strenuously opposing the dispatch of any additional aircraft to Singapore.

To pacify Page, Churchill simply repeated Britain's pledge to accept 'supreme responsibility' for Australia's defence and, if necessary, to abandon the Middle East.[26] It would not be long before the responsibility was put to the test, though Page seems to have been largely convinced by Churchill's account of Britain's difficulties and by news of the *Prince of Wales* being included in the proposed Eastern fleet. On a train journey with Churchill two days later, Page tried again to argue the case for Singapore's reinforcement, conceding in his diary that he 'did not make such wonderful progress'.[27] But he did not tell Curtin that, providing instead an optimistic assessment of his efforts. He reported that Churchill had 'made public the dispatch of [a] heavy British fleet to protect British interests in the Pacific and Indian Ocean and has also promised all necessary aid to ensure [the] safety of Australia'.[28] The Australian government had expected much from Page in his role as its special envoy to London, but it received only bland assurances that could have been sent equally well by Bruce or, for that matter, by Churchill himself. And time was running out.

NOTES

[1] Letter, Cross to Cranborne, 20 January 1942, ADD. MS. 58240, Emrys-Evans Papers, BL.

[2] *Argus*, Melbourne, 11 October 1941.

[3] See Note by Evatt, 27 July 1943, 'War — Matters Relating to — Australia', Evatt Collection, FUL; Cabinet Minutes, 17 October 1941, CRS A2703, Vol. I[B], NAA.

[4] Cable No. 653, Fadden to UK Government, 7 October 1941, PREM 3/63/1, PRO.

[5] Cable, Churchill to Fadden, 30 September 1941, and Cable, Fadden to Churchill, 4 October 1941, *DAFP*, Vol. 5, Docs 73 and 77; War Cabinet Minutes, 15 October 1941, CRS A2673, Vol. 8, Minute 1404, NAA.

[6] PREM 3/63/2 and War Cabinet Conclusions/Confidential Annex, 16 October 1941, CAB 65/23, W.M. 103(41), PRO.

[7] War Cabinet Minutes, 30 October 1941, CRS A2673, Vol. 9, Minute 1462, NAA; War Cabinet Conclusions/Confidential Annex, 27 October 1941, CAB 65/23, W.M. 106(41), PRO.

[8] Cable, Churchill to Curtin, 27 November 1941, VI/I, Ismay Papers, KC.

[9] War Cabinet Minutes, 15 October 1941, CRS A2673, Vol. 8, Minute 1407, NAA.

[10] Defence Committee (Operations) Minutes, 17 October 1941, CAB 69/2, D.O. (41)65, PRO.

[11] Defence Committee (Operations) Confidential Annex, 20 October 1941, CAB 69/8, D.O. (41)66, PRO; Letter, Admiral Ralph Edwards to Grenfell, 15 December 1951, GREN 2/2, Grenfell Papers, CC.

[12] War Cabinet Conclusions/Confidential Annex, 20 October 1941, CAB 65/23, W.M. 104(41), PRO; Letter, Seymour to his wife, 21 October 1941, SEYR 2/5, Seymour Papers, CC.

[13] War Cabinet Conclusions/Confidential Annex, 16 October 1940, CAB 65/23, W.M. 103(41), PRO.

[14] Advisory War Council Minutes, 16 October 1941, CRS A2682, Vol. 3, Minute 533, NAA.

[15] War Cabinet Agenda No. 317/1941, 7 October 1941, CRS A5954, Box 483, NAA.

[16] War Cabinet Minutes, 15 October 1941, CRS A2673, Vol. 8, Minute 1412, NAA.

[17] The government agreed on the 'urgency of the matter' and offered to 'co-operate to the fullest possible degree as regards bases in its territories'. War Cabinet Minutes, 18 October 1941, CRS A2673, Vol. 8, Minute 1416, NAA; See also War Cabinet Conclusions, 23 and 27 October 1941, CAB 65/19, W.M. 105 and 106(41), PRO.

[18] War Cabinet Minute No. 1419, 22 October 1941, CRS A5954, Box 495, NAA.

[19] Brooke-Popham cited the British order for Wirraway aircraft from Australia which, he claimed, had left the impression of it being 'only given to keep them quiet and not that their Wirraways were essential to the Empire war effort'. Letter, Brooke-Popham to Sir Arthur Street, Air Ministry, 28 October 1941, V/2/16, Brooke-Popham Papers, KC.

[20] The diplomats in the various posts were: in London, the former conservative prime minister S. M. Bruce; in Washington, the former UAP treasurer Richard Casey; in Tokyo, the former UAP deputy prime minister Sir John Latham; in Ottawa, the former conservative defence minister Sir William Glasgow; and in Chungking, the former conservative politician Sir Frederick Eggleston.

[21] Cabinet Minutes, 7 October 1941, CRS A2700, Vol. 1, Minute 2, NAA; Page diary, 31 October 1941, MS 1633, Folder 2345, Page Papers, NLA.

[22] For the meeting with Eden, Bruce and Page had decided to join together to 'insist on [the] story of British foreign policy ever since Roosevelt's and Churchill's meeting ... and [to] see how far [the] Foreign Office had receded from its old position of a few months ago [of] being ready to abandon [the] Far East'. Page diary, 31 October 1941, MS 1633, Folder 2345, Page Papers, KC.

[23] War Cabinet Conclusions/Confidential Annex, 3 November 1941, CAB 65/24, W.M. 108(41), PRO.

[24] Cadogan diary, 5 November 1941, ACAD 1/10, Cadogan Papers, CC; War Cabinet Conclusions/Confidential Annex, 5 November 1941, CAB 65/24, W.M. 109(41), PRO.

[25] King diary in King, *With Malice Toward None*, p. 142. For details of the Norway plan, see Pownall diary, 2 October 1941, in Bond (ed.), *Chief of Staff*, Vol. 2, p. 44; Harvey diary, 3 October 1941, ADD. MS. 56398, Harvey Papers, BL; 'Notes on my Life', p. 296, by Lord Alanbrooke, 3/A/iv, Alanbrooke Papers, KC.

[26] War Cabinet Conclusions/Confidential Annex, 5 November 1941, CAB 65/24, W.M. 109(41), PRO.

[27] See Page, *Truant Surgeon*, p. 312; Page diary, 7 November 1941, MS 1633, Folder 2345, Page Papers, NLA.

[28] Cable P.1, Page to Curtin, 10 November 1941, CRS CP 290/8, Bundle 1, 'Sir E. Page — cables from', NAA.

SEVENTEEN

'a pawn in the game'

The Australian government learned of the prospective Eastern fleet as it was hosting the visit of Alfred Duff Cooper, a British minister whose mission was to create a sense of heightened British activity in the Far East. He was welcomed in Sydney by a government minister, Senator Richard Keane, who hoped that Duff Cooper would be able to 'clarify any doubts we may have had about the support we may expect in the event of aggression'. The visitor duly complied, assuring a meeting of the advisory war council on 7 November that Britain would resist any Japanese attack on the NEI, despite Churchill's refusal to give a public guarantee to this effect. Although Curtin expressed satisfaction at the dispatch of the *Prince of Wales*, feeling that it 'altered the whole position', Evatt remained suspicious. He demanded that Duff Cooper set out 'the real plans of the United Kingdom Government in relation to Far Eastern and Pacific defence'. Rather than responding directly, Duff Cooper resorted to the familiar Churchillian declaration that Britain would 'abandon the Mediterranean altogether if this were necessary in order to hold Singapore'.[1]

It was the conservative members of the council who doubted the value of this assurance, although only because they could not countenance a British abandonment of the Mediterranean and the 100 000 Australian troops based there. Curtin, though, seemed satisfied by Duff Cooper's restatement of the grand British assurance now that it was accompanied by the dispatch of the *Prince of Wales*. As Curtin saw it, the basing of a fleet at Singapore was the 'core of the whole problem and the essential factor in determining the limits of our action'. He had been misled into believing that the forthcoming fleet was to be based at Singapore when, in fact, it was meant to cover the north-western triangle of the Indian Ocean and only have Singapore as its furthest reach. Nevertheless, buoyed by news of the ship, the council supported the sending of a Buffalo squadron from Malaya to China, manned by Australian crew. The council left it to Brooke-Popham to 'determine the limit to be placed on numbers of personnel and the consequent reduction in air strength in Malaya which would be entailed'.[2] After calling for air reinforcements for Malaya, the Australian government was now agreeing to reduce them to ridiculous levels without producing a commensurate advantage for China. Instead of concentrating their strength to meet an imminent threat, Australia was continuing to dissipate its forces across the globe in penny packet contributions at Britain's whim. In this case, the Japanese attacked before effect could be given to the decision.

As the decision over the Buffaloes indicated, Australia retained confidence in Brooke-Popham as British commander-in-chief at Singapore. But he quickly lost the confidence of Duff Cooper, who recommended to Churchill that the hapless commander be replaced. When this was announced to the Australian government, it caused a storm of protest. Curtin immediately telephoned Duff Cooper in Singapore demanding an explanation, only to have the minister profess ignorance. This caused Curtin to blame Churchill for it. And his attitude darkened even further when Brooke-Popham's announced replacement was changed within days. It was all done without any reference being made to Australia, despite the dominion providing much of Singapore's defence. Even Bruce thought the situation was 'intolerable' and told Curtin that he had 'left little unsaid' in complaining to the British government.[3] Again, a matter largely of form succeeded in spurring Bruce into action where matters of greater substance had failed to do so.

To an extent, Churchill was caught in the middle. His fault was his usual one of not consulting Australia on matters of mutual interest. As he complained to Ismay, there had been no consultations over the original appointment of Brooke-Popham. Angrily he denounced the Australian government as being 'out to make the most trouble and give the least help' and instructed Ismay to tidy up the situation, though there was 'no need to answer them in a hurry, as we are in the battle and they are not'.[4] In his own attempt to calm the storm, Churchill instructed Duff Cooper to 'privately explain' to Curtin why he thought the elderly Brooke-Popham was unsuitable.[5] One of the unfortunate effects of this latest dispute was to leave Singapore with a 'lame duck' commander when the Japanese attacked just over a week later.

While Curtin was arguing for last-minute reinforcements for Singapore, Page was doing likewise in London. On 12 November, he called on the war cabinet to increase Singapore's air strength 'even at the expense of other theatres' and argued against Churchill's policy of following the American lead in the Far East. Again he held out the prospect of Australia making an even greater contribution to imperial defence if only Britain would strengthen the defence of Singapore. In reply, Churchill explained how Japan lacked the strength to actually invade Australia but, if Australia was 'menaced with invasion', Britain remained 'resolute to help'. This did not mean necessarily that Britain would immediately abandon the Mediterranean and rush to Australia's assistance, as had been promised in the past. Such a decision to abandon the Mediterranean, said Churchill, was 'not one to be taken lightly'. Letting this pass, Page pronounced himself 'content' that his requests would be considered. In reporting the meeting to Curtin, Page promised to continue arguing the Australian case for the immediate reinforcement by aircraft of Singapore and Malaya. But British ears were deaf to his appeal. Despite Page's failure, Curtin agreed to spread Australia's defence forces even more thinly by allowing four RAN destroyers to join Britain's skeletal Far Eastern force.[6]

Although the downgrading of the Far East represented a reversal of the interwar strategy of imperial defence, and left Singapore, Australia and other British eastern interests in a position of considerable peril, it was justified in

Whitehall by reference to the obvious fact that there was, as yet, no war in the Pacific. British military and political leaders also had an overconfident belief in their own racial and military superiority to the Japanese. Thus, Field Marshal Wavell assured Brooke-Popham after inspecting Malaya's defences in mid-November that 'you ought easily to be able to deal with any Japanese attack on Malaya provided that you get the necessary air reinforcements when required'. Wavell was 'most doubtful' that the Japanese would ever attack and, if they did, he was 'sure they will get [it] in the neck if they do'.[7] Wavell's reference to air reinforcements was the other justification for the weakness at Singapore. There was a belief that, even if the Japanese entered the war, there would be sufficient time to move aircraft across the world to defend Malaya. It was a dangerous strategy of bluff by Britain in a game of poker where its hand was revealed and the eastern parts of its empire, including Australia, were very much at stake.

Although Britain was averse to specifying the level of assistance that Australia could rely upon in case of a Japanese attack, it was not so backward in making such specific commitments to neutral Turkey in the event of a German attack. Both Churchill and Eden were transfixed by the possibility of winning the numerically strong, but poorly equipped, Turkish army to the British cause. This had provided much of the rationale for the disastrous campaign in Greece and it continued to be a top British priority. While Page was in London reminding the British of their obligations to Singapore, Eden was reminding the war cabinet of Whitehall's commitment to Turkey and of his anxiety 'lest in concentrating on the needs of the Soviet Union the importance of continuing our supplies to Turkey should be overlooked'. In the event of a German attack, Britain had offered to provide Turkey with four infantry and two armoured divisions, two tank brigades and 24 squadrons of aircraft. In the meantime, Eden suggested that Britain supply Turkey with 'non-specialised equipment' and reserve for Turkey 1 per cent of Britain's allocation of munitions from the United States.[8] As a rather bitter irony, much of the British assistance earmarked for Turkey was to be provided by the Australian troops in the Middle East. At the end of November, Australia gave its conditional agreement in principle to such a commitment.[9]

There was one last opportunity for keeping the peace in the Pacific. The United States and Japan were holding talks in Washington from which a Pacific settlement might have been reached. Churchill looked to the talks as a breathing space for Britain and as a positive indication of a greater willingness in Washington to contemplate hostilities with the Axis powers. From the sidelines in London, Bruce urged that, if the talks were seriously intended by Roosevelt to find a basis of settlement, the British empire should be involved so that it could influence the nature of the settlement and the economic concessions that would have to be made to Japan to secure it.[10] But Churchill was happy for the United States to conduct the talks alone, confident in the belief that no settlement would be reached and therefore that there was no reason to discuss the economic concessions that the British empire might be called upon to concede.[11]

In Canberra, there was increasing suspicion that Britain would look favourably on the outbreak of a Pacific war provided that it also brought the United States into the war. There was also mounting impatience with Britain's refusal to commit itself to any action in the event of Japan attacking only non-British territories, such as the Netherlands East Indies or Portuguese Timor. However, Australia's legacy of defence weakness and its continued dependence upon Britain only allowed for an outburst of impotent anger. A report by Evatt on 22 November complained of Churchill's refusal to declare various Japanese moves as being sufficient to cause war with Britain. He claimed that London 'clearly recognised' that a breakdown of the Washington talks could lead to war with Japan and noted that 'it seems that the United Kingdom is willing to run the risk for the good prospect of active American participation'.[12]

Like Churchill, Evatt was prepared to countenance a war with Japan provided that it also brought the United States into the war, but he was worried that such a war would come before Britain was ready. That is, before the arrival of the naval squadron at Singapore. Accordingly, he urged that Australia should 'try very hard to gain time until the arrival of the battleships at Singapore'. Japan, he wrote, should be allowed the chance of a 'diplomatic retreat without inflicting upon her unnecessary humiliation'. This would not constitute 'appeasement of Japan', argued Evatt, 'but merely a commonsense expedient of war at a crucial moment in our history'. He suggested starting talks with the Japanese minister to Australia 'for the purpose of gaining time' and with the proviso that nothing was done 'to suggest that we are acting contrary to the desires of the U.S.A.'.[13] The problem was that Australia had no bargaining chips of any consequence. The concessions that might have satisfied Japan, such as the ending of the Anglo–American trade embargo, were not within Australia's power to concede.

Evatt's attempt to find a basis of agreement with Japan caused a flurry of opposition from conservatives in the defence department, with Shedden warning Curtin against taking any independent initiatives. Although Shedden agreed that Australia should try to keep Japan out of the war, he claimed that the initiative must rest with the United States. Like Churchill, he was afraid of venturing out on a limb with Japan without the all-important security of an American safety net. He maintained that there was 'no choice but to leave the main initiative to [the] U.S.A., whilst at the same time maintaining contact as to what is happening and expressing opinions where asked for or where it is deemed prudent to suggest a word of advice'. Shedden claimed that Britain was leaving a way out for Japan and was equally anxious to play for time.[14]

Curtin supported Shedden, preferring to trust in Britain's good faith. On the one hand, he hoped for positive results from the Washington talks, while on the other he was reassured by the developing defence cooperation in the Pacific. Like Evatt, Curtin regarded the British squadron steaming toward Singapore as a 'major redistribution of naval forces' but, unlike Evatt, he could 'understand the reluctance of the United Kingdom Government to do anything to anticipate the outcome of the [Washington] conversations'.[15] Curtin was relying more than ever on the forthcoming arrival of the British ships. He had just learned on 24 November that the Australian cruiser *Sydney* had been sunk off Western Australia five days earlier after an engagement with a German armed merchant cruiser. Both ships were sunk, and all of the crew of the *Sydney* were lost. Its sinking only came to light when German survivors fetched up on the Western Australian coast. Curtin waited until 30 November before announcing the loss to a shocked nation.

While Australia waited for the Washington conversations to conclude, Churchill helped to ensure that they would collapse without agreement. On 26 November, when the possibility of a limited agreement seemed in sight, Churchill cabled Washington to stiffen Roosevelt's resolve, claiming that the Japanese were 'most unsure of themselves' and reminding him of America's responsibility to support the Chinese in their resistance to Japan.[16] That same day, the Japanese fleet left on its deadly voyage across the north Pacific to take up a position off Pearl Harbor. Churchill's cable helped to destroy the last chance for recalling them from their mission and preserving peace in the Pacific. On 27 November, messages warning of war were sent to US fleet commanders. Although Casey made a last-minute effort to act as an honest broker to restart the Washington talks, his efforts came to nothing.[17]

Right to the end, Australia seemed remarkably confident about the prospects for peace. On 5 December, three days before the Japanese launched their attack against Pearl Harbor, the war cabinet authorised the return to Qantas Empire Airways of a flying boat requisitioned by the RAAF for reconnaissance work but which Qantas now wanted back to handle the pre-Christmas rush of passengers and mail.[18] It was also proposed to close the Australian information office operating on the American west coast.[19]

Australia's defences remained insufficient to meet a serious attack. All the promises by Churchill of providing three months' notice of Japan's belligerency, and reinforcing the Far East to meet such a threat, were not fulfilled as far as Australia was concerned. On the ground, it still had only ten light tanks for training purposes. In mid-November, Britain had planned to increase this number with the delivery of 80 tanks by March 1942. But these were also designated for training purposes and were meant for the armoured division that Australia proposed to form for the Middle East. The division would only receive its operational tanks after it arrived in the Middle East. As part of the same allocation discussions that day, the British defence committee considered the distribution of some five thousand tanks that were expected to be produced by the following March. Russia was to receive about a thousand, nearly two thousand were destined for the Middle East and over three hundred for India. Almost two thousand were to be retained in Britain for home defence, so that by June 1942 there would be 3500 tanks deployed in Britain.[20]

Up to the last minute, Churchill steadfastly refused to make any guarantees in the event of war with Japan, except in the case of an attack upon British possessions. He still feared the possibility of the American public refusing to defend Britain's imperial interests in the Far East and pinned his hopes on them reacting 'favourably to a war which America has entered in defence of her own interests'. Churchill did undertake to declare war on Japan if it attacked a British territory such as Hong Kong, but he did not specify the assistance that would be forthcoming as a result.[21] As chief of the air staff, Sir Charles Portal was more forthright. In a conversation with Page on 18 November, he shocked the Australian envoy by admitting that 'if Singapore were lost we would pick it up again' and that Britain might not fight 'if the Dutch East Indies were invaded'. Moreover, Portal acknowledged that Singapore was inadequately defended because of a 'political question, not a military one, and that he could, if necessary, get 6 Blenheim Squadrons . . . from the Middle East without completely damaging their prospects'.[22]

Portal's view conflicts with the conventional British justification for the weakness of Singapore. This argued that it was an unavoidable result of Britain being overstretched and unable to cover all possible threats. When General Sir Alan Brooke (later Lord Alanbrooke) took over effective control from Dill as Britain's army chief on 1 December, he was told by Dill that he had 'done practically nothing' to meet the threat from Japan. According to Alanbrooke's later account, Dill justified the inaction by arguing that Britain was 'already so weak on all fronts that it was impossible to denude them any further to meet a possible threat'. Although Alanbrooke agreed with this view, he conceded that 'it left us in a lamentably dangerous position on the entry of Japan into the war'.[23] This was the official British view, and it has been repeated ever since by an army of historians. But it overlooks the fact that the parlous position of Singapore in late 1941 had been reached due to a succession of deliberate choices that Britain had made about its relative defence priorities.

Those choices having been made, and despite last-minute promises about reinforcing Singapore by air, Britain did little more than watch and wait during those last days of peace in the Pacific. On 1 December, the British war cabinet refused to respond to reports of Japanese troop movements towards the south. There were fears that Japan was about to occupy the Kra isthmus, the narrow strip of land in southern Siam that connected it with Malaya. Although the chiefs of staff conceded that such a move would 'only be with the object of attacking Singapore', they argued nevertheless that it would not 'by itself be an attack on our vital interests' and that Britain should not react without a guarantee of American support. Australia wanted the imperial forces in Malaya, including its own 8th Division, to make a pre-emptive move to occupy the Kra isthmus and foil the likely Japanese plans. But Britain held back, allowing the Japanese to occupy it and gain the advantage in their assault on Malaya.[24]

Churchill had feared that the Americans would hold back if the Japanese bypassed the US-held Philippines and went straight for British and Dutch possessions. But he was encouraged by comments made by Roosevelt on 1 December to the British ambassador, Lord Halifax. The US president assured Halifax of American support if the Japanese attacked either Malaya or the NEI. When Halifax asked two days later whether this support would include armed American intervention, the usually rather enigmatic Roosevelt replied in the affirmative. His talks with the Japanese had produced no agreement and intelligence decrypts of Japanese signals indicated that troop convoys had been sent south.[25] Apparently oblivious of all this, Evatt cabled Australia's overseas representatives on 4 December in appreciation of their efforts to preserve the peace. He claimed that it was 'now obvious that our efforts have not been without some measure of success'. He called on them to continue their work, reminding them that 'Australia will feel [the] first impact of a war against Japan' and 'does not wish to become a pawn in the game'.[26] If the talks proved fruitless, Evatt could take some confidence from the well-publicised arrival in Singapore on 2 December of the *Prince of Wales* and the *Repulse*, the presence of which gave the deliberately misleading impression of British preparedness.

Discussions continued in London on how to ensure the entry of the Americans into a Pacific war. Despite Roosevelt's encouraging words to Halifax, Churchill had been misled before by the Delphic US president as to future American moves and he remained reluctant to confront the Japanese without the certainty of having the Americans alongside. As Oliver Harvey observed from the Foreign Office in the wake of Roosevelt's second meeting with Halifax, Churchill was steadfast in his desire to 'see a Jap–American war start ... rather than a Jap–British war which the Americans might or might not enter'.[27] At the same time, he strenuously opposed Australian suggestions that Britain seek mutual defence guarantees from Russia in the case of a Japanese attack on either party.[28] Australia wanted such a pact to provide an additional deterrent to the Japanese, hoping that it would compel them to keep their forces in the north Pacific to meet a possibly hostile Russia. But Churchill had no interest in diverting Russia from the struggle against Germany. Instead, as Japanese forces spread stealthily across the Pacific, Churchill busily assembled a package of promised assistance that Eden could present to Stalin during forthcoming talks in Moscow, hoping that it would encourage the Russians to concentrate against Germany. Even Australian troops were considered as possible reinforcements for the plucky Russians, although the idea was rejected by Churchill because of the likely opposition from the Australian government. He decided to offer the Russians ten RAF squadrons instead.[29]

The deteriorating situation in the Far East intruded on Eden's plans for his Moscow trip. Although it did not diminish the British offer of ten squadrons, the probability of Britain incurring defeats in the Pacific, together with setbacks to Auchinleck's military offensive in the Middle East, prompted Eden's political supporters to urge a reconsideration of his trip. With Eden as the likely successor to Churchill as prime minister, the conservative MP Richard Law told Eden that it would be 'appalling' for him to be out of reach in view of the domestic political situation which, Law confided, 'I don't like the smell of at all'.[30] Eden brushed off the advice, confident that the talks with Stalin would produce sufficient political credits to make worthwhile his absence from London at that critical time.

On 6 December, the British chiefs of staff were advised from Singapore that two Japanese troop convoys, escorted by cruisers and destroyers, had been sighted south-west of Saigon, possibly heading for the Kra isthmus. They waited for news of a second sighting so that the Japanese intention could be determined. The reconnaissance aircraft failed to locate them.[31] A last-minute peace initiative in Washington had failed and war was inevitable. At the Foreign Office, Sir Horace Seymour wondered what the 'horrid little Japs' would do, predicting that it would be 'something v[ery] tiresome'.[32] The Australian war cabinet took what comfort it could from a report by its air minister, Arthur Drakeford, who advised on the delivery schedule for the aircraft that Australia had on order for the RAAF. According to Drakeford, if the aircraft were delivered on schedule, Australia would have a fair measure of air defence by the end of 1942.[33] Unfortunately, Japan was working to a different timetable.

NOTES

[1] *Sun-Herald*, Sydney, 6 November 1941; Advisory War Council Minutes, 7 November 1941, CRS A2682, Vol. 3, Minutes 560–3, NAA.

[2] Advisory War Council Minutes, 7 November 1941, CRS A2682, Vol. 3, Minutes 560–3, NAA.

[3] See Cable No. 102, Bruce to Curtin, 19 November 1941, CRS M100, 'November 1941'; War Cabinet Minutes, 17 November 1941, CRS A2673, Vol. 9, Minute 1500, NAA; Minute, Churchill to Ismay, 28 October 1941, PREM 3/52/4, PRO; Letter, Duff Cooper to Brooke-Popham, 3 December 1941, V/5/22, Brooke-Popham Papers, KC.

[4] Minute D300/1, Churchill to Ismay, 24 November 1941, PREM 3/52/4, PRO.

[5] Cable, Churchill to Duff Cooper, 26 November 1941, 'The Prime Minister's Personal Telegrams 1941', VI/I, Ismay Papers, KC.

[6] War Cabinet Conclusions/Confidential Annex, 12 November 1941, CAB 65/24, W.M. 112(41), PRO; Cable P.5, Page to Curtin, 15 November 1941, and Cable, Curtin to Page, 20 November 1941, CRS A5954, Box 475, NAA.

[7] Letter, Wavell to Brooke-Popham, 13 November 1941, V/5/13, Brooke-Popham Papers, KC.

[8] 'Supplies to Turkey', Memorandum by Eden, 10 November 1941, CAB 66/19, W.P. (41)265, PRO.

[9] War Cabinet Minute, 26 November 1941, CRS A2676, Item 1519, NAA.

[10] Cable No. 99, Bruce to Curtin, 15 November 1941, CRS M100, 'November 1941', NAA.

[11] See David Carlton, *Anthony Eden*, London, 1981, pp. 189–90.

[12] 'Memorandum', by Evatt, 22 November 1941, CRS A5954, Box 475, NAA.

[13] ibid.

[14] 'The Pacific Situation', Memorandum by Shedden, 24 November 1941, CRS A5954, Box 475, NAA.

[15] Advisory War Council Minute No. 573, *DAFP*, Vol. 5, Doc. 132; Advisory War Council Minute No. 574, 28 November 1941, CRS A5954, Box 475, NAA.

[16] The British ambassador to China ensured that Chiang Kai-shek cabled to Roosevelt with similar comments. Cable, Churchill to Roosevelt, 26 November 1941, VI/I, Ismay Papers, KC; Kimball, *Forged in War*, p. 118.

[17] Casey, *Personal Experience*, pp. 57–8.

[18] The War Cabinet decision was immediately rescinded after the entry of Japan into the war. War Cabinet Agendum No. 397/1941, 25 November 1941 and Minute, Shedden to Director General of Civil Aviation, 8 December 1941, CRS A5954, Box 230, NAA.

[19] Letter, Watt to Hodgson, 9 December 1941, MS 3788/1/1, Watt Papers, NLA.

[20] The following week, India's allocation of tanks was more than doubled so that it could equip two armoured divisions and one tank brigade. Then New Zealand's allocation was more than halved, from 110 to just 44. 'Production and Allocation of Tanks between Different Theatres', Defence Committee (Operations) Committee Memorandum, 17 and 23 November 1941, and Memorandum, 1 December 1941, CAB 69/3, D.O. (41)27, 30 and 33; PRO.

[21] Cable No. 112, Bruce to Curtin, 1 December 1941, CRS M100, 'December 1941', NAA.

[22] Page diary, 18 November 1941, MS 1633, Folder 2345, Page Papers, NLA.

[23] Danchev and Todman (eds), *War Diaries*, p. 205.

[24] War Cabinet Conclusions/Confidential Annex, 1 December 1941, CAB 65/24, W.M. 122(41), PRO; See also Harvey diary, 2 December 1941, ADD. MS. 56398, Harvey Papers, BL; 'Far Eastern Policy', Memorandum by Eden, 2 December 1941, CAB 66/20, W.P. (41)296, PRO.

[25] Kimball, *Forged in War*, p. 119.

[26] Cable No. 369, Evatt to Bruce, 4 December 1941, CRS M100, 'December 1941', NAA; See also Cable No. 140, Evatt to Casey, 6 December 1941, CRS A3300, Item 100, NAA.

[27] Harvey diary, 3 December 1941, ADD. MS. 56398, Harvey Papers, BL.

[28] Defence Committee (Operations) Minutes, 3 December 1941, CAB 69/2, D.O. (41)71, PRO.

[29] In fact, the Australian opposition would not have been as certain as Churchill believed. On 4 December, Australia's air minister, Arthur Drakeford, publicly called for all-out aid for Russia, arguing that the 'more aid we can give Russia the further will Hitler's dream of embroiling the Pacific in war recede from the realms of possibility'. 'Supplies for Russia', speech by A. S. Drakeford at Essendon Town Hall, 4 December 1941, MS 987/5/191–8, Dedman Papers, NLA; 'Russia' Directive, Churchill to Eden, 6 December 1941, CAB 66/20, W.P. (41)298, PRO; War Cabinet Conclusions/Confidential Annex, 27 October 1941, CAB 65/23, W.M. 106(41), PRO; Alanbrooke diary, 2–5 December 1941, in Danchev and Todman (eds), *War Diaries*, pp. 205–08.

[30] Minute, Law to Harvey, 5 December 1941, ADD. MS. 56402, Harvey Papers, BL.

[31] Alanbrooke diary, 6 December 1941, in Danchev and Todman (eds), *War Diaries*, p. 208.

[32] Letter, Seymour to his wife, 5 December 1941, SEYR 2/5, Seymour Papers, CC.

[33] War Cabinet Agendum No. 410/1941, by Drakeford, 6 December 1941, CRS A5954, Box 230, NAA.

EIGHTEEN

'up to the neck and in to the death'

On Saturday 6 December 1941, the Japanese naval task force steamed to within striking distance of the anchored American battleships at Pearl Harbor. The following morning, flight after flight of Japanese planes struck at their tethered quarry. When they were done, and the six Japanese aircraft carriers had steamed away, they left in their wake six American battleships sunk at their moorings, effectively crippling the much-vaunted might of the US Pacific fleet. Less dramatically, but just as efficiently, Japanese forces launched attacks on poorly defended colonial outposts from Hong Kong to Manila, from Malaya to Singapore. Britain's bluff had been called, but it was at a time of Churchill's choosing. When news of the Japanese attacks was announced on the wireless that night in London, Churchill was elated, expressing himself 'well content with Sunday's developments in the Far East'.[1] It was Monday morning when Curtin was woken in his Melbourne hotel room and told of the attack, reportedly replying with a sense of resignation: 'Well, it has come.'[2]

Although Churchill later conceded that there would be 'terrible forfeits' to be paid in the Pacific, he dismissed it as 'merely a passing phase' that was outweighed by having the United States actively in the war 'up to the neck and in to the death'. Churchill went to bed that night and 'slept the sleep of the saved and thankful'.[3] His simple calculation of Allied superiority, now that America was on board, was correct so far as its ultimate conclusion was concerned. Total victory against Germany was no longer a pipedream. However, the intervening struggle would produce Australia's darkest days and sound the death knell of the British empire rather than provide its salvation. With little left standing between Australia and the oncoming Japanese, it was time for the dominion to call on the system of imperial defence to work in Australia's interest, as it had done in Britain's.

Churchill's optimism was reflected widely among Britain's political and military leadership. Six months before, the British empire had been standing alone against the combined might of Germany and Italy; now it was in alliance with both the Soviet Union and the United States and ultimate victory seemed certain. The Foreign Office had disputed Churchill's methods for drawing the Americans into the war, but not his aim. Its officials therefore could regard the events of Pearl Harbor with satisfaction. As Sir Horace Seymour observed with his usual aplomb, the 'Japs went off as I expected' and 'seem to have started very well'. He admitted that 'the little beasts are going to be a serious menace' but 'that of course was inevitable'. Admiral Somerville, soon to be commander-in-chief of the Eastern fleet, had a more down-to-earth desire to 'give the little sods a real kick', although the Admiralty's weekly intelligence report was more sympathetic to Japan's plight. It acknowledged that, 'had she not gone to war now, Japan would have seen such a deterioration of her economic situation as to render her ultimately unable to wage war, and to reduce her to the status of a second-rate Power'.[4]

When the Australian war cabinet met in the wake of the Pearl Harbor attack, it was forced to confront the awful reality of its predicament. After more than two years of war, it remained unprepared for a conflict in the Pacific. As Shedden stressed to the meeting, the army supposedly had seven divisions in Australia but not one of them was sufficiently trained or equipped to be deployed 'as a good fighting force' to resist invasion. But there was no sense of panic just yet. Curtin announced that he was not intending to bring back the Australian divisions from the Middle East. After all, the United States was now in the war and the British naval squadron was secure in Singapore. As Evatt advised, with the productive resources and manpower of the United States in the war, eventual victory must be all but certain for the Allies.[5]

Still, the Australian government did make some important decisions that day which would have long-term ramifications. For one thing, it declared war against Japan without waiting to take its lead from London as Menzies had done against Germany. Curtin also accepted the advice of Shedden that the war against Japan should be regarded as 'a new war', rather than simply a development in the existing war against Germany, and thereby required a strong response from the Allies.[6] This attitude would set Australia against both Britain and the United States in the coming months, as Curtin pushed hard for the Pacific war to be fought with as much vigour as the European war. After all, this was just the situation he had long predicted, with wars on opposite sides of the world keeping British forces in Europe and leaving Australia vulnerable to invasion. As Curtin told the 'men and women of Australia' in a wireless broadcast on 8 December, it was now Australia's turn to endure its 'darkest hour', with the nation itself being at stake in the war. He called for an 'all-in' effort to ensure that they could 'hold this country, and keep it as a citadel for the British-speaking race and as a place where civilisation will persist'.[7]

It took some time for the awful extent of the damage suffered by the Americans at Pearl Harbor to be publicly known. When the details became clear to the British government, the implications were worrying. As General Brooke observed, the success of the strike had 'entirely upset the balance in [the] Pacific and leaves Japs masters of the ocean ...'.[8] Despite the devastation suffered by the American battleships, their aircraft carriers had been away from Pearl Harbor when the Japanese struck and had emerged unscathed. Although it was not yet fully appreciated, it would be carriers rather than battleships that would be the key to victory in the Pacific. Indeed, Japan had already proven their worth at Pearl Harbor, with the carrier-borne aircraft rather than the covering battleships being the vital weapon in the success of their attack.

Some Australians shared Churchill's relief at the entry of the United States into the war. At the Australian legation in Washington, one official claimed that the 'main purpose' of the legation had been achieved: Australia had avoided being 'drawn into a major war in the Pacific area without the armed support of the United States'.⁹ It was certainly some consolation to have the Americans as allies against the Japanese, but it would not be any consolation if the Americans proved unable or unwilling to provide the level of assistance that could guarantee Australia's security. The sudden and successful strokes by the Japanese had left Australia much more vulnerable than had been anticipated. Only the British battle squadron at Singapore, and the mixed force of British, Indian and Australian troops defending Malaya, provided any hope that the southward thrust of the Japanese towards Australia could be stemmed.

It was time for Britain to fulfil its side of the imperial defence bargain and to reinforce the Far East with the promised ships and aircraft. There were certainly no illusions in London that Singapore could be held with the existing forces. But Churchill was determined that Britain retain its pre-existing agreement with the Americans to concentrate their joint efforts against Germany and fight only a 'holding war' in the Pacific. He was worried, though, that Washington might react with such fury to the attack on Pearl Harbor that it would divert a disproportionate amount of its munitions and forces to the Pacific and allow the war against Germany to languish. It became Churchill's urgent priority to ensure that this did not happen. Within hours of the attack on Pearl Harbor, the British war cabinet met and declared war on Japan. It decided to allow Eden, who was in Scotland preparing to leave by ship for Moscow, to proceed with his mission while Churchill announced to his colleagues that he would leave for Washington so that the world war could be 'concerted at the highest level'.¹⁰

Churchill wanted Roosevelt to reconfirm the agreed Anglo–American strategy and to ensure that the United States not overreact to the humiliation of Pearl Harbor. There were 'already indications', Churchill warned his colleagues, 'that the United States Naval authorities proposed to make certain re-dispositions of their Naval forces which would vitally affect us. There was also a risk that they would wish to retain, for their own forces, munitions of war which they had promised to allocate to us.'[11] Page was at the meeting but seems to have made no plea on Australia's behalf, although he did later ask Curtin for an increase in his status to ensure that he and Bruce were 'kept fully informed and consulted' by Britain.[12] As if it all came down to a question of status and lack of consultation.

Any protest by Page would have been brushed away as easily as Churchill brushed away the serious opposition to his Washington trip. Objections from Eden, from other war cabinet colleagues, from the American ambassador, John Winant, and even from Roosevelt himself were dismissed by Churchill, whose long campaign for American involvement in the European war had finally come to fruition. Now that it had happened, he had to ensure that the Americans were not overly distracted by the Japanese. Eden's secretary, Oliver Harvey, was one of those opposed to Churchill's trip, partly because he feared that it would threaten the political triumph that Eden might otherwise achieve in Moscow, with Churchill's talks with Roosevelt inevitably upstaging Eden's talks with Stalin. However, while still wanting it delayed, even Harvey conceded that there was good reason for Churchill's mission, observing that it was a 'poor look-out if the Americans are going to get into a flat spin and concentrate entirely on Japan'.[13]

Britain suffered its own naval humiliation with the sinking by Japanese torpedo bombers of the *Prince of Wales* and the *Repulse* off the east coast of Malaya on 10 December when the ships went to investigate reports of a Japanese landing. It was only by chance that they were at Singapore on the outbreak of the Pacific war, with Churchill never intending that the powerful vessels should remain there or confront the Japanese. His plan had been either to withdraw them to a safe distance in the Indian Ocean or to join them to the remnants of the US Pacific fleet. In either case, the role of the ships would be to exercise a distant and 'vague menace' that Churchill hoped would inhibit the scope of Japanese expansion. Events moved too fast for Churchill to control. Apparently without his permission or knowledge, the Admiralty allowed the vessels to steam beyond the range of covering fighter aircraft to search for the reported Japanese convoy. It was a risky operation that saw the British ships sunk in one stroke. When the news reached London, Churchill reported to the war cabinet that 'the Admiralty had known that it was intended to use these ships to attack the Japanese forces landing on the coast of Malaya, but they had not intervened to stop the operation'. By his comment, Churchill implied that he would have intervened had he known of it.[14]

Now there was little in the Pacific to prevent Japan from exercising its power wherever it wished. As Brooke observed in his diary on learning of their sinking, from 'Africa eastwards to America through the Indian Ocean and the Pacific, we have lost command of the sea'.[15] There was certainly nothing of any consequence that could be immediately interposed between the Japanese navy and the Australian continent. As Seymour observed from the Foreign Office, the Japanese navy would have 'control of the sea in the E. hemisphere for a long time to come now, which will be very tiresome'.[16] The loss of the ships provided further grim confirmation for Curtin of his long-held view that air power provided the key to Australia's defence. However, it was little consolation to be proved right in such circumstances. It was more important to use the disaster to shock Australians into making a greater effort for the war and to set aside their peacetime pursuits and concerns. Accordingly, Curtin called for 'an absolute concentration on war production' and for an end to Menzies' attitude of 'business as usual'.[17]

Churchill later claimed to have suffered nightmares from the shock of losing the *Prince of Wales* and the *Repulse*, with the ships having been sent at his insistence even though he had been forewarned that they were 'far more likely to act as a bait than as a deterrent'.[18] The Admiralty had regarded their dispatch on a flag-waving voyage to Singapore as a 'major strategical blunder fraught with the gravest of risks'. As such, the sinking of the ships did not come as a surprise to naval planners, although the 'speed and completeness of their destruction' was unexpected. According to one Admiralty official, the task now was to 'build up sufficient forces quickly enough to counter the eventual threat to Australia and New Zealand'. However, Churchill still refused to concede that Australia was exposed to invasion and tried to calm the dominion with the thought that was uppermost in his own mind: that the 'accession of [the] United States as [a] full war partner makes amends for all and makes the end certain'.[19]

The dramatic loss of the ships did have one benefit for Britain, allowing it to deny the charge of betraying its obligations in the Far East. It could always point to the two warships as evidence that it had made a real effort to resist the advance of the Japanese on Singapore. Without them, Britain was now less capable than ever of dispatching a strong fleet to the Far East, even had Churchill wanted to form one. Instead, his efforts were directed at stemming the Japanese landward advance towards India, preventing the loss of the 'imperial jewel' and stopping the possible joining of Japanese and German forces at the strategic Middle East crossroads.

At the war cabinet meeting that discussed the shocking loss of the ships, Churchill declared that Britain would not send more ships to take their place but instead would 'develop a different kind of warfare', whatever that meant. He did not explain that Britain intended to fight a holding war and to accept the forfeits that would have to be paid in the Far East as a result of this strategy. Ignorant of Churchill's intentions, Page suggested that aircraft and submarines be used to 'keep the Japanese out of the Indian Ocean', while its expansion elsewhere was checked by giving more assistance to China and encouraging Russia to declare war on Japan. Churchill was not about to do any of these things, and particularly dismissed the dangerous notion of having Russia declare war on Japan, pointing to 'the enormous service which Russia was giving to us by hammering the German Army'.[20] Not that there was much chance that Stalin would threaten his struggle with Hitler by declaring war on Japan. Like Churchill, he recognised that the national interest of his country depended in the first instance on the defeat of Germany rather than Japan. Indeed, on the day that Page proposed that Russia should turn against Japan, Stalin unleashed a large-scale offensive against the Germans along the length of the eastern front.

On 12 December, the eve of his departure for Washington, Churchill made some slight concessions to those wanting a more forthright reaction in the Far East. He informed the war cabinet that Eden's planned offer to the Russians of ten RAF squadrons had been withdrawn. Moreover, Eden had been advised by the chiefs of staff that 'it would be a great advantage if Russia should declare war on Japan', although the Russians 'should not do so until they felt strong enough to take this action without imperilling the maintenance of their European front'.[21] It might have been thought by this that Churchill had reversed his attitude to the appeal made by Page just two days earlier along these lines. That would be a mistake. As Churchill made clear to Eden, his attitude had not changed. To ensure that Eden did not press Russia to join the war against Japan, Churchill reminded him that 'victory on the European battlefield must have priority in our minds'. While Churchill acknowledged the 'evident strong wish of [the] United States, China, and I expect Australia, that Russia should come in against Japan', he cautioned Eden against doing anything to pressure Stalin in either direction. Churchill obviously wanted to leave it to Stalin's sense of national preservation, which could be presumed to oppose any immediate action against Japan.[22]

With Russia being kept out of the Pacific war, and the Americans still reeling from the damage caused at Pearl Harbor and the Philippines, Australia looked to Britain to provide the long-promised fleet. Some officials in the Admiralty were prepared to consider such a course in the wake of the sinking of the *Prince of Wales* and the *Repulse*. On learning of their loss, the Admiralty's initial reaction was to replace them with ships from Admiral Cunningham's fleet at Alexandria. But Cunningham was a long-time opponent of such a course and stuck to his guns even in the after-shock of the *Prince of Wales* sinking. Describing the proposal as a 'gambler's stake', Cunningham said that he would only accept it with the 'most serious misgivings'.[23] He need not have worried. Churchill would never accept such a diversion. Although he recalled the loss of the ships as being the most 'direct shock' he suffered during the war,[24] it did not cause him to change his strategy. Instead, Churchill took heart from the Russian offensive against Germany, the military success in Libya and, most importantly, the entry of the Americans. As he told his war cabinet, 'these developments far outweighed the immediate consequences of the position in the Far East, serious as they were'.[25]

If not ships, surely Australia could rely upon the reinforcements of aircraft that Menzies had been promised during his London visit to cover just such an eventuality that Australia was now facing. These promises to reallocate air strength from the Middle East to the Far East had been repeated by

British officials almost up to the eve of Pearl Harbor. And Australia had repeatedly relied upon them, and had continued to commit their forces overseas according to the accepted precepts of imperial defence long after such commitments should have ceased. Australia now put these promises to the test. The first-line combat strength of the RAAF was just 179 aircraft, but twenty of the 53 Hudson bombers had been sent off to the NEI. A further 57 of the aircraft were Wirraways, which had been lauded by the Menzies government as fighter-bombers but were now acknowledged to be just training aircraft.[26] As a direct result of Australia's compliance with British defence imperatives, there were no aircraft in the country capable of meeting the Japanese on anywhere near equal terms.

On 11 December, Curtin reminded Churchill of the assurances given to Menzies and called for an 'immediate review of air resources'. It noted that the dominion had supplied the RAF with nine thousand men, had scattered five squadrons to Britain, the Middle East, Malaya and the NEI and was left with the inadequate Wirraways as the core of its first-line striking force. Despite this parlous defence position, the Curtin government did not recall its squadrons from overseas, although it did request from Britain an equivalent number of aircraft.[27] It also banned the departure by ship to Canada of any more aircrew, off to complete their training before posting to RAF squadrons in Britain or the Middle East. The ban was strenuously opposed by Australia's chief of the air staff, Sir Charles Burnett, who warned that it would mean 'that the crews of ten squadrons will not be forthcoming to [the] U.K. every four weeks'. It was not as if there were any planes for them to fly in Australia. Rather, the ban seemed to have been imposed out of concern about the dangers of shipping personnel across an ocean that was now controlled by the Japanese. After further pressure from Burnett, the ban was eventually lifted in February 1942.[28]

While Curtin was demanding that Britain make good on its repeated promises regarding aircraft, Page reported from London that he had pressed Churchill to make the 'maximum aircraft available from the Libyan fight' to be 'flown over to the Burma Road or to Malaya'. Australia's special envoy did not call for any aircraft to be sent to Australia, requesting instead that the existing Australian production program of Beaufort bombers be accelerated and that 'the machine tools for this programme, if not procurable immediately in America, should be taken out of factories in Britain'. It did not seem to occur to Page that, while the dispatch of fighter aircraft might be too late to protect Malaya, their immediate dispatch from Britain could provide a good deal of security for Australia. Instead, he took comfort from the planned transfer of US battleships to the Pacific and the availability within seven or eight months of three new British battleships that were being constructed. He counselled Curtin to 'hold fast unfalteringly for the next few months'.[29] Few could foresee the speed of the Japanese advance that would soon have enemy forces on Australia's doorstep.

The Australian government accepted Page's recommendation to boost the local production of aircraft, which was now given the 'first degree of priority'. Unfortunately, the production program was that handed on to Curtin as a last-minute legacy from Fadden's outgoing administration. Its principal asset was the Beaufort bomber, which had been designed to attack the troopships of any invasion force. Because of innumerable production delays caused by the non-delivery of parts and tools from Britain and America, the Beaufort program was far behind schedule. As for the main aircraft being produced, the Wirraway, it had been retained in the production program at Britain's suggestion. Although Australia tried to convert them into fighter aircraft as an urgent stopgap measure, the effort proved lengthy, costly and ultimately fruitless. By the time they were produced in late 1942, superior American aircraft were arriving in large numbers.[30] In the interim, Australia was defenceless in the air.

John McEwen had been minister for air under Fadden and was instrumental in shaping the aircraft production program. He had privately defended the policy of relegating fighter aircraft to the lowest priority in the RAAF while publicly claiming that it was being given a high priority. Now that his policy had been revealed as woefully misconceived, he pressured Curtin to increase the provision for fighter aircraft in the RAAF. McEwen claimed that the previous policy had been based on the assumption that Australia and its allies would have command of the sea but that the situation had now changed with the Japanese naval successes.[31] In fact, the command of the sea had been effectively lost after the fall of France in June 1940. Ever since that time, and with steadily decreasing justification, McEwen and his colleagues had been recklessly banking on the Pacific remaining peaceful while they concentrated on the rapid development of Australian secondary industry under the impetus of the wartime economic boom. Dominion defence was left principally in the hands of Britain. That policy was now demonstrably bankrupt as Australia faced the looming prospect of Japanese attacks without being able to mount an effective defence.

Churchill's reaction to the run of Japanese successes in the Pacific held little hope for Australia. As he reminded Curtin, Germany was 'still the main enemy'.[32] Although Churchill had previously surrounded Singapore with so much imperial rhetoric, his initial response to its present plight was not to reinforce this distant and largely defenceless bastion but to make a stand on the Indo–Burmese border. On 12 December, he ordered the diversion to Bombay of the British 18th Division, then en route to the Middle East, for 'use in stiffening the Indian Divisions now on the Burma frontier'. Four squadrons of fighter aircraft, also on their way to the Middle East, would be sent to India. Churchill told Auchinleck in Cairo, who would have to make do without these reinforcements, that their diversion was 'required by [the] grievous need of strengthening long-starved India and enabling a stronger resistance to be made to [the] Japanese advance against Burma and down [the] Malay Peninsula'.[33]

While Churchill steamed off to Washington to focus the Americans on Europe, General Brooke was left in London to preside over the chiefs of staff committee and coordinate the defence of the Far East. Brooke was strongly committed to Britain's Mediterranean strategy and was most averse to weakening the Middle East in order to shore up the defences in the Far East. Like Churchill, his priority lay in defending India and preventing the Japanese spreading too far into the Indian Ocean. As for Britain's possessions in the Pacific, just a week after Pearl Harbor he doubted in his diary 'whether Hong Kong will hold out a fortnight and Malaya a month'.[34] There would be little point therefore in squandering reinforcements of men or aircraft on their futile defence. As for Australia, Brooke made no mention in his diary. But the overriding 'Germany first' strategy ensured that it would continue to have a low priority in the allocation of resources. Moreover, Churchill dismissed the idea that the Japanese had either the inclination or the capacity to invade Australia. In his view, they were aiming instead to encircle and subdue China, where their troops were still meeting stiff resistance, and perhaps overrun India as well. As Churchill later conceded, he was much mistaken in this estimation and was surprised when the Japanese pursued what he described as the 'bad strategy' of making 'threatening thrusts at Australia'.[35]

During his voyage across the Atlantic aboard Britain's newest battleship, the *Duke of York*, Churchill maintained daily contact with his war cabinet, ensuring that there would be little opportunity for independent strategic initiatives during his absence.[36] As for the expected parliamentary criticism of the disaster in the Far East, Churchill instructed that any debate in the House of Commons must be in secret session, which would limit its impact on his public popularity and his standing in Washington, and that any strong criticism should be 'resolutely dealt with'.[37] While refusing to send a fleet to the Far East, Churchill was able to appropriate Britain's most modern battleship to transport him across the Atlantic. On board the *Duke of York*, Churchill cabled Curtin with news of British plans to organise a fleet of four aircraft carriers with cruisers 'for action in the Indian Ocean in a form of novel warfare designed to repair our lack of modern capital ships', while the four elderly *Royal Sovereign* battleships would be available as convoy escorts.[38] This cable bore little resemblance to the reality of the plans Churchill actually finalised two days later.

Ensconced in his cabin, Churchill planned the distribution of Britain's navy to meet the new circumstances. His first priority remained that of retaining six battleships and two aircraft carriers in European waters to cover the one modern battleship that Germany still had in operation. His second priority remained the Mediterranean, where the battleships *Queen Elizabeth* and *Valiant* would be retained by Admiral Cunningham at Alexandria since, according to Churchill, their dispatch to the Far East would 'make the victualling of Malta far more difficult, and would exercise a disastrous effect upon Turkey'. Churchill even proposed adding another battleship, then under repair, to Cunningham's fleet. He did, of course, repeat the rather tattered assurance that in a 'supreme emergency, or for a great occasion', these three battleships would be available for use in the East.[39]

So, despite the entry of Japan into the war in a far more dramatic and successful manner than had been anticipated, the Far East remained Britain's lowest priority. Even then, the force proposed for the Far East was really designed to cover the Middle East from attack by the Japanese. The ships for Churchill's Eastern fleet were not destined for the Pacific or even for Singapore, but for the western shores of the Indian Ocean from where they would provide a 'very powerful deterrent effect upon the movement of Japanese heavy ships into the Indian Ocean or in the waters between Australia and South Africa'.[40] In the event, these limited plans were never put into operation. No matter how serious the setback suffered in the Far East, Churchill never felt it sufficiently imperative to send a fleet.

In a daring operation on 18 December, one day after Churchill drew up his grand naval design for the future conduct of the war, Italian frogmen attached limpet mines to Admiral Cunningham's two battleships moored in Alexandria harbour. The following morning they exploded, causing extensive damage that kept the ships out of action for many months. It made no difference. Cunningham held the Mediterranean and Malta without them. Had they been released to the Far East following Pearl Harbor, as Cunningham had reluctantly agreed to do in principle, they could have been used in the defence of Britain's eastern empire. Churchill now really could claim with some justification to have insufficient ships for a Far East fleet, and it was his own strategy that had produced such a predicament. Australia was not informed until much later of the damage to the ships, remaining ignorant of the fact that the closest available British battleships were at Gibraltar rather than Alexandria.

Australia had spent over two years of the war relying on a succession of increasingly tenuous British assurances. Despite Churchill's attempt to continue the dominion's dependence on such assurances, the Curtin government proved less willing to cooperate than its predecessors. Even Page seemed to question British sincerity after being fobbed off at successive meetings of the British war cabinet. On 16 December he advised Canberra that he was 'taking every opportunity [to] emphasise [the] Australian point of view' but suggested that a 'strong telegram' from Curtin insisting on the 'maximum earliest air support in Malaya' may cause Britain to accelerate the efforts it was making.[41] At the same time, he urged the Australian newspaper publisher Sir Keith Murdoch, who was then visiting London, to return to Australia to use his influence to 'force the pace of Britain's assistance'.[42] Nevertheless, Page accepted British plans for the Indian Ocean as being for the defence of Australia. On 18 December, he reported to Curtin that 'very substantial naval, air and army reinforcements [were] already on the way or arranged for the Far East'.[43] That was only true if India was regarded as being part of the Far East. As far as Singapore was concerned, the British had already given up on it and were concentrating instead on trying to hold Burma.[44]

Although Page seemed at times to realise that Britain was not taking sufficient measures to defend Singapore, he put aside any anxiety that he may have had and complied with British needs. At a meeting of the defence committee on 19 December, chaired by the Labour leader, Clement Attlee, Page supported the dispatch to Malaya of an Australian division from Palestine and even suggested that, 'if the air support were forthcoming, a division might even be found from Australia itself'. And this at a time when General Brooke had privately given up Malaya and Singapore as lost. Although Page pressed for the transfer of aircraft from the Middle East to Singapore, his arguments went largely unheeded. He was left to complain rather resignedly that 'it looked as if Australian troops would be required to fight once again without adequate air support'.[45] His concerns were dismissed, with Brooke later complaining that Page, who had 'the mentality of a greengrocer, wasted a lot of our time'.[46] Page seemed oblivious of the low regard in which he was held in London and was careful to present a positive account of his activities to Canberra, cabling Curtin with an assurance that the defence committee was anxious to reinforce Singapore to the extent that it was physically possible.[47]

Page squandered any opportunity that he might have had to direct British strategy away from its single-minded concentration on Germany. With Churchill absent, there could have been a chance for an able Australian envoy, assisted by Bruce, to mobilise dissident political and military opinion in a campaign for a greater British effort in the east. Unfortunately, Page was not the person to wage such a campaign. Two days after reporting his anxiety over Singapore and claiming credit for the minor contributions that

Britain was proposing for the Far East, Page left London for a six-day holiday in Belfast to spend Christmas with relatives. Upon his return on 28 December, he noted in his diary that 'Bruce came at 6.30, v[ery] worried, showed me cables'.[48] Abandoning his mission at such a vital time was hardly the action of a responsible envoy, even if he had little to show for his activity to date. As the dominion's military representative in London later reported, Page 'created a deplorable impression' while in London and 'exerted little influence in so far as Pacific Strategy and Australia's needs were concerned'.[49]

Apart from his personal shortcomings, Page's ability to extract concessions in London was hampered by Australia's continuing low reputation among British military and political leaders, mainly as a result of the drawn-out dispute over the relief of Australian troops in Tobruk. In mid-December, Churchill was so angered by comments from Curtin about the Greek debacle that he drafted a vituperative rebuttal of Curtin's charges. Still aboard the *Duke of York*, he showed the draft cable to General Dill, asking whether it should be strengthened even more. Anxious about the effect on Anglo–Australian relations, and the continuation of Australia's cooperation with Britain's war effort, Dill urged Churchill to ignore what he called the opportunity for 'rubbing in how the political leaders in Australia have cramped our efforts in the Middle East', specifically 'Tobruk and our inability to throw Australians into the Western Desert as and when required'.[50]

Despite some wavering, Britain's strategy remained fixed in the simple terms set out by Oliver Harvey: 'the Germans are our principal enemy and whatever it means losing elsewhere, we should concentrate on them'.[51] The problem for Australia was that its survival could depend on this strategy being given a flexible interpretation by Allied planners. But the dominion seemed to be only dimly aware that the 'Germany first' strategy still held sway in London and Washington, apparently assuming that the prearranged strategy would be reconsidered in view of the unexpected force and suddenness of the Japanese attacks across the Pacific.[52]

Evatt certainly acted on this assumption and campaigned for Allied leaders to ensure the protection of Australia. With Churchill about to arrive in Washington for talks with Roosevelt, Evatt instructed Casey to insist on separate representation for Australia in any Allied conference 'even though it may appear unpracticable at first sight'. As Evatt pointed out, the 'views of the United Kingdom representatives will differ from our own both in relation to supplies and forces' and it was crucial for Australia's security that its point of view was 'continuously stressed or our great needs will be overlooked'.[53] Not that Britain was ignorant of Australia's 'great needs', or the possible implications for the empire of neglecting to rectify them.[54] But Churchill was determined that Australian needs should not be addressed at the expense of his war with Hitler. That was the whole point of his visit to Washington.

NOTES

[1] Cable, Churchill to Smuts, 9 December 1941, 'Prime Minister's Personal Telegrams 1941', VI/I, Ismay Papers, KC.

[2] Day, *John Curtin*, p. 430.

[3] Churchill, *The Second World War*, Vol. 3, pp. 539–40, 608.

[4] Letters, Seymour to his wife, 8 and 9 December 1941, SEYR 2/5, Seymour Papers, CC; Letter, Somerville to H. MacQuarrie, 8 December 1941, ADD. MS. 50143, Somerville Papers, BL; Weekly Intelligence Report, No. 92, 12 December 1942, DRAX 5/10, Drax Papers, CC.

[5] Horner, *Inside the War Cabinet*, pp. 77–80, 216–22.

[6] ibid.

[7] *Sydney Morning Herald*, 9 December 1941.

[8] Alanbrooke diary, 9 December 1941, in Danchev and Todman (eds), *War Diaries*, p. 209.

[9] Letter, Alan Watt to Hodgson, 9 December 1941, MS 3788/1/1, Watt Papers, NLA; Casey, *Personal Experience*, p. 76.

[10] War Cabinet Conclusions, 8 December 1941, CAB 65/20, W.M. 125(41), PRO.

[11] ibid.

[12] Cable P9, Page to Curtin, 8 December 1941, CRS A1608, H33/1/2, NAA.

[13] Harvey diary, 8 and 10 December 1941, ADD. MS. 56398, Harvey Papers, BL.

[14] War Cabinet Conclusions, 12 December 1941, CAB 65/20, W.M. 127(41), PRO.

[15] Alanbrooke diary, 10 December 1941, in Danchev and Todman (eds), *War Diaries*, p. 210.

[16] Letter, Seymour to his wife, 11 December 1941, SEYR 2/5, Seymour Papers, CC.

[17] Not that Menzies had persisted with that attitude once the 'phoney war' had finished in April 1940. Press statement by Curtin, 11 December 1941, A5954, Box 69, Item 2205/3, NAA.

[18] Moran, *Winston Churchill*, p. 101; Letter, Admiral Somerville to H. MacQuarrie, 3 January 1943, ADD. MS. 50143, Somerville Papers, BL.

[19] Cable, Churchill to Curtin, 12 December 1941, VI/I, Ismay Papers, KC.

[20] War Cabinet Conclusions/Confidential Annex, 10 December 1941, CAB 65/24, W.M. 126(41), PRO.

[21] War Cabinet Conclusions, 12 December 1941, CAB 65/20, W.M. 127(41), PRO.

[22] Cables, Churchill to Eden, 12 December 1941, 'The Prime Minister's Personal Telegrams 1941', VI/I Ismay Papers, KC.

[23] Cable No. 842, Pound to Cunningham, 10 December 1941, and Cable, Cunningham to Pound, 11 December 1941, ADD. MS. 52567, Cunningham Papers, BL.

[24] Churchill, *The Second World War*, Vol. 3, p. 55.

[25] War Cabinet Conclusions, 10 December 1941, CAB 65/20, W.M. 126(41), PRO.

[26] Advisory War Council Minute No. 586 (extract), 9 December 1941, CRS A5954, Box 230, NAA.

[27] War Cabinet Minutes, 11 December 1941, CRS A2673, Vol. 9, NAA.

[28] Minute, Burnett to Drakeford, 22 December 1941, and other documents in this box. CRS A5954, Box 236, NAA.

[29] There was some support in the air ministry for implementing the promise to send substantial air support from the Middle East now that war had erupted in the Far East. Portal, as chief of the air staff, broached such an idea during a meeting of the chiefs of staff committee on 11 December. Alanbrooke records in his diary that: 'With some difficulty we calmed him down' and Portal's plan was quashed. Cable P11, Page to Curtin, 11 December 1941, CRS M100, 'December 1941', NAA; Alanbrooke diary, 11 December 1941, in Danchev and Todman (eds), *War Diaries*, p. 210.

[30] Statement by Curtin in House of Representatives, 16 December 1941, CRS A5954, Box 313; War Cabinet Minutes, 18 December 1941, CRS A2673, Vol. 9, Minute 1584, NAA.

[31] Advisory War Council Minute No. 625, 23 December 1941, CRS A5954, Box 230, NAA.

[32] Cable No. 817, Dominions Office to Curtin, 11 December 1941, PREM 4/43B/2, PRO.

[33] War Cabinet Conclusions, 12 December 1941, CAB 65/20, W.M. 127(41), PRO; Cable No. 977, Churchill to Auchinleck, 12 December 1941, 'The Prime Minister's Personal Telegrams 1941', VI/I, Ismay Papers, KC; See also Cable No. 978, Churchill to Wavell, 12 December 1941, ibid.

[34] Alanbrooke diary, 15 December 1941, in Danchev and Todman (eds), *War Diaries*, p. 211.

[35] Report of Churchill's Press Conference for British correspondents in Washington, enclosed in Letter, C. Thompson to Beaverbrook, 23 May 1943, BBK D/182, Beaverbrook Papers, HLRO; See also Mackenzie King diary, 29 December 1941, CUL.

[36] The air and naval chiefs, Portal and Pound, accompanied Churchill to Washington.

[37] War Cabinet Conclusions, 12 December 1941, CAB 65/20, W.M. 127(41), PRO.

[38] Cable No. 1014, Churchill to Curtin, 15 December 1941, 'The Prime Minister's Personal Telegrams 1941', VI/I, Ismay Papers, KC.

[39] 'Future Conduct of the War', Memorandum by Churchill, 17 December, CAB 69/4, D.O. (42)12, PRO.

[40] ibid.

[41] Cable P13, Page to Curtin, 16 December 1941, CRS M100, 'December 1941', NAA; See also Cable P12, Page to Curtin, 16 December 1941, ibid.

[42] Page diary, 16 December 1941, MS 1633, Folder 2345, Page Papers, NLA.

[43] Cable P14, Page to Curtin, 18 December 1941, CRS M100, 'December 1941', NAA.

[44] On 17 December, Brooke confided in his diary that he did not think 'there is much hope of saving Singapore, but feel that we ought to try and make certain of Burma'. On 20 December, he was resigned to suffering 'many more losses in the Far East'. Alanbrooke diary, 17 and 20 December 1941, in Danchev and Todman (eds), *War Diaries*, pp. 212–3.

[45] Defence Committee (Operations) Minutes, 19 December 1941, CAB 69/2, D.O. (41)73, PRO.

[46] Alanbrooke diary, 19 December 1941, in Danchev and Todman (eds), *War Diaries*, p. 212.

[47] Cable, Page to Curtin, 20 December 1941, *DAFP*, Vol. 5, Doc. 209.

[48] Page diary, 23–28 December 1941, MS 1633, Folder 2345, Page Papers, NLA.

[49] Note by Shedden, 'Mission of Sir Earle Page to the United Kingdom 1941–42', 17 March 1943, CRS A5954, Box 14, NAA.

[50] Minute, Dill to Churchill, 17 December 1941, PREM 3/206/2, PRO.

[51] Harvey diary, 18 December 1941, ADD. MS. 56398, Harvey Papers, BL.

[52] Day, 'H. V. Evatt and the "Beat Hitler First" Strategy: Scheming Politician or an Innocent Abroad?', *Historical Studies*, October 1987.

[53] Cable, Evatt to Casey, 16 December 1941, *DAFP*, Vol. 5, Doc. 196.

[54] General Sir Henry Pownall, on his way to Singapore to relieve Brooke-Popham, worried in his diary that the loss of Singapore could 'well mean losing Australia, if not New Zealand'. Pownall did not fear losing the dominions 'to the Japanese, but to the Empire, for they will think themselves let down' by Britain. He claimed that Dill had 'regarded the Middle East as less vital than Malaya' but that Churchill 'had the priority of these two the other way round'. Pownall diary, in Bond (ed.), *Chief of Staff*, Vol. 2, pp. 66–7.

NINETEEN

'no one is more responsible than I'

While Australia had contributed its best forces to the European war, it had been taking serious risks with its own defence. With the Japanese on the attack throughout much of the Pacific, these risks were now starkly apparent. Although the war cabinet called up an additional 114 000 men for the army on 12 December 1941, the force would still be less than 250 000 strong at a time when the British army had about two million men based in Britain alone. With a much greater area to defend, the Australian numbers would only be sufficient to defend against serious raids rather than being able to prevent a full-blown invasion. No wonder that the army chief, General Iven Mackay, urged the government to prepare Australians for the likely eventuality of Japanese forces enjoying initial success in any invasion of Australia while reminding the population that they 'may still win in the end'.[1] For its part, the government looked to Washington and the forthcoming meetings between Churchill and Roosevelt to ensure that Australia did not have to confront that daunting eventuality.

On the eve of Churchill's arrival in Washington, Attlee sent him a report resulting from the defence committee's meeting on 19 December. It included a proposal to build up an Eastern fleet of nine battleships and four aircraft carriers. According to the Admiralty, Britain's sea communications in the Indian Ocean ranked second in priority after the Atlantic because on the security of these communications 'rests our ability to supply our armies in North Africa and the Middle East, to supply Russia through Persia, to reinforce Singapore if the local situation permits and to proceed to the assistance of Australia and New Zealand'. This strategy largely accorded with Churchill's thinking. The Admiralty did not expect to be able to base a fleet at Singapore in the near future, and it envisaged the initial role of the Eastern fleet as being to secure the imperial triangle that had the Middle East at its apex and for it only to proceed to Australia's assistance 'if a real threat' arose. Still, this was more than Churchill was prepared to do. He had only promised to send a fleet *after* Australia had been seriously invaded. And he remained opposed to weakening the Mediterranean forces for the sake of the Indian Ocean.[2]

Without capital ships at Singapore, and preferably also at Sydney, there was little possibility of any British fleet being able to provide for Australia's security. Nevertheless, in the absence of definitive orders from Churchill, the Admiralty dusted off its prewar plans to provide for a Far East fleet, instructing that Sydney and Fremantle be prepared for possible use as eventual bases.[3] In fact it would be years before these ports would see a British ship. And that was largely due to Churchill, whose discussions in Washington ensured that the pre-existing Allied strategy to concentrate on Germany remained in place. He also ensured that Australia would have little influence in shaping the overall war effort.

Churchill had been warned by his colleagues in London that 'the Dominion Governments, especially Australia, will expect to be brought more fully than in the past into any machinery set up for the higher direction of the war'. Unlike Churchill, they were relatively sympathetic to this view, recommending that coordination with the dominions be retained in London, rather than Washington, and that measures be introduced to accord the dominions a higher level of representation in British decision making.[4] Though this proposal was an improvement on the existing situation, it was still a plan for giving the dominions little more than token representation.

The issue would become a growing source of friction between Australia and Britain until Churchill finally agreed to the establishment of Pacific war councils in both London and Washington.

In preparing for his talks in Washington, Churchill sought ways in which he could focus the attention of the Americans on the European war while still allowing them to avenge the humiliation of Pearl Harbor. He urged his defence chiefs, in their meetings with the US chiefs of staff, to encourage the American navy to concentrate on Japan while ensuring that the army would be primarily directed against Germany. Although Churchill privately acknowledged that an early Allied invasion of Europe was unlikely, he advised his chiefs to 'speak with confidence and decision' to the Americans about just such an invasion and request that they make the forces and equipment available for it. He realised that the 'Germany first' strategy would be imperilled if it was widely known that an invasion was unlikely before the summer of 1944, particularly 'if all the time Japan is "running wild" in the East Indies and Northern Australia'.[5] Churchill's anxiety about the American intentions was quickly put to rest when, at the first joint meeting in Washington on 22 December, the US chiefs of staff reiterated their commitment to the 'Germany first' strategy despite the events in the Pacific.

The relief that Churchill would have felt on having the American commitment reconfirmed was threatened almost immediately by a cable from Curtin calling on both Churchill and Roosevelt to devote greater resources to fighting the Pacific war. Curtin had already been advised by Casey that Roosevelt intended to create a regional command in the Pacific and that General Douglas MacArthur, then fighting a vain struggle against the Japanese in the Philippines, might be made commander of it. Casey suggested that it would be in Australia's interest to accept the situation gracefully, 'even to the extent of making the suggestion ourselves, in the interests of future harmonious working together'.[6] That might secure things in the long term for Australia. But it was immediate help that Curtin was desperate to obtain for Singapore and the 100 000 or so imperial troops trying to hold it.

In his cable to Roosevelt and Churchill, Curtin predicted that the campaign in Malaya would end in a disaster along the lines of Greece and

Crete and urged them to press for Russian entry into the Pacific war. He complained that Britain's planned reinforcements for the Far East, particularly of aircraft, were 'utterly inadequate' and that Malaya's ability to resist the Japanese would 'depend directly on [the] amount of assistance provided by the Governments of the United Kingdom and the United States'. Although Curtin promised that Australian troops would 'fight valiantly', he pointed out that they could only do so if they were 'adequately supported'.[7] This was an implicit attack on Churchill, who had sent the Australians into Greece and Crete without such adequate support. And was now doing so at Singapore.

The cable was sent to Casey, who passed it on to Churchill following a meeting that Churchill had with dominion representatives in Washington. According to Casey, Churchill gave the representatives a number of general assurances about reinforcements for the Far East and of the 'urgent necessity to maintain Singapore even if British forces were slowly driven southwards out of northern Malaya ...'. He also was said to have asserted Britain's 'determination to get naval, land and air reinforcements to Malaya and Singapore by diversion from other theatres'.[8] This was hardly what Churchill was planning. Indeed, he remained as determined as ever to prevent other than token reinforcements being sent to buttress the forces in Malaya and Singapore. And he was more buoyed than dismayed by the war situation. As he proclaimed to the dominion representatives, 'on balance, we could not be dissatisfied with the turn of events'.[9]

Whatever the assurances emanating from Washington, the reports from Singapore were alarming the Australian government. Its diplomatic representative on the island, the trade commissioner, V. G. Bowden, reported on Christmas Eve that the collapse of the defence situation in Malaya was assuming 'landslide' proportions. Bowden dismissed Britain's planned reinforcement of Singapore with 50 unassembled Hurricane fighters and the limited additions to the troop strength as being useless gestures. Instead, he argued for the 'immediate dispatch from the Middle East by air of powerful reinforcements, large numbers of the latest fighter aircraft with ample operationally trained personnel'.[10] Casey went to the White House on Christmas Eve to alert Churchill and Roosevelt about Bowden's disturbing report and pass on his call for urgent reinforcements. This first-hand and, as it would prove, accurate assessment was a considerable embarrassment to Churchill. It arrived while he was still trying to divert American attention from the Pacific war and it effectively demolished his confident assertions about the defence of Singapore. But still he would not bend.

In a Christmas Day message to Curtin, Churchill simply denied the truth of Bowden's assessment and repeated Britain's determination to defend Singapore with the 'utmost tenacity'. At the same time, he defended his decision not to strip the Middle East of resources for the sake of the Far East until the situation in Libya was secured. He tried to calm the Australian anxiety by holding out the prospect of reinforcements flowing from America through Australia to the Philippines and Singapore, and even basing American forces in Australia. He also set out the British reinforcements that were planned for Singapore, including his proposal that Australia withdraw one division from Palestine to go either to India or Singapore. Again, he rejected Australian pressure to get Russia into the Pacific war, with Curtin having suggested that Russia be offered territorial inducements if it did so. Curtin had urged that Britain should recognise Russian territorial claims over the Baltic states and, as part of the postwar peace settlement, that Britain should indicate its support for 'Russian strategical and territorial requirements in the Far East (i.e. Northern Korea, Southern Saghalien and possibly the neutralisation of Manchuria) and also to the longstanding Russian objective of an outlet to the Indian Ocean by way of Iran'. Churchill later would make his own territorial deals with Stalin, but this one could threaten the war against Germany and he rejected it absolutely.[11]

Curtin's cable could not be dismissed so easily, particularly when it was buttressed to some extent by a similar cable from South Africa's prime minister, Jan Smuts, who argued for a more forceful response to the Japanese. In contrast to just about all the Australian representatives, Smuts enjoyed a special place of respect and affection in the minds of British political and military leaders and his views were given close attention. His message may have been prompted by concern that the Japanese might reach all the way across the Indian Ocean to South Africa. Unless they were 'countered by very large scale action', argued Smuts, 'they may overrun the

Pacific ... and the recovery of this vast area would be a most difficult and prolonged affair'. Like Curtin, he opposed the idea of sending 'small aid in doles of ships or aircraft or troops to Malaya' and he suggested that Churchill impress upon Roosevelt the urgent need to 'plant the American fighting fleet opposite to that of Japan'.[12]

Perhaps in response to this combined pressure, and anticipating the political price that might have to be paid if Singapore fell, Churchill sent a Christmas Day cable to Auchinleck in Cairo requesting him to dispatch a force of American tanks and four squadrons of Hurricane fighter planes to Singapore. He suggested also that Auchinleck send his damaged tanks to India for repair and then use them as a training nucleus for the armoured divisions being formed there. As far as Singapore's defence was concerned, they remained token contributions designed to appease his critics rather than to provide the formidable reinforcements that Singapore needed. And they were only suggestions for Auchinleck. As Churchill made clear, Auchinleck was not to divest himself of anything that would prevent the planned capture of Tripoli.[13] So nothing was sent. The Middle East remained the higher priority, with a victory in north Africa compensating for the looming disaster in Singapore.

While Churchill was trying to fend off the pressure from Australia, he was faced with another problem concerning his restless dominion. Oliver Lyttelton, Britain's minister to the Middle East, had become so tired of Blamey's forceful representation of the Australian interest in Cairo that he pushed Churchill to have Blamey replaced. In recognition of Australia's military contribution to the Middle East, Blamey had been made deputy commander there and insisted that he be treated as such. He was also instrumental in warning Curtin, during a visit to Australia in November, against allowing Australian troops to be used in future operations without proper support, as they had been in Greece and Crete. It was this warning, and other similar communications from Blamey, that partly lay behind what Attlee described as a spate of 'critical and querulous' cables from Canberra. Together with Blamey's role in the relief of the Australians in Tobruk, it had earned him the enmity of British officers. Indeed, the dispute over Tobruk had prompted Lyttelton in September to urge Churchill to push for the relief of the feisty Australian commander. Churchill had rejected the idea then, claiming that any complaint to Canberra could 'injure the foundation of the Empire'. Now Lyttelton complained that Blamey had become 'very little short of being insufferable' after resisting Auchinleck's order to have one of the Australian divisions moved from Palestine to Syria and at the same time demanding to be on the Middle East war council and defence committee. Attlee passed Lyttelton's cable to Churchill in Washington, suggesting that he 'persuade Curtin to arrange for Blamey's employment in some other sphere' rather than make 'any bleak demands for Blamey's dismissal' that would, 'at this juncture, create a first class row'. Attlee pointed to the 'disquieting impression' that had been created in London by recent 'critical and querulous' cables from Australia, and again advised Churchill to increase the level of consultation with the dominions, although not to the extent of giving them independent representation at international conferences.[14]

Churchill's initial reaction was to support Attlee's suggestion while trying to prevent any adverse effect on the already strained relationship between the two countries. In a draft cable to Curtin, Churchill proposed that, because of the antagonism between Blamey and Auchinleck, Blamey be transferred to Australia and that Menzies be appointed as Australia's representative on the Middle East war council. In a second and more imperious draft, Churchill removed the reference to Menzies and claimed it was a 'matter of urgency ... that Blamey should be transferred elsewhere as soon as possible'. In the event, neither draft was sent. Churchill delayed its dispatch in order to 'get the bigger things settled first' and 'until other difficulties with Mr. Curtin had been disposed of'. Eventually, the Australian government relieved Churchill of the need to request Blamey's transfer when they made the request themselves in late February 1942 after most of the AIF was transferred to the Far East. Churchill was grateful that it had been achieved without any effort on his part, privately noting that Blamey had been a 'more ardent politician than soldier'.[15] As for Churchill's difficulties with Curtin, these were more fundamental and refused to disappear. Australia was challenging the core of Churchill's strategy.

All the assurances from Churchill about reinforcing Singapore and securing Australia counted for nought in Canberra. On 26 December, Evatt sent further anxious cables to both Bruce and Casey, declaring that the 'stage of gentle suggestion has now passed' and dismissing the promised reinforcements for Singapore as being insufficient to restore the situation. Again he called for the transfer of aircraft from the Middle East.[16] Australia was no longer blindly accepting London's lead on foreign and defence policy and intended to boost its pressure independently on both London and Washington for a greater effort in the Pacific. However, it continued to be hampered by having representatives overseas more concerned with pursuing British rather than Australian interests, or prepared to be too easily convinced by British arguments and protestations. In the wake of Evatt's cable to Bruce, General Brooke recorded in his diary how Attlee tried to organise a meeting of the defence committee for 26 December 'to keep Australians quiet as they were fretting about reinforcements to Singapore'. Instead of a meeting, Brooke saw Bruce privately and told him of what Britain was planning. Which was not much. But, according to Brooke, Bruce 'went away satisfied'. He cannot have been totally satisfied as, the following day, the defence committee had a meeting that was 'intended to satisfy Bruce and keep him quiet'.[17]

From Washington, Casey tried to placate Australian anxiety with assurances that Churchill lacked the means rather than the will to reinforce Singapore.[18] This was not true. The Middle East was continuing to enjoy priority over the Far East in the allocation of equipment. More importantly, Casey, Bruce and Page all neglected to inform Curtin that Britain and the United States were going to adhere to the prearranged 'Germany first' strategy, despite the humiliation of Pearl Harbor, and that this would mean the Allies fighting just a holding war in the Pacific. This had important implications for Australia's defence, but Curtin and Evatt were only dimly aware of them. As Opposition MPs, they had not been told of the strategy in early 1941 when the Anglo–American staff talks in Washington had first agreed to it, and they continued in ignorance of it even after they were in government.[19] Although there were sufficient indications to show that Roosevelt and Churchill regarded Germany as the main enemy, Curtin and his colleagues could not comprehend that the Allies were set on fighting such a limited war against Japan. After all, the rhetoric emanating from

Washington and London, and the repeated assurances from Churchill regarding Australia's defence, seemed to belie such a conclusion.

Who knew what and when they knew it regarding the 'Germany first' strategy remains somewhat of a puzzle. In the fog of war, and being so distant from the decision-making capitals, the 'Germany first' strategy seems to have been particularly indistinct from the vantage point of Canberra. As secretary of the defence department and of the war cabinet, Frederick Shedden had the clearest appreciation of the strategic situation and had been aware of the Washington staff talks. He should have alerted the Labor government to the implications for Australia of those talks, but he too seems to have been misled by the subsequent reassuring messages from London. He also perhaps assumed that the 'Germany first' strategy would no longer apply in all its rigour given the unexpected and swift success of the Japanese. He would have assumed that the Americans would respond with all the force they could muster to the attack on Pearl Harbor.[20] But they did not. Had Curtin been properly aware of the Allied strategy, his government would presumably have reacted by adopting a defence policy based on even greater self-reliance. Instead, Australia simply turned more towards America rather than Britain for its defence.

This was the thrust of a Boxing Day report by Shedden who now advised Curtin of the situation facing the Australian government as a result of the Pacific war. Knowing the attitude of his new political masters, and remembering the frustration of his trip with Menzies to London earlier that year, Shedden argued that Australia should be involved in the determination of Allied strategy since the allocation of resources and disposition of forces 'should have regard to the degrees of the threat in the various theatres in order to provide for equality of defence'. This is what Churchill would never concede. Under his plan, there would be no equality of defence; countries in the Far East simply had to accept a greater degree of threat while trusting in their ultimate salvation from the depredations of the Japanese. In stark contrast, Shedden was challenging Churchill's central thesis that the Japanese war was an incident in the present war, arguing instead that it was a new war in which Australia had a 'very real and vital link' with the United States.[21]

The following day, 27 December, the Melbourne *Herald* published a New Year message by Curtin to the Australian people. To the dismay of many Australian conservatives, it expressed sentiments along similar lines to Shedden's report. The message has been interpreted as signalling a turning point in Australia's modern history, with an Australian prime minister looking to America 'without any inhibitions of any kind' and 'free of any pangs as to our traditional links or kinship with the United Kingdom'.[22] Although Curtin tried to placate subsequent domestic criticism of the statement with protestations of loyalty to the empire, he was not simply turning from Britain to America to 'preserve Australia as part of the British empire'.[23] He was challenging the agreed Allied strategy just as Churchill was obtaining a renewal of the American commitment to that strategy. Most dangerously for Churchill, Curtin was publicly calling for Russian entry into the war with Japan and announcing Australia's refusal to 'accept the dictum that the Pacific struggle must be treated as a subordinate segment of the general conflict'. Curtin called instead for a 'concerted plan evoking the greatest strength at the Democracies' disposal, determined upon hurling Japan back'.[24]

Not only was Curtin challenging the 'Germany first' strategy, he was also threatening to break up the alliance between Churchill and Roosevelt with his claim that the Pacific was a theatre 'in which the United States and Australia must have the fullest say in the direction of the democracies' fighting plan'.[25] This was dangerous talk, at least for Britain, and perhaps even for Churchill personally given the degree of political dissatisfaction in Westminster. After a rowdy House of Commons debate about the war on 18 December, Conservative MP 'Chips' Channon considered that Churchill's government was 'doomed' in its present form. Of course, Churchill was not present in London to stiffen the ranks of his supporters. But even one of his own ministers, Hugh Dalton, was worried at the 'very bad spirit, pessimism and discontent with the conduct of the war' that was evident in the debate. Although the opposition to Churchill lacked a clear leader, Dalton thought that 'Malaya now is a little like Norway in May, 1940' when Chamberlain was pushed from power.[26]

Although it was directed at the Australian public, Curtin's message reverberated around the world when it was picked up and carried by the wire services. There was a possibility that Curtin's public championing of a more vigorous Pacific strategy could mobilise the large body of opinion in the United States and, to a lesser extent, in Britain that questioned the Anglo–American concentration on Germany. Neither Churchill nor Roosevelt wanted this to become an open debate, as the great majority of Americans would probably have agreed with the Australian view. To guard against this, Roosevelt had ensured that the Allied strategy would not become a partisan political issue in the US Congress.[27] Curtin's New Year message meant that the issue now was very public indeed, threatening to undo all of Roosevelt's careful efforts to control any public debate on how to react to Pearl Harbor.

If Curtin thought Roosevelt would look favourably on Australia 'turning to America', he was mistaken. According to Maie Casey, the president thought that Curtin's message smacked of panic and disloyalty.[28] As for Churchill, he condemned Curtin's statement in 'strong and outspoken' terms when he learned of it just prior to addressing a meeting of the war committee of the Canadian cabinet in Ottawa. He cabled his own war cabinet, telling his colleagues that he had been 'deeply shocked' on hearing of Curtin's 'insulting speech[29] and [was] vexed by his hectoring telegrams'. Churchill claimed that it had been badly received in Washington and Ottawa and warned that Australia must not be allowed to 'impede the good relations' between Britain and America. So alarmed and outraged was Churchill that he threatened to make a public broadcast over Curtin's head to the Australian people in order to bring the undisciplined dominion to heel. The British war cabinet shared Churchill's anger, although the dominions secretary, Lord Cranborne, argued that they should not focus their anger on Australians as a whole. He explained that Curtin's views 'represented those of his party only and had already caused strong reactions from other quarters' in Australia. To prevent a repetition of these recurring crises, Cranborne reiterated the case for giving 'the Dominions stronger representation in London in some form or another'.[30]

Churchill was not so understanding. He instructed Cranborne to take a 'firm stand against this misbehaviour' and ordered that there be 'no weakness or pandering to them'. It was as if the Australians were naughty schoolboys as far as Churchill was concerned and he was the strict schoolmaster. He seized upon Curtin's statement as effectively releasing Britain from its formal obligation and repeated promises to defend the dominion.[31] As for the deteriorating situation in Malaya revealed by Bowden, Churchill remained unrepentant about the series of actions and inactions that had brought the vaunted British bastion to such a state. He informed his colleagues in London that: 'If [the] Malay Peninsula has been starved for [the] sake of Libya and Russia, no one is more responsible than I, and I would do exactly the same again.'[32]

Curtin's New Year message had thrown down the gauntlet to Churchill. The harsh reality of the large-scale Japanese attacks, and the limited opposition that rose to meet them, caused the fanciful delusions that had previously provided the touchstone for Australia's defence to dissipate while increasing to fever pitch the dominion's anxiety for its own security. The years of imperial rhetoric were laid bare for the first time as Australia lay defenceless before the approaching Japanese. It was the terrible force of these circumstances that had prompted Curtin to place Australia's home defence at the top of his government's agenda. However, it was too late for this switch of priorities to guarantee, by itself, that Australian survival would be ensured. The dominion had been neglectful of its defence for so long that it could not make good the glaring deficiencies overnight. While Curtin's message posed a challenge to Churchill, as well as to Roosevelt, it also was meant as a general plea for help. It was Churchill's task to ensure that the plea went largely unanswered.

NOTES

[1] Report, Mackay to Minister for Army, 17 December 1941, MS 3939, Box 31, Lloyd Ross Papers, NLA.

[2] The Admiralty informed Cunningham on 24 December that it was almost certain that his damaged battleships would have to proceed east after being repaired and asked him to estimate the air strength that he would need to compensate for the absence of the ships. 'Far East Policy', Note by Attlee, 20 December 1941, with attached memoranda, Defence Committee (Operations) Memorandum, CAB 69/3, D.O. (41)40, PRO; See also Cable No. 305, Assistant Chief of Naval Staff (F) to Cunningham, 24 December 1941, ADD. MS. 52567, Cunningham Papers, BL.

[3] Cables, Admiralty to Commander in Chief, Eastern Fleet, 27 and 29 December 1941, REDW 2/10, Edwards Papers, CC.

[4] 'Allied Co-ordination', War Cabinet Memorandum, 20 December 1941, CAB 66/20, W.P. (41)303, PRO; See also War Cabinet Conclusions, 20 December 1941, CAB 65/20, W.M. 132(41), PRO.

[5] 'Most Secret', Note by Churchill, 21 December 1941, in Martin Gilbert, Road to Victory, London, 1986, pp. 21–2.

6   Cable No. 1188, Casey to Department of External Affairs, 21 December 1941, CRS A3300, Item 101, NAA.

7   Cable No. 1103, Curtin to Casey, 23 December 1941, CRS A3300, Item 101, NAA.

8   Cable No. 1199, Casey to Department of External Affairs, 23 December 1941, CRS A3300, Item 101, NAA.

9   Washington War Conference, 23 December 1941, in Gilbert, *Road to Victory*, p. 25.

10 Cable No. 1106, Evatt to Casey, 24 December 1941, CRS A3300, Item 101, NAA.

11 Cable, Churchill to Curtin, 25 December 1941, CRS A3300, Item 101, NAA; Cable, Curtin to Churchill, 22 December 1941, *DAFP*, Vol. 5, Doc. 212.

12 War Cabinet Conclusions, 24 December 1941, CAB 65/20, W.M. 135(41), PRO.

13 Cable No. 1071, Churchill to Auchinleck, 25 December 1941, VI/I, Ismay Papers, KC.

14 See PREM 3/63/3, PRO; Horner, *High Command*, pp. 118–28.

15 Cable No. 4038, Lyttelton to Churchill, 23 December 1941; Cable, Attlee to Churchill (no date); Two drafts of a cable, Churchill to Curtin, 27 December 1941; Cable No. 212, Churchill to Attlee, 5 January 1942; Minute, J. M. Martin to Ismay, 19 January 1941; Cable No. 152, Australian Government to Dominions Office, 27 February 1942; Minute, Attlee to Churchill, 28 February 1942; Note by Churchill, 1 March 1942; all in PREM 3/63/3, PRO.

16 Cable No. 8231, Evatt to Bruce, 26 December 1941, CRS M100, 'December 1941'; Cable No. 164, Evatt to Casey, 26 December 1941, CRS A3300, Item 101, NAA.

17 Alanbrooke diary, 26 and 27 December 1941, in Danchev and Todman (eds), *War Diaries*, pp. 214–5.

18 Cable No. 1220, Casey to Evatt, 26 December 1941, CRS A3300, Item 101, NAA.

19 David Horner, *Defence Supremo*, p. 124.

20 David Horner is probably right in suggesting that Shedden and others in Canberra simply 'lost sight' of the significance of the Washington staff talks and of the conclusions emanating from those talks. ibid., pp. 124–25.

21 'The War Situation from the Australian Viewpoint', Report by Shedden for Curtin, 26 December 1941, CRS A5954, Box 587, NAA.

22 'The Task Ahead', by Curtin, reprinted in F. K. Crowley (ed.), *Modern Australia in Documents*, Vol. 2, Melbourne, 1973, pp. 49–52; For other views of Curtin's statement, see for example, P. G. Edwards, *Prime Ministers and Diplomats*, p. 156, and N. Harper, 'Australian Foreign Policy', in W. S. Livingston and W. R. Louis (eds), *Australia, New Zealand, and the Pacific Islands since the First World War*, Austin, 1979, p. 86.

23 *Argus*, Melbourne, 30 December 1941.

24 'The Task Ahead', by Curtin, reprinted in Crowley (ed.), *Modern Australia in Documents*, Vol. 2, pp. 49–52.

25 ibid.

26 See Channon diary, 18 December 1941, in James (ed.), *Chips*, p. 315; Dalton diary, 19 December 1941, I/25/177, Dalton Papers, LSE.

27 Kimball, *Forged in War*, pp. 124–5.

28 M. Casey, *Tides and Eddies*, London, 1966, p. 83.

29 Curtin's New Year message was in the form of a newspaper article, rather than a speech. However, it has often been mistakenly referred to as a speech, both then and since.

30 Among the criticism that Curtin had to endure in Australia, one Sydney woman wrote to him claiming that, since his New Year message, there had been 'an increase of vice in every shape and form, a deliberate indifference to the things of God and Righteousness, and bitter recriminations against England, for which you, sir, know yourself to be responsible'. War Cabinet Conclusions, 29 December 1941, CAB 65/20, W.M. 137(41), PRO; Draft cable (not sent), Churchill to Curtin, 29 December 1941, PREM 3/154/3, PRO; Letters, Miss D. Cameron to Curtin, 13 and 30 January 1942, CRS CP 156/1, Bundle 1, Item C, NAA.

31 Roger Bell, *Unequal Allies*, Melbourne, 1977, p. 48.

32 Cable Grey No. 172, Churchill to Attlee, 30 December 1941, in Gilbert, *Road to Victory*, p. 34.

TWENTY

'hold out to the last'

The beginning of 1942 saw Australia's recurrent nightmare turn to reality. The Japanese were sweeping through the colonial outposts of Europe and America as they rushed southwards towards Australia's northern coastline. By 1 January, the Japanese had captured Hong Kong, Manila, much of Malaya, parts of the NEI and were thrusting into Burma. The massive battleships that might have blocked their path now lay on the ocean bottom of Pearl Harbor and the South China Sea. Despite the threat to their homeland, Australian forces remained scattered throughout the world. Three divisions of the AIF were in the Middle East, while many of Australia's best airmen were employed on costly and largely futile bombing raids against Germany. The ships of the Australian navy were deployed from the Mediterranean to Singapore, while the 8th Division of the AIF was in Malaya alongside other imperial troops in a hopeless defence of Britain's empty naval 'fortress'.

In Washington, Churchill had secured Roosevelt's renewed commitment to the previously agreed strategy to fight Germany first. Although Australia was vitally concerned with this strategy, it was neither consulted nor informed about its reaffirmation. The Washington meeting also agreed to establish a supreme command in the south-west Pacific under the direction of Britain's former army commander in the Middle East, General Wavell. With Brooke-Popham's successor, General Pownall, as his chief of staff, Wavell was given the task of halting the Japanese advance in South-East Asia. While the task was easy to define, the means were never provided for its accomplishment. It was Roosevelt who had suggested that Wavell be given the command, probably because it was considered to be a hopeless task that should fall on British rather than American shoulders. As well, it was British rather than American forces that largely would bear the brunt of the Japanese onslaught until the Americans were able to regroup their shattered forces, train their soldiers and airmen and deploy them around the edges of the newly created Japanese empire.

This time, Churchill did make some attempt to consult Australia about the arrangements which, so he claimed, were largely for the dominion's 'interest and safety'. Although his colleagues in London had serious misgivings about Wavell's command, the British war cabinet felt compelled to accept it. Ironically, the misgivings were prompted by a fear that the command would attract resources away from the fight against Germany. The chiefs of staff acted to forestall such a possibility by pressing for a joint Anglo–American body to allocate resources between the various theatres so as to avoid any undue concentration on the Pacific.[1] Australia felt compelled to agree to Churchill's plan,[2] although it did insist on Australian representation in the command and requested details of the forces intended for the south-west Pacific. It also continued its ban on the dispatch of Australian airmen for the Empire Air Training Scheme until the 'whole question of Australia's present position in relation to manpower requirements' was examined.[3]

Curtin was suspicious of Anglo–American intentions in the Pacific. As his New Year message had indicated, he realised there were strong forces in both London and Washington wanting to direct the Allied war effort mainly against Germany and that, if left unchallenged, their view would hold sway. Therefore, he called for the formation of an Anglo–American fleet in the Pacific superior to that of the Japanese.[4] This call was buttressed by the advisory war council, which joined in condemning the Allied plan to have 'two inferior fleets, one in the Indian and the other in the Pacific' which 'at the best will impose on us a defensive and not an offensive strategy'.[5] Although Curtin was not yet aware of the full extent of American losses at Pearl Harbor or of the damage to British battleships at Alexandria, there was much to commend his plan, even with the Allied naval forces that remained. A forceful, combined response might have dealt the Japanese navy such a blow as to prevent it establishing a firm grip on the south-west Pacific. Instead, Churchill did as Curtin feared, pitching his inferior naval forces against the Japanese in a pointless exercise of self-annihilation.

Although Australia could acknowledge that imperial defence was not working in the manner it had envisaged, it was another matter to set it aside and adopt a policy of greater self-reliance. It was much easier simply to shout ever louder for Whitehall's help. It was Churchill, not Curtin, who first suggested withdrawing Australian troops from the Middle East for the fight against Japan.[6] This sometimes has been depicted as a move by Churchill designed to secure Australia's defence. However, Churchill never intended that the Australian troops should return to their homeland. Rather, he suggested that they be sent either to India or Singapore. His idea was to place the Australians athwart the westward thrust of the Japanese towards India, rather than have them try to block the southward thrust towards Australia. They would do on land what the Eastern fleet was designed to do in the Indian Ocean. By deterring Japanese progress westward, there was the prospect of their forces being deflected southwards towards Australia. Churchill made little provision to prevent such an eventuality. Indeed, it almost seemed to be his deliberate aim.

Despite the shock of the Japanese advance, the Australian government had not requested the return of its troops from the Middle East. At the war cabinet meeting on 30 December, Churchill's proposal to withdraw one of the three divisions for use against Japan was received with some degree of puzzlement. The Australian chiefs of staff had recommended that the Australian forces in the Middle East be maintained at their present level of three divisions, along with a reinforcement pool of 11 000 men. Although this was approved by the war cabinet, it was now subject to review in light of Churchill's proposed transfer of one division. His suggestion could have been grasped as an opportunity to demand the return of all the divisions now that they were needed for the defence of Australia. But Curtin let the chance pass, simply advising that he opposed the idea of the one division being sent to India. Instead of calling for all the divisions to return, the war cabinet requested Bruce to 'ascertain definitely what is proposed' and 'to submit information as to dates of movement and arrangements for transport and escort'.[7]

Australia's continuing failure to mobilise its forces in its own defence can be partly explained by the conflicting signals being received in Canberra. Although Churchill was busily ensuring that Australia would not see a British fleet, the Admiralty was preparing plans that included the possibility of basing the proposed Eastern fleet at various Australian ports. On 29 December, the Admiralty requested that Australia agree in principle to make the 'necessary arrangements to enable [the] Eastern Fleet or part thereof to be operated from Australian bases'. At the same time, the government was informed by General Gordon Bennett, commander of the 8th Division in Malaya, that Singapore could be defended successfully, provided he was sent sufficient reinforcements. The government responded to these encouraging signals by approving British arrangements for the Eastern fleet and by dispatching a further 1800 ill-fated and half-trained men to Singapore.[8] Australia would have done better to take its cue from what the British government was actually doing to reinforce Malaya, rather than from what it said it was going to do.

Australia was brought back closer to reality on 31 December when Casey advised that Wavell's area of responsibility now was planned to exclude Australia and Papua New Guinea altogether. As well, the battered US Pacific fleet would not extend its area of responsibility to cover the Australian eastern seaboard. Australia was to have self-reliance thrust upon it, but not the resources to fulfil such a responsibility. As Curtin immediately pointed out to Churchill, the effect of these decisions was to offer Australia up as a sacrifice to the Japanese, who were being practically invited to 'avoid [the] main allied concentration in [the] South West Pacific Theatre and attack [the] Australia Area which will be weakly held'. He dismissed Churchill's assurance that Wavell's new command was designed to protect Australia, claiming instead that the Australian chiefs of staff were 'unable to see anything except [an] endangering of our safety by [the] proposal to exclude [the] Australian mainland and territories from [the] South West Pacific Area'.[9] Although this was certainly the effect of Churchill's strategy, he could not afford either to admit it or have it claimed against him.

In a cable quite as strong as Curtin's, Churchill rebutted the claim that Australia was being deliberately endangered. However, as with most of Churchill's cables, it was stronger on rhetoric than specific information. He claimed to be working night and day to 'make the best arrangements possible in your interests and for your safety, having regard to other theatres and other dangers which have to be met from our limited resources'. Australia was excluded from Wavell's command, declared Churchill, because it lay outside the fighting zone. Moreover, he denied Curtin's claim that a 'main allied concentration' was being assembled under Wavell, nor was there any intention to make such a concentration.[10] This should have heightened rather than reduced the Australian concern. Curtin's fears for Australian safety were certainly not allayed by Churchill's cable and he repeated his call for Australia to be included within Wavell's command and for the US navy to be given responsibility for the defence of the Australian east coast.[11]

It was nearly a month since the Japanese attack on Pearl Harbor and Curtin was increasingly frustrated by the brick wall he was encountering in Washington and London whenever he tried to alert the Allied leaders to the desperate situation in Australia's region. Writing to his wife, Elsie, in Perth on 5 January, Curtin confided that the war was going 'very badly and I have a cable fight with Churchill almost daily. He has been in Africa and India and they count before Australia and New Zealand. The truth is that Britain never thought Japan would fight and made no preparations to meet that eventuality.' Curtin was clearly acting under some misconceptions. It was not because Churchill had not visited Australia that he was neglecting its defence. Nor had Churchill believed that Japan would not fight. Indeed, Churchill's war strategy had rested on the Japanese being goaded into war, although he had not expected them to fight so effectively. Curtin, though, did have a fairly clear appreciation concerning the level of assistance that

Australia might expect, telling Elsie that the Allies would 'not risk ships uncovered by air support and there is no early probability of air support'. As a result, Australia would have to produce its own aircraft. After 'two years of Menzies', wrote Curtin, 'we have to really start production'.[12]

Curtin's latest appeal to Churchill was supported by Evatt, who warned Casey that there would be a 'very hostile' reaction if Australia was not given a position of responsibility within Wavell's command. He instructed Casey to push this view in Washington with the 'utmost vigour' in order to achieve 'true and equal collaboration'. Evatt could not understand how Australia's desperate defence needs could be overlooked by Churchill and Roosevelt. He could not reconcile their loudly professed commitment to defend Australia as a base against Japan with their tardy response to the Australian appeal for war resources. Rather naively, Evatt concluded that Australia's short-wave propaganda broadcasts must have 'produced the impression [in London and Washington] that we are far stronger from a military point of view than is the actual case'. To correct this apparent misconception, Evatt suggested that Casey make 'some frank confession of the true position' to Roosevelt, confiding to the president that Australian resources had been 'devoted to theatres other than the south-west Pacific'.[13] This was in vain. There were few illusions in London or Washington about Australia's defence strength.

Churchill, who was spending six days in the Florida sun, rejected Australia's attempt to be represented on any joint body charged with controlling the war against Japan. Moreover, he continued to describe Australia as lying outside the fighting zone and dismissed any suggestion that it was in immediate danger of invasion. While he conceded that Australia might experience Japanese air attacks, he observed that the British had had a 'good dose already in England without mortally harmful results'. Churchill remained determined to leave the defence of Australian soil to the dominion itself, although he did suggest that the United States would be willing to send forty or fifty thousand troops there. He asked Curtin to give him a week's grace to formulate a proper scheme for the direction of the Pacific war while assuring him that he was thinking of Australia's interest 'at every moment'.[14]

Churchill was exasperated with Australia and his mood was not helped by the relative humidity of his beachside retreat. His cable to Curtin had to be toned down considerably before it was sent. Churchill's medical adviser, Charles Moran, was worried by his 'belligerent mood' and his display of wild, childish temper at the Australians, with Churchill complaining that the situation had made Australia 'jumpy about invasion'. Although Churchill felt that Curtin's government did not truly represent the Australian people, he had been similarly irked by other Australians, from Bruce to Blamey and Page to Menzies. Under the pressure of it all, Churchill allowed his class and ethnic prejudices to surface, observing that 'the Australians came of bad stock'.[15] This angry jibe was more than an off-hand comment expressed in a fit of anger. Insecure to some extent in his own aristocratic background, and with his mixed Anglo–American parentage, Churchill could not help being dismissive of a country established originally as a convict colony and subsequently settled by large numbers of working-class Irish. His views would have been shared widely within Britain's ruling class, if only subconsciously, and would have exacerbated the prevailing British resentment towards Australia.

In contrast to his attitude towards Australia, Churchill was much more solicitous about New Zealand's defence, a dominion that did not have a convict past and which had experienced a much lower level of Irish migration. Australia's neighbour also had been less forthright in requesting assistance and Churchill had responded in kind, observing on 2 January that New Zealand had 'behaved so well and deserve[s] every help possible'. Accordingly, New Zealand was promised increased supplies of various military items, although not on such a scale as to detract from the Allied concentration against Germany. Churchill thanked the New Zealand Labour prime minister, Peter Fraser, for the 'splendid courage and loyalty to the Mother Country shown by New Zealand under stress of danger'.[16] Unlike Australia, New Zealand's plight had his sympathy and even some limited practical support.

Australia's pleas were probably responsible for Churchill now suggesting that two of the AIF divisions in the Middle East be transferred to meet the Japanese threat in the Far East. He probably also had in mind that it would lead inevitably to the removal of the 'insufferable' Blamey from the Middle East. The Australian war cabinet readily agreed to Churchill's suggestion, with the 6th and 7th Divisions being selected for transfer, not to Australia but to the NEI. It also suggested that Blamey consider joining the remaining 9th Division to the New Zealand division so that an Anzac corps, with all its historical associations, could operate in the Middle East.[17] In view of Churchill's refusal to make an adequate British contribution to the Pacific war and thereby jeopardising Australia's security, it really was time for all the AIF to return home, along with other Australian contributions to the European war. But the Australian government still shrank from such a drastic course.

Australia's willingness to follow London's lead despite the deteriorating war situation was shown in its reaction to the garrisoning of Portuguese Timor. It was feared that this territory, situated so close to Australia and lightly held by Portuguese forces, would be the logical launching pad for a Japanese assault on northern Australia. In order to pre-empt a Japanese takeover, and at the instigation of the British government, Australia moved troops to the island. When the Portuguese objected strongly, raising the possibility of them allowing German forces into the Iberian Peninsula and thereby threatening Gibraltar and the British hold on the Mediterranean, the British government decided to retreat. Once again, the possible threat to the British position in the Mediterranean outweighed in British minds any threat to Australia. Although Australia had a vital interest in keeping the Japanese out of Timor and away from Australia's northern shores, it again complied with British needs and priorities by agreeing to withdraw its force as soon as Portuguese reinforcements could arrive to boost the territory's defences. It did so even though it acknowledged that the reinforcements were 'unlikely to provide [an] adequate or effective defence'.[18]

European considerations had determined the British reaction to the diplomatic spat with Portugal. And European considerations had returned to the fore in the minds of those planners at the Admiralty who had been considering the dispatch of strong forces to rush to Singapore's succour and avenge the sinking of the *Prince of Wales*. They had come to terms with the shock of the Japanese advance, and now allotted that distant war to second priority behind the European war. Admiral Cunningham, who had earlier agreed to the withdrawal of his ships from the Mediterranean, now argued for their retention at Alexandria. Although he admitted that the Far East needed to be 'restored and stabilised', he agreed with Churchill that the war could only be won by beating Germany, which would bring in its train the defeat of Japan.[19] His colleagues at the Admiralty also agreed with this view, believing as Churchill did that the Japanese would reach the limit of their expansion before they had overrun Australia. A naval planner recalled how the Admiralty in early January expected an 'unrelieved succession of disasters' including the loss of Malaya, Singapore, the Philippines, the NEI and New Guinea 'as the first stage of a threat to Australia'. But naval planners 'guessed contrary to some opinions expressed in Australia that at this stage it was unlikely any attempt would be launched to capture Australia'.[20] Not that the Australian government should have relied on the judgment of the Admiralty, which had been rather unreliable concerning the intentions and ability of the Japanese.

The British confidence about Australia's relative security was partly caused by Churchill's misguided confidence in Singapore's ability to withstand attacks from the Japanese force that was fast working its way along the Malayan peninsula to the island. On 14 January, he finally conceded to Curtin that the loss of Malaya had been inevitable 'once the Japanese obtained command of [the] sea and whilst we are fighting for our lives against Germany and Italy'. However, Churchill implied that the loss of Malaya would be of little consequence since the only vital point was the 'Singapore Fortress and its essential hinterland'. He rejected Australian criticism of Britain's effort in the Far East, pointing to the 'agonising loss of two of our finest ships which we sent to sustain the Far Eastern War'. Even in its watery resting place, the *Prince of Wales* was proving to be a potent force, though as a defence against Australian criticism rather than against Japanese expansion. In this cable, Churchill also confessed to Curtin that the United States would only contribute one cruiser to the defence of Australian waters. Instead of the powerful Anglo–American fleet that Curtin demanded, Australia would have to get by with a single vessel of little more than symbolic power. But it was the symbolism that was important according to Churchill, for it confirmed America's formal undertaking to accept the naval responsibility for the Australian area.[21] Only time would tell whether that would prove to be sufficient to repel a Japanese invasion. After all, the American responsibility for the Philippines was not proving to be of much value, with MacArthur's embattled forces being bottled up on the Bataan peninsula and headed for certain defeat.

Although the Australian government remained unimpressed by Churchill's stout defence of British efforts in the Far East, it still had not realised that the British government had adopted a deliberate strategy that would see Singapore abandoned to its fate. Australia preferred to believe that the defence deficiencies at Singapore, about which Bowden was continuing to send alarming reports, were due to British complacency rather than anything more sinister. So, like an importuning relative, Curtin reminded Churchill once again of the imperial defence principles that had guided Australian defence policy during the interwar period and which had prompted it to contribute so lavishly to Britain's war against Germany. Now it wanted those principles applied to Australia's benefit. Curtin wanted the promised fleet sent to the Far East and he wanted the defence of Singapore guaranteed. If these two things could not be guaranteed, Australia would be forced to concentrate more land and air resources in Australia itself to guard against invasion.[22]

Churchill was greeted with Curtin's cable soon after he arrived back in London on 17 January, forcing him to deal with an Australian attack concerning the Far East when he was more consumed with the greater issue of coordinating Anglo–American energies against Germany and planning a campaign with the Americans to take north Africa. He tried to deflect Curtin's latest attack by alluding to the great victories then being won against Germany, both in Russia and the Middle East, and by claiming that the 'blame for the frightful risks we have had to run and will have to run rests with all those who, in and out of office, failed to discern the Nazi menace and to crush it while it was weak'. This was presumably a jibe at Curtin, whose Labor Party had opposed rearmament during the early 1930s. He also now informed Curtin of the damage to the Mediterranean battleships that had occurred a month before. Had they not been damaged, claimed Churchill, he would have sent them to the Far East. This was far from the truth but Curtin was not to know it. In place of immediate reinforcements, Churchill offered Australia another dose of rhetoric in which he held out the prospect of being able to turn the balance of sea power against the Japanese. He counselled Curtin not to be 'dismayed or get into recrimination' nor to doubt his 'loyalty to Australia and New Zealand'. He optimistically proclaimed himself 'hopeful as never before that we shall emerge safely and also gloriously from the dark valley'.[23]

Although Churchill continued to assure Australia about the strength of the Singapore 'fortress', about which he seemed to harbour some illusions that were not shared by his defence advisers, he actually had given it up as a lost cause. This was indicated in a cable that Churchill sent to Wavell on 14 January in which he confided that it had 'always seemed to me that the vital need is to prolong the defence of the Island to the last possible minute', though he still hoped that it would not come to that.[24] Five days later, and back in London, Churchill's attention was focusing less on Singapore and more on Burma, the gateway to India and China. He told his war cabinet that the Singapore garrison must 'hold out to the last' and emphasised the 'importance of maintaining the Burma Road in operation'. Cadogan left the war cabinet meeting with the impression that Churchill 'seems prepared for the worst in Malaya ...'. The following day, Churchill set out the scenario he expected for Singapore when he informed Wavell that he wanted 'every inch of ground to be defended, every scrap of matériel or defences to be blown to pieces to prevent capture by the enemy and no question of surrender to be entertained until after protracted fighting among the ruins of Singapore City'.[25]

Churchill's concern with the security of the Burma Road, along which China was being supplied with British and American munitions, was twofold. The loss of this tenuous supply route would cause great concern to the Americans and possibly lead China to capitulate to the Japanese. The latter result, Churchill feared, could lead to a pan-Asiatic movement, presumably also including the Indians, that would be capable of expelling the European nations from their colonies across Asia. As he warned Wavell, 'behind all looms the shadow of Asiatic solidarity, which the numerous disasters and defeats through which we have to plough our way may make more menacing'. It seemed that Singapore's remaining utility had been reduced to one of delaying the Japanese from capturing the Burma Road and unleashing this spectre.[26]

This fear of Asiatic solidarity was not confined to Churchill. Occupying a sparsely populated continent on the edge of Asia, Australians mostly shared the fear of such solidarity and the threat of Asian invasion was rooted deep in their national psyche. The White Australia policy of 1901, which excluded non-European immigrants and deported some of those non-Europeans already in Australia, was the most dramatic expression of this latent insecurity. The Japanese entry into the war had brought the Australian fears to the surface. In the wake of Pearl Harbor, Curtin had called on Australians to make an 'all-in' war effort to preserve the country as 'a citadel for the British-speaking race' and 'to resist those who would destroy our title to Australia'.[27] Now he was confronted with the ironic prospect of white Australia being defended, at least partly, by black American troops. Initially, Australia refused to countenance such a prospect for fear of compromising its racist immigration policy and asked that Washington not include black troops in any force that it was planning to send to Australia.[28]

After being advised by the United States legation that such black troops would be used in Darwin on construction work 'for which they are peculiarly fitted', Curtin overruled the advisory war council and left it to the discretion of the United States. The council reluctantly concurred on the express understanding that the US authorities, 'being aware of our views, would have regard to Australian susceptibilities in the numbers they decide to dispatch'. At the same time, the United States was planning to send 1600 black troops as part of a larger contingent to New Caledonia. Although Curtin gave permission for the troops to call at Australian ports en route to New Caledonia, permission was only given on the proviso that the 'coloured troops are on no account to be stationed in Australia' in the event of enemy action preventing them landing in New Caledonia.[29] When an American convoy did steam into Melbourne at the end of January, the black troops on board were prevented from stepping ashore by officious customs officers enforcing the racial provisions of the immigration act. It took another decision of the war cabinet for the ban to be overturned.[30]

Australia was also faced with the question of providing a safe refuge for Asians fleeing from the Japanese, with the Malayan authorities requesting Australia to accept up to five thousand Chinese and Eurasian refugees. Only after strong protests from the Malayan administration did the government relax its initial decision to restrict the number of refugees to just 50, and only on condition that they were self-supporting or maintained by Malaya. It also provided sanctuary for 580 Chinese miners evacuated from Nauru and Ocean Island where they had been employed in the extraction of phosphate for the ultimate benefit of Australian farmers. They were now sent to mine tungsten in the harsh conditions of central Australia, where they were paid a pittance and segregated from white miners in order to 'avoid any suggestion of exploitation of cheap labour for private interests'. The US government posed an additional challenge to the White Australia policy when it proposed to import 25 000 labourers from Java on a short-term basis to construct airfields in northern Australia. However, Java was captured by the Japanese before the plan could be implemented. It was made clear that these relaxations of the White Australia policy were temporary expedients and did not represent an abandonment of the policy. Nevertheless, they provided a graphic illustration of the desperate straits to which the dominion was reduced if the previously sacrosanct racial provisions of the Immigration Restriction Act could be waived, even temporarily.[31]

While the Australian government agreed under American pressure to relax the provisions of its White Australia policy, and while it had allowed an American air route across the Pacific, it was more reluctant to allow such a route across the Indian Ocean. The Americans feared that their recently established trans-Pacific route could be cut by the Japanese and wanted to establish an alternative route from southern Africa to Western Australia. Instead of giving its immediate approval, the government referred the question to London where it was discussed at a meeting between Bruce, Page and officials of Britain's air ministry. They agreed to give conditional approval so long as the route was 'regarded as supplementary and did not interfere with the existing route from Britain to Rangoon'. Despite this conditional approval, opposition from Qantas kept it in abeyance until such time as the Japanese had made the route untenable. Qantas feared that the American plan would lead to the eventual takeover of Australia's overseas air routes by Pan American Airways to the detriment of the joint

Anglo–Australian service, in which Qantas had a stake, and that it ignored the 'needs of the British war effort'.[32] No matter that it could have proved vital for the Australian war effort.

Australian protectiveness towards the British-controlled air route to Rangoon was rather curious at a time when Rangoon was about to fall to the Japanese. Although British planners had believed that Japan eventually would turn its attention towards Burma, they mistakenly believed that it would not happen until Malaya and Singapore had been captured. On 20 January, the Japanese proved them wrong when they moved across the Siamese border in a major thrust towards Rangoon. Britain now had the invidious problem of deciding whether to concentrate on defending Singapore or Rangoon. The day before the attack, the governor of Burma, Sir Reginald Dorman-Smith, had warned London that it would have to choose between the 'competing demands of [the] Mideast, Burma and Singapore'. Dorman-Smith wanted them to choose Burma. Describing it as the 'last remaining operational base against the Japs', he warned that it was 'dangerous to think in terms of reinforcing Singapore at the expense of Burma for purposes of prestige'.[33] Churchill agreed absolutely, as did General Brooke, but there were dominion and domestic critics who could not accept so easily the effective abandonment of Singapore.

NOTES

[1] War Cabinet Conclusions, 29 December 1941, CAB 65/20, W.M. 137 and 138(41); 'Command in the South West Pacific', Report by the Chiefs of Staff, 29 December 1941, CAB 66/20, W.P. (41)307, PRO.

[2] Churchill's plan was much less than that mooted to Casey by Dill, which had held out the possibility of Wavell being based in Australia and of an Australian regional commander being responsible for northern Australia. Cable No. 1237, Casey to External Affairs Department, 29 December 1941, CRS A3300, Item 101, NAA.

[3] War Cabinet Minutes, 30 December 1941, CRS A2673, Vol. 9, Minutes 1631 and 1634, NAA.

[4] Cable No. 166, Curtin to Casey, 29 December 1941, CRS A3300, Item 101, NAA.

[5] Cable No. 171, Curtin to Casey, 31 December 1941, CRS A3300, Item 101, NAA.

[6] Curtin later helped to create the myth that he had initiated the withdrawal of the troops from the Middle East. In 1944, he informed a meeting of the Empire Parliamentary Association in London that 'the Australian Government asked for the return of the men who were fighting overseas'. That was not strictly true, although what he had done was no less significant by insisting that the troops withdrawn at Churchill's suggestion from the Middle East be sent to Australia rather than to Burma. Address by Curtin, 17 May 1944, BEVN 6/21, Bevin Papers, CC.

[7] The advisory war council also shrank from interfering with Churchill's plans, other than by endorsing Curtin's opposition to the troops being sent to India. War Cabinet Minutes, 30 December 1941, CRS A2673, Vol. 9, Minute 1636; Advisory War Council Minutes, 31 December 1941, CRS A2682, Vol. 4, Minute 635, NAA.

[8] Advisory War Council Minutes, 31 December 1941, CRS A2682, Vol. 4, Minute 634; War Cabinet Minutes, 30 December 1941, CRS A2673, Vol. 9, Minutes 1631 and 1636, NAA.

[9] Cable, Curtin to Churchill, 1 January 1942, *DAFP*, Vol. 5, Doc. 247.

[10] Cable, Churchill to Curtin, 3 January 1942, *DAFP*, Vol. 5, Doc. 254.

[11] Cable, Curtin to Churchill, 6 January 1942, *DAFP*, Vol. 5, Doc. 259.

[12] Article by Lloyd Ross, *Sunday Australian*, Sydney, 9 January 1972.

[13] Cable, Evatt to Casey, 7 January 1942, *DAFP*, Vol. 5, Doc. 259.

[14] Cable, Churchill to Curtin, 8 January 1942, *DAFP*, Vol. 5, Doc. 262.

[15] Moran diary, 9 January 1942, in Moran, *Winston Churchill*, p. 21.

[16] See PREM 3/150/1, PRO.

[17] War Cabinet Minutes, 5 January 1942, CRS A2673, Vol. X, Minute 1667, NAA.

[18] In the event, a Japanese invading force arrived at Dili before the Portuguese reinforcements and quickly overwhelmed the small Australian force, forcing it to retreat into the hinterland. Radio Message 2, Department of External Affairs to David Ross, 20 January 1942, *DAFP*, Vol. 5, Doc. 284; See also War Cabinet Conclusions, 1 January 1942, CAB 65/25, W.M. (42)1, PRO.

[19] Letter, Cunningham to Vice Admiral Moore, 9 January 1942, ADD. MS. 52561, Cunningham Papers, BL; See also Speech by Lord Croft, Under Secretary of State for War, 15 January 1942, CRFT 2/8, Croft Papers, CC.

[20] 'My Life', Memoirs of Admiral Davis, p. 283, WDVS 1/3, Davis Papers, CC.

[21] Cable No. 50/2, Churchill to Curtin, 14 January 1942, VI/2, Ismay Papers, KC.

[22] Cable, Curtin to Churchill, 17 January 1942, *DAFP*, Vol. 5, Doc. 278.

[23] Cable, Churchill to Curtin, 19 January 1942, *DAFP*, Vol. 5, Doc. 281.

[24] Cable No. 62/2, Churchill to Wavell, 14 January 1942, VI/2, Ismay Papers, KC.

[25] Cable No. 82/2, Churchill to Wavell, 20 January 1942, VI/2, Ismay Papers, KC; Cadogan diary, 19 January 1942, in Dilks (ed.), *The Diaries of Sir Alexander Cadogan*, p. 428; War Cabinet Conclusions/Confidential Annex, 19 January 1942, CAB 65/29, W.M. (42)9, PRO.

[26] Robert Sherwood (ed.), *The White House Papers of Harry L. Hopkins*, Vol. 1, London, 1948, p. 478; Cable No. 101/2, Churchill to Wavell, 23 January 1942, VI/2, Ismay Papers, KC; See also Mackenzie King diary, 19 January 1942, CUL; War Cabinet Conclusions/Confidential Annex, 17 January 1942, CAB 65/29, W.M. (42)8, PRO.

[27] *Sydney Morning Herald*, 9 December 1941.

[28] In making this request, the advisory war council said that it was concerned at the 'probable repercussions of the use of coloured troops on the maintenance of the White Australia policy in the post-war settlement'. Advisory War Council Minutes, 12 January 1942, CRS A2682, Vol. 4, Minute 673, NAA.

[29] Teleprinter message, Hodgson to Secretary, Army Department, 13 January 1942; Notes of Discussion with Curtin (extract), by Shedden, 14 January 1942; Cable No. 86, Casey to Commonwealth Government, 16 January 1942; all in CRS A5954, Box 287; Advisory War Council Minutes, 20 January 1942, CRS A2682, Vol. 4, Minute 685, NAA.

[30] 'Presence of United States Coloured Troops in Australia', CRS A2676, Item 1848, NAA.

[31] War Cabinet Minutes, 25 January 1942, CRS A2673, Vol. X, Minute 1759; War Cabinet Agendum Nos. 11/1942 and 126/1942, CRS A2670, 11/1942 and 126/1942; War Cabinet Minute No. 1839, 1 February 1942, CRS A5954, Box 287, NAA.

[32] Page diary, 12 January 1942, MS 1633, Folder 2345, Page Papers, NLA; Hudson Fysh, *Qantas at War*, Sydney, 1968, pp. 127–8.

[33] Cable No. 63, Dorman-Smith to Amery, 19 January 1942, 'Secret Telegrams of Sir R. Dorman-Smith', Photo-Eur. 11, IOL.

TWENTY-ONE

'dark days'

For about twenty years, Australia had placed its faith in the ability of a powerful British fleet based at Singapore to protect it from the attentions of a hostile Japan. Throughout that time, there had never been a fleet based at Singapore, and the naval base to support such a fleet had only been completed just prior to the Second World War. Even without a fleet, Britain had proclaimed that the forces at Singapore would be able to hold out against a besieging force for up to 90 days, time enough for a British fleet to be organised and steam across the world to the rescue. It was now just over 30 days since the beginning of the Pacific war and the defences of Singapore were close to collapse, with Churchill wanting to abandon the island altogether and concentrate British resources on shoring up Burma and India.

When news reached London on 21 January 1941 of the Japanese offensive into Burma, the defence committee immediately weighed the competing demands of Singapore and Rangoon. Whatever illusions Churchill may have harboured about Singapore, he now knew from Wavell that it was not a fortress and that the battle to defend the island and its empty naval base might well be lost sooner than he expected. As such, he pressed the case for making the reinforcement of Burma a higher priority, arguing that 'taking the widest view, Burma was more important than Singapore'.[1] But he could not abandon Singapore without Australia's agreement, since the dominion had so many of its personnel involved in the island's defence. Churchill complained that Australia had not expressed a view on the possibility of its abandonment, an issue that was now a matter of some urgency. In fact, Curtin had cabled to Churchill ten days before, urging that everything possible should be done to reinforce Malaya, where Australia's 8th Division was then poised to fight the decisive battle for Johore, and warning that a 'repetition of the Greek and Crete campaigns would evoke a violent public reaction' in Australia. Page reinforced this point when he now assured Churchill that the Australian government would 'never consent to the desertion of its fighting men'.[2]

Churchill reluctantly bowed to this view, which was supported by several of his ministers, and delayed the planned diversion of British reinforcements from Singapore to Rangoon. After being pressured by Australia into making what he considered to be a wasteful contribution to the likely lost cause of Singapore, Churchill's mood was not enhanced when the late-night meeting of the defence committee concluded with the receipt of another cable from Curtin, this time rejecting Churchill's plan for Allied coordination in the Pacific. Curtin wanted instead a seat for Australia in the British war cabinet along with the formation of a combined policy-making body in Washington on which Australia would also be represented. On reading this, Page recalled that 'Churchill slammed the telegram on the table and declared that he had said his last words — Australia could go to Washington if she wished'.[3]

Churchill still could not believe that the Japanese might have both the resources to invade Australia, as well as the incentive to do so in order to neutralise Australia's potential as the most suitable base from which to launch an eventual Allied counterattack. From the Australian viewpoint, they had always regarded their lightly peopled continent as inherently desirable in the eyes of other peoples, particularly the densely populated societies of Asia. So it was easy for them to believe that the Japanese would have the conquest of Australia as a high priority, while it was difficult for them to accept how Britain could not have the defence of Australia, and its supposedly outlying bastion of Singapore, as a high priority. While Churchill saw the Japanese lunge into Burma as confirmation of his prediction about Japanese intentions, the Australian government interpreted the overwhelming Japanese attack on the Australian garrison at Rabaul in New Britain on 23 January, along with massive bombing raids on other Australian bases in New Guinea and its offshore islands, as confirmation that the Japanese were heading their way and intent on invasion.[4]

Curtin had informed Churchill on 21 January of his conviction that a Japanese invasion of Australia was likely. And he had accepted Churchill's suggestion to use American troops to help defend Australia. Not that any were immediately available, as US commanders concentrated on trying to shore up MacArthur's position in the Philippines and secure his reinforcement route. Therefore Singapore still seemed to be Australia's best hope of staving off the Japanese. Hence Curtin's continuing pressure on Churchill to reinforce Singapore and maintain the fight in Malaya. He warned Churchill that it was a 'race against time in Malaya in which the enemy will do everything possible by air and submarine attacks to prevent our reinforcements getting through'.[5] But Churchill had already given up on Singapore.

For Curtin, the stress of it all proved too much. Under pressure from his concerned cabinet colleagues, he was prevailed upon to take a recuperative break in Perth, leaving Melbourne by train on 21 January. Before departing, he made a statement to the press about a bombing raid on the Australian outpost at Rabaul, warning of the 'immediate menace which this attack constitutes for Australia ...'.[6] While his train slowly trundled across the Nullarbor Plain towards his home city of Perth, an emergency meeting of the war cabinet in Melbourne's Victoria Barracks was handed a cable from Page advising the worrying news that Churchill was considering the evacuation of Singapore. With the ineffectual army minister, Frank Forde, chairing the meeting, the outraged ministers decided to protest to Churchill in the strongest of terms. Without Curtin's moderating influence, little was left unsaid. As amended by Evatt, the subsequent cable blasted any evacuation of Singapore as 'an inexcusable betrayal'. Describing the island as a 'central fortress in the system of Empire and local defence', the cable complained angrily that Australia had 'acted and carried out our part of the bargain' and now wanted Britain 'not to frustrate the whole purpose by evacuation'. Moreover, if any reinforcements were to be diverted from Singapore, they should be sent to the Netherlands East Indies, from where they might still protect Singapore and Australia, rather than to Burma.[7]

Apart from pressing Churchill to reinforce Singapore, the war cabinet discussed the implications of the Japanese attack on Rabaul. A single battalion of Australian troops, supported by a handful of Wirraway and Hudson aircraft, had been left to face the Japanese. On 23 January, more than five thousand Japanese troops had stormed ashore to capture Rabaul, with its strategic harbour and two landing strips that would allow the Japanese to extend their air power into the Coral Sea as far as Port Moresby and the towns along Queensland's northern coastline. Two aircraft carriers, eight cruisers, twelve destroyers and nine submarines had supported the invasion, while plaintive messages from the RAAF commander at Rabaul for modern fighters to be sent and for American bombers to attack the massing enemy ships were rejected. 'If we had them you would get them,' came the reply from Melbourne. As for the defending Wirraways, they were vastly outnumbered and proved no match in the air against the superior Japanese fighters.[8]

So Australia's first-line fighter strength, the much-vaunted Wirraways, were confirmed as useless in combat against the best Japanese fighters. Australia could no longer pretend that it had even the semblance of an air defence force. Equally worrying, the chief of the naval staff, Admiral Royle, advised that there was 'no prospect of concentrating a battleship force of sufficient strength to defeat the Japanese before May'. As a result, Australia was wide open to invasion, although Royle thought that Australia did not offer a very attractive target to the Japanese. If it was invaded, though, he urged that Australians be told to 'remain in their homes and ... keep the roads clear'. The government was so worried that it announced that the forthcoming Australia Day on 26 January would not be a holiday, at least for the munitions industry and war-related government departments.[9]

When Churchill read the Australian cable describing an evacuation of Singapore as an inexcusable betrayal, he immediately rounded on the hapless

Page, who had unwittingly helped to instigate it, reminding him that Britain was not planning to evacuate Singapore, only to divert its reinforcements to Burma. These reinforcements included Britain's 18th Division, then crossing the Indian Ocean in troopships and available to be deployed where it was most needed. As a result of the Australian pressure, that division would now be landed at Singapore. Poor Page defended his report as being fact mixed with observations and partly intended, so he said, to serve Britain's purposes. He claimed that he was trying to buttress the arguments for the proposed Far Eastern Council to be established in London as Churchill wanted, rather than in Washington as Curtin wanted. When Page then attempted to put Australia's case for reinforcements, the war cabinet simply instructed that reports be drawn up which set out their plans for the Far East. Much of the meeting had been taken up with demands from Australia: for a seat in the war cabinet; for a Pacific War Council to be established in Washington; and for reinforcements for Singapore. Such was the British exasperation with its demanding dominion at this meeting, ironically held on Australia Day, that one cabinet member scrawled an angry note to a colleague describing Australia as 'the most dangerous obstacle in the path of this Gov[ernmen]t', a description one would have thought more apt for Germany or Japan. According to Page, Churchill 'went off the deep end about the Australians generally, and said if they were going to squeal he would send them all home again out of the various fighting zones'.[10]

David Horner has argued that the Australian government should have kept an open mind about the possible need for the evacuation of Singapore, particularly by late January when the battle for Malaya had clearly been lost. What was the point of Australia refusing to consider evacuation and of insisting so trenchantly that Singapore still had to be reinforced when its hopes of holding out were fading fast? As a result of this insistence, thousands of troops, most of them British, were landed on the island at a time when it was too late for them to be able to affect the final outcome. Against his better judgment, they were sacrificed uselessly by Churchill to appease the clamour from Australia. Who should bear the responsibility for this? Should it be Curtin, who was so weighed down by the burden of his office that he had to seek relief in Perth at the very time that this question should have been explored? Or should it be Evatt, who employed the term 'inexcusable betrayal' that so inflamed Churchill and led to additional troops being deployed there?

Evatt, though, was clearly acting under the illusion, induced by a succession of British and Australian governments, that Singapore really was a 'central fortress' and had to be held at all costs. The Australian chiefs of staff and Frederick Shedden could have advised him otherwise, but did not. Menzies and Spender had visited Singapore and seen its parlous defences. They could have raised the question of evacuating the garrison once its fate was clear. Again, they did not. As Horner also points out, neither did Bowden or Bennett, with their first-hand knowledge, raise evacuation as a possibility. Indeed, the safe evacuation of the entire garrison would have been an impossibility, bearing in mind the shortage of shipping and the Japanese control of the sea and air. What was regrettable was the useless deployment of additional British and Australian reinforcements. And the responsibility for that must be shared between the British and Australian governments, and the imperial-minded politicians who established the circumstances during the 1930s that had the effect of investing the reinforcement decisions of January 1942 with a sense of tragic inevitability.[11] Churchill now had yet another stick with which to beat the Australian government.

From Canberra, the British high commissioner, Sir Ronald Cross, stoked the fires of antagonism towards Australia by urging his former cabinet colleagues in London to take a tough line with the dominion, arguing that Australia was 'so dependent on our good-will that we can use a big enough stick to get our way'. He blamed Evatt for various articles in Australian newspapers that were hostile to Britain's war effort in the Far East and he proposed that Britain should respond to the Australian demand for representation in the British war cabinet by demanding the same for him in the Australian war cabinet. He urged it also to counter Australia's nationalist trend by adopting an unaccommodating attitude towards Australia on economic issues.[12]

Cross' proposals were rejected by the dominions secretary, Lord Cranborne, who urged again that Britain should concede Australia's demand for a greater say in imperial decision making. He warned that it would be a 'great and possibly dangerous mistake' for Britain to ignore the rising tide of concern in Australia.[13] Cranborne did not have to remind his colleagues that the British press was also replete with calls for greater dominion representation in the war cabinet and that there was considerable sympathy for such a move within the House of Commons by the growing number of MPs critical of Churchill's handling of the war. An editorial in the London *Times* on 19 January had called for greater dominion participation in the formulation of imperial policy and the granting of such representation as the dominions themselves desired.[14] There was not only Australia to be considered. It could involve the future of the empire itself. As Cranborne warned his colleagues, a 'rot which started in Australia might easily spread to other Dominions', adding to the 'centrifugal tendencies' that were already apparent in the empire. Cranborne suggested that Australia be appeased by according its representative the right to attend the war cabinet whenever questions affecting the war as a whole were discussed, provided that the representative was empowered to commit the dominion on urgent matters.[15] Even though it was less than Australia had enjoyed in the First World War, Churchill had always refused to make such a concession. On 17 January, he had again dismissed it out of hand, observing sarcastically that first 'Australians ought to lay aside their Party feud and set up a National Government.'[16]

Just five days later, in the face of renewed pressure from within and without, Churchill relented and allowed Page to attend relevant war cabinet meetings as the accredited representative of the Australian government. Page would now attend as a matter of right rather than privilege, although it would still be Churchill who decided which meetings were relevant for Page to attend. And it did not mean that Page's voice would be listened to any more than it had been before. Brooke summed up the British attitude to Page when he observed in his diary after one meeting of the defence committee that Page 'as usual wasted most of our time!'. But the change to Page's attendance would appease Churchill's domestic critics as well as the distant and detestable Australians. As Ismay privately confessed, Churchill was 'having a pretty rough time at the moment with Australia bickering and a few elements in Parliament and the Press (not very important ones) snarling'.[17] Churchill would also have been more comfortable having the long-winded Page in the war cabinet rather than the brilliant and ambitious Menzies.

However much it might appease Churchill's critics, Australia's representation in the war cabinet would not guarantee that the dominion's urgent defence needs would be met. Tanks were essential if Australia was to defend itself against invasion. Menzies had authorised the production of an Australian-built tank, but the program relied on the supply of machine tools and other essential equipment from Britain and America. It proved no easier to extract these items of equipment than it had been to extract a supply of tanks themselves. Still the program pressed on, absorbing much-needed funds, material and manpower until being eventually ended by Curtin in 1943 without an operational tank being produced.

With the locally produced tanks still not in sight, and a Japanese invasion feared within weeks, the Australian government made a determined effort to obtain the tanks that it had on order overseas. On 21 January, Bruce wrote to Beaverbrook requesting the diversion to Australia of 775 cruiser tanks, the minimum requirement for Australia to have some chance of fighting off an invasion force. Meanwhile, the Australian government learned that the United States did not plan to make any deliveries of tanks to the dominion during January, while Britain only intended to dispatch 40. One-third of US tank production and much of Britain's was being sent to Russia, with Casey urging Curtin to suggest a temporary diminution in the Russian allocation to provide for Australia's immediate needs. The government took up Casey's suggestion, advising Bruce that the time needed for delivery and the imminence of the Australian danger justified the 'strongest possible pressure being exerted to secure immediate shipments'. Britain's intelligence chiefs now admitted that Japan had the capability to defeat and invade Australia, but they still disputed the immediate likelihood of this happening. They predicted instead that 'Japan will probably be content, at this stage, with trying to isolate Australia and New Zealand without embarking on a major operation to the Southward, except for an attack to capture Port Darwin.' As for the allocation of tanks, this was not discussed by the British government until 30 January, nine days after the first letter from Bruce to Beaverbrook and the day on which the hard-pressed troops in Malaya retreated across the causeway to Singapore Island.[18]

At the defence committee meeting, the urgent Australian requests for tanks and aircraft faced determined opposition from Beaverbrook and Eden. Churchill had scored a momentous victory in the House of Commons the previous day, when he saw off his critics and won a motion of no confidence by 464 votes to one. The vote was not an accurate reflection of his standing in the parliament after the run of disasters that Britain had been suffering, but it did reveal that he had no serious rival as yet. As a result of that vote, he was under little political pressure to respond to the Australian pleas for assistance. Perhaps for this reason, Churchill did not bother to attend that morning's defence committee meeting and sent Attlee to chair it in his place. At the meeting, Beaverbrook argued forcefully that the supply of tanks to Russia must be maintained despite the military situation on the Eastern front becoming more favourable for the Russians and Russia's own tank production being restored. Eden supported Beaverbrook while also reminding the committee of the needs of the Middle East, where Auchinleck's offensive had been checked by Rommel. Despite these arguments, Attlee thought that it was impossible to ignore Australia's appeal. Rather than sending the requested tanks, the committee agreed to make available 125 Kittyhawk fighter aircraft from British sources and to request a similar amount for Australia from US sources.[19] It was a minuscule proportion of the total Allied supply of operational aircraft, of which some nine thousand were produced during the first three months of 1942,[20] and would satisfy less than one-quarter of the Australian request. The dominion fared little better with regard to tanks.

Under a proposal from General Brooke, who was not normally sympathetic to Australia's needs, the supply of tanks to Russia would be reduced by more than half during February and March to allow 321 tanks to be sent to Australia, which was still less than half the number requested by Bruce. In urging this upon the committee, Brooke conceded that the rush of Japanese successes had made the threat to Australia 'a very real one'. He reported Churchill's view that the home forces should take last priority, although taking last priority under Brooke's plan still allowed them to receive 602 tanks to add to their stock of 2261. Beaverbrook and Eden attacked the idea of cutting Russia's supply, arguing that it would be 'wrong to approach Russia at the present time just when things were going so well there'. On this curious logic, it would never be the right time to tell Russia it would be getting less tanks since it could hardly be done if things were going badly. Brooke was livid at being outmanoeuvred by Beaverbrook, noting in his diary that it was 'quite evident that we are incurring grave danger by going on supplying tanks to Russia [but] it is Beaverbrook's firm intention that we should go on doing so, and he controls PM on such matters'. Ever crafty, Beaverbrook offered to find a solution that would satisfy both Russian and Australian requirements. The committee agreed, authorising Beaverbrook to meet the needs of the Far East 'as far as possible' but without reducing either Russian or Middle East shipments.[21]

Beaverbrook drew up a plan to provide Australia with 325 tanks and for India, Australia and New Zealand to receive about 50 per cent of their allocation after the February and March allocations to all theatres had been delivered.[22] In mid-March, Beaverbrook discovered that tank production was 400 units more than he had anticipated, but Australia was not the beneficiary of this unexpected good fortune. Instead, Beaverbrook asked Churchill to divert all of this bonus production to Russia.[23] So the supplies to Russia continued, as much for political reasons as for military ones, and at great cost. In July 1942, one ill-fated convoy to Russia was attacked so heavily by the Germans that ships carrying some 500 tanks and 260 aircraft were sent to the bottom of the Arctic Ocean.[24] As for Australia, Beaverbrook's plan meant that, with delivery times taken into account, the dominion would receive half its minimum requirement of tanks by mid-1942, which was some weeks after any invasion was likely to have occurred. It was a level of risk that Britain would not have found acceptable for itself. Indeed, by the beginning of May, most of the tanks had not arrived. Although Australia had 352 tanks on 9 May 1942, only 63 were of British origin, 138 were American, 149 were two-man tanks for training purposes only, and the remaining two were Australian-produced prototypes.[25]

Like Menzies in 1941, Page was taken in completely by the wily Beaverbrook, who gave the naive envoy the impression he had Australian needs uppermost in his priorities but who quietly slipped its requirements to the bottom of the list.[26] When Australia successfully sought Roosevelt's support to divert machine tools to Australia that originally had been destined for Britain, Churchill reluctantly agreed on the condition that no further diversions were made from British orders.[27]

As the discussion of tanks indicated, there was little sympathy for Australia's plight. Oliver Harvey was reflecting a view that was prevalent in British government circles when he almost seemed to take delight in the dominion's predicament. On 24 January, as the Japanese consolidated their hold on Rabaul and launched bombing raids on further island stepping stones towards Australia, Harvey wrote in his diary of Australia being 'in the greatest possible flap. Almost a panic over [the] Jap approach and our alleged failure to have helped them more and [not to have] prevented it.' Dismissing Curtin as a 'wretched second-rate man', Harvey questioned 'why Australia hadn't yet got conscription, why in the past she didn't contribute more to the Royal Navy and R.A.F. and so on'. Of course, Australia did have conscription for home defence and its defence effort had been geared above all to satisfy Britain's needs rather than its own. Many of the fighter planes defending London, and the bombers raiding Germany, were flown by Australians under the Empire Air Training Scheme. Cunningham's fleet in the Mediterranean was partly composed of Australian ships, while Auchinleck's army had 100 000 Australians making up its ranks. No dominion had been as cooperative as Australia in contributing to Britain's war effort, or had fought as hard as Australians in the battles to that time. Yet it got little credit for that in London, with no dominion being more criticised by British officials. As Harvey remarked, Australia's 'clamour compares unfavourably with the relative calm of New Zealand'. According to Harvey's rather smug analysis, Australia had lived for a century in a fool's paradise and it had taken the war for it to be 'suddenly woken up to the cold and hard fact that her very existence as a white country depends not on herself but on protection from Gt Britain'.[28] Not that there was much protection being offered from London, which was the whole point of the 'clamour' emanating from Canberra.

Similar criticisms were being voiced by Britain's high commissioner in Canberra. In a letter to a Conservative Party colleague on 3 February, Cross deplored the bluntness of the messages that the Australian government had been sending to London and described Australians as an 'inferior people' with poor nerves. Cross urged London to publicise the fact that it had begun to provide help from 'the moment Pearl Harbor was attacked and that our efforts have proceeded ... unaffected by rude squeals'. This would not be such an easy matter. Even Cross seemed concerned about Australia's security and questioned Churchill's judgment in publicly asserting that the Japanese were unlikely to invade Australia. As Cross pointed out, this could be read by the Japanese as an invitation to mount an invasion against the sparsely populated continent while at the same time encouraging Australians to be complacent.[29]

With Singapore set to fall, even New Zealand was worrying about its safety. Its Labour government under Peter Fraser had earlier assured Churchill that New Zealand had never allowed any fears about its own safety to come before what he called its 'primary duty of applying the greatest force that we could provide at the most useful point'. That meant keeping New Zealand forces in the fight against Germany, rather than having them return to fight the Japanese. When the question of their possible return was being discussed with London in late January, Fraser assured the British high commissioner in Wellington that he was 'most anxious to find [a] solution acceptable to Mr Churchill and not to play Australia's game'. So the troops stayed. It meant that New Zealand effectively would be defended during 1942 by the Australians and Americans fighting in New Guinea and the Solomons, while New Zealand troops provided a garrison on Fiji. But there was mounting disquiet in parliament about New Zealand's defence preparedness, particularly the lack of fighter aircraft and tanks.[30]

It was against this background that Fraser reacted with uncharacteristic dismay to the British plan to provide Australia with 125 Kittyhawks while allocating only eighteen to New Zealand. On 4 February, Fraser protested to Churchill that such a miserly allocation would leave the country defenceless. In fact, Churchill was taking grave risks with the security of both dominions but, as before, he responded with greater sympathy to New Zealand's plea, ordering that it should have priority over Australia for the rather curious reason that it was 'so much smaller'. In the event, the air ministry devised a delivery plan to satisfy the New Zealanders without detracting from Australia.[31]

With the Japanese continuing to extend their empire across South-East Asia and the south-west Pacific, there was no telling where they would stop. In contrast to his defence advisers who had given Singapore up as lost, Churchill claimed to still harbour a hope that the besieged island might yet hold out, as the garrison had in Tobruk and the island of Malta had in the Mediterranean. At least, that was what he told the Americans, holding out the prospect to Roosevelt on 7 February of 'severe battles' being fought to defend Singapore where the Japanese had to 'cross a broad moat before attacking a strong fortified and still mobile force'.[32] To suggest anything less would make a mockery of his recent decision, under Australian pressure, to send the additional British division to Singapore. However solid were his hopes, it took just 24 hours for them to be dashed, with Japanese troops crossing the narrow channel from Johore to Singapore Island where they overcame ineffective resistance from the Australian defenders and established a beachhead. Once the Japanese were ashore, and with their forces having almost total command of the air and the surrounding sea, the end was never in doubt. The myth of the Singapore 'fortress' was shattered.

After denying Singapore its much-needed aircraft and ships for so long, Churchill now instructed its hapless commanders to put aside any thought of surrender and to 'perish at their post'.[33] In a cable to Wavell on 10 February, Churchill instructed that the beleaguered officers in Singapore should abandon any

thought of saving the troops or sparing the population. The battle must be fought to the bitter end at all costs. The 18th Division has a chance to make its name in history. Commanders and senior officers should die with their troops. The honour of the British empire and of the British Army is at stake.[34]

After four days of fighting on the island, and with the Japanese in control of the water supply, the game was up for the defenders. Only then did Churchill finally relent and give Wavell the freedom to 'judge when further resistance would be useless' and a surrender could be negotiated.[35] The following day, 15 February, the lanky figure of Britain's General Arthur Percival had the ignominious task of walking with a white flag along the road to the Japanese lines. More than twenty years of fitful preparation had come to this.

In Singapore's final weeks, several thousand poorly trained and ill-equipped Australian troops, along with the men of Britain's 18th Division, had clambered down the gangways of their troopships in time to join the tens of thousands of their comrades who were forced to surrender to the numerically inferior Japanese forces. The reputation of Australia's troops suffered severely from their role in Singapore's defeat, and not totally without cause. It had been the Australian sector of the shoreline where the Japanese had managed to secure a lodgment. And some Australian troops were alleged to have acted disreputably in the dying hours of the struggle, forcing their way onto the last evacuation ships.[36] Their commander, General Bennett, set a questionable example himself by refusing to stay with his men, slipping away instead with several of his staff and making for Australia from where he blasted the British for the defeat. As if that was not enough, Churchill could never forgive the Australian government for pressuring him into sending the 18th Division to Singapore rather than to Rangoon. The division had been unable to stave off the defeat of Singapore but, according to Churchill, might well have been able to stave off the defeat of Rangoon.[37]

As General Brooke observed, they were 'black days' for Britain. Not only had Singapore fallen and its defending army been marched off into captivity, but Burma was looking as if it might be next to fall.[38] Back home, two German battle cruisers had steamed out of their temporary haven in a French port and defiantly swept along the English Channel to Germany. Neither the planes of the RAF nor the ships of the RN were able to prevent their passage, although Britain lost about forty planes in the attempt. In the Middle East, Rommel had turned the British advance on Tripoli into a headlong retreat in the other direction. The Libyan port of Benghazi changed hands for the fourth time in twelve months. As a result of this run of humiliating defeats, there were renewed calls for Churchill's almost dictatorial power to be curbed by the appointment of a defence minister to take over the direction of the war.[39] None of it provided any relief for Australia, with the strategic implications of Rommel's successes in the Middle East putting even more pressure on the limited British effort in the Far East.

NOTES

[1] Defence Committee (Operations) Minutes, 21 January 1942, CAB 69/4, D.O. (42)4, PRO; Gilbert, *Road to Victory*, pp. 46–47.

[2] Page, *Truant Surgeon*, pp. 326–7; Cable, Curtin to Churchill, 11 January 1942, *DAFP*, Vol. 5, Doc. 266; See also Dalton diary, 21 January 1942, I/26/29, Dalton Papers, LSE.

[3] According to Brooke's slightly less dramatic account of the incident, the meeting 'finished with a climax caused by arrival of wire from Australia disagreeing with the arrangements PM had with USA concerning higher direction of the war!!'. Alanbrooke diary, 21 January 1942, in Danchev and Todman (eds), *War Diaries*, p. 222; Page, *Truant Surgeon*, pp. 326–7.

[4] For details of the Japanese attacks on Rabaul and other northern islands, see Douglas Gillison, *Royal Australian Air Force, 1939–1942*, Canberra, 1962.

[5] Cable, Curtin to Churchill, 21 January 1942, *DAFP*, Vol. 5, Doc. 287.

[6] *Age*, Melbourne, 22 January 1942.

[7] A second cable was sent to Churchill on 27 January, again drafted by Forde and Evatt and buttressing the earlier appeal by pointedly reminding Churchill of the substantial Australian contribution to the RAF. Cable, Curtin to Churchill, 23 January 1942, *DAFP*, Vol. 5, Doc. 294; See also War Cabinet Minutes, 23 January 1942, CRS A2673, Vol. X, Minute 1741; Cable Johcu 22, Curtin to Churchill, 27 January 1942, CRS A5954, Box 229, NAA; Horner, *High Command*, pp. 150–5.

[8] Gillison, *Royal Australian Air Force*, Chap. 18.

[9] War Cabinet Minutes, 23 January 1942, CRS A2673, Vol. X, Minutes 1742–4, NAA.

[10] War Cabinet Conclusions/Confidential Annex, 26 January 1942, CAB 65/29, W.M. (42)11; War Cabinet Conclusions, 26 January 1942, CAB 65/25, W.M. (42)11 and 12, PRO; Note, apparently by the First Lord of the Admiralty, A. V. Alexander, 26 January 1942, AVAR 5/7/12, Alexander papers, CC; Page cited in Horner, *High Command*, p. 152.

[11] Horner, *High Command*, pp. 152–4.

[12] Letter, Cross to Cranborne, 20 January 1942, ADD. MS. 58240, Emrys-Evans Papers, BL; 'Relations with Australia', Minute, Cranborne to Churchill, 22 January 1942, CAB 66/21, W.P. (42)33, PRO.

[13] 'Co-operation with Dominion Governments', Memorandum by Cranborne, 21 January 1942, CAB 66/21, W.P. (42)29, PRO.

[14] Menzies had helped to inspire these calls in the British press during his 1941 visit to London and he did what he could to promote this renewed campaign for dominion representation, probably still hoping that he would be the dominions' chosen representative. Editorial, *Times*, London, 19 January 1942; Article by Menzies, *Times*, London, 21 January 1942; For the political situation in Westminster, see Harvey diary, 19 January 1942, ADD. MS. 56398, Harvey Papers, BL; and Channon diary, 20 January 1942, in James, *Chips*, p. 317.

[15] 'Co-operation with Dominion Governments', Memorandum by Cranborne, 21 January 1942, CAB 66/21, W.P. (42)29, PRO.

[16] War Cabinet Conclusions, 17 January 1942, CAB 65/25, W.M. (42)8, PRO.

[17] War Cabinet Conclusions, 22 January 1942, CAB 65/25, W.M. (42)10, PRO; Letter, Ismay to Harry Hopkins, 27 January 1942, IV/Hop/9, Ismay Papers, KC.

[18] On 30 January, Brooke received the news from Singapore with grim foreboding, doubting in his diary 'whether the island holds out very long'. Alanbrooke diary, 30 January 1942, in Danchev and Todman (eds), *War Diaries*, p. 225; 'Tanks for Australia', Notes by Hollis, 25 and 29 January 1942, Defence Committee (Operations) Memoranda, CAB 69/4, D.O. (42)7 and 8, PRO; See also BBK D/70, Beaverbrook Papers, HLRO; Joint Intelligence Sub-Committee memorandum, 25 January 1942, PREM 3/151/4, PRO.

[19] Defence Committee (Operations) Minutes, 30 January 1942, CAB 69/4, D.O. (42)5, PRO; See also Cadogan diary, 30 January 1942, in Dilks (ed.), *The Diaries of Sir Alexander Cadogan*, p. 430; 'Tank Allocation', Memorandum by Brooke, 26 January 1942, PREM 3/150/4, PRO.

[20] 'Munition Production, January–June 1942', Survey by Minister of Production, 3 September 1942, CAB 66/28, W.P. (42)393, PRO.

[21] Alanbrooke diary, 30 January 1942, in Danchev and Todman (eds), *War Diaries*, p. 225; 'Tanks for Australia', Notes by Hollis, 25 and 29 January 1942, Defence Committee (Operations) Memoranda, CAB 69/4, D.O. (42)7 and 8, PRO; See also BBK D/70, Beaverbrook Papers, HLRO.

[22] 'Tank Allocation', Note by Hollis, 31 January 1942, CAB 69/4, D.O. (42)11, PRO.

[23] Minute, Beaverbrook to Churchill, 15 March 1942, BBK D/94, Beaverbrook Papers, HLRO.

[24] Defence Committee (Operations) Minutes, 13 July 1942, CAB 69/4, D.O. (42)15, PRO.

[25] Weekly Progress Report by Chiefs of Staff, 9 May 1942, CRS A2670, 28/1942, NAA.

[26] See Letter, Page to Beaverbrook, 4 February 1942, BBK D/408, Beaverbrook Papers, HLRO; Cable P37, Page to Curtin, 9 February 1942, CRS M103, '1942', NAA.

[27] Cable No. 23A, Halifax to Foreign Office, 30 January 1942; Cable No. 2020, Foreign Office to Halifax, 6 February 1942; Cable No. 100, Curtin to Churchill, 6 February 1942; Cable No. 202, Churchill to Curtin (but drafted by Beaverbrook), 16 February 1942; all in PREM 3/44, PRO.

[28] Harvey diary, 24, 25 January and 1 February 1942, ADD. MS. 56398, Harvey Papers, BL.

[29] From Sydney, the governor of New South Wales, Lord Wakehurst, also worried that Britain was too complacent about Australia's security, observing to a British MP that he did not think there was 'any margin to gamble on. One must face the possibility of Singapore, Java, and New Guinea going. Then what about Darwin, New Caledonia and Fiji? The Japs might be satisfied with cutting our communications with the outside world, but the more significant Australia becomes as a base the more will it be worth their while to destroy whatever strength is gathered here.' Letter, Cross to Emrys-Evans, 3 February 1942; Letter, Wakehurst to Emrys-Evans, 16 February 1942; See also Letter, Parker Leighton MP to Emrys-Evans, 10 February 1942, ADD. MS. 58243 and 58263, Emrys-Evans Papers, BL.

[30] Michael Bassett and Michael King, *Tomorrow Comes the Song: A Life of Peter Fraser*, Auckland, 2000, p. 227.

[31] See PREM 3/150/2 and PREM 3/150/6, PRO.

[32] Cable No. 193/2, Churchill to Roosevelt, 7 February 1942, VI/2, Ismay Papers, KC.

[33] Alanbrooke diary, 9 February 1942, in Danchev and Todman (eds), *War Diaries*, p. 228.

[34] Cable No. 206/2, Churchill to Wavell, 10 February 1942, VI/2, Ismay Papers, KC.

[35] Alanbrooke diary, 14 February 1942, in Danchev and Todman (eds), *War Diaries*, p. 229.

[36] See Day, 'Anzacs on the Run: The view from Whitehall, 1941–42'.

[37] This was an opinion widely shared among British political and military leaders after the event. See, for instance, Danchev and Todman (eds), *War Diaries*, p. 222.

[38] On 18 February, Brooke noted in his diary that 'Burma news now bad. Cannot work out why troops are not fighting better. If the army cannot fight better than it is doing at present we shall deserve to lose our Empire!' Alanbrooke diary, 12, 13 and 18 February 1942, in Danchev and Todman (eds), *War Diaries*, pp. 229, 231.

[39] Harvey diary, 12, 14 and 15 February 1942, ADD. MS. 56398, Harvey Papers, BL; See also Letter, Harvey to Eden, 13 February 1942, ADD. MS. 56402, Harvey Papers, BL; Letter, Cranborne to Emrys-Evans, 13 February 1942, ADD. MS. 58263, Emrys-Evans Papers, BL; Alanbrooke diary, 17 February 1942, in Danchev and Todman (eds), *War Diaries*, p. 230.

TWENTY-TWO

'The Japs have bombed Darwin!'

The loss of Singapore had important psychological as well as military effects. The island had been touted in British propaganda as being a fortress capable of withstanding attack for many months until it could be relieved by a British fleet. Countless newsreel films had extolled Singapore as the linchpin of imperial defence in the Far East. Now it was gone, along with a division of Australian troops, and many more British and Indian troops, and nothing seemed to stand between the unexpected might of the Japanese armed forces and the relatively defenceless continent of Australia. Curtin had just returned from his recuperation in Perth and described the fall of Singapore as 'Australia's Dunkirk', although the troops in Singapore had been captured rather than successfully evacuated. Curtin warned that it would be followed by the 'battle for Australia' and called on Australians, as 'the sons and daughters of Britishers', to prepare for the worst.[1] A day of prayer saw Australians crowd into churches to seek divine help, while others dug furiously in their backyards to construct shelters for the air raids that they feared would soon come.

Australia's recurrent nightmare had become a reality. The 'yellow hordes' that had been so frequently conjured up in the popular press were now beating on the door and demanding admission. The late poet Dorothy Hewett was a university student in Perth and recalled the city being plastered with 'posters showing the Japanese as less than human, as fanged animals really, who were sort of coming to rape your sister, your mother, your grandmother or anybody else about the place ...'.[2] For Australia, the war suddenly had become a question of survival. After two and a half years of war, and more than two months after Pearl Harbor, the Australian government finally announced that the country was on a total war footing. It informed its worried citizens that the dominion now had to 'rely on its own resources' and was no longer able to provide 'substantial aid in countries outside Australia'. The war cabinet was empowered to 'take immediate steps for the total mobilisation of all resources' so that 'the defence of Australia may be provided for'. There was no longer to be any confusion with the state governments as to who was in charge, with the Commonwealth government declaring that its authority was to be supreme over that of the states and that the *whole* resources of the Commonwealth' were to be 'mobilised and utilised'.[3]

Armed with this authority, the war cabinet began preparing for the invasion that they feared was coming. If it was to be repelled, modern fighter aircraft would be vital. But none of the 125 Kittyhawks promised by Britain had yet been delivered and there was no guarantee that they would arrive before the threatened invasion began. So the war cabinet approved the production of a hundred improved Wirraway aircraft as a 'reinsurance against [the] failure of fighter aircraft to arrive in sufficient numbers from overseas'. This was despite advice from Burnett that the improved Wirraways, to be known as Boomerangs, could only be justified as a makeshift solution. In fact, the main rationale for the war cabinet decision was to absorb personnel who otherwise would be idle on completion of the existing Wirraway program.[4]

The effort would prove to be largely futile, but the government had little alternative. The existing Wirraways had proved to be no match for their Japanese opponents, while a faster Wirraway with heavier armament might be able to mount a more credible threat. There was certainly no way that Australia could plan and build a really modern fighter, such as a Hurricane, in the time frame that it had available. It simply had to press ahead, producing planes that would probably prove unsuitable. So desperate was the situation that a suggestion was made to draft in convicted criminals as labourers in the aircraft factories. As the aircraft production minister argued, Australia could not be too particular when it was struggling for its life, although he assured trade unions that the prisoners would only be used 'providing they do not come into competition with organised labor, and are not used to break down awards'.[5]

As the Boomerang decision indicated, a policy of defence self-reliance could not be adopted at the last minute. Had it been done in the mid-1930s, Australia could have been in a much stronger position in early 1942. Instead, it remained dependent on the promises of Britain and the United States being fulfilled, although past experience gave it little cause for confidence that they would be. Even now, Churchill's promise to provide Kittyhawks was proving to be much less than it appeared. He had promised to provide 125 aircraft from among those that Britain had on order in the United States, while also requesting Roosevelt to provide an equal number from America's allocation of the Kittyhawk production. But there was still no confirmation that Washington would agree to Churchill's suggestion, while the delivery dates of the British Kittyhawks continued to recede into the future. Yet the Japanese advance kept on coming, with even the unsympathetic Sir Ronald Cross conceding later that 'the military position had so worsened that Australia lay open to invasion whilst not possessing the means of effective resistance'.[6]

Desperate times demanded desperate measures, but the years of neglect and misdirection in defence spending could not be put right overnight. Curtin's New Year message had been a dramatic attempt to do this, but it had misfired and caused anger and resentment both in Washington and London. Now Evatt tried a different course by appealing to the rising political star in London, the maverick Labour MP Stafford Cripps, who had gained considerable public popularity as Britain's ambassador to Russia. When he returned to London in the midst of the disasters of early 1942, he was seized upon as a possible panacea for Britain's military ills. With the general public questioning Churchill's war leadership for the first time, his parliamentary critics were spurred into open rebellion.[7] On 17 February, Brooke met with Churchill in Downing Street and discovered him 'in a dejected mood', with Churchill reporting that 'he was just back from dealing with a troublesome House [of Commons]'. Brooke wrote in his diary that 'I am afraid that he is in for a lot more trouble'.[8]

While there were no calls for Churchill's removal, there were demands for the appointment of a defence minister to take over his central role at the helm of Britain's war effort. On his own initiative, Australia's high commissioner became involved in schemes to promote Cripps into the war cabinet to act as a restraining influence on Churchill.[9] At the same time, Evatt cabled from Canberra with encouragement for Cripps in any struggle with Churchill. In his remarkable message, Evatt linked his bitter criticism of Churchill and support for Cripps with an appeal for Cripps to help secure Australia's urgent defence needs. 'It is vital,' argued Evatt, 'that someone in England should realise that we must find greater air support from U.S. and U.K.' He told Cripps that Australia was 'short in everything because we have poured out our resources to help the common cause everywhere in the world'. There was much truth in Evatt's plaintive appeal, but it was made in vain. Cripps was never able to get his hands on the levers of power. Instead, Churchill brought him into a trimmed-down war cabinet as minister for aircraft production, while retaining his own control over the strategic course of the war. It is very likely that Churchill was made aware of this latest Australian attempt to reduce his power, which would only have added to his considerable feelings of enmity towards the dominion.[10]

Meanwhile, within Australia, there was increasing resentment directed at Britain for removing the defensive cover under which Australia had sheltered for so long. In the immediate aftermath of Singapore's surrender, Lord Wakehurst wrote to London from Sydney warning of the possible boost to Australian nationalism caused by Britain's failure to defend the dominion. Where were the British planes, ships or tanks when Australia was in dire need of them and why had the Singapore bastion been allowed to fall? These questions were causing Australians to confront their faith in the 'mother country'.[11] As Wakehurst observed from his gubernatorial residence on Sydney Harbour, 'deep in the Australian mind is embedded the belief that, come what may, Britain would look after Australia'. That belief was now under threat from a 'recognisable but not considerable minority that is inclined to say that Australia has been let down'. It was compounded by the widespread feeling that Britain had been fighting the war mainly with dominion forces.[12] Wakehurst's concern was taken up in a leaflet published by the Australian Association of British Manufacturers which tried to refute what it described as 'unfair and ill-informed criticism — including the "England-let-us-down" myth'.[13]

While Australian servicemen in the Middle East and Britain demanded to be brought back to defend their homeland,[14] the British government tried to assess the likely next moves of the triumphant Japanese. The chiefs of staff predicted that they would continue with their two-pronged approach into Burma and sealing the outer ring of the NEI. After that, they suggested that Japan would pause for reorganisation 'whether or not a subsequent attack on Australia or India had a place in Japanese plans'. The chiefs alerted Churchill to the grave situation facing Allied shipping, which could not cope with simultaneous movements to the Middle East and Far East, warning that a choice would have to be made between the two theatres. Since their advice was also intended for dispatch to the dominions, Cranborne urged that no mention of such a choice should be included in the dominion copies.[15]

Churchill immediately bridled at the implicit suggestion that Britain might not be supporting the dominions to the fullest extent possible. He claimed that Britain already had made a choice and that it was in favour of the Far East. He pointed out that Britain had denuded the Levant–Caspian front in order to protect the Far East and 'would have to rely on the Russians if the Germans advanced to the Caucasus in the Spring'. In fact, the chiefs of staff had reported that there was no risk of a German attack on that front for at least six or seven months by which time reinforcements could be sent. Certainly the choice had been made, but not in the direction Churchill claimed.[16]

Within the Far East theatre, the choices were also being made. The fall of Singapore doomed the NEI to share the same fate. The Japanese had already landed in Sumatra when the defence committee ordered on 16 February that no further reinforcements were to be sent to Java. British and Australian forces were ordered to fall back to what were termed the 'essential bases':

Burma, Ceylon, India and Australia. Among these four bases there was an order of priority, with Churchill making clear that Australia was the lowest priority. He agreed that it was 'urgent to reinforce Burma and Ceylon' but so far as Australia was concerned there was no urgency, just an acknowledgment that 'it would be difficult to refuse the Australians' request that their divisions should return home'. Of the two reinforcement divisions designated for possible use in Java, the committee instructed that Australia's 7th Division, then in troopships in the Indian Ocean, should proceed to Australia rather than to Java, and for the 70th British Division to proceed to Burma and Ceylon, if necessary using the ships designated for the second AIF division that was preparing to leave the Middle East.[17]

These plans were thrown into disarray by the continuing deterioration of the British defences in Burma, with the governor, Dorman-Smith, having reported on 14 February that contingency plans for the evacuation of Rangoon were being completed. Although Dorman-Smith hoped that such an eventuality could still be avoided, claiming that their 'tails are wagging hard', Churchill and Brooke were not confident about its prospects.[18] But they remained determined to hold Burma, much as Churchill had been determined to hold Greece and Crete. Churchill sent out a new commander, General Harold Alexander, to take over from the discredited incumbent, although Brooke worried in his diary whether Alexander would arrive in time to rescue the situation, which was 'becoming very critical. Troops don't seem to be fighting well there either which is most depressing.'[19] Even Churchill later conceded that never had he 'taken the responsibility for sending a general on a more forlorn hope'.[20]

Despite the 'forlorn' chances of success, Churchill decided that he would use Australia's 7th Division to beef up the crumbling defences around Rangoon. For that, he needed to obtain Australia's agreement. It seemed reasonable to Churchill, after he had bowed to Australia's urging and sent Britain's 18th Division to the defence of Singapore, even though he had wanted it to go to Rangoon, that Australia should now respond in kind for the defence of Rangoon.[21] Diverting an Australian division to Rangoon would compensate for that needless British loss and would assist in what he regarded as the all-important defence of Burma.

Churchill had three allies in his campaign to obtain the diversion of the Australian troops. The first was Roosevelt. Following the defence committee meeting on 16 February, Churchill informed Roosevelt that the Australians 'seem inclined to press for the return of their two divisions ... and probably their third division, now in Palestine, will follow'. Britain could not resist such pressure for long, advised Churchill, even though Rangoon and the Burma Road were the 'most vital point at the moment' and Wavell had 'very rightly already diverted our Armoured Brigade there'. The clear implication from this message was for Roosevelt to pressure Curtin to do likewise and allow the Australian troops to be used in Burma. Roosevelt promptly did so, offering to send US troops to Australia if Curtin would agree to send the two Australian divisions to India or Burma.[22]

Churchill's second ally was Page, who was persuaded to pressure the Australian government to divert their troops to Burma until they could be relieved by British troops. Page informed Curtin that diverting the troops to Burma would not only keep open the road to China but would 'indicate that the Australians were taking the widest co-operative attitude towards the war'. He assured Curtin that Britain had promised 'very substantial air reinforcements' for Burma that would avoid any repetition of the Greek, Crete and Malayan campaigns. Page was supported by Churchill's third ally on this question, Bruce, who also cabled Curtin using a variety of arguments ranging from moral blackmail to spurious strategic points. He claimed that it would strengthen Australia's position in demanding similar action for its defence and that Britain's recognition of Australia's importance as a base would ensure that it could 'confidently rely on the maximum support it is physically possible to get to us'. On the day these cables were sent, Dorman-Smith reported to London that there was 'no more than a 50% chance of holding Rangoon'.[23]

After watching with horror the swift collapse of the Singapore defences, and having followed Britain into Greece, Crete and Malaya, the Australian government was most averse to repeating the experience in Burma. It had no illusions about Rangoon being any sort of fortress. On receipt of Page's advice, Curtin immediately instructed him to ensure that the convoy should not be diverted to Burma, predicting that his war cabinet was likely to press for its return to Australia. The war cabinet promptly did so, despite opposition from the conservative representatives on the advisory war council. The war cabinet also asked for the early return of the third AIF division, the 9th Division, and for the diversion to Australia of the British armoured brigade that Wavell had already diverted to Burma.[24]

Despite clear instructions from Canberra, Page did not pass on his government's decision regarding the diversion to Rangoon, arguing instead that Australia should reconsider its decision in view of the offer of US troops from Roosevelt.[25] Page was conscious of the poor regard in which Australia was held in London and was anxious to cooperate with Churchill and thereby hopefully restore Australia's reputation. It might also help to restore his own standing. And it all seemed to make strategic sense, since using the Australians in Burma and sending Americans to Australia would make the most efficient use of scarce Allied shipping. But Curtin again insisted that his instructions be carried out. As he explained the position to Blamey, the loss of Malaya, Singapore and the NEI had left Australia 'bare' and that, because of the 'unsatisfactory strength of our defences in Australia, the destination of the A.I.F. should be Australia'.[26] Curtin was under pressure from some of his Labor colleagues, as well as from his army chief, General Sturdee, who threatened to resign if the troops were not returned to Australia. Yet it still had been a difficult question for him to resolve, with Curtin declaring it to have been 'the biggest and most important decision I have had to make since Japan entered the war'.[27]

Australia's resolve to recall the troops was confirmed by the Japanese bombing of Darwin on 19 February. Just as at Pearl Harbor, more than a hundred Japanese aircraft had been able to swoop down on Darwin, dropping their bombs and strafing the unsuspecting defenders before the alarm was sounded. More than two hundred people were killed among the ruins of that isolated northern outpost and on the ships crowding its harbour. As the aircraft flew away to their waiting carriers, nine ships lay sunk or burning in the harbour and 23 aircraft were left destroyed on the ground. The sudden attack caused mass panic in the town's small civilian population and within the ranks of its uniformed defenders. Looting and desertions were commonplace. The panic was understandable. The town was virtually cut off by distance from reinforcement, while the defenders lacked the necessary aircraft and guns to withstand the force of the Japanese attack, let alone repel the widely expected follow-up invasion. Fortunately for the shocked survivors, the Japanese were only intent on destroying Darwin's potential as a base from which to attack the southern flank of Japan's invasion of the NEI. They had no plans as yet to occupy Darwin.

The timing of the Darwin raid, just four days after the fall of Singapore, convinced the government to remain firm in its refusal of Churchill's renewed request concerning Burma.[28] The advisory war council was meeting to discuss Churchill's request when details of the devastation at Darwin began to clatter in over the teleprinter. Shedden later claimed that ministers behaved 'like a lot of startled chooks' when they heard of it. He may have been referring to Jack Beasley, who left the meeting to be given the awful news, and then rushed back in to exclaim: 'The Japs have bombed Darwin! That settles it!' No amount of appealing or threatening by Churchill or Roosevelt could shift the Australian resolve. Not even when Churchill suggested that Roosevelt might refuse support for Australia if Curtin did not bend to Churchill's will. Or when he claimed that the Australian division was the only force available to save the situation, arguing that a 'vital war emergency cannot be ignored, and troops en route to other destinations must be ready to turn aside and take part in a battle'. Churchill still hoped that he might prevail. However, with the troopships steaming across the Indian Ocean, it was imperative to get a quick decision from Curtin before the ships were past the point at which they could be diverted to Burma. Churchill pressed Curtin 'for the sake of all interests, and above all your own interests', to concede to the request.[29]

Churchill's final appeal to Curtin was dispatched at 9.13 p.m. on 20 February. Earlier that day, Churchill had chaired a meeting of his chiefs of staff at which it was presumed that Australia would refuse to back down. Accordingly, arrangements were made to send troops from India, Cyprus and the Middle East. Despite this, Churchill still sent off his appeal asking Curtin for 'an answer immediately, as the leading ships of the convoy will soon be steaming in the opposite direction from Rangoon'.[30] In fact, Churchill had already ordered the diversion of the ships to Rangoon just thirteen minutes before his cable to Curtin was sent. This was despite a chiefs of staff decision two days earlier that 'orders regarding the diversion of the leading Australian formations to Burma could not be issued until a telegram had been received from Australia agreeing to the proposal'. Malice then became mixed with liberal measures of incompetence when Downing Street failed to inform Page of the diversion, although it was known that Page had assured Curtin that no diversion had been made. In a note to Churchill, Ismay justified this omission by claiming that, 'amidst the exceptional preoccupations of that particular day, the matter did not seem of any great consequence' since it had been 'confidently anticipated that the reply of the Australian Government ... would arrive before any complications ensued'.[31] The exceptional preoccupations referred to by Ismay were Churchill's changes to his war cabinet and his preparations for a critical Commons debate on the war situation.

Churchill's cable reached Canberra on Saturday morning, 21 February, where it was promptly considered by a meeting of the war cabinet. Curtin was back in charge after having been in a Sydney hospital from 17 February, recovering from a bout of gastritis that had probably been brought on by the stress of it all. He had only left his hospital bed for Canberra to address a secret session of parliament on 20 February and now joined with his war cabinet colleagues in reaffirming the government's opposition to their troops being diverted to Burma. There was little indecision in the war cabinet. As Shedden observed, it was 'patronizing' of Churchill to pressure 'the Prime Minister of a self-governing Dominion about the diversion of its own troops returning for the defence of their own country'.[32] But it was not until after midnight that Curtin had composed a cable relaying the war cabinet's decision to Churchill. The troopships spent that day steaming on towards Rangoon. Curtin would have had some trepidation as to how his refusal would be viewed in London and Washington and what the implications might be in terms of future American assistance. He had received a further cable from Roosevelt urging him to comply with Churchill's wish and again offering to reinforce the dominion with American troops, although Roosevelt reassured Curtin that Australia's 'vital centres' were not in 'immediate danger'. Roosevelt also reiterated Churchill's claim that the

Australian division was the only force able 'to save what now seems a very dangerous situation'.[33] These were strong appeals that an Australian government normally would have been unable to resist. But these were not normal times.

The Australian government did not share the confidence that Churchill and Roosevelt claimed to have concerning Australia's relative security and there was never much doubt, even in Churchill's mind, that Australia would refuse this repeated request. Which of course it did, with Curtin's refusal being couched in terms that were sure to infuriate Churchill even more. He predicted that the diversion of the 7th Division would probably lead on to the diversion of the 6th and 9th Divisions and perhaps a 'recurrence of the experiences of the Greek and Malayan campaigns'. Curtin disputed whether the troops could be landed safely in Rangoon in view of the Japanese air and naval superiority in the Bay of Bengal and, perhaps more importantly, whether they could be removed later when the promised British reinforcements arrived to take their place. All told, argued Curtin, the diversion was not a 'reasonable hazard of war, having regard to what has gone before'. And if it led to another humiliating defeat for Australian troops, it would have the 'gravest consequences on the morale of the Australian people'.[34] The stage was set for the most bitter dispute between Australia and Britain.

NOTES

[1] Following this speech in Sydney's Martin Place, Curtin had to be carted off to hospital for several days' treatment for a bout of gastritis. *Sydney Morning Herald*, 17 February 1942; Speech by Curtin, 17 February 1942, A5954, Box 69, Item 2205/1, NAA.

[2] Joanna Penglase and David Horner (eds), *When the War came to Australia*, Sydney, 1992, pp. 70–3, 91.

[3] Cabinet Minutes, 17 February 1942, CRS A2703, Vol. 1[C], NAA.

[4] 'Aircraft Production Policy: Proposal to build Wirraway-Interceptors', 13 February 1942; 'Wirraway Interceptors', Report by Burnett, 16 February 1942; War Cabinet Minute No. 1908, 18 February 1942, CRS A5954, Box 216, NAA.

[5] *Herald*, Melbourne, 18 February 1942.

[6] Letter, Cross to Cranborne, 13 April 1944, RC/4/23, Cross Papers, IWM; See also CRS A5954, Box 229, NAA.

[7] King diary, 16 February 1942, in King, *With Malice Toward None*, p. 158; See also Day, 'An Undiplomatic Incident: S. M. Bruce and the Moves to Curb Churchill, February 1942', *Journal of Australian Studies*, November 1986.

[8] Alanbrooke diary, 17 February 1942, in Danchev and Todman (eds), *War Diaries*, p. 230.

[9] Talk with Cripps, 16 February 1942, CRS M100, 'February 1942', NAA.

[10] Cable (draft), Evatt to Cripps, 16 February 1942, DAFP, Vol. 5, Doc. 335.

[11] One Australian later recalled the 'feeling of resentment and anger that Singapore wasn't what it had been cracked up to be'. Another commented: 'Did we feel that Britain had let us down? Yes, yes absolutely ... The people of Australia in February and March of 1942 — they were devastated. That was Australia's lowest ebb of the war'. Penglase and Horner (eds), *When the War came to Australia*, p. 72.

[12] Letter, Wakehurst to Emrys-Evans, 16 February 1942, ADD. MS. 58243, Emrys-Evans Papers, BL.

[13] 'This Riddle, This Paradox, This England!', four-page leaflet by Australian Association of British Manufacturers, RC/1/56, Cross Papers, IWM.

[14] See CRS A1608, A.C. 45/1/1, NAA.

[15] 'The Shipping Situation', Memorandum by Chiefs of Staff, 13 February 1942, CAB 69/4, D.O. (42)16, PRO.

[16] Defence Committee (Operations) Minutes, 16 February 1942, CAB 69/4, D.O. (42)6, PRO.

[17] ibid.

[18] Cable No. 160, Dorman-Smith to Amery, 14 February 1942, 'Secret Telegrams of Sir R. Dorman-Smith', Photo. Eur. 11, IOL.

[19] Alanbrooke diary, 19 February 1942, in Danchev and Todman (eds), *War Diaries*, p. 231.

[20] The generals he sent off to Norway in 1940, to Greece in 1941 and to Java in 1942 would have had good grounds for disagreeing with Churchill's claim. Churchill, *The Second World War*, Vol. 4, p. 146.

[21] War Cabinet Conclusions, 16 February 1942, CAB 65/25, W.M. (42)21, PRO.

[22] Cable No. 241/2, Churchill to Roosevelt, 16 February 1942, VI/2, Ismay Papers, KC; Cable, Casey to External Affairs Department, 17 February 1942, *DAFP*, Vol. 5, Doc. 340.

[23] Cable P44, Page to Curtin, 18 February 1942, CRS M103, '1942', NAA; Page, *Truant Surgeon*, p. 332; Cable, Bruce to Curtin, 18 February 1942, *DAFP*, Vol. 5, Doc. 344; Cables No. 177, 180 and one unnumbered, Dorman-Smith to Amery, 18 and 19 February 1942, 'Secret Telegrams of Sir R. Dorman-Smith', Photo. Eur. 11, IOL.

[24] Menzies had written earlier to Curtin stressing the importance of holding the Burma Road, while at the same time urging that Australian forces should concentrate on a 'Continental defence' in northern Australia rather than in the NEI. Menzies had finally embraced the policy of local defence that Curtin had been propounding for years. As Curtin observed in his reply to Menzies, the conservative leader's 'evolution of opinion towards a policy which has long since been advocated by me, not without some opposition, is not without interest'. Letter (copy), Menzies to Curtin, 14 February 1942, and Letter (copy), Curtin to Menzies, 16 February 1942, MS 4936/31/497/8a, Menzies Papers, NLA; Cables, Curtin to Page, 18 and 19 February 1942, *DAFP*, Vol. 5, Docs 343 and 345; War Cabinet Minutes, 18 and 19 February 1942, CRS A2673, Vol. X, Minutes 1896 and 1914, NAA.

[25] Cable, Cranborne to Curtin, 19 February 1942, and Cable P47, Page to Curtin, 19 February 1942, *DAFP*, Vol. 5, Docs 346–7.

[26] Cable, Curtin to Page, 20 February 1942, and Cable, Curtin to Blamey, 20 February 1942, *DAFP*, Vol. 5, Docs 348–9.

[27] Lloyd Ross, *John Curtin*, Sun Books, Melbourne, 1983, p. 260; Day, *John Curtin*, p. 454.

[28] Page had been finally prevailed upon to submit his government's view to Churchill, only to have Churchill respond with a fresh appeal from himself and Roosevelt to Curtin, carrying with it an implicit threat if Australia did not reverse its decision. See *DAFP*, Vol. 5, Docs 352–6.

[29] Day, *John Curtin*, pp. 449–50; Cable, Churchill to Curtin, 20 February 1942, *DAFP*, Vol. 5, Doc. 352.

[30] Cable, Churchill to Curtin, 20 February 1942, *DAFP*, Vol. 5, Doc. 352.

[31] Note, Ismay to Churchill, 23 February 1942 and Letter, Page to Churchill, 22 February 1942, PREM 3/63/4; Chiefs of Staff Committee Minutes, 18 February 1942, PREM 3/154/3, PRO.

[32] Horner, *Defence Supremo*, p. 137.

[33] *DAFP*, Vol. 5, Docs 353–6; Horner, *Inside the War Cabinet*, pp. 105–7.

[34] Cable, Curtin to Churchill, 22 February 1942, *DAFP*, Vol. 5, Doc. 357.

TWENTY-THREE

'there are very hard forfeits to pay'

It was Sunday morning, 22 February, when Churchill received word of Curtin's refusal to allow Australian troops to reinforce Burma.[1] By then, the ships had gone too far from their course to be rediverted towards Australia without first refuelling in Ceylon. This delay would increase the peril of their journey considerably. Churchill had overreached himself. As he later recalled, following the decision not to reinforce the NEI, he 'now sought only to save Burma and India'.[2] Churchill was so desperate to achieve this that he was willing to put Australian security at greater risk and use any methods at his disposal. As for Australia, Curtin's refusal to reinforce Burma was an implicit admission that he lacked faith in the Anglo–American undertakings to secure Australia and provided confirmation of the government's increasing emphasis on defence self-reliance.

After repeated refusals from Curtin, it might have been thought that Churchill would finally abandon the attempt to have the Australians go to Burma. However, apart from his obstinate desire to get the Australian division after he had sent, at Curtin's urging, the British division into Singapore, Churchill had been receiving mixed signals from the beginning about the likelihood of Australia agreeing to the request. Page and Bruce had both supported his scheme and had tried to pressure the Australian government from London. Now Cross advised from Canberra that it might still be possible to convince Curtin to change the government's stance. He confided to Churchill that although Curtin agreed with his war cabinet's decision, it had been made by his colleagues while he was in hospital. With an advisory war council meeting scheduled for 23 February, and with its conservative members 'hotly in support' of Churchill's proposal and some government members said to be 'wavering', Cross advised Churchill to have one last try.[3]

With Curtin's latest refusal, Churchill was forced to confess his unilateral diversion of the troopships. Rather disingenuously, he justified his high-handed action by claiming that he 'could not contemplate that you would refuse our request, and that of the President of the United States'. He advised Curtin that the ships would now have to call at Ceylon for refuelling. Bearing in mind Cross' secret advice about the possibility of Curtin's decision being reversed, Churchill suggested that the few days it would take to refuel the ships would allow 'the situation to develop, and for you to review the position should you wish to do so'.[4] Meanwhile, Dorman-Smith graphically reported from Rangoon the collapse of public order as panicked civilians fled the city in the face of Japanese bombing and the encircling Japanese army. Fires were raging, advised Dorman-Smith, 'and looting has begun on a considerable scale. City is as pathetic as it is smelly. Only 70 police remain and military too few to take real charge ...'[5]

In London, Page and Bruce had supported Churchill's attempt to divert the Australian troops but now were dismayed on learning of his unilateral diversion of the troopships and of his 'arrogant and offensive' message. They feared the reaction in Canberra and quickly counselled Curtin to avoid recriminations which would, Page warned, 'only do harm to our getting the maximum co-operative effort in the Allied cause'.[6] Curtin would not be calmed. Said to be 'greatly shocked', he agonised over his reply, at one stage disappearing from his office in parliament to walk around the surrounding hills. Returning, he angrily denounced Churchill's treatment of Australia and placed on Churchill the responsibility for the convoy's safety now that its exposure to possible Japanese attack had been unnecessarily heightened and prolonged. All of Australia's 'northern defences are gone or going', declared Curtin, and the government now had 'a primary obligation to save Australia not only for itself but to preserve it as a base for the development of the war against Japan'. As such, it was 'quite impossible to reverse a decision which we made with the utmost care and which we have affirmed and re-affirmed'.[7]

Evatt tried to ameliorate the inevitable resentment in London by explaining in a cable to Cripps the reasons for Australia's action. Denouncing what he described as Churchill's 'insolent' request, Evatt told Cripps that Australia's defences were

in such a state and are known to be such [by the Australian public] that any decision by our government to permit the A.I.F. to fight in Burma and India would cause upheaval. Rightly or wrongly the people feel that having given all the assistance possible to the Allied cause they have been let down badly by Churchill. Indeed his message hardly conceals his own disinclination to help us.[8]

It was not as if Australia was withdrawing all its forces home. At the same time as it was refusing to reinforce Burma, the Australian government was allowing air force personnel to leave for Canada to complete their training under the Empire Air Training Scheme. Once trained, they would join thousands of other Australian personnel who had been assigned to RAF squadrons for use against Germany.[9]

Ironically, just as Curtin was refusing to reinforce Burma, so too was Churchill. When the chiefs of staff proposed that 72 Hurricanes be taken from Russia's allotment and be sent to India and Burma instead, Churchill and Eden combined on 25 February to kill the idea. Nothing was to be taken from Russia in order to shore up the British position in Burma, even though the chiefs complained that the Russians did not seem to value the deliveries of the British aircraft. Indeed, three weeks later, Churchill proposed that fifteen RAF squadrons be sent from the Middle East as additional contributions to the Russian front when he discovered that Auchinleck planned to remain on the defensive in the Middle East for the following few months.[10]

Undeterred by Australia's repeated refusal to reinforce Burma, and angered by Curtin's criticism of his war leadership, Churchill drafted a defiant and angry riposte which blamed the predicament of the troopships on Curtin's delayed reply. Churchill not only accepted full responsibility for his action in diverting the ships, but threatened to defend it in public if it ever became possible. He also claimed that the danger to the convoy was not appreciably increased by the diversion, a claim that was disputed by Admiral Pound, who advised Churchill of the presence of Japanese submarines off Colombo where the convoy now was destined to refuel. Cooler heads than Churchill's prevailed and his draft was much toned down before it was dispatched to Curtin.[11]

Meanwhile, the situation in Rangoon developed much as Curtin had anticipated. Its evacuation was ordered by Dorman-Smith on 27 February, which would have caught the Australians in the process of unloading their ships had they proceeded on to Rangoon. Although the evacuation order was countermanded by Wavell, his resolve to defend Rangoon only delayed its evacuation for a week and nearly resulted in the loss of all the British forces, which barely managed to fight their way past the Japanese and begin their long march to safety in India.[12] Dorman-Smith later absolved the Australians of any responsibility for Rangoon's fall. Had they arrived there, conceded its governor, it is difficult to know 'what we'd have done with them. They might have been thrown in "from ship to Jap" — with disastrous results. They'd have died gallantly or would have been rounded up by the Japs, as so many of our own and Indian troops were.'[13] Churchill, though, was unrepentant and later justified his actions when he wrote his account of the war.[14] Page also stood by his support for the diversion of the troops, making the serious and unwarranted allegation in his memoirs that Australia's refusal to allow the troops to be used in Burma had the effect of condemning the Australian prisoners of war in Singapore to three and a half years of needless incarceration. In fact, had Curtin followed his advice, thousands more Australians would have been thrown into the hands of the Japanese.[15]

At the same time as Churchill was trying to send the Australians to Burma, Whitehall was conceding privately that Australia was 'insecure', predicting that Darwin and perhaps Perth would be overrun by the Japanese.[16] Churchill too thought that Australia was endangered, informing King George on 24 February that 'Burma, Ceylon, Calcutta and Madras in India and part of Australia may fall into enemy hands'. But that did not prevent him issuing orders that same day for Dutch naval units in Java to be evacuated to Ceylon rather than have them 'tucked away in Australia'.[17] In Churchill's view, the populated south-east corner of Australia was probably still secure from invasion.

The Australian chiefs of staff were also concentrating their attention on the south-east corner. On 4 February, the commander of the home forces, General Iven Mackay, urged the government not to send reinforcements out of the Brisbane–Adelaide–Melbourne triangle. This so-called 'Brisbane Line' effectively left the bulk of the Australian continent open to Japanese attack while concentrating the dominion's limited forces on the protection of the country's productive heartland. Despite criticism of the strategy then and since, it was the most sensible response to the desperate situation in which Australia found itself. As the British chiefs of staff later admitted, Japan had up to eleven divisions available for a possible invasion of Australia. Even with the concentration of its forces, Australia had only five divisions in the Brisbane–Adelaide–Melbourne triangle. With their paltry level of equipment, and lacking proper air support, the Australian defence forces had little chance of repelling such an invasion force.

Facing the possibility of this dire outcome, and after having fought so hard to prevent Australian troops being squandered in Burma, Curtin now found himself under pressure to leave many of those troops in Ceylon, where the troopships were refuelling and where a Japanese attack was anticipated. And the pressure originated from Australia's own representatives in London. When the British war cabinet met to consider Curtin's refusal to allow the troops to reinforce Rangoon, Page expressed his personal regret at the Australian decision and suggested that they be used instead to garrison Ceylon 'for the present'. Acknowledging that Churchill might find it difficult to propose such a plan so soon after the Burma dispute, Page offered to propose it himself 'provided that the chiefs of staff furnished him with an appreciation, which he could quote, setting out the importance of this course'. Despite advice from the chiefs that such a stay would last at least four to six weeks, Page persisted with his offer. Anticipating a hostile reaction from Canberra, the war cabinet insisted that Page make the suggestion on his own responsibility.[18]

While Page was concocting his scheme with the war cabinet, Bruce was busily cabling Curtin to prepare the ground for Page's proposal. According to Bruce, the security of Burma was 'important' but the retention of Ceylon was 'vital'. He conceded that Australia had its own defence deficiencies and that the returning AIF provided the most immediate source of reinforcement for the dominion. However, Bruce argued, self-reliance was not an option for Australia. Only with Anglo–American assistance and cooperation could Australia be protected from Japan. He claimed that such assistance would be increased by Australia adopting a compliant attitude on the use of its troops, there being a 'vast difference between the help given because of necessity and that afforded out of gratitude and good feeling'.[19]

Maybe so, but that did not explain why the massive contributions that Australia had made to Britain's war effort since 1939 had not produced any defence dividends for Australia in 1942, and certainly no sense of 'gratitude and good feeling' from the members of the British war cabinet. Bruce's argument had more force with regard to Washington, where Canberra expected a well of sympathy might exist from which it could draw. The Australian Labor politicians felt closer to Roosevelt's New Deal politics than to Churchill's conservatism and believed America's strategic interest lay more in the Pacific than the Atlantic. They blamed Churchill for focusing American attention on Europe, which they mistakenly believed was against Washington's natural inclination.

Duly briefed by the British chiefs of staff, Page cabled his own call for the retention of the 7th Division in Ceylon. Although the chiefs had stipulated that it would involve a stay of *at least* four to six weeks, Page suggested to Curtin that it would involve a stay of four to six weeks *at the most*. He also passed on a list of largely spurious reasons from the chiefs of staff as to why such retention would be in the Australian interest.[20] Curtin was aghast at this further evidence of Page according higher priority to the defence of British colonies than the defence of his own homeland. As he scathingly commented, 'there are numerous geographical centres where an A.I.F. or any other Division would be useful' but, from Australia's viewpoint, 'there is none east of Suez of greater importance than Australia'. After all the trouble over Burma, Curtin was under no illusions about the difficulty in getting the AIF back to Australia, which is why he was stressing the importance of its return for the dominion's defence and the importance of Australia as a base for a future offensive against Japan. Vainly, he instructed Page to 'press this most strenuously'.[21]

Evatt adopted a similar tone in a corresponding cable to Bruce, although he felt Bruce's culpability was mitigated by his long absence from Australia and his consequent ignorance of the Australian defence position. As for Page, Evatt confided to Bruce that he 'seems to have acted in (direct) opposition to his instructions and matters can hardly continue in this way'.[22] Evatt must have realised that both of Australia's representatives were equally culpable but perhaps intended by his cable to Bruce to drive a wedge between them in the hope that Bruce at least would heed his instructions. However, Bruce was unrepentant.

Rather than retreating on the question of retaining the AIF, Bruce simply approached the British government in an attempt to apply more pressure on Canberra. Realising that Churchill's word no longer carried much weight in Canberra, Bruce appealed to Attlee and Cripps to help convince their Labor counterparts in Canberra that there was a 'real appreciation [in London] of the defence of Australia as a great base in the Pacific'. According to Bruce, Britain needed to set out a 'definite plan for the reinforcement of Australia' which would allay Australia's anxiety and allow for its continued commitment to imperial defence.[23] Although no such plan was forthcoming, Bruce still went ahead to argue for the retention of Australian troops in Ceylon.

Citing the opinion of Cripps, Bruce cabled to Curtin on 27 February with the rather tenuous argument that Ceylon was 'not only essential to our whole position but was of the utmost importance in relation to the defence of Australia'. Cripps asked for the 7th Division to remain in Ceylon for 30 days, claiming that Australia would create thereby 'an atmosphere of goodwill towards her that would have a very real value in overcoming in the

United States the difficulties in the way of sending adequate assistance to Australia in men and equipment'. In fact, according to Wavell, now Britain's commander-in-chief in India, the defence of Ceylon could only be achieved by the commitment of naval and air units rather than by additional troops. Pouring in more troops 'to provide against large scale invasion', advised Wavell, 'would involve locking up troops which could be better used in offensive operations elsewhere'.[24]

Curtin was not advised of Wavell's view, which was directed to the British chiefs of staff, and he therefore could not use it to reject the pressure from Page and Bruce and their British allies. Instead, and despite the defiance of his latest cables, Curtin suddenly relented and agreed on 2 March to Australian troops being used to garrison Ceylon. However, it would not be troops of the 7th Division, some of whom were then in Ceylon, but two brigades of the 6th Division that were about to board ships in the Middle East for their return to Australia. Curtin's about-turn remains something of a puzzle. Perhaps he and his colleagues were anxious not to alienate Cripps, who was tipped to be a possible future prime minister.[25] Australia was also intent on nurturing its relationship with Roosevelt and feared the apparent influence that Churchill had over him. By agreeing to leave two brigades of the 6th Division in Ceylon, Australia at least was assured of obtaining the 7th Division immediately and the other brigade of the 6th Division. It might also reduce the total time the troops would be in Ceylon before the promised British reinforcements arrived to take their place. The government made its agreement conditional on the two brigades being 'escorted to Australia as soon as possible after their relief' and for the remaining 9th Division in the Middle East to be returned 'under proper escort as soon as possible'.[26]

Curtin was acting on the advice of the Australian chiefs of staff who claimed that the temporary retention of the troops in Ceylon would not expose Australia to undue risk since Japan would have to control both New Guinea and New Caledonia before it could invade Australia.[27] In proffering that advice to Curtin, the chiefs were acting on the assumption that the troops would be in Ceylon for four to six weeks, as promised by Page and Churchill, and that they would only remain until the British 70th Division could take their place. Unbeknown to the Australian chiefs of staff, as soon as Australian agreement was cabled to London, Churchill instructed his chiefs of staff to ensure that the two brigades of the 6th Division stayed in Ceylon for seven or eight weeks and that 'the shipping should be handled so as to make this convenient and almost inevitable'. At the same time, he cabled to Wavell offering two of the three brigades of the 70th Division for use in Burma or India, rather than have them relieve the Australians in Ceylon.[28]

In fact, it took six weeks for the Australian troops just to unload their equipment from the ships in Colombo's harbour, which had been deserted by its normal labour force.[29] Then the Australians became hostages to fortune, garrisoning an island with its important naval base at Trincomalee that they could not defend properly without strong air and naval forces. In fact, the commander of the Eastern fleet was instructed to retreat with his weak force back across the Indian Ocean in the face of any Japanese attack on Ceylon. The Admiralty told him in such circumstances to 'accept [the] possible loss of Ceylon' and thereby preserve his ships so they could 'defend our communications to [the] Middle East and India'.[30] Churchill ensured that the Australian troops remained there until mid-July, after the crucial battle of Midway put the Japanese navy on the defensive and effectively ended the threat of an invasion of Ceylon. Then they were loaded aboard a convoy of eleven troopships for the voyage to Australia, escorted by just one British cruiser and an armed merchant cruiser, which was an inadequate level of protection for such an important convoy, with battleship cover usually being provided in such circumstances.[31] The two brigades did not arrive back in Australia until August 1942, which was too late for them to be used in the crucial battle for Port Moresby. Moreover, their absence had increased the Australian dependence on United States forces, while their use in Ceylon had failed to earn any discernible credit in London.

Indeed, the British antagonism towards Australia was only increased by a concomitant dispute over the use of its troops in Java. With Singapore's capture by the Japanese on 15 February, the Pacific war council in London had recommended that no more reinforcements be sent to the NEI where Wavell commanded a mixed force of Australian, Dutch and British troops. The forces already in place were instructed to remain and fight it out with the Japanese until they were overwhelmed.[32] But 3400 Australian troops of the 7th Division had been landed on Java on 19 February, despite Wavell having received the recommendations of the Pacific war council advising against such reinforcement. In contrast to Curtin's forceful stand against the reinforcement of Burma, and despite contrary advice from Australian commanders on the spot, the Australian government allowed Wavell as supreme commander to determine the fate of this force.

Only after they had been landed and their capture seemed certain did the Australian government insist on 21 February that all the AIF, including those on Java, should be returned to Australia. Armed with the recommendations of the Pacific war council, Wavell refused to comply. At the same time, he busily organised the evacuation of his own staff from the island, the fall of which would signal the end of his short-lived command of the theatre. His deputy, General Pownall, blasted the Australians for their 'damnable attitude' in demanding a similar withdrawal for their recently landed troops. He wrote in his diary of the Australians having been

shown up in their true colours. Not so much the troops and commanders themselves ... as their Government, actuated presumably by a mixture of public opinion in Australia and common funk. Winston had little enough use for them before, especially after they demanded to be relieved at Tobruk, to everyone's great inconvenience. He'll be madder still now ...

Pownall had been in London during the dispute over Tobruk and now gave renewed vent to his anger, describing Australians as 'the most egotistical conceited people imaginable' who were 'so damned well pleased with themselves all the time, and so highly critical of everyone else ...'.[33] In the event, the Australians remained in Java, where they were captured by the Japanese after the island's surrender on 12 March.

By early March, after just three months of war with Japan, the invasion of Australia was being freely predicted. Observers in London mostly thought that such an invasion would be restricted to the relatively unpopulated northern and western portions of the Australian continent. Others were not so sure. On 8 March, the commander of Britain's Eastern fleet, Admiral

Somerville, was advised by his deputy, Vice Admiral Willis, that an attempted Japanese invasion of Australia 'must be expected' once the NEI and New Guinea had been mopped up. Willis expected that the total occupation of Australia would be completed once the initial invasion had been consolidated and sufficient Japanese forces had been amassed for the purpose.[34] His view was shared by the Australian chiefs of staff, who predicted on 9 March that the Japanese timetable would include an attempt to capture Port Moresby in mid-March, Darwin in early April, followed closely by New Caledonia and, some time in May, an attack upon the east coast of Australia.[35]

This timetable of Japanese ambitions was not something to which Churchill could afford to give any credence. Both his political position and his strategic priorities depended on a more limited view of Japanese capabilities. So he was concerned when his own chiefs of staff put forward a gloomy view of British prospects in the war against Japan and he tried unsuccessfully to prevent it going to the dominions. The chiefs held out little hope of immediate relief in the Pacific and admitted that Australia was 'insecure' and dependent on the United States for reinforcements. It was important to Churchill that the dominions be kept in the dark on the present pessimistic position in the hope that a 'very different picture and mood may be with us in a couple of months'. His own view of the situation was probably best summed up in a cable to Roosevelt on 5 March when he confided that it was 'not easy to assign limits to the Japanese aggression. All can be retrieved in 1943 or 1944, but meanwhile there are very hard forfeits to pay.'[36] It should not have been surprising in London, although it seems to have been, that Australia might not want to be one of those 'forfeits'.[37]

It was ironic that Australia's first major battle after the loss of Singapore should have been a battle of words with Britain over Burma. By its resolute determination to resist the diversion of Australian troops to Burma, the government had struck a blow for self-reliance. But the troops were not all home. The 6th and 7th Divisions were scattered across the Indian Ocean in poorly protected convoys from Suez to Fremantle, while the 9th Division remained in Palestine and the 8th Division was imprisoned in Singapore.

Most of the 6th Division was destined to be off-loaded in Ceylon, when they would have been better employed defending their homeland. Despite Washington accepting the strategic responsibility for Australia's defence, the first US division had still not arrived and the supply of aircraft and munitions remained insufficient to forestall or repel the expected invasion. The devastation of Darwin and the capture of Rabaul suggested that such an invasion might not be far off.

NOTES

[1] Curtin also informed Roosevelt of his decision, claiming that Australia would not be sufficiently defended without the troops and reminding him that Australia only had a small population which occupied 'the only white man's territory south of the equator'. *DAFP*, Vol. 5, Docs 357–9.

[2] Churchill, *The Second World War*, Vol. 4, p. 128.

[3] Cable No. 160, Cross to Dominions Office, 21 February 1942, PREM 3/63/4, PRO.

[4] Cable, Churchill to Curtin, 22 February 1942, *DAFP*, Vol. 5, Doc. 362.

[5] Cable, Dorman-Smith to Amery, 22 February 1942, 'Secret Telegrams of Sir R. Dorman-Smith', Photo. Eur. 11, IOL.

[6] Cable, Page to Curtin, 22 February 1942, and Cable, Bruce to Curtin, 23 February 1942, *DAFP*, Vol. 5, Docs 364–5.

[7] Cable, Curtin to Churchill, *DAFP*, Vol. 5, Doc. 366; Horner, *Defence Supremo*, p. 138.

[8] Cable, Evatt to Cripps, 22 February 1942, *DAFP*, Vol. 5, Doc. 360.

[9] See CRS A5954, Box 236, NAA.

[10] War Cabinet Conclusions/Confidential Annex, 25 February 1942, CAB 65/29, W.M. (42)24, PRO; Gilbert, *Road to Victory*, p. 76; Cable No. 66094, Churchill to Wavell, 23 January 1942, PREM 3/154/1, PRO.

[11] Draft and final copy of cable, Churchill to Curtin, 23 February 1942, PREM 3/63/4, NAA.

[12] Cables No. 104 and 105, Dorman-Smith to Amery, 27 February 1942, 'Secret Telegrams of Dorman-Smith', Photo. Eur. 11, IOL.

[13] 'Australian War History', undated note by Dorman-Smith, MSS. Euro. E.215/1, Dorman-Smith Papers, IOL.

[14] Churchill, *The Second World War*, Vol. 4, pp. 136–48.

[15] Page, *Truant Surgeon*, pp. 341–2.

[16] 'Far East Appreciation', Report by the Chiefs of Staff, 21 February 1942, CAB 66/22, W.P. (42)94, PRO.

[17] King George VI diary, 24 February 1942, cited in Gilbert, *Road to Victory*, pp. 66–7; Minute, Pound to Churchill, 24 February 1942, PREM 3/163/8, PRO.

[18] War Cabinet Conclusions/Confidential Annex, 23 February 1942, CAB 65/29, W.M. (42)23, PRO.

[19] Cable, Bruce to Curtin, 23 February 1942, *DAFP*, Vol. 5, Doc. 369.

[20] Cable, Page to Curtin, 24 February 1942, *DAFP*, Vol. 5, Doc. 372.

[21] Cable, Curtin to Page, 25 February 1942, *DAFP*, Vol. 5, Doc. 374.

[22] Cable, Evatt to Bruce, [rec'd] 25 February 1942, *DAFP*, Vol. 5, Doc. 375.

[23] Talk with Attlee, 26 February 1942, *DAFP*, Vol. 5, Doc. 377.

[24] Cable, Bruce to Curtin, 27 February 1942, *DAFP*, Vol. 5, Doc. 382; Cable No. 4231/G, Wavell to Chiefs of Staff, 28 February 1942, PREM 3/154/2, PRO.

[25] Lord Milne confided to General Brooke over dinner on 19 March that he thought 'Winston is drawing near unto his end and that he won't last much longer as PM. Predicts that Stafford Cripps will succeed him soon.' Alanbrooke diary, 19 March 1942, in Danchev and Todman (eds), *War Diaries*, p. 240.

[26] Cable, Curtin to Churchill, 2 March 1942, *DAFP*, Vol. 5, Doc. 385.

[27] 'Defence of Ceylon', Report by the Chiefs of Staff, 28 February 1942, CRS A2670, 106/1942, NAA.

[28] Minute D.44/2, Churchill to Ismay, 4 March 1942, PREM 3/154/2, PRO; Cable No. 320/6, Churchill to Wavell, 4 March 1942, VI/2, Ismay Papers, KC.

[29] Cable India No. 10577/C, Wavell to Brooke, 30 April 1942, CAB 66/24, W.P. (42)184, PRO.

[30] Gill, *Royal Australian Navy 1939–1945*, Vol. 2, pp. 12–13; Roskill, *The War at Sea 1939–1945*, Vol. 2, p. 22; Cable No. 0288A, Admiralty to S.O. Force 'V', 18 March 1942, PREM 3/233/1–4, PRO.

[31] Gill, *Royal Australian Navy 1939–1945*, Vol. 2, p. 185.

[32] Cable, Page to Curtin, 18 February 1942, *DAFP*, Vol. 5, Doc. 341.

[33] Pownall diary, 25 February 1942, in Bond (ed.), *Chief of Staff*, Vol. 2, pp. 90–91; Horner, *High Command*, pp. 162–7.

[34] 'Policy and Strategy in the Eastern theatre', by Willis, 8 March 1942, WLLS 5/5, Willis Papers, CC.

[35] War Cabinet Agendum No. 143/1942, CRS A2670, 143/1942, NAA.

[36] Minute M.71/2, Churchill to Attlee, 4 March 1942, PREM 4/43B/2, PRO; Cable No. 323/2, Churchill to Roosevelt, 5 March 1942, VI/2, Ismay Papers, KC; Cable, UK Dominions Office to Cross, 2 March 1942, *DAFP*, Vol. 5, Doc. 386.

[37] Despite the bleak view of his chiefs of staff, Churchill steadfastly resisted pressure to have Russia relieve the Allied plight in the Pacific by attacking the Japanese flank. Cadogan diary, 1 March 1942, in Dilks (ed.), *The Diaries of Sir Alexander Cadogan*, p. 438.

TWENTY-FOUR

'the saviour of Australia'

The conflict with Churchill over the reinforcement of Burma left Curtin stressed and sleepless, with some observers fearing that he was headed for another breakdown. He was said to have spent one night praying with his religious-minded secretary, Fred McLaughlin, as the vulnerable troopships steamed across an area of Japanese-controlled ocean. On another occasion, the concerned clerk of the House of Representatives, Frank Green, came across Curtin late one night standing alone in the moonlit garden of the Lodge. Feeling personally responsible for the dangerous position of the troops, Curtin confessed to Green that he was unable to sleep 'while our transports are out in the Indian Ocean with the Jap submarines looking for them'. Only when the crowded ships had reached Fremantle, wrote one Labor MP, was Curtin 'released from great darkness and unhappiness'.[1] Not that Australia was secured from invasion by the safe arrival of one battle-hardened division.

The Japanese navy still held sway over the Pacific and much of the Indian Ocean. Although the United States had plunged into the war alongside Britain, it would be many months before it could provide much support for

Britain's floundering empire. During that time, there would be just one American cruiser stationed in Australian waters as a token of Washington's protection. The dominion's most potent defence would remain its distance and its size, with the island continent requiring a major invasion force if it was to be subdued and occupied. For this reason, an invasion of Australia had not been an initial Japanese aim, although its sequence of rapid victories, culminating in the capture of Singapore, caused them to include the isolation of Australia from the United States among their next objectives. Once that was done, the possibility of invasion and occupation could be reconsidered.

In London and Washington, the Allied strategy remained one of concentrating on the defeat of Germany while at the same time trying to set limits to the expansion of Japan. But everything seemed to be going wrong for the Allies. The battle of the Atlantic, on which ultimate success against Germany could depend, had turned against the Allies after the German U-boats changed their codes and thereby ended for a time Britain's ability to intercept their messages and learn their locations. As a result, the attacks on Allied shipping increased immediately and dramatically. On the Eastern front, the prospect of a massive German offensive being launched in the coming spring led Churchill to fear the possibility of Stalin making a separate peace with Hitler. To relieve the German pressure on Russia, British planners considered mounting raids or even heavier attacks and lodgments on the French coast. And in the Mediterranean, the British position in Malta seemed set to collapse under the weight of the Axis air attack, while the offensive in Libya, on which Churchill had staked so much, had been repelled by Rommel's tanks and artillery. Bruised and battered, both armies retired behind defensive lines to build up their strength for the decisive battle to come, while Churchill harried Auchinleck from London in his anxiety to see the clash of arms begin.

During those last two weeks of March 1942, General Brooke began for the first time to harbour 'a growing conviction that we are going to lose this war unless we control it very differently and fight it with more determination'. As he wrote in his diary, Britain had 'already lost a large proportion of the British empire' and it was 'on the high road to lose a great deal more of it!'.[2] It was against this gloomy background, and with no relief in sight for Australia, that Evatt left Sydney for Washington and London on 13 March, charged by Curtin with securing men and munitions from the Allies. In particular, Australia was anxious to obtain supplies of modern aircraft that would be capable of withstanding a Japanese attack in ways that had not been possible at either Darwin or Rabaul.

Unbeknown to Curtin and Evatt, the leaders of Britain and the United States had reconfirmed their earlier agreement to defeat Germany before taking the offensive against Japan. They had done so during the series of post-Pearl Harbor meetings in Washington between Churchill and Roosevelt and their military chiefs, known as the Arcadia conference, with the strategy being enshrined in a top secret document coded as 'W.W.I.', by which it was subsequently known. The terms of 'W.W.I.' were never made known to Australia. As a result, the Australian government was unaware that a formal agreement had been reached that committed the United States and Britain to fight just a holding war against Japan and that Australia's pleas for assistance would be answered strictly in accordance with the terms of that agreement.[3]

Despite this, it seems clear that Curtin and Evatt were aware that the weight of official Allied opinion favoured such a policy and that Australia would have to exert a supreme effort to ensure an adequate level of men and supplies to deal with the fast-approaching Japanese.[4] Although Churchill and Roosevelt kept Australia ignorant of the terms of 'W.W.I.', there were enough indications that a 'Germany first' policy was guiding strategic decisions in London and Washington. Churchill had informed Curtin on Christmas Day 1941 that the defeat of the German army was the 'dominant military factor in the world war at this moment',[5] while Curtin freely acknowledged in his reply that British naval priorities gave precedence to the Atlantic over the Indian Ocean.[6] At the same time, the world press was reporting the 'Germany first' policy as an accepted fact, although not in terms of a formal agreement. Picking up these stories, the Sydney *Daily Telegraph* reported that the 'British War Office still believe that the conflict in the Pacific is a minor segment of the main conflict in Europe'. From London, the *Times* reviewed Churchill's trip to Washington with the observation that the Allies had not been diverted by the 'crucial distractions of the Japanese war' and that 'victory means first and foremost the defeat of Germany'. According to the *Times*, there was 'complete unity of view upon the fundamental aim' in London, Washington and Moscow.[7]

If these indications were not sufficiently explicit, Churchill had informed the defence committee upon his return from Washington on 21 January that 'the Americans were completely in agreement with ourselves that the main enemy was Germany'. Page had attended this meeting but failed to report Churchill's comment to Canberra, perhaps because he overlooked its important implications for Australia's defence after being strenuously reassured by Churchill about the reinforcements for the Pacific. Churchill also told him that the Allied strategy would 'not mean that the war in the South West Pacific would be allowed to languish'.[8]

While the Australian government remained ignorant of Churchill's comment, a public statement in Washington by the US navy secretary, Frank Knox, that Hitler must be defeated first should have alerted Australia to the substance of the Allied strategy. However, it seems that Curtin and Evatt viewed the statement by Knox as just a broadside in a continuing war between Allied planners. They remained convinced that the policy was not fixed and that Australia still could press for changes to decisions concerning the south-west Pacific. Casey helped to confirm this impression when he passed on an assurance from Knox that 'there would be no slackening of American effort in relation to [the] war against Japan'.[9] It was on the assumption of there being a continuing strategic debate that Evatt left Sydney to argue the Australian case for urgent assistance to meet the threat from Japan.

According to the assessment by the Australian chiefs of staff, Japan could be expected to launch an invasion of Australia's east coast in about eight weeks' time. There was little to prevent them from succeeding. The British position had collapsed with the capture of Singapore, and the American position in the Philippines had become untenable. The Japanese were occupying the islands of the Netherlands East Indies from where their aircraft were laying waste to Australia's northern defences. Little American assistance had yet arrived in Australia, and General Douglas MacArthur had not yet made his dash to Darwin when Evatt flew out of Sydney on 13 March. With Australia's future looking grim, Evatt was acutely conscious that time was at a premium. His urgent message for Churchill and Roosevelt was for the maximum assistance necessary to prevent a Japanese invasion. And he was prepared to confront his desperate fear of flying to ensure that the message was heard.[10]

The portents for the success of Evatt's mission were not good. On the day of his departure, Churchill had received an intelligence report of Japanese troop movements which, according to Churchill's interpretation, indicated that an 'immediate full scale invasion of Australia' was 'very unlikely'.[11] Although his chiefs of staff seemed to share his assessment, they conceded that the evidence on which it was based was 'scanty and in some cases lacks confirmation'. For good reason, the Australian government could not be so sanguine about the prospects for their country and an imminent invasion continued to be widely expected. Even General MacArthur, who had arrived on 17 March, considered that an invasion of Australia would be a strategic 'blunder' by the Japanese, although he conceded that they 'might try to overrun Australia in order to demonstrate their superiority over the white races'.[12]

Whatever the conflicting views and the value of the evidence on which they were based, there was no prospect of Britain changing its priority for the war against Japan, particularly in view of the imminent renewal of the German offensive against Russia. It was essential to Churchill that Russia be kept fighting for the many months that it would take the United States to organise and deliver its overwhelming might against Germany. This meant that the supply of war materials to the Soviet Union had to proceed without interruption and that there remained no question of enticing it into the Pacific war. Previously, Curtin had suggested that the Allies should offer secretly to recognise Russia's 1941 borders as a means of bringing it into the Pacific war. Invoking the moral principles of the Atlantic Charter, Churchill had stoutly resisted these suggestions that would have threatened his grand strategy.

Now, with the possibility of Stalin concluding a separate peace with Hitler, Churchill suggested to Roosevelt that the Allies should recognise

Russia's 1941 borders, arguing that the 'principles of the Atlantic Charter ought not to be construed so as to deny Russia the frontiers she occupied when Germany attacked her'. What had been morally unthinkable as a means of drawing Russia into the Pacific war became a sensible expedient to keep Russia in the European war. Although Roosevelt baulked at this suggestion, Churchill did ensure that Stalin received other encouragement in the form of uninterrupted war supplies and the resumption of the British air offensive against Germany. Both moves would severely limit the amount of assistance that theoretically was available for the war against Japan.[13]

Although the full scope of Japan's territorial ambitions remained unclear, Britain made little attempt to assuage the Australian fears of invasion or to guard against it happening. Among other things, there was an underlying feeling in Whitehall that Australia did not deserve being made secure against invasion. Australia's reputation had been practically destroyed in the minds of Britain's military and political leadership after the defeat of Australian troops in Greece and Crete and the drawn-out dispute over the relief of the Australians in Tobruk. Following Pearl Harbor, there was a feeling in London that Australia was squealing unreasonably for help and that its involvement in Britain's war effort was too hedged with conditions. The fall of Singapore confirmed Britain's worst fears about the reliability of Australia as an ally. It was Australian troops who had failed to keep the Japanese from crossing onto Singapore Island; it was Australian troops who were reported to have fled the fighting and forced their way onto evacuation ships; it was the Australian commander who had left his troops and then damned the British for Singapore's loss; and it was the Australian government that had forced Churchill, against his better judgment, to send the 18th Division into Singapore.[14]

Singapore had vied with India as the symbol of Britain's imperial strength, and the circumstances of its fall continued for months and even years to be an underlying source of grievance against Australia.[15] For reasons of wartime solidarity and, in the postwar period, to protect the Anglo–Australian relationship, the full depth of British anger towards Australia was never revealed. Churchill ensured there would not be a public inquiry into the causes of the disaster, for which he knew his own policies to be the ultimate cause. He prevented the publication of General Bennett's critical comments and, when his official report of the Malayan campaign was sent to London, Churchill pronounced it unfit for publication.[16] Churchill privately declared that Singapore's capture was the 'most shameful moment of his life', although he singled out the Australians as being primarily responsible.[17] It all contributed to British impatience with Australian requests for reinforcements. As Oliver Harvey observed from the Foreign Office, Australia was 'soft and narrow' and had 'screamed for help from the Americans, making it quite clear that they think us broken reeds'.[18] It did not bode well for the success of Evatt's trip.

Curtin had told Churchill that Evatt was being sent to Washington and London so that the Australian government's case could be put 'by a Minister who is fully familiar with its present problems and views thereon'.[19] Churchill regarded Evatt as a prime cause of the bitter disputes that had erupted between Britain and Australia and he was determined to prevent Evatt from achieving any modification of the 'Germany first' policy during his forthcoming talks in Washington. This may well have been Churchill's primary motivation in dropping a political bombshell on the eve of Evatt's departure from Sydney, proposing that the Australian minister in Washington, Richard Casey, be appointed as British minister in the Middle East, with a seat in the British war cabinet.

Until now, Casey, along with Bruce and Page in London, had accepted the dictates of the 'Germany first' strategy and played down the urgency of Australia's position. Casey saw his role as being to act in tandem with the British ambassador, and regarded the close cooperation of the British countries as being of prime importance. Page had a similar view, later recalling how he was 'prepared to stake everything to keep the Empire intact' and complaining that Curtin and Evatt had tried to obtain assistance from Washington without regard for the future consequence to the empire of wartime cooperation with the United States.[20] In attempting to be helpful to Britain, Page had ignored his government's request for the return of the 9th Division from the Middle East, suggesting to Churchill that it be retained while its place in Australia was taken by untested American troops.[21] Page also opposed Australia's defence becoming the strategic responsibility of the

United States. There seemed to be no recognition by Page that the interests of Australia and the empire, or Australia and Britain, might be capable of conflict.

Although Casey, like Bruce and Page, supported the 'Germany first' policy, he was more concerned than his colleagues in London with the security of Australia. He was critical of the planned reinforcement of the Far East and had exchanged harsh words with Churchill during the latter's visit to Washington.[22] With the strategic control of the Pacific war shifting to Washington, Casey's role could be crucial in Australia's efforts to secure greater assistance from the Americans, particularly if Casey could be stirred by Evatt into using his American contacts and influence more for Australia's benefit than for Britain's. By taking Casey from Washington, Churchill would leave Australia without effective representation in the American capital. The appointment, with its seat in the war cabinet, would also go some way towards satisfying those domestic critics of Churchill who had been demanding greater dominion involvement in imperial decision making as well as the call by Canberra for an Australian to be made a permanent member of the war cabinet.[23] For all these reasons, Casey was perfect for Churchill's purposes and he was determined to have him despite attempts by Curtin to prevent the appointment.

Curtin's initial reaction was to refuse permission for Churchill to approach Casey, asking that he not make the request 'at this juncture' in view of the value to Australia of Casey's contacts in Washington and the difficulty of finding a suitable replacement.[24] But Churchill had been trying to fill the Middle East post for nearly four weeks and he remained under great political pressure in Westminster. Moreover, his standing within the country had slipped for the first time since his taking over as prime minister, while the press were becoming openly critical of his leadership. As Churchill later shamefully admitted, the forced changes to his war cabinet were a 'concession or rather submission to Press criticism and public opinion'. While 'certainly not my Finest Hour', wrote Churchill, he claimed in retrospect to have been 'strong enough to spit in all their faces'.[25]

Despite this retrospective bravado, the political pressure was real enough and had to be appeased. Immediately rejecting Curtin's objections, Churchill pressed his case even harder. Citing the support of his colleagues, the chiefs of staff and Casey's own desire for a change of post, Churchill claimed that the appointment 'strikes the note of bringing Statesmen from all over the Empire to the highest direction of affairs'. Taken aback by the news of Casey's wish to leave Washington, Curtin agreed to Churchill offering him the appointment, asking only that Casey remain long enough to meet with Evatt and brief him on the American situation.[26] Accordingly, Churchill made his offer of the Cairo post to Casey, informing him that Curtin was 'very sorry to lose your services' but 'interposes no bar'.[27] This was technically correct. Curtin was not going to demand that Casey remain in Washington if he did not want to be there. But this did not mean that he was happy with Churchill using Casey to fill the Cairo post. Curtin would leave it to Casey's better instincts to refuse the offer and not place the Australian government in the predicament of having to find a replacement. However, after consulting with Roosevelt and the British ambassador, Lord Halifax, Casey accepted Churchill's offer, telling Curtin that they, along with top US officials, had unanimously urged him to accept the appointment and, subject to Curtin's agreement, he would do so. Casey assured Curtin that his 'judgment, as an Australian, is of great moment to me in what is for me a decision of great importance'.[28] If the relatively young Casey retained hopes of one day resuming his political career in Australia, it was important that he could not later be accused of deserting his post during such a vital time for the dominion. Curtin was not about to ease his path to Cairo.

Far from giving his agreement, Curtin set out the 'great difficulty and embarrassment' that Casey would cause to Australia. Not only would it be difficult to find a replacement, but Australia would be put at a 'serious disadvantage' if it lost the many contacts Casey had made in the United States and the 'familiarity which you have acquired as Minister with the many urgent and weighty matters now current in our relationship with the United States'. Although Curtin again left the final decision to Casey's better judgment, he obviously hoped that his arguments would cause Casey to reconsider.[29] Which Casey might have done, had Evatt not arrived in Washington and encouraged him to go. Evatt believed that Casey had not pushed sufficiently the views of the Australian government and that anyway the appointment of MacArthur would reduce the importance of the Washington post. He believed that Curtin would now only have to communicate Australia's needs to MacArthur, who would then pass them on to Washington.

Armed with Evatt's support, and apparently oblivious of Evatt's jaundiced view of him, Casey told Curtin that his appointment to Cairo would not cause Australia's interests to suffer. Taking up Evatt's point, Casey claimed that the 'Australian cause is now so bound up with the American cause ... that our interests are their interests and MacArthur's representations as to our Australian needs will be a much stronger voice in all matters of importance.' Everything considered, he proposed to accept.[30] So much for the weight he promised to place on Curtin's judgment.

Casey's decision should have been the end of the matter. But the question had been dragging on for six days and Churchill was anxious to announce the appointment to his critics in the House of Commons. Never overly particular about the courtesies due to a dominion, Churchill made the announcement as soon as he heard that Casey proposed to accept but before the proper formality of Casey's resignation from Australia's service had been concluded. To compound the insult, Curtin heard the announcement from a BBC news bulletin that was broadcast before he had received Casey's cabled notification. Curtin was furious and was only just persuaded not to publicly blast Churchill over the incident, although he did reveal that his government had opposed the appointment.[31] This was sufficient to ignite a chain reaction of explosive cables that blew the issue into a very public dispute between Curtin and Churchill, both of whom rightly felt aggrieved.

Churchill believed that he had Curtin's agreement to the appointment, however reluctant it may have been. On the other hand, Curtin obviously had hopes of retaining Casey's services but found his hopes dashed by Churchill's precipitate announcement, which had left him with no opportunity to make a fresh and more direct appeal to Casey. Casey then joined in the fray on Churchill's side, supplying London with copies of the cables passing between himself and Curtin. This led to Curtin and Churchill publishing their versions of the dispute along with the transcript of the cables passing between the Allied capitals. Roosevelt became embroiled when it was disclosed that he had advised Casey to accept the British post. The dispute could not have come at a worse time for Evatt, who found that the spat overshadowed the purpose of his desperate mission. And it made it more difficult for him to obtain a reasonable hearing in Washington or London. In the latter capital, official opinion was firmly against Curtin, with officials believing that he was 'behaving deplorably' and engaging in a 'childish fit of temper'.[32]

Churchill tried to use the dispute to neutralise Evatt's six-week mission in Washington. In a cable of explanation to Roosevelt on 23 March, he blamed the unseemly bickering on 'Australian party politics, which proceed with much bitterness and jealousy, regardless of national danger'. Having just survived his own political crisis in the House of Commons, this was a bit rich. But Churchill pressed on, telling Roosevelt that Evatt was an Australian politician who had made his way in politics by 'showing hostility to Great Britain'. With Evatt now pursuing his mission in Washington, Churchill asked Roosevelt for his 'personal impressions of Evatt and how you get on with him'.[33] He also advised his ambassador in Washington, Lord Halifax, to keep in close touch with Evatt, warning that he was 'reputed to be one of the least friendly of the Australian Ministers, and most eager to throw himself into the arms of the United States'.[34] The irony was that Evatt had made strenuous efforts to support Casey's appointment to Cairo and had earned Casey's thanks for the 'friendliness and personal help' extended during the time prior to the latter's departure for London. In return, Casey promised to 'prepare the ground for [Evatt] with Churchill and the others'.[35]

Churchill was right to be wary of Evatt, who quickly staked out a challenge to the 'Germany first' policy by pressing Britain to make a substantial sacrifice for the sake of securing Australia against invasion. On 23 March, he warned Bruce of the effect on imperial solidarity caused by the 'continuous rowing over unfortunate things and attempt to hector over more important things'. Evatt urged that Britain should make a dramatic gesture towards Australia in order to regenerate the previous warmth of their relationship. Pulling out his shopping list, Evatt then asked Bruce to request the immediate delivery to Australia of six weeks' worth of Britain's allocation from United States war production: aircraft, tanks, guns, the lot.

This, he claimed, would make Churchill 'the saviour of Australia'. Evatt also asked for the return of the 9th Division, Australia's last remaining troops in the Middle East, as previously agreed.[36] Churchill was not going to agree to make Evatt's dramatic gesture. Nor was he prepared any longer to release the 9th Division.

On 11 March, Churchill suggested to Curtin that Australia accept an extra American division in exchange for leaving the 9th Division in the Middle East. Citing support from Roosevelt, he argued that it would economise on shipping, with the Allies being hard-pressed to cope with the increased sinkings by U-boats and the effect on shipping of the American entry into the war. Acceptance of the American division would also, Churchill argued, increase the United States stake in Australia and thereby 'emphasize to the United States the importance of protecting that area by its main sea power and also of accelerating the equipment of existing Australian forces'. There was some sense in these arguments but they paid little heed to Australia's national sensitivities and ignored the dominion's loss of faith in Britain's good intentions. In addition, it was not a simple swap of divisions: the 9th Division was much more valuable to Australia, being fully trained and battle-hardened and, if returned to Australia, it would be fighting for its homeland. If it was left in the Middle East, it would continue to drain Australia of reinforcement troops which would have to be sent to replace losses.[37]

In agreeing to the retention in Ceylon of the two brigades from the 6th Division, Australia had tried to establish a clear understanding with Churchill that such retention would be conditional on the prompt return of the 9th Division. Now Churchill not only called for retention of the 9th, but also implied that a refusal from Canberra would lengthen the stay of the brigades in Ceylon. Australia once again felt betrayed, and not without cause. It might have sparked another angry dispute had Churchill's cable not been closely followed by the secret arrival in Australia of General Douglas MacArthur. With his army in the Philippines fighting a doomed battle against the Japanese, MacArthur had been ordered by Roosevelt to abandon his command and make the risky journey to Australia where he would take charge of the Allied effort in a newly created South West Pacific Area command. At Roosevelt's urging, this most theatrical of generals was promptly nominated by Curtin as its supreme commander, with control over all Australian forces. Although Australians would comprise the majority of MacArthur's forces for about a year, with only about 25 000 Americans being based in Australia at the time of his arrival, the symbolism of his presence in Australia was priceless.

NOTES

1. Day, *John Curtin*, p. 457.
2. Alanbrooke diary, 31 March 1942, in Danchev and Todman (eds), *War Diaries*, p. 243.
3. For a discussion of these points, see Day, 'H. V. Evatt and the "Beat Hitler First" Strategy: Scheming Politician or an Innocent Abroad', *Historical Studies*, October 1987.
4. Cable No. 1079, Evatt to Casey, 16 December 1941, CRS A3300, Item 100, NAA.
5. Cable, Churchill to Curtin, 25 December 1941, CRS A3300, Item 101, NAA.
6. Cable No. 166, Curtin to Casey, 29 December 1941, to be passed on to Churchill in Washington, CRS A3300, Item 101, NAA.
7. Cable No. 402, Curtin to Bruce, 16 January 1942, CRS M100, 'January 1942', NAA; *Times*, London, 19 January 1942.
8. Defence Committee (Operations) Minutes, 21 January 1942, CAB 69/4, D.O. (42)4, PRO.
9. Cable No. 119, Casey to External Affairs Department, 20 January 1942, CRS A3300, Item 219, NAA; See also Cable No. 11, Evatt to Casey, 25 January 1942, CRS A3300, Item 219, NAA.
10. The Australian businessman, W. S. Robinson, who accompanied Evatt, described how the nervous minister reacted to turbulent weather on one section of the flight by not only donning his life jacket but inflating it and, during a visit to the toilet, 'found himself wedged in the door — it took the steward and I to release him'. Letter, W. S. Robinson to L. B. Robinson, 1 November 1950, 'L. B. Robinson 1946–1956 (Personal and General)' Folder, W. S. Robinson Papers, UMA; See also Letter, Evatt to his wife, undated but probably 1942 or 1943, 'Evatt — Family Correspondence, M. A. S. Evatt to Evatt' Folder, Evatt Collection, FUL.
11. Gilbert, *Road to Victory*, p. 74.
12. Joint Intelligence Committee Appreciation, 14 March 1942, REDW 2/8/22 and 29, Edwards Papers, CC; Advisory War Council Minutes, 26 March 1942, CRS A2682, Vol. 4, Minute 869, NAA; See also 'Appreciation of the Defence of New Zealand 25th March 1942', 71/19/4, Parry Papers, IWM; Memoirs of Lord Wakehurst, Chap. 18, pp. 6–7, Wakehurst Papers, HLRO; Letter, Wakehurst to Emrys-Evans, 6 April 1942, ADD. MS. 58263, and Letter, Cross to Emrys-Evans, 26 April 1942, ADD. MS. 58243, Emrys-Evans Papers, BL.
13. Gilbert, *Road to Victory*, pp. 73–7.
14. Day, 'Anzacs on the Run: The View from Whitehall, 1941–2'; War Cabinet Minute No. 1931, 2 March 1942, CRS A5954, Box 264, NAA; Cable SC1, Evatt to Eggleston, 26 February 1942, 'External Affairs — Far East — Cables — 1942–45', Evatt Papers, FUL; Nicolson diary, 24 and 27 February 1942, in Nicolson, *Diaries and Letters*, Vol. 2, pp. 213–14; Edwards diary, 5 March 1942, REDW 1/4/40, Edwards Papers, CC; Letter, Rear Admiral Boyd to Admiral Cunningham, 14 March 1942, ADD. MS. 52570, Cunningham Papers, BL.
15. Two months after Singapore's fall, the Conservative MP wrote in his diary of the events going 'round and round in the head like some horrible obsession'. Nicolson diary, 10 April 1942, in Nicolson, *Diaries and Letters*, p. 221.
16. Presumably, the British ban was because of Bennett's criticism of the Indian troops and of the British military leadership. Ironically, his report also contained implicit admissions of wholesale desertions by Australian troops. War Cabinet Conclusions, 16, 18 and 30 March, 6 April 1942, CAB 65/25, W.M. (42)34, 35 and 38 and CAB 65/26, W.M. (42)42, PRO; See also CRS A5954, Box 264, NAA.
17. 'Notes for History', Talk with Air Marshal Richard Peck, 21 March 1942, by Liddell Hart, 11/1942/20, Liddell Hart Papers, KC; King diary, 23 March 1942, in King, *With Malice Toward None*, p. 170; Nicolson diary, 26 March 1942, in Nicolson, *Diaries and Letters*, p. 221.

18 Harvey diary, 21 March 1942, see also diary entry for 16 April 1942, ADD. MS. 56398, Harvey Papers, BL.

19 Letter, Curtin to Evatt, 11 March 1942, and Cable Johcu 24, Curtin to Churchill, 13 March 1942, CRS A5954, Box 474, NAA.

20 Page, *Truant Surgeon*, p. 356.

21 Churchill willingly grasped this suggestion and thrust it upon Curtin. Talk with Cripps, 5 March 1942, and Cable SL 4, Evatt to Bruce, 8 March 1942, CRS M100, 'March 1942', NAA; War Cabinet Conclusions/Confidential Annex, 9 March 1942, CAB 65/29, W.M. (42)32, PRO; Cable No. 359/2, Churchill to Curtin, 10 March 1942, VI/2, Ismay Papers, KC.

22 Casey diary 4, 6 and 18 January 1942, in Casey, *Personal Experience*, pp. 83, 86; Letter, Casey to Evatt, 17 January 1942, CRS A1608, D.41/1/5, NAA; Cable, Curtin to Churchill (rec'd) 13 March 1942, *DAFP*, Vol. 5, Doc. 409.

23 Churchill had already gone some way towards appeasing those critics who wanted him to appoint a defence minister by instead appointing Attlee as deputy prime minister, while also making him dominions secretary in place of Lord Cranborne, thereby bringing the dominions post within the war cabinet. Cable, Churchill to Curtin, 12 March 1942, *DAFP*, Vol. 5, Doc. 406; Cadogan diary, 5 March 1942, in Dilks (ed.), *The Diaries of Sir Alexander Cadogan*, p. 440; Day, *Menzies and Churchill at War*, Chap. 15; Day, 'An Undiplomatic Incident: S. M. Bruce and the Moves to Curb Churchill, February 1942'; Channon diary, 20 February 1942, in James (ed.), *Chips*, p. 322; King diary, 25 February 1942, in King, *With Malice Toward None*, p. 160; Harvey diary, 27 February 1942, ADD. MS. 56398, Harvey Papers, BL; Dalton diary, 5 March 1942, I/26/93, Dalton Papers, LSE.

24 Cable, Curtin to Churchill, (rec'd) 13 March 1942, *DAFP*, Vol. 5, Doc. 409.

25 Talk by Bruce with Eden, 19 March 1942, CRS M100, 'March 1942', NAA; Harvey diary, 16 and 20 February, 3, 9 and 14 March 1942, ADD. MS. 56398, Harvey Papers, BL; 'Notes 1942', Paper by Churchill, 12 July 1949, II/2/165, Ismay Papers, KC.

26 Not only was Churchill attempting to take one of Australia's representatives, but he also suggested who might be appointed in Casey's place, proposing that Menzies could fill the position in Washington. This was not motivated by a desire to see Australia have an effective representative there but by a desire to neutralise the continuing political threat posed by Menzies, who still was trying to secure his transfer to Westminster. See PREM 4/50/15, PRO; *DAFP*, Vol. 5, Docs 412–3.

27 Cable, Churchill to Casey, 14 March 1942, VI/2, Ismay Papers, KC.

28 Cable, Casey to Curtin, 15 March 1942, *DAFP*, Vol. 5, Doc. 414.

29 Cable, Curtin to Casey, 17 March 1942, *DAFP*, Vol. 5, Doc. 416.

30 Cable, Casey to Curtin, 19 March 1942, *DAFP*, Vol. 5, Doc. 423.

31 See *DAFP*, Vol. 5, Docs 426–7.

32 Harvey diary, 21 March 1942, ADD. MS. 56398, Harvey Papers, BL; Casey, *Personal Experience*, pp. 94–6; Cables No. 436/2 and No. 461/2, Churchill to Curtin, 21 and 23 March 1942, VI/2, Ismay Papers, KC; Cadogan diary, 23 March 1942, in Dilks (ed.), *The Diaries of Sir Alexander Cadogan*, p. 442; War Cabinet Conclusions, 23 March 1942, CAB 65/25, W.M. (42)36, PRO; Cabinet Minutes, 24 March 1942, CRS A2703, Vol. 1[C], NAA; *DAFP*, Vol. 5, Docs 431, 433, 435, 437 and 449.

33 Cable No. 458/2, Churchill to Roosevelt, 23 March 1942, VI/2, Ismay Papers, KC.

34 Cable No. 437/2, Churchill to Halifax, 21 March 1942, VI/2, Ismay Papers, KC.

35 Letter, Casey to Evatt, 2 April 1942, 'Evatt — Overseas Trip — 1942 — Correspondence', Evatt Papers, FUL; Dalton diary, 22 April 1942, I/26/145, Dalton Papers, LSE.

36 Cable No. 39, Evatt to Bruce, 23 March 1942, CRS M100, 'March 1942', NAA.

37 Cable, Curtin to Evatt, 20 March 1942, *DAFP*, Vol. 5, Doc. 428.

TWENTY-FIVE

'prepare to take the offensive'

With MacArthur's self-designed uniform dripping with gold braid, and his publicity people projecting his image across the newspapers and cinema screens of the United States, the strutting general was made to appear larger than life. Which was why he was selected by Roosevelt to take charge in Australia. MacArthur's presence alone would provide an image of American activity in the south-west Pacific that would conceal the relative paucity of the forces being sent to fight under his command.[1] And his rhetorical skills were put to good effect, helping to calm the Australian nervousness about invasion and instilling some confidence about the prospect for American reinforcements. As MacArthur declared to welcoming MPs in Canberra's parliamentary dining room on 26 March 1942, his presence was 'tangible evidence' of the 'indescribable consanguinity of race' between the two countries, proclaiming that he had come 'as a soldier in a great crusade' and pledging to the assembled diners 'all the resources of all the mighty power of my country and all the blood of my countrymen'.[2] They could ask for nothing more.

Evatt was quick to seize on MacArthur's appointment as a means of gaining additional leverage in Washington. Conscious of the public support in America for taking strong action against Japan, and of MacArthur's heroic public profile as the 'Lion of Luzon', Evatt urged Curtin to ensure that MacArthur made the strongest possible appeals for reinforcements. As Evatt confided, 'the [American] public would condemn the United States Government unless MacArthur is sufficiently supported'.[3] Evatt also made a renewed demand for the return of the 9th Division after Roosevelt made clear that the commitment of US troops was not conditional on Australia retaining the 9th Division in the Middle East as Churchill had claimed. Then, in an apparent change of heart, Evatt suggested to Churchill that Australia would leave the division in the Middle East in return for a British or American armoured division being sent to Australia. When this offer was rejected, Evatt went back to urging Curtin to press Churchill for the recall of the 9th Division, only to be rebuffed again by Churchill, who was determined to hang on to the division for as long as he could.[4]

Apart from trying to extract the 9th Division from Churchill's grasp, Evatt also renewed his call for Britain to increase the flow of munitions to Australia. Holding out the spectre of a full-scale Japanese invasion, Evatt pleaded for Churchill to make 'some immediate sacrifice ... to protect two of His Majesty's Dominions from violation by the enemy'. If Britain made a moderate contribution now, argued Evatt, it could prevent an invasion altogether and thereby save Britain from having to make a much heavier contribution once an invasion had occurred. Evatt also asked Bruce to approach any other British ministers who might be sympathetic to Australia's plight.[5] The problem was that Bruce was not all that sympathetic. He was not convinced that Australia was in danger of invasion nor that it warranted a large diversion of resources that would otherwise go to the European theatre. In fact, on 8 April Bruce privately raised with Eden the idea of Britain abandoning the Indian Ocean to the Japanese and opening a second front against Hitler in Europe.[6] Such a second front in 1942 would have consumed such a large proportion of Allied resources that the Pacific war would have been ceded almost by default to the Japanese.

Bruce's main concern was not the security of Australia but the growing rift in Anglo–Australian relations and the possible implications of this for the future of the British empire. Accordingly, when he met with Churchill on

31 March his priorities were not those of Evatt. He had already given copies of Evatt's cables to Churchill, not just the gist of them as Evatt had instructed, and he now used them to urge Churchill to improve the atmosphere of Anglo–Australian relations. He did not raise Evatt's request for six weeks' allocation of Britain's supplies from America, nor did he ask for British fighter planes. Instead, Bruce merely suggested that Churchill seize Evatt's proffered hand of friendship and put an end to the ceaseless disputes. Bruce admitted that some of the Australian cables had been 'somewhat ill-advised and certainly irritating' but asked him to make allowance for the inexperience of the Labor ministers and the circumstances in which they found themselves. Disinterring Churchill's promise of August 1940 to defend Australia if it was seriously invaded, Bruce suggested that Churchill resuscitate this commitment and provide a renewed undertaking to divert British divisions en route to the Middle East and India if Australia was invaded on a large scale.[7]

As it happened, Churchill had already made such a promise to Curtin on 17 March in response to the appointment of MacArthur. At that time he had been anxious to assure Curtin that MacArthur's arrival would not mean that Britain no longer felt any responsibility for Australia. So he restated the British government's

determination and duty to come to your aid to the best of their ability, and if you are actually invaded in force ... we shall do our utmost to divert British troops and British ships rounding the Cape, or already in the Indian Ocean, to your succour, albeit at the expense of India and the Middle East.[8]

Now he seized upon Bruce's suggestion with alacrity and proceeded to invest his recent promise to Curtin with more precision so that it might placate Evatt and limit the possibility of the promise being called upon.

Churchill promised Evatt that he would divert to Australia the two British divisions then rounding the Cape of Good Hope if Australia was invaded by at least eight Japanese divisions. This was three more than the Japanese had used to capture Malaya and Singapore and two more than British intelligence chiefs considered likely for a Japanese invasion of Australia.

Moreover, the dispatch of two divisions of British troops would hardly be sufficient to expel the Japanese, nor would they be likely to be able to break through the Japanese naval supremacy that such an invasion would entail. It was another questionable promise made to secure continued Australian contributions to Britain's war effort. Churchill also advised that removing the 9th Division would be a 'mistake' and that Australia could not have the six weeks' production of munitions that Evatt had requested. He claimed that he had denuded the Mediterranean of its heavy warships and carriers and had already amassed a 'respectable' naval force in the Indian Ocean. He assured Evatt that Britain had Australia's interests at heart, and that 'not a day passes when we do not think of Australia'.[9] This was certainly true, although not in the sense that Churchill was trying to convey. As for the much-vaunted Eastern fleet, it looked much better on paper than in reality.

Although the Eastern fleet had the responsibility for defending the west coast of Australia, it did not have the means to do so. As the returning Australian troops discovered, the weak and ill-balanced fleet could not even provide adequate escorts for convoys. Churchill was more honest with Roosevelt, admitting that the fleet was 'to a great extent [composed] of old ships with short-range guns', these being the four *Royal Sovereign* battleships that Churchill had earlier dismissed as floating coffins. Such was the weakness of the fleet that its commander's main weapon was deception, keeping the Japanese guessing as to its location and strength.[10] When the Japanese called the British bluff and sent a powerful Japanese fleet steaming towards Ceylon in early April, the British were forced to scurry back to the east African coast where the fleet sheltered in the relative safety of Mombasa harbour. Several British ships were not so fortunate and were quickly sunk when the Japanese chanced upon them in the Bay of Bengal. They included two cruisers, one small aircraft carrier and two destroyers. As one of the naval officers wrote at the time, the Japanese fleet could 'polish us off in a matter of minutes'.[11] The Admiralty was determined that would not happen, although it meant keeping their ships well out of harm's way and consequently well away from Australia. As Vice Admiral Willis observed, the strategic withdrawal of the Eastern fleet 'concedes control of the Bay of Bengal to the enemy, uncovers Ceylon and increases the threat to India'.[12]

Although the Japanese ships withdrew back to Singapore, Japan now effectively ruled the waves of both the Indian and Pacific Oceans.

The Japanese naval incursion caused panic and dismay in London, where General Brooke worried in his diary on 7 April that the empire 'has never been in such a precarious position throughout its history!'. He hoped for a Dunkirk-like miracle and wondered 'how we are to keep going through 1942!'.[13] Brooke and his fellow chiefs of staff retracted previous undertakings to supply Australia with aircraft. The promised delivery of 125 Kittyhawks had been increased to 205 aircraft, of which none had yet been delivered. The additional 80 planes were now subtracted from the commitment and diverted instead to the Middle East. At the same time, the chiefs decided that India had 'prior claim' to British Vengeance dive-bombers requested by Australia and awaiting shipment from US factories. This decision meant that India would receive three-quarters of the production, with the remainder going to Australia. Churchill agreed to the change despite a warning from General Ismay that the Australian reaction was 'likely to be violent'.[14]

At sea, Britain responded to the humiliation of its Eastern fleet in the Indian Ocean by seeking United States naval action in the Pacific Ocean to draw the Japanese away. Despite the increasing danger to its interests there, the Far East still remained low on the list of British priorities. It was mainly the shipping route along the east African coast that Churchill was concerned to defend. It was vital for supplying British forces in the Middle East and India, for the shipping of oil from the Arabian Gulf and for supplying munitions to Russia by way of Iran.[15] The Eastern fleet was kept in its weakened state, thereby allowing India, Ceylon and Western Australia to remain exposed to Japanese attack. With Britain also having lost control of the air, Brooke privately conceded that India's defence was now a 'gloomy prospect'.[16] From his new headquarters in Delhi, Wavell was as frantic as the Australian government about the situation. He was advised by the Eastern fleet's commander, Admiral Somerville, that he could not expect any naval assistance to resist a Japanese attack against India before June 1942 at the earliest. Meanwhile, Somerville continued his strategy of subterfuge, intending to 'remain at sea as much as possible and use unfrequented anchorages in order to make the Japanese uncertain of my movements' and thereby 'deter them from attempting any interference with our Middle East and Indian communications, except with a heavy Fleet concentration'.[17]

Just as Britain was faced with demands to reinforce the Eastern fleet, a competing demand arose that left no doubt about the place of the Far East in British priorities. The island of Malta was under heavy air attack and desperately needed supplies to avert disaster. Churchill's planned solution was to send a fast, heavily protected convoy through the Suez Canal and across the hazardous waters of the Eastern Mediterranean to Britain's embattled fortress. On 22 April, the defence committee approved this plan, intending to use much of Admiral Somerville's Eastern fleet for the task in the knowledge that it could well involve 'paying forfeits' in the Indian Ocean. Although the plan was never implemented, it was, as Britain's official naval historian later noted, 'important historically' for revealing the 'lengths to which the British Government was prepared to go to save Malta' and, in contrast, the risks it was still prepared to run in the Far East despite the rush of Japanese successes.[18]

The Malta plan caused dismay in Delhi, with Wavell warning the British war cabinet of the 'very grave risks' being taken with the defence of Ceylon and India. Like Australia, India had sent its best troops to fight for Britain in the Middle East and now clamoured for their return. Wavell confided that he had 'so far been able to resist this and to do something to maintain [the] sinking Indian morale by assurances that H[is] M[ajesty's] G[overnment] are determined to give every possible assistance to [the] defence of India'. He warned that he could not 'honourably continue to give these assurances if reinforcements for India are constantly diverted or deferred like this'.[19] Even without the diversion of naval forces to Malta, the situation remained grave. As one officer with the Eastern fleet noted at the end of April, the 'whole of the Indian Ocean [was] open to attack if the Japanese should move strong forces this way and India and Ceylon [where two brigades of Australian troops provided much of the garrison] are completely and absolutely undefended'.[20]

Churchill ensured that the Indian Ocean would remain in that state when he refused Wavell's request for naval assistance. He claimed as justification the need to retain sufficient naval forces in British home waters, noting the maxim that the 'first duty of any Government is to its own country'.[21] If India could be left undefended by the Royal Navy, it was not surprising to find that successive Australian requests for British naval assistance during March and April were similarly refused by Churchill.[22] Despite his refusal to provide Australia with practical insurance against invasion, Churchill's renewed pledge to rush to Australia's defence in the event of such an invasion gave 'great satisfaction' to Evatt.[23] The mercurial external affairs minister was getting even greater encouragement from the Americans, with Evatt taking heart from MacArthur's directive from the chiefs of staff which instructed MacArthur to 'hold the key military regions of Australia as bases for future offensive action against Japan' and to 'prepare to take the offensive'.[24]

Evatt seems hardly to have noticed that MacArthur's directive could be interpreted in different ways, and that it could involve the United States fighting a holding war in the Pacific for the immediate future. Instead, he seized on the apparent US commitment to defend Australia's key military regions, and the commitment to take the offensive against Japan, and called for MacArthur to be given the means to achieve those purposes. With his legal background, Evatt seems to have regarded the directive as being akin to a contract and he set about ensuring that its provisions were enforced. In a memorandum to Roosevelt on 5 April, Evatt called for munitions to be allocated on a theatre rather than a government basis, claiming that the relative importance of the Pacific theatre had not yet been assessed.[25] How wrong he was.

Not that Evatt was unaware of the danger to Australia posed by the European theatre staking a claim on US war resources. He warned Curtin on 6 April about an impending visit to London by the US army chief, General George Marshall, who was off to discuss with his British counterparts the prospects for a second front in Europe. This idea of a second front in 1942 had originally been raised in Washington by Churchill as a ploy to retain the US commitment to Europe and prevent any backsliding by US military chiefs wanting to push against Japan after the humiliation of Pearl Harbor. Evatt correctly recognised Marshall's visit as a threat to his own attempts to boost Allied activity in the Pacific, although it was still in terms of a continuing debate in which, Evatt urged, Curtin should make his views known to Churchill before a commitment was made.[26]

The proposal to invade Europe had never been a viable option for 1942. During Marshall's meetings with Churchill and the chiefs of staff, the plan was deferred until 1943 and replaced by the more realistic objective, and the one preferred by the British all along, of capturing north Africa. At a defence committee meeting on 14 April, Churchill reported with satisfaction the Anglo–American agreement to mount the north African operation, which would continue their 'concentration against the main enemy'. Although it would ensure that no major diversion of forces was possible for the war against Japan, Churchill did stipulate that India and the Middle East must be safeguarded and that Australia must not be completely captured or isolated from America. However, the US representatives made clear that, while they would discharge their obligations to Australia, their 'whole heart would be fully engaged' in the struggle against Germany. Marshall assured Churchill that he had made 'careful calculations' of Australia's requirements and would provide them, but he 'did not want to divert further forces to these places'.[27] Churchill had been concerned that the scrapping of the invasion plan for Europe might turn the attention of the Americans towards the Pacific. So he was relieved to have Marshall's confirmation that the 'Germany first' policy remained firmly in place.

Despite his discussions in Washington, Evatt was still unaware of 'W.W.I.', the terms of which were determining the decisions of both Roosevelt and Churchill. He was aware, though, of the considerable pressure in Washington to concentrate on Germany and he did what he could to counter that pressure. During a brief visit to Canada on 9 April, Evatt publicly declared that the dramatic Japanese gains in the Pacific had 'transformed the entire strategy of the war'. Arguing for the 'interdependence of all the theatres of the war', Evatt contended that the Allies 'can't "beat Hitler first", or "beat Japan first". You've got to beat them both together.'[28] So certain was Evatt that his discussions in Washington had been successful that he reported to Curtin on 17 April that he had substantially achieved his purpose and would proceed to Britain on 22 April where he was hopeful of obtaining 'a number of high performance modern fighters'.[29] The following day, Evatt told Curtin triumphantly that the 'accepted position' in Washington accorded Australia a 'major place in the general strategic scheme' and that he had ensured that the allocation of equipment to Australia would 'accord with the strategical necessity so clearly shown' in MacArthur's directive. Evatt claimed that 'this broad line of approach has been acceptable both to the President and to the military and naval chiefs'.[30]

Curtin had dispatched Evatt to Washington to secure sufficient men and resources to repel the invasion that his military chiefs advised was imminent. Rather than accepting Evatt's confident assurances at face value, Curtin met with MacArthur on 20 April to get his assessment of Evatt's claims. It was two days since MacArthur had formally taken control of Allied forces in the South West Pacific Area and he was anxious to implement the terms of his directive. But he questioned how he was meant to prepare to take the offensive against Japan with the forces then under his command and those promised to him. Rather than accepting Evatt's optimistic assessment of Australia's position in the general strategic scheme, MacArthur and the Australian chiefs of staff compiled a list of resources that Washington would have to supply before he could give effect to his directive. With the backing of MacArthur, Blamey and the war cabinet, Curtin instructed Evatt to remain in Washington until he had received this military shopping list and had obtained from US authorities a definite program for its delivery. With the utmost reluctance, Evatt agreed to do so.[31]

With MacArthur firmly in charge, and the prospect of American assistance forthcoming, Curtin finally buckled under the British pressure and offered to allow the 9th Division to remain in the Middle East for the time being. At the same time, he made a rather half-hearted attempt to make his agreement conditional on the provision by Britain of naval and air reinforcements for Australia. Curtin's change of mind was probably motivated partly by the fear of what might happen to a troop convoy trying to cross the Indian Ocean in the present circumstances of Japanese naval superiority. He had been worried enough by the return of the previous convoys prior to the entry of the Japanese navy into the Indian Ocean.[32] If there were conditions attached to Curtin's agreement, Churchill tried not to notice them. At Bruce's suggestion, he simply thanked Curtin for the decision, claiming impudently that Curtin had 'always been and will be perfectly free to decide the movement of all your troops'.[33]

Australia would have to confront any invasion force with the strength that it had on hand. If such a force managed to get ashore on the Australian coastline, the Australian defence forces would be hard placed to dislodge them. At a meeting in Melbourne with state premiers on 23 April, Blamey conceded that the army was 'by no means ready to fight. The infantry was not much more than 50% equipped, we were very short of motor transport and had practically no tanks, though these were arriving. There was no non-divisional artillery and we were deficient in engineering and similar units.' But the premiers doubtless were encouraged by the braid-encrusted MacArthur, who predicted that the Japanese were unlikely to invade Australia, although he acknowledged that such an eventuality was not impossible.[34] If it did occur, the experience at Darwin did not bode well for the fortitude likely to be shown by ill-equipped Australian servicemen and panic-stricken civilians. Reinforcements of men and supplies were imperative if Australia was to be assured of remaining inviolate.

With Casey gone from Washington, it was Evatt's responsibility to ensure that Australia's needs were met. He was loath to stay and do so, probably because he was misled into believing that the terms of MacArthur's directive would dictate the level of supplies that would be sent to Australia. In his view, the only problems now were of an organisational nature and these were best left to officials to handle. As he informed Curtin on 23 April, any attempt by him to argue Australia's needs at meetings of the newly created Pacific war council only produced a free-for-all, with each representative competing to argue the needs of their particular country. According to Evatt, it had become a matter for Australia's military and supply officials to resolve along the lines of the overriding directive. He therefore asked to be released from the instruction to remain in Washington, claiming to have 'driven myself and my colleagues almost to a standstill in order to get the results we have obtained. MacArthur at your end and our officers here can now exploit these results.'[35]

In order that the Australian public should also learn of his supposed achievements, and Evatt reap the political benefit, he briefed an Australian reporter with this version of his visit. The correspondent, George Warnecke, cabled the Melbourne *Herald* on 28 April claiming that Evatt had ensured that 'Australia's strategic importance and political consequence have been realised', this recognition being embodied in MacArthur's directive. Openly acknowledging the resolve of the Arcadia conference to 'rate Hitler still as [the] chief enemy', Warnecke argued that the 'Evatt Roosevelt Parleys have resulted in drastic revision' of the Allied strategy, with America now 'binding herself to direct cooperation with Australia and other Pacific countries in an offensive policy against Japan'. Warnecke apparently submitted a draft of his cable to Evatt, with the draft describing the appointment of MacArthur and the terms of his directive as creating a 'formal bond between America and Australia'. In place of 'formal bond' was inserted, apparently by Evatt, the words 'binding formal agreement', which reflected his legalistic interpretation of MacArthur's directive. If, as it seems, this report was inspired and edited by Evatt, it reveals him to have been a rather naive actor on the international stage. He would soon have his illusions shattered.[36]

Indeed, four days before Warnecke sent off his approved version of Evatt's achievements, Bruce had cabled Evatt with disturbing news from London that should have alerted him to the likely futility of his task. He advised Evatt of his failure to obtain greater priority for Australia in the allocation of munitions from Britain, with the chiefs of staffs having rejected his request on strategical grounds. This decision could not be altered except 'by the intervention of the Prime Minister and the President'. Bruce told Evatt that he doubted, in the present instance, whether Australia's case was strong enough to warrant such intervention.[37] This should have indicated to Evatt that, despite the perilous situation in the south-west Pacific and the terms of MacArthur's directive, Australia remained a low priority and the Allies would be slow to give much practical effect to MacArthur's instructions. But Evatt either could not, or would not, acknowledge the failure of his mission. It was Curtin who confronted him with that reality.

On 28 April, the day that Warnecke sent his optimistic story from Washington, Curtin reported that MacArthur absolutely rejected Evatt's achievements in Washington as providing adequate resources for the fulfilment of his directive. He advised Evatt that MacArthur was 'bitterly disappointed with the meagre assistance', which was not only 'entirely inadequate to carry [out] the directive given him but [would] leave Australia as a base for operations in such a weak state that any major attack will gravely threaten the security of the Commonwealth'. Curtin instructed him to remain in Washington until MacArthur could be assured of receiving an adequate supply of forces. He also asked Evatt to get an appreciation from the combined chiefs of staff so that Australia could understand the 'general strategic basis governing [the] allotment [of] forces and equipment to various theatres'.[38] It seems that Curtin was still oblivious of 'W.W.I.', although he might have suspected that some such agreement must have existed in light of the relatively slender resources being allocated to MacArthur.

Rather than remaining in Washington, Evatt flew on to London where he arrived on 2 May. Before leaving the American capital, he had passed on copies of Curtin's cable to Roosevelt's close adviser, Harry Hopkins, asking that Roosevelt intervene to speed up the flow of supplies to Australia. But Evatt did not comply with Curtin's instruction to stay until this had been achieved. As Evatt blithely told Hopkins, the 'strategy for the area is absolutely fixed by the directive' and the 'question is merely one of assessing what is required to carry out this agreed strategy'.[39] After six weeks in Washington, Evatt had left with little to show for his time there. His attempts to ensure that Australia was secure from invasion had been in vain. He had encouraged Casey to take the Cairo post at a time when his services were more important in Washington. Evatt had helped to get the Pacific war council established by Roosevelt, but it had no executive powers and quickly degenerated into a forum for discussion rather than decision.[40] His greatest failure in Washington was in not discovering the existence of 'W.W.I.' and his persistent misreading of MacArthur's directive in a legalistic light. Evatt's refusal to ensure personally that its terms were fulfilled and his abrupt departure for London were not calculated to serve Australia's interests.

Curtin's instruction for Evatt to remain in Washington was sent in the context of a deteriorating security situation for Australia, with Churchill having acknowledged the loss of British naval control in the Indian Ocean and conceding that there was little prospect of it being regained in the near future. There was also no sign of the air and naval reinforcements requested from Britain in return for the retention of the 9th Division. Although American reinforcements were beginning to arrive, the equipment position remained poor. Of the 494 American aircraft in Australia on 26 April, only 237 were in a serviceable condition. Moreover, MacArthur advised that the US air force units in Australia required four months of intensive training before they could even be considered as 'effective first-line units'. Of the 210 tanks held by the Australian army, 80 were light two-man tanks diverted from delivery to the Dutch forces in the NEI. In these circumstances, and with nearly two divisions of the AIF still in British hands, Curtin requested that Churchill divert the two British divisions shortly due to round the Cape of Good Hope en route to India. Churchill had promised to divert them in the event of Australia being seriously invaded but, as Curtin had pointed out, in such an event there was little chance of reinforcement convoys being able to reach Australia.[41]

As they had done previously, British officials dismissed Curtin's appeal as an overreaction. Although some recognised that an invasion of the dominion figured among the various options open to the Japanese,[42] the more common feeling was much less sympathetic, refusing to admit the possibility of Australia falling within the ambit of Japanese territorial ambitions. Thus, the Japanese thrust through the Solomon Islands and New Guinea, which was designed to isolate Australia from American reinforcements, was seen in London as merely a diversionary thrust. As such, Curtin's appeals for assistance were dismissed as 'frightened squeals'.[43] Cranborne, now the colonial secretary, privately berated the Australians for assuming that Britain 'could protect them under all circumstances', an assumption that he had been instrumental in helping to foster. He regarded with considerable equanimity the consequent Australian anger at Britain's betrayal of its defence pledge. Cranborne acknowledged that Australians 'have suddenly to face unpleasant facts, and the process is very painful. But perhaps taking a long view, it is better that our relationship [should] be put on a realistic basis.'[44] With the Japanese assembling their forces in Rabaul for attacks on Port Moresby and the Solomons, it was rather late in the day for Britain to point out the small print on its defence guarantee for Australia.

As for Curtin's request for the two British divisions, this was immediately and forthrightly rejected by Churchill. He argued that the threat to India was greater than that to Australia and that Britain would 'certainly be judged to have acted wrongly if we sent to an uninvaded Australia troops needed for an invaded India'.[45] Not that India was any more invaded at that time than Australia. Churchill then moved swiftly to stop Curtin making any more such requests based on recommendations from MacArthur. The amplification that MacArthur provided for Australia's voice alarmed Churchill, who saw it as a threat that could undermine the Anglo–American commitment to the 'Germany first' policy. He quickly moved to silence it. In a pointed message to Roosevelt on 29 April, Churchill set out the details of MacArthur's recommendations and asked whether the publicity-conscious supreme commander had 'any authority from the United States for taking such a line'. Whether or not he had, wrote Churchill, Britain was 'quite unable to meet these new demands, which are none the less a cause of concern when put forward on General MacArthur's authority'.[46] Churchill's message had the desired effect, producing a strong rebuke from Washington for MacArthur and helping to mute Australia's voice once again.

On the day of Churchill's cable to Roosevelt, Britain's defence committee had reaffirmed its commitment to the 'Germany first' policy and, as a result, the overriding priority for Russia when deciding on the allocation of aircraft. Although Churchill expressed regret at the cost to British commitments elsewhere, he successfully argued that 'it was in our own vital interests to do so, as the Russians would shortly be engaged in mortal combat with our main enemy'.[47] Three days later, Evatt arrived in London with the aim of obtaining aircraft for Australia. Meanwhile, Australia's main enemy completed its preparations for the capture of Port Moresby. The next few weeks would be the most crucial in the dominion's modern history.

NOTES

[1] Roosevelt's military aide suggested that MacArthur's presence was 'worth five army corps'. Day, *John Curtin*, p. 463.

[2] Horner, *Inside the War Cabinet*, pp. 111–3.

[3] Cable PM2, Evatt to Curtin, 22 March 1942, CRS A5954, Box 474, NAA.

[4] Cable No. 39, Evatt to Bruce, 23 March 1942, CRS M100, 'March 1942'; 'Aide Memoire for discussion with Hon. Harry Hopkins', by Evatt, 24 March 1942, and Cable, Evatt to Curtin, 28 March 1942, CRS A3300, Folder 233; Advisory War Council Minutes, 8 April 1942, CRS A2682, Vol. 5, Minute 894; Cable PM14, Evatt to Curtin, 29 March 1942, and Cable 16, Curtin to Evatt, 1 April 1942, CRS A5954, Box 474; Minutes of Prime Minister's War Conference, 8 April 1942, CRS A5954, Box 1, NAA; Cable No. 508/2, Churchill to Evatt, 1 April 1942, VI/2, Ismay Papers, KC.

[5] Cable No. 44, Evatt to Bruce, 26 March 1942, CRS M100, 'March 1942', NAA.

6   Talk with Eden, 8 April 1942, CRS M100, 'April 1942', NAA.

7   Bruce composed such a conciliatory cable to Evatt from himself, sending a copy to Churchill, apparently as a guide for Churchill's own reply to Evatt. Talk with Churchill, 31 March 1942, CRS M100, 'March 1942'; Letter, Churchill to Bruce, 3 April 1942, CRS M100, 'April 1942', NAA; See also PREM 3/151/2, PRO.

8   Cable No. 401/2, Churchill to Curtin, 17 March 1942, VI/2, Ismay Papers, KC.

9   Cable No. S20, Evatt to Curtin, 2 April 1942, CRS A5954, Box 474, NAA; Joint Intelligence Sub-Committee Memorandum, 25 January 1942, PREM 3/151/4, PRO.

10   In the words of Vice Admiral Willis, the fleet had to practise 'strategical evasion with the object of preventing the enemy knowing precisely where it is for any length of time'. Cable No. 400/2, Churchill to Roosevelt, 17 March 1942, VI/2, Ismay Papers, KC; 'Policy and Strategy in the Eastern Theatre', Paper by Vice Admiral Willis, 8 March 1942, WLLS 5/5, Willis Papers, CC; Roskill, *The War at Sea*, Vol. 2, p. 23; Gill, *Royal Australian Navy 1939–1945*, Vol. 2, p. 4.

11   Edwards diary, 6–10 April 1942, REDW 2/7, Edwards Papers, CC; 'General Remarks', by Willis, undated, WLLS 5/5, CC; Roskill, *The War at Sea*, Vol. 2, p. 32.

12   Letter, Willis to Moore, 13 April 1942, WLLS 5/5, Willis Papers, CC; See also 'The Naval Situation in the Indian Ocean', Memorandum by Rear Admiral Tennant, 12 April 1942, TEN 25, Tennant Papers, NMM; Harvey diary, 9 April 1942, ADD. MS. 56398, Harvey Papers, BL.

13   Alanbrooke diary, 7 April 1942, in Danchev and Todman (eds), *War Diaries*, p. 245.

14   Minute, Chief of Air Staff to Churchill, 9 April 1942; Minute, Ismay to Churchill, 9 April 1942, PREM 3/150/9, PRO.

15   Cables No. 570/2 and 591/2, Churchill to Roosevelt, 15 and 19 April 1942, VI/2, Ismay Papers, KC; See also PREM 3/163/8, PRO.

16   Alanbrooke diary, 10 April 1942, in Danchev and Todman (eds), *War Diaries*, pp. 246–7.

17   Memorandum, Somerville to Wavell, 21 April 1942, SMVL 8/7, Somerville Papers, CC; See also PREM 3/142/2, PRO.

18   Roskill, *The War at Sea*, Vol. 2, p. 60; See also Cable No. 618/2, Churchill to Roosevelt, 24 April 1942, VI/2, Ismay Papers, KC.

19   'The Defence of India', Note by Bridges for War Cabinet, 1 May 1942, CAB 66/24, W.P. (42)184, PRO.

20   Edwards diary, 28–29 April 1942, REDW 2/7, Edwards Papers, CC.

21   Cables No. 660/2 and 661/2, Churchill to Wavell, 30 April 1942, VI/2, Ismay Papers, KC.

22   Cables No. 428/2, 546/2 and 658/2, Churchill to Curtin, 20 March, 5 and 30 April 1942, VI/2, Ismay Papers, KC.

23   Cable S20, Evatt to Curtin, 2 April 1942, CRS A5954, Box 474, NAA.

24   Cable, Evatt to Curtin, 3 April 1942, CRS A3300, Item 233, NAA.

25   Memorandum, Evatt to Roosevelt, 5 April 1942, CRS A3300, Item 233, NAA.

26   Cable, Evatt to Curtin, 6 April 1942, CRS A3300, Item 233, NAA.

27   Defence Committee (Operations) Minutes, 14 April 1942, CAB 69/4, D.O. (42)10, PRO.

28   'Speech for Canadian Club Luncheon, Chateau Laurier, Thursday, April 9th, 1 pm', 'War — Statements and Articles' Folder, Evatt Collection, FUL.

29   Cable, Evatt to Curtin, 17 April 1942, CRS A3300, Item 233, NAA.

30   Cable ES9, Evatt to Curtin, 18 April 1942, CRS A3300, Item 233, NAA.

31   Minutes of Prime Minister's War Conference, 20 April 1942, CRS A5954, Box 1; Cables No. 49 and 50, Curtin to Evatt, 20 and 21 April 1942; Cable ES12, Evatt to Curtin, 20 April 1942, CRS A5954, Box 474, NAA; See also *DAFP*, Vol. 5, Docs 468–70.

32   Cable No. 245, Curtin to Churchill, 14 April 1942, CRS A5954, Box 474, NAA.

33   Cable No. 571/2, Churchill to Curtin, 15 April 1942, VI/2, Ismay Papers, KC; Note, Attlee to Churchill, 15 April 1942, PREM 3/63/10, PRO.

34   Minutes of Prime Minister's War Conference, 23 April 1942, CRS A5954, Box 1, NAA.

35   Australia's senior diplomat in Washington, Alan Watt, noted the effect of Evatt's temperamental presence, with all senior officials being '*trodden on, discarded, not used*' by the difficult minister. Although Watt admitted the need to shake up Australia's supply organisation in Washington, he complained that 'other things have occurred which I can scarcely put on paper'. Letter, Watt to Hood, 16 April 1942, MS 3788/1/1, Watt Papers, NLA; Cable ES17 Part 1, Evatt to Curtin, 23 April 1942, CRS A5954, Box 229; Cable ES17 Part 2, Evatt to Curtin, 23 April 1942, CRS A5954, Box 474, NAA.

36 Cable (copy), Warnecke to *Herald*, 28 April 1942, 'Evatt — Overseas Trip — 1942', Evatt Collection, FUL.

37 Cable No. 48, Bruce to Evatt, 24 April 1942, CRS A3300, Item 233, NAA.

38 Cable SW34, Curtin to Evatt, 28 April 1942, CRS A3300, Item 233, NAA.

39 Letter, Evatt to Hopkins, 29 April 1942, CRS A3300, Item 233, NAA.

40 For a discussion of the Pacific war council in Washington and Australia's failure to maximise its value, see Warren Kimball, '"Merely a Facade?" Roosevelt and the Southwest Pacific', in David Day (ed.), *Brave New World: Dr H. V. Evatt and Australian foreign policy*, Brisbane, 1996, Chap. 2.

41 Advisory War Council Minute No. 914 (extract), 28 April 1942, CRS A5954, Box 229; War Cabinet Agendum No. 275/1942, CRS A2670, 275/1942; Advisory War Council Minutes, 28 April 1942, CRS A5954, Box 537; Minute, Shedden to Curtin, 2 May 1942, CRS A5954, Box 3, NAA; Cable, Curtin to Churchill, 17 April 1942, *DAFP*, Vol. 5, Doc. 467 and note 5, p. 720.

42 'The Problem of Allied Strategy for the Defeat of Japan', Paper by Captain French, undated, pp. 4, 11, GDFR 2/3, French Papers, CC.

43 Harvey diary, 30 April 1942, ADD. MS. 56398, Harvey Papers, BL.

44 Letter, Cranborne to Emrys-Evans, 25 April 1942, ADD. MS. 58243, Emrys-Evans Papers, BL.

45 Cable No. 658/2, Churchill to Curtin, 30 April 1942, VI/2, Ismay Papers, KC.

46 Cable No. 653/2, Churchill to Roosevelt, 29 April 1942, VI/2, Ismay Papers, KC.

47 Defence Committee (Operations) Minutes, 29 April 1942, CAB 69/4, D.O. (42)13, PRO.

TWENTY-SIX

'a thoroughly unpleasant type of individual'

On 2 May, Evatt flew into Britain with the determined intention of obtaining the forces and supplies that would secure Australia from invasion and occupation by the Japanese. Even as the crumple-suited external affairs minister alighted from his aircraft, the Japanese forces were moving steadily south along the jungle-clad and mountainous Solomon Islands in their bid to sever the sea and air route between Australia and the United States. At the same time, a Japanese armada, complete with a convoy of troopships, was preparing for a seaborne assault on Port Moresby. Although the Americans knew of the impending attacks and were preparing to resist them, their naval strength in the Pacific was insufficient to give them the necessary preponderance of power. On Australia's western flank, much of Britain's Eastern fleet was hugging the coast of Africa for fear of discovery by the Japanese. The Indian Ocean, which had been a British 'lake' for so long, was now effectively under the control of the Japanese.

Australia remained ill prepared to fend off any Japanese attack, with its army composed mainly of a numerically strong but poorly trained militia operating with rudimentary equipment. Of the four battle-hardened divisions of the AIF, only the 7th Division, together with a brigade of the 6th Division, had returned from overseas. Australian air and naval support were almost totally lacking, with the RAAF continuing to contribute aircrew for Britain's use under the Empire Air Training Scheme while almost half the Australian navy had been destroyed in the previous twelve months, mainly in the hopeless defence and evacuation of the NEI. American combat aircraft were beginning to arrive in Australia, but they were equipping the US forces rather than the RAAF and they were still far from constituting an adequate front-line air defence force. Although the seas surrounding Australia were almost devoid of Allied warships, Australia was busily following British Admiralty advice by preparing its harbours to berth the warships of the Eastern fleet. However, Australian eyes could see on the horizon only the smokestacks of the Japanese fleet.

Evatt's purpose in London was to secure Australia from invasion, but he now appeared less confident of his prospects and openly conceded the difficulty of getting Australia's voice heard in the Allied councils of power. As he observed shortly after his arrival in the bomb-damaged capital: 'Australia had very little if any share in the formulation and direction of the general policy of the war.'[1] And it would be some days before Evatt even discovered the agreed thrust of that general policy. As in Washington, Evatt seems to have operated under the mistaken assumption that the Allied strategic direction of the war remained at least a partially open question that was susceptible to Australian pressure. He was determined to boost the priority of the Pacific theatre in the plans of Allied defence chiefs. In an initial discussion with Bruce on 3 May, the high commissioner was surprised to find that Evatt was ignorant of Allied strategy and 'too inclined to think in terms of Australia only'.[2] As if Churchill was not inclined to think in terms of Britain only, or Roosevelt in terms of the United States. The surprising thing is that Bruce did not feel it incumbent upon him as Australian high commissioner to mirror Evatt's concern, or to alert Evatt to the settled nature of the 'Germany first' policy about which he appeared ignorant. Instead, Bruce was more concerned with smoothing over the recent difficulties in Anglo–Australian relations and preserving Australia as a loyal imperial partner. Bruce had already approached the cabinet secretary, Sir

Edward Bridges, to stress the importance of Churchill avoiding any row with Evatt. Although Bridges was sympathetic, he warned of possible difficulties due to the 'peculiarities of the Prime Minister'.[3]

After his meeting with Bruce on 3 May, Evatt went to Chequers to press Australia's case with Churchill, but without much success. It was obvious to Bruce that Evatt had still 'not got the whole picture too clearly in his head' and they agreed to 'have a serious couple of hours' conversation on these strategic problems before he made any move with regard to them'.[4] Bruce wanted Evatt to take a wider view of the war, rather than simply concentrating on Australia's defence. This wider view essentially meant viewing the war through British eyes. Before the two men could have their conversation, Evatt attended a meeting of the munitions assignment board where he launched an attack on the amount of supplies reaching Australia and called for greater priority for the Pacific in the Allied strategic plan.

Evatt had Bruce and four Australian service advisers alongside him when he confronted the board of British and American service representatives which was chaired by Britain's minister of production, Oliver Lyttelton. Confessing that he 'did not even know whether there was any strategic plan', Evatt questioned 'how strategy could be considered separately from supply'. In front of the board members, Bruce then pointed out to Evatt that strategy was not within the purview of this meeting, which was simply to allocate resources according to the master strategy that had been decided by the combined chiefs of staff. He then tried to divert Evatt into the sidetrack of deciding where the Australian demands should be put: London or Washington. But Evatt ploughed on, dismissing Bruce's argument as 'a matter of detail' and complaining instead that there 'seemed to be a gap between strategy and allocation'. Realising that he was not making any headway, Evatt abruptly quit the meeting, leaving Bruce to settle the minor matters being decided by the board.[5] In the wake of the meeting, Lyttelton warned Churchill that Evatt was 'considerably aggrieved' after having spent six weeks in Washington without discovering 'how the strategy of the war ... was conducted'. Lyttelton assured Churchill that he had continued to keep Evatt in the dark and 'did not, of course, enter into any discussions on the purely strategical points'.[6]

Evatt went straight from the munitions assignment board to a meeting of the British war cabinet where he asked for a 'reassessment of the general strategical situation' which, he predicted, might provide 'good grounds for strengthening the forces available for the defence of Australia'. In particular, Evatt pleaded for aircraft with which to beat off, or even deter, a Japanese attack. Evatt had held out to Curtin the prospect of him being able to achieve such a commitment of aircraft, which would provide a valuable addition to Australia's armoury and be a valuable political asset for Evatt. But Churchill merely reassured him as to Britain's continuing commitment to 'do all in our power to defend our kith and kin in Australia' and suggested that Evatt meet with the relevant officials to assure himself about the flow of supplies. At no point did Churchill enlighten Evatt about 'W.W.I.' or the consequent low priority accorded by the Allies to the Pacific theatre.[7] In the eyes of those around the war cabinet table, the demanding Evatt cut a poor figure, with one observer complaining that 'Evatt wasted a lot of our time' while Brooke thought him to be 'Not very attractive at first sight!'.[8] It might have been expected that Bruce would be more sympathetic towards Evatt, but he cynically believed Evatt was more concerned with securing a privy councillorship for himself than with anything else.[9] And he continued to keep him in the dark.

Still none the wiser about 'W.W.I.', Evatt attended a press conference the next day hosted by the minister of information and close confidant of Churchill, Brendan Bracken. When the journalists closely questioned Evatt about his attitude to Allied war strategy, asking whether he objected to 'the theory that the Pacific is a side show', Evatt pounced on this chance to argue his case. Relying on MacArthur's directive, he blissfully assured his audience that the Allied strategy does 'not contemplate concentration on one enemy' and there was 'great danger to the common cause in talking along the line, "Let us beat Hitler first"'. Pointing to MacArthur's directive, Evatt repeated his argument that it 'has been laid down, must be carried into effect, and will be carried into effect by providing him with the necessary supplies to carry out his mission'.[10]

Bracken seems to have been sufficiently alarmed by Evatt's outburst at the press conference to mount a determined effort to divert him from his campaign to safeguard Australia. Describing Evatt as 'a dreadful fellow' who 'drinks a good deal too much', Bracken later claimed to have 'dined with him at least 20 times to get him better educated on viewing the War from the point of view of the world and not the fruitless parochial angle of one Dominion alone'. Churchill also was heavily involved in this systematic attempt to make Evatt see the world through British eyes, although he too found this duty an onerous one. On one occasion at Chequers, Churchill reportedly took Bracken aside and appealed to him to take Evatt away, complaining that 'I simply can't *bear* this fellow.' Despite their distaste, the efforts of Bracken and Churchill met with some success. As a British intelligence operative later observed, they did

a great deal to educate and mellow this parochial, restless, rude, ambitious, indefatigable and by no means unintelligent creature whose brain and energy one cannot help respecting and to some extent liking, in spite of his drab appearance, dreary droning voice with its nazal [sic] whine, and his unattractive personality.[11]

For all his pugnacity, Evatt got no closer to discovering the existence of 'W.W.I.' during his London meetings. Instead, it was Curtin who first was alerted to it in distant Australia.

While Evatt was proclaiming the supposed Allied commitment embodied in MacArthur's directive, MacArthur was finally concluding from the paucity of forces being committed to his charge that Roosevelt and Churchill must have come to an agreement to defeat Germany first. If so, he predicted that Evatt would be unable to change it. Whatever the rhetorical promises issuing from London and Washington, MacArthur was convinced that 'little assistance was to be afforded the Southwest Pacific Area'. Blaming Churchill for this, MacArthur claimed that 'the President and General Marshall were under the influence of Mr. Churchill's strategy'. He told Shedden that an officer recently arrived from the United States had reported that General Marshall, in referring to assistance to Australia, had said that if the Japanese overran the Commonwealth 'it would be just too bad. He could help the Australians no more than he could help MacArthur in the Philippines.'[12] In the face of this advice, MacArthur asked Marshall to specify the offensive action envisaged for the south-west Pacific and with what forces it was to be accomplished. He advised that the US forces arriving in Australia required several months' training before they would be ready to face the Japanese and that, although there were about 400 000 troops in Australia, the level of training, equipment and air and naval support left them incapable of withstanding a major attack. As a result, he urged Australia to demand the return of the 9th Division.[13]

After alerting the advisory war council of MacArthur's conclusions, the conservative MPs accepted that Australia would not be supplied with sufficient forces to mount an offensive against the Japanese and that its 'predominant concern' must be 'the security of Australia'. Armed with the unanimous support of MacArthur, Blamey and both sides of parliament, Curtin had the curious task of enlightening Evatt about the strategy that was being followed in the Allied capitals that he was visiting. He informed Evatt of MacArthur's scepticism about 'the degree of assistance that will be extended to the South West Pacific area' and about how 'it would be very difficult to get the President or Mr. Churchill to deviate from the view that all efforts have to be concentrated on knocking out Germany first'. In view of this, concluded Curtin, Australia's 'predominant consideration and objective' had to be its own security 'whether or not it is to be used as a base for offensive action'. He would advise Evatt of the forces necessary to achieve this more limited objective, although warning that imminent naval action by Japan might hinder any further reinforcement of Australia.[14]

Even after receiving Curtin's cable, Evatt continued to place his faith in the terms of MacArthur's directive. Although he agreed to press for the return of the 9th Division, he refused to scale down his demand that the Allies must find the means to carry out the directive in full. Far from reflecting the pessimism emanating from Australia, Evatt was positively optimistic, although he conceded that 'continual propaganda and persuasion' were needed in London to prevent the 'Pacific front from being regarded as a side show'. He ascribed this, not to an overriding Allied strategy, but to Anglo–American authorities who had 'grossly under-estimated Japan's strength' and who now found it difficult to accept their blunder and 'face up to the true position'. Nevertheless, Evatt claimed that the position had improved and he urged MacArthur to continue pressing for sufficient forces not only to 'successfully defend Australia' but 'to operate offensively within a reasonable time'. Describing this as MacArthur's 'present mandate', Evatt claimed that it was 'binding upon all the Governments concerned'. Evatt advised Curtin that he would be meeting with Churchill and the chiefs of staff to discuss the 'general strategy of war'.[15] Evatt's illusions would then be suddenly shattered.

In the meantime, from 5 to 8 May, American and Australian naval and air forces confronted a Japanese invasion force in the Coral Sea that was intent on capturing Port Moresby, the largest town in Australia's colony of New Guinea. Forewarned of the Japanese move by the deciphering of its communications, the United States was able to dispatch sufficient warships across the Pacific to pre-empt the Japanese strike. In a new type of naval warfare in which the two fleets never came within sight of each other, carrier aircraft searched the tropical seas for the opposing ships and attacked on sight. In this game of hide and seek, luck played a major part in the eventual outcome. Although the two fleets were evenly matched, the Allies' major loss was a fleet carrier compared to the loss of a light carrier by the Japanese. In fact, the Japanese retired from the battle confident that they had sunk two American carriers. The Japanese troopships had also managed to escape unscathed back to Rabaul. So it could be counted as a victory of sorts for the Japanese. However, the loss of the light carrier caused Japan to postpone its seaborne attack against Port Moresby, with subsequent events forcing Japan to abandon it altogether. Instead, an ill-fated landward attack would be launched later across the jungle-covered heights of the Owen Stanley mountains.

Although the battle of the Coral Sea represented a strategic defeat for Japan, and has since been celebrated as such, the powerful thrust at Port Moresby seemed at the time to confirm Australia's worst fears which were heightened by the scale of the Allied losses. At best, the battle was seen as providing a breathing space for Australia, with MacArthur warning Curtin that its forces had to be ready to repulse further attacks. He told Curtin that the US aircraft carriers which had stopped the Japanese fleet had since left

Australian waters, leaving just two cruisers to protect the continent. To be sure of repelling a further attack, MacArthur argued that Australia desperately needed aircraft, both seaborne and land-based, since no amount of troops would be sufficient 'if the enemy has superior naval and air power'.[16] From Washington, Roosevelt also warned that Australia faced the possibility of further Japanese attacks as part of its campaign to isolate the dominion from American assistance.[17] But Churchill remained determined to resist calls to secure Australia from such attacks, claiming that the Japanese were trying to force the Allies to 'lock up as many troops as possible in Australia'. Rather than reinforcing Australia, the build-up of the Eastern fleet was delayed even further, although Australia continued to remain ignorant of the fleet's weakened state.[18]

While the battle of the Coral Sea was being fought, Evatt was trying to make sense of the British response to his appeals for reinforcements. With a possible invasion of Australia just weeks away, Evatt seemed genuinely puzzled by Britain's reluctance to send help to fend it off. Suspecting the worst, he suggested to Curtin that Britain had effectively wiped its hands of Australia after transferring the strategic responsibility for the Pacific to the United States and now regarded the defence of India as its 'primary interest' in that war. Indeed, Evatt claimed that Britain was prepared to put Australia at risk in order to ensure that the Japanese were kept out of India. He warned Curtin that there was 'reason to believe that one of the objectives of the concentration of [British] aircraft carriers in the Indian Ocean is to force the Japanese to operate on the Pacific side of Singapore', which 'immediately adds to the danger of Australia'. Despite his suspicions, Evatt took comfort from the restatement by Churchill of his promise to divert the two British divisions rounding the cape if Australia was 'heavily invaded' and to 'throw everything possible into the defence of Australia preferring it to the defence of India'. It is difficult to understand how Evatt could attach any credibility to this promise. But he seems to have done so, also holding out to Curtin the possibility of Britain supplying Australia with additional aircraft and raising Australia's priority in the allocation of munitions.[19]

On 12 May, ten days after his arrival in London, Evatt was finally going to meet with the British chiefs of staff to discuss the strategy of the war. Bruce was concerned to learn from his military adviser, Brigadier Wardell, that the chiefs had prepared briefing papers for Evatt which had explicitly spelt out the 'Germany first' policy. Although he met with Evatt prior to the morning meeting, Bruce gave him no forewarning of what he was about to learn.[20] Had he done so, of course, it would have prompted Evatt to question why the high commissioner had been keeping him in the dark. So Bruce kept quiet.

Evatt was at his most demanding when he strode in to meet the chiefs, who had doubtless been briefed about Evatt's supposed anti-British proclivities. Brooke had not been impressed by his first meeting with Evatt some days before and his impressions were not improved by this meeting. Brooke considered him to be 'a thoroughly unpleasant type of individual with no outlook beyond the shores of Australia'. British officials could not comprehend how Australian ministers were less than enthusiastic about putting their country at risk for the greater good. Brooke complained in his diary that Evatt had

produced 3 strong blackmail cards and then asked for greater allocation of aircraft from America to Australia. In fact, if we did not ensure that MacArthur's requests were met we should probably be forced to part with the 9th Aust[ralian] Div[ision] from [the] Middle East, or the Australian Squadron from England, or the diversion of 2nd Inf[antry] Div[ision] and 8th Armoured Div[ision] to Australia!

Although Brooke tried 'to make him listen to a short statement of the global situation', he claimed that Evatt 'refused to listen', leaving Brooke with 'the impression that as far as he was concerned he did not mind what happened to anybody else as long as Australian shores could be made safe'.[21] Despite Evatt's bluster, Bruce was relieved to learn after the meeting that Evatt had not sighted the papers and had allowed himself to be fobbed off with the usual British promises. However, that night Bruce was horrified to hear from Wardell that some time after the meeting one of the papers had been shown to Evatt, who had 'reacted very violently'.[22]

It is unclear how Evatt came to see the offending paper and thereby learn of the relatively fixed nature of the 'Germany first' policy. But it is clear who was responsible for concealing the policy from him. Australia's firm allies, Britain and the United States, must take much of that responsibility, with a careful campaign orchestrated by Churchill and connived at by Roosevelt to conceal the reality of Allied strategy. They were aided and abetted by Australia's representatives in Washington and London who did a grave disservice to their duty when they became involved in this campaign and withheld vital information from their political masters. As former or present conservative MPs, Page, Bruce and Casey proved ill-suited to serve the needs of a more nationalistic Labor government. Bruce provided an interesting insight into his own patrician attitudes when he calmly recorded for posterity his deliberate deceit of Evatt, watching as the uninformed Australian minister was humiliated in a succession of meetings with British officials.

Armed with the briefing paper, an angry Evatt demanded that the chiefs provide him with a copy of 'W.W.I.', which they finally did. It is clear that the existence of the document came as a shock to Evatt and that he was not feigning surprise as has been suggested by one historian.[23] It should not have been a surprise. Evatt had adequate warning of the strong pressure in London and Washington to concentrate Allied resources on the defeat of Germany. In fact, the whole tenor of his trip was pitched to counter this pressure. Evatt's surprise was caused by his misplaced confidence in the terms of MacArthur's directive, which seemed to contradict the existence of a written agreement to the contrary between Britain and the United States. His belated discovery of 'W.W.I.' finally revealed to Evatt the rigidity of a strategy that he had believed was fluid. The limitation of MacArthur's directive was now painfully apparent as was the failure of Evatt's prolonged trip to achieve a substantial improvement in Australia's defence capability.

NOTES

[1] Cable, Evatt to Curtin, 7 May 1942, CRS A3300, Item 234, NAA.
[2] Talk with Evatt, 3 May 1942, CRS M100, 'May 1942', NAA.
[3] Talk with Bridges, 2 May 1942, CRS M100, 'May 1942', NAA.
[4] Talk with Evatt, 4 May 1942, CRS M100, 'May 1942', NAA.
[5] London Munitions Assignment Board Minutes, 4 May 1942, PREM 3/44, PRO.
[6] Note, Lyttelton to Churchill, 6 May 1942, PREM 3/44, PRO.
[7] War Cabinet Conclusions, 4 May 1942, CAB 65/26, W.M. (42)56, PRO.
[8] Cadogan diary, 4 May 1942, ACAD 1/11, Cadogan Papers, CC; Alanbrooke diary, 4 May 1942, in Danchev and Todman (eds), *War Diaries*, p. 255.

9   Bruce claimed that Evatt was bitter at Curtin for not pushing Churchill hard enough to make him a privy councillor. In fact, Churchill was blocking the move because he thought Evatt had not been a minister for sufficient time to become a privy councillor. Talk with Evatt, 4 May 1942, CRS M100, 'May 1942', NAA.

10 Transcript of Evatt's press conference, 5 May 1942, 'War — Matters Relating to — Australia', Evatt Collection, FUL.

11 War Journal of Gerald Wilkinson, 15 April 1943, WILK 1/2, Wilkinson Papers, CC.

12 'Notes of Discussion with General MacArthur, Commander-in-Chief, Southwest Pacific Area, 2–5–42', Minute, Shedden to Curtin, 2 May 1942, CRS A5954, Box 3, NAA.

13 This was supported by Blamey who also 'emphasized the number of inquiries that are being received from relatives regarding the return of the troops'. ibid; 'Notes of Discussion with General Sir Thomas Blamey, Commander, Allied Land Forces — Monday, 4th May, 1942', by Shedden, 4 May 1942, CRS A5954, Box 4, NAA.

14 Cable PM 57, Curtin to Evatt, 6 May 1942, CRS M100, 'May 1942', NAA.

15 Cable E4, Evatt to Curtin, 8 May 1942, CRS M100, 'May 1942', NAA.

16 Minutes of Prime Minister's War Conference, 11 May 1942, CRS A5954, Box 1; 'Weekly Resume', 28 May — 4 June 1942, CAB 66/25, W.P. (42)237, NAA.

17 Cable No. 135, Smith to Curtin, 20 May 1942, CRS A3300, Item 229, NAA.

18 Cable No. 691/2, Churchill to Auchinleck, 5 May 1942, and Cable No. 687/2, Churchill to Wavell, 5 May 1942, VI/2, Ismay Papers, KC; Gill, *Royal Australian Navy 1939–1945*, Vol. 2, pp. 185–6.

19 Cable, Evatt to Curtin, 6 May 1942, *DAFP*, Vol. 5, Doc. 484.

20 Talk with Evatt, 12 May 1942, CRS M100, 'May 1942', NAA.

21 Alanbrooke diary, 12 May 1942, in Danchev and Todman (eds), *War Diaries*, p. 257.

22 It is unclear who was responsible for bringing 'W.W.I.' to Evatt's attention. It may have been revealed by his unofficial adviser, W. S. Robinson, who enjoyed a friendship with Lyttelton. Or it may have been one of Australia's service advisers in London in an act of conscientiousness or by simple inadvertence. Or it could have come from one of Evatt's British Labour Party counterparts with whom he dined on the evening of his meeting with the chiefs of staff. Talk with Evatt, 12 May 1942, CRS M100, 'May 1942', NAA; Dalton diary, 12 May 1942, I/26/183, Dalton Papers, LSE.

23 Carl Bridge, 'R. G. Casey, Australia's First Washington Legation and the Origins of the Pacific War, 1940–42', *Australian Journal of Politics and History*, 1982, Vol. 28, No. 2.

TWENTY-SEVEN

'entirely captured by Winston'

For six months, the Australian government had operated under the mistaken assumption that its urgent defence needs would be met by Churchill and Roosevelt if only sufficient pressure could be brought to bear on them. All along, the Allied war policy had been determined by the pre-existing strategy to defeat Germany first, as set out in the Anglo–American document 'W.W.I.'. Despite Evatt's belated discovery of this document, and despite the vital implications of it for Australia's defence, he waited fifteen days before cabling its full details to Curtin.[1] The reason for the delay seems clear. He needed to find a way to portray his mission as a success. After all, he had claimed at the conclusion of his stay in Washington to have had a great personal victory. That would now prove to be hollow with the divulging of 'W.W.I.'. So he delayed cabling the contents of 'W.W.I.', except in the most general terms, until he could offset this embarrassing discovery with a dramatic and visible success.

Evatt had already held out the hope to Curtin of achieving an allocation of fighter aircraft from Britain. He now set about fulfilling this objective and paid less attention to pressing the issues raised by Curtin, including the return of the 9th Division. Although the 'Germany first' policy made the return of Australian troops even more vital, Evatt appears to have realised that the

328

policy also made these issues more difficult to achieve and he was unwilling to have a showdown with Churchill over them. It was now that Churchill's efforts in assiduously cultivating Evatt's favour began to pay dividends, with Evatt moderating his stance to protect the special relationship that he mistakenly believed he had developed with the British prime minister. He would be deaf to the renewed calls from Canberra for British reinforcements.

The battle of the Coral Sea might have been expected to relieve Australia's anxiety about invasion but the results of the battle were regarded as being 'rather disappointing'. The advisory war council thought it was a missed opportunity to strike a decisive blow against the Japanese. With all the advance information about the movement of the Japanese fleet, the council considered that the Allies 'should have been able to concentrate the superior strength necessary to have ensured a complete victory'.[2] Backed by the council and the support of MacArthur, Curtin again appealed to London for reinforcements. He acknowledged to Evatt that any captured Australian territory would probably be recovered in the long term, but by then the 'country may have been ravished and the people largely decimated'. Quoting Churchill's own threats back to him about the judgment of history, Curtin warned that it would 'gravely indict such a happening to a nation which sacrificed 60 000 of its men on overseas battlefields in the last war and at its peril has sent its Naval, Military and Air Forces to fight overseas in this one'. And contrary to British opinion, Curtin claimed that Australia was more attractive to the Japanese as an immediate objective than India. As such, its defence deficiencies had to be made good. To do so, the resources 'must come from somewhere', argued Curtin, 'and come quickly'.[3]

Evatt received this message on 14 May and immediately passed it on to Churchill, who in turn referred it to the war cabinet. That night, Evatt left with Churchill on a two-day train tour of Yorkshire and Durham. Ensconced in a carriage with the champagne-swilling Churchill, the experience proved to be a turning point in Evatt's advocacy of the Australian case. Armed with his new-found knowledge of 'W.W.I.', it might have been expected that Evatt would take Churchill to task for not informing Australia of it and for placing the dominion in consequent peril. There is little evidence that he did so. Instead, his tour of northern England impressed upon Evatt the strong hold that the British prime minister had on the affections of his national constituency. A few months before, Evatt had entertained hopes of Churchill being replaced by a leader more sympathetic to Australia's plight and, to this end, had given encouragement to Cripps. Now he realised these hopes were forlorn, that whatever critics Churchill had in the House of Commons, he had 'popular backing everywhere outside Parliament'.[4] It was clear that Australia would have to deal with Churchill for the foreseeable future, which made Evatt less inclined to pressure him unduly. He also seems to have been captivated by Churchill's mesmerising personality.

Returning from his tour on 17 May, Evatt immediately cabled Curtin to confirm the rigidity of the Allied strategy and to explain how difficult it was to press for reinforcements 'without being importunate'. Believing that he had developed a special relationship with Churchill, Evatt confided to Curtin his fear that making a strong demand to Churchill might 'adversely affect the relationship which has built up during my fortnight here and thereby injure Australia'. He assured Curtin that Churchill was 'impressed' with Australia's argument and was anxious to do more for the dominion but was 'perplexed as to the source from which it should come'.[5] Evatt did not draw the obvious implication from Churchill's supposed dilemma: that the Australian claim on British resources was outranked in priority by almost every other claimant.

Evatt had been greeted on his return to London with a letter from W. S. Robinson, a businessman and adviser, which strongly urged him that his strident attitude could be dangerous to the Australian cause. Arguing that such an attitude was no longer appropriate, Robinson reminded Evatt of the 'generous hospitality' and the 'tremendous reception' that he had received in Britain. Having received Churchill's promises of help, it was now time to moderate his tough approach and become

warmly appreciative of all that has been done in the past for Australia — all that has been promised and you hope Britain can do today. I know you will not carry in your mind the slightest suspicion that promises are now being made to you that cannot or will not be fulfilled or that there is the least desire to neglect Australia and Australians or that the utmost Britain can do herself and can influence the United States to do will not be done.[6]

Evatt had already reached this conclusion himself. His discovery of 'W.W.I.', and his recognition of Churchill's entrenched political position, had made him realise that a confrontation over Australia's defence would be futile and could even detract from the limited assistance already offered.[7]

On the same day that Robinson was counselling moderation, Evatt was assuring Bruce that, because of Churchill's grip on the British public, 'it would be a bad thing for us to have a quarrel with Winston [on the issue of Australian representation in the war cabinet] as it might hurt Australia's interests in obtaining reinforcements and supplies we need if we antagonise him'. Bruce was taken aback by this dramatic change from Evatt's previous 'blood and thunder' attitude and found himself in the curious position of trying to encourage Evatt to take a stronger line. Bruce downplayed the public demonstrations of support for Churchill, arguing from personal experience that the 'people's favour was notoriously a somewhat uncertain quantity'. But Evatt would not budge, leaving Bruce to remark privately on how Churchill had obviously 'exercised his charm and unquestionable astuteness upon Evatt'.[8]

Although Evatt's raised hackles were being smoothed down by Churchill's beguiling touch, the Australian remained desperate to obtain a commitment of fighter aircraft. He had held out to Curtin the prospect of such an achievement even before he left Washington, while Robinson had suggested to Curtin on 18 May that most of the problems facing Evatt in London would soon be solved and that the 'results of his firm and persistent pressure' would 'give great satisfaction to your Government and the Australian people'.[9] MacArthur had provided Evatt with arguments to use in his appeal, noting that Britain had only supplied 316 of the 2087 aircraft requested from it for the RAAF. In fact, between January and August 1942, Britain supplied just 77 combat aircraft for the RAAF from its own production, although there were a further 366 training aircraft supplied. These combat aircraft had been ordered by Australia prior to the Japanese attack on Pearl Harbor.[10]

On 20 May, Evatt achieved his objective, at least in the political sense, when Churchill finally relented and agreed to support the dispatch of three Spitfire squadrons to Australia. Two of them were to be drawn from RAAF units based in Britain. It was Churchill's wife, Clementine, who was instrumental in Evatt's largely symbolic success, intervening in a lunchtime argument between himself and Churchill and prevailing upon her reluctant husband to at least concede Evatt his planes. Evatt later thanked her for these comments, noting that afterwards 'the Prime Minister was most helpful'. In fact, Churchill was predisposed to making a token contribution to Australia's defence. Just three days before his lunch with Evatt, he had pointed to the importance of Britain's 'permanent relationship with Australia' and observed how 'it seems very detrimental to the future of the Empire for us not to be represented in any way in their defence'.[11] In this instance, Churchill had been referring to the absence of any British warships in Australian waters. The commitment of Spitfires would allow his admirals to keep their ships well away from the Japanese while providing the equally symbolic commitment of Britain's renowned fighter aircraft, even if most of them were flown by Australian pilots.

Despite Churchill's support, the commitment faced opposition from the air ministry when it came before the war cabinet on 21 May.[12] With Evatt looking on, the chief of the air staff suggested that Australia forgo the Spitfires and instead accept Kittyhawk fighters from the United States. That would allow the abundant personnel within Australia to crew them and save having to ship whole squadrons of Spitfires complete with aircrew and ground staff. But it would not allow Evatt to return with his political trophy. So, in accordance with his agreement with Evatt, Churchill intervened to countermand the air ministry argument and to do so in a way that allowed Evatt to squeeze the maximum political benefit from the decision. Churchill instructed the air ministry to draw up a plan for the dispatch of the Spitfires, which Evatt could use in a cable to his colleagues in Canberra. In the meantime, Churchill instructed that no other announcement be allowed to emanate from the British government concerning the Spitfires. Evatt would be permitted to reap all the political plaudits. To ensure that the plan did not go awry, Evatt got Churchill to promise that the dispatch of the two Australian squadrons would not be publicly portrayed as being done at Australia's behest and, most importantly, that the commitment of the three squadrons would not detract from the planes already promised from the United States.[13]

As an added precaution, Evatt was provided with a written statement by Downing Street listing the various undertakings of the British government to provide for Australia's defence. They did not amount to much. Apart from the Spitfires and the accelerated delivery of certain military supplies, the other undertakings were restatements of previous pledges, the value of which could only be tested in the event of Australia being invaded.[14] The experience to date would not have given an observer much confidence in the pledges being fulfilled.

The pledges were probably prompted by the rather frantic cable from Curtin that Churchill had referred to his war cabinet for discussion. When it came before the meeting on 21 May, Evatt advised that it had been dispatched before he had alerted Curtin to the existence of 'W.W.I.'. Nevertheless, Evatt went through the motions of arguing Curtin's case for reinforcements, which seems to have aroused little heat around the cabinet table. Churchill merely responded by repeating the previous assurances regarding the possible diversion of British troops in the event of a large-scale invasion. He also claimed that, notwithstanding Australia's appeal for help to the United States and the dominion's subsequent allocation to the American strategic sphere in the Pacific, Britain did not regard its traditional obligation to help Australia 'as being lessened in any way'. However, Churchill refused to commit British forces prior to an actual invasion of Australia, although he was doing so in the case of India. In Australia's case, the immediate assistance was limited to the dispatch of the Spitfire squadrons. Although Evatt also raised the need for naval forces, none were offered. The meeting concluded with Evatt expressing his 'gratitude to all the War Cabinet for the help which they had given him'.[15]

On 28 May, Evatt finally cabled to Curtin with the full terms of 'W.W.I.'. He blamed Page and Casey for keeping knowledge of the agreement from the Australian government, while he also claimed that Wardell, but not Bruce, had known the substance of 'W.W.I.'.[16] So Bruce largely escaped Evatt's wrath, which now was tempered by a conviction that even 'W.W.I.' could be made to help the dominion since it called for the security of Australia as a base against Japan. Evatt's emphasis, therefore, shifted from his previous stance of opposition to the 'Germany first' strategy to one of grudging acceptance provided that its clause relating to Australian security was applied to the letter. In fact, he went on at great length in his cable to place Australian demands in a global context, much in the way that Churchill must have argued during Evatt's visits to Chequers, and Bracken during those interminable dinners.[17]

Apart from reporting on 'W.W.I.', Evatt repeated the promises given by Churchill for the diversion to Australia of British land forces if Australia was heavily invaded. He reported that the two brigades of Australian troops temporarily garrisoning Ceylon would be returned to Australia 'at the very earliest possible moment'. Instead of pressing for the return of the 9th Division from the Middle East as instructed by Curtin, Evatt passed the matter back to Canberra on the dubious pretext that it was 'a matter of the highest Government policy'. It is difficult to escape the conclusion that Evatt had done a deal with Churchill whereby the Spitfires would be traded for Britain's retention of the 9th Division. As for the accelerated delivery of military supplies from Britain, Evatt admitted that they 'fall short of full requests' but reassured Curtin with the fanciful British claim that 'the Australian army will very shortly be the best equipped in the world'.[18]

To compensate for the disappointments, Evatt announced with a flourish his great victory with regard to the promised delivery of three Spitfire squadrons leaving Britain by the end of June as an additional allocation of air strength for Australia. He described them as 'two crack R.A.A.F. squadrons' and 'a first class R.A.F. squadron' with planes of the 'most modern character' which together comprised a 'small air expeditionary force'.[19] This description of the rather minuscule force of 48 second-hand aircraft served its purpose and allowed Evatt to claim a victory from his trip that would fudge the harsh reality of 'W.W.I.'. Although Curtin expressed his gratification at the news of the Spitfires, he also suggested that Evatt use the continuation of Australia's participation in the Empire Air Training Scheme as a bargaining counter to ensure the provision from Britain of aircraft for the RAAF. This suggestion came too late and was not sufficiently explicit for Evatt to act upon. Moreover, given Evatt's change of heart, it is doubtful whether he would have agreed to the use of Australian contributions to imperial defence as a means to force Britain to fulfil its obligations to the dominion's defence.[20]

Whitehall celebrated Evatt's departure from London. Although generations of British officials had become used to dealing with importuning colonial politicians and were adept at sending them away empty-handed, they had regarded the arrival of Evatt with some trepidation. Rushing to count Britain's stock of military hardware on his departure, they were relieved to find him leaving the imperial capital with such light luggage.[21] According to Wardell, any additional assignments of munitions gained by Evatt were subsequently subtracted after his departure from London, thereby leaving Australia with no improvement in its net position.[22]

Despite Evatt's shouting and stamping, nothing had changed. Churchill made this clear to General Ismay after being asked whether the commitment given to Evatt would affect the order of British priorities whereby 'the Middle East is regarded as having priority over Australia, India and Ceylon' in the allocation of resources. Churchill confirmed that the order of priorities remained unchanged, that the promise to abandon the Mediterranean in the event of a serious invasion of Australia 'related only to a contingency ... regarded as highly improbable, and that it was not intended to have any bearing on the immediate problem of allocation of resources'. Churchill's private feelings were revealed by the changes he made to the draft commitment drawn up for Evatt. He cut out the reference to Australia's 'unswerving' support of Britain and scrawled his pen through Britain's promise to 'cut her losses in the Mediterranean'.[23]

Prior to Evatt's arrival in Washington, Churchill had warned Roosevelt to be on guard against the anti-British Australian but now informed the president that Evatt had 'shown himself most friendly, especially to me personally, and I think you will find that he will help in every way'.[24] This was confirmed by a well-placed observer in London who reported that Evatt had been 'entirely captured by Winston' and departed 'much better disposed and less anti-British after getting his wool prices and the Spitfires'.[25] The New South Wales governor, Lord Wakehurst, later reported to London that Evatt had returned 'full of Winston and genuinely impressed by the war effort in London. His trouble is that although he has brains he has neither courage nor integrity. One should make use of his ability without putting too much strain on his reliability.'[26]

Evatt's three-month mission had added little to Australia's security. Admittedly it is difficult for a small power to coerce great power allies into ensuring its protection. But there is little evidence, despite the complaints of Brooke, that Evatt made any serious attempt at arm-twisting in Washington or London. As a lawyer, and then a leading jurist, he was accustomed to words having a precise meaning. This ill served him in his new role as a politician where words had shades of meaning, meant different things to different people and were open to sudden reinterpretation. Although, like Lewis Carroll's Alice, he sensed that things were not quite as they seemed, the dominion's historic dependence on Britain curbed his independent inclinations.[27] Ultimately, Australia had more to lose than Britain from any open breach in their relations, which also would have carried a political cost for the Labor Party. So Evatt returned with a semblance of achievement and in the apparently genuine belief that Churchill had Australia's interests at heart.

Although Evatt was able publicly to proclaim his mission a triumph,[28] there were few such illusions in Canberra. Throughout Evatt's trip, Shedden had been keeping track, presumably at Curtin's request, of Evatt's claimed achievements and comparing them with confirmed improvements in the supply of personnel and equipment from Britain and the United States. The trend of these reports generally disparaged Evatt's efforts and concluded that his trip had done little to improve Australia's security position. Similarly, General MacArthur informed Curtin that, based on information from Evatt's own cables, the external affairs minister had 'no doubt evoked a sympathetic hearing from Mr. Churchill and other Ministers, but from the practical military point of view little had been achieved'.[29] Evatt's most symbolic triumph, the three Spitfire squadrons, would arrive more than six months later than promised after the original consignment was diverted to the Middle East. And then the United States simply subtracted an equivalent number of aircraft from their allocation to Australia, despite Churchill's assurance that this would not occur. Australia was therefore no better off for having the Spitfires, apart perhaps from the possible boost to Australian morale from their presence.[30]

After his weeks in Washington and London, knocking on doors in the confident belief that he was reshaping Allied strategy, Evatt realised that all the doors he had pushed at were of the revolving type. He had played the part of the rough colonial but was really an innocent abroad in the care of his worldly-wise cousins from the imperial *métropole*. Like innumerable Australian politicians before and since, Evatt then became preoccupied with making a display of personal achievement rather than in promoting national interests. By the end of his stay in London, he had become a virtual apologist for the 'Germany first' policy. There was certainly little in this trip to sustain the concept of him being the father of a distinctive Australian foreign policy. The reverse could well be argued: that his visit reconciled him to the reality of Australia's dependence on powerful and distant allies and that any distinctiveness in Australian foreign policy would lie in its details rather than its substance.

While Evatt had been concluding his stay in London, the Japanese navy had been assembling a massive assault force of two hundred ships that was scheduled to descend upon the American-held island of Midway in the first week of June. The north Pacific island was one of the most westerly of the Hawaiian islands and provided a possible launching pad for future American attacks on Japan. As such, it was essential to the Japanese that it be captured and neutralised. In the process, Tokyo hoped to destroy the remaining vestiges of US naval power in the Pacific and thereby make the expanded Japanese empire virtually invulnerable for several years. By that time, American war weariness might have set in and a compromise peace have been possible whereby the Japanese could negotiate from a position of strength. Although Australia would take no part in this decisive naval battle erupting far from its shores, its outcome would determine the fate of the dominion.

NOTES

[1] Cable ET30, Evatt to Curtin, 28 May 1942, CRS A3300, Item 228; Talk with Evatt, 28 May 1942, CRS M100, 'May 1942', NAA.

[2] Advisory War Council Minutes, 13 May 1942, CRS A2682, Vol. 5, Minute 938, NAA.

[3] Cable, Curtin to Evatt, 13 May 1942, *DAFP*, Vol. 5, Doc. 487; See also 'Defence of Australia', Note by Bridges, 18 May 1942, CAB 66/24, W.P. (42)210, PRO.

[4] Cable, Evatt to Curtin, 17 May 1942, *DAFP*, Vol. 5, Doc. 490.

[5] ibid.

[6] Letter, W. S. Robinson to Evatt, 18 May 1942, 'Robinson, W. S., 1942–45(a)' Folder, Evatt Collection, FUL.

[7] On the day that Evatt discovered the terms of 'W.W.I.', he apparently decided instead to make a stand on wool prices, telling Bruce that he would demand a threepence a pound increase rather than the twopence a pound previously contemplated. He was determined to have at least one popular victory from his mission. Talk with Evatt, 13 May 1942, CRS M100, 'May 1942', NAA.

8   Talk with Evatt, 18 May 1942, CRS M100, 'May 1942', NAA.

9   Cable No. 4503, Robinson to Curtin, 18 May 1942, CRS A5954, Box 474, NAA.

10 Letter, MacArthur to Curtin, 16 May 1942, CRS A5954, Box 229; Teleprinter message, Polglaze to Shedden, 1 October 1942, CRS A5954, Box 229, NAA.

11 Letter, Evatt to Mrs Churchill, 20 May 1942, 'Evatt — Overseas Trips — 1942 — Correspondence' Folder, Evatt Collection, FUL; Minute, Churchill to Alexander and Pound, 17 May 1942, PREM 3/151/4, PRO.

12 Evatt was attending what he thought would be his last meeting with the British war cabinet before his departure for Australia. However, his departure was subsequently delayed for a week.

13 War Cabinet Conclusions/Confidential Annex, 21 May 1942, CAB 65/30, W.M. (42)65, PRO.

14 Cable No. 46, Evatt to Smith (Washington), repeated as ET33 to Curtin, 28 May 1942, CRS A3300, Item 228, NAA.

15 War Cabinet Conclusions/Confidential Annex, 21 May 1942, CAB 65/30, W.M. (42)65, PRO.

16 On his return to Canberra, Evatt succeeded in having Wardell removed from his London posting. See CRS A5954, Box 461, NAA.

17 Cable ET30, Evatt to Curtin, 28 May 1942, CRS A3300, Item 228, NAA.

18 ibid.

19 ibid.

20 Curtin duly cabled back with his 'warmest congratulations', assuring Evatt that the news of the squadrons was 'very gratifying'. Cable PM76, Curtin to Evatt, 29 May 1942, CRS A3300, Item 228, NAA.

21 After his final meeting with the chiefs of staff on 28 May, Brooke complained that Evatt had spent three-quarters of an hour 'pleading that Australia should be crammed full of forces at the expense of all other fronts. However he left with no more than he had come!' Alanbrooke diary, 28 May 1942, in Danchev and Todman (eds), *War Diaries*, p. 261.

22 Wardell's allegation was made during the course of a conversation with Shedden, neither of whom had much affection for Evatt. Nevertheless, his claim is borne out by other evidence. 'Mission Abroad of Dr Evatt ...', Report of Talk between Shedden and Wardell, 17 March 1943, CRS A5954, Box 14, NAA.

23 Note, Ismay to Churchill, 30 May 1942; Draft note, Ismay to Evatt, 26 May 1942, PREM 3/151/4, PRO.

24 Cable No. 785/2, Churchill to Roosevelt, 30 May 1942, VI/2, Ismay Papers, KC.

25 Letter, Emrys-Evans to Lord Wakehurst, 23 July 1942, ADD. MS. 58243, Emrys-Evans Papers, BL; See also War Journal of Gerald Wilkinson, 30 March 1943, WILK 1/2, Wilkinson Papers, CC; Cable, R. D. Elliott to Beaverbrook, 23 December 1942, BBK C/131, Beaverbrook Papers, HLRO.

26 Letter, Lord Wakehurst to Emrys-Evans, 30 September 1942, ADD. MS. 58243, Emrys-Evans Papers, BL.

27 See Talk with Evatt, 28 May 1942, CRS M100, 'May 1942', NAA.

28 See Advisory War Council Minutes, 1 July 1942, CRS A2682, Vol. 5, Minute 978; Statement by Evatt in House of Representatives, 3 September 1942, CRS A5954, Box 474, NAA; Text of radio broadcast by Evatt, 7 March 1943, 'War — Speeches by Evatt '43(a)', Evatt Collection, FUL.

29 See CRS A5954, Box 474, NAA.

30 See Day, 'H. V. Evatt and the "Beat Hitler First" Strategy'.

TWENTY-EIGHT

'every ditch a last ditch'

The first six months after the Japanese attack on Pearl Harbor and Singapore had seen territory after territory fall to the Japanese. The island of Timor, almost within sight of northern Australia, had been occupied while a substantial Japanese base was being developed at Rabaul off the north-east coast of New Guinea. Although the Japanese seaborne assault on Port Moresby had been repulsed during the battle of the Coral Sea, the Japanese still retained naval superiority in the Pacific. They planned to use that superiority in the forthcoming attack against the island of Midway in early June, during which they hoped to draw the US fleet out and deal it a decisive blow. If the Americans suffered another defeat, losing their aircraft carriers at Midway as they had lost their battleships at Pearl Harbor, then there would be little to prevent an invasion of Australia. Australian leaders were acutely conscious of this and waited anxiously for the crucial battle to begin.

Australian fears had been heightened by an attack launched against Australian and American warships in Sydney Harbour. On 29 May, five Japanese submarines managed to arrive undetected off Sydney Heads from where they dispatched midget submarines into the harbour to attack what they believed to be battleships and cruisers. In fact, there was just one US cruiser and one Australian cruiser at anchor in the harbour when the submarines struck. And the midgets were either caught up in submarine nets or otherwise failed to hit their intended targets, the torpedoes missing one cruiser by just a few feet and hitting instead a harbour ferry that had been taken over for the accommodation of naval ratings. The attack caused some panic in the city, which was exacerbated by the submarines offshore lobbing shells into beachside suburbs, though not to any great effect. A week later, Newcastle was shelled. Harbourside homes in Sydney suddenly became more affordable, with one Sydneysider later recalling how people were 'selling them for a song and moving up to Bourke to get away from the Japs. They panicked and away they went, couldn't get out quick enough.'[1] Most, though, stayed and regaled anyone who would listen with stories of where they were when the shells had come over or what they had seen on the darkened harbour as the confused defences swung into action.

Curtin had sent Evatt on a mission to obtain the resources that might make Sydney and the rest of Australia secure. There was little to show for his weeks abroad. When Curtin met with MacArthur on 1 June, he showed the American general copies of Evatt's cables from London and Washington in order to get his assessment. MacArthur was not impressed, describing the results of the trip as 'distressing' and bitterly criticising Britain's failure to provide for Australia's security. Since his arrival in March, declared MacArthur, Australia had not received from Britain 'an additional ship, soldier or squadron'. Although MacArthur acknowledged that the United States also had been niggardly with its reinforcements, he pointed out that America had 'no sovereign interest in the integrity of Australia' and was only sending forces there because of its 'utility as a base from which to hit Japan'. By promising forces in the event of an invasion, argued MacArthur, Britain was conceding that the forces within Australia were insufficient to withstand a serious attack. He described such a promise of reinforcements as 'an extremely weak reed on which to rely' and he berated Britain for not returning in kind the 'assistance Australia had rendered overseas with naval, military and air forces'. MacArthur contrasted Britain's recent thousand-bomber raid against Cologne with the 40 bombers allocated to his command, most of them now unserviceable.[2]

MacArthur advised Curtin that a Japanese victory at Midway would lead quickly to the isolation of Australia. Although Australia could not influence the outcome of the distant battle, the dominion could act to protect itself against the consequences of an adverse result. MacArthur recommended that Curtin insist on the return of the 9th Division from the Middle East and obtain Britain's support for the supply of aircraft to the RAAF. As he argued, 'in Australia's hour of peril she was entitled at least to the use of all the forces she could raise herself'. Those forces that could not be returned should be replaced with equivalent British forces. These were matters that Evatt's mission should have resolved but had failed to do. In this regard, MacArthur was particularly derisive about Evatt's principal achievement — the three Spitfire squadrons — noting that 'Churchill was only giving back to Australia part of her forces and one R.A.F. squadron as a gesture'. He criticised Evatt for regarding them as a 'favour and a concession' when 'they and more should be forthcoming as a right'.[3]

On 3 June, as the opposing fleets were positioned for battle across the disputed expanses of the north Pacific near Midway Island, the advisory war council met to consider the dominion's position in the wake of Evatt's failure in London and Washington. Although the council supported the worried outlook of Curtin and MacArthur, the distant sound of the decisive naval battle stopped them giving effect to their view. Instead of the US navy suffering another defeat, and losing more of its vital aircraft carriers, its carrier aircraft had instead chanced upon the Japanese fleet and sunk four of the enemy carriers. It would prove to be the most crucial battle of the Pacific war, effectively forcing Japan onto the defensive for the remainder of the conflict.

With an invasion of Australia no longer a practical possibility for Japan, there was a radical reappraisal of Australia's urgent calls for reinforcements. As MacArthur advised Curtin on 11 June, 'it would now be interpreted as a timid cry for help, if we were to persist in demands for assistance for the defence of Australia'.[4] The struggle now was to obtain sufficient forces to take the offensive and expel Japan from its Pacific conquests. Australia could look with greater confidence towards ultimate victory, for which planning was immediately begun. With MacArthur advising Curtin that 'the defensive position of Australia was now assured', the Australian cabinet effectively acknowledged its fortuitous rescue by establishing a committee just three days after the battle of Midway to examine the problems of demobilisation. Three weeks later, the war cabinet approved a reduction in Australia's army by one or two divisions.[5]

While defeat was no longer regarded by Australia as a serious possibility,[6] Japan remained in a strong defensive position. Its naval force remained the most powerful in the Pacific in terms of battleships and cruisers, and its land-based air strength partially compensated for the loss of the four fleet carriers at Midway. The decisive difference after the Midway defeat was that Japan could no longer afford to gamble its fleet on offensive actions that might, if they failed, lay Japan itself open to Allied attack. So Tokyo conserved its strength for a long war, while it tried to wear down the American will to avenge the humiliation of Pearl Harbor. There were many more battles to be fought, with an ultimate Japanese defeat remaining a formidable and costly prospect for the Allies, who had to find ways of projecting their power across the immense distances of the Pacific.

There were three strategies that the Americans could adopt in taking the war to Tokyo. One was to join with the Chinese and strike from bases on the Chinese mainland; another was to use Australia as a base from which to strike towards Japan by way of the Philippines; and the third was to strike west across the Pacific from America itself, leapfrogging from one distant island to another until Japan came within reach. Each had its difficulties and each had its champions within the US armed forces. But none could be attempted until the US navy had made good its losses. And all were constrained by the overriding Allied strategy to defeat Germany first before mounting large-scale offensives against Japan. In the meantime, the Japanese tried to thwart these strategies by strengthening the outer perimeter of their new empire and by capturing a further string of islands off the east coast of Australia in an attempt to sever the reinforcement route from the United States.

Australia was anxious that the Allies follow up the success at Midway by attacking Japan's developing bases in the islands to the north of Australia. China too was critical of Britain's effort in Burma which had allowed

Japanese forces to threaten China from the south. Their ambassador in London, Dr Wellington Koo, had complained to Britain's foreign secretary, Anthony Eden, about British 'ineptitude' in the Far East, with Eden later warning Churchill that the Chinese attitude towards Britain had changed from 'hostility to contempt'. Eden advised that the Chinese were hoping to assume the postwar leadership in Asia and to 'help their neighbours to throw off the yoke of western imperialism'.[7] This accorded with Churchill's fear of an Asiatic bloc expelling western influence from the region[8] and he quickly assured Koo on 3 June of Britain's aggressive intentions against the Japanese while simultaneously instructing Wavell to take the offensive in Burma. Not that Churchill had done an about-face and was going to send an army of reinforcements to the Far East. Although he did hold out the possibility of British forces in the Middle East being drawn upon to help in the task, he was careful to stress the overriding importance of the war against Germany. Only when that was won, Churchill told Koo, would the full weight of British forces be turned against Japan.[9]

While trying to appease the Chinese, Churchill did not deviate from his earlier instruction to the chiefs of staff that no further troops should be committed to the war against Japan. As he informed them on 1 June, he had 'never suggested sending any further troops to the East than those now on the sea or under orders'.[10] This hardly allowed for any offensive to be mounted in Burma, as Wavell quickly advised him. Undaunted, and desperate to keep up the appearance of action, Churchill continued to pressure his chiefs to plan for an early offensive there.[11] As commander of the Eastern fleet, Admiral Somerville would have had to use his ships to support any Burmese operation. And they were already being drawn upon for the prospective capture of French Madagascar. This latter operation was designed to deny that Vichy-controlled island to the Japanese, with Churchill fearing that the Japanese would try to send naval forces there to threaten Britain's sea links to India and the Middle East. With his forces stretched so thin, and conscious of the weakness of Wavell's land and air forces, Somerville was most dismissive of Churchill's plan for a Burmese offensive, commenting caustically that Churchill was 'cut out as a figurehead but *not* as a military war winner ... His strategical intuition is disastrous.'[12]

Churchill was once again facing political criticism and was anxious to divert the attention of his critics by the sound of battle, whether it be in Burma, north Africa or even Norway.[13] There were also the Americans to be considered. After seven months' involvement in the war, their forces were still not engaged on land against Germany. The Americans had talked wildly of invading Europe in 1942 but had been convinced by the British that such a massive operation was premature. The British chiefs of staff wanted the Americans to join in capturing north Africa and regaining control of the Mediterranean. The hard-pressed Russians also wanted action in Europe to relieve the pressure on their armies in the east. This pressure from Moscow, along with the popular pressure to do something, led Churchill into approving the ill-conceived and costly raid on Dieppe. And he maintained his pressure on Wavell, his former commander in the Middle East who had been shifted by Churchill for being too cautious. Churchill now disparaged his planned offensive for Burma, dismissing it as being 'very nice and useful nibbling' and calling on Wavell to make 'war on a large scale' and seize the initiative from Japan 'instead of being through no fault of your own like clay in the hands of the potter'.[14] Wavell was unmoved, pointing to the lack of sea and air power in his command, and the poor condition of his mostly Indian troops, and suggesting instead that he transfer some of his forces to the Middle East where Rommel was rapidly turning Auchinleck's long-awaited offensive into another headlong retreat by the British back into Egypt.[15]

The mounting problems in the Middle East, where the massive British army was being out-generalled and out-gunned by the Germans, put paid to Churchill's wilder fancies in Burma and Norway. His concern shifted instead to the Pacific where Roosevelt was suggesting that Britain's Eastern fleet mount a joint operation with the US Pacific fleet, either against the islands off Burma or against Timor, as a way of easing the Japanese pressure on New Guinea and northern Australia.[16] Although this was knocked on the head by Britain's naval chief, Admiral Dudley Pound, Churchill also faced a call from Somerville, who wanted the ships that were being assembled for the operation against Madagascar to steam across the Indian Ocean once Madagascar was secure and help to defend Australia, a proposal that Churchill firmly rejected.[17] In Churchill's view, these were dangerous distractions that had to be nipped in the bud, particularly as they seemed to be gaining some ground in Washington. So he proposed to Roosevelt on 13 June that he visit Washington again to discuss the future of Allied plans. As Churchill confided to Brooke, 'Roosevelt was getting a bit off the rails and some good talks as regards western front were required.'[18]

It was not just because these proposed diversions of warships to Australian waters would detract from the 'Germany first' policy that disturbed Churchill. It was also because a succession of bitter disputes with a succession of Australian prime ministers had left Churchill so resentful towards the dominion that any proposal intended for Australia's benefit was likely to be rejected by him. He was almost at the stage of refusing to deal with Australia at all and was leaving most of the communicating to the dominions secretary. Whereas Churchill had sent 43 personal cables to Curtin during the first three months of 1942, he sent just 33 during the last nine months of that year.[19] Disputes over Tobruk, Singapore, Burma and Casey, along with a multitude of other issues, had combined to turn Churchill, as well as some of his ministers, against Australia. To make matters worse, refugees from Singapore began to trickle back to Britain around this time, bringing with them highly coloured stories of Australian cowardice. So worried was Bruce by reports of these refugee accounts, and their possible effect on British opinion, that he visited the War Office about the matter. As he feared, the war minister, Sir James Grigg, was well aware of the reports, although he assured Bruce that it was all 'hearsay' and applied to British and Indian troops as well. Nevertheless, Grigg had thought it sufficiently serious to raise the matter already with Churchill who decided that 'it was better not to approach the Australian Government on the matter'.[20]

But the stories kept spreading and the poisonous British opinion of Australia continued to fester. Lord Croft, an under-secretary at the War Office, described the Australians as being 'terribly disappointing — I won't say more about them'.[21] From Canberra, Cross confided to Attlee about widespread stories of Australian troops 'having "broken" in Greece, Crete, Libya and, above all, at Singapore'.[22] Further reports filtered through to Australia House in London, but there was little that could be done about them. As Bruce's secretary noted, it required delicate handling.[23] British officials were unwilling to admit that these stories influenced their treatment of Australia and Bruce's attempts to combat them may only have lent credence to the stories and widened the circle of officials who were privy to the details. Although he could do little to stop their spread, Bruce did warn Curtin of the 'undercurrent of resentment' against Australia and of the 'feeling in some quarters that Australia is entirely selfish and out to get what she can for herself irrespective of the common interest and the wide strategical necessities of the war'.[24]

This underlying resentment may have affected a series of decisions by British officials concerning Australia. The first one was a proposal to divert to Ceylon eight British motor torpedo boats that had originally been destined for Australia.[25] At the same time, Churchill tried to retain the two Australian brigades in Ceylon despite Australia's urgent need for them. And he ignored various Australian requests for the return of the 9th Division from the Middle East or for the provision of equivalent forces in their stead.[26] In mid-June, Britain's joint planning staff recommended that, in the case of conflicting demands for the war against Japan, 'priority should be given to supplies to India and Siberian Russia rather than to Australia'.[27] Then Britain diverted to the Middle East the first consignment of 42 Spitfire aircraft that Evatt had secured from Churchill and which were en route to Australia. The day after their ship had left Britain, the 33 000 strong British garrison in Tobruk surrendered to Rommel's forces, marking the most ignominious British defeat since Singapore. Rommel's tanks with their powerful guns pushed on towards the Egyptian frontier and the British naval base at Alexandria. The Spitfires were diverted to shore up the whole British position in the Middle East, which now was in danger of collapsing.

Bruce had supported the diversion of the Spitfires. He accepted the British military opinion that Australia was not seriously threatened and he supported Britain's policy of concentrating on the Middle East.[28] Ironically, it was Bruce, rather than Churchill, who was most roundly condemned by Evatt when Australia heard on 24 June about the unilateral diversion of the aircraft. Evatt had just been congratulated by Curtin on the success of his mission, with Curtin claiming that Australia was now 'assured of the certainty that all our needs are known to our allies and [we] will be afforded greatly increased strength of armaments'.[29] Not surprisingly, Evatt was furious when he heard that he had lost his cherished planes. He refused to accept the British decision, bursting into a meeting at Parliament House between Curtin and Cross where he pressured Curtin to reverse his previous acceptance of the decision, suggesting instead that Britain should consider evacuating the Middle East.[30]

Absolving Churchill of personal blame for the diversion, Evatt accused the British air ministry and Bruce for conspiring to take his aircraft. He told Curtin that Bruce was ready to 'let us down at the slightest pretext'. Unwilling to concede their loss, Evatt sent a private cable to Brendan Bracken threatening 'considerable trouble' if the Spitfires were diverted. He pleaded with Bracken to use his influence with Churchill to ensure 'the bargain made with Australia' was implemented. Even suggesting their diversion, declared Evatt, was 'calculated to open old wounds'. Apologising for the directness of his protest, Evatt claimed to be 'utterly disgusted to find that people can be so forgetful of their obligations as to rob us of aid which is en route solely because of our foresight'.[31]

Evatt's hopes of gaining a sympathetic hearing in London were much misplaced. The Labour leader, Clement Attlee, who served as dominions secretary, might have been expected to be helpful to his Australian comrade. But Attlee dismissed Evatt's plea, explaining it to Churchill as an attempt by the politically ambitious Evatt to undermine Curtin, with Evatt being 'violently upset' at the diversion of the Spitfires because it 'delays his presenting to Australia the fruits of his visit'.[32] British politicians were often quick to ascribe political motivations to the actions of their Australian counterparts while claiming that their own actions were motivated by questions of high policy or the greater good. In this case, Attlee failed to appreciate Evatt's frustration at finding his only gain being threatened, after braving the perils of flying across the war-torn world to obtain it. And Churchill concurred with Attlee's advice, noting that the diversion of the Spitfires would not involve 'any substantial departure from what was agreed with Evatt'.[33]

Evatt was left with no option but to agree 'with a heavy heart' to the diversion, telling Bracken that it was 'solely as a result of [Churchill's] personal intervention that we are consenting to one month's postponement of delivery of [the] first instalment of Spitfires'.[34] There the matter rested for the time being, although Churchill later punished Evatt by refusing to intercede with the Americans to have the Spitfires treated as an extra allocation of aircraft. The Americans simply reduced by an equivalent number the aircraft they promised to send to Australia, thereby destroying the defence advantage for Australia and some of the political advantage for Evatt.[35]

The failure of Evatt's mission was only partly due to Anglo–American resentment of the importuning dominion. It was also due to the personal antagonism of Anglo–American policy makers towards Evatt. The distaste of Churchill, Bracken and Brooke for Evatt has already been noted, with Evatt apparently failing to notice the low regard in which he was held by people with whom he believed he had developed a close friendship. Another British minister, Lord Cranborne, later expressed relief at losing office in 1945 since it meant that he would no longer have to deal with Evatt, who he described as 'particularly repulsive'.[36] Although they could not help acknowledging his obvious intellect, they were repelled by the defects of his character. The American Supreme Court judge Felix Frankfurter was also a case in point. Evatt regarded Frankfurter, who was a trusted adviser to Roosevelt, as one of his best allies in Washington. However, Frankfurter freely admitted to Menzies in 1941 that he was 'a little disillusioned about [Evatt's] character'.[37]

Evatt's task was not made any easier by the common knowledge of his ambition, something that he found impossible to conceal. His rivalry with Curtin created the appearance overseas of Australia speaking with two voices. The British government exploited this division in Canberra and sometimes circumvented the hostility they anticipated from Evatt by approaching Curtin directly. The rivalry was exacerbated by the fact that all top-level cables passed through Evatt's department, allowing him to oversee them and even intervene to change their contents. This included cables to and from Bruce in London, whose post as high commissioner had traditionally been kept within the purview of the prime minister.[38]

Despite Evatt's belated discovery of the 'Germany first' policy, Australia remained determined to obtain reinforcements from London and Washington.

With the battle of Midway removing the threat of an imminent Japanese invasion, Australia now wanted sufficient resources for MacArthur to be able to take the offensive. With Japan thrown off-balance by its strategic defeat at Midway, and with no prospect in 1942 of the Allies invading Europe, MacArthur argued that it was time to strike at the Japanese. In an address to the advisory war council on 17 June, MacArthur warned that the situation in the Pacific remained unstable and it was still possible for Japan to win the Pacific war even if Germany lost in Europe. As such, it was essential that an offensive was launched against them as soon as possible. If Japan could be knocked out of the war, argued MacArthur, it would free up Russian forces in Siberia for use against the Germans. Moreover, an early offensive in the Pacific was vital for the 'prestige of the white races' and to prevent the 'coloured races' from consolidating behind Japan and making its position 'unassailable'.[39]

This was just the sort of dangerous talk that Churchill was determined to counter as he tried to concentrate the attention of the Americans on the European war and keep Roosevelt on the rails. Fearing that they might be enticed into switching their attention to the Japanese for want of seeing some action that year, Churchill flew off to Washington by flying boat with Brooke on 17 June, the same day that MacArthur was meeting with Australia's advisory war council and arguing that an offensive against Japan did not have to conflict with the 'Germany first' policy. Churchill's talks confirmed that the Americans and British remained of one mind concerning the strategy for 1942 and 1943, which was to concentrate on taking north Africa before mounting a full-scale invasion of Europe. In the interim, the south-west Pacific would be left largely to languish.

Some feared that Australia might be lost to Britain, not because of the Japanese but because of the Americans. It was suggested that the American presence, combined with Australian resentment at the absence of British forces, could see Australia leave the empire and join with the United States. The Anglican archbishop of Brisbane tried to defend British actions with the publication of a small book entitled *Has Britain let us down?* which appealed to 'the vast bulk of loyal opinion' to make clear that Australians would be 'forever a British people'.[40] The former Australian prime minister

Billy Hughes was now leader of the United Australia Party and shared the archbishop's concern about the threat posed by the Americans to British influence in Australia. Cabling to Churchill, he warned that the position in Australia was

not good. Nearly 90 000 American troops ... crowd the streets producing great impression on the public mind. MacArthur's confidential report to the Government strongly anti-British. He is highly thought of, is Government adviser, his soldiers are here, the Government leans naturally to America. Strangely forget what they owe to Britain.

To counter the American influence, Hughes urged Churchill to send a 'substantial number' of British troops to the dominion.[41] Apart from the symbolic British Spitfire squadron, Churchill and his chiefs were determined to do no such thing.[42]

Following the division of the Pacific and Indian Oceans into spheres of American and British control, Britain tended to view the Pacific as an area solely of American interest. It was an attitude that the Americans were happy to encourage. When Britain's Admiral Cunningham was sent to Washington to deal with the US naval chief, the 'rather truculent and didactic' Ernie King, he confided to a colleague about his horror at encountering 'all the jealousy and suspicion' between the British and American naval staffs as they each fought their separate wars. Cunningham reported that

nowhere are our two staff sitting together and studying war problems on a broad basis. We have divided the world into spheres of influence and each country is fighting its own war in its own sphere and resents the other poking his nose into or even examining the problems in the sphere in which he is predominant.[43]

The division suited Churchill, allowing him to wipe his hands of Australia and the Pacific.

Churchill's attention was elsewhere. He had survived the fall of Greece and Crete and then the fall of Singapore. No one in the House of Commons had yet dared to stand up and call upon Churchill to depart in the wake of these disasters as they had with Neville Chamberlain after the Norwegian fiasco of 1940. But they were becoming rather bolder, particularly after the unexpected fall of Tobruk to Rommel's forces, with Churchill being informed of the disaster on 21 June as he was meeting in the White House with Roosevelt. Brooke was in the room when the message arrived and recalled how neither he nor Churchill 'had contemplated such an eventuality', which he described as 'a staggering blow'.[44] With Rommel pushing on towards Cairo, the American press carried stories from London predicting Churchill's imminent political downfall. So worried was Churchill by these reports that he rang from Washington and woke Eden for confirmation, only to be assured by Eden that he 'had not heard one word of this'.[45] But the challenge was laid down for Churchill when his critics issued notice on 25 June that they would be calling for a parliamentary vote of no confidence in Churchill's leadership.

Churchill was back in London on 27 June, immediately seeking to shore up his political position while also trying to shore up the military position in the Middle East. He talked wildly of flying out to Cairo to lean on Auchinleck, but was convinced by Brooke to postpone any such visit until the situation had clarified. Instead, he sent a stirring message to Casey, now the resident British minister in Cairo, instructing Casey to organise the

defence to the death of every fortified area or strong building, making every post a winning post and every ditch a last ditch. This is the spirit you have to inculcate. No general evacuation, no playing for safety. Egypt must be held at all costs.[46]

Churchill had sent a message in similar terms to Wavell just before the fall of Singapore and the prospects for Cairo looked equally bleak. According to stories in Whitehall, Casey panicked and 'blotted his copy book badly in Cairo by completely getting the wind up when Rommel was advancing, and issuing all sorts of notices advising flight'.[47]

Curtin viewed the situation in the Middle East with as much alarm as Churchill. The 9th Division, which Curtin had been unable to have returned to Australia, was about to be thrown into the defence of Egypt. Curtin was aware that his own political fate might hang on the fate of that division. If it met with disaster, like the 8th Division in Singapore, Curtin could be held to account by his colleagues for allowing it to remain there. According to one well-placed observer, Curtin believed that Evatt's reluctance to press for the division's return during his visit to London was due to him anticipating just such a military reverse occurring. And now Curtin suspected that the ambitious Evatt was waiting to profit politically from any calamity befalling the division.[48]

In confidential briefings to prepare the press for a possible disaster, Curtin warned that the situation in the Middle East might 'entail some sacrifices by Australia, and the taking of some more risks by Australia'. Hunched down in his leather chair among the huddle of scribbling journalists, the haggard prime minister warned that Australia must expect a 'harder and longer war' and that 'he would have to commence his fight for strength in the Pacific all over again'.[49] Even then, the Japanese army was planning to attack Port Moresby from the northern coast of New Guinea across the daunting terrain of the Owen Stanley mountains, while the Japanese navy was preparing to strike out from its base at Rabaul and extend its control along the length of the Solomon Islands.

NOTES

[1] Penglase and Horner (eds), *When the War came to Australia*, p. 129.

[2] Prime Minister's War Conference, Minute 23, 1 June 1942, *DAFP*, Vol. 5, Doc. 510.

[3] ibid.

[4] Prime Minister's War Conference Minutes, 11 June 1942, CRS A5954, Box 1, NAA.

[5] Advisory War Council Minutes, 11 June 1942, CRS A2682, Vol. 5, Minute 960; Cabinet Minutes, 9 June 1942, CRS A2703, Vol. 1[c]; Letter, Blamey to Curtin, 29 June 1942, and War Cabinet Minute No. 2224, 30 June 1942, CRS A5954, Box 261, NAA.

[6] 'War Situation from the Australian Viewpoint. A Review at 1st July 1942', Report by Shedden for Curtin, 10 July 1942, CRS A5954, Box 587, NAA.

[7] War Cabinet Conclusions, 1 June 1942, CAB 65/26, W.M. (42)70; Memorandum by Eden, 3 June 1942, CAB 66/25, W.P. (42)236, PRO.

[8] For an expression by Churchill of such a fear, see Robert Sherwood, *The White House Papers of Harry L. Hopkins*, Vol. 1, p. 478.

[9] Conversation between Churchill and the Chinese Ambassador, 3 June 1942, PREM 3/158/6, PRO.

[10] Minute, Churchill to Chiefs of Staff, 1 June 1942, PREM 3/143/9, PRO.

[11] Cable, Wavell to Churchill, 3 June 1942, PREM 3/143/9; Extract from C.O.S. (42) 51st Meeting (0), 8 June 1942, PREM 3/143/9, PRO.

[12] Letter, Somerville to MacQuarrie, 1 June 1942, ADD. MS. 50143, Somerville Papers, BL.

13 As one critic, Sir Edward Grigg, privately opined to the newspaper proprietor, Lord Astor, 'Winston ... has lost the power to give us moral strength — he just stimulates and titivates, and makes everyone feel that things are going better than they really are'. Grigg thought that Churchill could soon face a political crisis when Britain once again had 'to be steered through another patch of great disillusionment'. Letter, Grigg to Lord Astor, 12 June 1942, MS 1066/1/823, Astor Papers, RUL.

14 Cable, Churchill to Wavell, 12 June 1942, PREM 3/143/9, PRO.

15 Wavell was also faced with a deteriorating security situation in India when Gandhi launched a mass campaign of disruption, the so-called Quit India movement. Cable, Wavell to Churchill, 14 June 1942, PREM 3/143/9, PRO.

16 Letter, Kirke to Pound, 10 June 1942, PREM 3/163/8; Cable, Little to Pound, 12 June 1942, PREM 3/163/4, PRO.

17 Cable, Pound to Little, 18 June 1942, PREM 3/163/4, PRO; Cable, Churchill to Wavell, 5 June 1942, VI/2, Ismay Papers, KC.

18 Gilbert, *Road to Victory*, p. 122; Alanbrooke diary, 13 June 1942, in Danchev and Todman (eds), *War Diaries*, p. 265.

19 For Churchill's cables to Curtin, see ISMAY VI/2, Ismay Papers, KC.

20 Talk with Sir James Grigg, 16 June 1942, CRS M100, 'June 1942', AA.

21 Letter, Croft to Percival, 6 August 1942, CRFT 1/17, Croft Papers, CC.

22 Letter, Cross to Attlee, 16 September 1942, Rc/4/12, Cross Papers, IWM; See also Dalton diary, 11–14 September 1942, I/27/66, Dalton Papers, LSE.

23 Letter, Norman Douglas to Bruce, 25 June 1942, and letter, Official Secretary to Douglas, 3 July 1942, AA 1970/559/2, 'High Commissioner Bruce — Miscellaneous Papers — 1939–1945', NAA.

24 Cable, Bruce to Curtin, 26 June 1942, CRS M100, 'June 1942', NAA.

25 Minutes of Prime Minister's War Conference, 11 June 1942, CRS A5954, Box 1, NAA.

26 Minute, Churchill to Chiefs of Staff, 12 June 1942, PREM 3/151/4, PRO.

27 Report by the Joint Planning Staff, 17 June 1942, PREM 3/158/3, PRO.

28 Despite this, Churchill never trusted Australia's high commissioner and former prime minister. He condemned Bruce for his prewar association with Neville Chamberlain's appeasement policies and his later support for a compromise peace that would avoid a total war. And he disliked him for his occasional straight talking and his continuing support for Churchill's political opponents. War Cabinet Conclusions/Confidential Annex, 22 June 1942, CAB 65/30, W.M. (42)79, PRO; Talk with Attlee, 28 June 1942, CRS M100, 'June 1942', NAA; Day, 'An Undiplomatic Incident: S. M. Bruce and the Moves to Curb Churchill, 1942'.

29 Despite the effusiveness of Curtin's letter, both men realised that his mission had largely been a failure. Letter, Curtin to Evatt, 23 June 1942, and Memorandum, Shedden to Curtin, 23 June 1942, CRS A5954, Box 474, NAA.

30 Churchill's reaction to the suggestion of evacuating the Middle East, after Evatt had been adamant that Britain must not evacuate Singapore, can only be imagined. Cables, Attlee to Churchill, and Commonwealth Government to Dominions Office, both 25 June 1942, PREM 3/150/7, PRO.

31 Cable, Evatt to Bracken, 25 June 1942, PREM 3/150/7, PRO.

32 Minute, Attlee to Churchill, 26 June 1942, PREM 3/150/7, PRO.

33 Cable, Churchill to Curtin, 27 June 1942, VI/2, Ismay Papers, KC.

34 Cable, Evatt to Bracken, 30 June 1942, PREM 3/150/7, PRO.

35 Cable, Churchill to Curtin, 3 September 1942, CRS A5954, Box 229, NAA.

36 Letters, one undated but probably late 1945 and the other 17 September 1945, Cranborne to Emrys-Evans, ADD. MS. 58263, Emrys-Evans Papers, BL.

37 Menzies 1941 trip diary, p. 197, Menzies Papers, MS 4936/13/3, NLA.

38 Shedden's draft memoirs, Chap. 57, pp. 6–7, CRS A5954, Box 771; Cable, Evatt to Bruce, 15 November 1941, CRS M100, 'November 1941', NAA.

39 Advisory War Council Minutes, 17 June 1942, CRS A2682, Vol. 5, Minute 967, NAA.

40 The book became a bestseller. Rev. J. W. C. Wand, *Has Britain let us down?*, Melbourne, 1942.

41 Cable, Hughes to Churchill, 20 June 1942, PREM 3/150/7, PRO.

[42] The deputy commander of the Eastern fleet proposed in late June to form an Anglo–American fleet in Australian waters that would be equal in strength to the Japanese main fleet. Despite being supported by the South African prime minister, General Smuts, the plan was quashed in Whitehall. Appreciation by Willis, 19 June 1942, WLLS 5/5, Willis Papers, CC.

[43] Letter, Cunningham to Willis, 21 June 1942, CUNN 5/9, Cunningham Papers, CC.

[44] Alanbrooke diary, 21 June 1942, in Danchev and Todman (eds), *War Diaries*, p. 269.

[45] With Eden being canvassed as the most likely successor to Churchill, it was hardly possible that the increasing political disquiet had not been drawn to his attention. Gilbert, *Road to Victory*, p. 131; Cecil King diary, 9 July 1942, in King, *With Malice Toward None*, pp. 181–2; Unsigned paper, probably by Waldorf Astor, 23 June 1942, canvassing possibility of replacing Churchill as minister for defence, Astor Papers, MS 1066/1/823, RUL; Day, 'An Undiplomatic Incident'.

[46] Gilbert, *Road to Victory*, p. 137.

[47] Dalton diary, 27 August 1942, Dalton Papers, LSE.

[48] Shedden's draft memoirs, Chap. 57, p. 6, CRS A5954, Box 771, NAA.

[49] Background briefing by Curtin, 1 July 1942, MS 4675, Smith Papers, NLA.

TWENTY-NINE

'the nastiest of the entire war'

The first days of July saw Churchill confront his worst political crisis of the war, as Britain's Eighth Army dug in outside Cairo in a desperate attempt to bring the powerful tanks of Rommel's Afrika Korps to a shuddering halt. From Westminster, Churchill's critics watched with alarm as British forces were pushed back almost seven hundred kilometres into Egypt and more than thirty thousand of their troops were led off from Tobruk into captivity. In Cairo, smoke hung over the British headquarters as soldiers hurriedly burnt secret files in anticipation of the city's fall. In Russia, Hitler's panzer divisions were engaged in a massive offensive towards the south-east, attempting to strike out for the oil supplies of the Caucasus with one arm of their advance while the other arm struck at Stalingrad before turning to encircle Moscow. That at least was the plan, and it looked like it might succeed as spring turned into summer and the initial attacks brushed aside all Russian resistance.

The German offensive through the Caucasus, along with Rommel's push from Libya, threatened to create a pincer movement on the embattled British Middle East position. If the Germans succeeded in their rush to the

Caucasus, there was little to stop them moving into Persia and capturing the oil supplies upon which Britain's war effort was largely based. The Germans then would have almost encircled Turkey, making it difficult for the Turks to maintain their neutrality and ending Churchill's vain hope of drawing Turkey in on the Allied side. The Middle East and the Mediterranean could then become untenable for Britain. That, at least, was the worst case scenario that Churchill held out as he tried to shore up the Russians by shipping convoys of tanks and aircraft through the Arctic Ocean. But that could only be done at great cost, with one convoy being almost totally destroyed by the patrolling German aircraft and submarines. As a result, future convoys were temporarily suspended.

The deteriorating military situation in Europe and the Middle East had worrying implications for Australia. The 9th Division was threatened by the German onslaught in the Middle East and its continued presence there would be vital for any British recovery. As a result of the British reverse, it would be even more difficult for Curtin to extricate the division from Churchill's grasp. At the same time, the Spitfire aircraft that had been destined for Australia had been diverted to the Middle East, while the Eastern fleet was drawn upon to restore the position in the Mediterranean rather than being used to form a strong Anglo–American fleet in the Pacific. Although the prospect of an imminent Japanese invasion of Australia had receded, the dominion remained in considerable peril. Having established two secure bases on the north New Guinea coast, the Japanese were planning a landward attack against Port Moresby while other forces were advancing southward through the Solomon Islands.

It was a time for taking stock in Canberra. In a report drawn up for Curtin, Shedden claimed that the setbacks suffered by Japan ensured Australian security for the time being. Nevertheless, he warned that Japan remained potentially dangerous to Australia. Like MacArthur, Shedden argued that Japan should be dealt a series of heavy blows while it was still off-balance, thereby driving its forces away from northern Australia and demolishing the hastily constructed defences of its new empire before they could be consolidated. But no early offensive could be launched against Japan while the 'Germany first' strategy dominated Allied thinking. To overcome this, Shedden urged Curtin to shout even louder and to instruct Australia's representatives on the Pacific war councils and in the British war cabinet to make the most 'vigorous presentation of the Australian viewpoint ...'. And he berated the British for expecting Australia to defend British possessions in Malaya, Burma and Ceylon, areas from which 'large revenues had been derived by British trade and commerce, but the defence of which had been largely neglected'.[1]

It is difficult to imagine how Australia could have done more than it had done in early 1942, when its desperate appeals for assistance had simply led to anti-Australian feeling in Whitehall while producing few reinforcements for the embattled dominion. Although there was no reason why that would change now, there was good sense in Shedden wanting the Allies to hit Japan hard. The Pacific was a much more decisive theatre than the Middle East and the effect of knocking Japan out of the war at an early stage would have been of immense assistance to the Russian fight against Germany. So long as Japan remained in the war, Russia was forced to fight Germany with one hand tied behind its back, maintaining considerable forces in Siberia to guard against a Japanese attack from the rear.

Shedden's report also had important implications for Australia's attitude towards its own security. However, he failed to recognise that Britain's refusal to provide for Australian defence was a result of its declining imperial power and a calculated decision to concentrate that power in the Middle East. Shedden was mindful that America was guided by self-interest in extending assistance to Australia rather than by any innate sense of protectiveness. Therefore, argued Shedden, Australia had to continue building up its land and air forces to the 'highest degree possible'. As he reminded Curtin, it remained the 'obligation of every sovereign State to provide for its national defence to the maximum degree possible'.[2]

Despite Shedden's reminder, there were worrying signs that the lessons of the war had not been learnt. Already the government had approved the formation of a cabinet committee to plan for postwar demobilisation, while General Blamey was reorganising the army so as to reduce the number of its fighting units.[3] The demands of Australia's war effort, combined with the growing demands of MacArthur's forces, was beginning to place intolerable strains on the economy and the country's limited manpower. In early July, Curtin suggested that Australians should have a hundred days of austerity which, along with rationing, would help to maximise Australia's war effort.[4] When his cabinet submitted plans to increase expenditure from £320 million to £500 million, Curtin demanded that they be trimmed in accordance with the country's capacity to fulfil them while also keeping the war and civilian economies in balance.[5] The demands of the postwar period were also starting to impinge upon Curtin's attention, with the tariff board urging the establishment of a reconstruction authority, noting that 'some effort must be diverted from waging the war if reconstruction planning is to be effective'.[6]

At the same time, the United States was moving to prevent Australia from playing a full part in any offensive organised from its shores. In early 1942, the RAAF, which was being amalgamated with American squadrons as they arrived in Australia, was placed under the control of an American, General George Brett, who had been charged with controlling the US effort in Australia prior to the arrival of MacArthur. Brett had an uneasy relationship with the new supreme commander, with MacArthur finally moving to sack him after it was clear that Washington had also lost confidence in him. In late July, Brett was replaced by another American, General Kenney, who proceeded to divide the Allied air force along national lines, reserving for the Americans the role of pursuing the offensive against Japan. Australia's air force became a second-line, and very much second-rate, defence force.[7]

Australia was conscious of the problem but unable to influence events. By welcoming MacArthur as the saviour of the nation and making him supreme commander, Australia lost an opportunity to maximise its sense of self-reliance. For the duration of the war it became a *de facto* American colony, just as it had been a British colony since 1788 and a *de facto* colony of London since federation in 1901. The dependent mentality nurtured by a century and a half of colonialism, and buttressed by the difficulties of defending the island continent with a population of just seven million people, remained (and still remains to some extent) a barrier to the full exercise of its nationhood.

While the defence links between Britain and Australia were strained by the 'Germany first' policy, and considerable resentment was felt by many

Australians over the British failure to hold Singapore, there were many more who continued to hold tight to the 'mother country'. Still operating as a minority government, Curtin acknowledged the political influence of these staunch Anglo-Australians when he overlooked his party's commitment to having an Australian as governor-general and asked the King instead to extend the term of the present incumbent, Lord Gowrie.[8] By doing so, Curtin was postponing the task of choosing a replacement and perhaps earning additional credit in London by retaining a Briton as the King's representative. There was also the personal advisory role that Gowrie provided for Curtin, with the prime minister often calling at Gowrie's residence at Yarralumla to unburden himself of the cares of office.

Evatt was also keen to repair relations with Britain. Since his return from London in June, his antagonistic attitude towards Whitehall had softened somewhat. As the parliamentary under-secretary at the Dominions Office later observed, Britain's relations with Australia, the 'most difficult' of all the dominions, 'seem to be a little happier than they were and I think that the Evatt visit was useful, not that he created an altogether happy impression here but he learned something ...'.[9] Certainly Evatt gave an upbeat assessment of his talks in London when reporting back to his parliamentary colleagues in Canberra on 1 July, even going so far as to claim that Britain was 'coming round to the view ... that there should be a concentration of naval forces against Japan'.[10] This first-hand account from a forthright politician with a reputation for being anti-British would have assuaged some of the resentment felt by his Labor colleagues at the absence of British reinforcements.

Evatt's attitude towards Britain had softened partly due to the efforts of his businessman-adviser, W. S. Robinson, who had accompanied him to London and was adept at playing to Evatt's vanity. Robinson was a leading figure in Australia's metal industry and had been an important adviser to Prime Minister Billy Hughes during the First World War. He had an impressive array of business and political contacts across the world, although his loyalties were to Britain and the empire rather than simply to Australia.[11] Robinson now proposed to Evatt that he be allowed to return to London by way of the United States, claiming that he could be useful to Australia in London, where 'my voice might add a little weight to the claims of the Pacific Front'. He assured Evatt that he would not interfere with Bruce's role as high commissioner and might even be able to help Bruce's staff through his 'personal relations with the various ministers and departmental heads ...'.[12]

Indeed, Evatt would have been happy for Robinson to replace Bruce as high commissioner, but the office was not within his gift. So he used Robinson as a *de facto* ambassador in London, providing an alternative line of communication with the British government. Robinson was on close terms with Brendan Bracken and Oliver Lyttelton, respectively ministers for information and production, and was often invited for weekends with Churchill at Chequers. And there is no doubt that Robinson sometimes served Australia well, helping to smooth over rough patches in the often stormy wartime relationship with Britain.[13] But he also allowed his imperial perspective to affect the manner in which he presented the arguments of the Australian government while playing down demands of a more nationalistic nature. His presence also undercut Bruce's effectiveness as Australian representative, since it made clear to the British government that the high commissioner did not enjoy Evatt's confidence. Certainly, Bruce resented Robinson's presence, observing that he 'would not trust him a yard' and counselling visiting Australian politicians and British officials to stay well clear of him.[14]

One of the proposals pushed hard by Robinson concerned a planned survey of an alternative air route across the south Pacific. The idea for the route had originated with an Australian pioneer aviator, P. G. Taylor, who had run foul of MacArthur and American officials in Washington who regarded the route as a threat to America's trans-Pacific monopoly. By using the isolated and unpopulated Clipperton Island off the west coast of Mexico, Taylor planned to avoid refuelling in Hawaii, thereby overcoming the American monopoly and creating a secure air route far from the reach of the Japanese.[15] It might also fill the last gap in a round-the-world air route controlled by Britain, thereby giving Britain a considerable advantage in postwar aviation. There was much to commend the Clipperton route as far as Australia was concerned and Evatt and Robinson combined to support Taylor's endeavour. First, though, Taylor had to secure a long-range flying boat to survey the route at a time when such aircraft were sorely needed for the war. And his plans were prepared without the knowledge of MacArthur, whose authority as supreme commander was required before such a survey could be undertaken.[16]

On 2 July, Australia's defence committee had agreed to give MacArthur power to allocate all supplies within the South West Pacific Area (SWPA). This meant that MacArthur had the power to starve Australian defence forces of aircraft and munitions and direct them instead to the American forces. Indeed, as the chief of the air staff, Air Vice Marshal George Jones, advised Shedden, even the Spitfires that Evatt had secured from Britain could now be allocated by MacArthur to American squadrons if he so wanted. Australia would have to rely upon the supreme commander's sense of fair play to ensure that Australian forces were given a proper role in the defence of their homeland and the wherewithal to perform that role. Although these issues were vital to Australia, Jones warned that they would have to be circumspect in raising them with MacArthur 'lest any impression be created that we feared his powers would not be exercised in a manner which would give the R.A.A.F. a fair deal'.[17] In fact, the problem was insoluble once the supreme command for the country's defence had passed out of the control of its political leaders.

MacArthur might have enjoyed control over Australia's defence forces and the country's productive capacity, and he might have had Curtin's support for him taking the offensive against Japan, but he still had to contend with the Anglo–American attachment to the 'Germany first' policy. Churchill was as determined as ever to keep American eyes fixed upon the struggle against Germany. To do that, he had to devise some operation that would occupy the troops accumulating in Britain since there was no prospect of them invading France for at least another year. The destruction of the British convoy in the Arctic Ocean spurred him to repeat his earlier suggestion of invading Norway so as to neutralise the German bases there and protect the northern convoy route. He had bungled such an invasion in 1940 and had risen to the prime ministership from the ashes of that disaster. Although the chiefs of staff resisted being bitten twice, Churchill was adamant that the operation presented 'such attractive possibilities from so many points of view'.[18] It would not only soak up some of the forces massing in Britain but would maintain the offensive spirit among the Allies and deflect criticism from the dire situation in Egypt.

Churchill had fought off his critics in the House of Commons on 1 and 2 July when they had debated his running of the war. With some of these critics being people of considerable influence, the parliamentary situation was judged by Churchill's most recent biographer to be 'the nastiest of the entire war', with the radical Labourite, Aneurin Bevan, accusing Churchill of winning 'debate after debate' while losing 'battle after battle'.[19] But what was to be done to solve the situation? Fortunately for Churchill, his critics were disunited and could not even agree as to what sort of changes they wanted to impose on him. The mover of the motion caused the house to burst into 'ribald laughter' when he suggested that the King's ineffectual brother, the Duke of Gloucester, should be made commander-in-chief. Not that MPs were relaxed about the disastrous trend of the ongoing battles and the production side of the war effort. But, as one Conservative backbencher observed in his diary, 'the censure motion was so stupidly framed' that it was almost impossible to support. Moreover, to vote for it would have 'meant the fall of the Government in the middle of a great battle ...'. And that simply could not happen despite the atmosphere of 'all-pervading gloom'. Churchill's critics might have rallied around Cripps or Eden, but both men stood by Churchill and once more saved the day for him. The motion was defeated by 475 votes to 25, with about twenty abstentions.[20] The massive majority was certainly comforting, but Churchill would have noticed that the number of MPs prepared to vote against him was on the rise.

With his domestic critics silenced, at least for a time, Churchill could concentrate on killing the American plan for the Eastern fleet to attack Timor while the Americans sent their fleet to attack Rabaul.[21] The plan had been devised by the US naval chief, Ernie King, who effectively led the pro-Pacific group in Washington and who was critical of Britain's north African strategy. Even the US army supported King as it became clear that Churchill had been misleading Washington about the chances for a cross-Channel operation in 1942, and perhaps even in 1943. However, the Americans were hopelessly divided on the best way to mount an offensive against Japan.

King wanted to use his warships and marines to mount a thrust across the central Pacific rather than adopt the army plan to launch a major offensive from Australia, which would reduce his Pacific fleet to an appendage of MacArthur's force. Nevertheless, there was mounting support in Roosevelt's cabinet for doing something in the Pacific now that no cross-Channel operation was in prospect.

The US war secretary, Henry Stimson, privately expressed his exasperation with the British, complaining in his diary that they 'won't go through with what they agreed to' regarding an invasion of Europe. In retaliation, Stimson thought that the Americans should 'turn our backs on them and take up war with Japan'.[22] A concerned General Dill reported the drift of American thinking to Churchill, warning that the Americans might be so disappointed that they would withdraw to 'a war of [their] own in the Pacific, leaving us with limited American assistance to make out as best we can against Germany'.[23] To sort out the growing division in Anglo–American opinion on Allied strategy for the coming year, Roosevelt dispatched Marshal and King, along with Harry Hopkins, to London to try to reach an agreement with the British. Although a showdown with Churchill seemed inevitable, the meeting instead forced Roosevelt finally to concede that a cross-Channel operation was impossible in 1942. Accordingly, he instructed his naval and army chiefs to support the north African campaign rather than push for their preferred option in the Pacific.[24] As a result, the Pacific war was needlessly prolonged, and Australia remained under the shadow of the strengthening Japanese empire.

As for the suggested naval attack on Timor, Churchill tried to remove the Eastern fleet from consideration by having its heavy units pass through the Suez Canal into the eastern Mediterranean so that they could interpose themselves between Britain's hard-pressed forces in the Middle East and any German thrust that might be launched from across the Mediterranean from Greece. Given the weak state of Axis sea power in the Mediterranean, such a German thrust was most unlikely. But Churchill persisted, arguing that the presence of the warships would also provide an 'invaluable distraction' for the supply convoy that the Admiralty was planning to sail through the Strait of Gibraltar to Malta while also helping to 'steady things in Turkey'. As well, if British land forces could repel Rommel, the simultaneous return of the British fleet would 'very nearly restore our prestige in the Eastern Mediterranean'.[25] While the Admiralty joined with Churchill in opposing the Timor proposal, it also opposed as 'an unjustifiable risk' his alternative of sending the ships into the Mediterranean. Given Axis air superiority in the Mediterranean, it was aircraft rather than ships that were required to restore British power there. So the ships stayed put, while the Americans were told that the Royal Navy was fully occupied with its present commitments and could not contemplate the Timor operation within the time frame suggested by Washington.[26]

Realising that Britain could be the target of American criticism when it became known that the Eastern fleet, now strengthened with two modern aircraft carriers and a modern battleship, had been 'doing nothing for several months', Churchill warned the Admiralty that 'we cannot really keep this fleet idle indefinitely'.[27] However, instead of backing the American strategy of launching simultaneous strikes against Timor and Rabaul, Churchill wanted Wavell to use his limited resources in India to launch a combined operation against the Japanese forces in Burma. In various guises over the next couple of years, this would be Churchill's grand strategy for the war against Japan as he pressed his generals in India to launch offensives in Burma or Sumatra without providing them with the means to guarantee victory. In this instance, Wavell required landing ships for the operation suggested by Churchill, but they were taken instead for use in the Mediterranean. Consequently, Wavell's plans were postponed to 1943 and the Eastern fleet remained relatively idle.[28]

Given that the Allies were unable to invade Europe, the Mediterranean remained Churchill's principal focus. It was there that he wanted to introduce the Americans to the fighting against Germany, provided that Auchinleck could hold the line against Rommel that he had established at El Alamein, about a hundred kilometres west of Alexandria. For this, Auchinleck would need all the troops and tanks that he could get. So Churchill was not pleased to receive a cable from Curtin intimating that Australia would soon have to ask for the return of its 9th Division. Even though the two AIF brigades of the 6th Division were on their way back to

Australia from Ceylon, the dominion was struggling to provide the manpower for its own national defence while also servicing the growing American forces. Leaving the 9th Division in the Middle East meant that a continual flow of reinforcements had to be sent from Australia to keep it up to strength, something that was becoming increasingly difficult to do. Claiming that Australia was still open to a Japanese invasion, and pointing to the eight thousand air force personnel serving in Britain and the three thousand sailors serving with the Royal Navy, Curtin informed Churchill that it was time for the AIF to be concentrated in Australia 'for home defence and for participation with our American allies in offensive action against Japan when this becomes possible'. However, rather than making a demand for their return, Curtin asked Churchill for his views on the matter. Not surprisingly, Churchill's view was clear, as it always was when the question arose of subtracting forces from the effort against Germany. 'We must try to stop this,' he told his chiefs of staff, instructing them to prepare a 'short, definitive opinion ... setting forth the dangers of withdrawing this division at the present time or, indeed, during this year'.[29]

With such a clear brief, the chiefs duly submitted advice setting out the dangers of withdrawing the 9th Division from the Middle East. It was not only Rommel's forces in the west that concerned them. They were also worried by the possibility of German forces that were then pushing through southern Russia reaching as far as Persia from where Britain and Australia drew much of their oil supplies. As well, the withdrawal of the 9th Division, and the sending of a division to take its place, 'would involve an unjustifiable and dangerous shipping commitment'.[30] There was some sense in these arguments, although the Germans would never get close to capturing the Persian refining facilities. Nevertheless, shipping was in short supply, with all available troopships being used to carry American forces across the Atlantic, or British and Indian reinforcements to the Middle East. On the other hand, Australia needed all the troops that it could get, with a land battle about to begin with Japanese forces for control of New Guinea. Curtin was also advised by MacArthur on 17 July that his plans for mounting an offensive against Japanese forces in the Solomons, New Guinea and New Britain had been rejected by Washington. Instead, MacArthur would be allowed only to mount a limited offensive in the Solomons. As a result, warned MacArthur, the outlook had become so grave that it had become a question 'as to how we could save the war'. Moreover, the low priority accorded to SWPA by Allied planners had resulted in him being supplied with inferior aircraft and tanks.[31] They would soon be put to the test.

Although Washington had not approved an offensive for New Guinea, it would come anyway. First, though, the Australians had to defend the positions they held. Port Moresby was the prize that the Japanese wanted and the Australian defenders were determined to deny it to them. A small company of Australians had managed to traverse the rugged trail from Port Moresby over the Owen Stanley mountains to establish an outpost at the town of Kokoda in central New Guinea. To pre-empt a Japanese landward offensive, Blamey ordered on 17 July the occupation of Buna on the island's north coast, where MacArthur was planning to establish an important air base. But it was too late. Before they could get there, and with little opposition from the air, the Japanese landed troops at nearby Gona on 21 July and began quickly to push south towards the strategically important Kokoda and its small airfield. Using tactics perfected in Malaya, within a week of landing at Gona the lightly equipped Japanese had forced the base at Kokoda to be abandoned before its defenders were encircled.[32]

As the Australians struggled back towards more defensible positions closer to Port Moresby, Curtin learnt from Churchill that the promised delivery of Spitfires had been delayed further, this time by an administrative mix-up when only twelve of the promised 50 aircraft scheduled for dispatch during July were actually sent. It was a sign of the strained relations between London and Canberra that Churchill felt impelled to advise Curtin personally of the news, while promising that 46 aircraft were being loaded onto a ship that would leave for Australia on 5 August.[33] It was fortunate for Churchill that Curtin, rather than Evatt, responded to this latest setback to the arrival of the Spitfires. Curtin not only took the news calmly but agreed to the further retention of the 9th Division in the Middle East and the dispatch of a further draft of reinforcements from Australia to keep the division up to strength. When tackled by members of the advisory war council, Curtin assured them that the dispatch of the reinforcements did not

AWM SUK10355

Britain's information minister, Brendan Bracken (*centre*), looks on well satisfied as Australia's external affairs minister, Dr H.V. Evatt (*left*), and his adviser, W.S. Robinson, take their leave of London in May 1942 without the commitment of aircraft and munitions that they had hoped to get.

AWM P02018.083

The president of the USA holds forth during a meeting at the White House of the Pacific war council in April 1942.

AWM 157901

Desperate American sailors abandon the aircraft carrier *Lexington*, as it burns furiously after being attacked by Japanese aircraft during the battle of the Coral Sea in May 1942. The battle effectively secured New Guinea by forcing the Japanese to call off their seaborne capture of Port Moresby.

From left to right: T.V. Soong (China), Walter Nash (New Zealand), H.V. Evatt (Australia), Lord Halifax (Britain), Franklin D. Roosevelt (USA), Hume Wrong (Canada), Alexander Loudon (Netherlands) and Harry Hopkins (USA).

AWM P02018.106

While Evatt (*second from right*) and the dapper British foreign secretary, Anthony Eden (*far right*), look on, Churchill and the Soviet foreign minister, V.M. Molotov (*far left*), conclude a twenty-year treaty of friendship between their two countries in May 1942.

AWM 041439

Australia's former minister in Washington, and now Britain's minister in the Middle East, Richard Casey (*centre*), stands alongside the bearded South African prime minister, Jan Smuts, as they wait for Churchill during his visit to the Middle East in August 1942. Britain's General Auchinleck is on the far left and the British ambassador to Egypt, Sir Miles Lampson, is on the right.

AWM MED0522

With General Auchinleck as his guide, an impatient Churchill takes stock of the British position in Egypt in August 1942.

AWM P01977-1

During his visit to British positions on the El Alamein front, Churchill interrogates
Australia's General Leslie Morshead, commander of the 9th Division.

AWM MED0522

An Australian soldier tends the grave of Private Bruce Kingsbury, killed on 29 August 1942 during the battle of Isurava that helped to slow down the Japanese attack on Port Moresby. His lone charge at the Japanese lines earned him a Victoria Cross.

AWM 013572

The flag is raised at Kokoda on 14 November 1942 to mark its reoccupation by Australian troops.

The governor-general, Lord Gowrie, chats with Prime Minister John Curtin in Perth as they wait to review a parade of AIF troops in November 1942.

Presumably oblivious of the light naval protection provided for their convoy across the Indian Ocean, officers of the 9th Division enjoy a carefree game with nurses on their voyage home in February 1943.

Former Australian prime minister Billy Hughes tries on one of Evatt's Spitfires for size during a visit to their base at Darwin.

Chinese leader Chiang Kai-shek seems pleased after meeting in Cairo in November 1943 with Roosevelt and Churchill and getting a commitment of greater Allied activity against Japan. Behind them (*from left*): Generals Marshall and Dill, Air Chief Marshal Portal, Admirals Leahy, King, Brown and Cunningham, Generals Ismay and Brooke, Admiral Lord Louis Mountbatten, Shang Cheng and General Stilwell.

AWM 082279A

AWM 128480

denote any 'departure from the principle that the A.I.F. Forces abroad should ultimately return to Australia to fight in this theatre'.[34]

In his conciliatory message to Churchill agreeing to the retention of the 9th Division, Curtin had attempted to get in return an agreement from Churchill for Australia to have sufficient aircraft to build the RAAF up to 73 squadrons. He also wanted the regular transfer from Britain of Australian squadrons with operational experience in Europe. With the 9th Division secured, Churchill had no need to concede either of these requests and merely trotted out the usual assurances about Britain's protectiveness towards Australia. As for the aircraft, Churchill directed Curtin to approach the combined chiefs of staff in Washington, who would shortly be deciding on the allocation of aircraft for the SWPA. He assured him that the Americans had agreed that 'adequate measures would be taken to ensure the safety of Australia and the provision of the necessary equipment'.[35]

Churchill had more important things on his mind. On 1 August he had flown out to Cairo to meet with Auchinleck, whose cautious approach and inept subordinates were causing him serious concern. Auchinleck had dug his forces into a defensive line at El Alamein and delayed plans for a counterattack against Rommel until at least September. Churchill was desperate for a victory in the Middle East to compensate for the humiliation of Tobruk's surrender. Moreover, he was aware of Rommel's supply problems across the Mediterranean and feared that any delay would allow the Germans to regain the initiative and move on to overwhelm Egypt.[36] More importantly, Churchill was planning to fly on to Moscow for his first meeting with Stalin. He would try to soothe the Russian leader's anger at the British refusal to launch an invasion of Europe that year and thereby relieve the enormous German pressure bearing down on the Russian front line. This would be one of the most important meetings of the war. Upon it might depend the continued existence of that most peculiar alliance of convenience between Russia, Britain and the United States. Churchill's own political future was also bound up in the coming talks with Stalin. If he could cement a working relationship with Stalin to complement the one he had developed with Roosevelt, it would eclipse the rash of recent military defeats and make his political position practically unassailable.[37]

NOTES

1   Report by Shedden, presented to Curtin on 10 July 1942 and to MacArthur on 20 July 1942, CRS A5954, Box 587, NAA.

2   ibid.

3   Letter, Blamey to Curtin, 29 June 1942, CRS A5954, Box 261; Cabinet Minutes, 9 June 1942, CRS A2703/1[C], NAA.

4   Cabinet Minutes, 7 and 8 July 1942, CRS A2703/1[C], NAA.

5   Letter, Curtin to his Ministers, 18 July 1942, CRS A5954, Box 375, NAA; See also Background briefing, 29 July 1942, MS 4675, Smith Papers, NLA.

6   A new ministry of postwar reconstruction would be established later that year with the treasurer, Ben Chifley, in charge. Preliminary report by Tariff Board, 23 July 1942, CRS A2700/4/318, NAA.

7   Horner, *High Command*, pp. 353–7.

8   See MS 2852/4/21/24, Gowrie Papers, NLA.

9   Letter, Emrys-Evans to Wakehurst, 23 July 1942, MS 58243, Emrys-Evans Papers, BL.

10 Advisory War Council Minutes, 1 July 1942, CRS A2682/V/978, NAA.

11 As late as 1963, he wrote of being unable to 'think or refer to Britain as other than "Home"'. Letter, Robinson to Earl of Drogheda, 21 February 1963, Robinson Papers, 'Interesting Letters' Folder, UMA.

12 Memorandum, Robinson to Evatt, 20 July 1942, Evatt Papers, 'Robinson, W. S., 1942–45 (a)' Folder, FUL.

13 Draft cable, Robinson to Bracken, undated but, according to a note, written between 20 July 1942 and January 1943, Robinson Papers, 'Wars' Folder, UMA; War journal, 15 April 1943, Wilkinson Papers, WILK 1/2, CC; See also Lord Chandos, *The Memoirs of Lord Chandos*, London, 1962.

14 Talk with Spender, 19 November 1942, CRS M100, 'November 1942' and Talk with Robinson, 6 July 1943, CRS M100, 'July 1943', NAA.

15 Day, 'P. G. Taylor and the alternative Pacific air route, 1939–45'; See also P. G. Taylor, *Forgotten Island*, New York, 1946.

16 On 13 July, Robinson wrote to Evatt urging that 'when the necessary machine and other equipment, plus personnel, can be released [the survey of the Clipperton route] should be done and let us pray that it will be possible to do it quickly'. Letter, Robinson to Evatt, 13 July 1942, Evatt Papers, 'Robinson, W. S., 1942–45 (a)' Folder, FUL.

17 Note by Shedden, 6 July 1942, CRS A5954, Box 229, NAA.

18 War Cabinet Minute, 7 July 1942, cited in Gilbert, *Road to Victory*, p. 143.

19 Roy Jenkins, *Churchill*, London, 2001, pp. 693–98.

20 Headlam diary, 2 July 1942, in Stuart Ball (ed.), *Parliament and Politics in the Age of Churchill and Attlee: The Headlam Diaries 1935–1951*, Cambridge, 1999, p. 323.

21 Minute, Churchill to Alexander and Pound, 4 July 1942, PREM 3/163/4, PRO.

22 Bryant, *Turn of the Tide*, p. 421.

23 Gilbert, *Road to Victory*, p. 149.

24 Alanbrooke diary, 20–24 July 1942, in Danchev and Todman (eds), *War Diaries*, pp. 282–5.

25 Minute, Churchill to Alexander and Pound, 4 July 1942, PREM 3/163/4, PRO.

26 Minute, Alexander to Churchill, 14 July 1942, PREM 3/163/4; Cable, Pound to Little, 12 July 1942, PREM 3/163/5, PRO.

27 Minute, Churchill to Alexander and Pound, 13 July 1942, PREM 3/163/5, PRO.

28 See PREM 3/143/9, PRO.

29 Cable, Curtin to Churchill, 16 July 1942, and Minute, Churchill to Ismay, 18 July 1942, PREM 3/63/10, PRO.

30 Cable, Churchill to Curtin, 24 July 1942, PREM 3/63/10, PRO.

31 Minutes of Prime Minister's War Conference, 17 July 1942, CRS A5954, Box 1, NAA.

32 Gillison, *Royal Australian Air Force 1939–1942*, pp. 565–7.

33 See CRS A5954, Box 231, NAA; PREM 3/150/7, PRO.

34 Advisory War Council Minutes, 30 July 1942, CRS A2682/5/1009, NAA.

[35] MacArthur was singing a more discordant song in Curtin's ear and the parlous situation on the ground tended to bear out the words of the supreme commander. In early August, a statement of Allied air strength in MacArthur's command showed a notional complement of nearly seven hundred aircraft, but only three hundred were listed as being in a serviceable condition. Gillison, *Royal Australian Air Force 1939–1942*, pp. 574–5; Cable, Curtin to Churchill, 31 July 1942, PREM 3/63/10; Cable, Dominions Office to Australian Government, 6 August 1942, PREM 3/150/9, PRO.

[36] Gilbert, *Road to Victory*, p. 160.

[37] If Churchill could establish a viable relationship with Stalin, it would overshadow the position of Cripps whose role in Moscow had made him a political danger to Churchill. It would also overshadow the success of Eden's mission to Moscow some six months before.

THIRTY

'the perils of a common cause'

Churchill flew into Cairo on 3 August, determined to reorganise Auchinleck's Middle East command and bring on the offensive against Rommel. Churchill's political future could well depend upon it.[1] Before heading off to Moscow, he dumped Auchinleck as commander-in-chief and ordered General Bernard Montgomery out from England to take over the Eighth Army. They were fateful decisions that would finally tip the balance irrevocably against Rommel. Flying on to Moscow, Churchill had several late-night meetings with Stalin, who accepted under bitter protest the inability of his Anglo–American allies to mount an invasion of Europe that year, with landings in north Africa being staged instead. Returning to London on 23 August, Churchill could be well satisfied with the results of his long and dangerous journey. The value of his changes to the Middle East command would be known when Rommel launched his renewed offensive, with intercepted German cipher traffic suggesting it would occur within days.

Australia's 9th Division, which Churchill had visited during his time in Egypt, would be in the forefront of the coming battles. Churchill knew from his signals intelligence that Rommel's forces were starved of fuel and that the forthcoming German offensive would depend on a quick British collapse and the capture of their fuel dumps. With German tankers across the Mediterranean being harried by British submarines, and his forces operating at the end of a long line of communication, Rommel had no room for error. As Churchill confided in a letter to his wife: 'The more I study the situation on the spot the more sure I am that a decisive victory can be won if only the leadership is equal to the opportunity.' As his new commander of the Eighth Army, Montgomery was 'disagreeable to those about him' but, as Churchill observed, he would 'also [be] disagreeable to the enemy'.[2]

While Churchill could be confident about the outcome of the forthcoming battle, no such confidence was seen in Australia, where Curtin was expressing alarm at the Australian casualties already suffered during the retreat into Egypt. Although he had just allowed Churchill to hold on to the 9th Division, Curtin spoke bitterly to journalists on 4 August of the Australians being 'butchered' in the Middle East when they should have been returned to the Pacific theatre with the other two divisions. 'He was angry,' he said, that the Australians 'had been made the "chopping block" although there were 900 000 other troops in the Middle East.'[3] This was a familiar and not unjustified complaint, but it was also true that Australian governments had made clear to Whitehall on several occasions that they wished their troops to be in the front line rather than in reserve where they believed the troops would be prone to discipline problems.[4] Moreover, by agreeing to further reinforcements for the 9th Division, Curtin had effectively committed the troops to the offensive that Churchill would soon be urging upon Montgomery.

Although Churchill concentrated his attention and his country's resources on the European theatre, a watching brief was also kept on the Pacific, partly to ensure that excessive Allied resources were not diverted there and thereby lost to the war in Europe. As part of this brief, Whitehall requested that Australia allow a military mission to be attached to the office of the British high commissioner in Canberra so that London could be kept informed of military developments in the South West Pacific Area. This seemed an innocuous request that could be to Australia's advantage since it would provide a direct channel to the British War Office. Australia had already conceded supreme control of its forces to the Americans so there seemed to be no basis for any objection to such a military mission being established, particularly as Australia already enjoyed such facilities in London. But Curtin was worried that the proposal would interfere with his relationship with MacArthur while Blamey, who had rankled under the control of a British commander in the Middle East, was keen to preserve his relative independence in Australia. Accordingly, Blamey urged that the government simply strengthen its representation in London so that Whitehall could be provided with all the information it needed through Australian channels.[5]

Blamey's objections caused dismay and disbelief in the War Office, with British officials finding it difficult to understand why facilities they extended to Australian officers in London could not be reciprocated to British officers in Australia. In fact, as Bruce informed Curtin on 20 August, Britain had expected Canberra to welcome its proposal as an indication of increased British interest and concern in the region. The matter was taken up at cabinet level where it was seen by British ministers as further evidence of Australian bloody-mindedness. Bruce pressed Curtin to withdraw his objections while there was still time and 'put an end to an episode which is tending to engender a quite unnecessary amount of friction'. In the face of Bruce's pleading, and armed with assurances that the British officers would not intrude on the triangular relationship between London, Washington and Canberra, Curtin finally consented to the plan in mid-September, although MacArthur still strenuously opposed it and granted the officers only the most limited access to his headquarters.[6]

The British proposal was not as innocent as it seemed. Its timing gave some indication of its intent. There had been no proposal for such a mission to Australia during the dangerous months leading up to the attack on Pearl Harbor, or during the first half of 1942 when Australia's survival had been at stake. Curtin and MacArthur had appealed for greater resources to be allocated to the SWPA, but such appeals, if they were successful, would threaten the British effort against Germany. London could guard against this with a military mission that could provide an independent, authoritative assessment of the needs of the SWPA and thereby undermine further appeals emanating from Australia. It had the potential, therefore, of muting Australia's voice in the international councils of war. Which is what Blamey had feared, and which seemed to be confirmed when he discovered later that the original proposal for three officers headed by a brigadier had been expanded into a full-blown mission led by a major-general. Blamey denounced this as a British trick designed to 'prevent as much as possible our direct dealing with America and to ensure British control of Australian requirements'. He urged Curtin to ban the mission from Australia's 'inner councils' and warned that it was capable of becoming a great 'thorn in our side'. He was too late. Curtin had taken Bruce's warning about British displeasure seriously and refused to reverse his consent to the mission.[7]

Unknown to Curtin, Bruce's support for the mission was motivated partly by his continuing involvement in two different issues. One concerned his efforts to achieve greater substance for his role as Australian representative in the British war cabinet, while the other involved him in a backstairs conspiracy against Churchill's leadership. For the previous two months, Bruce had been struggling to gain enough power to prevent his being excluded from the war cabinet when matters of interest to Australia were being discussed. Indeed, Bruce wanted to attend the war cabinet even when it was only discussing matters of purely British domestic interest. Now, just when he was confident of having developed a workable understanding with Attlee on this issue, the dispute over the military mission threatened to reignite British hostility towards Australia and disturb his position in the war cabinet.[8]

The issue also threatened to disturb his standing in British political circles and prevent his voice being heard on the question of a replacement for Churchill. Bruce had interfered in British politics before and, with Churchill away in Cairo and Moscow, he did so again as renewed criticisms of Churchill swept through Westminster. With the war situation appearing critical in the Middle East and Russia, the influential newspaper proprietor Lord Astor dispatched an emissary to Wales to sound out Lloyd George and check on the rumours of his increasing senility. The elderly statesman, who had been waiting in the wings for just such a call, declared himself ready to join in a move against Churchill and willing to serve under Eden if he became prime minister, but not to serve under Cripps.[9] Bruce, though, was using his position as high commissioner and Australian representative in the war cabinet to support Cripps. Part of the strategy was to attack Churchill where he was vulnerable, criticising his concentration of air resources on the bombing of Germany to the detriment of the war against the U-boats in the Atlantic and the defence of Ceylon.

When Churchill was on his way to Moscow, Bruce took advantage of his absence to submit a memorandum to the war cabinet urging that aircraft be diverted from the bombing of Germany to the war at sea. He also wanted the defence of Ceylon to be given the high priority in the allocation of aircraft that it was accorded on paper by British defence planners. Bruce did not suggest diverting part of the bomber force to the defence of Australia, where it was sorely needed.[10] Instead, his call had a political barb with its suggestion that the vital war against the U-boats was being neglected. Had it been echoed in the war cabinet, it would have seriously undermined Churchill's leadership since he had staked so much on the bombing offensive and had already deflected moves for some of the aircraft to be used as long-range patrols over Britain's vital north-western approaches. But Churchill's colleagues were unwilling to challenge his strategy, merely responding to Bruce's memorandum by requesting details concerning the allocation of aircraft.[11]

Bruce was undeterred by the setback in the war cabinet. On 17 August, with Churchill back in Cairo after his successful visit to Moscow, Bruce met with Cripps, ostensibly to discuss the diversion of aircraft to the war at sea. However, the meeting soon degenerated into a diatribe against Churchill's leadership. According to Bruce's account, they

both agreed that while the Prime Minister had been an invaluable asset in what might be described as the emotional period following on Dunkirk he was not temperamentally suited to running the war in the planning and organising period in which we now are.

It might have been the discussion that prompted a serious tilt by Cripps at Churchill's leadership. However, almost immediately after being ushered from Cripps' presence, Bruce was handed various cables from Moscow reporting on the progress of Churchill's difficult talks with Stalin.[12] They prompted one of the fastest about-turns in political history.

Churchill realised that his political future could rest on the outcome of his talks with Stalin. So, in a cable to Attlee written while he was resting in Tehran on the return journey, Churchill quickly claimed his trip had been a personal triumph, arguing that 'the disappointing news I brought could not have been imparted except by me personally without leading to really serious drifting apart. It was my duty to go. Now they know the worst, and having made their protest are entirely friendly ...'[13] The political implication was clear. Combined with his relationship with Roosevelt, it was apparent that only Churchill could carry the war forward and manage these vitally important relationships with Moscow and Washington. And Bruce freely acknowledged this once he had read Churchill's account of the Moscow meetings.

Rather than being a liability, Bruce now considered that Churchill was 'an asset of incalculable value [who] has established his position with Stalin in an amazing way and in doing so has re-affirmed his position, vis-a-vis the U.S.A.'. As a result of Churchill's apparent prestige in Russia and the United States, Bruce's commitment to support Cripps would have to be withdrawn since 'any idea of action which might lead to his displacement as Prime Minister is quite out of the question'.[14] As such, the trip had had its desired effect.[15] From that point onwards, as the war outlook slowly improved, Bruce's attitude towards Churchill changed from outright opposition to one of warm support. But it was too late. Bruce had destroyed his chances of wielding influence in Downing Street since nothing could convince Churchill that the high commissioner was not continuing to seek his political demise.[16] He also would have remembered Bruce as a supporter of Chamberlain's appeasement policies and of a negotiated peace in 1939–40. Although Lord Hankey lent his support to Bruce, proposing in a note to British ministers that Bruce should have access to 'all meetings, proceedings and documents, including those of the Defence Committee, of which he ought to be a member', Churchill would never allow it.[17] He was again sufficiently strong to ignore the high commissioner, even though Bruce now only wanted to be helpful.

While the battle for the Middle East and for control of the Caucasus continued to rage, Australia's attention was fixed on the battle closer to home as Japanese and Australian forces fought for control of the landward approaches to Port Moresby. With control of the airfield at Kokoda having been lost at the end of July, the forces trying to stem the oncoming Japanese had to rely on supplies dropped from the air or carried laboriously over the mountains by a line of New Guinean porters. There never seemed to be enough porters, nor enough transport aircraft to make air drops, to maintain sufficient supplies at the front line. And the fighting on the ground was left to a relatively small force of conscripted militia.

As the battle continued, the government tried to keep Australians focused on the war now that an imminent invasion had become less likely. On 3 August, Curtin met with his colleagues in Canberra where the cabinet decried the apathy of the Australian public. Curtin, the former alcoholic and anti-war activist, angrily pointed to the prevalence of drinking, gambling and strikes, and urged that the laws 'be invoked to put down these national abuses', reminding his cabinet that 'war could not be waged without ruthlessness'.[18] But Curtin and his colleagues were infected with the same apathy that was beginning to beset their fellow Australians. With 90 000 Americans having arrived by August, even Curtin's fears for Australia's survival had been largely allayed. And neither Blamey nor MacArthur believed that the Japanese were intent on capturing Port Moresby or had sufficient forces in New Guinea for that purpose. If they were intent on doing so, both Allied commanders were confident that the mountains of the Owen Stanley Range would provide secure positions from which to hold the attackers at bay.[19]

The elderly UAP leader and former wartime prime minister, Billy Hughes, was not so sure and presumably saw the southward advance of the Japanese as a chance also to beset Curtin's minority government. Concerned that MacArthur had been beaten into Buna by the Japanese, who had gone on quickly to capture Kokoda, Hughes issued an alarming statement on 5 August which predicted that Australia might mimic the recent experience of Malaya. Blasting Australia's military leaders, including presumably MacArthur, Hughes claimed there had been 'a lamentable lack of vision, of initiative, of co-ordination of control' by defence chiefs who had 'failed to anticipate the enemy's movements'. Rather than waiting for the 'death stroke', said Hughes, Allied forces must 'go out and sweep the enemy from his vantage ground'.[20] But his premonitions were dismissed, both by the government and by its military advisers, who remained confident about Moresby's position.

When Curtin gathered his chiefs of staff together to address a conference of state premiers in Melbourne on 10 August, Blamey assured the meeting that the fighting for control of Kokoda, which was splashed across the front pages of the nation's newspapers, was 'not of great importance'. As for the nation's security, Blamey claimed that 'there had been an immense improvement in Australia's position in recent months' and that, 'while one could not say definitely that Australia would not be attacked, he did not think it would be very easy for the enemy to attack on a large scale at present'.[21] That night, Curtin told the annual dinner of the Commercial Travellers' Association in a Melbourne hotel that the war was 'one which the men of our race are going to wage to a victorious end'. Mindful of Hughes' apparent scaremongering, Curtin called on Australians to 'share the perils of a common cause'.[22]

At least part of the government's confidence about the security situation was based upon a false understanding of the Allied naval position. Thus, Blamey had assured the premiers that Western Australia was secure because its two infantry divisions in Perth were augmented by the 'protection of the fleet stationed in the Indian Ocean'. Australia's naval chief, Admiral Sir Guy Royle, backed Blamey up, pointing to the Allied 'preponderance of naval power', including 'a substantial force in the Indian Ocean' that could reinforce those in the Pacific.[23] However, unknown to Blamey, and perhaps also to Royle, the major ships of Britain's Eastern fleet had been transferred to the Mediterranean to sustain the British bastion of Malta and support the forthcoming invasion of north Africa. As far as warships of any substance were concerned, there were just two modernised battleships and an aircraft carrier left in the Indian Ocean, and they were concentrated in the Cape Town–Ceylon–Aden triangle to protect the reinforcement route to the Middle East and the British hold on India. They may have posed a vague menace to the Japanese navy but they would have been insufficient to prevent an invasion in force of Australia.

Fortunately for the people of Perth, the Japanese were preoccupied with their conquest of the Solomon Islands, as they attempted to isolate Australia from the United States, and with consolidating their occupation of New Guinea by taking Port Moresby. Beating off these offensives was essential for the safety of Australia, although the government remained remarkably complacent about the deteriorating position in New Guinea and was slow to reinforce its embattled defenders. In the Solomons, the Americans had decided to resist the Japanese expansion when it became known that they were building an airfield on the island of Guadalcanal from where they would be able to attack Allied forces further south in the New Hebrides and New Caledonia. To prevent this, US marines were landed on Guadalcanal and Tulagi on 7 August, with a force of Allied warships, along with aircraft from MacArthur's command, protecting the operation. Among the ships was the Australian cruiser *Canberra*, which had been taken from SWPA without the knowledge of the Australian government and attached to the South Pacific Command for the duration of the operation. Along with three US cruisers, it was caught unprepared when a force of Japanese cruisers launched a night-time attack with torpedoes that sent all four ships to the bottom. Despite this disaster, the marines were ashore and in a position to contest the Japanese hold over the Solomons. The outcome of the struggle would hinge upon the ability of the opposing navies to keep their separate forces supplied.

Evatt was quick to congratulate Admiral Ernie King for the apparent success of the US naval landings on Guadalcanal, where the marines now outnumbered the Japanese defenders and were busy constructing an airfield that came to be dubbed Henderson Field. Of course, Evatt had another agenda. Australia had been advised by Bruce that the postponement until at least 1943 of the Anglo–American invasion of Europe had released 25 per cent of the American aircraft that had been destined for use in Britain. The planes could now be sent to the Pacific.[24] This news also would have boosted the confidence of Curtin and his commanders in the prospects for the SWPA. First they had to ensure that a substantial number of the aircraft were sent to

Australia. Accordingly, Evatt warned King that the Japanese would probably react to the Solomons landings with 'some spectacular counter blow, and probably at the mainland of Australia'. To guard against this, Evatt urged that Australia receive its share of the aircraft being diverted to the Pacific so that it might be 'secure against large scale invasion'. If Australia could be made secure, argued Evatt, Britain would not have to abandon the Mediterranean in the event of Australia being invaded.[25] Evatt was right to stress Australia's continuing vulnerability, but King knew enough about Japan's defence situation to realise that it was unlikely to attack, let alone invade, Australia.

In fact, the aim of the Australian government seemed to be less about securing the country from invasion and more about building up the long-term strength of the RAAF. As Curtin advised his minister in Washington, the eminent jurist Sir Owen Dixon, he wanted the RAAF to have an eventual strength of 71 squadrons. He recognised that it would have to be achieved in stages and suggested that the first stage could be the provision of modern aircraft for the seventeen existing RAAF squadrons that were operating with obsolete or insufficient aircraft. The second stage could be to supply sufficient aircraft by January 1943 to allow for the formation of 44 squadrons. Curtin suggested that Dixon enlist the help of British officials in his appeal to Roosevelt and link the request for aircraft to Australia's agreement to leave the 9th Division in the Middle East and its continuing commitment to supply Britain with aircrew under the Empire Air Training Scheme.[26]

Neither Britain nor the United States were willing to respond positively to Australia's pleading. While British officials made sympathetic noises in response to the Australian appeal, their aims were diametrically opposed.[27] As for the Americans, Curtin was aghast to learn that the US chiefs of staff proposed to allocate sufficient aircraft to Australia for just 30 squadrons instead of 44, and then only by April 1943 rather than January. The Americans also proposed to provide aircraft for another ten RAAF squadrons but to take them from the USAAF squadrons already in Australia. So Australia would gain ten RAAF squadrons at the expense of ten USAAF squadrons, producing little net benefit. As well, Evatt's three Spitfire squadrons were subtracted from the total allocation of American aircraft. Existing Australian squadrons would have to subsist with their outmoded types, for there would be few aircraft to replace them. Curtin also discovered that MacArthur intended to assign only secondary defensive roles to those squadrons.[28]

Evatt demanded to know how a proposal from Australia to increase the strength of the RAAF in return for leaving the 9th Division in the Middle East had been transformed into a proposal simply to transfer existing aircraft from American to Australian squadrons and leave SWPA no better off. Moreover, he told Dixon that the 'proposal to count in the special Spitfires which I obtained is quite opposed to the express agreement I made with Churchill', which he found 'most distressing'.[29] Evatt had already been taunted by Hughes when the first delivery of Spitfires had been diverted to the Middle East, with Hughes publicly querying 'the vaunted success of Dr. Evatt's mission, if as it now appears, we are not going to get the goods after all'. Desperate to keep counting them as a political success, Evatt gave an off-the-record briefing to journalists in which he tried to resurrect the planes as a great personal triumph.[30] But he received no joy from Washington, with Dixon simply reiterating the American argument about shortages of aircraft and informing Evatt that the US chiefs of staff 'appear to regard the result as defensively adequate'.[31] As this exchange revealed, the appointment of Dixon had not given Australia a particularly forthright representative in the American capital, with the Anglophile Dixon having a reserved and reflective nature that suited him as a High Court justice but hampered him as a diplomat in wartime Washington.[32]

While Evatt was shooting cables off to Washington, the Japanese were tightening their hold on New Guinea and continuing their steady push southwards towards Port Moresby. MacArthur had planned to occupy the north coast of New Guinea but had been pre-empted by the Japanese. Only at Milne Bay, on the far east coast of the island, had the Australians managed to establish a defensive position, complete with an airfield among the coconut trees and using steel matting to cope with the boggy ground.[33] As at Port Moresby, the defenders were drawn from the partly trained militia which had not yet been battle tested. They would soon have their chance, with the Japanese landing at Milne Bay on 25 August intent on capturing the newly constructed airfield. They managed to get ashore without serious interference from Allied aircraft.

As the events at Milne Bay were unfolding, Curtin made a fresh appeal to Churchill for naval and air assistance, claiming that there could soon be a 'naval clash which may well decide the course of the conflict in this theatre'. Not realising the weakened state of the Eastern fleet, Curtin again asked for its warships to join with the US Pacific fleet to create a naval force capable of defeating the Japanese main fleet. He also confronted Churchill with the aircraft situation and the miserly plan by the US chiefs of staff to equip just 30 squadrons of the RAAF. Reminding Churchill of Australian sacrifices for the Allied cause, Curtin argued that it was only right that the Allies should provide a proper 'degree of reinsurance', particularly as the 9th Division had been allowed to remain in the Middle East only on condition that British representatives in Washington 'would be instructed to do their utmost' to ensure the adequate supply of aircraft for Australia. Claiming that Australia was 'more vulnerable to invasion than any other part of the Empire', and that the proposed allocation would 'not ensure even the defence of Australia as a base', Curtin appealed to Churchill to intercede with Roosevelt while there was still time.[34]

Churchill would have none of it. He was willing to offer Australia the gift of a British cruiser to replace the *Canberra*, but he refused to intercede with Roosevelt.[35] He remained intent on keeping the Americans focused on the coming invasion of north Africa, with Brooke noting on 29 August that additional forces would be needed for it 'which can only be found by drawing on [the] Pacific. This will not suit Admiral King. We shall have again to remind the Americans that Germany must remain our primary concern and that the defeat of Japan must take second place.'[36] Meanwhile, Japan continued to strengthen the outer defences of its newly won empire.

MacArthur enlisted Curtin's help to coordinate a two-pronged appeal to the US chiefs of staff for more forces for the SWPA. In his message to Washington on 30 August, MacArthur warned of the crisis confronting his command and predicted 'the development within a reasonable period of time of a situation similar to those which produced the disasters that have successively overwhelmed our forces in the Pacific since the opening of the war'.[37] The supreme commander and the Australian government had finally realised the seriousness of the threat to Port Moresby, while the Japanese thrust south-east through the Solomons had the potential of cutting Australia's Allied lifeline and leaving the dominion isolated in a Japanese sea.

NOTES

[1] There was talk in the House of Commons at the beginning of August of political conspiracies directed by Beaverbrook with the aim of getting a new national government, although perhaps retaining Churchill as a figurehead. While supporting Churchill, the Conservative MP Sir Cuthbert Headlam thought that there 'never was such an opportunity for a man of grit as there is today — everyone on our side is looking for a leader — someone who will be ready to take control when Winston passes from the scene either during or after the war'. Headlam diary, 4 August 1942, in Ball (ed.), *Parliament and Politics in the Age of Churchill and Attlee*, p. 330.

[2] Gilbert, *Road to Victory*, pp. 168–9.

[3] Background briefing by Curtin, 4 August 1942, MS 4675, Smith Papers, NLA.

[4] Hasluck, *The Government and the People 1939–1941*, p. 225.

[5] Letters, Blamey to Shedden, 29 July 1942, and Curtin to Cross, 6 August 1942, CRS A5954, Box 463, NAA.

[6] Cable, Bruce to Curtin, 20 August 1942, CRS A5954, Box 463, NAA; See also other documents in this box.

[7] Letters, Blamey to Shedden, 30 November 1942, and Shedden to Blamey, 22 December 1942, CRS A5954, Box 463, NAA.

[8] Cable, Bruce to Curtin, 2 August 1942, CRS M100, 'August 1942', NAA.

[9] Secret memorandum, Jones to Astor, 7 August 1942, and Letters, Thomas to Jones, 13 August 1942, and Astor to H. Brooke MP, 17 August 1942, MS 1066/1/823, Waldorf Astor Papers, RUL.

[10] When the Japanese convoy landed its troops at Gona in mid-July, MacArthur was able to muster only five bombers to make an ineffectual attempt to prevent the landing. Gillison, *Royal Australian Air Force 1939–1942*, p. 568.

[11] War Cabinet Conclusions/Confidential Annex, 12 August 1942, CAB 65/31, W.M. (42)111, PRO.

[12] Talk with Cripps, 17 August 1942, CRS M100, 'August 1942', NAA.

[13] Cable, Churchill to Attlee, 17 August 1942, PREM 3/76A/11, PRO; See also G. Ross, 'Operation Bracelet: Churchill in Moscow, 1942', in David Dilks (ed.), *Retreat from Power*, Vol. 2, London, 1981.

[14] Talk with Cripps, 17 August 1942, CRS M100, 'August 1942', NAA; See also Paul Addison, *The Road to 1945*, London, 1975, Chap. 7.

[15] As one Conservative MP observed upon Churchill's triumphant return to London, 'these trips strengthen his position at home immensely ...' Headlam diary, 26 August 1942, in Ball (ed.), *Parliament and Politics in the Age of Churchill and Attlee*, p. 333.

[16] Note by Bruce, 6 October 1942, CRS M100, 'October 1942', NAA.

[17] Memorandum by Hankey, 3 September 1942, HNKY 11/7, Hankey Papers, CC.

[18] Cabinet Minutes, 3 August 1942, CRS A2703/1(c), NAA.

[19] Horner, *High Command*, pp. 215–8.

[20] ibid., p. 218.

[21] Minutes of Prime Minister's War Conference, 10 August 1942, CRS A5954, Box 1, NAA.

[22] This was a far cry from Curtin's calls to Roosevelt and Churchill during April and May for Australia to be accorded special treatment as the last bastion of the white man in the southern hemisphere. *Sydney Morning Herald*, 11 August 1942.

[23] Minutes of Prime Minister's War Conference, 10 August 1942, CRS A5954, Box 1, NAA.

[24] Cable, Bruce to Curtin, 8 August 1942, *DAFP*, Vol. 6, Doc. 20.

[25] Cable, Evatt to King, 14 August 1942, *DAFP*, Vol. 6, Doc. 24.

[26] Cable, Evatt to Dixon, 11 August 1942, CRS A5954, Box 229, NAA.

27 As leader of the British admiralty delegation in Washington, Admiral Cunningham described the agreement allowing for the diversion to the Pacific of some American air force units as being 'a most poisonous document ...' Letters, Cunningham to Pound, 31 July and 12 August 1942, ADD. MSS. 52561, Cunningham Papers, BL.

28 Cable, Dixon to Evatt, 20 August 1942, CRS A5954, Box 229, NAA.

29 Cable, Evatt to Dixon, 25 August 1942, CRS A5954, Box 229, NAA.

30 Background briefing, 25 August 1942, MS 4675, Smith Papers, NLA.

31 Cable, Dixon to Evatt, 25 August 1942, CRS A5954, Box 229, NAA.

32 Letter, Watt to Hood, 10 August 1942, MS 3788/1/1, Watt Papers, NLA.

33 Gillison, *Royal Australian Air Force 1939–1945*, pp. 564–5, 605.

34 Cables, Curtin to Churchill, 25 August 1942, *DAFP*, Vol. 6, Docs 27 and 28.

35 Churchill suggested that 'it might have a lasting effect on Australian sentiment if His Majesty's Government gave [a cruiser] freely and outright to the Royal Australian Navy ...' Note, Churchill to War Cabinet, 28 August 1942, CAB 66/28, W.P. (42)384, PRO.

36 Alanbrooke diary, 29 August 1942, in Danchev and Todman (eds), *War Diaries*, p. 315.

37 Horner, *High Command*, p. 219.

THIRTY-ONE

'while the enemy thunders at the gates'

By the beginning of September, the Australian forces defending Port Moresby were being pushed back towards the town. The militia troops proved no match for either the Japanese or the punishing terrain. Their commander, General Rowell, appealed for reinforcements of battle-tested AIF troops from Australia who could stand steady in the face of the Japanese assaults.[1] But even the troops of the battle-tested 7th Division were unable to stem the remorseless advance of the lightly equipped Japanese. When the Australians established fixed positions blocking the tortuous and muddy track, the Japanese would melt into the surrounding jungle and reappear behind the Australians in successive outflanking movements that sent the defenders rushing backwards in a desperate attempt to maintain their grip on the tenuous supply line to Port Moresby.

With too few aircraft to keep the troops supplied from the air, they had to rely upon lines of local porters to struggle through with the food and munitions and to carry out the sick and wounded. Although the situation was certainly critical, and Port Moresby's capture seemed imminent, every retreat by the Australians lengthened the lines of communication for the

Japanese and reduced the advantage of their troops, who found themselves subsisting on the most meagre of rations. A ten-kilometre retreat brought the Japanese closer to Port Moresby but it also added ten kilometres of mud over which porters had to transport ammunition and supplies from the Japanese base at Buna. Conversely, every retreat made the supply situation of the Australian defenders that much less critical. Whether that would be sufficient to save Port Moresby remained to be seen.

As for the other Japanese thrust, there were pitched battles between American marines and Japanese troops on Guadalcanal, with both sides becoming entrenched in strong positions and neither having the ability or the numbers to overwhelm the other. Unknown to the Japanese, the Americans had about 20 000 men dug in a protective circle around Henderson Field, the rudimentary airfield from where they were struggling to establish air superiority in the difficult climatic conditions. With the Japanese enjoying superiority in the air and surrounding seas, it would be a long and costly campaign to eject them from the two hundred-kilometre-long island.

Following the Japanese naval success in the Solomons, and the steady advance of their troops towards Port Moresby, Allied assurances of Australian inviolability were called into question. Each battle required the United States to learn of Japanese intentions through its interception of their naval signals and then to rush its aircraft carriers from Hawaii to thwart those intentions. As the Americans discovered at Midway, there was a large element of luck involved as to which navy would emerge supreme from each engagement. And each side had its submarines lurking along the likely reinforcement routes, waiting to pick off enemy warships. On 31 August, the American carrier *Saratoga* was damaged near Guadalcanal by a torpedo from a Japanese submarine and forced to retire to Pearl Harbor for lengthy repairs. Two weeks later, the carrier *Wasp* was sunk by another submarine. For the following month, there was just one American carrier operating in the Pacific. During this time, there was little to prevent the Japanese doing what they pleased in the south-west Pacific. As the former chief of Britain's committee of imperial defence, Lord Hankey, observed from London, the loss of Singapore 'has enabled the Japanese to sprawl all over the Far East', providing them with 'an embarrassing choice of attractive offensives open to them — China, Eastern Siberia, Australia, New Zealand and India'.[2]

The situation was not quite as dark as the elderly Hankey was inclined to paint it. The Japanese had postponed plans for further offensives, other than those that were designed to shore up the boundaries of its hastily won empire. Mounting a scaled-down offensive to cut Australia's lifeline to the United States remained one of Tokyo's top priorities. If that could be achieved, Australia would again be vulnerable to invasion. And if Port Moresby fell, a door into northern Australia would be forced wide open. From his newly established headquarters in Brisbane, MacArthur now conceded the seriousness of the situation in New Guinea. His previous complacency had been shattered by the success of the Japanese landings on its north coast and by their push on Port Moresby. The critical public statements by Billy Hughes would have also put him under pressure to retrieve the position and so avoid another disaster like that which he had experienced in the Philippines.

MacArthur encouraged Curtin to make yet another appeal for reinforcements. On 31 August, the day the *Saratoga* was torpedoed, Curtin cabled to Roosevelt expressing concern about the Allies' ability to defend Australia and emphatically rejecting the plan to withdraw US airmen from Australia and transfer their aircraft to the RAAF. Once again, Curtin 'respectfully' pointed out to Roosevelt that Australia was still contributing about 48 000 service personnel to the Allied war effort against Germany. If Australian casualties incurred in that distant theatre were added to this number, the total Australian contribution to the war against Germany would total about 85 000, not much less than the total American force of about 98 000 that was then in Australia. The implication of this was clear: that the Allies had so far contributed little more to Australia's security in the Pacific than Australia had contributed to the Allied effort in the European war. Curtin concluded with an appeal for Japan's defeat to be made the 'first priority' of the Allies, claiming that intelligence reports indicated that an intense Japanese offensive was imminent in the SWPA.[3]

A copy of Curtin's cable was sent to Churchill along with a request for the British to support Australia's case in Washington. Instead, Churchill challenged the basis of Curtin's fears and refused again to intercede with Roosevelt to increase the supply of American aircraft or to have the Spitfires counted as an additional allocation. As usual, Churchill expressed his 'entire sympathy and anxiety' to help in strengthening Australia's defences, but claimed that the Americans were not neglecting their responsibilities. He told Curtin to trust that their plans would provide sufficient resources 'to ensure Australia's defence' while conceding that such resources would not be sufficient for MacArthur to mount the strategic offensive that had been envisaged in his original orders.[4] Churchill's cable had been drafted by the air ministry and approved by Churchill without reference to the chiefs of staff. Despite Australia's wholehearted involvement in the Empire Air Training Scheme and the service of so many Australian airmen in the European theatre, the ministry was most reluctant to release aircraft to the distant dominion. As the chief of the air staff, Air Chief Marshal Sir Charles Portal, confided to Churchill, 'the danger ... is not that the forces sent to that area will not be large enough, but that they will be greater than is necessary'. Moreover, they would be provided at the expense of operations in the European theatre, where Portal was a great proponent of the strategic bombing of Germany.[5]

Bruce had been taken unawares when the draft reply to Curtin's cable was approved and dispatched during one of Churchill's late-night sessions. In an attempt to soothe the anticipated anger in Canberra, Bruce claimed that the cable 'was not really considered by the Prime Minister[,] who at the moment is almost entirely preoccupied with the battle in the Middle East ...'.[6] So concerned was Churchill with the battle, and with the concurrent German thrust through the Caucasus and around the eastern shore of the Black Sea, that he proposed sending 200 tanks to the Turks, who remained stubbornly neutral despite repeated British blandishments. Churchill feared that the German advance through the Caucasus would pressure Turkey into joining with Germany, with the tanks being an attempt to avert such an eventuality.[7] At the same time he was shipping a huge convoy of munitions through the Arctic Ocean to Russia. Despite the protection of a full fleet of 77 warships, thirteen of the 44 heavily laden cargo ships were sunk by the German aircraft swarming above, or the submarines waiting below, its icy surface.

Bruce promised that he would try to enlist Churchill's 'personal interest' in making a fraction of this effort for Australia, although Bruce had earlier called on Curtin to drop the demand about the Spitfires being considered as an additional allocation of aircraft.[8] This Curtin readily agreed to do.[9] Since most of the political kudos for the Spitfires would accrue to his rival Evatt, there was not much incentive for Curtin to maximise their value.[10] Anyway, for reasons of maintenance and American prestige, MacArthur's command was not enthusiastic about having Spitfires in the SWPA, suggesting that they be stationed in Perth, a proposal described as 'absurd' by the chief of the RAAF.[11] In the end they were sent to Darwin where they performed useful duty for a time before being left to languish when the front line moved away from Australia's northern shores and the Japanese air attacks on Darwin abated.[12]

As Bruce had indicated, Churchill's attention was fixed on the Middle East where Rommel launched his long-awaited offensive towards Alexandria on 30 August. It was a do-or-die attempt by an army running critically short of fuel and ammunition. Within three days, Churchill had the success he was seeking when the German attack was broken off to conserve fuel. Within a week, the Germans had been pushed back to where they had started their offensive. The British forces under Montgomery, including Australia's 9th Division, regrouped for an offensive that Churchill was keen to begin almost immediately. As Brooke observed, it was 'a regular disease that [Churchill] suffers from, this frightful impatience to get an attack launched!'.[13] However, Montgomery counselled patience, mindful of previous hasty offensives mounted at Churchill's behest and ending in defeat for the army and dismissal for the commander. Despite Churchill's badgering during September, his commanders carefully gathered their forces for a counterstroke that would repel Rommel once and for all. The Middle East campaign had been seesawing for two years and had served its purpose of keeping British forces actively engaged with the enemy on the ground, and thereby appeasing British and American public opinion, while the Russians were taking the brunt of the German effort. Now, with the Anglo–American landings along the north African coast planned for early November, the time for a final push against Rommel was approaching.

With so much hanging in the balance in the Mediterranean, it was not the time for Churchill and Roosevelt to be distracted by more appeals from Australia. Churchill would not risk the Middle East for the sake of Australia, with his repeated pledges to protect Australia being made with fingers crossed, in hopeful expectation that they would never be tested. In any event, they were so hedged about with conditions that only an invasion in force by the Japanese would have triggered a British response. Roosevelt was no more sympathetic than Churchill, replying, two weeks after receiving Curtin's request, that the planned aircraft allocation would not be altered. Already Roosevelt was considering the US navy's plan for an island-hopping strategy that would enable the US to sidestep Australia, with the navy wanting to leave MacArthur marooned while its marines stormed on towards Tokyo.

Australia received another body blow on 8 September when Churchill finally informed Curtin that he could not arrange for the Eastern fleet to join with the US Pacific fleet and thereby achieve a concentration of Allied naval power in the Pacific. As he now admitted, the Eastern fleet existed in little more than name only. On 30 August, an Australian intelligence report had claimed that the fleet comprised five battleships, three aircraft carriers, three heavy cruisers, sixteen light cruisers, nine armed merchant cruisers and about twenty-five destroyers. In fact, the core of the fleet consisted of just two battleships and an aircraft carrier, and they were engaged in the protection of the Middle East reinforcement route along the east coast of Africa.[14] Australia's western shores had been protected for the past three months by a figment of Curtin's imagination.

As Curtin digested the news from Churchill, more depressing news was received from Port Moresby where the Australian troops had been unable to stem the Japanese advance. Blamey's headquarters reported 'heavy and confused fighting' in which one AIF battalion had been outflanked by the Japanese and cut off from retreat. It was three weeks before the exhausted troops stumbled into the comparative safety of Port Moresby after an epic and circuitous trek across the forbidding terrain.[15] Curtin despondently announced in a secret briefing to journalists that Australians faced 'a long struggle ... to hold this place', suggesting that they 'might have a 100 years war'. He railed in frustration against Australia's allies who were only too willing to provide 'plenty of ships to transport reinforcements to the 9th Division in the Middle East' but not 'to reinforce our men in Port Moresby'.[16]

Curtin was depressed by his continuing failure to extract defence resources from either London or Washington, and by the deteriorating situation in New Guinea. On 7 September, Blamey had advised him of more bad news when they met in Canberra. Not only was Australia being denied aircraft and ships but the Americans did not intend to increase their existing commitment of two divisions until at least April 1943. Moreover, these two divisions were 'green' and still training for active operations. Blamey reported that he had only two Australian divisions in his command that were capable of being used in offensive operations against the Japanese, while the division defending the Townsville area of north Queensland was under strength by two thousand men who had been released to cut sugar cane. Although Australia would soon have a nominal strength of eleven divisions, Blamey calculated that at least fourteen were needed to ensure the security of the Australian continent. Nevertheless, when Curtin suggested demanding the withdrawal of the 9th Division from the Middle East, Blamey argued that it should be left there if the Americans could be persuaded to provide three more divisions.[17]

Blamey understood the difficulty of withdrawing the division when it was committed to the offensive against Rommel. However, his suggestion that it be left there indefinitely was foolish considering the drain that it would cause on Australia's military manpower. Blamey may have been prompted in part by a desire to keep the 9th Division's commander, the highly regarded General Leslie Morshead, occupied in a distant theatre and unable to threaten his position as land forces commander in Australia. Blamey was facing a tough time in New Guinea and the fewer close rivals the better for his survival at the pinnacle of the Australian army. Apart from the possibility of defeat in New Guinea, Blamey's Falstaffian figure was assailed by journalists making pointed references about his private life, which was marked by an overindulgence in drink and women. Curtin, having shared at least one of Blamey's failings, shielded him from attack, pointing out to his attackers that, in originally appointing Blamey, he 'was seeking a military leader not a Sunday School teacher'.[18]

Curtin had more important things to worry about. On 11 September, he took up Blamey's call for the United States to send three divisions of troops in return for the retention of the 9th Division in the Middle East.[19] And he sent another forceful message to Churchill demanding for Australia the same level of protection that Britain was providing for India and its other possessions in the Indian Ocean. He pointed out that, without the necessary naval forces to intercept and destroy a Japanese invasion force, Australia was reliant on its air and land forces being able to repel such an invasion as it was being landed ashore. Since these forces were seriously deficient, Curtin warned that the Japanese capture of Port Moresby would leave the way open for 'a direct attack on the mainland under cover of land-based aircraft, which may well defy all naval attempts to interrupt their line of communication and dislodge them'. Churchill was unconcerned by Curtin's anxious missive, simply passing it to his chiefs of staff to consider 'at leisure'.[20]

Curtin had no better luck in Washington, with Field Marshal Dill reporting to Churchill that Roosevelt had referred Curtin's cables to the combined chiefs of staff and asked for guidance from London to ensure that the replies of both leaders were along 'parallel lines'. So Churchill instructed his chiefs of staff to prepare a reply for him along the lines that 'we do not think there is danger to Australia and we do not intend to move the Eastern Fleet there'.[21] Meanwhile, the Japanese pushed to within eighty kilometres of Port Moresby, brushing aside the ineffectual Australian resistance.

Although Blamey continued to issue confident assurances about the defenders of Port Moresby being able to hold off the attack, MacArthur had become seriously concerned by the deteriorating situation, which affected his plans for using bases in New Guinea to mount an eventual offensive against Japanese forces in Rabaul and elsewhere. He confided to Curtin that he had lost confidence in the hapless Australian commanders in New Guinea, who had had to make do with the limited forces and supplies that MacArthur and Blamey had deigned to send them and who now had to take the responsibility for it all. MacArthur advised that he was planning to send

American troops there to stiffen the resistance and urged that Blamey be sent to Port Moresby to take personal command of the defence so as to save both the strategic town and Blamey's position as land forces commander. On a more confident note, MacArthur told Curtin that he had discerned a change in Washington's attitude towards the Pacific war which would eventually increase the flow of supplies and reinforcements for the SWPA. In the meantime, said MacArthur, 'the problem is one of fending the enemy off for some months'. He assured Curtin that support was coming, although he could not help wondering, 'will it be too late?'.[22]

The concerns of MacArthur and Curtin were shared by Sir Earle Page, who had recently returned from London where he had served briefly and ignominiously as Australia's special representative. Now, as a member of the advisory war council and with the full support of Curtin, he sent an urgent and almost hysterical message to Bruce imploring the high commissioner to exert maximum pressure on Churchill for the sake of Australian security. He warned that Britain risked 'precipitating an Empire political crisis that will leave indelible scars for generations'. Page declared that even his own 'intense Empire patriotism' would be tested to the utmost. If the dominion's appeals were ignored, Page predicted that 'the heart will largely have been taken out of Australia'.[23] It was dramatic stuff, and it stirred Bruce in a way that Curtin had been unable to do.

On receiving Page's message, Bruce asked for an immediate meeting with Churchill. However, he was rebuffed with the excuse that Churchill had a heavy round of engagements and was suffering from a sore throat. Bruce was directed instead to meet with the acting dominions secretary, Lord Cranborne. Bruce was not put off so easily, although he agreed to meet with Cranborne out of deference to Churchill's 'slight throat trouble'. At the same time, he repeated his request, as Australia's representative in the war cabinet, for 'an opportunity to discuss with you at the earliest possible moment a matter of the greatest consequence'.[24] Cranborne supported him, assuring Churchill that Bruce was not out to make trouble and rather was 'really anxious to help'. In fact, wrote Cranborne, Bruce accepted that 'there is no immediate danger of invasion to Australia' but he needed to be able to tell Curtin and Evatt that 'he has put their views to you personally'.[25]

The two men finally met after a war cabinet meeting on 21 September, five days after Bruce's initial request. Bruce acknowledged that no one in London or Washington believed that Australia was in danger of a full-scale invasion, but he maintained nevertheless that it was his 'duty to put the case as we saw it'. That is, as the Australian government saw it rather than Bruce himself. The high commissioner made clear to Churchill that he did not share Curtin's fears. Indeed, he told Churchill that there was no need to strengthen the forces in the Pacific until after the forthcoming Anglo–American invasion of north Africa. When Churchill then began to dispute some of the points made by Curtin in his cable, Bruce refused to respond, declaring that 'nothing was to be gained by pursuing the argument at this stage'. But he advised Churchill that, of course, he 'would have to continue to press him upon the question'.[26]

After having sought to undermine, or even overthrow, Churchill, Bruce now regarded him as indispensable. He was anxious that Churchill recognise him as a political convert, assuring him of his loyalty following the success of Churchill's talks with Stalin and declaring that it was 'unthinkable that he should go' from Downing Street. This did not mean that Bruce had become an uncritical admirer or that he supported the way Churchill was directing the war. In fact, he spent most of his meeting with Churchill arguing the case for diverting aircraft from the bombing offensive against Germany into the war against the U-boats in the Atlantic. Bruce might have argued for some of these long-range bombers to be used in the Pacific against Rabaul, the strategic centre of Japanese power in the SWPA, but he did not pursue Canberra's case in this regard. He was pursuing his own agenda. While Bruce acknowledged that Churchill was essential as an inspirational figurehead, he still believed that his government should be reorganised. There remained much support for this view in Westminster, with one Conservative MP even approaching Bruce to be put forward as first lord of the Admiralty in place of the rather ordinary incumbent, A. V. Alexander. But nothing came of it. If Bruce harboured such aspirations, it was essential to have the support of Churchill. So he would have been pleased to hear Churchill concede at the conclusion of their meeting that Bruce had been 'discreet and ... had sent a number of most helpful telegrams to Australia'.

Bruce came away from Downing Street confident that the meeting had marked the beginning of a new and promising chapter in their previously stormy relationship.[27]

That same day, the dozen or so journalists of the Canberra press gallery gathered in Curtin's office for a solemn briefing about Australia's situation. After nine months of beseeching and cajoling Churchill and Roosevelt, and after Evatt's fruitless mission to London and Washington, Curtin had no illusions about what he could expect in the way of reinforcements. Even with the support of MacArthur, there never seemed to be enough to meet the scale of threat that Australia was facing. Now he had been rebuffed again. He told the journalists that he was profoundly disturbed by the replies from Churchill and Roosevelt and could only conclude that it was 'vain to appeal for these places to be made a major theatre'. All the warnings that he made during the 1930s of such an eventuality seemed to have been borne out. As he told the scribbling throng, 'You were told all this when I was in Opposition. The bloody country was told what would happen long before the war came.' With only limited reinforcements of men and munitions being forwarded to Australia, the country would have to endure the continuing peril largely alone. Anxious to dispel any sense of Australian complacency, Curtin announced that they had 'six months' menace to survive' and could only do so with 'blood and sweat and hard work'.[28]

With the war effort and the civilian economy competing for scarce supplies of resources and manpower, the government wanted Australians to adopt an attitude of austerity so as to cool the overheated economy. At a public meeting in Brisbane's town hall in late August, Curtin had called for a 'season of austerity' during which he wanted Australians to defer their spending on 'intoxicants, holidays and theatres'.[29] As part of the austerity campaign, Curtin introduced 'raceless Saturdays': one day in each month when Australians could not gamble on horses. An enterprising Sydney promoter promptly announced that he would hold a boxing match on those Saturdays when the horses were not running. It undermined everything that Curtin was trying to achieve and seemed to him to be symptomatic of the lackadaisical attitude towards the war that had been adopted by many Australians now that the threat of invasion appeared to have receded.

Shocked and angered by this deliberate attempt to subvert the government's intention, Curtin railed against the idea of holding 'alternative assemblages for the purposes of fun while the enemy thunders at the gates'.[30]

The outcome of the battle for Port Moresby still hung in the balance when Curtin issued his impassioned press statement. On 17 September, Australian troops had been forced back to Imita Ridge, one of the last defensive positions protecting the township. Unlike the desert warfare in the Middle East, where some of the troops had first experienced fighting, the war in New Guinea was fought as if in slow motion, where men might slog through mud for days to gain an advantage of metres. Aircraft were often useless in these battles, with the weather keeping them grounded or the vegetation and the terrain making it impossible to discern the front line. It was a war fought out on the ground by men with their rifles and their machine-guns, all the time searching for snipers in the jungle canopy waiting to pick them off or anxiously watching and listening for Japanese units trying to outflank them. They were fighting the formidable terrain, the tropical weather and the disease-carrying mosquitoes as much as the Japanese. More troops fell victim to malaria than to enemy bullets. Such was the terrible rate of sickness that it was necessary to have three men in reserve to keep one in the field.

At Port Moresby, a few thousand Australians were dug in to make a last-ditch stand, with orders from General Rowell to 'fight it out at all costs'.[31] Blamey had tried to stay well clear of the battle. It would not do to be implicated in a defeat, if that were to occur. He was also reluctant to intrude on the command of Rowell, with whom he had had a falling out during the battle for Greece in 1941. And the rather sybaritic Blamey could not hope to enjoy in Port Moresby the type of nightlife that he enjoyed in Australia's southern cities. But he was ordered there by Curtin after MacArthur expressed concern on 17 September that the town might fall and advised that Blamey should take personal control of its defence. Five days later, Blamey had got no further north than Brisbane, where Curtin phoned him, warning that, if he valued his position he should 'not remain in Brisbane another day'. So Blamey headed off to Port Moresby where he soon took charge from the testy Rowell, who regarded the arrival of Blamey as signifying a lack of confidence in himself.[32]

Instead of supervising the withdrawal of the Australians, Blamey found Rowell's regrouped forces ready to advance. For the first time, Australian artillery was brought to bear against the approaching Japanese. But the climactic battle never came. Instead, the Japanese troops were ordered to relinquish their hard-won gains and retreat northwards back across the mountains to the coast. They had battled their way to within sight of the sea and were now forced gradually to give it all back. With their counterparts at Milne Bay having failed to capture the staunchly defended Australian airfield, and with the Americans on Guadalcanal making the contest for that island a test of wills, the Japanese found themselves overstretched. With instructions to make Guadalcanal his primary objective, the Japanese commander, Lieutenant-General Hyakutake, was forced to cut his losses in New Guinea and withdraw to his bases on the north coast.

The Japanese had been trying to do too much with too little and the capture of Port Moresby became one commitment too many. Just when victory was so close that their half-starved and exhausted troops could sense its sweet taste, the prospect was whipped away. With their backs to the wall, the Australians suddenly found that they could advance. On 28 September, they reoccupied the abandoned position on Ioribaiwa Ridge, the final redoubt of the Japanese offensive. Instead of a cleansing bath in the captured town, the retreating Japanese now faced many more days trudging back along the muddy trail and more nights in the jungle, fighting a difficult delaying action against Australians who were enjoying the advantage of their artillery and the increasing air support. The battle had been won by default. But there was still much more fighting to be done before the war would be over.

NOTES

[1] Letter, Rowell to Vasey, 1 September 1942, in John Robertson and John McCarthy (eds), *Australian War Strategy 1939–1945*, Brisbane, 1985, Doc. 328.

[2] Hankey's observation was made before the loss of the *Wasp* left Allied naval forces seriously weakened in the Pacific. Report by Hankey, 3 September 1942, sent to British and dominion ministers and officials including Bruce and Shedden, HNKY 11/7, Hankey Papers, CC.

[3] Cable, Curtin to Churchill, 31 August 1942, PREM 3/163/4, PRO.

[4] Cable, Churchill to Curtin, 1 September 1942, ISMAY VI/2, Ismay Papers, KC.

[5] Minute, Portal to Pound, 28 August 1942, PREM 3/150/9, PRO.

[6] Cables, Bruce to Curtin, 1 and 2 September 1942, *DAFP*, Vol. 6, Docs 36 and 38.

[7] Gilbert, *Road to Victory*, p. 222.

[8] Cables, Bruce to Curtin, 1 and 2 September 1942, *DAFP*, Vol. 6, Docs 36 and 38.

9   Cable, Curtin to Bruce, 5 September 1942, CRS A5954, Box 229, NAA.

10 In a speech to the House of Representatives on 3 September, Evatt had lauded the Spitfires as 'another splendid contribution, which Britain agreed to, [that] will be of inestimable value to our defence'. Curtin, Shedden and MacArthur knew otherwise. Statement by Evatt, 3 September 1942, CRS A5954, Box 474, NAA.

11 Letter, Jones to Shedden, 3 September 1942, CRS A5954, Box 231, NAA.

12 Letter, Dewing to Ismay, 18 August 1943, ISMAY IV/DEW/1b, Ismay Papers, KC.

13 Alanbrooke diary, 8 September 1942, in Danchev and Todman (eds), *War Diaries*, p. 319.

14 Cable, Churchill to Curtin, 8 September 1942, PREM 3/163/6, PRO; Gill, *Royal Australian Navy 1942–1945*, pp. 185–7; Roskill, *The War at Sea*, Vol. 2, pp. 236–7.

15 'Operations in New Guinea — Review of 23rd November, 1942', CRS A5954, Box 587, NAA.

16 Background briefing by Curtin, 9 September 1942, MS 4675, Smith Papers, NLA.

17 Minutes of Prime Minister's War Conference, 7 September 1942, CRS A5954, Box 1, NAA.

18 Curtin's support could not be vouchsafed forever, with some Labor MPs critical of Blamey's right-wing associations during the 1920s and 1930s and with more recent whispers about him heading a future military administration in place of the government. Talk by Bruce with Irvine Douglas, 8 September 1942, CRS M100, 'September 1942', NAA; Background briefing, 23 July 1942, MS 4675, Smith Papers, NLA; Memoirs of Lord Wakehurst, Chap. 18, p. 9, Wakehurst Papers, HLRO.

19 Cable, Curtin to Roosevelt, 11 September 1942, *DAFP*, Vol. 6, Doc. 43.

20 Cable, Curtin to Churchill, 11 September 1942, PREM 3/163/6, PRO.

21 Cable, Dill to Chiefs of Staff, 12 September 1942, PREM 3/163/4, PRO.

22 Note of Secraphone Conversation between MacArthur and Curtin, 17 September 1942, *DAFP*, Vol. 6, Doc. 47.

23 Advisory War Council Minute, 24 September 1942, CRS A5954, Box 261, NAA; Cable, Page to Bruce, 14 September 1942, *DAFP*, Vol. 6, Doc. 45.

24 Letters, Bruce to Churchill, 16 and 17 September 1942, PREM 3/163/6, PRO.

25 Note, Cranborne to Churchill, 18 September 1942, PREM 3/163/6, PRO.

26 Note by Bruce, 21 September 1942, *DAFP*, Vol. 6, Doc. 51.

27 ibid; Talk with Austin Hopkinson, 17 September 1942, CRS M100, 'September 1942', NAA; For the contemporary accounts of the continuing disquiet in Westminster, see King, *With Malice Toward None*, pp. 189–90; Moran, *Winston Churchill*, Chap. 9.

28 Background briefing, 21 September 1942, MS 4675, Smith Papers, NLA.

29 *Courier-Mail*, Brisbane, 20 August 1942.

30 Press statement by Curtin, 23 September 1942, CRS A5954, Box 305A, NAA.

31 John Robertson, *Australia at War 1939–1945*, Melbourne, 1981, p. 143.

32 David Horner, *Crisis of Command: Australian Generalship and the Japanese Threat, 1941–1943*, Canberra, 1978, pp. 154–70, 181–4.

THIRTY-TWO

'great possibilities and great dangers'

When asked in retrospect to nominate the most difficult months of the war, Churchill immediately chose September and October 1942.[1] Not surprisingly, the fact that Australia's security was safeguarded during this period did not figure as a factor in his assessment. It was only the events in the European theatre that were noteworthy. During those two months, the German offensive in southern Russia seemed set to overwhelm Stalingrad and spread through the Caucasus to threaten the eastern flank of Britain's Middle Eastern fortress. At the same time, Montgomery was planning a massive offensive westward from his base in Egypt that was designed to catch Rommel's Afrika Korps while it was still reeling from its failed lunge towards Alexandria. Other British forces were assembling with their American allies for a large-scale invasion of French north Africa. Together with Montgomery's forces, they were designed to drive Rommel back to Europe and provide a springboard for an Allied invasion across the Mediterranean.

Upon the success of these various enterprises might depend the fate of the entire Allied war effort as well as the political fate of the Allied war leaders.

Stalin's personal prestige was locked into the battle for Stalingrad; Roosevelt was facing an important congressional election that would test public support for his handling of the war; and Churchill's political position hinged on the forthcoming battle for control of north Africa. As he told Eden on 1 October, the failure of the Allied operation would mean that he was 'done for' and would have to 'hand over to one of you'.[2] This was not the rambling of a depressive, but an assessment of the political reality in Westminster. The Conservative MP Victor Cazalet was expressing a widespread opinion in the House of Commons when he told Lord Halifax on 2 October that there would 'come a day, unless a victory intervenes, in which it will not be a question of who is to succeed Winston, but the conviction that with him as P.M. we cannot win the war'.[3] Had there been an obvious successor to Churchill, it is likely that he would have been deposed long before then. However, as Sir Cuthbert Headlam observed, 'when one looks round for someone to succeed Winston there is literally nobody of any stature'.[4] This was Churchill's strength when the war was not going his way, and he played on it for all it was worth.

Churchill also went to great lengths to produce a much-needed victory. He threw everything into the struggle. To sustain the Russian resistance, he ordered ships full of munitions across the Arctic Ocean before the protective winter darkness set in. They would sail independently, unprotected by the huge fleet that had been assembled to little effect for the previous convoy. The new strategy was no more successful. Of the thirteen ships that set out during October, only five reached Russia.[5] Despite this loss, the Russian resistance did not collapse, but simply recoiled before the German summer offensive and then sprang back in mid-November when German strength was spent and cold was besetting Hitler's attenuated lines of supply and communication. Rather than relying upon the Arctic convoys, hundreds of tanks and aircraft and masses of armaments poured from Russian factories deep in the distant Ural mountains.[6] Allied efforts to sustain Russia and keep it in the fight were of little practical assistance and, to Churchill's annoyance, even prompted Stalin to complain that the aircraft and tanks being sent to him were outdated British rejects.[7] Had they been sent to Australia instead, the aircraft would have been particularly useful in repelling the Japanese and providing Australia with an important measure of security against invasion. But Churchill remained as unsympathetic as ever towards Australia's plight.

Curtin's appeals for assistance during September were passed to Washington for comment, since it was from there that any additional help would have to come. When the Dominions Office asked Churchill on 3 October whether he was planning to reply to Curtin, he followed his secretary's advice to stay silent. This was in accord with advice from General Dill in Washington, who urged that Britain avoid answering Australia's appeals and allow any Australian criticism to be directed at the United States. As for answering Curtin's question regarding Britain's much-depleted Eastern fleet, and its capacity to deter or repel a Japanese attack against Western Australia, Churchill instructed the Admiralty that it should 'leave it for a while' before preparing an answer.[8]

Churchill had earlier instructed the chiefs of staff to draw up a draft reply to Curtin's questions at their leisure, which they certainly did. It was not until 9 October, almost a month after receiving Curtin's cable, that the chiefs approved the Admiralty reaction, which was to make no reply at all. They pointed out that Roosevelt had already effectively answered Curtin's cables in the negative. As for an attack on Western Australia, that was 'most unlikely to take place' and was anyway 'an entirely hypothetical question'.[9] It was, however, a hypothetical question to which Curtin was keen to know the answer. Curtin's electorate and home were in Western Australia and he was well aware of Perth's isolation from the populated south-east of the continent, with a single-track railway across the desolate Nullarbor Plain providing its main means of supply and reinforcement. If Japan decided to capture Perth, there was little that the Allied forces in eastern Australia would be able to do to prevent it. The dominion really was relying upon Britain's Eastern fleet to prevent such an invasion of its western capital.

Fortunately for Australia, no invasion was ever attempted for it is doubtful whether Britain would have responded to it with any force. Not only because Britain's forces were already hard-pressed to cope with their existing responsibilities, but also because the official attitude towards Australia remained deeply critical within both Westminster and Whitehall. The dominion's reputation had been tainted by the succession of disputes that had embittered wartime relations between the two countries and by continuing Australian attempts to dilute the Anglo–American commitment to the 'Germany first' strategy. The depth of the bitterness was seen in late October when Eden's private secretary, Oliver Harvey, wrote in his diary of the Australians 'running screaming to America' after having 'behaved like sillies, if not worse. Witness the withdrawal [a year earlier] of the Australian Division from Tobruk on the eve of the battle.'[10]

Australia's reputation with Churchill was further damaged by Bruce's continued political meddling. He still sought to change the political composition of the British war cabinet so that Churchill's almost untrammelled power would be curbed and his own role enhanced. Following what he believed was an amicable meeting with Churchill in September, Bruce naively believed that he could propose such a change directly to Churchill. This was a major political *faux pas* at a time when Churchill was being beset by Cripps and waiting anxiously for the events in the Mediterranean to retrieve his political fortunes. If Bruce thought Churchill was thereby weakened and would bend to his pressure, he was much mistaken. When the two met on 6 October, Bruce found that Churchill not only rejected his proposal but 'became somewhat violent on the subject'. Churchill later dictated a 'fairly acid' letter to Bruce pointing out that it was the responsibility of the House of Commons and not the Australian high commissioner to decide on the composition of the British war cabinet. It was only the timely arrival of W. S. Robinson at Chequers that dissuaded Churchill from sending the angry missive. Robinson could not prevent Churchill excluding Bruce from future war cabinet meetings and ignoring his repeated protests on the matter. Bruce even threatened to resign on the issue of his exclusion, but eventually learned to live with the situation he had created.[11]

Australia's reputation was also damaged in Washington, where the desperate fighting by the defenders of Port Moresby was looked at askance. Roosevelt asked why Australian troops were not able to defeat the smaller Japanese force that had to cope with operating at the end of an extended line of communication that stretched over some of the most difficult terrain in the world.[12] MacArthur had inspired this criticism with adverse reports to

Washington about the fighting ability of the Australians. The dire situation in Port Moresby had been caused partly by MacArthur's complacency and his slowness to react to the Japanese offensive despite clear warnings from Allied intelligence. Anxious to avoid such a responsibility, MacArthur tried to shift the blame to the troops on the ground. When Curtin questioned the size of the relatively small garrison in Port Moresby, which comprised about 40 000 personnel, MacArthur responded that even '140 000 men would be no good unless they'd fight'.[13] MacArthur told his British liaison officer, Gerald Wilkinson, that the 'whole senior officer class in Australia [was] too complacent and easily pleased with work 1/2 done'. He complained that they lived 'off but not up to the name Anzac', with General Gordon Bennett, the commander who had fled Singapore, being dismissed as a 'cantankerous crab — a low Australian type' while Blamey was a 'tough commander' but also 'sensual, slothful and [of] doubtful moral character'.[14] Such aspersions, when transmitted to London and Washington, exacerbated the already jaundiced view in those capitals regarding the martial quality of the Australians.

For their part, Australian officials and politicians continued to harbour resentment towards Britain for its failure to make good on its historic defence guarantee and to fulfil its repeated promises during the war to provide for Australia's protection. There were no illusions in Canberra that such protection had not been forthcoming. In early October, the defence department provided Shedden with a report listing the number of British aircraft received by Australia during the first eight critical months of 1942. Of the 449 aircraft, 366 were for training under the Empire Air Training Scheme and of no use for defence against the Japanese. There were only 83 operational aircraft and 77 of those were from previous contracts and not sent in response to Australia's plight. The only special British contribution were the six Spitfires that had so far arrived, and these had been subtracted from the American allocation, leaving Australia with no net benefit.[15] While Churchill had so far sent Australia just six Spitfires, British factories produced about 13 500 aircraft, and American factories more than 18 000 aircraft, during those first eight months of 1942.[16] Few made it as far as Australia. The figures reveal much about Australia's place in Britain's system of imperial defence and put Churchill's oft-repeated pledges in proper perspective.

Despite the feelings of resentment harboured by both sides, there was a recognition in Canberra that Australia's postwar relations, both economic and diplomatic, would continue to centre upon Britain. As such, the bitterness would have to abate if the relationship was to be resuscitated. The inept British high commissioner, Sir Ronald Cross, claimed there had indeed been 'a steady improvement in the feelings [of Australians] towards the United Kingdom'. Having himself been 'pricked into sensitiveness on the subject', Cross assured Attlee in mid-September that he now had the 'pleasurable sensation of basking in the sunshine of restored amity'.[17] There was at least the appearance of increased amity. However, it was also the time when Evatt moved to ratify the Statute of Westminster, the 1931 Act of the British parliament that recognised the dominions as nations largely independent of Britain. It is one of the several dates when it could be said that Australia became an independent nation. For more than a decade, Australia had refused to ratify the statute and, even now, Evatt denied that ratification would indicate any break with Britain. He was anxious not to stir up any opposition from those many Australians, probably the great majority, who would have been disturbed by any suggestion of cutting ties with the mother country. So he argued that it was simply a technical measure that was required 'to remove threats of invalidity which now hang over important Commonwealth laws and regulations'.[18]

Menzies, who had tried unsuccessfully when he was attorney-general in the 1930s to ratify the statute, agreed with Evatt that it was of 'relatively minor importance', with its 'chief interest' being as a reminder that 'in our Empire relations we have by no means reached either finality or certainty'.[19] However, the combative Billy Hughes was not one to allow an opportunity for political grandstanding to go unexploited. So he seized on the ratification as indicating Labor's disloyalty to the mother country. Ignoring appeals from Evatt not to couch his arguments in terms of 'Australia v. Britain', Hughes fought in vain against the bill's passage through the parliament.[20]

Although the Australian government was resigned to resuming a postwar place within the British empire, Curtin and his ministers were determined that Australia should play a much more independent and greater part within that empire, and particularly within the Pacific. Following the 1930s depression, there was recognition by some Australian politicians that the policy of imperial preference, whereby Britain and its dominions gave preferential tariff treatment to each other's goods, was not workable. Britain was unable to absorb Australia's agricultural surpluses and Australia was unwilling to accept second-rate industrial goods from Britain. These were sometimes foisted upon them by British manufacturers who knew that their American competitors were effectively excluded from the Australian market by the discriminatory tariff. Even Bruce with his strong imperial predilections accepted that Australia's postwar economic revival would depend on an expansion of world trade generally, rather than returning to the restraints of the economic empire of the 1930s. When a British cabinet minister warned him that 'Australia would have great difficulty in getting rid of the Americans after the war', Bruce retorted that Australia would 'welcome the maximum co-operation by the Americans both financially and by their exports in developing industry in Australia'.[21] Not that Bruce or the Australian government expected the Americans to provide a substantial market for Australian goods. That was going to be found closer to home.

Following on from prewar attempts by the conservative government to boost the country's industrial development, the Labor government pursued a vision developed and promoted by the globe-trotting Australian businessman W. S. Robinson for Australia to become a regional industrial power. With the connivance of the government, Robinson had dispatched a mission of business colleagues to Britain and the United States with secret orders to seek out new industrial processes that could benefit the war effort and, in the longer term, the companies that Robinson controlled. Describing the mission as 'an urgent necessity if Australian industrial progress is to be maintained', Robinson proposed to Evatt that he would finance the trip out of his companies' funds if the government would provide the necessary American dollars.[22]

With the government's backing, Robinson arranged visits for his colleagues to aircraft plants and aluminium smelters where they were expected to acquire valuable information on the latest scientific advances and industrial processes. He warned them not to send by ordinary mail to Australia any such information that they gleaned during their travels, since it was illegal to send it outside of the United States. Instead, they were to use official channels at the Australian legation in Washington, where they would not be subject to American inspection. Robinson told his industrial spies that they should put aside any outdated ideas and 'think in terms of the new world now being created — one in which the light metals — aluminium, magnesium, beryllium and their alloys will reign supreme with the aid of the internal combustion engine, oil and aircraft'.[23] Robinson wanted Australia to control the resources, produce the metals and develop the industries to which they would give rise. He wanted Australia, as part of the British empire, to reign supreme in its own region. And he convinced the government to support his vision.

The vision conjured up by Robinson was for an Australian economic empire that could replace the vanquished prewar European empires in the Pacific as well as Japan's co-prosperity sphere. It would not be a formal empire, but an informal empire based upon Australia's enhanced economic power and enforced, if necessary, by its enhanced military power. Robinson proposed 'a new map of the possible "sphere of influence" of Australia in the new world ...'. He envisioned that this area of Australian influence would extend for thousands of miles north and east 'in arcs from the big centres of population on the east coast of Australia'. Robinson left their precise coverage undefined, but declared that they would include 'unlimited resources' within them. It was a matter of the dominion's survival, warned Robinson, that these resource-rich areas should be developed by Australia and be 'under the protection of Britain and the United States and their Allies'. If they were 'controlled by those antagonistic to Australia', Robinson predicted that 'Australia will not long survive'.[24]

Evatt was certainly convinced by Robinson's vision, telling the House of Representatives in early September that Australia had 'a particular interest in closer economic relations with its nearer neighbours'. Prior to the war, it had been difficult to pursue such interests due to the protective tariffs and other measures imposed by the European powers controlling the region. To achieve Robinson's vision, those European powers would have to be dislodged or have their colonies brought under the control of an international body. Accordingly, Evatt argued for the former colonial arrangements to be converted to a doctrine of trusteeship that would guarantee the territories their economic and political freedom. While he genuinely supported the granting of political freedom to the native inhabitants of these European colonies, he did not believe that they were ready immediately for self-government and would have to be trusteeship territories for some years or decades. In the meantime, the territories would be thrown open for Australian investment and trade. Evatt cited the Australian mandated territory of New Guinea as an example of the doctrine of trusteeship in practice.[25] Evatt's proposal, based on seemingly idealistic underpinnings, threatened Britain's hold over its colonial interests while enhancing Australia's position in the Pacific. In time, it would develop into a new dispute that would increasingly trouble relations between Canberra and London.[26]

While Evatt was working towards this postwar vision of a sub-empire for Australia, the mainly Australian forces in New Guinea and the Americans on Guadalcanal still had some way to go before they could claim mastery over their enemy. As Lord Gowrie observed from Canberra on 20 October, Australia was still going through 'pretty hectic and anxious times'. Following the Japanese retreat from Port Moresby, attention was fixed on Guadalcanal, with the outcome not being decided for some months yet. Until that time, Australian security could not be assured. Even Roosevelt was concerned, confiding to Churchill that there was 'no use blinking at the fact that [in the SWPA] we are greatly outnumbered' as Japan and the United States continued their test of strength in the region.[27] Australia too was having problems coping with all the demands being placed upon its manpower, both to provide troops and people to support the growing American presence.

Curtin cast around for a solution to Australia's immediate security problem and its looming manpower problem, as demands were made for more and more troops to be sent to New Guinea. Every person sent out of Australia was one less for the nation's defence. Curtin's nightmare was that the Japanese might succeed in the Solomons and leapfrog to the north Australian coastline, leaving the Allied forces in New Guinea isolated and doomed to defeat. By early October the troops faced the arduous task of pursuing the Japanese back from Port Moresby. With tremendous supply problems across the mountainous terrain, there would be no easy victory for the Australians but rather a slow, hard slog. Anxious not to lock up too many troops in New Guinea, Curtin rejected calls for the campaign to be conducted with greater speed, telling journalists that he

was not going to be driven by public demand to send men to form suicide squads in New Guinea ... New Guinea wasn't Australia. It was only a place of military strategy and if we took it entirely it would not affect the war greatly because the situation was dependent on factors far removed from New Guinea.[28]

Despite Curtin's reluctance to commit more men to New Guinea, any prolonged campaign in those tropical conditions would inevitably soak up further precious manpower.

With manpower at a premium, the question again arose of retrieving the 9th Division from the Middle East. After first assuring himself of the support of MacArthur, the Australian chiefs of staff, the advisory war council (except for Menzies) and his own war cabinet, Curtin called on 17 October for the return of the division. At the same time, he announced that Australia's contribution to the Empire Air Training Scheme would continue much as before. In justifying his new demand for the return of the division, Curtin told Churchill that the looming manpower crisis and the campaign in New Guinea and the Solomons meant that Australia could no longer supply reinforcements for it. Since the government would not allow it to lose its national identity by being broken up into smaller units and distributed among British formations, the only alternative was for it to be returned to Australia as soon as practicable.[29]

Curtin's cable was sent just six days before the planned British counterattack against Rommel's forces at El Alamein for which, apparently unbeknown to Curtin, the 9th Division had been assigned a front-line position. In Churchill's view, it would have been reminiscent of the previous year's withdrawal of Australian troops from Tobruk. That had caused deep and prolonged feelings of resentment in the minds of Churchill and his colleagues. This time, while there was no possibility of releasing the Australian division prior to the coming battle, Churchill did concede that it 'seems important' to release the Australians once the battle had concluded. He even suggested to the chiefs of staff, more in exasperation at the Australians than out of concern for the dominion's defence, that the RAF could release the Australian airmen serving within its ranks despite Curtin's willingness to allow them to remain.[30] Churchill could presumably foresee that there would be demands eventually for the return of the airmen as well. With the Americans arriving in large numbers, the Australian troops and airmen were no longer so necessary and their return home would have the considerable benefit of removing the issue as a continuing source of conflict between London and Canberra. But Churchill held back from replying to Curtin for fear of jeopardising the security of the Middle East operations.

The fact that this latest demand for the return of Australian forces did not provoke a sharp response from Churchill may also have been due to the visit of W. S. Robinson in early October. His visit was part of Robinson's mission to gather information on the latest industrial processes but he also met with Churchill, spending two weekends at Chequers, as well as with other British ministers in his role as Evatt's unofficial emissary. He wanted to break down the climate of hostility and mistrust between the two countries and provide Churchill and his colleagues with 'a slightly more intimate expression of the views of some of the Leaders than is possible through official channels'.[31] There is little evidence, though, of him doing much to promote the Australian government's demands. Quite the reverse. He came away from his weekends with Churchill convinced of the British case and anxious to rein in the Australian appeals for assistance.[32]

Bruce was also anxious to prevent a further deterioration in Anglo–Australian relations. He met with Attlee on 20 October to urge that Churchill reply to Curtin's three-day-old cable concerning the 9th Division and that Churchill also take him into his confidence about the coming counterattack at El Alamein. Bruce hoped that this information would allay any Australian opposition to the retention of the troops until the battle was done. Although Attlee nodded his agreement, Bruce was 'doubtful if he will do anything about it'. So that same day Bruce sent a cable of his own to Curtin in which he advised that the withdrawal of the division was complicated by its imminent involvement in operations, but that Australia's manpower problems were 'fully recognised and the necessity for the return of the 9th Division [was] fully appreciated'. He advised that Whitehall was 'examining the problem with a view to [the division's] return at the earliest possible date'.[33]

Instead of satisfying the Australian government, Bruce's secret news about the division's involvement in the forthcoming offensive only caused alarm in Canberra. Australia needed the division returned in good shape for use against Japan. Moreover, if it was badly mauled in the Middle East after earlier calls for its return had been ignored, Curtin could face political problems. There was talk of Evatt mounting a challenge against Curtin if the offensive went badly and ended in another disaster for Australian troops.[34] Curtin quickly did what he could to avert such a calamity, immediately cabling to Bruce to stress that no more reinforcements would be forthcoming for the division and instructing that it must not be reinforced by its ancillary units. This message, dispatched on the eve of battle, was intended to prevent the division's use in the front line, since any casualties it suffered could not be made good. To drive this point home, Curtin instructed Bruce to 'emphasise the crucial importance' of the Australian government's view to Whitehall and ensure that the British commander-in-chief in the Middle East, General Alexander, 'should have regard to this position in his use of the Division'.[35]

On the afternoon of 23 October, just a few hours before the battle began in Egypt, Bruce called in General Brooke, commander of the imperial general staff, to pass on Curtin's instructions. Brooke was not amused by this last-minute attempt to keep the 9th Division out of harm's way. With considerable restraint, he wrote in his diary that Australia's 'shouting' for the division had come 'just as the attack was starting!!'.[36] Curtin's message was duly relayed to Whitehall and passed on to Alexander in Egypt, although it was not brought to his notice prior to the battle commencing.[37] Even if it had been, it was too late to alter the disposition of the Australian troops as they waited for the artillery barrage from one thousand British guns to light up the freezing moonlit night and so signal the beginning of the long-awaited offensive. Brooke wrote that night in his diary of the 'great possibilities and great dangers' that awaited British forces at El Alamein. 'It may be the turning point of the war,' he wrote, 'leading to further success combined with the North African attack, or it may mean nothing. If it fails I don't quite know how I shall bear it . . . '[38]

Rommel was recuperating in Austria when the battle began. Under orders from Hitler, he rushed back to take charge of his command. There was little he could do against the overwhelming odds that he now faced. As he wrote to his wife on 29 October, 'I haven't much hope left. At night I sleep with eyes wide open, unable to sleep, for the load that is on my shoulders.'[39] Churchill slept much more soundly, knowing the German supply difficulties and confident that decoded German wireless messages would allow the RAF to sink tankers if they attempted to cross the Mediterranean with the lifeblood for Rommel's army. With only three days' supply of fuel in reserve, Rommel's freedom to manoeuvre was all but gone. If his desperate counterattacks failed, his only hope lay in a timely retreat to a defensible position in Libya.

On 27 October, Churchill reported to Curtin on the opening of the 'great battle in Egypt', noting that 'you will have observed with pride and pleasure the distinguished part which the 9th Australian Division are playing in what may be an event of [the] first magnitude'.[40] In his reply, Curtin did not miss the opportunity of reminding Churchill of the 'vital importance' to Australia of the 9th Division being returned 'as soon as possible' and 'in good shape and strength'.[41] At this stage, the British chiefs of staff had still not considered when, how, or even if, this would be done. General Alexander only learned of the Australian government's instructions regarding the division after he was visited by its commander, General Morshead, prompting Alexander to inform London that it would be 'quite impossible to lose their magnificent services until present operations are brought to a successful conclusion'.[42] Only then did Churchill, who previously had seemed committed to the return of the division, prod the chiefs of staff into submitting their advice on the matter.[43]

It had all seemed like plain sailing for the division once the present battle was concluded. Instead, there was a renewed attempt, supported by

Roosevelt, to retain the Australian division in the Middle East. On 29 October, Roosevelt offered to dispatch to Australia a US division from Hawaii if the Australian government would agree to leave its division in the Middle East and thereby serve the 'common cause'. Churchill told Roosevelt that he was 'deeply grateful' for his help and, while acknowledging that the division would have to be returned later 'if Curtin insists', he hoped that Roosevelt's telegram would be 'decisive' in convincing Curtin otherwise.[44] In the event, it was far from decisive, particularly after MacArthur advised Curtin that the American division had already left Hawaii and was committed to the theatre anyway.[45] Meanwhile, the British chiefs of staff advised that five fast liners could be made available in January 1943 to take the Australians home. The ships had been scheduled to pick up 30 000 Polish refugees, recently released by the Russians and waiting in Persia for transport to Mexico. If Curtin insisted, the ships could take the Australians instead. However, the chiefs advised Churchill first to wait for Australia's response to the pressure from Roosevelt. Churchill readily complied, noting 'There's no hurry'.[46]

Australia would not have agreed. As Britain's joint staff mission reported from Washington on 27 October, Allied operations in the SWPA had entered a 'critical phase'. The previous day, the Americans had fought another carrier battle with the Japanese as part of their campaign to hold on to Guadalcanal. During the battle of Santa Cruz, the US aircraft carrier *Hornet* was sunk and another carrier damaged. Once again, the US Pacific fleet had only one operational aircraft carrier left to cover that entire ocean. As the British report observed, it made the American navy's 'ability to command the seas problematical'. If Guadalcanal fell to the Japanese, the Americans could be forced back to New Caledonia and Fiji. If this happened, warned the report, 'Australian fears will be multiplied and [the] difficulties of a renewed American offensive will be increased'. Most worrying of all from London's point of view, the 'drain of aircraft and shipping to the Pacific will increase'.[47]

To cover their sudden weakness in the Pacific, the Americans appealed for British assistance. Such appeals had been ignored by Churchill when they originated from Australia, but he could not afford to offend the Americans on whom his war strategy depended for its success. Not that his assistance was of any practical value. Although Churchill sent the carrier *Victorious* steaming to the rescue, it was not until March 1943 that it arrived in Hawaii where it had to remain for two months being refitted. By that time, the danger in the Pacific had long passed. Nevertheless, its symbolic voyage allowed the Royal Navy's official historian, Captain Stephen Roskill, to make the spurious claim that 'in spite of its overriding responsibilities in connection with the defeat of Germany, the British Government were anxious to contribute to the Pacific struggle'.[48] The minutes of the Pacific war council that met under Churchill's chairmanship in London provided a clearer reflection of Britain's concern for the Pacific struggle. The council brought together representatives from all the countries involved in the war against Japan. But it rarely met. When it did so, such as on 21 October, it was to little effect. As the permanent head of the Foreign Office, Sir Alexander Cadogan, caustically observed in his diary, 'Had to attend Pacific War Council at 6. Review by P.M. (they hadn't met since May!) but no business done.'[49]

Churchill continued to stall on Australia's demand for the return of the 9th Division. In line with the advice from his chiefs of staff, Churchill had instructed Attlee, as dominions secretary, to 'await the effect of the President's telegram and do nothing meanwhile'.[50] But Attlee was concerned that Churchill's refusal to respond to Curtin's cable would do fresh damage to Anglo–Australian relations. He assured Churchill that Curtin's cable was 'nothing more than a general, and rather out-of-date, repetition of his wish to have the Division back in Australia as soon as practicable and a request for your personal interest in the matter'. As such, it could be answered without giving any commitment regarding the return of the troops. Which is what Churchill did, simply assuring Curtin of his 'personal interest in the question'.[51]

Although the fighting in the Solomons remained on a knife edge, the war of attrition on Guadalcanal would increasingly favour the Americans as they were progressively gearing up their war production. During October and November, nearly nine thousand Allied combat aircraft were produced, most of them American.[52] From November, American Lightning fighter aircraft began to be dispatched to the Pacific, providing Allied pilots with aircraft capable of meeting the Japanese Zeros on more than equal terms. And escort carriers that were being mass-produced in American shipyards would soon steam out across the ocean to tip the naval balance irrevocably in the Allies' favour. Before the arrival of these modern aircraft and warships, there still could be no certainty that Australia would not face invasion.

On 2 November, while Australian troops recaptured the airstrip at Kokoda, their counterparts in Egypt remained in the forefront of the fighting against Rommel, playing a crucial part in Montgomery's military victory and helping to ensure Churchill's political survival. Australian city dwellers rushed home from work, snatching a glimpse of newspaper headlines that told of these battles and of the fight for supremacy on Guadalcanal where troops, ships and aircraft were remorselessly thrown into the ongoing struggle. As they fought their daily battle for a seat on the limited number of trains and trams, the seas and swamps of the nearby Pacific island ran red with the blood of the combatants. It was one of the most fiercely contested battles of the entire war and on its outcome Australia's security could still depend.

NOTES

[1] Moran, *Winston Churchill*, p. 90.

[2] Harvey diary, 2 October 1942, cited in Gilbert, *Road to Victory*, p. 237.

[3] James (ed.), *Victor Cazalet*, p. 281.

[4] Headlam diary, 12 September 1942, in Ball (ed.), *Parliament and Politics in the Age of Churchill and Attlee*, p. 334.

[5] Gilbert, *Road to Victory*, p. 236.

[6] A good account of the Russian campaign is given in B. Liddell Hart, *History of the Second World War*, Chap. 18.

[7] Alanbrooke diary, 13 August 1942, in Danchev and Todman (eds), *War Diaries*, p. 300.

[8] Minute, Peck to Churchill, 3 October 1942, PREM 3/163/6, PRO.

[9] Memorandum by Pound, 9 October 1942, PREM 3/163/6, PRO.

[10] Harvey diary, 31 October 1942, ADD. MS. 56399, Harvey Papers, BL.

[11] Note, Martin to Bridges, 4 October 1942, PREM 3/163/6, PRO; See also various documents in CRS M100, 'September 1942' and 'October 1942', NAA.

[12] Cable, Dixon to Curtin, 17 September 1942, *DAFP*, Vol. 6, Doc. 49.

[13] War journal of Gerald Wilkinson, 19 October 1942, WILK 1/1, Wilkinson Papers, CC.

[14] ibid, 22 September 1942.

[15] Teleprinter message, Polglaze to Shedden, 1 October 1942, CRS A5954, Box 229, NAA.

[16] Survey by the Minister of Production, 3 September 1942, CAB 66/28, W.P. (42)393, PRO.

[17] Letter, Cross to Attlee, 16 September 1942, RC/4/12, Cross Papers, IWM.

[18] Cabinet agenda No. 335, 22 September 1942, CRS A2700, Box 4, NAA.

[19] Broadcast by Menzies, 9 October 1942, MS 3668, Folder S4, Tonkin Papers, NLA.

[20] Letter, Evatt to Hughes, 29 September 1942, 'Hughes, W. M. Folder', Evatt Papers, FUL.

[21] Talk with Sir Henry Self, 19 October 1942, CRS M100, 'October 1942', NAA.

[22] Memo, Evatt to Robinson, undated, 'Dr H. V. Evatt Folder', Robinson Papers, UMA.

[23] Memorandum by Robinson, 7 September 1942, 'Robinson, W. S., 1942–45(a) Folder', Evatt Papers, FUL.

[24] ibid.

[25] New Guinea was not a good example to cite. It was a plantation society where native land had been expropriated, and native labour ruthlessly exploited for the profit of a few Australian and British companies, and little had been done to prepare its people for self-government. Statement by Evatt, 3 September 1942, CRS A5954, Box 474, NAA.

[26] Bruce, who also supported the idea of trusteeship, had predicted earlier that the issue of colonial trusteeship would be one where Australia and America would have to combine to force a 'realistic' attitude upon Whitehall. Cable, Bruce to Curtin, 28 August 1942, and Talk with Lord Cranborne, 28 August 1942, CRS M100, 'August 1942', NAA.

[27] Letter, Gowrie to Colonel Bankie, 20 October 1942, MS 2852/4/22/28, Gowrie Papers, NLA; Letter, Roosevelt to Churchill, 19 October 1942, in Warren Kimball (ed.), *Churchill and Roosevelt*, Vol. 1, p. 633.

[28] Background briefing by Curtin, 6 October 1942, MS 4675, Smith Papers, NLA.

[29] Advisory War Council Minutes, 15 October 1942, CRS A2682/6/1087; War Cabinet Minutes, 14 and 15 October 1942, CRS A2673/XII/2428 and 2446, NAA; Cable, Curtin to Churchill, 17 October 1942, PREM 3/63/10, PRO.

[30] Minute, Churchill to Ismay, 18 October 1942, PREM 3/63/10, PRO.

[31] Letter, Robinson to Evatt, 12 August 1942, 'Robinson, W. S. 1942–45(a) Folder', Evatt Papers, FUL.

[32] Letter, Robinson to Evatt, 16 October 1942, 'Robinson, W. S. 1942–45(a) Folder', Evatt Papers, FUL.

[33] Talk with Attlee, 20 October 1942, and Cable, Bruce to Curtin, 20 October 1942, CRS M100, 'October 1942', NAA.

[34] Shedden's draft memoirs, Chap. 57, p. 6, CRS A5954, Box 771, NAA.

[35] Cable, Curtin to Bruce, 22 October 1942, *DAFP*, Vol. 6, Doc. 64; Cable, Bruce to Curtin, 23 October 1942, CRS M100, 'October 1942', NAA.

[36] Alanbrooke diary, 23 October 1942, in Danchev and Todman (eds), *War Diaries*, pp. 332–3.

[37] See documents in PREM 3/63/10, PRO.

[38] Alanbrooke diary, 23 October 1942, in Danchev and Todman (eds), *War Diaries*, p. 333.

[39] Liddell Hart, *History of the Second World War*, p. 316.

[40] Cable, Churchill to Curtin, 27 October 1942, PREM 3/63/10, PRO.

[41] Cable, Curtin to Churchill, 29 October 1942, *DAFP*, Vol. 6, Doc. 66.

[42] Cable, Alexander to Brooke, 28 October 1942, PREM 3/63/10, PRO.

[43] Minute, Churchill to Ismay, 28 October 1942, PREM 3/63/10, PRO.

[44] Dispatch, Roosevelt to Curtin, 28 October 1942, *DAFP*, Vol. 6, Doc. 68; Cable, Churchill to Roosevelt, 29 October 1942, PREM 3/63/10, PRO.

[45] Horner, *High Command*, p. 221.

[46] Note, Hollis to Churchill, 29 October 1942, PREM 3/63/10, PRO.

[47] War Cabinet paper, 30 October 1942, CAB 66/30, W.P. (42)491, PRO.

[48] Roskill, *The War at Sea*, Vol. 2, p. 229.

[49] Cadogan diary, 21 October 1942, in Dilks (ed.), *The Diaries of Sir Alexander Cadogan*, p. 485.

[50] Cable, Curtin to Churchill, 29 October 1942, and Note, Churchill to Attlee, 30 October 1942, PREM 3/63/10, PRO.

[51] Note, Attlee to Churchill, 30 October 1942, and Draft cable, Churchill to Curtin, PREM 3/63/10, PRO.

[52] Cable, Dixon to External Affairs, 20 November 1942, CRS A5954, Box 229, NAA.

THIRTY-THREE

'determined to dominate the world'

Following the Japanese naval victory off Santa Cruz on 26 October 1942, in which the US Pacific fleet was reduced to just one operational aircraft carrier, the battle for Guadalcanal was turning into what one Japanese officer termed the 'decisive struggle between America and Japan'.[1] In early November, General Imamura was ordered from Tokyo to take command of Japanese headquarters in Rabaul, with orders to overcome the disruption to Japanese ambitions caused by the American landings on Guadalcanal and to complete the capture of the Solomons. He was also instructed to prepare his forces for a major offensive in New Guinea. Clearly, the Japanese retreat from Port Moresby and back across the mountains towards their bases on the north coast had not signalled the end of their plan to capture the island.

Australian forces pursuing the Japanese along the treacherous Kokoda trail were assisted by their capture of the airstrip at Kokoda on 2 November. They could now be assured of greater fighter support against their stubbornly resisting foe as well as greater supply by air of much needed food and munitions to sustain their struggle. Despite these advantages, expelling the Japanese from New Guinea remained a most formidable task. They had built up a strongly fortified bastion at Rabaul from where their warships controlled the seas north of New Guinea and their aircraft fought for control of the air. However, in both men and machines, the Allies were fast surpassing them, with Japan being unable to make good the huge losses of highly trained airmen and their aircraft. Tokyo desperately needed another major victory to provide it with the time and means to secure its empire, hoping thereby to make it so difficult and expensive to conquer that the Allies would agree eventually to a negotiated peace.

There was certainly no pressure on the Allies to conclude a negotiated peace in the Middle East where the overwhelming might of Britain's Eighth Army was swamping the German forces with the sheer number of its troops, tanks and aircraft. The patient preparation by Auchinleck before his sacking by Churchill was paying off, as was the appointment of Montgomery to direct the attack. Although Montgomery lost nearly two hundred tanks during the course of one battle compared to a much smaller German loss, the Germans had so few to begin with that the war of attrition was working in Britain's favour. By 2 November, there was a ratio of twenty British tanks in the battle for every one German tank. Faced with these odds, Rommel had no alternative but to retreat. On 3 November, his forces began their withdrawal back into Libya. They stopped briefly when Hitler, who still had delusions of another victory in the desert, ordered that a stand be made, enjoining Rommel's troops to select between 'death and victory'.[2] But it could not be done, although Rommel displayed his skill as a commander by withdrawing in such order that he left the British forces far behind.

Rommel's retreat was a political victory for Churchill after the run of defeats that had begun with the falls of Hong Kong and Singapore and culminated with the German capture of Tobruk. Prior to the battle, Bracken had advised Churchill's doctor, Charles Moran, that 'Winston is finding the suspense almost unbearable', with Bracken predicting that another British failure would mean 'the end of Winston'. However, once the German retreat had begun, Moran recorded how Churchill 'breathed again'. His political position once again was secure. 'This victory will silence criticism,' observed Moran, 'and it seems that for the moment all his troubles are at an end.'[3] Especially when the El Alamein victory was followed on 8 November by successful Anglo–American landings in north Africa. Anxious not to make people complacent, but at the same time wanting to confirm that eventual victory was assured, Churchill told an audience at London's Mansion House two days after the north African landings that Britain had now reached 'the end of the beginning'. To emphasise the magnitude of Montgomery's military victory, and to ensure that it translated into a political victory of similar magnitude, Churchill instructed that the church bells of Britain be rung in celebration on 15 November. Apart from being rung at the end of the battle of Britain, they had been kept silent and retained as alarm bells to signal the news of a German invasion.[4]

Australia's 9th Division played a large part in the fighting at El Alamein. When Curtin received a triumphant cable from Churchill advising of the British victory against Rommel, and of the part played by the Australians, he shot off a worried cable to Bruce noting how it was 'very difficult to reconcile' the division's leading role in the fighting 'with the observance of the steps necessary to give effect to our repeated instructions for the return of the Division'.[5] Despite Curtin's concern to have the division returned home as soon as possible, and his attempt to prevent it being used up in the fighting, Churchill had advised General Alexander on 5 November not to feel hampered by the conditions that Curtin was attempting to impose on its use. Instead, ordered Churchill, the Australians were to be used 'freely' and 'no further reference to Australia [was] needed'. Once the battle was over, continued Churchill, 'we will make the best arrangements possible to send them home *if their return is still demanded*'.[6]

The 9th Division had already incurred more than two thousand casualties in the first ten days of the fighting and had just four thousand reinforcements in reserve. There would be more to come before the division was done with fighting in the Middle East. Not that Churchill would make it easy for the division to leave. And he was supported in this endeavour by Australia's former minister to the United States, and now British minister in Cairo, Richard Casey, who warned Churchill that the return of the Australians would put pressure on the New Zealand government to withdraw its division too. Moreover, the South African infantry division was about to be withdrawn from the front line so that it could be converted to an armoured division. If all these moves occurred, declared Casey, it would be 'a serious matter for this Theatre'. Apparently unaware of Roosevelt's proposal to send an American division to Australia, Casey suggested that the sending of an American division might allow the 9th Division to be retained.[7]

As always, Churchill's attention was more focused on the fighting against Germany than on the more distant struggle against Japan. Although Mongomery had dealt Rommel a heavy blow, the Afrika Korps had withdrawn beyond Montgomery's immediate reach and was being reinforced from across the Mediterranean. At the same time, the Anglo–American landings in north Africa had seen the quick occupation of Casablanca, Algiers and Oran. For their part, the Germans had reacted by rushing into Vichy-controlled Tunis to protect the narrow strait to Sicily, which might otherwise act as an Allied stepping stone into Europe. They had also occupied those parts of France that had remained under the control of the Vichy government, although they were not quick enough to seize the French warships in Toulon harbour which were scuttled by their crews. The rest of the French fleet was in north Africa and joined with the Allies. With the Germans reeling, Churchill was anxious to maintain the momentum that Montgomery had begun. He urged his military chiefs to press on with plans for an invasion of France in 1943 and not allow their forces to be 'stuck in North Africa'. It was, he thundered, meant to be 'a springboard and not a sofa'.[8] When they disparaged the chances of such a landing in 1943, Churchill warned that their conclusions would 'probably encourage the "Japan first" elements in America'.[9] Churchill was adamant that Allied resources should not leak away from the struggle in Europe, where the Russian army had broken the siege of Stalingrad on 19 November and besieged the Germans instead in their frozen fortifications.

It was at this point that Curtin rejected Roosevelt's proffered division and insisted that Churchill return the 9th Division. He claimed that Australia's attitude regarding the return of the division had always been 'quite definite and clear'.[10] This was hardly true. Churchill could be excused for doubting the strength of Curtin's convictions and for playing on it. Initially, though, Churchill appeared to relent once again, informing his chiefs of staff on 18 November that they would 'have to let them go', although only if shipping was not 'unduly deranged'.[11] This was an important rider, but the chiefs had shown previously that they had been able to find the shipping if it were required. Then came confirmation of Casey's warning concerning the implications for the New Zealand division.

The British high commissioner in Wellington advised that New Zealand, under pressure from Curtin, was likely to demand the return of its division as well. Churchill was concerned but hoped that the issue could be delayed sufficiently to 'enable us to see more clearly'.[12] His prayers were answered almost immediately when Roosevelt refused to countenance the withdrawal of Australia's division before victory was achieved in north Africa and, even then, only after the combined chiefs of staff in Washington had given approval. As Roosevelt confirmed to Churchill, the 'primary consideration' was the Africa campaign, while 'building up the Australian strength for use north of Australia' was only a 'secondary consideration'.[13] Armed with Roosevelt's support, Churchill immediately ordered the chiefs of staff to take no action about the withdrawal of either the Australians or the New Zealanders.[14] In fact, they had already met that morning to discuss the transfer, with General Brooke concluding from Curtin's cables that it was 'clear' that the Australians 'must return', although he called for a last-minute examination of the implications for Britain of the division being withdrawn. He also stipulated that the motor transport and equipment must remain in the Middle East and be replaced from American sources once the division reached Australia.[15]

Churchill was heartened to learn that the combined chiefs of staff in Washington had also discussed the issue, with the US army chief, General Marshall, being 'strongly opposed' to the return of the division and disputing Curtin's argument that it was needed to defend Australia. But Churchill was not pleased to learn that General Dill, the British army representative on the combined chiefs committee, had argued on behalf of Australia, pointing out Australia's difficulty in maintaining the division's strength if it was retained in the Middle East. Dill had also alluded to the battle-hardened division's value as a 'highly trained nucleus' if it was returned to the SWPA. Marshall eventually relented to Dill's persuasion on condition that the move would not unduly inconvenience personnel shipping. When he received Dill's report of the discussion, Churchill pointedly highlighted Marshall's initial objections while ignoring Marshall's final, albeit conditional, approval. Churchill could comfort himself with the thought that Marshall's comments still left room for manoeuvre if it could be shown that shipping would be seriously disrupted.[16]

Seizing on this rider to Marshall's approval, which had also figured in Roosevelt's comments on the issue, Churchill asked Roosevelt to delay replying to Curtin until the issue had been studied in London, 'especially in its shipping aspect'. Churchill also alerted Roosevelt to the possibility of the New Zealanders also being withdrawn.[17] Meanwhile, the chiefs of staff reconsidered the issue in accordance with Churchill's instructions, now concluding that they had 'grave objections' to the withdrawal of the divisions and claiming that there would be 'no question of their relief' if they were British troops. This was the same point that had been made by British commanders regarding the relief of the Australians in Tobruk in 1941. Then it had some point, but it was not appropriate in this case. Curtin was not calling for the Australians to be relieved from a besieged town but to be withdrawn from the Middle East altogether to meet the danger at home and to help in solving the manpower problem that was besetting the Australian government. But the chiefs of staff could only see the Australian request in the light of Tobruk, which still rankled with them, and believed that the demand for the return of the 9th Division was due to domestic political pressures in Australia. As such, and despite the military reasons for retaining the division, they conceded that 'political and Imperial considerations may be overriding'.[18]

Curtin certainly seems to have believed that, after his months of requests, he would finally get the troops back home. Before receiving a definitive reply from London or Washington, Curtin held one of his regular background briefings for journalists on 23 November, confidently telling them the 'news' that 'negotiations for the return of the 9th Division from the Middle East had been successful'. In justification of their return, Curtin claimed that Washington had refused to provide Australia with the three additional divisions that were considered necessary to ensure Australia's defence and therefore 'he must get back as many of our own men as he could'.[19] It is difficult to know on what information Curtin was basing his confident pronouncement. It may have been a deliberate leak to put pressure on Britain to allow the division's return. For Curtin was under pressure of his own, with Australian troops having pushed the Japanese back to the northern coast of New Guinea only to find them dug in for a determined battle. The untested American troops who were thrown in by MacArthur to help with the fight had recoiled at their first taste of battle.[20] At the same time, the Americans on Guadalcanal were still locked in bitter fighting for control of that island. On a world view, and particularly looking from London, these were small-scale battles. But their outcome was of vital importance for Australia.

When Churchill referred to the issue of the 9th Division during a war cabinet meeting on 23 November, Bruce was surprised to find that the British prime minister seemed to acquiesce to Curtin's demand while making clear that he was 'very unhappy about it'.[21] Bruce was mistaken. Despite Churchill's apparent acquiescence, the wily politician remained intent on blocking the division's return while ensuring that the responsibility for it was shifted to Washington. On 24 November, he informed Roosevelt that Britain could not oppose the Australian demand in principle but that Roosevelt certainly could, and should do so. Churchill claimed that Roosevelt had 'every right to express an opinion, more especially as American armies are also engaged in North Africa and it is arguable their position might be affected. Moreover there is a great case against the uneconomical use of our limited shipping.'[22] The chiefs of staff had not yet presented their report on the shipping implications, but Churchill was clearly going to play his trump card for all it was worth.

While Churchill assured Curtin that the decision was for Australia to make, he warned that the removal of the 9th Division could prompt Washington to withdraw an American division from Australia so as to make up the deficiency in the Middle East. Moreover, the removal of the Australian division as an isolated shipping movement could only be done at the 'expense of our general power to move troops about the world', which raised questions that could only be settled by the combined chiefs of staff in Washington. As for himself, Churchill declared disingenuously that he would not oppose Curtin's wishes but pointed out that the 'common cause' would best be served 'if fresh troops were moved from the United States into the Pacific' rather than remove the Australians from the Middle East and then have to move another division to take their place.[23] Churchill's opposition was not entirely bloody-minded. The situation in the Mediterranean was not proceeding as smoothly as he had hoped. German troops were reinforcing Tunisia on a large scale and holding up the Anglo–American forces trying to attack Rommel's rear while Montgomery's pursuit of Rommel was bogged down by bad weather.[24]

When Bruce was given a copy of Churchill's cable, he realised the reaction that it could cause in Canberra and immediately rushed in to smooth the ruffled imperial relationship. Bruce told Curtin that he was surprised at the harsh tone of Churchill's cable given Churchill's apparent attitude at the war cabinet meeting. Bruce suggested that Churchill must have discussed the matter with Roosevelt who, Bruce claimed, was very opposed to the division's withdrawal. In fact, the cable had been drafted prior to the war cabinet meeting. Contrary to Bruce's suggestion that Churchill had been 'fortified by the President's attitude' into expressing objections based 'to a considerable extent upon American views and wishes', it was Churchill who had been doing the fortifying of Roosevelt and of his chiefs of staff.[25]

Regardless of Churchill's attitude, his war office went ahead with planning in case Churchill's efforts failed and the troops had to return. As military commander in the Middle East, General Alexander was asked whether the Australians could be released in January 1943 and the New Zealanders in March 1943 'without prejudice [to the] completion of operations in Tripolitania'. Churchill was disconcerted when he learned of this question being put to Alexander, perhaps because he feared that the process of bureaucratic planning would make the troops' return inevitable. Depending on the answer from Cairo, it could also expose as fallacious his claim about the troops being indispensable to Alexander's operations. To try to influence the answer from Alexander, Churchill immediately informed both the War Office and his distant commander that he was 'still steadily resisting' such a move. While he might lose the Australians, he hoped at least to 'save the New Zealanders'.[26] His message arrived too late. Alexander had already admitted to the War Office that the Australian and New Zealand divisions could be removed without harming his ongoing military operations.[27]

Alexander's message was received at the War Office around midnight on 24 November. When Churchill learned of it the following day, he realised that his own officials were undercutting his efforts, albeit unwittingly. In a forthright memo to General Brooke, Churchill set out his opposition to any break-up of the Middle Eastern army. If the dominion troops were to go, asked Churchill, 'what is going to be left? It seems to me that we have got to think of the whole picture in relation to the next six months. Please report. I am disquieted.'[28] Part of Churchill's disquiet may have been caused by the need to maintain the relative strength of British forces as American troops poured into a region over which the United States previously had little influence. Similarly, when the time came to move back into Europe, the more divisions that could be counted as British, the more influence Britain would have on the European peace settlement.

Like Alexander, Brooke was not as 'disquieted' as Churchill. He advised that, even without the dominion troops, the Middle East Command would have sufficient troops for its 'minimum defensive requirements' and could draw on those British troops presently fighting alongside the Americans in their bid to capture Tunisia. Churchill would have none of this. He instructed Brooke that 'We must resist strenuously. Let nothing slip off without my knowing. Let no measures be taken to facilitate dispersion. Watch it and warn me in good time.'[29] The chiefs of staff had actually considered the issue that morning, before Brooke had received Churchill's peremptory instructions. They had discussed a paper by Brooke which had opposed the withdrawal from a 'purely military point of view' but which recognised that 'political pressure from the Dominions will be difficult to resist and may therefore be an overriding consideration'. As such, he recommended that the Australians be withdrawn in January 1943 when five fast passenger ships were available to make a speedy and economical move.[30]

The irresistible political pressure that Brooke had anticipated finally came in a cable from Curtin on 30 November which allowed for no further prevarication by Britain. He told Churchill that he 'had hoped ... this matter was finally settled' and that Churchill would have actively supported Australia's case in Washington. He disputed the importance of the shipping factor since the victories in north Africa and the opening of the Mediterranean route were expected to release about two million tonnes of Allied shipping. Although the withdrawal of the troops would affect Allied operations elsewhere, Curtin claimed that it would not be crucial whereas for Australia the availability of the 9th Division 'may in certain circumstances mean everything to us'. As for Churchill's threat to withdraw an American division from Australia, Curtin was unfazed, threatening to support and stimulate the 'Pacific first' elements in the United States if sufficiently provoked. He also insisted that the division be returned along with its transport and other equipment.[31]

Curtin's cable clinched the matter. But it also further embittered the British attitude towards Australia. Churchill drafted a 'very stiff' reply that might have done considerable damage to relations with Curtin had Attlee not intervened to have it modified. Even then, Churchill still insisted that the troops be returned without their equipment, again enlisting Roosevelt's help to bring the dominion to heel. Meanwhile, the New Zealanders backed down and agreed to allow their division to remain in the Middle East, although advising that its eventual return would still be required since 'it would be neither wise nor proper' to permit the Pacific war 'to be conducted entirely by the Americans without substantial British collaboration'.[32] Churchill was relieved by the New Zealand decision, although he had suspected they would prove more malleable than the Australians. Churchill told Fraser of his feelings of 'admiration for New Zealand and all that she stands for', while Roosevelt said simply that he was 'delighted' that New Zealand had 'done the right thing' which was 'altogether generous'.[33] Both leaders left no doubt that their attitude towards Australia was plumbing new depths.

In the midst of all these disputes, and against the background of the ongoing battles, the Australian aviator P. G. Taylor persisted with his campaign to survey an alternative air route across the Pacific linking Australia with North America. Although the governor-general, Lord Gowrie, and Evatt had both encouraged Taylor's efforts, Curtin had bowed to the opposition of MacArthur, who had opposed any British route that might compete with the existing American monopoly. Effectively blocked in Canberra, Taylor was undeterred and left for London where he hoped to persuade British officials to support his plan and provide him with a long-range flying boat to implement it.[34] Arriving in London in late October, Taylor made a strong appeal to the air ministry, claiming the support of Evatt and advising that the Australian government was concerned about the safety of the existing Pacific route. Taylor warned that the American air transport command, with its strong commercial representation, was 'determined to dominate the world'. Although Australians were grateful to the United States for defence assistance, Taylor claimed that 'they had no intention of becoming Americanised'. Instead, Australians were predominantly 'pro-British, and there was every intention that it should remain in the British empire'. While British officials gave Taylor a sympathetic hearing, they pointed to the practical difficulties that would prevent them assisting his proposal.[35]

Despite this setback, Taylor hoped that the under-secretary of state at the air ministry, Harold Balfour, who had been Taylor's flying instructor in the First World War, might still approve the plan. But Balfour feared the route would divert scarce resources away from the war effort.[36] And Bruce did not help matters when he pressed for a quick decision, confiding to Balfour that if the air ministry 'wish to throw cold water on it — that is all right by him', provided they decided quickly.[37] Bruce was confirmed in his opposition to the plan when Curtin informed him that Taylor had no government backing for his mission.[38] With no support from the high commission, and the air ministry opposing it as a war measure, Taylor's mission crashed to the ground. Balfour accepted the advice of his planning staff that, since the Pacific was an American sphere of strategic interest, 'it is up to them to develop it'.[39] The day after Taylor's interview with Balfour, the Admiralty advised Churchill that American naval inferiority in the Pacific had reached such an alarming level that 'the security of the trans-Pacific air and sea routes may be endangered'.[40] But this brought no reprieve for Taylor, who had to wait until 1944 before his proposal was eventually accepted when it was seen to be in Britain's postwar interest to develop such an imperial route across the Pacific.

Taylor was unsuccessful in 1942 largely because of Britain's 'Germany first' strategy, which was also the basis of Churchill's opposition to the withdrawal of dominion troops from the Middle East. Churchill was also convinced that Australia did not face the imminent prospect of a Japanese invasion and that risks could therefore be taken with its security, even though they were risks that he would not have accepted taking in the case of Britain. Nevertheless, he was sensitive to criticism about Britain abandoning parts of its empire or not playing a sufficient part in the Pacific war. So, when Roosevelt requested the transfer of a British aircraft carrier to the Pacific to cover their temporary deficiency, Churchill offered to send two carriers there, provided that an American carrier was provided to cover British convoys in the Atlantic. Such moves, Churchill assured Curtin, would 'provide an additional and important reinsurance for the safety of Australia'.[41] This had not been the rationale for the move, but he claimed it nonetheless. In fact, it was planned to take the Eastern fleet's aircraft carrier to provide one of the ships, so that what Australia gained in one ocean it would lose in the other. As it happened, the transfer of one of the carriers never went ahead after the Americans declined to let Britain have the use of an American carrier in the Atlantic.[42]

Churchill was still concerned to fix American attention on Europe, despite the impossibility of mounting an invasion of France in 1943. He feared that the Americans, when they realised that an invasion was off for the coming year, would turn to the Pacific instead. To the annoyance of Brooke, Churchill even joined the Americans in November to press for a cross-Channel invasion in 1943, only abandoning the idea when German resistance in Tunisia promised a longer campaign in north Africa than he had anticipated.[43] It was all part of the ongoing struggle by Churchill to ensure continued American adherence to the 'Germany first' strategy. In his view, any large diversion of resources to the Pacific could only be done at the expense of the Allied effort in the European war, even if that effort would be relatively muted for the next eighteen months or so.

Although Australia had not seen one ship of the Eastern fleet since the beginning of the Pacific war, it proceeded with work to accommodate such ships in Sydney. The British Admiralty had requested the construction of berthing facilities at Australian ports shortly after the attack on Pearl Harbor, when Churchill was absent in Washington. Although the works had been approved in principle, it had taken ten months of discussions between Canberra, London and Washington before the plans finally resurfaced in mid-November 1942, for the approval of the Australian war cabinet.[44] The fact that the expenditure was approved at a time when there was little sign that British warships would use the facilities, indicates the dominion's responsiveness to the tug of empire even after all the events of 1942. While Australian officials hoped that the close Anglo–American relationship would continue into the postwar period, they wanted Australia to remain firmly within the British rather than the American orbit.[45] For all his conflicts with Churchill, Curtin wanted the judgment of history to record that his leadership had been one of 'successful struggle to assert Australian sovereignty as a Self-Governing Dominion'.[46] It was not a struggle by Curtin to assert independence, but a struggle for a greater place for Australia within the empire. In this, he would have been supported by Shedden, who had long served the imperial cause and who later recorded with regret the effect of 'Churchill's dictatorial attitude which implied that Australia was still a colony, and [which] eroded rather than strengthened sentiment in the British Commonwealth'.[47]

Even in retrospect, Shedden failed to grasp the inevitability of this conflict. With his Victorian conceptions of empire, Churchill was predisposed to trample Australian sensitivities. But such behaviour was not confined to Churchill. Curtin and his colleagues found little sympathy for Australia even among anti-imperial counterparts in the British Labour Party. The simple fact, particularly after the outbreak of the Pacific war, was that British and Australian interests were diametrically opposed as Britain pursued its national interests and concentrated its resources in the European theatre to the detriment of its distant dominion. Australia was reluctant to question the imperial propaganda that equated British interests and imperial interests. Whenever a clash developed between London and Canberra, it was treated as an aberration rather than taken as evidence of a fundamental clash of interests. It was ascribed instead to a flaw in the personalities of the decision makers or a flaw in the decision-making process itself, which prevented Britain from pursuing its 'real' interests.

The official blindness was in Canberra rather than in London, with Evatt providing a graphic example at the end of 1942. In a secret Christmas message to Churchill in which he sent 'deep and affectionate greetings', Evatt promised that when Australia had 'finished with the Japs with his assistance we shall put our full force into Europe'.[48] The message was clearly sent in an end-of-year attempt to appease the resentment that Churchill would have felt after the months of disputation between the two capitals. But it was based on a rather curious misconception by Evatt. Despite the failure of his mission to London and Washington, and his discovery of the 'Germany first' strategy, Evatt still did not seem to get it. As his message indicated, he still assumed that the Pacific war would finish first and that Australian forces would then be transferred to Europe to finish off the Germans. Churchill, of course, had the opposite idea. And he would use his power to ensure that his vision, rather than Evatt's, came to fruition.

NOTES

1 Cited in Spector, *Eagle Against the Sun*, p. 211.

2 British intercepts of Rommel's wireless messages to Berlin allowed Churchill to know of the commander's plight. On 3 November, Brooke was handed a decrypted German message in which Rommel 'practically stated that his army was faced with a desperate defeat from which he could extract only remnants!'. Alanbrooke diary, 3 and 4 November 1942, in Todman and Danchev (eds), *War Diaries*, p. 338.

3 Moran, *Winston Churchill*, pp. 95–6.

4 Sir Cuthbert Headlam confided in his diary that many of his fellow MPs were 'a bit dubious about ringing the church bells next Sunday', presumably for fear that it might spread a sense of complacency when a long war still remained to be fought. But they were rung anyway. Headlam diary, 11 November 1942, in Ball (ed.), *Parliament and Politics in the Age of Churchill and Attlee*, p. 341.

5 Cable, Curtin to Bruce, 4 November 1942, CRS M100, 'November 1942', NAA.

6 Minute, Churchill to Brooke, 5 November 1942, PREM 3/63/10, PRO (author's emphasis in italics).

7 Cable, Casey to Churchill, 3 November 1942, PREM 3/63/10, PRO.

8 Churchill, *The Second World War*, Vol. 4, p. 583.

9 Defence Committee (Operations) Minutes, 16 November 1942, CAB 69/4, D.O. (42)17, PRO.

10 Cable, Curtin to Bruce, 16 November 1942, CRS M100, 'November 1942', NAA; Cable, Curtin to Churchill, 16 November 1942, PREM 3/63/10, PRO.

11 Cable, Curtin to Churchill, 16 November 1942, and attached note by Churchill, 18 November 1942, PREM 3/63/10, PRO.

12 Minute, Dominions Office to J. Martin, 18 November 1942, and other documents in this file, PREM 3/63/10, PRO.

13 Cable, Roosevelt to Churchill, 20 November 1942, PREM 3/63/10, PRO.

14 Cable, Chiefs of Staff to Joint Staff Mission, 20 November 1942, PREM 3/63/10, PRO.

15 Chiefs of Staff Meeting Minutes, 20 November 1942; Cable, Fraser to Churchill, 20 November 1942, PREM 3/63/10, PRO.

16 Cable, Joint Staff Mission to Chiefs of Staff, 21 November 1942, PREM 3/63/10, PRO.

17 Cable, Churchill to Roosevelt, 23 November 1942, PREM 3/63/10, PRO.

[18] Note, Ismay to Churchill, 23 November 1942, PREM 3/63/10, PRO.

[19] Background briefing by Curtin, 23 November 1942, MS 4675, Smith Papers, NLA.

[20] Letter, Blamey to Curtin, 4 December 1942, CRS A5954, Box 262, NAA.

[21] Bruce shared Churchill's anger and assured him that he had relayed all the British objections to Curtin. Note by Bruce, 23 November 1942, and Talk with Spender, 17 November 1942, CRS M100, 'November 1942', NAA.

[22] Cable, Churchill to Roosevelt, 24 November 1942, PREM 3/63/10, PRO.

[23] Cables, Churchill to Curtin, and Churchill to Fraser, 24 November 1942, PREM 3/63/10, PRO.

[24] The concern about the Mediterranean was short-lived. While Brooke was worrying in his diary on 23 November that Rommel was being given too much time to re-establish himself, three days later the intelligence intercepts of German communications confirmed that 'there should be a chance of pushing him into the sea before long'. Alanbrooke diary, 23 and 26 November 1942, in Danchev and Todman (eds), *War Diaries*, pp. 337–38.

[25] Cable, Bruce to Curtin, 25 November 1942, CRS M100, 'November 1942', NAA.

[26] Cable, Churchill to Alexander, 24 November 1942, and Cable, War Office to Alexander, 23 November 1942, PREM 3/63/10, PRO.

[27] Cable, Alexander to War Office, 24 November 1942, PREM 3/63/10, PRO.

[28] Minute, Churchill to Brooke, 25 November 1942, PREM 3/63/10, PRO.

[29] Note, Brooke to Churchill, 25 November 1942, with attached note by Churchill to Brooke, 27 November 1942, PREM 3/63/10, PRO.

[30] Memorandum by Brooke, 26 November 1942, PREM 3/63/10, PRO.

[31] Cable, Curtin to Churchill, 30 November 1942, PREM 3/63/10, PRO.

[32] In the event, the New Zealanders allowed their division to remain for the duration of the European war. Note, Attlee to Churchill, 1 December 1942; Cable, Churchill to Roosevelt, 1 December 1942; Cable, Churchill to Curtin, 2 December 1942; Cable, Fraser to Churchill, 5 December 1942, PREM 3/63/10, PRO.

[33] Cable, Churchill to Fraser, 6 December 1942; Cable, Roosevelt to Churchill, 6 December 1942, PREM 3/63/10, PRO.

[34] See Day, 'P. G. Taylor and the alternative Pacific air route, 1939–45'.

[35] Memo, W. P. Hildred to Balfour, 27 October 1942, BBK D/208, Beaverbrook Papers, HLRO.

[36] Note of Captain P. G. Taylor's Interview, 4 November 1942, BBK D/208, Beaverbrook Papers, HLRO.

[37] Memo, Balfour to Vice Chief of Air Staff, 28 October 1942, BBK D/208, Beaverbrook Papers, HLRO.

[38] Cable, Curtin to Bruce, 30 October 1942, CRS A2676, Box 2200, NAA.

[39] Memo, Assistant Chief of Air Staff (Plans) to Balfour, 31 October 1942, BBK D/208, Beaverbrook Papers, HLRO.

[40] Memo, Pound to Churchill, 5 November 1942, PREM 3/163/1, PRO.

[41] Cable, Churchill to Curtin, 2 December 1942, VI/2, Ismay Papers, KC.

[42] See PREM 3/163/1, PRO.

[43] Bryant, *Turn of the Tide*, pp. 525–35.

[44] See CRS A2670/461/1942, NAA.

[45] For an example of this view, see Letter, Watt to Hood, 20 July 1942, MS 3788/1/1, Watt Papers, NLA.

[46] Shedden's draft memoirs, Chap. 57, CRS A5954, Box 771, NAA.

[47] Shedden's draft memoirs, Chap. 56, CRS A5944, Box 771, NAA.

[48] Minute, Bracken to Churchill, 16 December 1942, PREM 3/150/7, PRO.

THIRTY-FOUR

'one horrible gamble'

By December 1942, twelve months after Pearl Harbor, the Japanese empire in the Pacific had not been seriously challenged. Although its naval forces had been checked at the battle of Midway, its warships still remained superior to the American Pacific fleet and its forces remained in control of all the territory they had captured so swiftly. Moreover, its ships had inflicted heavy losses on the Americans in successive battles. But the Americans could afford to lose warships since their massive ship-building program would soon be replacing them faster than they were being sunk. The Japanese had no such productive advantage and had to husband their depleted naval forces to guard against any attack that might be launched on their home islands. Their cautious commanders could no longer afford to risk their forces in aggressive main fleet actions against the Americans. Nevertheless, they still controlled the seas around Australia and they remained intent on preventing the Americans from using Australia as a base from which to launch offensives against their empire.

Japanese efforts in the south-west Pacific continued to be concentrated on the battle for control of that otherwise insignificant backwater of British colonialism, the island of Guadalcanal. For four months, each side had upped the ante by sending in successive reinforcements of men and supplies in the hope that it finally would tip the balance their way. In October, Roosevelt had instructed that the island must be held at whatever cost, while the Japanese were equally adamant that the outcome of the battle was as much a matter of national pride as strategic necessity. Almost daily, the Japanese sent waves of aircraft from Rabaul to destroy the American planes on Henderson Field, only to find that the American losses were quickly replaced. When fresh reinforcements of Japanese troops were sent south to overrun the American positions, the Japanese supply ships were attacked and sunk by Allied aircraft. The Japanese were forced to resort to sending men and supplies by fast destroyers and, as a measure of their increasing desperation, even by submarine. Their outnumbered troops fought tenaciously but to little effect, and now were close to starving due to constant American attacks on their naval supply line. Had they sent in sufficient forces, the Japanese might have won the battle in August or September but by October or November it was too late. And the demands of Guadalcanal were bleeding forces from New Guinea and even from China. It could not continue. At the end of December, after heated arguments in Tokyo, the Japanese military finally called a halt and planned for an evacuation. The Japanese headquarters at Rabaul would concentrate its attention on New Guinea instead.[1]

The Allied forces in New Guinea had pursued the Japanese back to Gona and Buna on the north-east coast where the Japanese had retreated behind heavily defended fortifications in some of the most difficult country imaginable, a mixture of 'thick jungle, kunai grass, sago swamps and mangrove swamps'.[2] Supplies for the Australian and American troops had to be either flown in over the Owen Stanley Range, carried laboriously from Port Moresby by local porters, or shipped by barge along the northern New Guinea coast. As a result, heavy weapons were scarce and the battles were fought in hand-to-hand struggles in which the Japanese put up a determined resistance. Battle fatigue and malarial mosquitoes took a heavy toll of the Australian troops, many of whom were men of the 6th and 7th Divisions who had gained their battle experience in the very different conditions of the

Middle East. After fierce battles, Gona finally fell to the Australians on 9 December while Buna fell three weeks later to mainly American forces. With thousands of soldiers laid low by disease and the rigours of the fighting, Blamey was relying on the early return of the 9th Division from the Middle East to provide relief for his hard-pressed troops.[3]

The hard-won successes in New Guinea and on Guadalcanal signalled the eventual end of the Japanese empire. But it would not come quickly or cheaply. Although the Allies were gradually gaining the ascendancy in the air, with even the slow and vulnerable Wirraways being brought back into action in New Guinea, MacArthur was unable to take full advantage of the weakening Japanese position. As always, he was still hampered by the overriding Allied commitment to defeat Germany first, with Churchill determined to keep Washington concentrated on the European struggle and not distracted by the calls from the south-west Pacific for reinforcements. As part of this strategy, Churchill proposed in early December 1942 that there be a cross-Channel invasion of France in 1943. The planning for such an invasion would ensure that there was no undue leakage of shipping and armed forces to the Pacific and it would satisfy the Russian demands for an Allied landing to occupy German forces in western Europe. However, when Churchill suggested a summit meeting with Stalin and Roosevelt to settle plans for the coming year,[4] Stalin declined the invitation. He was too preoccupied with prosecuting his own successful offensive against the Germans, which he planned to continue right through the winter.

Undaunted, Roosevelt proposed that he and Churchill meet in Casablanca, formerly the Vichy French capital of Morocco. Churchill intended to use the meeting to confirm Britain's commitment to an invasion of Europe in August 1943. However, the prospect of mounting such an invasion gradually faded as the German and Italian resistance in Tunisia toughened, with German reinforcements from as far away as Russia pouring across the narrow strait from Sicily and the 'toe' of Italy. Churchill's hopes for an easy victory in north Africa were disappointed, with his forward troops retreating in the face of overwhelming odds and both armies becoming bogged down in the winter mud. At a meeting with his chiefs of staff on 16 December, Churchill was finally forced to acknowledge that a cross-Channel invasion of Europe in 1943 would be impossible.[5] In the absence of such an invasion until 1944 at the earliest, there would inevitably be calls for Allied resources to be diverted to the Pacific. To pre-empt such calls, Churchill and his chiefs of staff devised amphibious operations for the Mediterranean in order to tie Allied resources to that theatre once victory in north Africa had been secured.

The conference between Churchill and Roosevelt at Casablanca from 14 to 23 January 1943 was very different to the conference they had held in Washington in the wake of Pearl Harbor just a year before. Whereas the Allies then had been facing the prospect of widespread defeats, culminating in the fall of Singapore and Burma, they now were facing the prospect of widespread victories. If only they could agree where the battles would be fought and the victories won. After much argument, the British delegation believed they had convinced their American counterparts that a cross-Channel invasion of France could not be mounted that year and that their focus should remain fixed on the Mediterranean, with the next operation, after north Africa was secured, to be an invasion of Sicily. General Brooke complained in his diary that it was 'a slow and tiring business which requires a lot of patience', with the Americans having to be 'made gradually to assimilate our proposed policy'. However, that still left open the question of the Pacific war, with America's Admiral Ernie King wanting the Allies to commit 30 per cent of their war effort to that theatre. According to Brooke, this would amount to them fighting an 'all-out' war in the Pacific rather than the holding operation that had previously been agreed upon. Indeed, wrote Brooke, the Americans now 'did not agree with Germany being the primary enemy and were wishing to defeat Japan first!!!'.[6] This was a considerable exaggeration of the American position.

Although King was naturally keen for his naval forces to be given the resources to push home their growing advantage against the Japanese, the Americans had not rejected the fundamental strategy of concentrating on Germany. But they had thought out the implications for the United States of a two-stage ending to the war. Once Germany was defeated, the Allies would have to gather their strength to defeat Japan at a time when governments would be under pressure to devote resources to domestic reconstruction. The devastation of Britain's cities meant that Britain faced more domestic reconstruction and might be less inclined to see the war against Japan through to the end. Moreover, if it could convert its industries to peacetime production while the United States was shouldering most of the burden of defeating Japan, Britain could quickly take advantage of the expected postwar boom in world trade and perhaps regain at least some of their former dominance. Both London and Washington suspected each other's economic motives and imperial ambitions.[7]

Britain's war secretary, Sir James Grigg, had warned the war cabinet in November 1942 that the Americans were pursuing an 'Imperialistic policy which aims at the building up of American power and prestige in various parts of the world ... under the guise of the war effort ...' Australia was one of the places mentioned by Grigg as a target of this American imperialism.[8] Grigg's report confirmed existing British suspicions. And they were buttressed the following month by a similar report from the production minister, Oliver Lyttelton, who returned from a trip to Washington having been struck by the attention American industry was devoting to planning for postwar trade. He claimed that the Ford Motor Company had new models ready for production as soon as the war ended and that 'the aircraft industry, and in particular Pan American Airways, are largely engaged in preparing for post-war Civil Aviation'.[9]

Likewise, American suspicions of Britain were very widely expressed and were probably rooted in the country's colonial past as much as anything. Eisenhower's chief of staff, General Bedell Smith, confided to Churchill's military adviser, General Ismay, in December 1942 that the American military opposed heavy involvement in the Mediterranean because they regarded it as serving purely British interests. General Dill had earlier warned from Washington of the many leading Americans 'who feel that we have led them down the Mediterranean garden path and although they are enjoying the walk are fearful of what they might find at the end of it'.[10] Partly to allay such suspicions, the British delegation at Casablanca supported Eisenhower being made supreme commander of Allied forces in the Mediterranean.[11] To further allay such suspicions, Churchill assured the Americans that Britain would not leave them to fight Japan alone, declaring that both Britain's 'interest and our honour were alike engaged' and that Britain would 'devote their whole resources to the defeat of Japan after Germany had been brought to her knees'. Roosevelt accepted the assurance and rejected as unnecessary Churchill's offer to formalise the pledge in a treaty between the two countries. Churchill also promised to mount a major operation in Burma to reopen land communications with China. The two leaders then announced that they would continue their struggle until they had forced the unconditional surrender of Germany, Italy and Japan.[12]

At the conclusion of the Casablanca conference, Brooke could be relatively satisfied with the outcome. As he observed in his diary, he had ensured 'that Germany should continue to be regarded as our primary enemy and that the defeat of Japan must come after that of Germany'.[13] This reassertion of the overriding Anglo–American strategy had important implications for Australia and for the ongoing fighting in New Guinea and elsewhere. But Curtin was neither informed nor consulted about the discussions. When rumours reached him suggesting that a meeting between Churchill and Roosevelt was about to take place, Curtin tried to have Australia's viewpoint considered, appealing this time for two thousand additional aircraft for MacArthur's command. However, such was the secrecy surrounding the meeting that Curtin wrongly believed the conference was being held in the United States. Accordingly, he sent his cabled appeal to Washington, while confiding to a group of Australian journalists on 19 January that the meeting was taking place and asserting that he was 'taking a hand in the conversations'.[14] He was too late. By the time Curtin's message was received by Roosevelt and Churchill, they had already reaffirmed the 'Germany first' strategy. Not that Curtin's cable would have swayed them towards a greater concentration on the Pacific.

It was another example of Australia's needs and viewpoints being ignored by its more powerful allies. Curtin had earlier complained to journalists of being 'fed up with the way [Churchill and Roosevelt] played ball with one another, quite regardless of the world at large'. Events during 1942 had convinced him, he said, that both Allied leaders had 'made their minds up that if the British Empire in the Far East had to go then it had to go'.[15] If necessary, it all would be sacrificed for the sake of the war in

Europe. As MacArthur had explained to him, and despite their warm personal relations, the United States could not be relied upon, any more than Britain could, to treat Australia with any consideration. Curtin discovered as much when he tried to oppose a plan by Roosevelt to replace the American minister in Canberra, a respected career diplomat who had become close to Curtin, with a political crony. In an off-the-record briefing to journalists at the end of December 1942, Curtin had declared: 'I'm not having him.' Two days later, journalists found him 'very downcast' when he was forced to back down after learning that Roosevelt would be 'deeply offended' if Australia refused to accept his chosen nominee.[16] The Casablanca conference came in the immediate wake of this humiliation for Curtin. Hence his concern to be seen as having some input into the discussions.

Although Australia no longer faced the likelihood of a Japanese invasion, it did face the tough task of defeating and expelling the Japanese forces that had secured such a firm hold on the islands to its north. Not just New Guinea and the Solomons, but also the more strategically important Netherlands East Indies and the naval base at Singapore. And it could not achieve this without greater resources from Britain and the United States. Although most of Australia's forces had returned home from the Middle East, its manpower was stretched to the limit with all the demands being placed upon it. The number of Australian army units that had been created during the first three years of war now exceeded the ability of the population to sustain them. Moreover, men were increasingly reluctant to enlist for the expeditionary AIF rather than for the home-based militia. By March 1943 the Australian army would be under strength by 79 000 and require a monthly injection of 12 500 personnel. With the competing demands of the civilian economy, the production of food for Britain and elsewhere, the growing munitions industry and the support of the American forces, these numbers simply were not available.[17]

With pressure from his conservative political opponents, as well as from a chorus of American commentators, to abolish the distinction between the AIF and the militia, Curtin had announced in mid-November 1942 that conscripted militia troops would be liable for service in the region north of

Australia. This was a momentous decision for Curtin, given the strong anti-conscriptionist tradition of the Labor Party and his own involvement in the anti-conscription movement of 1916 and 1917. Before the First World War, the Labor government had introduced compulsory military training, which was designed to provide an American-style militia for local defence. But the party had split in two in 1916 when the Labor prime minister, Billy Hughes, had attempted to introduce conscription for the European war. Curtin had been one of the leaders in that fight and it had become an article of faith that Labor would not introduce conscription for overseas service. In the context of 1942, though, conscripted militia troops fighting in New Guinea were clearly fighting for the defence of Australia and it was nonsensical if those troops fighting in the Australian colony of Papua were debarred from crossing the unmarked border to Dutch New Guinea in pursuit of the Japanese. Or, as Curtin argued, it was incongruous that 'a man could be sent to Darwin, where he could be bombed, but not to Timor to save Darwin from being bombed'. Against the trenchant opposition from some of his own colleagues, Curtin managed to remove this anomaly in a way that did not greatly enlarge the area in which conscripted service personnel could be forced to serve. Curtin thereby satisfied his American critics and neutralised the issue as a political problem for Labor. With a federal election due in 1943, it became instead a problem for the Opposition, which soon split apart as it attempted to react to Curtin's carefully crafted system of limited conscription.[18]

As the debate over conscription indicated, along with the faltering enlistments for the AIF, the Australian government was facing increasing difficulties in maintaining the tempo of its war effort. Despite the most strenuous fighting close to Australian shores, the society seemed to be slipping back into its prewar apathy.[19] With free-spending American troops thronging the pavements of Australian cities, many seized upon the chance to turn a few 'quid' into a small fortune. Horse-racing continued to captivate so many Australians that Curtin complained of not being able to make a phone call on a Saturday because the lines were tied up with punters placing their bets with illegal bookmakers.[20] In December 1942, Curtin had complained bitterly to journalists of the

buggers in Australia who won't work. Coal mines are idle, and everyone is
thinking about holidays just at a time when a few extra tons in our war
effort would have a crucial effect. We are like people who have just got
contagion out of the house, and just over the back fence. Apparently we are
not worrying how dirty the yard is.

It was no good, Curtin said, looking to a great power for the country's
salvation. In fact, Australia's plight earlier that year had been 'the proper
fate of any country that thought it could fight anybody's war before it made
its own position safe'.[21]

It was not just Australia's defence that Curtin was anxious to secure.
Along with Evatt, he wanted to see Australia emerge from the war as the
leading power in its region. To this end, the Australian government sought to
change the relationship between European powers and their colonial
territories, with regional committees of interested nations supervising the
administration of the European colonies and helping to steer them towards
independence. From London, Bruce was a leading advocate of such a course,
fearing that China would otherwise come to dominate South-East Asia,
which he described as 'probably the richest prize in the world'. From
Canberra, and to the considerable consternation of Whitehall, Evatt backed
independence for India and sought greater Australian influence within the
Netherlands East Indies and British-controlled Malaya.[22] This might not
have mattered had Roosevelt not also been a persistent proponent of
independence for India and other European colonies.[23] While it might have
been possible for Churchill to ignore Evatt's views on the future of the
British empire, it was not so easy to ignore the views of the US president.

In a ringing declaration in November 1942, Churchill had proclaimed
that he had not become prime minister to preside over the break-up of the
British empire. His remark had been intended to kill speculation about a
new post-imperial world order along American lines. Churchill rejected any
change to the colonial status of Britain's territories not only because of his
romantic Victorian notions of empire but because Britain needed the empire
if it were to join with America as an equal partner in any postwar
relationship. He was supported by a number of pro-imperial conservative

MPs led by Leo Amery, the secretary of state for India, who fought a vigorous delaying action against the forces of change. Amery went further than Churchill, arguing that Britain should keep clear of any postwar alliance, whether with America or the countries of Europe, 'so long as our main interests, our primary obligations and our instinctive loyalties are concerned with our partners in the British Commonwealth'.[24] In a letter to the governor of Burma, now cooling his heels in India, Amery declared that he was

at least as Colonel Blimpish as you are, and 'By Gad! Sir' am not at all prepared that anyone, Yank or Chink, should poke either projecting or flat noses into the problem of the reconstitution of Burma. In that we shall certainly have Winston behind us and I think increasingly the Cabinet as a whole.[25]

But it was not only Roosevelt and the Australians who wanted to break down the old European empires, along with the rising nationalist tide in India and elsewhere. The British Labour Party was also reluctant to pay the price of retaining an empire that Britain no longer had the will or power to defend.[26]

The question of Britain's future world role was one of the factors influencing the ongoing debate about its participation in the Pacific war. Gerald Wilkinson, a British security agent and businessman, was concerned that Churchill's neglect of the Pacific would lead to Britain losing its economic influence there. For this reason, Wilkinson felt it to be vitally important that he continue as British liaison officer with MacArthur and that Britain should contribute forces to MacArthur's command. In February 1943, while passing through Washington on his way to London for consultations, Wilkinson impressed upon the British ambassador, Lord Halifax, the danger of MacArthur making his expedition against Japan a 'Pan-American' one, 'in which case British status in the eye of the Native peoples of the areas under MacArthur's command, would not increase with the defeat of the enemy, as would American status'. This could mean Britain finding itself 'not only in an inferior position to take advantage of the immediate opportunities of post-war reconstruction, but of the greater reaching opportunities [when those areas] become due for a great economic and social up-surge'.[27]

While Evatt worked to expand Australia's regional role and sought the end of colonial empires, former prime minister Robert Menzies sought to restore the British empire in all its tarnished glory. From his position on the advisory war council, Menzies tried to have Australia join in Britain's battle in Burma, rather than remain committed to MacArthur's campaign in the islands to Australia's north. Menzies had wanted Australian troops sent to Burma in early 1942 and, like many of his fellow conservative MPs, was concerned at the implications for the empire of Australia's close wartime relations with Washington. Loudly predicting a gloomy future of stringency and belt-tightening after the war, and uncertain of his own political future after the humiliation he suffered in 1941, Menzies used W. S. Robinson to ask Churchill in February 1943 to sanction his permanent return to London. In contrast to his role in 1941 as a rival to Churchill, Menzies would go this time as 'an out-and-out supporter of Winston and as a Britisher devoted to Australia and the Empire'. However, it seems that Churchill would not take the risk and Menzies was forced to remain in Australia.[28]

Nearly all Australians expected Britain to continue to play a large part in Australian life after the war, differing only on the degree of British involvement. Curtin, as Menzies had done before him, blamed Churchill personally rather than Britain for Australia's shabby treatment in 1942. Menzies had concluded after his trip to London in mid-1941 that Australia was simply too far away for Churchill to give it his proper attention. Curtin took a similar view, suggesting to journalists in late 1942 that Australia was Churchill's 'forgotten land'.[29] They preferred to believe that Britain's failure to fulfil its defence guarantees was more a result of misguided leadership rather than the inevitable result of it pursuing its national self-interest. Hence the various attempts by Menzies, Bruce and Evatt to change the composition of the British war cabinet in ways that might curb Churchill's largely untrammelled power or cause his complete downfall.[30] There was an assumption that Churchill's fall from power would see Australian interests come more to the fore in London.

With Churchill having seen off all these challenges, Curtin tried to woo him, or one of his ministers, to visit Australia in the hope that it might help to restore amicable relations between the two countries and increase British sympathy for Australia. But the suggestion went no further than the British high commissioner, Sir Ronald Cross, who petulantly decried it as betraying a lack of confidence in him by the Australian government.[31] Failing such a ministerial visit, Curtin asked in February 1943 for 'some demonstration by the United Kingdom of its interest in the Pacific by the despatch to Australia of a token force, e.g., a Brigade or a naval unit'. He watched enviously as Britain sent hundreds of bombers in almost nightly raids over Germany but, as he complained, 'by Christ you can't get any here'. All Britain had on offer were superannuated Lancaster bombers which it planned to convert into civil aircraft after the war and provide free to the dominions so as to shut out the superior American machines that then would be available. Australia was no longer prepared automatically to accept aircraft just because they were British. Not even if they were free. It asked London how the Lancasters compared with 'American designed passenger aircraft embodying comfort and speed'.[32]

Anxious to develop its own aircraft industry, and not wanting to forgo superior American aircraft, Australia tried to hedge its bets. The Australian air minister proposed instead that Australia should manufacture one hundred American C-47 transport aircraft, the sturdy military version of the versatile DC-3 aircraft that were being used to such good effect in New Guinea transporting troops and supplies to the front line. These American workhorses would not only be put to good use during the war but would be able to service Australia's postwar air transport needs. If Australia was able to manufacture such large aircraft, it would be less dependent on either the United States or Britain for its civil aviation needs in the future and would have less need to go begging again for aircraft in the event of a future war.[33]

While making moves to reduce its dependence on either Britain or the United States, Curtin was anxious to avoid further acrimonious disputes with Britain. Partly for this reason, Curtin deferred the appointment of a new governor-general to replace the ageing and ailing Lord Gowrie. Ever since the Scullin Labor government had insisted in 1930 that its Australian-born nominee, Sir Isaac Isaacs, be appointed, the Labor party had been committed to having Australians, rather than British aristocrats, as governor-general. The conservatives had appointed the Duke of Kent to take over from Gowrie in 1939, but his arrival had been postponed for the duration of the war. The duke's death in a plane crash in August 1942 raised the issue of finding a replacement. Rather than appointing an Australian, and thereby risk provoking Britain over a matter of symbolism when matters of survival were at stake, Curtin did nothing, hoping that the elderly Gowrie would soldier on indefinitely. As Gowrie confided to his counterpart in India, the duke's death had 'made it more difficult for me to retire — as Labor policy is that an Australian should be G.G., and as there are several candidates but nobody suitable, Curtin does not want to be faced with the problem'.[34] It would take more than these gestures to restore Anglo–Australian relations to their former state of amicability.

More importantly, Britain would continue to risk Australian lives and interests for the sake of its overriding commitment to the defeat of Germany and the protection of its own interests in Europe. This was seen when the troops of the returning 9th Division, who had played such a leading role in the recent British victory at El Alamein, had to face the hazard of crossing the Indian Ocean in early 1943. Curtin had fought hard for the return of the division, but the victory almost became pyrrhic when the troopships set off from Cairo with the lightest of naval escorts. It had been axiomatic that troopships should have what the British official naval historian Captain Stephen Roskill called 'special protection'.[35] As far as Australia was concerned, this meant that troop convoys should be escorted by at least a battleship. In March 1941, the acting prime minister, Artie Fadden, had rejected a suggestion that it was sufficient for troop convoys in the Indian Ocean to have capital ship 'cover'; that is a capital ship force in the general area providing protection from a distance. Fadden insisted that 'capital ship escort should be provided for the larger troop convoys, in accordance with the principle agreed to at the 1940 Singapore Defence Conference'.[36] This was the level of protection considered necessary in the Indian Ocean prior to the entry of Japan into the war.

In the case of the 9th Division, five fast passenger liners were allocated for its voyage across the Indian Ocean. The speed of the ships provided considerable security, allowing them to outpace submarines and reducing the risk of them being torpedoed. This was all right for the western part of the Indian Ocean, where only isolated enemy raiders might be encountered. However, the convoy would pass within reach of the Japanese naval and air forces stationed at the former British bastion of Singapore. The division's departure from Egypt could hardly be kept secret and its destination could be easily guessed by the Japanese. As such, there was a very real danger that a Japanese force of cruisers, or even a battleship or aircraft carrier, might intercept and annihilate the convoy with its thirty thousand troops.

Initially, the chiefs of staff had considered sending the division back completely unescorted. Only later did they agree that the convoy would have to have a naval escort, although without specifying the strength of that escort.[37] When the troops of the 9th Division lined the rails of their camouflaged ships as they sailed from Suez in mid-January, they found they had two escorts for the voyage, the British cruiser *Devonshire* and an armed merchant ship, as well as destroyers for their passage through the narrow waters of the Red Sea. There was no battleship to provide certain protection against raiding cruisers. Although Roskill's official history noted how 'this large movement took place without any untoward incidents',[38] this was more through good fortune than good management.

At the time of the convoy's passage across the Indian Ocean, a German armed merchant raider was also present in that ocean, sinking or seizing any merchant ships it encountered. Fortunately for the Australians, the heavily armed raider, complete with spotter planes, arrived in Batavia on 10 February without sighting the convoy. If it had, it may itself have been sunk by the *Devonshire*, which had sunk a similar German raider fourteen months earlier.[39] But there was no certainty in naval warfare, as the sailors aboard the Australian cruiser *Sydney* learned when their ship was destroyed by just such a raider in 1941. Japanese submarines were also active across the Indian Ocean, while a German U-boat 'wolf pack' sank 23 ships off the west coast of Africa in early 1943 as it tried to cut the British supply line to the Middle East.[40]

The commander of Britain's hard-pressed Eastern fleet, Admiral Somerville, did what he could to provide protection for the convoy. He was hampered by losing the aircraft carrier *Illustrious*, which was transferred to the Pacific in response to an American request for assistance.[41] Although Somerville protested at this depletion of his strength, it was to no avail. Even with the aircraft carrier, the fleet did not amount to much. As one of its officers observed, if the Japanese 'really go for us they'll put in forces which would eat us'.[42] When Somerville received orders in mid-January to 'cover' the passage of the Australian convoy, he was also ordered to dispatch two of his destroyers to South Africa to help deal with the German submarines. It was not until 3 February that the much-reduced Eastern fleet raised anchor in the Kenyan port of Kilindini and set course for the Seychelles, where they were due to rendezvous with the troop convoy. The force of three battleships, one cruiser and six destroyers was calculated to impress the returning troops, who would not have realised that two of the battleships were of First World War vintage and had been described by Churchill as 'floating coffins' unfit for use against the Japanese.[43]

By 6 February, the ships were in the Seychelles waiting for the overdue Australians. Ralph Edwards, a captain in the Eastern fleet, vented his anxiety in the pages of his diary, writing that 'I don't like this convoy and I'm thankful at all events that Jap'n major forces appear to be fully engaged to the Eastward ... It's one horrible gamble ...'[44] Just how horrible a gamble was made plain the following day when a report was received of a Japanese submarine in the area, with the fleet having few ships capable of dealing with it. Somerville's plan was to fool the Japanese into thinking that a substantial British fleet was operating in the central Indian Ocean, hoping that would cause the Japanese to retain their surface fleet at Singapore.[45] The other part of his plan was to impress the passing Australian troops with a false sense of British strength. He had hoped, he told Admiral Pound, 'to steam close past them and give them a good chuck up'. However, just over an hour before the convoy sailed into sight on 10 February, another submarine was detected. The convoy was immediately ordered to change course while keeping to its zigzag pattern. As a result, Somerville's ships could not get any closer than a few miles to the convoy as the troops strained to catch sight of the distant specks before they sank away below the horizon and the darkness of the tropical night descended to cover the fleet's inadequacies.[46] Apart from the light escort, the thirty thousand troops were now on their own for the four thousand miles of ocean that separated them from their homeland.

Fortunately, Somerville's subterfuge seems to have worked. The convoy arrived in Western Australia unscathed on 18 February. The single railway line across the continent would take months to transport them in a slow shuffle of steam trains, and Australia could not afford the delay. So the troops were sent on by sea, this time with all the escorts, both sea and air, that the country could muster. Curtin confessed to journalists that he had not slept well for three weeks while awaiting the arrival of the convoy.[47] Somerville was similarly relieved at its safe return, confiding to Pound that 'we took a bit of a chance over this since it is unlikely the Japanese were unaware of the movement of the Australian Division from Egypt, and its probable destination must have been obvious'. If they had sent out a cruiser force and an auxiliary carrier, observed Somerville, 'they would have had no great difficulty in locating the convoy, and would have made hay of it if they had found it'.[48] So, by a stroke of considerable luck, Australia had most of its forces returned to its control.

While the 9th Division had been steaming across the Indian Ocean, the fighting on Guadalcanal had suddenly stopped in a completely unexpected way. The remaining Japanese troops, exhausted and half-starving, had quietly left the island in a daring night-time operation reminiscent of the brilliant Australian evacuation from Gallipoli in the First World War. When the American trap clanged shut on the Japanese positions, there was not a live Japanese in sight. More than twenty thousand men had died fighting for control of the island, with the Americans incurring seven thousand casualties and losing hundreds of aircraft and 24 ships to achieve a victory that mattered little in the final defeat of Japan, but which did remove the threat of Japanese air attacks on Australia's eastern cities. Nevertheless, because of the concentration of Allied bomber strength in Europe, the core of Japanese strength in the south-west Pacific stayed intact at Rabaul. While MacArthur remained unable to launch an offensive against Rabaul, the victories in New Guinea and Guadalcanal marked the beginning of the end for the Japanese empire.

NOTES

1 Edwin Hoyt, *Japan's War: The Great Pacific Conflict*, Hutchinson, London, 1987, pp. 305–13, 318–9; Gillison, *Royal Australian Air Force, 1939–1942*, pp. 579–85.

2 'Operations in New Guinea', 30 January 1943, in Robertson and McCarthy (eds), *Australian War Strategy 1939–1945*, Doc. 351.

3 Gillison, *Royal Australian Air Force, 1939–1942*, Chap. 31.

4 Gilbert, *Road to Victory*, p. 272.

5 ibid., pp. 281–2; Alanbrooke diary, 16 December 1942, Danchev and Todman (eds), *War Diaries, 1939–1945*, p. 349.

6 Alanbrooke diary, 13–23 January 1943, in Danchev and Todman (eds), *War Diaries*, pp. 358–68.

7 For discussion of this mutual suspicion and manoeuvring for economic advantage, see David Reynolds, *The Creation of the Anglo–American Alliance, 1937–41*; W. R. Louis, *Imperialism at Bay*; and Christopher Thorne, *Allies of a Kind*.

8 Note by Grigg, 9 November 1942, CAB 66/30, W.P. (42)515, PRO; See also Harvey diary, 1 December 1942, ADD. MS. 56399, Harvey Papers, BL.

9 Note by Lyttelton, 16 December 1942, CAB 66/32, W.P. (42)591, PRO.

10 Letter, Bedell Smith to Ismay, 15 December 1942, IV/Smi/1a, Ismay Papers, KC; Letter, Dill to Cunningham, 1 December 1942, ADD. MS. 52570, Cunningham Papers, BL.

11 Eisenhower was nonetheless wise to British intentions, noting how he was 'not so incredibly naive that I do not realize that Britishers instinctively approach every military problem from the viewpoint of the Empire, just as we approach them from the viewpoint of American interest'. Warren Kimball, *The Juggler: Franklin Roosevelt as Wartime Statesman*, Princeton University Press, Princeton, 1991, pp. 66–7.

12 Just as Churchill had made repeated pledges to Australia about Singapore and the sending of a Far East fleet, he would often repeat this pledge to the Americans over the succeeding years until it began to haunt him as the time approached to put it into effect. Cable, Churchill to Attlee, 20 January 1943, CAB 65/37, W.M. (43)12, PRO; See also Gilbert, *Road to Victory*, Chap. 18; Bryant, *The Turn of the Tide*, Chap. 11.

13 Alanbrooke diary, 22 January 1943, in Danchev and Todman (eds), *War Diaries*, pp. 366–7.

14 Press conference, 19 January 1943, MS 4675, Smith Papers, NLA; Cable, Curtin to Dixon, 19 January 1943, *DAFP*, Vol. 6, Doc. 105.

15 Background briefing, 30 December 1942, MS 4675, Smith Papers, NLA.

16 Background briefings, 30 December 1942 and 1 January 1943, MS 4675, Smith Papers, NLA.

17 Perry, *The Commonwealth Armies*, pp. 168–9.

18 Peter Love, 'Curtin, MacArthur and conscription, 1942–43', *Historical Studies*, October 1977; Day, *John Curtin*, pp. 489–94.

19 The British intelligence operative, Gerald Wilkinson, feared that the Australian government might not bother to continue fighting Japan once its own continent was secure. This was never a possibility, with the government being committed to fighting Japan to the finish. War Journal, 18 and 19 October 1942, WILK 1/1, Wilkinson Papers, CC.

20 Press Statement by Curtin, 7 December 1942, CRS A5954/305A, NAA.

21 Curtin was reaffirming the Labor Party's defence policy of the 1930s which called for the defence of Australia to be secured before contributions were made to imperial defence. Background briefing, 30 December 1942, MS 4675, Smith Papers, NLA.

22 See Thorne, *Allies of a Kind*, p. 259; Talk with Cripps, 29 December 1942, CRS M100, 'December 1942', NAA; See also Memorandum by Attlee, 4 January 1943, CAB 66/33, W.P. (43)6, PRO.

23 Kimball, *The Juggler*, pp. 127–57.

24 Memoranda by Amery, 12 November 1942, CAB 66/31, W.P. (42)524, and 25 January 1943, CAB 66/33, W.P. (43)39, PRO.

25 Letter, Amery to Dorman-Smith, 29 December 1942, MSS Eur E 215/2, Dorman-Smith Papers, IOL.

26 Carlton, *Anthony Eden*, p. 211; CAB 66/33, W.P. (43)33, PRO; Cable, Dixon to External Affairs Department, 9 December 1942, CRS A3300/229, NAA; Memorandum by Bruce, 5 January 1943, CRS M100, 'January 1943', NAA.

27 In late 1942, Wilkinson had floated a plan for Britain to support MacArthur's promotion to the command of all Pacific land forces while ensuring that MacArthur was made 'unofficially aware' of the British support 'so that we might hope for his friendship and understanding in future Anglo–American matters such as Pacific and Asiatic post-war settlements'. Although MacArthur at first gave guarded approval, the paranoiac general later backed down, warning Wilkinson on 1 November 1942 that 'Roosevelt has his spies right down to the kitchen sink' and that the time was not ripe for such a move. MacArthur also decided that Wilkinson, with his top-level contacts in Whitehall, should no longer be attached to his headquarters. Despite strenuous efforts by Churchill and Wilkinson, MacArthur refused to let him return. War Journal, 10 and 24 October, and 1 November 1942, WILK 1/1, and 22 February 1943, WILK 1/2, Wilkinson Papers, CC; Letter, Dewing to Gowrie, 31 January 1943, MS 2852/4/22/28, Gowrie Papers, NLA. For Churchill's attempts to have Wilkinson returned to MacArthur's headquarters, see PREM 3/158/5, PRO.

28 Letter, Robinson to Evatt, enclosing letter, Robinson to Bracken, 11 February 1943, 'Dr H. V. Evatt' folder, Robinson Papers, UMA; See also Day, *Menzies and Churchill at War*, Chap. 15; War Journal, 29 October 1942, WILK 1/1, Wilkinson Papers, CC.

29 Background briefing, 30 December 1942, MS 4675, Smith Papers, NLA.

30 See Day, 'An Undiplomatic Incident'; and Day, *Menzies and Churchill at War*.

31 In fact, both the British and Australian governments regarded Cross as an embarrassment that had to be borne stoically.

32 Advisory War Council Minutes, 9 February 1943, CRS A2682/6/1138, NAA; Background briefing, 30 December 1942, MS 4675, Smith Papers, NLA; Talk with Lord Brabazon, 6 January 1943, and Cable, Commonwealth Government to Bruce, 22 January 1943, CRS M100, 'January 1943', NAA.

33 In another move designed to increase Australia's flexibility and maintain its wartime links with the United States, Curtin ensured that the wartime communication links established across the Pacific would be continued into the postwar period, thereby ending British attempts to keep Australia committed solely to British-owned communication links. This was a move of considerable symbolic and practical importance and one that had been resolutely resisted by the former Menzies government. Submission by Curtin, 1 January 1943, CRS A2700/5/412, and documents in CRS A2670/42/1943, NAA.

34 Letter, Gowrie to Linlithgow, 14 January 1943, MS 2852/4/21/24, Gowrie Papers, NLA.

35 Roskill, *The War at Sea*, Vol. 1, p. 349.

36 War Cabinet Minutes, 26 November 1940 and 22 March 1941, CRS A2673/4/632 and A2673/6/909, NAA.

37 Minute, Hollis to Churchill, 29 October 1942; Minutes of Chiefs of Staff Meeting, 20 November 1942; Memorandum by Brooke, 27 November 1942, PREM 3/63/10, PRO.

38 Roskill, *The War at Sea*, Vol. 2, p. 433.

39 ibid., p. 481.

40 In February 1944 a lone Japanese submarine chanced upon a British troop convoy, albeit a slower one, and succeeded in evading its naval escort. One of the troopships was torpedoed, with almost all of its complement of 1500 servicemen and women being killed. The subsequent inquiry concluded that the number of escort vessels available in the Indian Ocean was 'totally inadequate for the protection of valuable convoys on widely separated routes'. Gill, *Royal Australian Navy, 1942–1945*, pp. 295–6, 383–4.

41 Roskill, *The War at Sea*, Vol. 2, p. 425.

42 Somerville shared this concern, observing that 'We have formidable antagonists and if you start taking liberties … you are bound to come a cropper sooner or later.' Letter, Somerville to H. MacQuarrie, 3 January 1943, ADD. MS. 50143, Somerville Papers, BL; Edwards diary, 7 January 1943, REDW 1/5, Edwards Papers, CC.

43 Edwards Diary, January — February 1943, REDW 1/5, Edwards Papers, CC.

44 ibid.

45 Letter, Somerville to Harold Guard, 6 February 1948, Misc. Box 30/557, Somerville Papers, IWM.

46 Letter, Somerville to Pound, 11 March 1943, SMVL 8/1, Somerville Papers, CC; Edwards Diary, 8–11 February 1943, REDW 1/5, Edwards Papers, CC.

47 Press conference, 24 February 1943, MS 4675, Smith Papers, NLA.

48 Letter, Somerville to Pound, 11 March 1943, SMVL 8/1, Somerville Papers, CC.

THIRTY-FIVE

'what queer people'

The sudden Japanese withdrawal from Guadalcanal in February 1943 secured Australia's reinforcement route from the United States. It meant that the country would no longer face the threat of isolation, or the possibility of a future invasion. The steady build-up of American forces and supplies could continue, troubled only by the submarine attacks on the Allied shipping off Australia's east coast. Australia's security was not only guaranteed by the presence of the American forces, as well as by the concentration of its own forces at home, but also by the ongoing war in China which was tying down so much of the Japanese army and limiting Tokyo's ability to expand its recent conquests in the south-west Pacific. Japan also had to keep forces on hand to guard against a possible Russian move in Manchuria.

Although the threat of invasion was lifted from Australia, the threat of attack remained. Repelled from Guadalcanal, and defeated at Buna and Gona, the Japanese still planned on capturing New Guinea. Their forces were deeply entrenched at Rabaul, within striking distance of northern Australia and of the Allied forces in New Guinea. Across the Pacific, Tokyo stuck to its original strategy of trying to make the war too expensive in men and machines for the Allies to prosecute to a conclusion. Although Churchill and Roosevelt at Casablanca had demanded the unconditional surrender of the Axis powers, the Japanese still hoped to reach a compromise that would allow them to retain their conquests and which would recognise the western Pacific as a region in which they could reign supreme. It was a vain hope that ignored the overwhelming American intention to make good the humiliation of Pearl Harbor and assert their own supremacy across the entire Pacific. Australia likewise was determined that the Japanese empire should be destroyed and the threat of a future invasion removed.

From mid-1942, MacArthur had planned to mount an offensive to dislodge the Japanese from Rabaul. It could have worked if he had been provided with the wherewithal to do it, but the necessary long-range bombers were almost exclusively restricted to the so-called strategic bombing offensive against Germany, spreading death and destruction and terrifying both civilians and soldiers alike. In the absence of a cross-Channel invasion, and in order to appease the Russians, Churchill and Roosevelt had agreed at Casablanca to increase the weight of the bombing offensive. This blunt instrument bludgeoned entire populations senseless and sent the stench of death wafting across Europe. Unlike the gas ovens of Treblinka and Auschwitz, it was death delivered from a distance. But it was no less 'scientific' and cold-blooded. Entire cities were laid waste by incendiary bombs designed to cause firestorms that would maximise civilian casualties. Despite the slaughter, the bombing did not produce the quick victory that its eager advocates predicted or remove the need for a large-scale military campaign in western Europe. However, its costly use of aircraft did prevent an early and strong blow being directed against the Japanese.

Following the Casablanca conference, Curtin realised for the first time that the Allied strategy would necessarily involve a two-stage ending to the war. As he explained to a group of reporters on 2 February 1943, it meant that Australia 'will be at war in the Pacific when we have ceased to be at war anywhere else'. In a burst of prescience, Curtin suggested that he might not live even to see out the war. The two-stage ending to the war also threatened the reconstruction effort that his government had begun planning once the battle of Midway had tipped the balance in the Allies' favour. It meant that

Australia would have to fight Japan and provide supplies for the Allies long after Europe had returned to peacetime pursuits. Although Curtin could no longer claim that Australia needed additional forces to ensure its defence, he was frustrated that the Allied strategy of fighting Germany first had left Australia in a military backwater and unable to deal the Japanese a decisive blow. He bemoaned Russia 'getting more planes in a week than we got in almost a year', although he had to concede that 'they were of course doing a useful job' and that Russia and China 'probably had stronger claims than Australia'. Despite the apparent logic of Allied strategy, Curtin complained that Australia deserved better: that Australians were 'the only white race in the southern hemisphere and almost the only Empire country doing anything'.[1]

The experience of the past year had engendered in Curtin an acute sense of Australia's relative inability to have its voice heard when decisions were being made concerning its destiny by powerbrokers in London or Washington. In the 1930s, the Labor Party had criticised Australia's reliance on Britain and on the system of imperial defence and had argued instead for a strong Australian defence force capable of resisting invasion. The experience of war, with the nation fully mobilised and substantial American forces stationed in the country, revealed the limits of Australia's power to influence events in the region by force of arms. As Curtin now conceded, with a population of just seven million the country could never raise more than five divisions for service overseas, and could not tackle a great power by itself.[2] Accordingly, once the war was won, Australia would have to return to the protective umbrella of a great power.

The Australian government was resigned to accepting the decisions reached by Churchill and Roosevelt at Casablanca, which reconfirmed the Allied strategy of fighting a holding war in the Pacific. It did not stop Curtin though from quickly requesting additional forces to ensure that the holding strategy could be implemented.[3] As well, both MacArthur and Curtin asked Churchill to visit Australia in the confident, but mistaken, expectation that the British leader 'could not fail to be impressed if he saw our difficulties'.[4] Not that Churchill was unaware of Australia's difficulties, or the peril which, until recently, it had endured. However, he was far from the fighting and ignorant of the conditions in which the battles had to be fought. So he tended to discount the danger, believing anyway that a 'taste' of the bombing that Britain had endured would do Australia good.

Instead of agreeing to visit Australia, Churchill invited Curtin to visit Britain. Churchill had succeeded in transforming the normally irascible Evatt into somewhat of a simpering lapdog, and he was keen to exert his influence on Curtin. But Curtin would not be wooed, claiming that parliamentary business prevented him from leaving Australia. The Labor Party had to fight a federal election that year and Curtin was keen to consolidate his government's tenuous grip on power. He would also have been mindful, in view of his morbid dread of flying, that the arduous trip by plane would not help his failing health. Curtin could only watch in amazement Churchill's 'energy' and 'enterprise' as he flew on from the Casablanca conference to Cairo and then to Turkey before returning to London by way of Cyprus, Cairo and Algiers, braving the dangers of wartime flights and the considerable discomforts of unpressurised aircraft.[5]

Not having the benefit of meeting with Curtin, Churchill had to rely on reports from those who had in order to get his measure of the man. So when Churchill lunched with the recently returned Gerald Wilkinson on 15 March, he asked him to 'dilate' on the 'question of Mr. Curtin'. Wilkinson confirmed Churchill's pre-existing view of Curtin, and buttressed his general prejudices towards Australians, describing Curtin as 'a small and parochial man' who was 'obviously not equipped by experience and environment to take naturally to a global view of strategy'. Nevertheless, Wilkinson urged that Churchill 'should forgive him any waverings that might have occurred in connection with Australian overtures to Washington last year', arguing that Britain 'might manage [Curtin] more easily than we might manage some of his less scrupulous associates'. But Churchill was unrepentant, with Wilkinson reporting that he merely 'chuckled rather grimly' at this suggestion, saying that the dominion had paid the price for its disloyalty when Washington rebuffed its advances in early 1942.[6]

In the wake of the Casablanca conference, MacArthur dispatched his chief of staff, General Sutherland, to Washington to seek a commitment of forces that would enable an assault on the Japanese headquarters at Rabaul.[7]

If that enemy redoubt could be taken, it would assist the campaign in New Guinea and remove a formidable obstacle in the path of MacArthur's triumphant return to the Philippines. To achieve the conquest of Rabaul, MacArthur asked for an additional 1800 aircraft, including a number of long-range bombers. When Washington was slow to respond, MacArthur asked Curtin to add his weight to the appeal, although warning Curtin that any political pressure from Canberra should be made in such a way that 'it does not lay itself open to the suspicion of definite collusion'. He suggested that Curtin approach Roosevelt via Churchill, claiming that it was 'astonishing' that Churchill had not yet replied to Curtin's appeal of 19 January.[8]

Curtin's cable in January had been intended to influence the outcome of the Casablanca conference, which Curtin mistakenly thought was taking place in Washington. His cabled appeal for further reinforcements had been passed on to Roosevelt in Casablanca, who had handed it in turn to Churchill, who promptly tossed it aside without bothering to reply.[9] Churchill was too concerned about getting the Americans to reconfirm their commitment to the 'Germany first' strategy. When that was done by the end of the conference, he may have thought that there was little to be gained in replying to Curtin with yet another refusal to send reinforcements. But events in the south-west Pacific were sufficiently worrying to impel Curtin to insist on a reply. There were indications that the Japanese presence to the north-west of Australia was being boosted, with intelligence reports suggesting that the Japanese intended to invade Darwin and perhaps launch a Pearl Harbor-scale attack against Perth. Australia remained ill-equipped to ward off any such large-scale assaults. Its best troops had been exhausted by the fighting in New Guinea, its naval protection remained meagre and the arrival of aircraft from the United States during the previous six months had barely kept pace with Australian and American losses. And there were still many battles to be fought in New Guinea where the Japanese were intent on shoring up their position.[10]

At the end of February 1943, a convoy of eight Japanese troopships was dispatched from Rabaul with thousands of reinforcements for New Guinea. On 2 March the slow-moving ships and their destroyer escorts, with Zero fighters providing protection high overhead, were located in the Bismarck Sea by a combined force of Allied aircraft that had been training for just such an eventuality. After Flying Fortress bombers dropped their load on the scattering craft, Mitchell bombers flew in at little more than mast height to complete the destruction while Lightning fighters dealt with the Zeros. All the troopships were sunk, while Australian Beaufighters followed up over the following days by strafing those survivors who managed to take to their life rafts.[11] Although the reinforcement attempt had been repulsed, the incident increased Australian fears about Japanese intentions, while it made the Japanese commander, Admiral Yamamoto, determined to overcome the growing Allied ascendancy in the air.

Australian fears were compounded on 15 March when more than twenty bombers, escorted by Zero fighters, raided Darwin. It was the fifty-third attack on the town. Although the Japanese aircraft were beaten off by the Spitfire fighters that now defended the town,[12] MacArthur warned Curtin that the raid was part of a general Japanese build-up in the region to the north-west of Australia, perhaps in preparation for a serious attack on northern Australia in a few months. The Japanese were developing 67 airfields within reach of Australia, from which they could operate up to two thousand aircraft, although MacArthur admitted that there was no sign that such numbers of aircraft were yet being deployed. In fact, the Japanese moves were of a defensive rather than an offensive nature. MacArthur was deliberately exaggerating the danger to Australia while assuring Curtin that he was asking Washington for only enough forces to defend what the Allies already held, rather than to mount an offensive against Rabaul. He told Curtin that the south-west Pacific was no longer threatened, but that the north-west approaches to Australia were threatened by the apparent Japanese movements of aircraft and construction of airfields.[13]

On 18 March, the day after MacArthur's warning, Curtin sent cables to both Churchill and Roosevelt reminding them that his request on 19 January for additional aircraft was still unanswered. Curtin claimed that the attacks on Darwin indicated the 'paramount importance' of maintaining air superiority to the north and west of Australia. 'Of particular importance,' he wrote, was 'the vital base of Fremantle [Curtin's constituency] where owing to the depletion of the Eastern Fleet a heavy attack of the tip and run variety might be carried out by naval bombardment and carrier-borne aircraft.'[14] Even though there were calls in the American press for making a greater effort in the Pacific, there was never much chance of the appeals from Curtin and MacArthur getting a receptive hearing in Washington. For one thing, American service chiefs rejected MacArthur's proposed assault on Rabaul in deference to the Casablanca agreement for an all-out bombing offensive against Germany. It was not only the aircraft that could not be found for such a major enterprise. With all of MacArthur's divisions needing rest and reorganisation after the rigours of the fighting in New Guinea, there was no way that the shipping could be found to move the massive number of fresh troops to Australia that the Rabaul plans called for.[15] So the assault was deferred. But Curtin's repeated requests for reinforcements still demanded an answer, particularly as he intended to dispatch Evatt on another mission to the Allied capitals to support the Australian demands.

Sensing another storm in Anglo–Australian relations, Bruce approached General Ismay on 20 March for a response that he could pass on to Curtin. Australia's high commissioner was dismayed to find that Ismay knew nothing of Curtin's request; apparently Churchill had not passed it on to the chiefs of staff for consideration. Bruce urged Ismay to dissuade Churchill from sending any intemperate reply to Curtin's renewed request until the chiefs of staff had considered the issue. In the meantime, Bruce put the Australian case to Ismay so that he might gauge the likely British reaction. Bruce then agreed with Ismay that he should 'telegraph to Australia and raise all the points that were discussed between us, and see what reaction I got'. By unofficially advising Curtin of Britain's objections, Bruce might thereby forestall the inevitable blow to Anglo–Australian relations that would be caused by Britain blankly refusing the Australian request. At the least, it would soften Churchill's blow when it came.[16]

And come it certainly did. On 27 March, Churchill rebutted Curtin's claim that Australia was insufficiently protected by the aircraft already allotted to the region. In rejecting Curtin's argument, Churchill pointed to the large number of aircraft in the Pacific, including not only the aircraft in MacArthur's command but also those in the adjacent South Pacific

Command and carrier-borne aircraft throughout the Pacific. Counting aircraft in New Zealand and Fiji was akin to counting aircraft in London as part of the force available for the defence of Moscow. If the reassuring arithmetic was somewhat questionable, Churchill reminded Curtin of the overriding Allied strategy which had the war in Europe as the 'first charge on the forces of the United Nations'. Once that war was won, declared Churchill, 'every man who can be carried and every suitable ship and aircraft will be concentrated on Japan'.[17] This undertaking was similar to the one he had given to Roosevelt at Casablanca, and was reminiscent of the succession of promises Churchill had made about the defence of Singapore and about abandoning the Mediterranean to defend Australia. Once again, events would see this new undertaking only partially fulfilled.

With intelligence reports from the south-west Pacific indicating that MacArthur was gaining the ascendancy over the Japanese, particularly in the air, it must have seemed to Churchill that Australia would never be satisfied. It was more reason for him to continue harbouring resentment towards it. Yet the difficulties in Anglo–Australian relations were more than partly caused by his own high-handed approach and his generally dismissive attitude towards the dominions. In a revealing remark during the course of a cabinet meeting, Churchill referred to the 'troublesome attitude of the Colonies' when he was actually referring to the dominions. It was almost as if the gradual moves towards independence by the various dominions had not happened.[18] Churchill continued to treat them like colonies, as he had done as colonial secretary before the First World War. Although he treated Canada and South Africa with much more consideration than Australia, New Zealand was also treated rather dismissively. Its mostly compliant attitude towards Whitehall's wishes, particularly over the continuing use of New Zealand troops in the Middle East, only encouraged Churchill in his Victorian ways.[19]

As a former conservative prime minister, Bruce might have helped to soothe Churchill's anger. But Churchill's anger continued to be directed towards Bruce, as much as towards Australia, and Bruce continued to be sidelined in Downing Street as a result. His role as a prewar supporter of appeasement would always affect Bruce's reputation as far as Churchill was concerned. As

Bruce's naval adviser and former chief of the Australian navy, Admiral Colvin, confided to Lord Gowrie, 'Winston has no use for people who got on well with Chamberlain'. Although Bruce's admission to meetings of the British war cabinet 'promised better things ... it all came to nothing and [Bruce] only attends the weekly War Cabinet meetings which decide nothing of importance'. According to Colvin, when British officials were confronted with Australian views, they 'simply shrug their shoulders, say "what queer people" and pass on to the next business'. Colvin suggested that Curtin visit London to correct the poor impression that Evatt had created in 1942 and also to imbue Curtin with 'a better conception of the magnitude and scale of the system of Government and of running the war'.[20] In other words, Curtin could be given the 'world' view of the war, which meant the view from Whitehall.

Curtin refused to be diverted by Churchill's vague promises and platitudes. Australia had not, he said, agreed to the 'Germany first' strategy. Instead, it had been 'confronted with a *fait accompli* and we had no alternative but to accept the decisions, much as we disliked them'. He also disputed the Allies' confident assessment of the situation in the south-west Pacific, pointing out that there were only 1450 modern aircraft in the region, of which less than half were in a serviceable condition. Curtin informed Churchill that promised delivery dates for aircraft from the United States were not being met, while the aircraft on hand were being put out of service faster than they could be repaired or replaced. It was not enough, Curtin argued, for Australia to have a few more planes than the Japanese. What was needed was the 'provision of such air power as will enable the forces in the South-West Pacific Area to prevent the consolidation of the Japanese in their positions to the north of Australia and so render reasonably feasible the task of ultimately defeating them when the war in Europe ends'.[21]

Although the construction of Japanese airfields, the movements of enemy aircraft and the attacks on Darwin seem to have genuinely alarmed Curtin, it was increasingly clear that Allied supremacy in the air amounted to more than having 'a few more planes than the Japanese'. As Douglas Gillison observed in his official history of the RAAF, by early 1943 the balance was shifting decisively in favour of the Allies as their air forces were progressively strengthened and the Japanese were weakened in both relative and absolute terms. The arrival of the American Lightning fighters, as well as the Spitfires, gave the Allies a clear technical advantage over the Japanese, with both planes being able to fly at a higher altitude than the Japanese Zeros and thereby have at least the initial advantage in their encounters. The quality of the Japanese pilots was also declining sharply as their more experienced men were lost in combat. As for bombers, some of the formidable Flying Fortresses, which were mostly destined for use over Europe, were sent to the south-west Pacific for MacArthur to use in bombing Japanese concentrations at Rabaul and elsewhere. Even in the case of transport aircraft, while MacArthur would never have enough for all his needs, he had sufficient planes to move some troops and supplies from Australia to the front line in New Guinea, whereas the Japanese had the more dangerous task of moving their troops by sea under skies dominated by Allied aircraft.[22]

Curtin's appeal for additional aircraft was not only designed to keep the Japanese off-balance but also part of a grander ambition to build up Australia's air strength, both for the present war and for the postwar period. Curtin had been a long-time proponent of air power as being the most effectual means to defend the far-flung reaches of the continent. And the government was under intense political pressure to ensure Australia's security by obtaining commitments of modern aircraft from the United States. The issue also had industrial ramifications, with both the Labor government and its conservative predecessor being keen to augment the local aircraft production industry, not only for its own sake but as a precursor to the establishment of an automobile industry. Curtin was also conscious of the civil aviation aspect, in a country of Australia's size and relative isolation, of gaining transport aircraft for the RAAF that could later be used for civil purposes. A strengthened RAAF would also be able to hold sway over the region in the postwar period, while in the interim making a substantial contribution to the Pacific war and thereby gaining a greater say for Australia at the peace table. While the war cabinet in March 1942 had authorised an eventual strength for the RAAF of 73 squadrons, it had just 31 operational squadrons in April 1943. Although aircrew were being trained for additional squadrons, the aircraft were not arriving from the United States in sufficient numbers to allow those squadrons to be formed.[23]

Curtin hoped that Evatt's trip to Washington and London would see Australia's requests for aircraft fulfilled. However, Evatt regarded the trip at least partly as another opportunity to display his prime ministerial qualities, with rumours already circulating about his willingness to change sides and lead a 'national' administration as Billy Hughes had done during the First World War. Evatt had made such a proposal to Menzies in 1941 without success and there is no reason to suppose that he had dropped the idea. There were even suggestions that Evatt, with the support of the businessman W. S. Robinson, might switch sides and lead the conservative opposition.[24]

Evatt's mission had been announced by Curtin on 24 February, at a time when Australia was encountering opposition over the size and future role of the RAAF. Evatt was meant to overcome this American and British opposition and obtain a greater diversion of Allied resources for the Pacific war, although the limited results of his previous trip did not hold out much hope for him being successful.[25] Churchill was particularly concerned that the Americans should not pander to the importuning Australian minister. At the same time, Churchill was anxious to allay American suspicions about British intentions in the Pacific by finally boosting his country's war effort against Japan.

The Casablanca conference had approved a British offensive to recapture Burma, but resources to ensure its success were not made available, with Churchill being loath to divert any forces from the Mediterranean. Rather than sending additional forces, Churchill wanted Wavell to use the 'very great forces' that Churchill claimed were standing idle in India.[26] Certainly, the Indian forces were numerically strong but they were not well equipped to mount the required offensive into Burma. As Wavell pointed out, the 'natural and climatic conditions' and the 'poverty of communications' in India made it necessary to have such 'very great forces', which after all were responsible for defending a country two-thirds the size of Europe.[27] Although the war office supported Wavell's view, Churchill refused to accept the report.[28] It was only when it became clear in early April that the Burma offensive could not be mounted without impinging on the planned invasion of Sicily that Churchill relented and called Wavell and Somerville to London for more talks about British options in the Far East.[29]

Churchill was acutely conscious that America would hold Britain responsible if China fell because insufficient Allied support had reached it by way of Burma. As Churchill told his war cabinet, the recapture of Burma had been agreed to by him at Casablanca 'largely as a concession to United States opinion'.[30] In Washington's view, keeping China in the Pacific war was almost as important as keeping Russia in the European war. The United States and Britain were relying on both these countries to keep wearing down their respective enemies until the Americans could deliver the coup de grace. If the Chinese were defeated, or made peace with the Japanese, this strategy would be in tatters. The Japanese would be able to strengthen their Pacific forces, thereby forcing Washington to withdraw forces from Europe. They might even attack the Russians with forces previously tied down in China. It was for these reasons that Churchill was also anxious to secure the Burmese lifeline to China. The implications in Europe of the defeat of China were simply too terrible to contemplate.

Roosevelt had agreed that the Burma operation could be dropped and China sustained with supplies by aircraft flying over the mountainous 'hump' from India to Chungking. However, Churchill refused to let the planned offensive fizzle out. In a withering message to his chiefs of staff in early April, he complained that Wavell's campaign in India was going from 'bad to worse', with British forces being 'completely outfought and out-manoeuvred by the Japanese'. Churchill warned that there would be political problems if public opinion ever focused upon 'this lamentable scene'. Rather than tackling him head-on, Churchill's military advisers recommended that the Burma operation be postponed for practical reasons rather than be cancelled altogether.[31]

In north Africa, Montgomery's Eighth Army had been battling its way westward from Libya into Tunisia where the last of Rommel's forces were holding out. The Americans under Eisenhower were moving in from the other direction after their successful capture of Algeria. On 7 April, the British and American armies finally linked up to close the ring on the Axis army. There was still much fighting to be done before victory could be declared. Once Tunisia was secured, the next step was to leapfrog across to Sicily and thence perhaps to Italy itself. To ensure the success of these operations, sufficient shipping and landing craft would have to be on hand in the Mediterranean. This not only precluded an amphibious offensive in Burma but also the American plan to capture a bridgehead on the northern French coastline in the autumn of 1943.[32]

Although the Allies were clearly winning the battle for Tunisia, the fighting was more prolonged and bitter than they had anticipated after Hitler reinforced his shattered Afrika Korps with fresh divisions and armour. With their backs to the Mediterranean, these troops resisted so strongly that Eisenhower questioned whether the invasion of Sicily was feasible for 1943. In Washington, General Marshall scotched Eisenhower's fears and ordered plans for an invasion of Sicily even if the Germans still held on in Tunisia. This was 'splendid', Churchill cabled, and on 17 April he invited Marshall to London to set their joint stamp upon the decision. But Marshall begged off, confiding that he had to travel to the Pacific theatre to 'orient the various people concerned, who [were] reacting to public clamour for intensification of [the] war effort in that theatre'.[33] This news only helped to confirm the British suspicion that the Americans would not adhere to the commitment to the European war that Roosevelt had made during his meetings with Churchill at Casablanca. As Brooke observed in his diary, 'recent telegrams from America show that we are just about back where we were before Casablanca! Their hearts are really in the Pacific ...'[34]

The American public had been outraged by news that the Japanese had executed two American aircrew who had taken part in a bombing raid against Tokyo and other Japanese cities in April 1942. The daring attack by sixteen B-25 bombers had been mounted from an aircraft carrier that had steamed within reach of the Japanese mainland to launch the planes which, after dropping their bombs, were meant to fly on to airfields in China. When the planes were forced to ditch in the darkness over China, two of the crews fell into the hands of the Japanese army. The raid was a considerable psychological blow to the Japanese, catching them unprepared at a time when they believed their homeland was beyond the reach of the Americans. The execution of the two men was intended to avenge that humiliation. But when news of their execution reached the United States, it prompted renewed calls for a greater American effort in the Pacific. As Roosevelt's influential adviser, Harry Hopkins, warned Anthony Eden on 23 April, the 'shooting of our fliers in Tokyo has started all the isolationist papers promoting the war in the Far East as against Germany'. Hopkins thought that the public still supported Roosevelt, and that even the 'Australians or Mme Chiang [the persuasive wife of the Chinese leader]' could not change the strategy, but the danger could not be dismissed.[35] The combination of MacArthur, Ernie King, the 'isolationist' press and the governments of Australia and China was potentially a formidable one.

With the Americans pushing for a greater effort in the Pacific, and the prospects for the Mediterranean remaining in some doubt, Churchill withdrew his support for the operation in Burma. With Wavell and Somerville in London, the practical difficulties of the Burmese offensive and its possible effect on his Mediterranean plans were impressed upon Churchill. As a result, when Wavell, Churchill and the chiefs of staff gathered to discuss the Burmese operation on 22 April, it was Churchill who put the case against it, proposing instead an operation against north Sumatra as a stepping stone to an eventual assault on Singapore. Although Wavell argued that Burma was 'the only possible plan particularly in view of the political necessity of gaining touch with China', Churchill now likened it to 'munching a porcupine quill by quill'. Churchill argued that Japan would only be defeated by a bombing offensive from bases in China and Russia, and this could not be done until after the fall of Germany when resources would be released and Russia joined the war against Japan. Until then, said Churchill, the Allies should sustain China in its struggle against Japan by adopting Roosevelt's proposed aerial lifeline over the Himalayas from India. Burma could then be bypassed and the danger of embroiling large numbers of British troops in jungle warfare could be avoided. In the absence of a major Burmese land offensive, Churchill suggested that sea power could be used to tackle Japan elsewhere. The effect would be more dramatic than a land campaign and the cost would be much less. As for Wavell's forces in India, they could still be used, either in Burma or Sumatra, but any such offensive during the next two years 'must be reduced to a very minor one'.[36] That still left the Americans to be appeased.

The US chiefs of staff wanted Wavell and his fellow Far Eastern commanders to go on to Washington to discuss Allied plans for the war against Japan. However, Churchill feared that the 'Pacific first' elements in Washington might use the presence of Wavell and his colleagues to push for a greater effort against Japan. As the British chiefs of staff warned Churchill on 28 April, if Wavell was allowed to accept the invitation, it 'might well give the Americans the impression that we were weakening on the "Germany first" policy' and prompt the US chiefs of staff to push for 'a more forward policy in the Pacific'.[37] Churchill needed no urging. He was feeling politically vulnerable over the inactivity of the sizeable British forces in India and had already prevented Wavell visiting Australia on his way to London, partly out of fear that Wavell might support Curtin's call for more Allied resources. He would have had even greater fears about letting Wavell loose in Washington.

Churchill was in a difficult position. As he confided to his war cabinet on 29 April, the US commanders in India and China, Generals Stilwell and Chennault, had accompanied Wavell's team to London and were going on to Washington. It would be 'awkward', Churchill said, if the British officers refused to go with them. On the other hand, any such visit carried the 'grave danger that the main strategy of the war would be altered and greater emphasis put on the Pacific'. The only solution, Churchill argued, was for himself, his chiefs of staff and the minister of war transport, Lord Leathers, to accompany Wavell and the others to Washington.[38]

The luxury liner, the *Queen Mary*, now converted to a troop transport, was ordered to be prepared to take Churchill and his chiefs once more across the Atlantic to set the Americans right about the Pacific. Bunks were ripped out of several cabins and some of its former luxury appointments restored for its important passengers while pest exterminators worked at ridding its recesses of vermin. On 5 May, Churchill and his large party of military officers boarded the ship at the Scottish naval base at Greenock, while about three thousand troops were accommodated in its lower decks. As the ship and its escorting cruiser headed out into the heavy Atlantic seas, Churchill and his chiefs worked on ways of recommitting the Americans to the 'Germany first' strategy and defeating attempts by Evatt to secure resources for Australia.[39]

NOTES

1. Curtin told the journalists that he would like to have half a million pounds available to spend surreptitiously in a public relations campaign in the United States, presumably so that Americans might feel racially responsible for Australia's defence. His claim that Australians were 'the only white race in the southern hemisphere' was part of this pitch for American sympathy. Background briefing, 2 February 1943, MS 4675, Smith Papers, NLA.

2. ibid.

3. Advisory War Council Minutes, 2 February 1943, CRS A2682/6/1129, NAA.

4. Press conference, 2 March 1943, MS 4675, Smith Papers, NLA.

5. In fact, travel also took its toll on Churchill, who was left struggling with a serious bout of pneumonia, the so-called 'old man's friend'. Cables, Churchill to Curtin, 12 February 1943, and Curtin to Churchill, 17 February 1943, DAFP, Vol. 6, Docs 119 and 120; Moran, Winston Churchill, p. 108.

6. War Journal, 15 March 1943, WILK 1/2, Wilkinson Papers, CC.

7. The Anglo–American agreement reached at Casablanca had provided for MacArthur's forces to 'continue the advance from Guadalcanal and New Guinea until Rabaul had been taken ...' But there was no time limit stipulated and no forces were provided for it to be achieved. George Odgers, Air War Against Japan 1943–1945, Australian War Memorial, Canberra, 1957, p. 4.

8. Teleprinter message, MacArthur to Curtin, 17 March 1943, DAFP, Vol. 6, Doc. 138.

9. Talk with Ismay, 20 March 1943 and Cable, Bruce to Curtin, 23 March 1943, CRS M100, 'March 1943', NAA.

10. Odgers, Air War Against Japan, 1943–1945, p. 38.

11. The presence of the British-built Beaufighters allowed Britain's official naval historian to declare that, 'for all our acute needs for them at home and in the Mediterranean, [Beaufighters] had been sent out to Australia on the British Government's orders'. In fact, they had only been sent after a tough and largely unsuccessful struggle by Menzies and after Britain had advised Australia against producing the aircraft itself. Roskill, The War at Sea, Vol. 2, p. 422; Gillison, Royal Australian Air Force 1939–1942, pp. 139–40, 690–7.

12. Evatt had claimed the political credit when the Spitfires finally arrived. In a radio broadcast from Sydney, he declared that they represented the 'greatest qualities of the British race — their engineering genius, their refusal to be satisfied with anything less than the best, and above all their dauntless courage in the face of adversity'. He described their temporary diversion to the Middle East, which he had bitterly resisted, as an 'excellent' move that had 'played a vital part in the battle for Egypt'. Broadcast by Evatt, 7 March 1943, 'War — Speeches by Evatt 43 (a)' folder, Evatt Papers, FUL.

13. Notes of telephone conversation, 16 March 1943, CRS A5954, Box 229, NAA.

14. Cable, Curtin to Churchill, 18 March 1943, PREM 3/142/7, PRO; Cable, Curtin to Roosevelt, 18 March 1943, CRS A5954, Box 229, NAA; See also Background briefing, 23 March 1943, MS 4675, Smith Papers, NLA.

15. Spector, Eagle against the Sun, pp. 223–6; Odgers, Air War Against Japan, 1943–1945, pp. 20–2.

16. Talk with Ismay, 20 March 1943 and Cable, Bruce to Curtin, 23 March 1943, CRS M100, 'March 1943', NAA.

17. Attlee, probably on the advice of Bruce, had warned Churchill that Curtin would not be satisfied by a blank refusal, and had suggested that Churchill promise to discuss the whole question with Evatt once the external affairs minister arrived in London. Cable, Churchill to Curtin, 27 March 1943, DAFP, Vol. 6, Doc. 145; Note, Attlee to Churchill, 25 March 1943, PREM 3/142/7, PRO.

18. Note by Bruce, 22 March 1943, CRS M100, 'March 1943', NAA.

19. Canada was regarded with some respect because of its special position vis-à-vis the United States. As for South Africa, it was led by the venerable General Smuts, the former Boer leader whom Churchill and the rest of Whitehall came to regard as a fount of imperial and strategic wisdom. See Granatstein, Canada's War, p. 119; for some of the innumerable and favourable references to Smuts, see Cadogan diary, 4 August and 14 October 1942, in Dilks (ed.), The Diaries of Sir Alexander Cadogan, pp. 467, 483, and Alanbrooke diary in Danchev and Todman (eds), War Diaries, pp. 289, 194, 312, 336, 542.

20. Letter, Colvin to Gowrie, 19 January 1943, MS 2852/4/21/24, Gowrie Papers, NLA; See also Talks with Attlee, 13 January and 15 February 1943, and Letter, Bruce to Curtin, 5 March 1943, CRS M100, 'March 1943', NAA.

[21] Cable, Curtin to Churchill, 30 March 1943, PREM 3/142/7, PRO; See also Cable, Curtin to Bruce, 29 March 1943, CRS M100, 'March 1943', NAA. Roosevelt had also rejected the Australian request, claiming that while the Japanese had the 'capability of massing 1,500 to 2,000 aircraft in the South West Pacific theatre ... the United Nations have even greater capabilities'. Cable, Roosevelt to Curtin and Evatt, 29 March 1943, CRS A5954, Box 229, NAA.

[22] For details of the shifting balance of air power, see Gillison, *Royal Australian Air Force, 1939–1942*, Chap. 32.

[23] Gillison, *Royal Australian Air Force, 1939–1942*, pp. 703–7; Odgers, *Royal Australian Air Force, 1943–1945*, pp. 4–8.

[24] Talk with Sir Campbell Stuart, 31 March 1943, CRS M100, 'March 1943', NAA; Letter, Lord Wakehurst to Emrys-Evans, 22 March 1943, ADD. MS. 58243, Emrys-Evans Papers, BL.

[25] Evatt's ability to convince Allied leaders of Australia's case was seriously questioned by Bruce's military liaison officer, Colonel Wardell, who had been recalled to Canberra at Evatt's insistence. On his arrival back in Australia, Wardell told Shedden that Evatt's previous visit to London had been a disaster, with Evatt having 'created a very poor impression ... due to his bad manners in discussion with people'. The diaries and letters of British political and military figures bear out Wardell's assessment. Talk with Colonel Wardell, 17 March 1943, CRS A5954, Box 14, NAA.

[26] Cable, Churchill to Wavell, 3 February 1943, PREM 3/143/10, PRO.

[27] Cable, Wavell to Churchill, 4 February 1943, PREM 3/143/10, PRO.

[28] Minute, Churchill to Ismay, 11 February 1943, PREM 3/143/3/4, PRO.

[29] See documents in PREM 3/143/10, PRO.

[30] War Cabinet Conclusions, Confidential Annex, 29 April 1943, CAB 65/38, W.M. (43)61, PRO.

[31] See documents in PREM 3/143/10, PRO.

[32] It remains a matter of dispute whether the British preoccupation with the Mediterranean delayed the D-day landings in Normandy and thereby unnecessarily lengthened the war.

[33] As it happened, Marshall's inability to go to London was fortunate for Churchill since the British chiefs of staff did not share Churchill's view about the advisability of invading Sicily while the Germans remained undefeated in Tunisia. Brooke thought the plan was 'quite mad and quite impossible' and had a long and heated row with Churchill on the telephone over it. ibid; Gilbert, *Road to Victory*, Chap. 21; Alanbrooke diary, 17 April 1943, in Danchev and Todman (eds), *War Diaries*, p. 394.

[34] Alanbrooke diary, 15 April 1943, in Danchev and Todman (eds), *War Diaries*, p. 393.

[35] Carlton, *Anthony Eden*, p. 212.

[36] Chiefs of Staff meeting, 22 April 1943, PREM 3/143/7, PRO; Alanbrooke diary, 22 and 28 April 1943, in Danchev and Todman (eds), *War Diaries*, pp. 395–6.

[37] Minute, Ismay to Churchill, 28 April 1943, PREM 3/143/10, PRO.

[38] War Cabinet Conclusions, 29 April 1943, CAB 65/34, W.M. (43)62, PRO.

[39] Brooke recorded in his diary how the chiefs of staff met on 7 May to discuss 'lines of action to take at our impending meeting with Dr Evatt of Australia who will be in Washington when we get there endeavouring to extract additional forces for the security of Australia'. Alanbrooke diary, 7 May 1943, in Danchev and Todman (eds), *War Diaries*, pp. 399–400.

THIRTY-SIX

'Australia has failed us'

In early May 1943, as the blacked-out *Queen Mary* took Churchill and his chiefs of staff across the Atlantic to Washington, his military planners worked away in their cabins on arguments that Churchill could use to refute Australia's call for further reinforcements of aircraft.[1] In the resulting strategic appreciation presented to Churchill, the planners acknowledged Australia's concern that Japan was intent on making its newly won empire 'impregnable to Allied assault'. However, they argued that the existing commitment of Allied forces to the south-west Pacific was sufficient to maintain the 'holding war' against Japan and prevent Australia from being seriously attacked, let alone invaded.[2]

In fact, the Australian government no longer feared an invasion. What Curtin wanted, and what Evatt was charged with achieving during his visit to Washington, was a commitment of sufficient forces to mount a sustained and timely offensive against the Japanese concentrations to Australia's north so that they could be kept off-balance after the quick succession of defeats that had recently been inflicted upon them. Britain, though, assumed that the Australian government still feared an invasion, with Churchill and his advisers being intent on allaying this fear rather than dealing with the Australian desire to increase pressure on the enemy. As Churchill realised, an Allied commitment to keep the Japanese off-balance would require a greater diversion of resources from the European war than he was prepared to concede. For this reason, it was essential that Evatt's trip to Washington should end in failure.

The danger posed by Evatt, in Churchill's view, centred upon the possibility of him being able to mobilise pro-Pacific elements within the American military, as well as within the media, such that it could cause Roosevelt to renege on his commitments at Casablanca. It was to neutralise such forces that Churchill was travelling to Washington with his high-powered entourage. As he informed Stalin in a cable from the *Queen Mary* on 8 May, his talks with Roosevelt would concentrate upon the Allied plans for Europe and would also 'discourage undue bias towards the Pacific'.[3] Churchill was particularly concerned that the scarce supplies of landing craft and amphibious shipping would threaten operations planned for the European theatre. The operations in Tunisia and the planned invasion of Sicily had drawn off so much shipping from Britain that a cross-Channel operation was now impossible for 1943. This meant that the American troops accumulating in Britain would have to cool their heels until at least the spring of 1944. As Churchill realised, this would increase the pressure in Washington to divert even more American forces to the Pacific where they could at least grapple with the enemy.

Before Evatt had left for Washington, MacArthur had suggested that he concentrate on trying to obtain a commitment of sufficient aircraft to more than double the size of the RAAF. However, even as a nervous Evatt, his wife and an American nurse were flying across the Pacific in a converted Liberator bomber (assured by MacArthur to be the 'best and safest' aircraft available), Roosevelt was signalling from Washington that Evatt's trip would be in vain. Although Roosevelt promised that additional forces would be provided for the south-west Pacific, they would not be sufficient to mount an assault on Rabaul. But they would be sufficient, Roosevelt assured Curtin, 'to preclude any serious attack on the continent of Australia'.[4] Anxious to rebut Roosevelt's implication that Australia was exaggerating its vulnerability and 'squealing' for help, Curtin told Roosevelt that his primary concern was no longer to protect Australia from attack but to have sufficient aircraft for offensive action against the Japanese until the Allies were ready to deal them a final blow.[5]

While Australia was arguing for additional front-line aircraft, including heavy bombers, and finding itself blocked at every turn, the British air ministry was trying to persuade the dominion to accept superannuated British bombers for conversion to civil aircraft once the war was won. The proposal arose during the visit to London of an Australian mission investigating new types of aircraft suitable for production in Australia. This mission, under the leadership of Daniel McVey, head of the department of aircraft production, returned with recommendations for the production of Mustang high-altitude fighters and Lancaster heavy bombers, both British-designed planes. The choice of British aircraft was at least partly due, as Bruce observed, to McVey's personal commitment to 'maintaining the link with the United Kingdom',[6] although the choice of the Lancaster bombers had an additional significance for Australia.

The recommendation for Australia's burgeoning aircraft factories to produce Lancaster bombers reflected a shift in the dominion's view of its position in the postwar world. The bombers would not be ready until at least 1946, by which time the war might well be over. The role of the Lancasters would then be to extend Australian power over the adjacent Pacific region and increase the independence of its defence industry. The production of the bombers was also a partial repudiation of the country's prewar reliance on the Royal Navy, as well as laying the basis for a civil aircraft industry so that Australia could avoid its wartime position of being totally dependent on the goodwill of the United States for such planes. As Curtin told journalists, Australia had to be mindful that the war might end soon and therefore had to choose an aircraft for production 'the machinery and dies for which could without much trouble be turned to the production of civil aircraft'.[7] In 1941, Menzies had promoted aircraft production in Australia, intending it to be the precursor of a postwar automobile industry controlled by British capital.[8]

While Menzies had been effectively rebuffed by Britain when he had sought support for his plans in 1941, British authorities were now obsessed with the idea that the Americans were stealing a march on them in civil aviation and that they would emerge from the war in control of the Australian aircraft industry. Consequently, the British were keen to support the Australian program. Much time was spent by officials in London, Washington and Canberra debating the issues of civil aviation in the widespread belief that it would comprise a key sector of the postwar economy. Indeed, it was assumed that the rapid progress in aircraft development would eventually see aircraft superseding ships as carriers of people and goods. Hence the importance of Britain not being overtaken by the United States in the development of civil aircraft, even in wartime. In January 1943, Hugh Dalton, as president of the board of trade, pointed in alarm at the 'long start' the Americans had and the danger of Britain being 'at a great disadvantage in export trade, both of aircraft and of other goods'. He argued for an immediate diversion of some war resources to civil production.[9] Armed with this advice, the war cabinet agreed to new civil aircraft being designed so that Britain would be able, after the war, immediately to produce aircraft 'on a scale and quantity in keeping with our world position'.[10]

At the same time, there were officials who believed that Britain was doomed to lose any such race with American aircraft manufacturers and pushed instead for the internationalisation of civil aviation. They wanted the production and operation of aircraft, as well as the airfields themselves, controlled by an international authority. Some proponents went even further, arguing that an international air force should take the place of national air forces as a means of reducing the risk of future wars. There was considerable support in Britain for the concept, both for idealistic reasons and because, although Britain controlled many of the world's airfields, it could not compete with the Americans in aircraft production. As Anthony Eden's secretary observed, the alternative to internationalisation was 'cut throat competition between national lines, heavy subsidies for British lines and final defeat by the richer, more efficient Pan American Airways'. Yet he complained that there were 'fools here in the Government who cannot see it and are for starting up British national lines again'.[11]

Australia also supported internationalisation for idealistic and practical reasons. However, despite official support from Bruce and Evatt, there were important groups eager for Australia to go it alone, either as part of the British empire or as an independent initiative. The Qantas Empire Airways chief, Hudson Fysh, was in the forefront of these moves. Although the Japanese thrust in 1942 had effectively cut Australia's commercial air links with Britain, Fysh was soon seeking to restore his airline's prewar hold on these routes. When Britain proposed re-establishing an air route to Australia, with plans to fly from Ceylon to Perth using RAF planes, Fysh mounted strong objections, warning of the 'danger to post war Australian Empire aviation should the Commonwealth lose its interest and equity in the operation of the Indian Ocean section'.[12] With the backing of the British high commissioner in Canberra, Fysh flew to London to put the case for Qantas operating the route. To avoid arousing American suspicions, he was 'requested to travel as unostentatiously as possible'.[13] Fysh spent several months campaigning successfully in London, where he also added his support to the moves for the immediate development by Britain of civil aircraft. Fysh warned British officials of American encroachment in Australia and called for a 'strong and virile lead from the United Kingdom'.[14]

Although Fysh won the right for Qantas to operate the Indian Ocean route, there were few aircraft available for him to use. Australia's prewar stock of civil aircraft had dwindled away to such an extent that the American air transport command was forced to provide the limited civil air service that still operated within Australia. The Americans also maintained Australia's only air links with the outside world. There were concerns that America's wartime stranglehold on Australia's civil aviation industry would continue even when the war was won. As civil aviation minister and former train driver Arthur Drakeford observed in April 1943, Australia faced the awful prospect of the 'total loss of Civil Aviation in this country to American airline companies'. For a decade before the war, Australia had refused landing rights to any American airlines. Now, to its dismay, 'every day large United States airliners arrive in Australia operated on behalf of the U.S. Air Transport Command by personnel of American companies such as Pan American and United Airline Companies'. To prevent these companies dominating Australia's postwar civil aviation, Drakeford urged that Australia either secure its own transport aircraft from overseas sources or build them itself, suggesting that 24 such aircraft might be built from wood, plywood and plastic. But the war cabinet thought better of it, opting instead to approach MacArthur for an allocation of American aircraft.[15]

In order to avoid any dispute with MacArthur, Shedden also informed him of the forthcoming arrival of the Lancaster bomber and its British sales mission. Shedden believed that MacArthur sympathised with Australia's position.[16] MacArthur certainly responded sympathetically, informing Shedden that Australia's civil aviation should be left at the end of the war 'in at least the same condition, in so far as the number of up to date aircraft was concerned, as it was at the beginning'. But he did not make clear how this was to be achieved. As he warned Shedden, 'powerful influences were at work [in Washington] in regard to the post-war civil aviation position and these may have exercised some influence on the refusal of the request for transport aircraft from America'. As for Australia producing them itself, MacArthur opposed the production of such aircraft within Australia in case it used resources that might otherwise be used for his command.[17]

In sending out the Lancaster and its accompanying sales team, Britain had to be wary of not alerting the Americans as to the real intentions of the flight. Yet, because of the difficulties of a flight across the disputed reaches of the Indian Ocean, Britain would have to send it across the Pacific and seek American permission to land at Hawaii for refuelling. In order to disguise the purpose of the mission from the Americans, Australia was asked to request the aircraft 'to assist in the raising of subscriptions for the next War Loan'.[18] Bruce suggested that Evatt make the request while he was in Washington. However, Evatt was unaware of the British plan and almost caused it to become unstuck when he asked suspiciously 'under what circumstances [the] loan of the bomber has been obtained from [the] British Government and how the idea originated'. If it was going to be used for publicising a war loans campaign, observed Evatt, it was 'far too early as there will be no loan appeal for several months'. An alarmed Bruce immediately alerted Evatt that the real reason for the Lancaster's flight was Britain's 'desire to show the flag in Australia in relation to transport aircraft'.[19]

Evatt needed no further prodding. W. S. Robinson had already bombarded Evatt with advice about the importance of air power underpinning Australia's place in the postwar world. In a paper submitted to Evatt in early June, Robinson had argued that Australia's future survival

depends more on strength in the air than on any other factor. A thousand million coloured people are her nearest neighbours — but a few hours flight from our shores. Not only for our defence but for the maintenance of our economic activities we must have efficient aircraft in sufficient supply — we must be able to build them and we must have trained men to fly them.

Robinson also believed that Australia must retain for its own use the 'vast oil reserves in New Guinea' to fuel the large air force and the extensive civil air services that he envisaged would link various parts of the continent to each other and to the outside world. 'It is not too much to say,' wrote Robinson, 'that the areas of Australia's geographical markets after the war which it will be necessary to cover by air will be twice as large as the Continent of Australia is today.' Defending this area would require a greater degree of Australian self-reliance. According to Robinson, the most important lesson from the war was that 'we cannot rely on others to make and sell us aircraft when they are in danger themselves'.[20]

Surprisingly, it was Churchill who had the most realistic ideas about postwar civil aviation despite his well-known aversion to considering peacetime matters during the heat of battle. He argued with some accuracy in June 1943 that 'there is no industry which will undergo a more intense and severe contraction than the aircraft industry'. Although he conceded that, 'for strategic and political reasons' Britain must develop 'large, efficient air lines binding the British Commonwealth and Empire together', he did not believe that these routes would be profitable. Instead, argued Churchill, British aviation 'should make a strong British effort to excel in the profitable European traffic'.[21]

While Britain was trying to give away one Lancaster bomber to induce Australia to use them as civil airliners in peacetime, Churchill was ensuring that Evatt would not get any such bombers for wartime use. On 12 May, the day after Churchill arrived in Washington, Evatt sent him a note asking for a commitment of sufficient aircraft to allow the RAAF to be built up to

45 squadrons by the end of 1943. Although the Americans were most averse to using the RAAF as a striking force, and generally relegated it to the defence of base areas and the servicing of American squadrons, MacArthur nevertheless wanted to maximise the forces under his command and had suggested that Evatt try to secure some of the American aircraft that had been allotted to Britain. If successful, this would mean that the Australian aircraft under MacArthur's command would be increased without detracting from his own air forces.[22] So desperate was Evatt to achieve such a commitment that he pitched his appeal in terms that were difficult to refuse. 'All that is asked for,' he informed Churchill, 'is that the United States and the United Kingdom agree to equip the additional 27 squadrons over such a period and at such a rate as is regarded as reasonable.' Evatt followed up this note with a long talk with Churchill at the White House after which he confided to Curtin that he was 'hopeful of securing Churchill's support at any rate for a substantial part of the programme'.[23]

If Britain agreed to support Australia over the aircraft, Evatt proposed to Churchill that Australia would represent Polish interests in the Soviet Union. At the time, the relations between London and Moscow were strained after Stalin broke off contact with the London-based Polish government-in-exile because the Poles publicly, and correctly, accused the Russians of the notorious Katyn Forest massacre of Polish officers. In order to raise its own international profile, as well as help Britain out of a sticky situation, Evatt put this proposal to Churchill during their White House meeting, adroitly linking it to his proposal for additional aircraft. He was pleased to find that Churchill was 'greatly impressed' with the Australian approach to the Polish problem.[24]

Evatt also requested that the Allied leaders consult Australia in making their war plans. Australian leaders had repeatedly been caught in the humiliating position of learning of Allied war plans from the newspapers. Evatt readily admitted that the Australian tail could not expect to wag the British dog, but pleaded that the dog at least keep the tail informed as to its future movements. Citing the decisions at Casablanca, in which Australia had no part but which vitally concerned it, Evatt reminded Churchill that *high morale can best be maintained if the people feel that their government is fully consulted in advance of major decisions vitally affecting them. From the Empire point of view the public appearance of consultation is almost as important as the fact of prior consultation.*[25]

In other words, token consultation would do so long as the public could be beguiled into believing that Australia was playing a full part in the councils of war.

Evatt's entreaty marked a switch in Australian tactics away from hectoring demands and fearful appeals. MacArthur had suggested the switch, claiming that it would be inadvisable simply to repeat previous Australian demands 'unless specifically called for' by Roosevelt and Churchill. Accordingly, Curtin counselled Evatt to 'angle for an opportunity to represent our case rather than to awaken disfavour by a forcible intrusion'.[26] The silky voice of moderation worked. On reading Evatt's appeal for aircraft, Churchill instructed that his chiefs 'must do something for him. Observe that he has not asked for any timetable. Pray make me proposals.'[27] In other words, Churchill saw an opportunity to make another of his vague promises to Australia, this time to supply American aircraft on an extended timetable related more to their convenience than to Australia's need.

Just two days after his conciliatory note to Churchill, Evatt called upon Admiral Somerville, also in Washington with the British delegation, to discuss plans for the Eastern fleet. Australia still remained relatively oblivious of the Eastern fleet's weakened position. As Somerville had complained to Gerald Wilkinson before leaving for Washington, he was in the uncomfortable position of having to do too much with too little. Apart from defensively covering the Middle Eastern reinforcement route with his elderly battleships, he was also under pressure to go out and attack the Japanese. Being so overstretched, he resisted any proposal to transfer part of his fleet to Western Australia, arguing that Japan could do nothing more than a hit-and-run raid from the air or sea. In any event, Somerville confided to Wilkinson, his strength was simply not up to the task. He was still relying on deceiving the Japanese, citing with relish 'the fake photographs of absent British battleships which we are making in India and selling to the enemy'.[28]

Australia had been similarly deceived over the strength of the fleet and its recent failure to escort properly the 9th Division across the Indian Ocean.

During his discussion with Evatt, Somerville told the querulous Australian of his fleet's flag-waving meeting with the troop convoy, adding that he was sorry the Australians had not remained in the Middle East long enough to participate in the final victory that was then being celebrated in Tunisia. With some astonishment, Somerville observed Evatt's angry response, later warning Churchill that

Dr. Evatt immediately flared up and said this was the 'dirtiest crack that anyone could make'. I asked him to explain what he meant; then he embarked on a long rigmarole that neither I nor anyone else had the right to question Mr. Curtin's decision [to recall the 9th Division] and added once again that I had made a very dirty crack.[29]

Somerville's stance of injured innocence would have been at least partly contrived, but his remark was perhaps a further sign of the widespread sense of superiority among British officials.[30]

Somerville tried to repair the damage by limiting their talk to the Eastern fleet, but found that even this provoked a storm from the tempestuous Evatt, who now claimed that Britain had broken an agreement to maintain the strength of the Eastern fleet at no less than five battleships and three aircraft carriers and that, as a consequence, Western Australia had been exposed to Japanese attack. Certainly, Western Australia was vulnerable to such an attack, but there was no agreement along the lines that Evatt had claimed. In his report to Churchill, Somerville warned that Evatt was 'singularly ill informed of the general strategic situation, that he was anxious to pick a quarrel and that he took no trouble to avoid being offensive'.[31] According to Somerville, Churchill later expressed his approval for the manner in which the admiral had stood up to Evatt, although later he tried to smooth over the dispute. During a garden party at the White House, Churchill 'brought Evatt over to Somerville and proceeded to put their two hands together with his own over the top and said that they had all got to be friends in Washington'.[32]

Although Churchill wanted to placate Evatt over the aircraft and satisfy his vague appeal with an equally vague promise, he found that his air ministry head, Sir Charles Portal, had practical objections to such a course. Portal was unaware of Evatt's postwar vision of a virtual 'Greater Australian Co-Prosperity Sphere' enforced with air power, or of the other reasons for Australia wanting aircraft. He simply examined Australia's case for greater air power in the south-west Pacific and concluded that the facts did not support Evatt's case, at least as far as Britain was concerned. Allied air power in the Pacific far outweighed that of Japan and was more than sufficient for the agreed holding strategy. As for the Cinderella treatment of the RAAF, Portal saw this as a matter for the Australians to take up with Washington rather than London. He suggested to Churchill that Evatt should ask MacArthur to allow the RAAF to operate a greater proportion of the aircraft allocated to the SWPA.[33] Perhaps sensing the drift of British opinion on this issue, Evatt sent a letter that same day to Churchill advising that the proposed expansion of the RAAF had been 'committed to my charge by the Australian Government and I specially ask that you enable my mission to be fulfilled before your present conferences terminate'.[34]

Churchill was certainly anxious to prevent Evatt allying himself with the 'Pacific first' elements within Washington. At a meeting of the Pacific War Council on 20 May, which Evatt and Roosevelt attended, Churchill expressed his support for the RAAF's expansion. This was what Evatt had wanted to hear, but his legal background as well as his political sense demanded that it should be committed to writing if it were to have any effect. So he 'respectfully' called on Churchill to do just that and for the two Allied leaders then to make 'a suitable public announcement' that would, he claimed, 'create an excellent impression from an Empire point of view'.[35] For once, Churchill and the Australian government were as one, mainly because Australia was demanding something that would not affect the 'Germany first' strategy. As Churchill saw it, any increase in the strength of the RAAF would subtract from the aircraft allocated to the American forces in the SWPA and there would be no increase in the overall aircraft strength of the Allied forces in the Pacific. In fact, it might release American pilots for the fight in Europe.

Following the war council meeting, Churchill informed Portal that he had, 'with the President's permission, strongly urged the supply of this small number of aircraft from the vast American production in order that the Australian fliers might take a larger part in the defence of their own country'. Churchill thought that this was 'most desirable' and Roosevelt had 'promised to consider it sympathetically'. Most importantly, Evatt was 'extremely pleased'. Churchill urged Portal to 'get this matter moved forward on a lower level, as I wish to clinch it with the President before I leave'.[36] Evatt was elated. On 19 May he had watched Churchill address the US Congress, during which he had promised the somewhat sceptical American politicians that Britain would fight the Pacific war to a finish with all the resources of the empire once Germany had been defeated. Churchill was at the top of his form, easily casting a spell over Evatt, despite his failure during the speech to acknowledge Evatt's presence in the gallery or the effort of Australia while nevertheless making 'a pointed reference to the presence of Mr. Mackenzie King [the Canadian prime minister]'.[37]

Evatt was also encouraged by a meeting on 20 May when Churchill assembled various Commonwealth representatives at the White House for a discussion on the war. As the music of the military band died away, the counsellor at the Australian legation, Alan Watt, watched with approval as Evatt reined in his impetuous personality to address the meeting on the issues facing Australia. According to Watt, Evatt 'spoke firmly but politely, and I thought that his remarks were well received by Mr. Churchill and had some effect'. For his part, Churchill redressed the omission of the previous day and, in the privacy of this Commonwealth conclave, spoke warmly of 'our beloved Australia and New Zealand' and of the splendid work of the 9th Division.[38] Evatt seems to have been impressed, informing Curtin two days later that the British prime minister was 'far keener on Pacific activities than during last year' and was 'really anxious to join Roosevelt and push against Japan whenever it is practicable to do so'.[39]

In fact, there had been no change of heart by Churchill. His course was still set firmly against Germany.[40] As were his military advisers, headed by General Brooke, who described Evatt after the White House meeting as the

'Australian nuisance!'.[41] Churchill also remained deeply antagonistic towards Australia after the bitter disputes of the previous two years. Although he was careful to conceal his feelings from Evatt, Churchill revealed them to a colleague when the question arose of using the New Zealand division in the capture of Sicily. Using the New Zealanders, Churchill claimed, would provide 'a great opportunity for them to win honour, and the fact that Australia has failed us makes it all the more necessary'. If they refused, said Churchill, 'there is nothing more to be said. They will then place themselves on the same level as Australia. But I do not think they will refuse.'[42] Churchill was right. The New Zealanders left their troops in the European theatre despite Curtin's anger at them for failing to fight alongside the Australians in New Guinea.[43]

After all his problems in extracting aircraft from Churchill during his previous trip, Evatt remained rightly wary of being let down again. Accordingly, the day after his cautiously optimistic cable to Curtin, Evatt again approached Churchill asking that he intervene with Roosevelt to have the RAAF expansion program formally approved. Writing from Baltimore where his wife was recovering from an operation, Evatt blamed British service officials for dragging their feet over the proposal and declared that 'it would be heart-breaking to have the matter shelved further'. Churchill also wanted the matter concluded and Evatt sent away satisfied, telling Portal that he attached 'great importance to getting this settled now' and asking imperiously, 'What has happened?'[44]

Although Churchill threw his weight behind Evatt's plan, which envisaged most of the aircraft not being delivered until the first half of 1944,[45] Portal continued to oppose any scheme that would increase the level of aircraft in Australia. As Portal advised Churchill, MacArthur and the Australians seemed set on using the argument for an expanded RAAF as a cover 'to obtain a further overall increase of air forces in the Pacific for which neither the American nor the British Chiefs of Staff see any justification'. Only if Evatt was prepared to restrict himself to expanding the RAAF within the limit of the already agreed aircraft deliveries would Portal be prepared to dispatch by the end of 1944 sufficient aircraft to satisfy Australia's request.[46] But American agreement also had to be achieved.

Evatt had hoped to tie up the agreement before Churchill left Washington, realising that it might otherwise be lost in the labyrinth of American bureaucracy. On the eve of Churchill's departure, Evatt asked W. S. Robinson to make a personal plea to Churchill. From his temporary office in the Australian legation, Robinson informed Churchill that

Bert [Evatt] has just returned and told me of his most encouraging talk with you regarding aircraft ... Knowing what this means to the Empire and the justifiable anxiety of Bert to have it completed immediately, I trust that you and the President will be able to complete it before you leave.[47]

Although Churchill wanted to satisfy Evatt, the Americans had the final say. And he left it to them. Before boarding his flying boat for the journey to Newfoundland, Churchill told Evatt that he should direct his inquiries to Harry Hopkins, Roosevelt's close adviser, assuring Evatt that Roosevelt was 'very favourably disposed to your request'.[48]

Churchill could leave Washington content with the agreements he had made with the Americans. He and Roosevelt had agreed to share research into the atomic bomb, and he had diverted the Americans from switching the focus of the Allied war effort to the Pacific. However, he had failed so far to convince the Americans that, once Sicily was captured, the Allied armies should descend upon the Italian mainland and knock Italy out of the war altogether. To do so, Churchill left Washington via Newfoundland and Gibraltar for Algiers, for talks with the American supreme commander in the Mediterranean, General Eisenhower. Churchill prevailed upon Roosevelt to send the American army chief, General Marshall, to accompany the British group to secure a final decision on the issue. Churchill knew that Marshall, who was ambivalent about the Mediterranean strategy, had been about to visit the south-west Pacific, where he may well have become converted instead to MacArthur's case for reinforcements. By getting Marshall to visit north Africa first, Churchill ensured that the general did not waver from his attachment to the 'Germany first' strategy. Although no final agreement was reached in Algiers, Churchill left satisfied that his view about eliminating Italy would prevail as soon as Sicily had been conquered.[49]

Meanwhile, in Washington, Evatt was frustrated by his failure to obtain a formal agreement to provide specific numbers and types of aircraft for Australia. It had not been finalised despite him agreeing to allow the timetable for their delivery to slip back twelve months to the end of 1944.[50] On 4 June, as Churchill was travelling back to London from Algiers, Evatt again complained that service officials had not implemented the verbal promises made by Churchill and Roosevelt regarding the supply of aircraft for Australia. He advised Curtin that the success of his mission would now depend upon the support of the American air force chief, General Arnold, who was off duty until the following week. In order to await Arnold's decision, Evatt postponed his departure for London, while at the same time imploring Churchill to instruct British service officials in Washington to support the Australian case more actively and thereby 'clinch the matter'.[51]

After a month away, Churchill arrived back in London on the morning of 5 June after narrowly escaping death at the hands of the German air force, which shot down a flying boat taking the same route as Churchill and killed, among others, the British actor Leslie Howard. Churchill, though, made a last-minute switch, abandoning his flying boat for a converted bomber that avoided the German interceptors. That same day in Tokyo, there was a grand official funeral for Japan's naval hero, Admiral Yamamoto, the architect of the attack on Pearl Harbor who had been caught in a similar assassination attempt by the Americans but who had not been lucky enough to survive it. American intelligence had learned of Yamamoto's planned flight to Bougainville on 18 April, and ordered an ambush. His escort of Zero fighters was overwhelmed by eighteen American fighters which then turned upon Yamamoto's bomber, sending it crashing into the island's jungle-clad terrain.[52]

Before reading Evatt's message, Churchill presided over a lunchtime meeting of his war cabinet where he reported upon his prolonged trip. He informed his colleagues of his meeting with Evatt and of his hope that he 'had been of some help to Dr. Evatt in obtaining the aircraft which the Australian Government were anxious to obtain from the United States'. The bulk of Churchill's report centred upon his success in keeping official American attention fixed upon the European war. Claiming that the visit had been 'amply justified', Churchill reminded his ministers that American public opinion 'was much more concerned about the war against Japan — it was almost true to say that the American public would be more disturbed if China fell out of the war than if Russia did so'. Churchill added that his idea of forcing Marshall to accompany them to north Africa rather than Australia had been a triumph. 'It seemed likely,' Churchill crowed, that Marshall would 'return to the United States a convinced supporter of the projected operations in this theatre'.[53]

When Churchill finally did read Evatt's renewed appeal for help, he instructed General Dill in Washington to reach an agreement with the Americans on the RAAF expansion program and thereby prevent any further delay of Evatt's departure for Britain. Dill immediately promised to do all he could to help Evatt since, he said, 'we are equally anxious to speed Dr. Evatt on his way'. The problem remained, however, that 'none of us can justify his claims on strategical grounds'.[54] Since it was clear that Evatt would not leave without a piece of paper to wave in Canberra, Roosevelt finally relented and promised to supply 475 additional aircraft to Australia by the end of 1944, but with no commitment as to specific types of aircraft or by which dates they would be delivered. Evatt accepted Roosevelt's promise gratefully, realising that this rather vague commitment would have to suffice. When the combined chiefs of staff allocated future Allied aircraft production between the various theatres, Evatt hoped Australia would receive at least some of the heavy bombers it had requested. Without such aircraft, as Evatt informed Roosevelt, the long-range striking power of the RAAF was almost negligible.[55] This meant that Australia might be prevented from partaking in the final blows against Japan and would be denied adequate power to hold sway over the south-west Pacific in the postwar period.

On 12 June, Evatt trumpeted his success, informing Curtin that 'I cannot tell you how relieved and proud I am ... that I have discharged the sole mission entrusted to me by you in relation to aircraft'. He claimed that the initial American refusal of his request was only overcome when Churchill arrived in Washington and lent his support, despite the opposition of Portal who, Evatt confided, pointed out 'truly enough that my application was an indirect way of increasing the overall allocation to the theatre'. According to Evatt, it was only as he was about to leave for London that Roosevelt finally agreed to supply the aircraft and make them additional to those already committed to the south-west Pacific theatre. Lastly, in order to maximise the political benefit of his supposed victory, Evatt asked that Curtin 'make a public statement in Australia that I have fully carried out the mission entrusted to me'. W. S. Robinson sent a similar signal to Curtin proclaiming a 'major Australian victory' for Evatt and claiming that Evatt had 'endeared himself to Churchill and Roosevelt'.[56]

At the same time, Evatt cabled to Colonel Hodgson, the former intelligence officer heading the external affairs department, reiterating his call for Curtin to 'issue an appropriate[ly] worded statement marking the conclusion of my mission here and its complete success in relation to the outstanding object of obtaining equipment for the expansion of the RAAF'. Moreover, he suggested that Hodgson should 'discreetly' tell various key Australian political figures, as well as the editor of the influential *Sydney Morning Herald*, 'something of the fight I have had and of its ultimate success. I am happy to know that — whatever befalls us — something big has been done for Australia and the Empire.'[57] This final comment was presumably a last political testament in the event of his flight across the Atlantic ending in disaster, as a disturbing number of such flights did. To Evatt's chagrin, political kudos was denied him. Curtin sent his congratulations but refused to make any public statement. Curtin had Evatt where he wanted him: far from political conspiracies in Canberra and entrusted with a mission that was probably impossible to achieve.[58]

Evatt also claimed as a success Churchill's announcement at a Washington press conference that the war against Japan would be prosecuted with the same vigour as the war against Germany. In fact, Churchill had reportedly said that Britain and the United States were 'talking of waging war with equal force on both the European and Asiatic fronts'.[59] Which was not quite the same as actually doing it. Nevertheless, his message was interpreted in Australia as meaning that resources would be equally provided to both wars. Even the normally sceptical MacArthur, while withholding final judgment on the statement's significance, argued that it 'cannot be ignored by those who made it'. In a week-long series of meetings at his headquarters in Brisbane with Shedden, MacArthur suggested that the political pressure on Roosevelt, whom he lambasted as 'utterly ruthless and unscrupulous', might reach the point where he would pull American forces out of Europe altogether in order 'to save his own position'. The presidential election of 1944, according to MacArthur's cynical assessment, would concentrate Roosevelt's energies upon gaining a military victory somewhere and avoiding too many casualties.[60] This might be good news for the war in the Pacific.

Following Shedden's return from Brisbane, and with Evatt's advice that he express cautious optimism, Curtin announced to the press on 1 June that there had been a change in the Allied attitude towards Australia. The only problem remaining, said Curtin, was the 'physical problem of giving this theatre equality in strength'. As a consequence of Churchill's declaration concerning the Pacific, Curtin claimed that it was now 'possible to see daylight in the ultimate result ...'.[61] In an attempt to ensure that the declaration would be implemented, Curtin sent messages to Churchill and Roosevelt conveying Australia's 'appreciation of the deep significance of your public assurance that the war in the Pacific will be prosecuted with the same vigour as the war in Europe'.[62]

Four days later in Sydney, Curtin met MacArthur who talked of attacking the Japanese stronghold at Rabaul and forcing the Japanese back to their strategic naval base on the island of Truk in the central Pacific. Although MacArthur assured Curtin that he wanted Australian forces to accompany him as his campaign worked its way north towards Tokyo, he forecast that, with the fall of Rabaul, Australia would be able to

resume a more reasonable and rational basis of national activity, more closely harmonised with its normal structure and post-war aims. It was important that the National effort must not be so devoted to war as to result in the Commonwealth being left behind in the post-war situation.

Now that a Japanese invasion was no longer a realistic possibility, MacArthur told Curtin that Australia could alleviate its manpower shortage by reducing its land forces south of Brisbane.[63] As a result of this optimistic picture, and perhaps as another means of holding the Allied leaders to their supposed commitment, Curtin told journalists that the first stage of the Pacific war was over and that Australians should 'sit tight' as they awaited for the 'second phase which involves certain limited offensive action'.[64]

With his mission in Washington apparently concluded, Evatt cabled to Churchill with news of his victory, thereby enabling him to go on to London where he would be 'anxious to have the honour of conferring with yourself'.[65] Britain's air ministry representative in Washington also warned of Evatt's imminent arrival and confirmed that the Australian had extracted from Roosevelt a commitment of additional aircraft for the dominion. Although Evatt refused to show the British official the terms of Roosevelt's letter, Australia's air force representative did reveal the details of the American commitment, which were promptly passed on to London. As the British representative confided, there was still much opposition within the American services to Roosevelt's commitment. With American military opposition and the vague wording of the commitment, Roosevelt's promise might yet be circumvented.[66]

The British were particularly concerned that the Australians not be allowed to secure heavy bombers, which the British air ministry wanted to concentrate against Germany. As yet, the RAAF had no heavy bombers at all. Although Evatt had urged Roosevelt to provide 36 such aircraft during 1943 to allow two squadrons to be formed, and a further 126 aircraft in 1944 to allow a further seven squadrons to be formed, Roosevelt had refused to make any commitment as to what aircraft would be provided other than dive-bombers and fighter planes. Before leaving Washington, Evatt had asked British officials to continue pressing Australia's case for heavy bombers. They not only brushed off this request, but warned London that Evatt might demand British bombers instead.[67] Portal needed no warning on this point and was ready to rebut any argument that Evatt might mount. As the anxious Australian sat in his aircraft, rigid with apprehension about the long flight to London, he could at least be confident that Roosevelt's letter would compensate for the danger that he was forcing himself to endure. Or so he thought. Once again, Evatt would find that the political corridors of London and Washington were like halls of mirrors in which illusion could merge with reality to create a false sense of achievement.

NOTES

1. On 19 April, prior to leaving for the United States, Churchill had ordered a 'searching examination into the situation in the Pacific, with a view to establishing the extent to which the Australian demand for reinforcements is justified from the military point of view'. War Cabinet Conclusions, 19 April 1943, CAB 65/34, W.M. (43)56, PRO.

2. Aide memoire, 6 May 1943, PREM 3/151/4, PRO.

3. Gilbert, *Road to Victory*, p. 396.

4. Letter, Curtin to Evatt, 1 April 1943, Teleprinter message, MacArthur to Shedden, 25 March 1943, and Cable, Roosevelt to Curtin, 6 April 1943, CRS A5954, Box 474, NAA.

5. Cable, Curtin to Roosevelt, 13 April 1943, CRS A5954, Box 474, NAA.

6. Talk with McVey, 6 April 1943, CRS M100, 'April 1943', NAA.

7. Butlin and Schedvin, *War Economy*, pp. 410–3; Press Conference, 14 June 1943, MS 4675, Smith Papers, NLA; See also documents in CRS A5954, Box 219, NAA.

8. See Day, *Menzies and Churchill at War*.

9. Letter, Dalton to Jowitt, 6 January 1943, II/7/5, Dalton Papers, LSE.

10. War Cabinet Conclusions, 25 February 1943, CAB 65/33, W.M. (43)35; Memorandum by Cripps and Sinclair, 24 February 1943, CAB 66/34, W.P. (43)83, PRO.

11. Harvey diary, 19 January 1943, ADD. MS. 56399, Harvey Papers, BL.

12. Letter, Fysh to Forde, 5 November 1942, CRS A461, T314/1/4/2, NAA.

13. Letter, M. E. Antrobus to Secretary, Prime Minister's Department, 23 February 1943, CRS A461, T314/1/4/2, NAA.

14. See, 'Evatt — Overseas Trips — 1943' folder, Evatt Papers, FUL; See also Fysh, *Qantas at War*, pp. 176–7; Talk with Fysh, 6 May 1943, CRS M100, 'May 1943', NAA; Cable, Dominions Secretary to Commonwealth Government, 28 April 1943, CRS A5954, Box 343, NAA.

15. Submission by Drakeford, 13 April 1943, CRS A2670/183/1943, NAA.

16. Note by Shedden, and Notes of discussion with MacArthur, 25–31 May 1943, CRS A5954, Box 2, NAA; See also Shedden's memoirs, Chap. 57, pp. 4–5, CRS A5954, Box 771, NAA.

17. ibid.

18. If Australia decided in favour of Lancasters, the bomber that had carried the sales team would be presented as a gift. Talk with McVey, 6 April 1943, CRS M100, 'April 1943', NAA.

19. Talk with Lord Burghley, 20 April 1943, Cables, Bruce to Curtin, 21 April 1943, Evatt to Bruce, 24 April 1943 and Bruce to Evatt, 24 April 1943, CRS M100, 'April 1943', NAA.

20. Although the memorandum is not signed, it is most likely that it was written by Robinson. Of course, subsidised postwar aircraft production would benefit Robinson's metal interests. Even so, his criticism of the British industry was well made. Even in 1943, the British aircraft companies only grudgingly accepted the Australian industry and urged the British government to keep all aircraft research and development work in British hands. Memorandum by the Society of British Aircraft Constructors, June 1943, BBK D/228, Beaverbrook Papers, HLRO; Memorandum to Evatt, 8 June 1943, 'Aviation — Post War' folder, Evatt Papers, FUL.

21. Note by Churchill, 22 June 1943, CAB 66/38, W.P. (43)257, PRO.

22. Letter, Curtin to Evatt, 1 April 1943, CRS A5954, Box 474, NAA.

23. Note, Evatt to Churchill, 12 May 1943, PREM 3/150/8, PRO; Cable, Evatt to Curtin, 13 May 1943, *DAFP*, Vol. 6, Doc. 191.

24. Cable, Evatt to Curtin, 13 May 1943, *DAFP*, Vol. 6, Doc. 191.

[25] Note, Evatt to Churchill, 12 May 1943, PREM 3/150/8, PRO.

[26] Advisory War Council Minutes, 13 May 1943, CRS A2682/6/1188, NAA.

[27] Note, Churchill to Portal, 13 May 1943, PREM 3/150/8, PRO.

[28] War Journal, 3 May 1943, WILK 1/2, Wilkinson Papers, CC.

[29] Note, Somerville to Pound, 17 May 1943, PREM 3/163/6, PRO.

[30] Even the rather patrician Bruce complained of British officials having a 'superiority complex'. Talk with Attlee, 24 May 1943, CRS M100, 'May 1943', NAA.

[31] Note, Somerville to Pound, 17 May 1943, PREM 3/163/6, PRO.

[32] Note by Bruce of Conversation with Somerville, 1 June 1943, *DAFP*, Vol. 6, Doc. 207.

[33] Minute, Portal to Churchill, 18 May 1943, PREM 3/150/8, PRO.

[34] Letter, Evatt to Churchill, 18 May 1943, PREM 3/150/8, PRO.

[35] Letter, Evatt to Churchill, 20 May 1943, PREM 3/150/8, PRO.

[36] Minute, Churchill to Portal, 21 May 1943, PREM 3/150/8, PRO.

[37] Letter, Watt to Hodgson, 24 May 1943, MS 3788/1/1, Watt Papers, NLA.

[38] ibid.

[39] Cable, Evatt to Curtin, 22 May 1943, 'Washington' folder, Evatt Papers, FUL.

[40] As Churchill told a group of British correspondents on 23 May, the Japanese air force was weakening so that it had become 'possible to hold Japan aggressively until the time is ripe for all out attack'. Again he promised that 'when the European war is over, Britain will send every available man against Japan to assist the Americans'. Letter, Thompson to Beaverbrook, 23 May 1943, enclosing precis of Churchill's press conference, BBK D/182, Beaverbrook Papers, HLRO.

[41] Alanbrooke diary, 20 May 1943, in Danchev and Todman (eds), *War Diaries*, p. 408.

[42] Minute, Churchill to Attlee, 8 April 1943, PREM 3/63/5, PRO.

[43] Cable, Batterbee to Dominions Office, 9 June 1943, PREM 3/63/5, PRO; See also *DAFP*, Vol. 6, Docs 198 and 206.

[44] Letter, Evatt to Churchill, 23 May 1943, PREM 3/150/8, PRO.

[45] Under Evatt's plan, the RAAF would reach its maximum strength at a time when the Japanese would probably be located far from Australian shores. But Evatt had more than wartime considerations in view. To the consternation of the Dutch government, he had already spoken publicly in New York of Australia's desire to be involved in a 'partnership' with the Dutch in the postwar development of the Netherlands East Indies and to take control of Portuguese Timor from Lisbon. Aide-memoire, Van Aerssen to Curtin, and Letter, Curtin to Van Aerssen, 14 May 1943, *DAFP*, Vol. 6, Docs 192–3; War Cabinet Conclusions, 15 June 1943, CAB 65/34, W.M. (43)85, PRO.

[46] Note by Portal, 24 May 1943, PREM 3/150/8, PRO.

[47] Letter, Robinson to Churchill, 25 May 1943, PREM 3/150/8, PRO.

[48] Cable, Churchill to Evatt, 26 May 1943, PREM 3/150/8, PRO.

[49] Gilbert, *Road to Victory*, Chap. 24; Bryant, *Turn of the Tide*, Chap. 12.

[50] To put the Australian request for less than five hundred aircraft in some perspective, the British and Americans supplied Russia, which already had a huge aircraft production industry, with more than eighteen thousand aircraft during the course of the war. For details of the Allied contribution to the Russian war effort, see III/4/9/4, Ismay Papers, KC.

[51] Evatt later told Curtin that he had 'never worked so hard or so untiringly on anything in my life. Indeed it is the most difficult job I have ever had.' Cable, Evatt to Curtin, 12 June 1943, in *DAFP*, Vol. 6, Doc. 222; Cable, Evatt to Churchill, 4 June 1943, PREM 3/150/8, PRO.

[52] Jenkins, *Churchill*, p. 713; Hoyt, *Japan's War*, p. 324; Gillison, *Royal Australian Air Force, 1939–1942*, pp. 701–2.

[53] War Cabinet Conclusions, 5 June 1943, CAB 65/34, W.M. (43)81, PRO.

[54] Cable, Churchill to Dill, 7 June 1943, and Cable, Dill to Churchill, 9 June 1943, PREM 3/150/8, PRO.

[55] Letter, Evatt to Roosevelt, 3 June 1943, *DAFP*, Vol. 6, Doc. 210; Cable, Dill to Churchill, 13 June 1943, PREM 3/150/8, PRO.

[56] Cables, Robinson to Curtin, and Evatt to Curtin, 12 June 1943, *DAFP*, Vol. 6, Docs 221 and 222.

[57] Cable, Evatt to Hodgson, 12 June 1943, *DAFP*, Vol. 6, Doc. 223.

58 Background briefing, 1 June 1943, MS 4675, Smith Papers, NLA.
59 *Sydney Morning Herald*, 27 May 1943.
60 Cable, Curtin to Evatt, 3 June 1943, 'Washington' folder, Evatt Papers, FUL; See also Notes by Shedden, 25–31 May 1943, CRS A5954, Box 2, NAA.
61 Background briefing, 1 June 1943, MS 4675, Smith Papers, NLA.
62 Cable, Curtin to Churchill, 3 June 1943, in *DAFP*, Vol. 6, Doc. 208.
63 Prime Minister's War Conference Minute, 7 June 1943, CRS A5954, Box 2, NAA.
64 Background briefing, 9 June 1943, MS 4675, Smith Papers, NLA.
65 Cable, Evatt to Churchill, 12 June 1943, PREM 3/150/8, PRO.
66 Cable, Courtney to Portal, 14 June 1943, PREM 3/150/8, PRO.
67 ibid.

THIRTY-SEVEN

'we cannot possibly give him any'

At the time that Evatt was flying across the Atlantic to London in mid-June 1943, the Anglo–American forces in north Africa were coping with more than a quarter of a million German and Italian prisoners caught in the hard-won defeat of the Axis armies in Tunisia. With the ending of German resistance in north Africa, preparations could now be advanced for an invasion of Sicily, set for early July, and thence to Italy itself. As for a cross-Channel invasion, that had been delayed at least until 1944, much to the chagrin of Stalin whose armies would be left for another year to bear the brunt of the fighting against German forces. Despite Stalin's continuing complaints about the Allies' failure to launch a cross-Channel invasion, his own forces were no longer on the defensive. They had pushed the Germans out of the Caucasus region and were mounting an offensive along much of the eastern front. At last, Russian numerical superiority was taking its toll of German technical superiority.

Churchill attempted to appease the Russian anger by reminding Stalin of the heavy Allied bombing campaign against German cities, which was tying up much of the German air force and hampering German operations in

Russia. As Churchill pointed out, that bombing campaign was being done at a heavy cost, both to men and machines.[1] It was those four-engine bombers that Evatt was particularly keen to obtain for Australia's use in the south-west Pacific, where MacArthur was continuing to work on plans for an eventual assault by Australian and American troops against the Japanese headquarters at Rabaul. MacArthur's plan was to fight a series of small battles to seize the whole north-eastern coast of New Guinea before encircling the Japanese fortress. Enjoying air superiority and moving with increasing boldness at sea, the Allied forces had the upper hand over the Japanese. However, such was the difficulty of the terrain in New Guinea, and the courage of the defenders, that each minor battle became a major struggle. Meanwhile, across in Burma, the Japanese had launched a pre-emptive strike against the British forces assembling on the Indian border for their own offensive. Churchill watched in disgust as his troops were forced into a further retreat, ending a sorry campaign that he described privately to General Brooke as 'one of the most disappointing and indeed discreditable which has occurred in this war'.[2]

Long-range bombers were also being deployed finally in the crucial battle of the Atlantic, providing air cover for convoys and seeking out submarines that tried to sneak out into the Atlantic from their bases on the Bay of Biscay. This prolonged battle, on which Britain's war effort ultimately depended, was won by mid-1943 when new Allied tactics forced the Germans to withdraw their submarines from the north Atlantic. As in the First World War, the submarine offensive had pushed Britain close to defeat by threatening to cut its essential lifeline to North America. However, the Allies were now building ships faster than the submarines were able to sink them. Moreover, the Allies were finding better ways of locating and sinking the German submarines at sea, while their bombers continued to destroy those being constructed in German yards. The Germans were losing their submarines faster than they could be replaced.[3] If that continued, the final victory against Germany was almost assured, with some now predicting that it would come before the end of 1944 while the war against Japan was expected to last for three or more years after that.

Along with sections of the American military, the Australian government was hoping that the Pacific war might be brought to an end sooner than that and was looking to Evatt to extract a commitment of resources that might help to achieve that aim. As he indicated in Washington, Churchill was prepared to satisfy Evatt's wish for aircraft provided that it did not detract from the war in Europe. On 16 June, the day after Evatt's arrival in London, Churchill cabled to Roosevelt thanking him for his 'kindness in meeting my wishes by giving additional help to the Australian Air Force'.[4] The commitment by Roosevelt had been deliberately vague, both as to delivery times and types of aircraft. No matter. Evatt seemed to be largely satisfied with it, although he remained intent on obtaining an additional commitment of aircraft from Britain, particularly the heavy bombers that Roosevelt had been so cagey about. Churchill agreed with Portal that Evatt must not be given any heavy bombers from Britain. This was despite Evatt using his presence at a British cabinet meeting to remind Churchill and his colleagues of the sizeable Australian contribution to the bombing of Germany.[5] About 21 500 Australian airmen served in Britain during the war, of whom approximately a quarter were killed. Despite the fighting in the south-west Pacific, the flow of such men was accelerating as Evatt spoke, with more than 10 000 arriving in Britain between July 1943 and June 1944.[6]

Portal warned Churchill that Evatt was likely to use the Australian contribution as the basis for a 'moral claim for the supply of British heavy bombers'. He called on Churchill to resist such a claim, arguing that it would harm the British effort against Germany, be a blow to the morale of Bomber Command and make it more difficult for Britain to obtain heavy bombers from America. Portal also resented stories apparently put about by Evatt after his visit in 1942, that the Australian had scored a victory over the air ministry with the commitment of Spitfire squadrons, which Churchill had approved after overruling opposition from Portal. 'I am sure,' wrote Portal, 'that you would not wish the Australians to think that there is any difference between us about the allocation of British Heavy Bombers.' He asked Churchill to support him in telling Evatt that 'we cannot possibly give him any'. Churchill agreed, but suggested that the air ministry at least help Evatt get his American aircraft.[7]

As Portal had predicted, Evatt suggested to Churchill during a stay at Chequers that Britain make a symbolic commitment of squadrons to the Australian theatre, linking his request to the great increase in Australian aircrew for the war in Europe. Evatt followed this up with a letter on 2 July which proposed that Britain dispatch three additional squadrons to Australia: one Lancaster bomber, one Sunderland flying boat and one additional Spitfire squadron. Two of them could be Australian squadrons serving in Britain and one a British squadron. Evatt made clear that any such commitment would be subtracted from the aircraft promised to the RAAF from American sources, leaving Australia's net position unaffected. In an attempt to circumvent the expected opposition from Portal, Evatt did not put his request on an official level. Instead, he described it to Churchill as 'a personal unofficial suggestion to the Empire's leader, upon which you are left free to take the initiative if you feel you can make a favourable response'.[8]

Churchill still referred it to Portal, who remained adamant that no such commitment could be made. It would mean, he claimed, that there would be 'nothing left for Turkey, Portugal or Russia'. Of course, neither Portugal nor Turkey were at war, although Churchill hoped to draw them into it. As a way of satisfying Evatt, Portal suggested instead that Britain could include a Sunderland and a Spitfire squadron among the allocation that America had committed to Australia, provided that Washington reimbursed Britain with equivalent aircraft. Portal made this suggestion in the knowledge that the Americans were retreating already from Roosevelt's commitment, with General Arnold having refused to provide any heavy bombers for the RAAF expansion program.[9]

Evatt seems to have believed that his relationship with Churchill, the rough patches of which had been partly smoothed over by Robinson, would see him emerge victorious with more 'trophy' aircraft to flourish on his return. At least, that is what he assured Curtin on 8 July, declaring that the purpose of his London mission had been 'completely achieved' and that Australia's stocks stood high in the British capital.[10] After more than three weeks in London, he took off for Washington, where his wife was still recuperating, confident that his relationship with Churchill would result in the air ministry objections being overruled once again. But no word was forthcoming from London, while in Washington he found that Roosevelt's vague commitment of aircraft had been used by American officials as a means to dump unwanted planes on Australia.

Air Marshal Williams, Australia's air force representative in Washington, informed Evatt that the promised American aircraft were outmoded types rejected by the RAF and USAAF. Moreover, they included five more squadrons of dive-bombers than Australia had requested. The United States was discontinuing such units, and the RAF wanted no more of them. Williams pointed to the irony of Britain being allocated heavy bombers from America that it was only able to accept because there were Australian aircrew to operate them, while Australia received no bombers at all. Evatt's supposed victory had been transformed into a farce. Australia would receive a numerically strong force, but it would be so unbalanced that it would hardly be able to defend the continent, let alone project its power over the adjacent Pacific region. As Williams warned, it would be 'madness and a waste of valuable manpower' for Australia to accept such aircraft, which would allow for an air force that would be 'incapable of little other than attending merely to the passive defence of its own possessions'. He urged Evatt to take the matter up with Roosevelt, and perhaps even with Churchill.[11]

Evatt met with Roosevelt on 13 July, and followed up the meeting with a letter that accused American officials of betraying the 'broad and generous spirit' in which Roosevelt had made the commitment to give the RAAF 'a great striking power'. As Evatt pointed out to the president, the RAAF could hardly hope to have such an offensive capacity if it continued to lack heavy bombers, not one of which was included in the American commitment. Although Evatt claimed to be reasonably satisfied with the planes scheduled for delivery in 1943, he asked for the 1944 allotment, which was the great bulk of the planes, to be reconsidered in consultation with Williams. If that was done, the unwanted dive-bombers could be ditched and heavy bombers put in their place.[12] At the same time, he kept up the pressure on Churchill for a commitment of British squadrons, telling him on 14 July that he would shortly be leaving the United States and hoped that 'it will be possible for you to tell me soon what I can put into my kit for Australia'.[13]

Churchill was certainly keen to do something for Evatt. Although he had refused to safeguard Australia in the critical days of early 1942, Churchill now wished to restore the imperial links that had been worn so thin by neglect. Accordingly, he overruled the objections of Portal to giving Evatt his squadrons, citing as justification the 'high importance for the future of the British Commonwealth and Empire that we should be represented in the defence of Australia and the war in the Pacific'.[14] Although it was too late to defend Australia, which now stood secure behind a solid barrier of American air and naval power, Churchill recognised a perfect opportunity to increase the symbolic, but high-profile, British presence in the Pacific at minimal cost to Britain, while maintaining the flow of Australian aircrew for the bombing of Germany.

As Churchill pointed out to Portal, the token RAF Spitfire squadron sent out to Australia in late 1942 had 'played a part out of all proportion to the size of the unit'. He now suggested that another three RAF squadrons be dispatched to Australia, using 40 or 50 of the 945 fighter pilots in Britain for whom serviceable aircraft were not available. The pilots would not be missed in Britain, and neither would the aircraft, since Churchill proposed to ask the Americans to subtract an equivalent number of fighter aircraft from their allocation to Australia and send them instead to Britain. If Churchill's plan worked, Britain would establish a significant presence in the Pacific with eight Spitfire squadrons, four of them with British pilots, and all without diminishing the war effort against Germany. 'It is my duty,' intoned Churchill, 'to preserve goodwill between the Mother Country and this vast continent of Australia, inhabited by six million of our race and tongue.'[15] He soon found, though, that it took more than rhetoric to shift the air ministry.

The air minister, Sir Archibald Sinclair, continued to claim that the dispatch of the squadrons was 'quite indefensible' from a military point of view, while also questioning whether a commitment of additional RAF squadrons could be guaranteed to reap an additional political benefit for Britain.[16] Churchill's staff suggested a compromise to satisfy both Evatt and the air ministry while 'taking into account the political importance of carrying Australia along with us'.[17] While the wrangling went on, Evatt was about to board his ship at San Fransisco for the voyage home and was fretting at the lack of any answer from Churchill. He cabled again on 23 July, confiding to Churchill that he was 'anxiously hoping to hear from you'.[18] Evatt's ship would arrive back in the middle of the federal election campaign, the outcome of which was somewhat uncertain. If he could make a dockside announcement about more Spitfires, it might swing the election Labor's way. It would certainly elevate his own position within the party and the nation.

With Evatt's appeal in hand, Churchill once more assailed his air ministry for at least one or two more Spitfire squadrons in addition to the extra aircraft proposed by the ministry. As Churchill pointed out, his proposal was 'going less than halfway towards meeting the Australian requests' and would not include any of the Lancasters or Sunderlands that Evatt had requested.[19] Still the air ministry resisted, with Sinclair begging Churchill not to help Australia 'at the expense of the Royal Air Force squadrons now closely engaged in the Mediterranean with a more formidable enemy than the Japanese'.[20] Lord Cherwell, Churchill's scientific adviser, agreed that it was 'a pity to deprive ourselves of the most modern types of Spitfires when almost any fighter could cope with the Japanese Zeros', a remarkably ignorant assessment that would have been hotly disputed by Allied pilots who had experienced combat with the Japanese fighters. At the same time, while Cherwell acknowledged that Britain 'must try to make a good showing in Australia', he suggested that Evatt's anxiety was probably motivated by the need 'to have some trophies to announce before the election'.[21] Churchill, who apparently was convinced that the Labor government would be tossed out of office by the election,[22] suddenly saw a way of helping to ensure such an outcome by withholding Evatt's vote-catching election trophy.

On 1 August, after Evatt arrived back in Australia and had again implored Churchill to 'please let me know whether you can help me along the lines discussed',[23] Churchill suggested to Portal and Sinclair that he offer Evatt two Spitfire squadrons on condition that Australia provide their ground crew. 'Far better sentimental results will be produced in this,' Churchill argued, 'than by giving even a larger quantity of Spitfires and pilots without the Squadron personality.' Churchill also agreed not to make any offer to Evatt until after the Australian election was over. Given the personal hostility between Portal and Evatt, it was unlikely that the air ministry would agree to anything that might allow Evatt to retain power in Canberra. Churchill too would have been happy to see the end of the Labor government. In the meantime, he assured Evatt that he had been doing his best and hoped 'shortly to have something to report to you'.[24]

Evatt was probably more relieved to touch Australian soil after his dangerous trip than he was to receive Churchill's encouraging news. In fact, he had already exaggerated the success of his mission. In a national radio broadcast on 2 August, just nineteen days before the federal election, Evatt claimed that he had convinced Churchill and Roosevelt to increase assistance for Australia and they could 'rely absolutely upon Mr. Churchill's statement that unremitting pressure of an offensive character is being and will be employed against Japan'. Evatt also sketched out for his audience a secure and prosperous future, based upon Australia's development of a local aviation industry that would 'provide industrial leadership in the South-west Pacific, where there was already a population of 130 millions'. Indeed, Evatt suggested that Japan had done Australia a favour. Because of the conflict, the 'lazy peaceful islands in the Pacific have become acquainted with the latest aircraft, with the means of mechanised warfare, and the products of industrial production'. As a result, 'demands have been created, markets have been made possible, and Australia has the machinery and resources to supply the demand'.[25]

The election, though, was more about the past, with both sides arguing about their respective roles in defending Australia. Earlier in the year, the combative Labor MP Eddie Ward had alleged that the Menzies government had been planning, in effect, to concede to the Japanese all of Australia north of a line running from Brisbane to Adelaide, the so-called 'Brisbane Line', and to concentrate its forces in the Adelaide–Brisbane–Melbourne triangle. The accusation had provoked political uproar and prompted demands for Curtin to sack his robust minister. But Curtin allowed the issue to run its course, confident that it would help to convince the public that the defence of Australia was best left to the Labor Party. The issue had come to a head in June 1943 when opposition leader Arthur Fadden had moved a no-confidence motion in the Labor government. Although the motion was

AWM IMG02

With the New Zealand prime minister, Peter Fraser, in the background, Evatt watches Prime Minister John Curtin sign his name to the Australia–New Zealand Agreement in January 1944 that attempted, among other things, to restrict the United States to the north Pacific.

AWM 072967

In the wake of the assertive Australia–New Zealand Agreement, Curtin welcomes General Douglas MacArthur to Canberra in March 1944 while Shedden brings up the rear.

NLA

In the shadow of New York's skyscrapers in June 1943, Evatt prepares to broadcast from Anzac Square while America's first lady, Eleanor Roosevelt, looks on, posy in hand.

AWM 077684

At a dinner in March 1944 to mark the second anniversary of MacArthur's arrival, Army Minister Frank Forde chats to the impassive guest of honour while Curtin seems lost in thought, perhaps worrying about his forthcoming trip to London. Two of Curtin's closest supporters, the treasurer, Ben Chifley, and former prime minister, James Scullin, are seated on the far left. At right, Nelson Johnson (USA) and H.V. Evatt.

AWM UK2415

Australian airmen line up along the wings of a Lancaster bomber at their English airbase in December 1944, just part of the Australian contribution to the British bombing of Germany.

AWM IMG01

Still recuperating from his heart attack, Curtin amuses an almost deaf Billy Hughes during a reception in Canberra for the new governor-general, the Duke of Gloucester (*right*), in early 1945.

AWM 128857

The first of the locally built Lincoln bombers that were meant to underpin Australia's postwar ambitions in the south-west Pacific.

AWM P02018.382

Outside the ruins of the Reichstag in July 1945, Churchill surveys the damage caused by his bombing campaign and the Soviet battle for Berlin.

NLA

Curtin's colleagues line up outside parliament on 6 July 1945 to await the passing of the prime minister's coffin. His soon-to-be-anointed successor, Ben Chifley, is second from the left.

AWM 40969

On board USS *Missouri* in Tokyo Harbour on 2 September 1945, MacArthur (*far left*) watches as General Sir Thomas Blamey adds his signature to the surrender documents.

AWM 112689

Until next time. Two children fly the flag outside Melbourne's Shrine of Remembrance as the last of the crowd leaves a memorial service on 16 August 1945 to mark the end of the Pacific war.

lost by one vote, Curtin immediately announced that he would be calling an election so that the people could pass their own judgment on the performance of his government and the past performance and present disunity of his opponents.[26]

When Australians went to the polls on 21 August, they gave the government, and Curtin's leadership, a resounding endorsement, with twice as many Labor MPs as conservatives being returned to the new parliament. Contrary to Churchill's expectation, Labor now had majorities in both houses of parliament for the first time since 1916.[27] In the wake of the election, the 80-year-old Billy Hughes resigned from the leadership of the UAP, while Menzies, who had been denounced by Hughes as 'the man behind the scenes in every intrigue, the fountain head of every whispering campaign, the destroyer of unity,'[28] took over as leader and began the laborious task of constructing a credible opposition.

The Labor campaign benefited from Evatt's timely return and his optimistic speeches, even though there was no confirmation from Churchill that would allow Evatt to announce a specific commitment of additional British Spitfire squadrons. Although Sinclair had agreed to Churchill's proposal on 13 August, Churchill maintained his silence during the election campaign in the vain hope that the Labor government might yet be tipped out of power. Evatt might have kept up the pressure on Churchill but he had been laid low by a bout of pneumonia. It was not until the day after the election that Evatt again cabled to Churchill asking for 'the results of your plans in relation to aircraft, as to which naturally I am still most anxious'. Only after the election results became clear did Churchill finally inform Evatt of Britain's commitment of two additional Spitfire squadrons.[29]

Instead of the three complete squadrons and ground crew — one Lancaster, one Sunderland and one Spitfire — that had been requested by Evatt, Britain would send just two Spitfire squadrons without their ground crew. Evatt's request for an increased flow of Spitfire aircraft to keep all the squadrons in the air was refused, which meant that an additional Spitfire squadron that Australia had formed for operations in New Guinea had to be disbanded. Despite this setback, Evatt assured Curtin that 'from the highest political and imperial angle, the result is eminently satisfactory'.[30] As in

1942, Evatt had been fobbed off with a largely symbolic contribution from Britain.

Churchill's half-hearted contributions to Australia's effort in the Pacific war reflected not only his view of how the war should be fought but also his view of Britain's postwar place in the world. While some British politicians and officials wanted to have the empire at the core of Britain's postwar political life, other voices called for Britain to concentrate on Europe and the Middle East. Churchill took a longer view of Britain's place in the world than many of his contemporaries. As a young man he had fought personally to seize and hold various parts of the empire. But the experience did not blind him to the fact that Britain's future greatness might reside, not with the empire, but in its strategic position off the coast of Europe and in its links with the United States. According to this scenario, the empire would buttress Britain's position in the world rather than provide its foundation. The war had certainly shown that the far-flung empire could not be held in its entirety forever.[31] As for the empire in the Far East, Churchill was content to leave the Pacific to the Americans. Despite prewar Anglo–American disputes about the sovereignty of various Pacific islands, Churchill now maintained that it 'should be the basis of our policy that we would not object to any American proposals to acquire further bases in this area'.[32]

While the question of America acquiring bases in the Pacific was of little moment to Churchill, there was a substantial body of British opinion that was less sanguine about America's territorial ambitions, particularly when they impinged on Britain's own ambitions for civil aviation. It was in civil aviation that Britain's empire bulked large, since its widely scattered colonies and dominions offered the landing fields for a web of British air routes that could cover the globe and undercut the American dominance in the manufacture of civil aircraft. The empire also offered a market that might underpin the postwar resurgence of the British aviation industry. As one junior minister observed in June 1943, a parliamentary debate on civil aviation had made it 'quite clear that the House in general, and the Conservative Party in particular, are taking a real and lively interest in the Empire'.[33] For all its wartime differences with Britain, Australia shared these views about the postwar importance of civil aviation and the part that the empire could play in boosting Britain's place in that industry. But only if Britain was able to produce aircraft that could compete with the currently superior American types.

As W. S. Robinson advised British officials in July 1943, Australia's future survival 'depends more on strength in the air than on any other factor'. In a widely circulated memorandum that Robinson claimed was in line with Evatt's views, the Australian businessman called for Australia to become a manufacturer of aircraft rather than just a fabricator of aircraft designed elsewhere or a purchaser of machine tools manufactured elsewhere. It would have to do so if it was to avoid 'quick death and destruction' in the future. Robinson reminded British ministers that there were

1 100 000 000 of the coloured races lying above Australia ... Today the ability of our enemies to produce and utilise the light Metals is fortunately limited. But the powers of the colonial races in this direction are capable of almost unlimited expansion within a single generation.

To ensure its future security, Robinson argued that Australia also would have to establish a defence perimeter some 2500 kilometres from northern Australia covering Singapore, the Netherlands East Indies, New Guinea and the adjacent island chains. According to Robinson, such an extended defence perimeter was necessary to prevent 'those opposed to our ideals of life and to our ways of living' from establishing air bases. It would also encompass those areas 'to which Australia and New Zealand must have free economic access if not economic direction and in the Government and control of which they must have a definite voice'.[34]

Like Robinson, Curtin also wanted Britain, America and Australia to combine as the 'policemen of the Pacific', taking over the defence of those islands that the controlling European powers had been unable to defend against Japan. He confided to journalists that he was even prepared to consider a postwar American military role in Australia's New Guinea territory.[35] But he would have to contend with a strand of isolationism that remained strong within the Australian population. According to the head of the British military mission, General Dewing, the support for isolationism was fuelled by the activities of 'Anti-British Irish Catholics and [the] worst elements in the Trades Union organisation'.[36] Despite Dewing's fears, this isolationist tendency had little influence on the formulation of Australian foreign policy, which was directed overwhelmingly at preventing a repetition of Pearl Harbor and the emergence of a future invasion threat to Australia. Moreover, as Dewing assured a relieved General Brooke during a visit to London in July 1943, the Australians were 'still above all desirous of remaining in the Commonwealth'.[37]

It was the fear of a future invasion that lay behind Robinson's call for Australia to dominate from the air the potentially threatening territories to its north. Such domination would also allow the resources of these territories to be exploited on a vast scale. Robinson painted a picture of undeveloped regions abundant with 'tropical products, plus oil, timber, water power, minerals and metals' that would 'provide opportunities for the enterprising Australian'. If Britain, America and Australia combined to exploit these resources, they could produce prosperity 'great enough to attract the millions of white people we so urgently require'. Seizing upon Churchill's vision of an English-speaking alliance, Robinson called on the 'White Races' to put aside their national rivalry and combine their aeronautical resources to ensure the 'future safety of the world'. While Australia would prefer to buy British aircraft, Robinson warned that it would only do so if they fitted Australia's needs and were competitive with American ones.[38] Qantas Empire Airways chief Hudson Fysh claimed in a talk with Beaverbrook at London's RAF club that although the Australian people were keen to develop air links with the empire, the government took a broader view. Qantas certainly wanted to resume the route to London, Fysh said, but also wanted to fly to China, the Soviet Union, and across the Pacific to North America.[39] Australian needs were arising in ways that would have been unthinkable even two years before.

As these various comments suggested, Australia wanted to play a greater and more independent role in the postwar world, preferably within the empire but, if necessary, outside of it. As it happened, this did not necessarily conflict with Britain's thinking on the shape of the postwar world. Even Churchill conceded that, as a declining imperial power, Britain should hive off those defence burdens capable of being borne by friendly powers such as America. In the Pacific, Australia could relieve Britain's burden by defending neighbouring parts of its battered empire, while India could perform a similar service in the Indian Ocean. Together they might conceal the relative decline in Britain's worldwide power. Ernest Bevin suggested that Indian forces should be built up to the point where they could provide protection for the arc of British territories that stretched from Burma to the Persian Gulf. With Russia being a possible postwar threat to Britain, India could also provide a base from which to threaten the Russian 'underbelly'.[40]

While Britain was keen to have Australian help in defending its empire, it was not keen to have Australian interference in the running of that empire, particularly when the Labor governments of Australia and New Zealand harboured disturbing views about the future of the European colonies. According to some, Australia was salaciously eyeing the Netherlands East Indies, Portuguese Timor, the New Hebrides, the Solomon Islands and New Caledonia, while there was talk of dissolving the European empires altogether.[41] Britain might have ignored such talk had Roosevelt not also been continuing his personal pressure in the same direction. According to Lord Cranborne, soon to succeed Attlee as dominions secretary, Britain somehow had to involve the dominions in the administration of the colonies so that they would cease to regard them as Britain's private property and instead come to regard the empire as 'an inter-dependent whole'. Cranborne claimed that the Australians were 'particularly bad about this. They want all the advantages of the Imperial connection without any responsibilities.'[42]

Apart from the opposition to his ideas within Whitehall, the problem with Cranborne's scenario for a new cooperative empire was that it ignored the relative decline of Britain's military and naval might. Historically, Britain's strength had largely guaranteed Australia's continuing adherence to the empire. Now that this strength had waned in the Pacific, there was no telling how much longer Australia would stick close to Britain. As General Dewing warned Whitehall, the future of Anglo–Australian relations would be 'greatly influenced by the extent to which [Britain] can within the next year or so, demonstrate in a manner which will get across to all Australians, her ability and desire to give practical help to Australia in the war against

Japan'.[43] However, there remained serious differences between Churchill and his chiefs of staff, and between the chiefs themselves, as to how Britain should contribute to the Pacific war.

It was only now that serious attention was directed towards the problem of motivating British service personnel to fight in the Pacific once the war with Germany was done and at a time when many of their colleagues would have been demobilised. British ministers recalled with trepidation the unrest within the British army following the First World War and the refusal of the troops to consider Churchill's plan to suppress the Bolsheviks in Russia. They worried that similar problems might arise once Germany was defeated such that, if British troops refused to fight, the empire might well be lost forever. This was the fear of the India secretary, Leo Amery, who together with the war secretary, Sir James Grigg, urged their colleagues to prepare the British people for the need to also fight Japan to the finish. He urged that servicemen fighting Japan once Germany was defeated should be rewarded with better wages and conditions. Since many of them would be Indian, the morale of the Indian army also needed attention.[44] The British people had to realise, said Grigg, that their country's 'destiny as a great Imperial power in the future as in the past, demands that we British should recover, stabilize and develop our Imperial possessions in the East'.[45]

As war secretary in 1919, Churchill had had the difficult task of keeping the lid on unrest within army ranks during demobilisation, and the memory bulked large when considering the future demobilisation. Churchill was also worried about Britain's discreditable war record in the Far East. With the Japanese pressing hard on India's eastern flank, Churchill considered sending his foreign secretary, Anthony Eden, off to India as viceroy in June 1943, lamenting to Eden 'how bad it would be if after doing so well in the West we lost India and boggled the war against Japan'.[46] Not that Churchill had been converted to the 'Pacific first' strategy. Indeed, when the invasion of Sicily went off much better than anticipated, he moved quickly to argue for the Allies to invade the Italian mainland rather than divert resources to the war against Japan. The British and Americans had been unable to agree on the next step in the Mediterranean campaign. With Sicily captured, a decision was urgently needed and Churchill proposed that he meet with Roosevelt in

Quebec in early August. As Oliver Harvey observed, Churchill was 'anxious to pin the Americans down before their well-known dislike of European operations except across the Channel gets the better of them again, and they pull out their landing craft and send their ships off to the Pacific'.[47] Such a meeting would also allow Churchill and Roosevelt to agree on the future British role against Japan.

Churchill had announced that there would be a partial demobilisation in Britain after the war against Germany, allowing part of the armed forces and the munitions industry to return to peacetime activities. But Britain could not plan for this until it knew exactly what its contribution would be to the war in the Far East. Already Churchill was hoping that he would not be held to his promise to send a great army against Japan. As he informed MacArthur on 20 July, there simply would not be the shipping 'to carry more than a portion of our total military forces to the Far East'.[48] So Churchill began to scale down his grand promise to devote Britain's 'whole resources to the defeat of Japan'.[49] Instead, he hoped Russia would declare war against Japan and allow its territory to be used for a great air onslaught against Japanese towns and cities. Perhaps also at the back of his mind was the thought of the atomic bomb, the American development of which he had so recently approved.

In a devious strategy to obtain American approval for British plans in Europe, Churchill intended to use the Quebec conference to raise the Pacific question himself rather than have the Americans force him to face it, as they had at the previous Washington conference. Churchill confided to his chiefs of staff that the Americans would be 'gratified at the interest we are taking in the Japanese war and at our making earnest preparations to undertake it'. More importantly, his 'introduction of this topic as a major issue' at Quebec 'will perhaps make other nearer decisions more easy'.[50] He had been criticised by the American press during his previous trip for not taking the Pacific war seriously.[51] Now, by raising the Pacific war himself, he could dodge this criticism and keep the Americans onside over Europe.

Churchill did not intend to translate the coming talk at Quebec into greater resources for the Pacific, at least not until Germany was defeated. In fact, by capitalising on the Sicilian success and invading the Italian mainland, any major operation in Burma would have to be postponed. The amphibious shipping and tank-landing ships would be tied to the Mediterranean and, given the cross-Channel operations planned for 1944, might never leave the European theatre. Churchill wanted more action from the forces already committed to India, rather than wanting to commit more forces to the region.

What Britain lacked in substance in the Far East would be made up for with symbolism. This was probably part of the reasoning behind an unsuccessful attempt by Churchill to have Wavell appointed as governor-general of Australia, where the unsuccessful general might oversee MacArthur from the comfort of Yarralumla, while also providing for Australia a decorated token of British military might.[52] However, the plan came unstuck. When Churchill suggested it to his dominions secretary, Labour leader Clem Attlee, he was reminded that dominion prime ministers 'nowadays advise on appointment to [the] Post of Governor General' rather than having them imposed from London. Undeterred by this, Churchill was not about to let Australian sensitivities block his plan to shelve Wavell and planned to 'enlist Evatt, who is in the most friendly mood, behind the proposition'. He petulantly informed Attlee that there was 'no harm in my asking Curtin what he thinks and I will do so to-day'.[53] Churchill's hopes were dashed when Curtin refused to accept Wavell, partly for fear of upsetting MacArthur, who was determined to keep British military representatives, even superannuated ones, at arm's length.[54]

As well as this, Curtin wanted a 'Royal' replacement for the Duke of Kent, who had been appointed governor-general in 1939 but who had been killed before taking up the post.[55] Although Labor Party policy stipulated that the governor-general should be Australian, Curtin wanted a royal appointment to allay public suspicions about his government's supposed hostility towards Britain and also to repair some of the damage to the Anglo–Australian relationship. The choice of governor-general was heavy with symbolism. Choosing an Australian would confirm how much the dominion's political life had matured during the war, and would have helped to re-establish its relations with the great powers on a more equal footing. With a British official in Yarralumla, it was no wonder that American leaders were confused about Australia's constitutional status, regarding it as a colony in principle and practice.

When Curtin rejected Wavell, the question of the governor-general was left in abeyance. Wavell was made viceroy of India while Churchill decided who might take his place and provide more forceful and vigorous leadership as supreme commander of a newly created South East Asia Command. While Churchill was not planning any time soon to increase the forces available to the new supreme commander, he needed the appointment to provide the appearance of British activity, while also establishing British authority over the American and Chinese forces using India as a base.[56] As Churchill informed his chiefs of staff on 26 July, he wanted a 'young, competent soldier, well trained in war, to become a Supreme Commander and to re-examine the whole problem of the war on this front so as to infuse vigour and audacity into the operations'. Despite the limited resources, pessimistic planning must be avoided, warned Churchill, for it would 'rightly excite the deepest suspicions in the United States that we are only playing and dawdling with the war in this theatre'.[57]

Once the supreme commander was appointed, Churchill wanted to plan a bold stroke against Japan using Britain's advantage in sea and air power to strike at a distant point such as the northern tip of Sumatra, rather than pursue Wavell's preferred option of pushing the Japanese back through the jungles of Burma. The plan was rather similar to Churchill's strategically unsound scheme for an invasion of Norway, which he periodically presented to the chiefs of staff for approval only to have it turned down. They were just as scathing about his Sumatran plan. During a meeting of the defence committee on 28 July, the chiefs of staff pointed out that such a stroke would have to be followed through in Malaya to capture the Japanese airfields that would otherwise dominate the British landing. This would, in turn, make necessary the recapture of Singapore. And resources were simply not sufficient to do all this until Germany had been defeated.[58] Game and set to the chiefs of staff. Or so they might have thought. But Churchill persisted. A week later, at a meeting of London's largely moribund Pacific war council, he was still speaking of launching 'a stroke more adventurous and further flung' than an offensive in lower Burma.[59]

The Chinese were pressing Britain for details of their much-mooted offensive in Burma. As Brooke observed after a meeting on 3 August with a 'very inquisitive' Chinese representative, this was a 'delicate problem' as 'there was a good deal to conceal from him'.[60] There was still no agreement with the Americans as to who should be the supreme commander of the area, and Churchill and his chiefs were increasingly at loggerheads over the strategy that the commander should pursue. As well, with Mussolini having abdicated on 25 July, and the new Italian government seeking an armistice, the portents for an Italian offensive looked promising. But any such Allied offensive would have implications for their future operations against Japan, as well as the prospects for a cross-Channel invasion of France. Churchill hoped that it could all be worked out in Quebec, with Roosevelt having finally succumbed to Churchill's pressure for an August meeting. Once again, Churchill and his chiefs of staff clambered aboard the *Queen Mary*, sailing down the Clyde for Canada on 5 August, with Churchill being determined to keep American attention concentrated on Europe while, in return, he was prepared to settle the nature and extent of the British contribution to the defeat of Japan.

NOTES

[1] Gilbert, *Finest Hour*, pp. 430–3.

[2] Minute, Churchill to Brooke, 21 May 1943, PREM 3/143/10, PRO.

[3] B. H. Liddell Hart, *History of the Second World War*, London, 1973, Chap. 24.

[4] Cable, Churchill to Roosevelt, 16 June 1943, PREM 3/150/8, PRO.

[5] Minute, Portal to Churchill, 16 June 1943, PREM 3/150/8, PRO.

[6] John Robertson, *Australia at War 1939–1945*, Melbourne, 1981, Appendices 2 & 3.

[7] Minute, Portal to Churchill, 16 June 1943, PREM 3/150/8, PRO.

[8] Letter, Evatt to Churchill, 2 July 1943, PREM 3/150/8, PRO.

[9] Minute, Portal to Churchill, 6 July 1943, PREM 3/150/8, PRO.

[10] Cable, Evatt to Curtin, 8 July 1943, CRS A5954, Box 474, NAA.

[11] Letters, Williams to Evatt, both 11 July 1943, CRS A3300, Box 258, NAA.

[12] Letter, Evatt to Roosevelt, 13 July 1943, *DAFP*, Vol. 6, Doc. 244.

[13] Cable, Evatt to Churchill, 14 July 1943, PREM 3/150/8, PRO.

[14] Minute, Churchill to Sinclair and Portal, 12 July 1943, PREM 3/150/8, PRO.

[15] ibid.

[16] Minute, Sinclair to Churchill, 19 July 1943, PREM 3/150/8, PRO.

[17] Minute, Hollis to Churchill, 21 July 1943, Draft cable, Churchill to Evatt, undated, and Minute, Hollis to Churchill, 22 July 1943, PREM 3/150/8, PRO.

[18] Cable, Evatt to Churchill, 23 July 1943, PREM 3/150/8, PRO.

[19] Minute, Churchill to Sinclair, 23 July 1943, PREM 3/150/8, PRO.

[20] Minute, Sinclair to Churchill, 26 July 1943, PREM 3/150/8, PRO.

21 Even the Spitfires could be sorely tested by the Japanese fighters. For a description of one such engagement between Spitfires and Zeros, in which eight Spitfires were destroyed, see Odgers, *Royal Australian Air Force 1943–1945*, pp. 46–50; Minute, Cherwell to Churchill, 29 July 1943, PREM 3/150/8, PRO.

22 When Australia's new minister to the United States, Sir Frederick Eggleston, met with Roosevelt in November 1944, the president told him that Churchill had predicted Curtin's certain downfall in the 1943 election. Letter, Eggleston to Evatt, 21 November 1944, CRS A5954, Box 293, NAA.

23 Cable, Evatt to Churchill and Note, K.H. to Churchill, 1 August 1943, PREM 3/150/8, PRO.

24 Minute, Churchill to Sinclair and Portal, 1 August 1943, and Cable, Churchill to Evatt, 2 August 1943, PREM 3/150/8, PRO.

25 *Sydney Morning Herald*, 2 August 1943.

26 Day, *John Curtin*, pp. 503–7. For discussion of the 'Brisbane Line' controversy, see Paul Burns, *The Brisbane Line Controversy: Political Opportunism versus National Security, 1942–45*, Allen & Unwin, Sydney, 1998.

27 During the election, Curtin had flown to Perth in the Lancaster bomber that was visiting Australia on its sales flight from Britain. It was only the second flight that the nervous Curtin had ever taken in an aircraft. Day, *John Curtin*, pp. 508–15.

28 Fitzhardinge, *The Little Digger 1914–1952*, p. 661.

29 In thanking Churchill for the belated commitment, Evatt asked that he ensure Portal provided the latest type of Spitfire 'tropicalised' for conditions in the Pacific. See PREM 3/150/8, PRO.

30 Letter, Curtin to MacArthur, 4 September 1943, and Message, Evatt to Curtin, 28 August 1943, CRS A5954, Box 231, NAA.

31 Note by Churchill, 10 June 1943, CAB 66/37, W.P. (43)233, PRO.

32 War Cabinet Conclusions, Confidential Annex, 13 April 1943, CAB 65/38, W.M. (43)53, PRO.

33 Letter, Emrys-Evans to Wakehurst, 4 June 1943, ADD. MS. 58243, Emrys-Evans Papers, BL.

34 Note by Robinson sent to various British ministers in July 1943, BBK D214, Beaverbrook Papers, HLRO.

35 Background briefing, 5 July 1943, MS 4675, Smith Papers, NLA.

36 Report by Dewing, 20 April 1943, enclosed in letter to Ismay, 18 November 1943, IV/Dew/3/2d, Ismay Papers, KC.

37 Alanbrooke diary, 7 July 1943, in Danchev and Todman (eds), *War Diaries*, p. 426.

38 Note by Robinson sent to various British ministers in July 1943, BBK D214, Beaverbrook Papers, HLRO.

39 Interview with Hudson Fysh, 15 July 1943, BBK D/214, Beaverbrook Papers, HLRO.

40 Draft war cabinet paper by Bevin, 21 June 1943, BEVN 2/4, Bevin Papers, CC.

41 Cable, Dixon to External Affairs Department, 25 March 1943, and Cable, Evatt to Dixon, 31 March 1943, CRS A3300/262, NAA. Evatt informed Dixon that the war had 'demonstrated that control or supervision of control over neighbouring territories will be vital to the security of Australia as well as to other Pacific countries; and we must have a full say in the determination of these questions'.

42 Letter, Cranborne to Emrys-Evans, 18 March 1943, ADD. MS. 58240, Emrys-Evans Papers, BL.

43 Letter, Dewing to Ismay, 18 November 1943, enclosing a report on 'Australia in Relation to the War', 20 April 1943, IV/Dew/3/2b, Ismay Papers, KC.

44 Memorandum by Amery, 5 June 1943, CAB 66/37, W.P. (43)232, PRO.

45 Memorandum by Grigg, 14 June 1943, CAB 66/37, W.P. (43)239, PRO.

46 Memorandum by Churchill, 21 July 1943, CAB 66/39, W.P. (43)327, PRO; Harvey diary, 7 June 1943, ADD. MS. 56399, Harvey Papers, BL.

47 Harvey diary, 16 July 1943, ADD. MS. 56399, Harvey Papers, BL.

48 Letter, Churchill to MacArthur, 20 July 1943, PREM 3/158/5, PRO.

49 See Day, 'Promise and Performance'.

50 Minute, Churchill to Ismay, 19 July 1943, PREM 3/143/8, PRO.

51 Letter, Somerville to MacQuarrie, 22 July 1943, ADD. MS. 50143, Somerville Papers, BL.

52 According to Oliver Harvey, Churchill was 'determined to oust Wavell from his command in India and Burma. He has never thought highly of [Wavell] and he says he is shocked at the lifelessness of our command there. He wants to put Wavell on the shelf as Governor General of Australia ...' Harvey diary, 30 May 1943, ADD. MS. 56399, Harvey Papers, BL.

[53] Cables, Churchill to Attlee, 29 and 31 May 1943, and Attlee to Churchill, 30 May 1943, PREM 3/53/5, PRO.

[54] The British intelligence agent, Gerald Wilkinson, had been attached to MacArthur's headquarters from his time in the Philippines and came to Australia with MacArthur in March 1942. When Wilkinson later left for consultations in London, MacArthur refused to allow him to return, despite pleas from Evatt and Churchill. Evatt had assured Wilkinson that he and Curtin would combine to get Wilkinson reattached to MacArthur's headquarters, but to no avail. General Dewing, the head of the British military mission to Australia, fared little better, with MacArthur according him only the most limited access to his headquarters. See War Journal, 23 and 29 July 1943, WILK 1/2, Wilkinson Papers, CC; Talk with Dewing, 30 June 1943, CRS M100, 'June 1943', NAA; and Documents in CRS A5954, Box 463, NAA.

[55] Cable, Curtin to Churchill, 7 June 1943, MS 2852/4/22/28, Gowrie Papers, NLA.

[56] Minute, Amery to Churchill, 27 April 1943, PREM 3/53/1, PRO; Edwards diary, 22 May 1943, REDW 1/5, Edwards Papers, CC; See also PREM 3/154/1, PRO.

[57] Minute, Churchill to Ismay, 26 July 1943, PREM 3/143/8, PRO.

[58] Minutes of Defence Committee (Operations), 28 July 1943, PREM 3/143/8, PRO.

[59] Cable, Bruce to Curtin, 6 August 1943, CRS M100, 'August 1943', NAA.

[60] Alanbrooke diary, 3 August 1943, in Danchev and Todman (eds), *War Diaries*, p. 435.

THIRTY-EIGHT

'we mean business'

On 6 August 1943, as the *Queen Mary* ploughed through the heavy seas of the north Atlantic towards Canada, Churchill and his chiefs of staff prepared for the coming conference with the Americans. Allaying the American concern about the British effort in Burma was high on their agenda. To this end, Churchill suggested appointing Lord Louis Mountbatten as supreme commander in South-East Asia. Although Mountbatten, Britain's head of combined operations, was not Churchill's first choice for the position, he was perfect for the task. As the young cousin of the King, he would be a dashing commander, projecting an image of daring onto what Churchill angrily described as 'this decayed Indian scene'.[1] A supreme command under British control would also debar the Americans from independent action within India and the adjacent British colonies.[2]

However, as Mountbatten would find to his dismay, he would have no more resources than Wavell for pursuing his allotted task. His war experience up until then had given little indication that he was even capable of fulfilling it.[3] Mountbatten had been a destroyer captain before being elevated to chief of combined operations, in which position he had supervised the disastrous commando raid on Dieppe in August 1942. To make this royal figurehead militarily effective would obviously be a problem, as General Brooke acknowledged when he observed that Mountbatten would 'require a very efficient Chief of Staff to pull him through'.[4] The most important consideration, though, was not Mountbatten's relative lack of qualifications but, as Churchill wrote, 'whether the Americans liked the idea'. His appointment would also, Churchill argued, 'command public interest and approval ...'[5]

The second strand of Churchill's plan for the Far East featured the rather eccentric figure of Brigadier Orde Wingate, who had led his so-called long-range penetration group into Japanese-occupied Burma in February 1943, where he had launched sudden guerrilla attacks on the Japanese lines of communication before being driven back into India. Wingate had arrived in London on the day of Churchill's departure for Quebec and was peremptorily ordered to join the *Queen Mary* along with the rest of the two hundred-strong British delegation. Churchill hoped to obtain American approval for Wingate's dramatic but low-cost operations and thereby cancel the major offensive that the Americans wanted the British to mount in Burma. Churchill also planned to put forward his scheme to capture the tip of north Sumatra, disputing his military advisers' argument that it would have to lead on to an invasion of Malaya.[6]

Although the Americans did not want the British to take a major part in the Pacific, they had expressed concern about the lacklustre campaign against the Japanese in Burma, which they believed was threatening the Chinese war effort and allowing Japan to concentrate its forces against the Americans in the Pacific. Washington suspected, not without cause, that Britain sought the recovery of its colonial territories more than the final defeat of Japan. If this suspicion was not allayed, the Americans would divert even more resources away from Europe to the Pacific. Accordingly, Churchill instructed his chiefs of staff to reach agreement with him on proposed operations against the Japanese so they could present a united front at Quebec and convince the Americans 'that we mean business'.[7] But the differences between Churchill and his advisers were too deep to be bridged.

Britain had sizeable forces in India but communication problems prevented them going into action against the Japanese on a large scale. Churchill wanted a bold stroke against Japan but could not provide the means to launch it. As he was preparing to meet with the Americans, an outbreak of serious flooding in India made a British offensive in Burma that much more difficult. Even without the impediment of the flooding, the major land offensive that the Americans and Chinese were urging upon the British would take all the forces in India and possibly require forces and equipment to be sent from Europe as well. Hence Churchill's idea of a limited but dramatic attack on northern Sumatra using a minimal number of troops and landing craft. From there, argued Churchill, the British would be able to bomb the Japanese at Singapore, which seems to have been the extent of his vision for the operation. He had no clear idea as to where the British would go once they had secured their lodgment in Sumatra. To his chagrin, his advisers would only countenance such an operation if it were mounted with sufficient forces and within the context of an overall strategic plan that made military sense.[8] For nearly two years this fruitless debate would go on, later prompting General Ismay to predict that the 'waffling' over Britain's Far Eastern strategy would be 'one of the black spots in the record of the British Higher Direction of War'.[9]

Although Brooke had been dreading the Quebec conference, several major points of contention with the Americans were settled prior to the conference convening. Along with his daughter Mary, Churchill had travelled by train to Roosevelt's country home at Hyde Park on the Hudson River. There the two leaders agreed that the Americans could command the coming cross-Channel invasion while Roosevelt accepted Mountbatten as supreme commander for the new South East Asia command. They also agreed to make the development of an atomic bomb a joint project of the two countries. Back in Quebec on 15 August, the two leaders relayed the gist of their agreements to their respective military chiefs and caught up with the state of the discussions on future Allied strategy for both Europe and the Far East. To the relief of the British, the Americans had agreed that Germany must still be defeated prior to the final victory over Japan. Over the following days, the chiefs and their political masters also agreed to press on with the planned invasion of Italy, in which they had good reason to expect Italian support. They also confirmed the cross-Channel invasion of France as the major operation for 1944, despite Churchill being nervous about its chances and wanting his chiefs to have plans ready for an invasion of Norway as an alternative.[10]

As for the Far East, British plans for the war against Japan remained a matter of conjecture. British military planners, for want of something better, continued to favour a large-scale offensive in Burma. Churchill, for want of something easier, continued to favour the capture of northern Sumatra while Wingate's guerrilla force was let loose in northern Burma to link up with the Chinese in Yunnan. Churchill was deliberately vague as to what would follow the British capture of northern Sumatra, while insisting that it need not be the first stage in the recapture of Singapore. Far from it, he claimed, warning that

Singapore would be regarded by the Americans as a purely British target and it is certainly divergent from the main line of advance into China. It is more probable that Singapore will be recovered at the peace table than during the war. For the present it should be ruled out altogether ...[11]

Churchill's disclaimer does not ring true. He was obsessed with the disgrace of Singapore's surrender and was determined that it be forcefully redressed. If he could win support for his Sumatra operation, the case for an attack on Malaya and Singapore could be argued afresh and with much more strength. Indeed, the attraction for Churchill of north Sumatra was that it would bring Singapore within the range of British bombers.[12]

British military planners had already proposed to the Americans the recapture of Singapore instead of Rangoon, claiming that it would 'electrify the Eastern world and have an immense psychological effect on the Japanese'. The Americans, who were intent on recapturing the Philippines and redressing their own disgrace, pressed for an Allied commitment to defeat Japan within twelve months of Germany's surrender. Otherwise, the Americans warned, the Allies would face the 'serious hazard that the war against Japan will not, in fact, be won by the United Nations'. Presumably they feared that a prolonged war against Japan would see public opinion in Allied countries force a compromise peace in the Pacific. Hence the need for a relatively swift victory against Japan once Germany was subdued. Hence the need also to have others share the burden of the fighting, with both Britain and the United States seeking to use dominion forces in their favoured campaigns.[13]

Despite the need for a swift victory, no agreement was reached at Quebec as to how Britain would contribute to such an outcome. With Churchill still fixed on his Sumatra operation, he was keen to ensure that his chiefs would not commit Britain to any alternative favoured by the Americans. Accordingly, he warned them not to make any agreement about the Pacific war, threatening if they did so that he would refuse to take any responsibility for it and would refer it to the war cabinet for decision upon their return to London.[14] The threat worked. Churchill was able to report to his colleagues in London that 'all difficulties have been smoothed away except that the question of the exact form of our amphibious activities in the Bay of Bengal has been left over for further study'. This did not stop him from claiming in a radio broadcast at the conclusion of the conference that its deliberations had been largely directed towards 'heating and inflaming the war against Japan'. Exhausted after the conference, Churchill took a few days' rest fishing for trout in the Canadian mountains before heading south by train to accept an honorary degree from Harvard University.[15]

After seven weeks away, Churchill returned to London on 20 September, content that he had achieved at least some of his goals. Mountbatten's appointment had been approved, and he had committed Britain to playing a 'full and fair' part in the war against Japan once Germany was defeated. He had been careful not to specify what this part would be and, once back in London, he continued to plan for a substantial demobilisation of British forces once the European war was won. As for European commitments, Churchill feared that the planned cross-Channel invasion could meet stiff German resistance and degenerate into the static trench warfare of the First World War. Nevertheless, the invasion was agreed upon for May 1944, with the proviso that it could be called off if Germany was believed to have sufficient divisions available in France to counter it. Only the Sumatra operation remained undecided, with Roosevelt siding with the British chiefs of staff and pointing out to Churchill, without success, that an attack on Sumatra 'would be heading away from the main direction of our advance to Japan'.[16] Despite division over this issue, Churchill had succeeded once again in committing America to Europe while convincing Roosevelt of his sincerity in the Far East. As Admiral Pound observed during the talks, the Americans seemed 'very gratified by the interest which we were taking in Far Eastern operations'.[17]

While Australian forces were included in the calculations made by both British and American planners for the Pacific war, its representatives were not invited to the discussions at Quebec, although Chinese and Canadian representatives were included in some of the talks. When news of this reached Canberra, Evatt cabled on 24 August to the high commissioner in Canada, Sir William Glasgow, instructing that he 'should appear in the picture as representing Australia' as it was 'most embarrassing for Canada and China to appear included whereas Australia makes no showing at all'. It was not only appearances that had to be kept up. Evatt also wanted Glasgow to report on what decisions had been taken, although he had no illusions that Australia would be consulted by Churchill or Roosevelt prior to those decisions being taken. In fact, his cable reached Glasgow on the last day of the conference, with the Americans leaving after lunch for Washington. Glasgow still did what he could to satisfy Evatt, calling upon Churchill and telling him of Evatt's cable. Unconcerned, Churchill refused to inform him of the decisions that had been reached, promising to provide them instead to a meeting of the Pacific war council in Washington.[18]

The Australian government accepted Churchill's public declaration about the Pacific war being fought with equal vigour, little realising that it would result in a largely cosmetic change at the top. The promise of future British activity in the Pacific seemed to be borne out by Churchill announcing the appointment of a general to MacArthur's headquarters, with Churchill telling Evatt that the appointment was 'important in view of my being drawn increasingly into the war against Japan'.[19] Perhaps more importantly, it would allow Churchill to keep a closer watch on American military activities in the Pacific so as to ensure there was not too great a diversion of forces from the European theatre. Certainly there was still much to be done in the Pacific, and great forces were required, both to cope with the stubborn resistance of the Japanese and the tropical diseases that decimated Allied formations in the field.

A year on from their Kokoda victory, Australian forces were still struggling to regain control of the north-east coast of New Guinea, which had to be captured prior to MacArthur's planned invasion of the Japanese bastion at Rabaul, where some 100 000 troops protected this major air and naval base. Other Allied forces, including some New Zealand troops, hacked away at the Japanese defences in the Solomon Islands on the south-east approaches to Rabaul. All this activity was being overshadowed in the central Pacific, where Admiral King's ships converged on successive Japanese islands, unleashing a lethal bombardment before the marines stormed ashore to confirm their capture with bullets and bayonets. Rabaul had been a base too tough to crack without the enveloping movements in New Guinea and the Solomons. With King's victories in the central Pacific, it was becoming a base not worth cracking. By March 1944 it would be effectively neutralised by intensive bombing and isolated by the Allied capture of the surrounding islands.

After his overwhelming election triumph, and with eventual victory in the Pacific war seeming ever more certain, Curtin confidently turned his attention to the shape of the postwar world and the nature of Australia's place within it. Ever since 1939, the dominion had been pursuing three different strands in defence and foreign affairs. One strand stressed greater Australian self-reliance, albeit under the protection of one, or more than one, great power; another strand encouraged stronger links between Canberra and Washington; while the final strand was aimed at preserving and strengthening the ties with Britain. All three strands operated concurrently, whether under a conservative or Labor government. Only the emphasis changed according to circumstances and the political colour of the government. Throughout 1943 and early 1944, it was the first strand that was emphasised, with Australia pushing hard to exercise greater power within its immediate region. The Australian people supported this mild surge of nationalism at the federal election despite conservative criticism that Curtin had turned his back on Britain.[20] The opposite was true.

Instead of turning his back on Britain and embracing the United States, Curtin was exploring ways of strengthening Australia's frayed links to the empire, albeit based on a new conception of the empire in which Australia would enjoy a greater and more independent role. He recognised that Australia's industrial and military strength had grown while Britain's relative strength had declined. Curtin therefore thought it logical that Britain should turn more towards the dominions for support, while Australia sheltered under the shadow of imperial defence arrangements and constructed a sort of 'sub-empire' in the Pacific. In pursuit of this aim, Curtin used the annual dinner in Melbourne of the United Commercial Travellers' Association to call for an empire council. No longer was it sufficient, argued Curtin, for Britain to 'manage the affairs of Empire on the basis of a Government sitting in London'. Instead, he said, the empire must establish a 'standing consultative body with all the facilities for communication and meeting'. He envisaged an empire of equal members consulting together to develop a common policy and meeting not only in London but doing the rounds of the dominion capitals.[21]

Curtin's devolutionary proposal was based on the Australian view of the empire as belonging to the whole British race, rather than to the British government. This view allowed the Australians at times to be bitterly critical of the British government while remaining staunch supporters of the British empire. While the Australians regarded the Churchill government as a transitory political entity, they saw the empire as a racial brotherhood that would endure. Of course, the view from Westminster was quite different, with the British regarding the empire as something owned by Britain, rather than simply led by it. In fact, the word 'possessions' was used interchangeably with 'colonies' to describe the territories under British control. While Churchill referred to the 'Empire', stressing possession, Australians preferred to use 'Commonwealth', stressing fraternity. While the Australians could envisage the leadership of the empire one day passing to one of the dominions, the idea was regarded as totally alien in London. This gulf in thinking would doom Curtin's proposal for an empire council, which also failed to take account of the opposition such proposals always met from South Africa and Canada, neither of which was anxious to be seen supporting closer integration of the empire.[22]

In Curtin's view, the British shield was needed as much against America as against the resurgent Japan. As he confided to journalists during a background briefing on 6 September, the government planned to build up the external affairs department so that it could send officers to the Pacific islands 'after the Japanese had been driven out to watch Australia's economic and commercial interests'. Curtin warned that Australia had to 'watch her interests very carefully' since there was already evidence that 'the Americans would not give up economic claims to some of the Pacific islands'.[23] He predicted that there would be a fierce economic war after the present military war was won and that Australia could not 'allow her economic position to be not known or misunderstood', particularly if the Pacific was 'studded by bases occupied by half a dozen nations' intent on using tariff walls to keep out Australian goods. To counter possible American expansionism in the Pacific, Curtin called for Australia to stake out its own Pacific claims, although the success of such claims would be more likely if Australia could count on the support of Britain.[24]

As a mark of Australia's resurgent attachment to the empire, Curtin made it clear that Bruce would remain in London as high commissioner, believing that Bruce enjoyed the confidence of the British government and was well placed to assert Australia's interests. In fact, the high commissioner continued to be sidelined by Churchill, a state of affairs that Bruce managed largely to conceal from Canberra. During October and November 1943, Bruce tried to bring matters to a head with Churchill, complaining of the prime minister's persistent refusal to consult with him. When Bruce threatened to resign as high commissioner, Churchill successfully called his bluff, refusing to meet with him and forcing him to make a humiliating backdown. Only afterwards did Bruce inform Curtin of the spat, glossing over its bitterness and the extent of his defeat.[25]

Relations between Evatt and Bruce had also been poor, with Bruce being convinced that Evatt and Robinson were conspiring to have him removed. During Evatt's visit to London in 1942, he had accused Bruce of being disloyal while, during his visit the following year, he and Bruce had engaged in a shouting match at Australia House over who was the ruder after Evatt had hung up on the high commissioner. Evatt was right to be suspicious of

Bruce. Although the well-connected high commissioner had developed a wide range of sources of information in London, Bruce did not pass on to Canberra all the intelligence he gleaned. Curtin was unaware of this, claiming that Bruce 'had been a marvellous man in the job and Australia had been well served by him'. With Curtin staunch in his support, Evatt was forced to express approval for keeping Bruce in London. This was an unfortunate outcome. By retaining the former conservative prime minister as high commissioner, and by pressing at the same time for a royal appointee as governor-general, Curtin was closing off important options for change in Australia's external relations.[26]

The prospect of Curtin achieving his goal of a 'practical fraternity' of the British Commonwealth was made plain within days of his announcement. Churchill had not consulted Canberra about the Allied discussions at Quebec, despite their having direct relevance to Australia and despite Evatt's plea that Churchill at least maintain the appearance of consultation with Canberra.[27] This was followed by the British war cabinet rejecting as 'impracticable' a suggestion from Australia that the British Commonwealth, rather than just Britain, be treated as one of the four Great Powers.[28] In Britain's view, such a 'practical fraternity' would be neither practical nor particularly fraternal. While Britain did not want to discourage closer Commonwealth cooperation, it was not ready to recognise a relative diminution in its own power. Curtin persisted, conscious that Australia needed the empire for protection and as a source of population and believing that the Anglo–Australian relationship would become increasingly symbiotic.

Curtin realised that Australia's ambitions and future security needs could not be achieved by a population of just seven million people occupying a continent that was greater than the size of Europe. Accordingly, a postwar immigration scheme was planned so that Australia would have a 'population requisite to its safety'.[29] Curtin assured Australians that the immigrants would be white, in line with Australia's 'principles and traditions'. Earlier, Curtin had been prepared to import thousands of Asian labourers to repair Japanese bomb damage in Darwin and Port Moresby.[30] But that emergency had passed and the strict colour bar was reinstated at Australian ports. After all, that is what the war was all about as far as many Australians were concerned. In his appeal for help from the United States in 1942, Curtin had consciously pitched his appeal in racial terms with his supposedly poignant picture of Australia as 'the only white man's territory south of the equator'.[31] And he was determined that it remain so.

With labour in short supply, the Americans had already resorted to using several hundred Chinese labourers in Brisbane. In July 1943, MacArthur sought Curtin's approval to import a 'substantial number' of labourers from India and China for use in the islands and perhaps in Cairns and Townsville, where Australian labour was difficult to recruit and Australian troops had to be deployed in the cane fields to ensure a sufficient supply of sugar to make ice-cream for the American troops.[32] MacArthur's request placed Curtin in a quandary. His government had been complaining of the manpower shortage and had been steadily reducing the number of Australians deployed to support the American forces. He could therefore hardly refuse MacArthur's request to import Asian labourers given his government's protestations about the Australian manpower situation. After deliberating for five weeks, he finally gave his approval provided that 'Asiatic labour should not be employed on the mainland of Australia south of the 20th parallel, nor permanently anywhere on the mainland'. Curtin also handed over to MacArthur those Chinese phosphate miners rescued in early 1942 from Nauru and Ocean Island and then banished to the hostile heart of Australia to mine tungsten. For obvious reasons, these Allied citizens had not been grateful for their treatment and proved to be troublesome as workers. Now they were placed in American custody for use outside Australia, with Curtin requesting that the Americans also take responsibility for disposing of them at the end of the war.[33]

The mounting manpower problem was an early indication that Australia's ambitions might well exceed its present ability to achieve them. Among other things, Evatt wanted to create a postwar ship-building industry; Robinson wanted the production of transport aircraft to be made a top priority; the RAAF wanted more manpower to expand the air force; General Blamey wanted more manpower to ensure that at least three divisions could be kept in the field at any one time in New Guinea; Britain and America wanted Australian manpower to concentrate on providing foodstuffs for export; and MacArthur wanted the Australians to service his forces. On the horizon, there was the daunting prospect of a British Pacific fleet being based in Australia and placing even further demands on the local population.[34] And there were the plans being drawn up in Whitehall to use Australian troops as part of a British force against Japan.

For its part, Australia was keen to have British troops based in the dominion, both for the symbolism of such a commitment and also to relieve the Australian army of part of its burden in New Guinea. The British high commissioner in Canberra, Sir Ronald Cross, had supported the idea of sending British troops to Australia, stressing to Churchill the political benefits for Britain of such a move.[35] His suggestion was supported by Sir Owen Dixon, Australia's minister in Washington, during a meeting with Churchill on 10 September. However, Churchill made it clear to Dixon that no British troops would be available before the end of the European war, by which time he predicted that they would be used 'far to the north and west of Australia'.[36] Instead of troops in the Pacific, Churchill suggested to his war cabinet that, with the imminent defeat of Italy, and the consequent reduction in Britain's naval commitments in Europe, it should build up the skeletal Eastern fleet. Churchill wanted to send these reinforcements to the Indian Ocean by way of the Panama Canal, so that the fleet could 'put in at least four months of useful fighting in the Pacific before taking up its Indian Ocean station'. It would help satisfy Britain's 'obligations to Australia and New Zealand', and 'it would surely give proof positive of British resolve to take an active and vigorous part to the end in the war against Japan'.[37] Over the following months, Churchill's suggestion was gradually whittled down before being finally abandoned.

To Churchill's horror, the announcement of Mountbatten's appointment had raised unrealistic public expectations about the scale of future British operations against Japan. In an effort to put a damper on such expectations, Britain's information minister, Brendan Bracken, met with press representatives on 30 September to quell talk of an early offensive in Burma. Bracken asked Churchill whether he should have Mountbatten beside him during the briefing. 'Better not,' replied Churchill, who wanted to kill the speculation without dulling Mountbatten's keenness for action.[38] Churchill still wanted Mountbatten to capture the northern tip of Sumatra, and was also reluctant to relinquish his idea of launching an offensive in Burma in 1944. He faced stiff opposition from Brooke and the other chiefs of staff, with Brooke claiming that Churchill's 'wild schemes can have only one result, to detract forces from the main front' in Europe.[39]

It all came to a head on 1 October, when Churchill and Mountbatten met with the chiefs of staff. According to Brooke, there was 'an hour's pitched battle between me and the PM on the question of withdrawing troops from the Mediterranean for the Indian Ocean offensive', with Churchill being 'prepared to scrap our basic policy and put Japan before Germany'. Churchill seems to have been seduced by the aggressive schemes and infectious optimism of the glamorous Mountbatten, and it was with some difficulty that the chiefs managed in the end to defeat 'most of his evil intentions'.[40] It was in the wake of this meeting, as Mountbatten set off for India, that Churchill instructed that Mountbatten's 'Order of the Day', an aggressive statement for the forces in his new command, must not be generally published since it would only 'draw more Japanese to this theatre'. He also warned the House of Commons of the long period of training that would be required before an offensive could be launched by Mountbatten, and stressed to Ismay 'the importance of damping down all publicity about this theatre for at least three months'.[41] Mountbatten was undaunted by these negative signals, exulting to a fellow officer: 'It's grand. They have promised me everything.'[42]

Although Mountbatten was destined to be disappointed, there were good reasons for optimism in the Allied camp concerning the course of the wider war. On 3 September 1943, Allied armies had crossed from Sicily to land on the continent of Europe for the first time since the expulsion of British empire forces from Greece two and a half years earlier. Despite an early setback when the Germans almost forced the Americans to mount a hurried withdrawal, they managed to capture their initial objective of Naples by 1 October and seemed set to move on to Rome. With the Italians throwing in their lot with the Allies, and with the Russians continuing to push the Germans back on the eastern front, the end of the war looked closer than ever. Deceptively so, as Churchill reminded people, warning them of the many battles before Germany could be expected to accept the Allied demand of unconditional surrender. Nevertheless, the increasing certainty of an eventual Allied victory inevitably focused official minds on the likely shape of the postwar world. Some policy makers in London predicted that it would see a war-ravaged Britain being unable to assert itself as a great power unless it had the support of the dominions. As Attlee warned his cabinet colleagues in June 1943, 'If we are to carry our full weight in the post-war world with the United States and the U.S.S.R., it can only be as a united British Commonwealth.'[43] With this in mind, the war cabinet decided to call a meeting of dominion prime ministers, the first such conference since 1937.

As dominions secretary, Attlee was eager for the prime ministers' meeting to proceed since so many postwar issues, such as trade policy and civil aviation, demanded discussion. Alarmingly, the divisions between Britain and the dominions on such issues seemed greater than those between Britain and the United States. If the British Commonwealth was to be a major force in the postwar world, it would have to develop a united view on these issues. However, as Attlee would discover, there were as many differences between the dominions on issues such as civil aviation as there were between the dominions and Britain. Nevertheless, even if agreement could not be reached, there was another compelling reason for a prime ministers' conference. As Attlee pointed out, there was 'the important question of the prestige which a meeting between the Heads of the Governments of the Commonwealth at this stage would have in the world generally'. In other words, it would emphasise to Russia and America, as their forces dominated the fighting and their leaders jockeyed for postwar supremacy, that Britain was more than just a small island off the coast of France.[44]

On the issue of trade policy, staunch supporters of the imperial idea, such as Leo Amery, called for a strengthening of the prewar imperial preference system to defend British industry and exporters against American economic penetration.[45] In London and Washington, there was mutual suspicion about each other's motives as both Allies used the war to position themselves for early access to postwar markets. When the Americans dragged their feet over the Italian armistice terms, the British war secretary, Sir James Grigg, wondered whether they were 'busily laying the foundations for post-war commercial penetration. Sometimes I think that Winston gives in to them too much, and we are certainly far too polite to the Russians.'[46] Churchill was more concerned with fighting the war than fighting for postwar economic advantage. Moreover, he had not relinquished his free trade beliefs and wanted trade barriers reduced after the war, combined with an expansionist economic policy. Australia agreed with this view. The 1930s had shown that the British empire could not provide sufficient markets for Australian exports, leading the government to believe that Australia's future prosperity would be better served by a general lowering of tariffs and an international agreement to raise living standards, both of which could be expected to cause an increase in the volume of world trade. Although Churchill and Roosevelt had agreed on a reduction in trade barriers as part of the 1941 Atlantic Charter, it was not until July 1943 that Britain and its dominions were able to agree that an expansionist commercial policy was preferable to a return to high trade barriers.[47] Australia wanted the world to go further, hoping that it could get a commitment to raise living standards and to full employment.[48]

A prime ministers' conference in London could set a political seal on the discussion of postwar problems and determine the postwar course of the Commonwealth. However, Curtin declared that he could not travel to London before April 1944, justifying his reluctance by pointing to Australia's worsening manpower problems and the military operations in New Guinea. He claimed that he was the only minister with 'precise personal knowledge' of these problems and consequently had to be on hand to sort them out. If Churchill could be absent from the helm in London for prolonged periods, maintaining contact with his colleagues by cable, it is difficult to see how Curtin, in the wake of his resounding election victory, could not be similarly absent from Canberra. The real reason for his reluctance was probably revealed at the conclusion of his cable, telling Attlee that he did 'not feel satisfied in leaving Australia until the results of the decision to carry on the war in the Pacific with the same vigour as the war in Europe are evident ...'[49] If this was meant to pressure Churchill, it had no discernible effect. Ignoring Curtin's reservations, the British government pressed ahead with its proposal for a conference by January 1944.[50]

After four years of war in Europe, many observers were predicting that peace might come during the course of 1944. Churchill was unconvinced, still worrying that the long-awaited invasion of France might miscarry and perhaps rob him of an unconditional victory against Hitler. Meanwhile, the competition between Britain and the United States intensified as they sought to mould the postwar world to their separate advantage. Australia was more concerned with ensuring its future survival. As the tide of Japanese invasion ebbed from its shores, Australia fervently wanted to prevent a repetition of 1942. A policy of greater self-reliance was called for, both industrially and militarily, although the protection of a great power would still be necessary. Britain, the likely protector, was needed to provide the security within which an Australasian co-prosperity sphere in the south-west Pacific could be developed. Australia would discover that Washington and London had their own plans for the Pacific.

NOTES

1. Cable, Churchill to Attlee, 11 August 1943, PREM 3/53/4, PRO.
2. Chiefs of Staff Committee Minutes, 7 August 1943, PREM 3/147/2, PRO.
3. Brooke noted with exasperation in his diary, after a chiefs of staff meeting with Mountbatten in attendance, that Mountbatten was 'quite irresponsible, suffers from the most illogical brain, always producing red herrings ...' Alanbrooke diary, 8 January 1943, in Danchev and Todman (eds), *War Diaries*, p. 357.
4. Alanbrooke diary, 6 August 1943, in Danchev and Todman (eds), *War Diaries*, p. 437; Pownall diary, 14 September 1943, in Bond (ed.), *Chief of Staff*, Vol. 2, p. 108; For a defence of Mountbatten, see Phillip Ziegler, *Mountbatten*, London, 1985.
5. Gilbert, *Road to Victory*, p. 467.
6. Minute, Churchill to Ismay, 7 August 1943, PREM 3/147/3, PRO; Bryant, *The Turn of the Tide*, p. 694; Gilbert, *Road to Victory*, pp. 460–1, 465.
7. Minute, Churchill to Ismay, 7 August 1943, PREM 3/147/3, PRO.
8. After one meeting with Churchill at Quebec, Brooke declaimed in his diary that Churchill was 'insisting on capturing the top of Sumatra Island irrespective of what our general plan for the war against Japan may be! He refused to accept that any general plan was necessary, recommended a purely opportunistic policy and behaved like a spoilt child that wants a toy in a shop irrespective of the fact that its parents tell it that it is no good!' Alanbrooke diary, 19 August 1943, Danchev and Todman (eds), *War Diaries*, pp. 444–5; Cable, Churchill to Chiang Kai-shek, 11 August 1943, PREM 3/143/10, PRO; See also documents in PREM 3/147/3, PRO.
9. Letter, Ismay to Pownall, undated but most likely 27 May 1944, IV/Pow/4/2a, Ismay Papers, KC.
10. Gilbert, *Road to Victory*, pp. 462–508.
11. Minute, Churchill to Ismay, 17 August 1943, PREM 3/147/3, PRO.
12. Brooke complained that Churchill 'had discovered with a pair of dividers that we could bomb Singapore from this point and he had set his heart on going there'. Danchev and Todman (eds), *War Diaries*, p. 445.
13. Memorandum by Combined Staff Planners, 18 August 1943, PREM 3/147/1, PRO.
14. Minute, Churchill to Ismay, 20 August 1943, PREM 3/147/3, PRO; See also other documents in this file.
15. Cable, Churchill to Attlee, undated, PREM 3/366/10, PRO; Gilbert, *Road to Victory*, p. 486.
16. Gilbert, *Road to Victory*, p. 478.

17 Roskill, *The War at Sea*, Vol. 2, pp. 420–1; Ziegler, *Mountbatten*, p. 221.

18 Cables, Evatt to Glasgow and Glasgow to Evatt, both 24 August 1943, *DAFP*, Vol. 6, Docs 260 and 261.

19 Cable, Churchill to Evatt, 26 August 1943, *DAFP*, Vol. 6, Doc. 265.

20 Letter, Robinson to Evatt, 13 August 1943, 'Dr H. V. Evatt' folder, Robinson Papers, UMA.

21 *Sydney Morning Herald*, 16 August 1943.

22 ibid., 7 September 1943.

23 Background briefing, 6 September 1943, MS 4675, Smith Papers, NLA.

24 *Sydney Morning Herald*, 7 September 1943.

25 Letter, Churchill to Bruce, 6 October 1943, Talk with Cranborne, 19 October 1943, Letters, Churchill to Bruce, 21 October 1943, Bruce to Churchill, 24 October 1943, Churchill to Bruce, 3 November 1943 and Bruce to Churchill, 8 November 1943, CRS M100, 'October 1943' and 'November 1943', NAA; See also Letter, Bruce to Curtin, 15 November 1943, CRS A1608/H33/1/2, NAA.

26 Background briefing, 6 September 1943, MS 4675, Smith Papers, NLA; Talk with Evatt, 16 June 1943, CRS M100, 'June 1943', NAA; Note by Bruce, 22 February 1943, CRS A1970/559/2, NAA; P. G. Edwards, 'The rise and fall of the High Commissioner', in A. F. Madden and W. H. Morris-Jones (eds), *Australia and Britain: Studies in a Changing Relationship*, pp. 48–9; Letter, Bruce to Officer, 6 August 1943, MS 2629/1, Officer Papers, NLA; Talks with Attlee, 22 April and 24 May 1943, CRS M100, 'May 1943', NAA.

27 Cable, Evatt to Glasgow, 24 August 1943, and Glasgow to Evatt, 24 August 1943, *DAFP*, Vol. 6, Docs 260–1.

28 Memorandum by Attlee, 22 September 1943, CAB 66/41, W.P. (43)412, PRO; War Cabinet Conclusions, 24 September 1943, CAB 65/35, W.M. (43)131, PRO.

29 Background briefing, 7 September 1943, MS 4675, Smith Papers, NLA.

30 Press conference, 9 June 1943, MS 4675, Smith Papers, NLA.

31 Cable, Curtin to Casey, enclosing message to Roosevelt, 22 February 1942, in *DAFP*, Vol. 5, Doc. 358.

32 Undated note by MacArthur, CRS A5954, Box 287, NAA.

33 Letter, Curtin to MacArthur, 5 August 1943, and other documents in CRS A5954, Box 306; See also CRS A2670, 126/1942, NAA.

34 Memorandum, Robinson to Evatt, 13 August 1943 and Radio broadcast by Evatt, 21 March 1943, 'War — Speeches by Evatt 43(a)' folder, Evatt Papers, FUL.

35 It was, perhaps, a measure of the British disregard for Australia that Cross was kept in Canberra throughout the war despite the most bitter denunciations of him. One highly placed British official returned from a visit to Australia in early 1943, and 'drew the most appalling picture of Cross's ineptitude and quite frankly suggested that he had got to be removed from Australia'. The official claimed that Cross was 'a complete snob, disliked Australia and the Australians, and the only associations he had were with the so-called "best people" in Melbourne and Sydney'. Talk with Sir Campbell Stuart, 31 March 1943, CRS M100, 'March 1943', NAA; Letter, Cross to Churchill, 11 August 1943, and Cable, Churchill to Cross, 2 September 1943, PREM 3/151/4, PRO.

36 Note by Churchill, 5 October 1943, CAB 66/41, W.P. (43)430, PRO; Cable, Dixon to Evatt and Curtin, 4 September 1943, CRS A3300/258, NAA.

37 Cable, Churchill to Attlee, 9 September 1943, PREM 3/163/7, PRO; See also other documents in this file.

38 Minute, Martin to Churchill, 29 September 1943, PREM 3/147/10, PRO.

39 Alanbrooke diary, 28 September 1943, in Danchev and Todman (eds), *War Diaries*, p. 456.

40 Alanbrooke diary, 1 October 1943, in Danchev and Todman (eds), *War Diaries*, p. 457.

41 Minute, Churchill to Ismay, 2 October 1943, PREM 3/53/16, PRO.

42 Ziegler, *Mountbatten*, p. 223.

43 In July 1943 Attlee had proposed that Britain promote the role of the dominions in the proposed United Nations organisation. 'Australia,' he wrote, 'might play a leading part among the countries of the Pacific Region ... if it were known that she would be backed by the full weight of the British Commonwealth, if the need arose.' Attlee also suggested that Britain dispense with the term 'Far East' as it was 'often taken in Australia and New Zealand to imply that the area is far from our thoughts and our plans'. Memoranda by Attlee, 15 June and 19 July 1943, CAB 66/37, W.P. (43)244 and CAB 66/39, W.P. (43)321, PRO.

44 Memorandum by Attlee, 17 September 1943, CAB 66/41, W.P. (43)404, PRO.

[45] Memorandum by Amery, 2 September 1943, CAB 66/40, W.P. (43)388, PRO.

[46] Letter, Grigg to his father, 9 September 1943, PJGG 9/6/24, Grigg Papers, CC.

[47] War Cabinet Conclusions, 8 April 1943, CAB 65/34, W.M. (43)50, PRO; Talk with Coombs, 23 June 1943, CRS M100, 'June 1943', NAA; Dalton diary, 6 July 1943, I/29/7, Dalton Papers, LSE; Note by Dalton, 23 July 1943, CAB 66/39, W.P. (43)334, PRO.

[48] For the Australian government's view on their full employment objective, see Cable, Commonwealth Government to Attlee, 7 September 1943, *DAFP*, Vol. 6, Doc. 273.

[49] Curtin's reluctance to have an early meeting may also have been prompted by his fear of flying. He had only flown in an aircraft twice, both times during election campaigns. He had not visited the troops in New Guinea and was even reluctant about going to Brisbane to see MacArthur, which he insisted on doing by train. A plane trip to London may have been more than he cared to think about. Cable, Curtin to Attlee, 14 September 1943, *DAFP*, Vol. 6, Doc. 277.

[50] War Cabinet Conclusions, 22 September 1943, CAB 65/35, W.M. (43)130, PRO.

THIRTY-NINE

'the maximum of which Australia is capable'

By the beginning of October 1943, the Allies were tightening their grip upon both Germany and Japan. Naples had been taken by the American Fifth Army under General Mark Clark while Montgomery inched his Eighth Army up the 'toe' of Italy in support. The mass of landing craft that had been retained in the Mediterranean could have been used with much greater effect to cut off the scattered German forces as they retreated northwards. The excessive caution of the Allied effort allowed these scanty German forces to hold back superior Allied armies; the Germans were even able to dispatch several of their stronger divisions to the eastern front, where a series of Russian offensives had drained the strength of the German army and brought the Russian army across the Dnieper River to threaten Kiev. In retrospect, it is clear that Hitler was living on borrowed time. But it was not so clear then, with his forces gradually retreating and gaining strength from shortened lines of communication.

In the Pacific, Hirohito's forces were outmanoeuvred as America avoided frontal attacks on Japanese strongholds such as Rabaul, and instead used its growing naval and air power to leapfrog from one lightly defended island to another. The bypassed Japanese garrisons would be isolated from reinforcement and kept under air and sea attack so as to minimise their offensive potential. With the great bulk of their army tied down in China and Manchuria, the Japanese had no effective answer to the Allied strategy. American sea and air superiority counted for everything. Churchill had tried to deter Japan from war by simple arithmetic, comparing Allied steel production to that of the Japanese. Now his sums were starting to make sense. In mid-September, the Japanese High Command conceded that its forces in the Pacific were stretched too thinly and ordered that they be contracted behind a line that ran from Malaya to western New Guinea and thence to the Caroline and Mariana Islands. They hoped that a smaller nut would prove harder to crack. In its factories and shipyards, America was assembling a formidable sledgehammer.

While the Americans assembled the forces for the coming thrust through the Japanese-held islands of the central Pacific, Australian and American troops continued to fight in New Guinea. Enjoying clear superiority at sea and in the air, as well as on the ground, the Allied forces managed to clear the Japanese from eastern New Guinea and to keep pushing them north-westward along the coast. The towns of Lae and Salamaua were captured by the Australian 7th and 9th Divisions in mid-September with little fighting and few casualties, while an air armada of more than three hundred aircraft was engaged in the dropping of American and Australian paratroops who quickly seized the airfield at nearby Nadzab. An elated MacArthur had watched the drop from a circling bomber and, emboldened by these successes, brought forward the capture of the entire Huon peninsula. At the same time he sent a force along the Markham and Ramu river valleys towards the Japanese base at Wewak. Although the Japanese were restricted to using barges and submarines to keep their New Guinea force supplied, there would be nearly two more years of fighting before Wewak was taken.

With the logistical and other difficulties of the New Guinea operations, only three Australian divisions were kept in the field at one time while eight divisions were undergoing training in Australia. Many more troops were engaged in garrison duties around the continent even though the danger of a Japanese invasion had passed. With disease taking a heavy toll of the troops in New Guinea, and with the flow of Australian aircrew continuing unabated to Britain, the country was facing a desperate manpower crisis. At the beginning of October, the Australian war cabinet finally resolved to reassess the country's war effort and to attempt to reconcile the impossible demands being placed upon its limited manpower. The army and the aircraft and munitions industries were ordered to release forty thousand men by June 1944, with fifteen thousand of them being transferred to rural industry. The men were being sent back to the farms. The plan to build up the RAAF to 73 squadrons, on which Evatt had spent so much time in London and Washington, was abandoned. Instead, Australia would make only that military effort sufficient to assure it 'an effective voice in the peace settlement'. It was an impossible balancing act that managed to upset everyone. The Australian public resented increased controls when the security threat was so obviously receding. Although Curtin did relax restrictions on horse-racing, he then introduced meat rationing. MacArthur objected to Australia limiting its support for his forces. And both Britain and America wanted Australian agricultural produce, but resented men being transferred from the army to harvest and process it. Curtin could only afford to confront these conflicting pressures now that he had a comfortable majority in parliament.[1]

The government's measures were in recognition of the changing nature of the Pacific war, with Australia's war effort being retuned to adjust to the change from a defensive to an offensive war. The country no longer needed such strong garrison forces, while the success of Admiral King's island-hopping campaign reduced Australia's role as the main base for the invasion of the Philippines and the final assault on Japan. Curtin also stressed the need to prepare the Australian economy for the postwar world. As Shedden made clear in a memorandum, Australia should concentrate on satisfying those Allied demands that best promoted the civilian economy. Thus the dairy industry, the products of which sustained American troops in the Pacific and the civilian population of Britain, should solve its manpower problem by taking men from the armed forces or from other war projects. The more that Australia could restore the 'peace characteristics of our specialized industries', argued Shedden, 'the more simple will be the transition from a war to a peace footing'.[2] In other words, it was time to start putting butter before guns. Britain had similar plans, and was busily stockpiling raw materials for its export industries and proposing large-scale demobilisation once Germany was defeated.[3]

When Curtin assembled his re-elected cabinet on 22 September, the new Australian priorities were made clear. His ministers found that the treasurer, Ben Chifley, had savagely cut expenditure for the service departments. Despite objections from Evatt and the service ministers, Chifley stood his ground, pointing to the economic dangers for Australia of a two-stage ending of the war.[4] Britain was also worried about a two-stage ending, conscious that it would be difficult to encourage its forces to fight if many of their compatriots had been released from the services. Moreover, British society would be reluctant to weather more hardships for the sake of a distant war in which many of them felt they had no stake. It was left to the Royal Navy, which would have to shoulder most of the burden of the Pacific war, to be 'appalled' at the failure to plan for the switch of resources to the Pacific once Germany had been defeated. The Admiralty warned Churchill of the likely political reaction from Washington if Britain failed to make good on its oft-repeated promises to fight the Japanese with all the strength that it could bring to bear.[5]

Australia's position was also difficult: while it was fighting alongside the Americans it was now planning to reduce its military numbers, which could give the impression that it was throwing more of the burden onto Washington. Despite this, MacArthur's initial reaction to the Australian plight had been surprisingly sympathetic. He conceded that Australia had been 'bled white' and he promised to 'nurse the A.I.F. Corps as much as possible' so as to reduce their casualties. However, his attitude stiffened when Australia sought to reduce not only its garrison troops, but also the manpower assigned to servicing the American forces. As MacArthur pointed out, if the American forces had to maintain themselves, then fewer American combat units could be shipped to the south-west Pacific. Although this was a consideration that Curtin could not easily dismiss, there were other factors that also had to be borne in mind.[6]

If the manpower servicing the needs of the Americans was to be maintained at its existing level, Australian military units would have to be disbanded to provide the numbers. Blamey warned Curtin that this could see Australia becoming so overwhelmed by American troops that 'it may find itself very much in the same position as an occupied country'. He told Curtin that it was up to the Australian government, rather than MacArthur, 'to determine the strength of the forces it is to maintain, and the extent to which its nationals may be employed by an Allied Force Command in Australia'. Blamey urged that, in the face of MacArthur's intransigence, Curtin should approach Washington directly to have the matter resolved.[7]

Relations between MacArthur and Blamey had never been good. MacArthur was critical of Blamey's boozing and womanising and suspected him of harbouring political ambitions. Although Blamey was meant to be Allied land force commander in the south-west Pacific and have control of Australian, American and other Allied troops, MacArthur now sought to confine his authority to the Australian mainland and to keep him away from the fighting. When this failed, MacArthur created special commands under his own control to which he allocated all the American troops, thereby removing them from Blamey's control altogether.[8] The relations between Curtin and MacArthur were also becoming cooler, with Curtin's increasing concern about postwar American ambitions in the Pacific affecting his view of MacArthur. Certainly, from this time Curtin began to be more forthright towards the American general. Although Curtin still consulted closely with MacArthur, he no longer deferred automatically to the supreme commander as he mostly had in the past.[9]

On 8 October, Curtin informed Churchill of Australia's problems, claiming that the country had 'overreached' itself by taking on more commitments than the available manpower could handle.[10] Australia had to meet the various demands placed upon civilian and military manpower, and still maintain a military effort in the Pacific sufficient to guarantee it a place at the peace table. If the divisions in the field had to be maintained at their present strength, other commitments would have to be reined in. One way of relieving the manpower shortage, as Curtin suggested to Churchill, was to bring back those thousands of Australians serving with British forces in Europe. After all, argued Curtin, the effort in the south-west Pacific was not just for Australia's sake but for the empire as a whole. As usual, Curtin did not demand the return of these Australians. He simply set out his conclusions and asked Churchill for his 'observations'.[11]

The tentative tone of Curtin's cable ensured that the observations would be slow in coming. Indeed, it took three and a half months before the chiefs of staff submitted a reply for Churchill to approve. It provided little solace for Curtin, with the chiefs demanding that Australia keep its army up to strength and advising Churchill that he should refuse to return the three thousand Australian sailors attached to the Royal Navy, or the twelve thousand Australian aircrew operating with the RAF. As always, they said, everything would depend upon the war against Germany, although even after that was won only those Australians immediately required for the war against Japan should be transferred to the Pacific. Not only should Australia's manpower shortage not be relieved by the return of its citizens, but the chiefs intended to advise Australia that British units arriving in Australia would add to its manpower crisis. They urged Churchill to send this negative cable in conjunction with advice about Britain's plans for the Pacific war. However, because these plans remained a matter of dispute between Churchill and the chiefs, the cable was never sent.[12]

Although Churchill was willing to return Australia's sailors and airmen when their transfer home would no longer affect the war against Germany, he wanted the chiefs to advise on the consequences of withdrawing the Australians from Europe. He also warned them against raising expectations in Australia about any imminent dispatch of British troops to the dominion, since there was no certainty that Germany would collapse in 1944. While offering no immediate relief for Australia's manpower problem, Churchill went further than his chiefs by suggesting that Australia should have more than just three divisions in action against the Japanese at any one time. 'There is really no excuse for this,' he wrote, 'and I should think the United States would complain.'[13] Churchill failed to understand the difficulties of jungle warfare, where disease took more casualties than fighting and logistics limited the numbers that could be brought to bear in the front line. In fact, maintaining three divisions in the field would require six divisions behind the lines. The British chiefs of staff were more understanding, having experienced the problems of Burma, and described the Australian military effort against Japan as 'a very remarkable achievement'.[14] Churchill's continuing hostility to Australia made him reluctant to concede this point, while Curtin's attempt to solve the manpower shortage would only exacerbate the tension between Canberra and London.

As was clear from the British reaction, Australia's manpower problems were likely to increase. While the Allies wanted Australia to maintain its war effort, Curtin wanted the dominion's limited manpower to turn increasingly towards laying the groundwork for the country's postwar ambitions. Prominent among these ambitions was a plan to build heavy bombers in Australia. Despite the additional demands that this would impose on Australian manpower, the plan was supported by Britain on condition that Australia resume its dependency on the British aircraft industry. However, the United States was opposed to Australia building anything larger than small two-engine aircraft. There was some sense in the American objection, since it would be wasteful of scarce wartime resources, although the peacetime benefit to America of restricting Australia's aircraft industry was doubtless not forgotten in Washington. Under an agreement with the Americans, Britain had largely concentrated on producing smaller aircraft while America had concentrated on larger types, such as the four-engine Flying Fortress bombers which could be built more efficiently in North American factories, away from German bombing, and then flown across the Atlantic. While this division made sense in wartime, it also gave America a virtual monopoly on the production of large civil aircraft in peacetime.

When MacArthur was asked to approve Australia's plan to manufacture Lancaster bombers, he refused on the grounds of it being inefficient.[15] This might have settled the matter in 1942, but MacArthur's word was no longer law. Daniel McVey, secretary of the aircraft production department and leader of the mission to Britain which had recommended the Lancaster, called upon Curtin not to give in to the Americans on this issue. McVey claimed that the issue was regarded as being of 'great importance' in Britain, with McVey arguing that it was also 'of the greatest importance that we should preserve the most intimate possible relationships — technical and commercial, as well as social and political — with Great Britain'. Curtin needed little convincing. He fully supported the development of an

Australian aircraft industry, believing that Britain and America were winning the aviation race and fearing for Australia if it were not independent in the air. Australia's wartime experience, when it had been denied heavy bombers and become dependent on the beneficence of MacArthur for its civil aviation needs, had shown Curtin the dangers of not having the capacity to manufacture large aircraft capable of being used for either civil or military use. As a result, when the Lancaster proposal came before the war cabinet on 11 November, Curtin drew upon McVey's arguments to convince his colleagues to approve the production of 50 Lancasters.[16]

Curtin also sought approval from the advisory war council, emphasising the importance of the Lancaster program to the postwar aircraft industry and stressing the 'potential use of these resources for the production of civil transport aircraft'. Not surprisingly, Menzies supported this commitment to British aircraft, particularly if it would allow the RAAF to enjoy operational autonomy and not be merely an adjunct of the USAAF. 'From the aspect of post-war defence,' said Menzies, 'it was important that the RAAF should have an opportunity of functioning as a complete air force during this war.'[17] Four days later, in a radio broadcast on civil aviation, Menzies called for a 'strong and well-knit British Empire' that could protect its aviation interests from American encroachments. Menzies pointed out that Britain and the two Pacific dominions had 'their own proper and vital flying interests in the South-west Pacific and in the Pacific generally' and should 'not lightly abandon those interests'.[18]

The Labor government had rather more ambitious plans that extended beyond aviation and envisaged a more exalted place for Australia within the empire. When Evatt reported to parliament in mid-October concerning his visit to London and Washington, he sketched out his vision of a future Australian sphere of influence. He argued that France and Holland could hardly remain responsible for the defence of New Caledonia and the East Indies if, as recent events had shown, they collapsed at the lightest touch by Japan. Instead, said Evatt, the region adjacent to Australia had to be regarded as 'a great zone of mutual interest which had to be grouped in the same defence area after the war, and be the subject of special efforts for economic betterment and aviation development'. The Pacific was where

'Australia's predominant interests' lay, and consequently where 'Australia had a leading part to play'. Pointing to the island territories to Australia's north, Evatt claimed that these European colonies should be recognised as 'coming within an Australian zone' so far as defence, trade and transport were concerned.[19] If Australia was going to assert its interest in this zone, it would need to use its membership of the British empire as a foil to fend off America's own ambitions in the Pacific. While British observers noted with satisfaction Australia's renewed interest in the empire, they did so without appreciating the underlying motivation.[20]

Curtin emphasised this renewed interest by arranging the appointment of the Duke of Gloucester as governor-general. While some of his cabinet colleagues deplored the betrayal of Labor Party policy and the lack of consultation with the cabinet, Evatt supported Curtin's move, arguing that the King's brother would act as 'a symbol in Australia of the whole Empire'.[21] The decision had the desired effect. It was widely acclaimed in both Britain and Australia, with one British newspaper suggesting that it 'effectively disposes of fears that Australia might cast in her lot with the United States'.[22] In another conciliatory move, Curtin roused himself from his sick bed to rebuke the information minister, Arthur Calwell, who had requested that cinemas begin their screenings by playing 'Advance Australia Fair' rather than 'God Save The King'. In rejecting this symbolic move, Curtin said that he did 'not know of any anthem other than the National Anthem, *God Save the King*'.[23]

Of more practical importance to Britain was Curtin's ready agreement to the appointment of a British liaison officer to MacArthur's headquarters who could act as a personal and direct link between Churchill and the American general. Curtin had attempted to resist such a suggestion in 1942 when the British agent, Gerald Wilkinson, had been put forward for the post. This officer would be in addition to the British military mission in Canberra. His opposition then had been partly out of deference to MacArthur, who opposed the idea, but also because he suspected Churchill's intentions and feared that Australia's connection, via MacArthur, to the decision-making councils of Washington and London would be diminished. Now he submitted meekly in the interests of the Anglo–Australian relationship, despite the opposition of Blamey, who believed such liaison officers would erode the imperial relationship between the British and Australian armies.[24]

At the end of November 1943, Curtin and Shedden travelled by train to meet MacArthur in Brisbane, telling him that the government planned to go ahead with the Lancaster proposal. It would do so despite MacArthur's opposition, and despite the crash in Australia of the Lancaster on loan from Britain and belated advice from Australia's air representative in Washington that the Lancasters were inferior to American bombers and not so easily converted for civil use. Curtin admitted to MacArthur that the Australian decision was motivated by its ambition to develop a local aircraft industry for the postwar period. It was essential, Curtin said, 'that the largest type [of aircraft] should be produced, even if it might not be manufactured in time to be of much use in this war. It was the price which had to be paid for the development of the industry.'[25] Curtin's admission to MacArthur was made despite advice that same day from McVey to conceal from MacArthur the civil dimension of the Australian plan. In fact, MacArthur again sympathised with Australia's plight regarding civil aviation and promised to do what he could to secure smaller DC-3 transport aircraft for immediate use within Australia.[26]

As their train trundled back towards Canberra, Curtin may have felt well satisfied with the results of his trip. But MacArthur was rather like Roosevelt in his approach to provincial politicians. He would express sympathy and appear to approve their requests but leave himself enough room to crawl out from under any commitment. His headquarters had, among its air force staff, various officers with interests in commercial aviation who were eager to claim the south Pacific for American aircraft manufacturers. While the supply of DC-3 aircraft would suit this purpose, an agreement to build British aircraft would not.

Aviation was a particularly touchy topic between Washington and London as they fought for postwar pre-eminence. Five powerful American senators had toured the world, including Australia, to report on national defence, returning to Washington in September 1943 with strong recommendations about combating economic competition from Britain. Claiming that the American troops they visited wanted jobs after the war, not Anglo–American collaboration, the senators alleged that Britain was using the war to promote its economic interests while the United States played the role of a 'global sucker', winning battles for Britain but not collecting the prizes. As proof of this, they cited the two million British soldiers in India confronting just sixty thousand Japanese in Burma while American soldiers slogged it out against the Japanese across the Pacific. They also pointed to the virtual British monopoly of the world's airfields. As Senator Owen Brewster bitterly observed: 'America has invested hundreds of millions of dollars in Britain, Africa, Australia and India, yet there is not a single spot in these countries where our planes can land after the war.'[27]

This was dangerous talk, exacerbating the rivalry between the two Allies and threatening the unity needed for victory. The progress of their tour was carefully monitored in London and Washington. Roosevelt's close adviser, Harry Hopkins, explained to a visiting junior minister from the British Foreign Office, Richard Law, that the 'real root of the trouble was the Pacific', where the 'old doubts about British actions and intentions' provided 'the real danger point'. Law reported Hopkins' comments to London, reminding Churchill of the appeal for British forces made by Sir Owen Dixon when Churchill was last in Washington. Once again, Churchill refused to send such forces. They were hard pressed in the Mediterranean and there was the forthcoming invasion of France to be considered. So Churchill dismissed the arguments as 'politics, and bad politics at that'. Anyway, asked Churchill, how could Britain divert forces to the Pacific when the Americans were insisting that all their forces be concentrated for the invasion of France?[28]

As for the territorial claims being asserted by the American senators, Britain was adamant that they should be resisted. It wanted to retain its prewar territorial advantage in relation to airfields, warning Washington that America could not retain any residual rights to airfields constructed by them in British colonies such as Fiji.[29] This was what the American senators had found so objectionable, that their government had shed the blood of their troops and expended the treasure of their people establishing airfields and other facilities in colonial territories to fight the Japanese and would have to hand them over to their colonial owners at the end of the war. Britain was also preparing itself for the expected postwar boom in aviation by developing an infrastructure that could quickly be converted into a web of British-controlled peacetime air routes, serviced initially by converted British bombers and later by new civil airplanes that were already appearing on the drawing boards of British factories. These plans, and the intensifying Anglo–American competition, would end the chances of Australia's preferred option for civil aviation — the internationalisation of aviation facilities — coming to fruition.[30]

From Canberra, Sir Ronald Cross tried to push this process along when he advised Churchill in August 1943 to use the transfer of British forces to the Pacific to justify establishing a British trans-Pacific air service 'on a scale if possible equal to those now operated by the United States'. He warned Churchill that 'employees of the big United States Air Lines have been put into naval and military uniforms ... and are in effect establishing their companies upon this route'.[31] However, Churchill was not prepared to allow competition over civil aviation to complicate the establishment of a structure of international relations which would see the three great Allied powers (or four, if China was included) dominate the postwar world and thereby preserve the peace.[32] Churchill had made this clear during a meeting with dominion representatives at the British embassy in Washington on 10 September, arguing that it would be 'a mistake to regard the future of civil aviation in terms of a competition between the United States and the United Kingdom'.[33]

Nevertheless, competition over civil aviation continued to disrupt the relationship between London and Washington. Lord Beaverbrook was placed in charge of civil aviation discussions and pushed British interests hard. In December 1943, he rejected plans for Britain to develop a superior civil aircraft for trans-Atlantic traffic. Such a plane, he argued, would take six years to develop, which would be far too late to beat the Americans. Instead, Beaverbrook proposed that existing bomber aircraft be redesigned for civil use. He claimed that Britain had to choose 'between having or abandoning British Civil Aviation after the war'. If it hoped to succeed, it had 'to provide British aircraft and British engines for the Dominions at the end of the War'. Otherwise, warned Beaverbrook, 'the leadership of air routes in the Empire must pass to the United States'.[34]

Although Beaverbrook's fears were well founded, the solution was not as simple as he imagined. Certainly if Britain spent years developing new types of civil aircraft, it would leave America with the advantage for the crucial first years of peacetime. However, if resources were ploughed instead into converting British bombers for civil use, the resulting aircraft would be inferior to the American planes, thereby still leaving Britain behind in the aviation race. If its dominions could be persuaded to take the inferior aircraft, Britain's problems might be reduced. But such easy acceptance could no longer be guaranteed, particularly as the dominions had their own aviation ambitions and were conscious of the relative inferiority of British planes.

Leo Amery urged Beaverbrook to stymie the dominions' ambitions by declaring all air traffic between Britain, Newfoundland, and the colonies as part of Britain's internal traffic and therefore reserved for its airlines alone. This would effectively prevent the dominions from operating international airlines. As Beaverbrook pointed out, it was too late for such a move. The Canadians were already flying by way of Newfoundland and could not be stopped, with Beaverbrook adding dryly that if he stopped the Canadians flying into Newfoundland he would 'never be able to go home again' to his native Canada.[35] Britain's predicament was no easier in the south Pacific, where its high commissioner in New Zealand echoed the call by Cross for Britain to increase its aviation presence so as to be prepared for postwar American competition. Britain rejected the proposal, advising that aircraft were simply not available for 'a purely prestige service', while there were also no existing British aircraft types that could carry a worthwhile payload of passengers or cargo between New Zealand and North America.[36]

It was not that Britain did not have ambitions for controlling the aviation traffic across the Pacific. In late October 1943, Beaverbrook had shown dominion representatives a map of the world on which was marked a future British air route, crossing the Pacific from Sydney by way of Manila and Vladivostok to Edmonton in Canada. Previously, plans for such a Pacific route had foundered on the need to obtain landing rights in American-controlled Hawaii, the vital stopping place in the final stretch across the Pacific. Prior to the war, the United States had used its control of Hawaii to demand that Britain cede landing rights in British colonies to American airlines. Beaverbrook's tortuous pan-Pacific route had the advantage of avoiding Hawaii altogether and would provide the final leg in an air route that would allow British airlines to 'girdle the globe'. To achieve his vision, Beaverbrook wanted Britain to swap its aviation interests in South America in return for the United States giving Britain a free hand in Europe, the Middle East and Africa.[37]

It was as if the two world wars had never happened: Britain would still enjoy its former pre-eminence and the growing dominance of the United States could be simply dismissed. If Beaverbrook thought that a British air route could circle the globe and bypass the United States, Australia certainly did not. As Beaverbrook conceded, Australia had plans of its own to establish a trans-Pacific route via Hawaii to the United States. Moreover, Beaverbrook's plan depended on the Americans being willing to trade a large part of their aviation interests in the northern hemisphere for lesser interests in the southern hemisphere. This was never likely to happen. But Beaverbrook pressed on, trying to compete with the United States in aviation while at the same time preventing the independent ambitions of its dominions from being realised. Bruce tried to have Britain concede the new realities of the world before it was too late, urging Beaverbrook in December not to abandon his efforts to reach an agreement with Washington on aviation. In the absence of such an agreement, warned Bruce, the US government would be under political pressure to claim rights unilaterally over the military airfields it had constructed. This would allow them to control most of the Pacific islands and even lead to claims within Australia, where American construction corps had built airfields across the far north. Britain was already moving to confront the Americans. On 9 December, Whitehall approved a surreptitious plan by New Zealand to use its weather reporting station on Pitcairn Island as a cover to ascertain if nearby Henderson Island was suitable for an airfield linking a possible postwar air route from New Zealand to Britain via South America.[38]

The United States was just as assiduous in seeking to re-establish its aviation interests in the Pacific, with Roosevelt taking a close personal interest in the construction of bases across the Pacific that would deter any future expansion by Japan. The president also tried to appropriate the plan of Australian aviator P. G. Taylor by dispatching the Antarctic explorer Admiral Byrd on an expedition to assess the potential of Clipperton Island, the key to Taylor's alternative trans-Pacific route that would bypass Hawaii and link Australia to Britain. Among Byrd's party aboard the USS *Concord* when he sailed from Panama to the Galapagos Islands and Clipperton Island on 5 September 1943 were representatives of six American airlines. After making his survey, Byrd reported that Roosevelt had been 'entirely correct about Clipperton and the strategic and commercial value of certain key islands in the Tuamoto, Marquesas and Society Groups, as well as about the feasibility of new air routes to the South Pacific'. Byrd urged Roosevelt not to allow the sovereignty of any Pacific island to be transferred without American permission. 'We have ahead of us,' he wrote, 'unparalleled opportunities which may never come again that this war has developed for the United States.' The American chiefs of staff had also drawn up a list of Pacific bases, from Alaska through to the Philippines, then south to the Solomon Islands and east to the Marquesas, which they considered Washington should control after the war. They planned to avoid any stigma of imperialism by leasing the bases rather than annexing them, and using the cover of the United Nations to do it. Roosevelt pronounced it 'excellent'.[39]

Meanwhile, Taylor continued his lonely campaign to survey the route by way of Clipperton, apparently unaware of the American survey. He attached himself to the RAF transport command, shuffling bombers from North American factories across the Atlantic to Britain. This allowed him to press his case in both Washington and London, which he did unremittingly. Eventually Taylor came into contact with some RAF officers from the air route planning section and, as Taylor subsequently described it, 'over a few beers in the local pub under Westminster Bridge they were soon very inspired with enthusiasm for the R.A.F. route to the Pacific'. Together they 'drafted a signal which ... we felt would produce the necessary results in Washington'.[40] It seemed that Taylor might finally get his chance to prove the viability of his trans-Pacific air route.

As Taylor pursued his personal odyssey, Curtin wrestled with the problem of Australian manpower while at the same time trying to position the dominion's economy so that it could benefit from the resumption of peacetime trade. The government had already decided in July 1943 to discontinue the attempt to produce tanks in Australia, after the Americans had refused to support it any longer. It had been a costly program, begun by Menzies in 1940 for political as much as military reasons, which had failed after three years to produce a single operational tank. The Labor government had persisted with it as much for postwar industrial development and future defence purposes as for wartime needs. Tanks might have been crucial to Australia's defence in 1942, had they been available, but they were of limited use in 1943 against the Japanese in the islands. Indeed, Blamey informed the advisory war council on 14 October 1943 that Australian armoured divisions were being broken up into brigades, and it was being considered whether their British and American tanks could be put into storage and the troops transferred to the infantry. If further tanks were required in the future, better ones than Australia had been planning to produce could now be secured from American factories. This decision would allow the eight thousand skilled personnel who were assigned to the local tank program to be diverted to more essential tasks.[41]

As a further move to reshape the Australian war effort while securing postwar markets, the government decided in October 1943 to increase the supply of food for Britain and reduce the supply for MacArthur's forces. Britain had always been Australia's main market for primary produce and Canberra was keen to ensure that its traditional share of that market was secured prior to the end of the Pacific war, when Britain might otherwise be forced to turn to alternative suppliers. As a further sign of the changing relationship with MacArthur, Curtin bluntly informed him that the primary reason for the Australian decision was 'the maintenance to some degree of markets which would be important to the Australian export trade in the post-war period'.[42] The government was beginning to realise that Australian forces might not accompany MacArthur on his triumphant march back to the Philippines and beyond. If the troops were to be relegated to a secondary theatre, or to garrison duties where they could neither win glory nor guarantee a voice for Australia at the peace table, they might as well be back on the farm or in the burgeoning factories. As Curtin revealed during a press conference on 17 November, 'the trend of things showed that despite the government's objections, the role which Australia would play [in future Pacific operations] was that of the "hewer of wood and carrier of water"'.[43]

Although MacArthur expressed the 'strongest protest' at the Australian decision, which amounted to a partial demobilisation, he agreed with Curtin that the final decision was Australia's to make and that he would comply with it. MacArthur also agreed to do what he could to help the Australian production of aircraft after Curtin announced that the dominion was pressing ahead with the program in the face of MacArthur's advice to the contrary. In a draft press statement describing their talks and meant for release by Curtin, it was claimed that Australia's war effort was entering a new phase in which its role would be 'a mighty one'. During this phase, the continent would be used as a base from which would be launched 'one of the major offensives of the war'.[44] The statement implied that the war effort was being built up rather than scaled down, with Curtin being quoted as claiming that MacArthur was 'a vital factor in all decisions to be taken not only along military lines but those of commerce, industry and economics' and that Curtin was 'indebted to General MacArthur for the high statesmanship and breadth of world vision he has contributed to the discussion'. High praise indeed, and no wonder considering the statement was drawn up by MacArthur's intelligence chief, General Willoughby, before the talks and then handed to Shedden for Curtin to issue on their completion.[45]

In 1942, the statement probably would have been issued to the press without question. But now Shedden warned Curtin that it was dangerous to suggest that the scale of the Australian war effort had been 'fixed' with MacArthur rather than, as it had been, simply communicated to him by Curtin. Moreover, wrote Shedden, the reference to a 'mighty' Australian effort in the future 'might prove embarrassing at some time', while describing MacArthur as a 'vital factor' in Australian manpower decisions was 'imprudent in view of the widespread comment at present being aroused about American imperialism being furthered under the cloak of the Military Command in the South West Pacific Area'. Shedden submitted a completely revised statement that made the 'fullest use' of MacArthur's verbal agreement to the Australian switch of resources in order to formally and publicly commit him to it. When it was finally issued by Curtin on 3 December, it announced that 'General MacArthur has expressed his full agreement with the general principles laid down by the Government' and that Curtin had 'assured General MacArthur that Australia's war effort, whatever shape it may take by this process of re-adjustment, will be the maximum of which Australia is capable'.[46]

While Curtin was seeking to reshape Australia's war effort, Churchill and Roosevelt were planning Allied operations for the coming year. The offensive in Italy had bogged down south of Rome and Churchill's wild scheme to capture several Greek islands from the Germans had backfired when the Germans had just as promptly recaptured them. With the Allied effort in Italy being restricted by the need to build up forces in Britain for the invasion of France, Churchill feared that their divided forces might be defeated in both places. To coordinate Allied policy on these issues, Churchill and Roosevelt planned to meet with their military chiefs in Cairo prior to their first meeting with Stalin in Tehran. As darkness fell on 12 November, Churchill and his small entourage sailed out of Plymouth on board the battleship *Renown*, bound for Alexandria. After meeting with officials in Gibraltar, Malta and Algiers, Churchill finally fetched up in Cairo in time to greet Roosevelt when he landed on 22 November. Also there was the Chinese leader, Chiang Kai-shek, and Mountbatten, with Britain's future operations in the Far East being high on the agenda for the Cairo conference.

The Americans had insisted on meeting first with Chiang Kai-shek, rather than leaving him and discussion of the Far East until after the meeting with Stalin. To Churchill's horror, Roosevelt also agreed without consulting the British to a Chinese request for an amphibious operation across the Bay of Bengal to Burma. Landing craft had already been diverted from Mountbatten's forces to the operations in Italy, and Churchill was obsessed with ensuring that the cross-Channel invasion of France would have sufficient resources to overwhelm the Germans and secure a lodgment on French soil. He also remained adamant that his cherished operation against Sumatra was preferable to footslogging through Burma. However, he was unable to prevent Chiang Kai-shek leaving Cairo with the commitment from Roosevelt.

Following their meeting, Churchill and Roosevelt flew to Tehran for a conference with Stalin, who promised to join the war against Japan once Germany was defeated. The British and the Americans, both overwhelmed by the prospect of defeating the Japanese, were relieved. Before the development of missiles, distance was a formidable barrier to the successful prosecution of war. There was no guarantee that the American atomic bomb would be ready in time or that it would work in the manner the physicists predicted. The Allies had to assume that Japan could only be defeated by an invasion of the Japanese home islands with the countless Allied casualties that this was likely to entail. So Stalin's offer was gratefully accepted. To Churchill's relief, it allowed him to convince Roosevelt upon their return to Cairo to cancel the commitment to China. As Eden reported to the war cabinet, with the removal of this 'great obstacle', the conference 'ended with complete agreement and general satisfaction'.[47]

At Cairo, Churchill also tried to convince a delegation from Turkey to join the war, offering them substantial British forces if they agreed. This dubious plan to enlist the Turks was a legacy of Churchill's thwarted ambitions during the First World War to defeat the German empire from the south-east, a strategy that came to grief at Gallipoli and cost him his post at the Admiralty, blighting his career and his reputation. Churchill, according to a close observer, 'persuaded himself that he can bring Turkey into the war and keeps turning over in his mind the consequences, just as if it had already happened. He does not stop to ask what the Turks themselves are thinking.'[48] Once again, his hopes were dashed when Turkey, still fearful of Germany, refused to cooperate.[49] It was further evidence that Churchill would consider the wildest schemes in the Mediterranean in preference to any commitment in the Far East.[50]

As at Quebec, there was much rhetoric about the importance of the Far East but little of substance was announced. Australia was angry that the Allies again had met and decided issues of importance to the dominion without any attempt at consultation and little information after the event. At a meeting with journalists on 6 December, Curtin made it quite clear that Australia had been left out in the cold by its Allies, remarking bitterly that 'They don't tell us anything'. Indeed, Australian newspapers received the text of the public communiqué from the conference before the government had sighted it.[51]

What particularly alarmed the Australian government were the terms of that communiqué, in which the Allies undertook to strip Japan of all its conquests and restore to China all those territories taken from it by the Japanese. Moreover, it proclaimed that the Allies 'covet no gain for themselves and have no thought of territorial expansion'.[52] This was not true of Washington or Moscow, and was certainly not true of Canberra, which was particularly angered by the news that Churchill had pressured Roosevelt to agree that the European empires in the Pacific would also have their territories restored to them. As Eden assured the British war cabinet, Churchill 'had on several occasions said that we asked for no increase of territory for ourselves at the end of the war, but likewise we were not going to give any up'.[53]

Australia had hoped to create a regional empire from the detritus of the European empires that would shield it from future threats and allow for its economic expansion. Even as the Allied leaders were meeting, Evatt had been planning his own conference with New Zealand leaders at which he intended to stake out Australia's territorial claims in the Pacific. Australia was also resisting Dutch attempts to establish an administrative structure within Australia, preparatory to the Dutch recapturing the Netherlands East Indies.[54] All these Australian plans were now threatened by the conclusions of the Cairo conference.

NOTES

[1] War Cabinet Minutes, 1 October 1943, CRS A2673/XIII/3065; Press release, undated, CRS A5954, Box 305A; Cabinet Minutes, 21 October 1943, CRS A2703/1(D), NAA.

[2] Memorandum by Shedden, 1 July 1943, CRS A5954, Box 301, NAA.

[3] Dalton diary, 9 December 1943, I/29/154, Dalton Papers, LSE.

[4] Cabinet Minutes, 22 September 1943, CRS A2703/1(D), NAA.

[5] Pownall diary, 2 October 1943, in Bond (ed.), *Chief of Staff*, Vol. 2, p. 109; Minute, Lambe to Cunningham, 3 November 1943, and Admiralty Board Minutes, 4 November 1943, ADM 205/33, PRO.

[6] Notes of Discussion with MacArthur, 25–31 May 1943, CRS A5954, Box 2, NAA.

[7] Letters, Blamey to Curtin, 2 June and 5 October 1943, CRS A5954, Box 306, NAA; See also Letter, Forde to Curtin, 31 July 1943, same file.

[8] Notes on discussions with MacArthur, 16–20 January 1943, CRS A5954, Box 2, NAA; Note by Sir Walter Layton, October 1943, PREM 3/159/2, PRO; Spector, *Eagle Against the Sun*, pp. 232–3.

[9] Notes on talk with Curtin, 22 October 1943, PREM 3/159/2, PRO; See also other documents in this file.

[10] Cable, Curtin to Churchill, 8 October 1943, *DAFP*, Vol. 6, Doc. 293. Many countries experienced similar manpower problems. The organisational structures drawn up at the beginning of the war were almost invariably over-optimistic and had to be scaled down when the flow of recruits proved unable to sustain them. For details of this, see Perry, *The Commonwealth Armies*. In the case of the German army, Hitler kept diminished divisions on the Russian front rather than amalgamating them to keep them up to strength. See Liddell Hart, *The Second World War*, pp. 507–8.

[11] Cable, Curtin to Churchill, 8 October 1943, *DAFP*, Vol. 6, Doc. 293.

[12] Note, Ismay to Churchill, 23 January 1944, and Note, Cranborne to Churchill, 21 January 1944, PREM 3/63/8, PRO.

[13] Minute, Churchill to Cranborne, 25 January 1944, PREM 3/63/8, PRO.

[14] Note by Chiefs of Staff, 1 May 1944, PREM 3/63/8, PRO.

[15] Letter, MacArthur to Curtin, 8 September 1943, CRS A5954, Box 218, NAA.

[16] Letters, Storey to Curtin, 4 October 1943, and Curtin to Storey, 11 October 1943, and War Cabinet Minute, 11 November 1943, CRS A5954, Box 218, NAA; War Cabinet Agendum by Curtin, 23 September 1943, CRS A5954, Box 345, NAA.

[17] Advisory War Council Minute, 11 November 1943, CRS A5954, Box 218, NAA.

[18] *Age*, Melbourne, 16 October 1943.

[19] *Age*, Melbourne, 15 October 1943; See also Cable, Commonwealth Government to Bruce, 8 October 1943, CRS A5954, Box 345, NAA.

[20] Letter, Dewing to Ismay, 18 November 1943, IV/Dew/3/3c, Ismay Papers, KC.

[21] Cabinet Minutes, 23 November 1943, CRS A2703/1(D), NAA.

[22] Cited in *Argus*, Melbourne, 17 November 1943; See also Letter, Campbell Stuart to Gowrie, 17 November 1943, MS 2852/4/21/24, Gowrie Papers, NLA.

[23] Calwell was 30 years too early. It was not until Gough Whitlam's Labor government in the early 1970s that the anthem was changed. Background briefing, 8 December 1943, MS 4675, Smith Papers, NLA.

[24] Cable, Churchill to War Cabinet Office, 25 August 1943, PREM 3/150/8, PRO; Message, Shedden to MacArthur, 27 August 1943 and Letter, Blamey to Brooke, 29 November 1943, and other documents in this file, CRS A5954, Box 463, NAA.

[25] Prime Minister's War Conference, 29 November–1 December 1943, CRS A5954, Box 2; Letter, Air Marshal Williams to Drakeford, 24 November 1943, CRS A3300/258, NAA; *Argus*, Melbourne, 27 October 1943.

[26] Prime Minister's War Conference, 29 November–1 December 1943, CRS A5954, Box 2; Letter, McVey to Colonel Wilson, 29 November 1943, CRS A5954, Box 218, NAA.

[27] *Herald*, Melbourne, 1 October 1943; Kimball (ed.), *Churchill and Roosevelt*, Vol. 2, pp. 527–30.

[28] Cable, Law to Eden and Churchill, 8 October 1943, and Minute, Churchill to Eden, 9 October 1943, PREM 3/158/7, PRO.

[29] 'Summary of Air Ministry Memorandum', British High Commission, Canberra, 16 September 1943, CRS A5954, Box 345, NAA. For an extensive file on British concern about the American development of air facilities in Fiji and their fear that the Americans would try to retain residual rights, see BBK D/214, Beaverbrook Papers, HLRO.

[30] Cable, Dominions Secretary to Commonwealth Government, 3 July 1943, CRS A5954, Box 345, NAA.

[31] Letter, Cross to Churchill, 11 August 1943, PREM 3/151/4, PRO.

[32] For the Anglo–American view of the future United Nations organisation, see War Cabinet Conclusions/Confidential Annex, 13 April 1943, CAB 65/38, W.M. (43)53, and 'United Nations Plan for Organising Peace', Memorandum by Eden, 7 July 1943, CAB 66/38, W.P. (43)300, PRO.

[33] See PREM 3/366/8, PRO.

[34] Memorandum by Beaverbrook, 3 December 1943, CAB 66/43, W.P. (43)537, PRO.

[35] Letters, Amery to Beaverbrook and Beaverbrook to Amery, 5 and 6 October 1943, BBK D/228, Beaverbrook Papers, HLRO.

[36] Letter, J. E. Stephenson to Batterbee, 28 October 1943, BBK D/274, Beaverbrook Papers, HLRO.

[37] Cable, Bruce to Commonwealth Government, 27 October 1943, CRS A5954, Box 345, NAA; War Cabinet Conclusions, 27 October 1943, CAB 65/36, W.M. (43)146, PRO.

[38] Talk with Beaverbrook, 22 December 1943, CRS M100, NAA; Cable, New Zealand Government to Dominions Office, 25 November 1943, and Cable, Dominions Office to New Zealand Government, 9 December 1943, BBK D/274, Beaverbrook Papers, HLRO.

[39] Cable (extract), Campbell to Foreign Office, 12 August 1943, BBK D/221, Beaverbrook Papers, HLRO; Cable, Dixon to Curtin, 11 August 1943, CRS A3300/264, NAA; Louis, *Imperialism at Bay*, pp. 269–73.

[40] Letter, Taylor to Bowhill, 11 November 1943, MS 2852/4/22/28, Gowrie Papers, NLA; P. G. Taylor, *The Sky Beyond*, pp. 159–61.

41 Advisory War Council Minute, 14 October 1943, CRS A5954, Box 261; War Cabinet Minute, 13 July 1943, and War Cabinet Agendum, CRS A2670/299/1943, NAA; Butlin and Schedvin, *War Economy 1942–1945*, pp. 70–9.

42 See documents in CRS A5954, Boxes 306, 309 and 843, NAA.

43 Press Conference, 17 November 1943, MS 4675, Smith Papers, NLA.

44 Draft press statement, 28 November 1943, CRS A5954, Box 306, NAA.

45 ibid.

46 Minute, Shedden to Curtin, 1 December 1943, and Message, Rodgers to Diller, 3 December 1943, CRS A5954, Box 306, NAA.

47 War Cabinet Conclusions/Confidential Annex, 13 December 1943, CAB 65/40, W.M. (43)169, PRO.

48 Moran diary, 5 December 1943, in Moran, *Winston Churchill*, p. 145.

49 Gilbert, *Road to Victory*, pp. 596–8.

50 The quick British capture and equally quick fall of the Italian-held islands of Leros and Samos off the coast of Turkey at the end of 1943 was an example of Churchill's eagerness to take wild gambles with forces in the Mediterranean in pursuit of distant and doubtful objectives. Harvey diary, 18 November 1943, ADD. MS. 56400, Harvey Papers, BL; Bryant, *Triumph in the West*, pp. 48–58.

51 Press Conference, 6 December 1943, MS 4675, Smith Papers, NLA.

52 Cable, Cranborne to Curtin, 1 December 1943, *DAFP*, Vol. 6, Doc. 340.

53 War Cabinet Conclusions, 13 December 1943, CAB 65/40, W.M. (43)169, PRO; *DAFP*, Vol. 6, p. 606, fn 1.

54 See *DAFP*, Vol. 6, Docs 330, 334, 347–9.

FORTY

'the evil genius of this war'

On 30 November 1943, a grand banquet was held at the British legation in Tehran for Churchill's 69th birthday. It also marked the end of the Allied conference between Churchill, Roosevelt and Stalin. Along with their respective military chiefs, the three leaders toasted each other across the table in the Russian manner, using Churchill's favourite champagne tipple as the lubricant. The British prime minister had much to celebrate. As he cabled to Attlee, 'relations between Britain, United States and USSR have never been so cordial and intimate. All war plans are agreed and concerted.'[1] They had agreed to defer the cross-Channel invasion of France until 1 June 1944, timing it to coincide with Stalin's spring offensive on the eastern front, and they had agreed to maintain the offensive in Italy. Only in the Far East was there any lingering disagreement.

With the possibility of Germany being defeated during the course of the coming year, the Allies needed to decide on their strategy for the subsequent defeat of Japan. The Americans had looked to China to play a large part in this, with Chinese airfields to be used as launching pads for a bombing offensive that would blast Japan into submission. China was also promoted by Roosevelt as one of the four great powers, along with Britain, the United States and the Soviet Union, which would underpin the future world organisation. To emphasise this, Roosevelt had made a point upon his arrival at Cairo of meeting first with the Chinese leader, Chiang Kai-shek, before he met with Churchill. Despite Roosevelt's agreement to the Burma operation at that first Cairo meeting, the Americans were starting to look beyond the obvious attractions of China and were beginning to realise that there were alternative and less costly approaches to defeating Japan. The naval thrust through the central Pacific, together with the production of increasingly long-range bombers, was likely to bring the Japanese mainland within reach of American air power without the need to rely on Chinese airfields, which were vulnerable to capture by the Japanese army. Moreover, the likelihood of the Russians declaring war against Japan as soon as Germany was defeated might allow their much closer territory to be used.

Under pressure from the British chiefs of staff at Tehran, and a few days later at the second Cairo conference in early December, the Americans finally relented and allowed the Burma operation to be deferred so that the landing craft could be concentrated against Germany. The decision confirmed again that the world was faced with two wars, not one, and that Allied strategy would concentrate on fighting the European conflict first. As General Ismay proclaimed with relief, Britain had resisted 'any resources of any kind that were required to beat the Boche being diverted at this juncture against the Yellow Man'.[2]

Although excluded from all these discussions, Australians who were anxious to see a larger British presence in their region could take some comfort from British plans to shift the weight of its naval effort from the Indian Ocean to the Pacific in early 1944. The British navy had always been keen to position its ships alongside the Americans in the Pacific, where the outcome of the war against Japan would be decided. The Eastern fleet commander, Admiral Somerville, had made several proposals to this effect and was finally rewarded in December 1943 with news from the first sea lord, Admiral Cunningham, that 'towards the end of March a large slice of your fleet will go to the Pacific'.[3] To boost the strength of Britain's prospective Pacific fleet, three battleships and four destroyers were dispatched on 30 December from Scapa Flow off the far north coast of Scotland. They were joined by two aircraft carriers and three more destroyers, with the squadron steaming into Colombo at the end of January 1944.[4]

Even before it had left British waters, Churchill had queried the cost of sending a fleet all the way to the Pacific. To sustain a modern fleet so far from any British base required a whole fleet of cargo ships, oilers and repair ships, known as a 'fleet train', shuttling supplies from Britain and elsewhere. After having managed to postpone Mountbatten's planned amphibious operations in Burma, Churchill now worried that the planned British Pacific fleet might be an equally heavy drain on the limited British resources and detract from the effort against Germany.[5] It might also doom the chances of the operation that Churchill still wanted to mount against northern Sumatra preparatory to an assault on Singapore.

At the beginning of January 1944, while recovering in Marrakech from an almost fatal bout of pneumonia, Churchill was asked to approve a cable to the dominions informing them of the tentative plans reached at Cairo with the Americans. He agreed, providing that these plans would not preclude the operation against Sumatra, his much-favoured Operation Culverin. The chiefs of staff conceded that dispatching forces to the Pacific would make Culverin more unlikely but argued that the Pacific strategy should take precedence over South-East Asia. To win Churchill over, the chiefs added 'one final point for your private ear which we have mentioned to no-one'. That was to have a large part of Britain's effort in the Pacific comprised of dominion land forces, buttressed with British forces and 'based on British possessions'. They also intended to insist that the command of this area be ceded to the British. With the addition of these dominion forces, Britain would give the appearance of making a mightier effort against Japan than it was in fact preparing to do. First, though, the dominions would have to be advised so that possible logistical problems could be investigated in Australia.[6]

Ensconced in his villa at Marrakech, Churchill was not convinced by the arguments of his advisers in London, although he conceded that Stalin's intention to enter the Pacific war once Germany had been defeated meant that Allied plans for the Pacific would have to be revised. While the chiefs wanted to shift the British effort from the Indian Ocean to the Pacific and join America and Russia in a joint thrust at the Japanese heartland, Churchill wanted to use the Russian assault on Japan as a cover for Britain's operations in South-East Asia, such as the one against Sumatra. Accordingly, he ordered that the dominions were to be kept in the dark until he had fully recovered his health and been able to review the whole issue of British strategy against Japan.[7]

Meanwhile, the British admiral in command of the Australian navy, Sir Guy Royle, was informed unofficially by Cunningham that a British naval squadron would arrive in Australia in March 1944. Ever since Pearl Harbor, the Australian navy had been awaiting the arrival of the British fleet and had made provision for its berthing and dry-docking. Its arrival now could help to restore the status of the Australian navy at a time when it was being squeezed by the manpower crisis and falling behind the army and air force in the scale of Australian priorities. Royle informed Somerville that a dry dock suitable for capital ships was being built at a cost of £7 million in Sydney Harbour and would be ready by July 1944. 'We should be flattered and pleased,' wrote Royle, 'if anyone would make use of that' as well as the facilities that had been developed at Darwin and Fremantle. The arrival of the British fleet would also strengthen Royle's campaign to have another British officer succeed him as Australian naval chief when his appointment came to an end. The Australian government had other ideas, having appointed the Australian officer Captain John Collins to command the Australian squadron at sea with a view to promoting him to Royle's post in twelve months' time.[8]

Despite this move to have an Australian naval commander, the government was not pursuing a defence policy based upon narrow nationalism and a blank rejection of the prewar system of imperial defence. Rather, it was trying to formulate a scheme of postwar defence that would guarantee Australian security. Although Curtin had been the leading proponent of local defence during the late 1930s, and the fall of Singapore had confirmed the mistrust of the labour movement with the system of imperial defence, Curtin realised that Australia's future defence needs could not be met from its own resources alone. Acting on Shedden's advice, Curtin set out to soften the justifiable antagonism of the labour movement towards Britain and to develop a defence policy that would provide for Australia's security within a redefined British empire.

Shedden proposed that Australia's future security would have to be based on a combination of its own defence effort, cooperation with the Commonwealth and collective security under any new international organisation that was formed out of the war. While Curtin would have no trouble convincing his party about the first and third options, he would face resistance in arguing the case for cooperation with Britain. The solution, suggested Shedden, was to stress the contribution that such Commonwealth cooperation would make to a new world order. This would mean Curtin partially repudiating the arguments in favour of local defence that he had used during the 1937 election campaign.[9] Curtin accepted Shedden's advice, telling a federal conference of the Labor Party in December 1943 that a narrowly nationalistic approach would not guarantee the country's security, that their new citizenship responsibilities involved being 'a good Australian, a good British subject and a good world citizen'. To clinch his argument, Curtin reminded the delegates of the 'teeming millions of coloured races to the north of Australia', which meant that the dominion must therefore be 'harnessed to other nations'. This did not mean Australia returning to its former position of dependence upon Britain. Instead, its own increased strength, combined with Commonwealth cooperation and regional cooperation with the United Nations, would allow Australia a 'pre-eminent position to speak with authority on the problems of the Pacific and have a primary interest in their solution'.[10]

With his bold vision of a postwar Pacific in which a more independent Australia would play a leading role, Curtin managed to convince the isolationists, the imperialists and the internationalists that Australia's future lay with Britain. After the Japanese had come so close to Australian shores, the spectre of a future Asian invasion also would have had deep resonance with his audience. Australians had long had an underlying feeling that they had yet to enjoy the sort of total control of their land that most nations take for granted.[11] In order to secure their possession and meet the future possibility of a hostile 'Asiatic bloc', Curtin planned a massive immigration program to bring settlers from northern Europe and Italy, although he rejected suggestions of a Jewish settlement being established in Australia's 'vacant' spaces. His immigration plans also did not extend to Asians, who would continue to be rigorously barred from the continent under the White Australia policy, although Curtin claimed defensively that it was because of their 'antagonism to the white man'.[12] With his background as an international socialist, Curtin never seemed comfortable when justifying the White Australia policy. As prime minister of a nation that looked partly to Asian markets to underpin its postwar economic recovery, Curtin also realised that it would be difficult to sell manufactured goods to 'Asiatics and other colored people, [while] at the same time strenuously refusing them access to an empty Australia'.[13] But he could see no way around this apparent conundrum.

The racial dimension was a very real consideration for the men directing the course of the war and shaping the postwar world.[14] Churchill was as susceptible to racism as any Australian. As Lord Moran observed, when Churchill thinks of the Chinese he 'thinks only of the colour of their skin; it is when he talks of India or China that you remember he is a Victorian'.[15] Similarly, Admiral Somerville was 'disgusted' to find that British nurses at a hospital in Ceylon were treating wounded Indian servicemen. He immediately ordered it to stop and for the 'segregation of Asiatics from Europeans'.[16] In 1941, Anthony Eden had objected to a plan for settling the problem in Palestine, observing to his secretary that 'the Arabs are neither as black as you paint them ... nor a Jew-filled Palestine so white a panorama ... If we *must* have preferences, let me murmur in your ear that I prefer Arabs to Jews!'[17] In 1943 his secretary noted that Eden 'loves Arabs and hates Jews'.[18] Beaverbrook had revealed similar sympathies when replying to an Australian friend who had likened Jewish refugees to 'a cancer developing in our midst'. Beaverbrook observed that Britain also had its 'share of the Jewish refugee problem' which he regarded as 'extremely difficult and disagreeable' and hoped that the war would 'relieve us of this cause of anxiety about the future'.[19] This sort of racism passed without comment at the time.

Curtin had other causes for anxiety at the end of 1943, with bureaucratic inertia and resistance from interest groups subverting the government's decisions about manpower. Instead of releasing forty thousand people from the services and munitions industries, a cabinet sub-committee had passed the matter back to Curtin for further decision. With harvest time approaching, primary producers were becoming restive about their promised labour supply. Shedden warned Curtin that *you are personally going to carry the responsibility* for deciding on cuts in war industries and finding the much-needed labour. It was time, urged Shedden, to be 'direct and ruthless'.[20] Curtin would have to confront MacArthur, who was resisting the government's attempts to limit the Australian manpower servicing his forces. While previously he had supported the construction of Lancaster bombers in Australia, MacArthur now informed Curtin that the matter was out of his hands due to a ruling from Washington that prevented resources going to projects that might not come to fruition during the course of the war.[21]

The Lancasters were an essential part of Australia's plan for asserting its supremacy in the south-west Pacific once the war was won, with Australia hoping to exercise both economic and military control over the array of colonial territories to its north and east. In a report to the Australian government on 5 January 1944, the defence committee advised that the 'best means of securing Australia from invasion is by taking strong offensive action from established and well defended forward bases'. It recommended that such bases be established in territories stretching from Java through Timor and the Solomons to New Caledonia and Fiji. The committee, composed of Shedden and the chiefs of staff, ignored the central lesson of the war: that Australia could not rely on a distant power to protect it from invasion. While it rejected the United States as a replacement for Britain, the report declared that the 'best assurance' of Australia's security was provided by a 'scheme of Imperial defence formulated and carried out by the members of the British Commonwealth in co-operation'.[22] It was as if the fall of Singapore had never happened, with Shedden and the chiefs of staff proposing that imperial defence remain the cornerstone of Australian defence policy, albeit with Australia playing a more forthright role.

With his troops battling both the Japanese and the tropical conditions in New Guinea, General Blamey was less convinced about Australia being able to man a string of island fortifications after the war. Such distant defences had proved untenable in 1941–42 and were proving similarly untenable for the Japanese. Australian forces in their island redoubts could be bypassed by a future invader in the same way as the Allies were presently bypassing the Japanese island strongholds. Rather than Australia requiring bases on Java, Blamey argued for the Dutch to be 'wholeheartedly' supported in retrieving the Netherlands East Indies which, although of 'vital interest' to Australia, was 'beyond the capacity of Australia to exert any direct influence [over]'. While Blamey rejected the defence committee's plan for a string of offshore fortresses, he did agree that Australia's postwar defence policy had to be based upon 'a closer degree of co-operation, and a closer alignment of common interest in the Empire than ever before in our history'. As for American bases in the Pacific, Blamey believed that these should only be encouraged where they could not pose a future threat to Australia. He also disparaged the idea of an alliance with New Zealand, claiming that there was little common interest between the two dominions, despite their close geographic position. In the event of a future invasion, they would not stand or fall together but one after the other, with Australia being first in line. Thus, Australia's defence effort had to be concentrated at home rather than in the islands or New Zealand. Blamey urged that 'a very close study of this position should be made ... before we commit ourselves to common action or agreement with that country'.[23] His advice was not heeded.

Curtin read Blamey's memo on 19 January, in the midst of his discussions in Canberra with the New Zealand prime minister, Peter Fraser, as to how their two countries could forestall America's territorial ambitions in the region. Their meeting came in the wake of the Cairo talks between Churchill, Roosevelt and Chiang Kai-shek, when discussions were had about the Pacific without Australia or New Zealand being consulted. So the Canberra talks were held without consulting either London or Washington, although their motive was certainly not anti-British. In a statement on defence to the Canberra conference, Curtin had proclaimed the need for a strategic naval base such as Singapore and a fleet that could command the seas of the region. Since neither dominion could provide such a base, or the fleet to go with it, cooperation with Britain was 'therefore essential', said Curtin. Since it would be easier to reach agreement on imperial defence than it would be to establish a system of collective security, which must await the creation of the United Nations organisation, it was essential 'that an understanding should be reached as quickly as possible in regard to closer co-operation in Empire Defence'.[24]

When their conference concluded on 21 January, Curtin and Fraser signed the Australia–New Zealand Agreement which, among other things, asserted their pre-eminent right to determine territorial changes in the region. Rejecting the Allied decisions in Cairo, they declared that the disposal of enemy islands in the Pacific 'should be effected only with their agreement and as part of a general Pacific settlement'. To begin the process of deciding the future of colonial territories in the Pacific, they called for a conference of Pacific powers that would include Australia and New Zealand. They also declared that the United States should not be able to retain control over US bases built on foreign soil during the course of the war and that the White Australia policy would not be subject to change by any future international organisation.[25]

With Roosevelt and Churchill having made promises to Stalin and Chiang Kai-shek at Cairo about the postwar carve-up of Japanese territories, the Anzac agreement was a belated attempt to assert Australia's right to share in the shaping of the Pacific. It was not, as is sometimes suggested, a trick pulled out of the hat by Evatt at the final meeting of the conference and signed by delegates too tired to notice its significance. Despite Curtin's later attempts to disown the agreement, its terms accorded with statements by both Evatt and Curtin stretching back for many months. In that sense, the agreement was not an aberration in Australian foreign policy but its logical outcome. The success of the agreement, though, depended on the willingness of Washington and London to accept its conditions. It also presumed that Australia and New Zealand had common interests. Although they were both primary producing countries, they mostly produced the same products and tended to compete for business within the same markets. As Blamey had noted, they also had different defence outlooks, as was seen by New Zealand keeping its troops in Europe rather than withdrawing them to fight alongside Australia in New Guinea.

When the agreement was cabled to Washington and London, it was regarded as another shrill scream for attention. Britain's dominions secretary, Lord Cranborne, tried to calm the hostility of his cabinet colleagues by explaining that, while the agreement had been reached without any consultation with Britain, Evatt had been careful to claim that it arose from anxiety

concerning the United States' attempts at infiltrating in non-American Pacific Islands south of the Equator and 'anxiety concerning similar tendencies in Australia and New Zealand'. A second motive, Dr Evatt said, derived from the view ... that the United Kingdom Government tended 'to concede too easily proposals made by the United States of America in relation to the Pacific'.

Britain too was worried by American encroachments in the Pacific, especially if they impinged upon British sovereignty in places such as Fiji where the Americans had built an air base. As such, Cranborne was prepared to overlook Evatt's criticism of Britain and the risk to the empire of such unilateral declarations, arguing that the assertion of defence responsibility by Australia and New Zealand 'may be extremely valuable when we come to arrangements for the post-war period'. In other words, Britain might be able to shift some of the responsibility for defending its Pacific territories onto Australia. At the same time, though, Cranborne dismissed the call for a Pacific conference since it would undermine the prerogatives of the Great Powers in settling the peace. Killing off this Anzac proposal had to be done carefully, said Cranborne, as Evatt would 'resent anything that he may regard as grandmotherly restraint by the mother country'.[26]

The war cabinet took Cranborne's advice, declaring that the 'offer to share in defence responsibilities in the Pacific [was] a notable landmark' and instructing that the British response to the Anzac agreement should 'be more cordial'.[27] The British attitude worked wonders, with Peter Fraser expressing his 'warm gratitude' for London's restrained response. It would have been 'a great mistake', said Fraser, for the British government to have 'shown any sign of soreness'. That would only have antagonised Evatt, 'who was now "on our side"'.[28] Not that Britain would countenance the right of their dominions to decide any postwar carve-up of colonial territories in the south-west Pacific. To ensure that could not happen, both Britain and the United States opposed the calling of a Pacific conference, which thereby neutralised a crucial part of the agreement. Arguing that such a conference could cause public disunity among the Allies if they clashed over the postwar allocation of Pacific territories, the US secretary of state, Cordell Hull, called on Curtin not to press for it. Hull suggested instead that Curtin discuss the issues personally in Washington while en route to the Commonwealth prime ministers' meeting in London, which was scheduled to begin in May.[29] That delay would ensure that it was kept on the backburner for several months, and perhaps lost to sight forever. Of course, Washington did not really fear disunity with its Allies, since the various informal talks between America, Britain, Russia and China would soon settle all the issues of sovereignty without Australia being involved. What America feared was that the two dominions might disturb Washington's plans.

Evatt had been more anxious than Curtin to hold the Pacific conference. He realised that the battle for control of the Pacific was being fought on two fronts: between the Japanese and the Allies on the ground; and between the Allies themselves. Australia was being sidelined by MacArthur in the military battle and was not involved at all in the secret discussions that were deciding the future shape of the Pacific. Without consulting Evatt, Curtin assured Hull on 3 February that 'it did not appear reasonable that there could be an early conference arising out of the Australian–New Zealand discussions'.[30] That was self-evident if it faced opposition from Britain and the United States. Moreover, it would need the participation of France, Portugal and the Netherlands, since it was the future of their territories, as well as Britain's and America's, that would be discussed at any conference. Yet Curtin allowed Evatt to reply to Hull's concerns in a way that kept his cherished conference idea alive.

In his reply, Evatt defended the Pacific conference as 'a helpful contribution to the maintenance of harmonious relations among the United Nations' rather than posing a threat of disunity. Moreover, argued Evatt, it was not a kneejerk reaction to the Cairo conference, with Evatt pointing out that he had first proposed such a conference two months before the meeting in Cairo had taken place. He insisted that the conference should still be held, if necessary after the talks in London between the Commonwealth prime ministers. He reminded Hull that Australia had not been informed of the Cairo decisions affecting the sovereignty of Pacific territories and complained that Roosevelt had been deciding these questions for some time. For instance, at the Pacific war council meeting in Washington on 12 January 1944, Roosevelt had said that France 'should not have New Caledonia back under any conditions and that he believed that in this view Australia and New Zealand would back him up'. Far from it, wrote Evatt, both Australia and New Zealand now wanted it returned to France. This would interpose a European power between Australia and the Americans, thereby preventing the stars and stripes from flying all over the Pacific.[31]

Evatt's conference never came. Moreover, as Warren Kimball has pointed out, his indiscreet reference to off-the-record statements made by Roosevelt during Pacific war council meetings was probably responsible for Roosevelt never again convening meetings of that council. As a result, Australia 'lost a mechanism valuable both as a window into American thinking, and as a means of putting ideas directly before the President'.[32] Of course, the forum that the council provided had not guaranteed that Australian views were heeded, but at least they had been heard in the place where it mattered most. Now that ready access to Roosevelt, and the opportunity for insights into his thinking, was closed.

Meanwhile, there was such widespread suspicion in Washington about British motives that the British naval representative, Admiral Sir Percy Noble, warned Whitehall on 12 January 1944 that the Americans were beginning to complain about providing resources to Britain 'when they don't seem to want to use them'. This anti-British hostility had arisen out of the Cairo conference. Noble reported that Admiral King 'quite openly said that it was his opinion that we were not trying our hardest ... in South-East Asia'. Another American admiral had claimed that Britain was going slow in the Far East to cripple China and prevent its postwar recognition as a great power. This admiral had welcomed Mountbatten's appointment but now 'felt like other Americans that the appointment was "a piece of window dressing" on the part of the British'.[33] When Cunningham referred Noble's report to the Admiralty's director of plans, Captain Charles Lambe, he was told that the American view was 'understandable', given the lack of British naval activity against Japan. Lambe urged Cunningham to order the immediate use of the Eastern fleet's aircraft carriers in an operation in the south-west Pacific 'against any target regardless of its importance'. Without such dramatic action, argued Lambe, the Americans and Churchill might combine to force the navy into mounting the operation against Sumatra 'because we *must do something* to save our faces'.[34]

Australia received news of this proposed British naval squadron when Admiral Royle informed the advisory war council that a task force comprising a battle cruiser, two aircraft carriers, four cruisers and twelve destroyers would move to Sydney and operate under the command of America's Admiral Nimitz.[35] Curtin took the news at face value, telling Churchill on 5 February that Australia 'looks forward with great pleasure and keenest anticipation to the arrival here of the first increment of the Royal Navy' which would 'provide a strong uplift to feelings of Empire solidarity'.[36] Churchill, however, ensured at a late night meeting of his defence committee that the plans were quashed. After returning to London on 18 January from his convalescence at Marrakech, Churchill had been advised by the chiefs of staff of their plans for the Pacific war, observing that it would necessarily 'restrict operations in the South-East Asia theatre', specifically Churchill's cherished Sumatran operation and the continuing British operations in Burma.[37] Churchill was furious, denying that he and Roosevelt had agreed to these Pacific plans at the conference in Cairo and expressing his dismay 'at the thought that a large British army and air force would stand inactive in India during the whole of 1944'. Switching the British effort against Japan to the Pacific, declared Churchill, would be 'casting away the substance for the shadow'. The 'substance' was the operation against Sumatra which he claimed 'would provide an important diversion and contain substantial Japanese forces in the Malayan area'.[38]

Now that Stalin had agreed to enter the war against Japan as soon as Germany was conquered, the Allies could attack Japan from that direction far earlier than they could from a naval advance across the Pacific. Churchill instructed the planners to recast their proposals, based on the assumption that Russia would enter the war on VE Day, which could occur any time after autumn 1944. When the chiefs of staff had planned to transfer resources to the Far East based on the assumption of a quick victory in Europe, Churchill had scotched the idea; now he argued *against* any such transfer of resources based on the same assumption of early victory.[39] And this time Churchill was not alone. Labour leader Clement Attlee assured Churchill of his support for what he described as the better strategy of an attack against Sumatra. In Attlee's simplistic assessment, the Sumatra operation would be doing to the Japanese what the Japanese had done to the British in 1942. 'I cannot see,' argued Attlee, 'why we cannot play the same game as effectively, provided we act with the same ruthless vigour.' With political support from Attlee and other colleagues, Churchill tried to remove the issue from the control of his military advisers and make it an issue for debate 'as between Governments'.[40]

Churchill suggested that the naval task force should go temporarily to the south-west Pacific in mid-1944, rather than be the first echelon of an eventual British Pacific fleet. In return, Britain should demand American logistical support for the operation against Sumatra.[41] Despite an assurance from Admiral King on 23 January that 'he personally had never gone back on the Sextant agreement [reached at Cairo], and that he contemplated the force being placed under Admiral Nimitz', Churchill informed his chiefs of staff that he refused to consider himself bound by the Sextant agreement, claiming that he had not been consulted about it. Even though he had initialled it, Churchill claimed that he 'was not even aware at all of what had taken place'. It was 'pretty clear', Churchill wrote, 'that Admiral King is by no means anxious to have the force we offer and we ought not to press it upon him unduly in view of the logistic difficulties'.[42] It was not, as most historians have suggested, that Britain was prevented from dispatching forces to the Pacific by implacable opposition from Admiral King. Certainly King was none too keen to have them if he thought he could defeat the Japanese by himself. But the real stumbling block was in Downing Street, where Churchill consistently refused to support a powerful British contribution for the Pacific.

Meanwhile, British forces languished in the Indian Ocean, receiving conflicting signals from different quarters in London and insufficient forces for any major operation. In Delhi, General Pownall wondered why there was any 'need to set up this command at all, with all the emphasis and publicity which, for political reasons, was put on it last September'. Although Pownall supported the Sumatra plan, he realised that it was a sideshow to the main thrust against Japan and that it was 'most unlikely' that Mountbatten would ever be given the resources to do it. Admiral Somerville agreed, complaining that the position was one of

complete chaos … because no-one appears to know what the policy is to be. I get signals from [Admiral Cunningham] asking me to reduce personnel in view of our reduced commitments and at the same time get proposals from Dickie [Mountbatten] at Delhi in connection with operations on a considerable scale. When I tax Dickie with these obvious conflictions of policy he tells me that he has received instructions direct from the P.M.[43]

Even Mountbatten eventually realised that Churchill's bold words would not translate into resources for his command. When he wrote to Beaverbrook expressing profound disappointment at the collapse of all the plans for the South East Asia Command (SEAC) that had been approved at Cairo, Beaverbrook simply instructed his secretary to 'answer at length and most agreeably because of course I am only too willing to give him the opportunity of engaging in correspondence with me in order to work out his disappointments'.[44] Realising that he was heading a command that might never mount a significant operation, Mountbatten retreated from Delhi to the more comfortable climate of Kandy in Ceylon where he planned to establish his headquarters with some seven thousand staff, complete with a private band.[45] If he could not have substance, at least he would have the style appropriate to his royal rank.

Churchill found support for his campaign to torpedo the British navy's plans for the Pacific when his envoy to MacArthur's headquarters, General Lumsden, arrived in London with stories of disunity within the American ranks. As Churchill trumpeted to his chiefs of staff on 13 February, there were two competing strategies put forward by MacArthur and King, with Lumsden's reports making him 'more than ever doubtful of Admiral King's scheme'. Churchill pointed out that King's capture of the Marshall Islands had required 'the largest armada ever assembled', with 100 000 men being used to attack the relatively small Japanese garrisons. 'The waste of effort involved in this kind of operation is indescribable,' wrote Churchill, with King being 'the evil genius of this war'. The following day, Churchill jibbed at Admiralty proposals for the deployment of the Pacific 'fleet train' of supply ships, instructing that 'no ships can be set aside now from merchant traffic for the purposes of the Japanese naval war'. He instructed the defence committee to re-examine the proposals in the light of the 'more promising plan put forward by General MacArthur' and involving the British forces in India.[46]

That evening, Churchill and Eden met with the chiefs of staff, Lumsden, and a representative of Mountbatten, to thrash out an agreed strategy. Mountbatten's envoy laid out a plan to mount the amphibious assault on Sumatra, knowing that this was Churchill's preference. But he made the mistake of requiring more men and resources than Churchill was prepared to concede. Nevertheless, Churchill stubbornly argued its merits, claiming that it would be a way of forcing Japan to make terms with the Allies. Although there was no question of Churchill making terms with Hitler, he never excluded the possibility with Hirohito. For their part, the chiefs of staff stuck to their Pacific plan, justifying it partly on the grounds that it would foster good relations with Australia and New Zealand and convert the SWPA into a British theatre of operations. They rightly regarded Mountbatten's South East Asia Command as a military backwater where no decisive result could be achieved. Instead, the chiefs urged that British forces should be based in Australia and strike north towards the heart of Japan in tandem with MacArthur.[47]

Churchill's intransigence on the issue left Brooke wondering 'whether he is really sane',[48] while British inaction in the Pacific was causing increasing damage to Anglo–American relations. Apart from the hostility within the American navy, the American chiefs of staff now alleged that Mountbatten was fighting a guerrilla war in Burma to conserve his main forces for an attack on Sumatra. They urged their British counterparts to order Mountbatten to extend his operations in north Burma. With Churchill's support, the British chiefs refused. London regarded it all as a conspiracy by the American representative in Chungking, the buccaneering General Stilwell. Meanwhile, Churchill pursued his own suspicions about American strategy in the Pacific, ordering a report on the American capture of the Marshall Islands. When it was received in Downing Street, Churchill denounced King's strategy as one 'of using a steam hammer to crack a nut'. When the first lord of the Admiralty, A. V. Alexander, pointed out that the overwhelming American force had saved both time and lives, Churchill observed laconically that there was 'no doubt that a steam cracker will crack a nut'.[49]

The chiefs of staff now faced opposition to the Pacific plans from Churchill and his war cabinet colleagues, from Mountbatten, Roosevelt and the US chiefs of staff. Undaunted, they returned to the charge on 23 February with a memorandum that dismissed the Sumatran operation as a diversion from the main effort in the Pacific. Its only effect, they argued, would be to lengthen the war since British forces would be unable to mount the operation before Germany had been defeated, which would mean a delay of about eighteen months. 'On purely military grounds,' concluded the chiefs, the Pacific strategy 'offers the best opportunities for the earliest possible defeat of Japan'.[50]

Anthony Eden now weighed in on Churchill's side, supporting the Sumatran operation and sending him a dispatch from a Foreign Office official, Esler Dening, who was acting as Mountbatten's political adviser. Dening argued that Britain would gain little by joining America's central Pacific thrust and had instead to defeat the Japanese army in South-East Asia if it were to recover its standing with colonial peoples and the dominions. 'The record of disaster,' Dening wrote, 'must be wiped out' and the 'British part in the Far Eastern war should be a principal and not a subsidiary one'. Anything less than this, he argued, and it would be 'no exaggeration to say the solidarity of the British Commonwealth and its influence in the maintenance of peace in the Far East will be irretrievably damaged'. Eden backed this up, warning Churchill that if the British were 'merely dragged along at the tail of the Americans in the Pacific, we shall get no credit whatever for our share in the joint operations'.[51]

Churchill sent Eden's and Dening's comments to his service advisers, observing that he was 'increasingly convinced that CULVERIN is the only step of importance which it is open for us to take, and I think we should take it even if we have to wait till April 1945'. Churchill could dismiss the convincing military arguments of his advisers and instruct them, on political grounds, to plan for an operation against Sumatra, but he was loath to do so for fear they would resign. Also, the Dardanelles disaster in 1915 and the Norwegian disaster in 1940, both warned against him mounting a hazardous operation on his own responsibility. So he continued to try to bring the chiefs around to his point of view.[52] On 25 February, he met with them to discuss their critical memorandum regarding the Sumatran operation. When they trooped in, the chiefs found Churchill buttressed by three of his colleagues and a clutch of representatives from Mountbatten's headquarters. Again, neither side was prepared to give way. With Churchill taking it all personally, and allowing 'his dislike for Curtin and the Australians' to determine his attitude towards cooperation with Australian forces, Brooke was left frustrated and angered by the lack of progress.[53] There would be many more arguments to come.

While the jousting went on in London, news was received of a powerful Japanese naval concentration at Singapore. Unclear as to the intentions of the Japanese fleet, Somerville's Eastern fleet prepared to scurry for cover, much as it had done two years previously. After two years of war against Japan and with the defeat of Italy and the virtual elimination of German surface ships, Britain was still unable to confront a force from the increasingly hard-pressed Japanese navy. In exasperation, Somerville wrote of finding himself 'in the same position now as I was two years ago, i.e. with a quite inadequate force which would be a gift for the Japanese if they came out in full strength'.[54] At Mountbatten's headquarters, General Pownall viewed the Japanese move with relative equanimity, believing that the Japanese would probably attack Darwin or Western Australia, or move against shipping in the Indian Ocean.[55] There was little to stop them. Only the caution engendered by repeated bloody battles with the Americans, and the need to conserve the still formidable remains of their fleet for the climactic battle for control of Japan itself, prevented the Japanese commanders from risking their ships in an attack against Australia.

NOTES

1 Alanbrooke diary, 30 November 1943, in Danchev and Todman (eds), *War Diaries*, pp. 486–9; Kimball, *Forged in War*, p. 255.

2 Letter, Ismay to Somerville, 20 December 1943, IV/Som/4b, Ismay Papers, KC.

3 Letter, Cunningham to Somerville, 19 December 1943, ADD. MS. 52563, Cunningham Papers, BL.

4 Gill, *Royal Australian Navy 1942–1945*, p. 358.

5 Cable, Hollis to Jacob, 31 December 1943, PREM 3/164/5, PRO; Gilbert, *Road to Victory*, p. 599.

6 Minute, Hollis to Churchill, 1 January 1944; Cable, Chiefs of Staff to Churchill, 13 January 1944, PREM 3/160/7, PRO; See also Letter, Dewing to Ismay, 8 February 1944, IV/Dew/6/1a, Ismay Papers, KC.

7 Cable, Churchill to Chiefs of Staff, 14 January 1944, PREM 3/160/7, PRO.

8 Letter, Royle to Somerville, 30 December 1943, SMVL 8/7, Somerville Papers, CC; War Cabinet Minutes, 4 February 1944, CRS A2673/XIV, NAA; Letter, Royle to Shedden, 6 January 1944, CRS A5954, Box 294, NAA; Bruce supported British pressure to appoint a British officer to replace Royle. Cable, Bruce to Curtin, 10 February 1944, CRS A5954, Box 509, NAA.

9 Minute, Shedden to Curtin, 10 December 1942, CRS A5954, Box 393, NAA.

10 Speech by Curtin, Canberra, 14 December 1943, CRS A5954, Box 294, NAA.

11 For an extended discussion of this point, see Day, *Claiming a Continent*.

12 Notes by a British press delegation, submitted to Churchill, 3 February 1944, PREM 3/159/2, PRO.

13 Background briefing, 25 November 1943, MS 4675, Smith Papers, NLA.

14 See Thorne, *Allies of a Kind*; and Dower, *War without Mercy*.

15 Moran, *Winston Churchill*, p. 131.

16 Somerville journal, 20 November 1943, SMVL 2/2, Somerville Papers, CC.

17 Minute, Harvey to Eden, with note appended by Eden, 7 September 1941, ADD. MS. 56402, Harvey Papers, BL.

18 Harvey diary, 21 April 1943, ADD. MS. 56399, Harvey Papers, BL.

19 Letters, ex-Senator R. D. Elliott to Beaverbrook, 21 September 1939 and Beaverbrook to Elliott, 25 October 1939, BBK C/130, Beaverbrook Papers, HLRO.

20 Shedden's emphasis; Minute, Shedden to Curtin, 21 December 1943, CRS A5954, Box 305, NAA; See also Letter, W. J. Scully to Curtin, 7 December 1943, same file.

21 Letter, MacArthur to Curtin, 4 February 1944, CRS A5954, Box 218, NAA; Letter, Dewing to Ismay, 31 December 1943, IV/Dew/4c, Ismay Papers, KC; Letter, Gowrie to Cranborne, 6 January 1944, MS 2852/4/21/25, NLA; Defence Committee Minutes, 23 February 1944, CRS A5954, Box 306, NAA.

22 Report by Defence Committee, 5 January 1944, CRS A2031/12/2/1944, NAA; See also Letter, Royle to Shedden, 6 January 1944, CRS A5954, Box 294, NAA.

23 Letter, Blamey to Shedden, 15 January 1944, CRS A5954, Box 294, NAA.

24 Statement by Curtin, 18 January 1944, CRS A5954, Box 294, NAA.

25 Agreement between Australia and New Zealand, 21 January 1944, *DAFP*, Vol. 7, Doc. 26.

26 Memorandum by Cranborne, 2 February 1944, CAB 66/46, W.P. (44)70, PRO.

27 War Cabinet Conclusions, 11 February 1944, CAB 65/41, W.M. (44)18, PRO.

28 Memorandum by Cranborne, 15 February 1944, CAB 66/47, W.P. (44)106, PRO.

29 Note by Curtin of Conversation with Johnson, 3 February 1944, *DAFP*, Vol. 7, Doc. 40.

30 Letter, Curtin to Evatt, 5 February 1944, enclosing Message, Hull to Curtin, 3 February 1944, CRS A1608/Y41/1/1, NAA.

31 Letter, Evatt to Johnson, 24 February 1944, and initialled by Curtin, CRS A1608/Y41/1/1, NAA. For details of the Pacific war council meeting on 12 January, see Cable, Dixon to External Affairs Department, 12 January 1944, CRS A3300, Box 265, NAA; See also Cable, D'Alton to Evatt, 8 January 1944, *DAFP*, Vol. 7, Doc. 8.

32 Warren Kimball, '"Merely a Facade"? Roosevelt and the Southwest Pacific', in Day (ed.), *Brave New World*, p. 27.

33 Letters, Noble to Cunningham, 12, 24 and 30 January 1944, ADD. MS. 52571, Cunningham Papers, BL.

34 Memorandum by Lambe, 5 February 1944, ADD. MS. 52571, Cunningham Papers, BL.

35 Advisory War Council Minutes, 20 January 1944, CRS A2682/7/1284, NAA.

36 Cable, Curtin to Churchill, 5 February 1944, PREM 3/164/5, PRO.

[37] Defence Committee (Operations) Minutes, 19 January 1944, CAB 69/6, D.O. (44)3, PRO.

[38] ibid; Letter, Churchill to de Wiart, 18 January 1944, PREM 3/159/14, PRO.

[39] Defence Committee (Operations) Minutes, 19 January 1944, CAB 69/6, D.O. (44)3, PRO.

[40] Note, Attlee to Churchill, 20 January 1944, and Minute, Churchill to Ismay, 24 January 1944, PREM 3/160/7, PRO.

[41] ibid.

[42] Minutes, Ismay to Churchill, 25 January 1944, and Minute, Churchill to Ismay, 31 January 1944, PREM 3/160/7, PRO.

[43] Pownall diary, 12 January and 5 February 1944, in Bond (ed.), *Chief of Staff*, Vol. 2, pp. 132, 139; Letter, Somerville to Tennant, 22 January 1944, TEN 25, Tennant Papers, NMM; See also Letter, Somerville to MacQuarrie, 27 January 1944, ADD. MS. 50143, Somerville Papers, BL.

[44] Letter, Mountbatten to Beaverbrook, 4 February 1944, BBK D/141, Beaverbrook Papers, HLRO.

[45] The local commander in Ceylon was aghast, noting that the headquarters increased in size as its prospective operations decreased, and exclaimed in exasperation, 'what the general effect on prices and servants' wages here is going to be I tremble to think!' Letter, Layton to Cunningham, 7 February 1944, ADD. MS. 52571, Cunningham Papers, BL; See also Letter, Ismay to Auchinleck, 2 February 1944, IV/Con/1/1Fa, Ismay Papers, KC.

[46] Minute, Churchill to Ismay, 13 February 1944, PREM 3/159/14; Minute, Churchill to Alexander and Cunningham, 14 February 1944, PREM 3/164/5, PRO.

[47] Draft memorandum by Churchill, 14 February 1944, and Minutes of a Staff Conference, 14 February 1944, PREM 3/160/7, PRO; C.O.S. (44)161(O), 14 February 1944, PREM 3/148/10, PRO; Alanbrooke diary, 14 February 1944, in Danchev and Todman (eds), *War Diaries*, p. 521.

[48] Alanbrooke diary, 14 February 1944, in Danchev and Todman (eds), *War Diaries*, p. 521.

[49] See documents in PREM 3/148/10, PRO; Note by Churchill, 17 February 1944, PREM 3/159/14, PRO; Note, Alexander to Churchill, 20 February 1944, PREM 3/164/5, PRO.

[50] Alanbrooke diary, 21 and 22 February 1944, in Danchev and Todman (eds) *War Diaries*, pp. 523–4; Report by Chiefs of Staff, 23 February 1944, PREM 3/148/2, PRO.

[51] Memorandum by Dening, 17 February 1944, and Minute, Eden to Churchill, 21 February 1944, PREM 3/160/7, PRO.

[52] Minute, Churchill to Ismay, 23 February 1944, PREM 3/160/7, PRO.

[53] Alanbrooke diary, 25 February 1944, in Danchev and Todman (eds), *War Diaries*, p. 525.

[54] Letter, Somerville to Mountbatten, 23 February 1944, SMVL 8/3, Somerville Papers, CC. One of Somerville's officers wrote in his diary that Britain had 'always taken the most appalling Risks in this Ocean and they're now terrified that their Bluff is to be called'. Edwards diary, 24 February 1944, REDW 1/6, Edwards Papers, CC.

[55] Pownall diary, 25 February 1944, in Bond (ed.), *Chief of Staff*, Vol. 2, pp. 145–6; See also Cable, Mountbatten to Chiefs of Staff, 25 February 1944, PREM 3/164/1, PRO; Gill, *Royal Australian Navy 1942–1945*, p. 388.

FORTY-ONE

'no commitments'

The arrival of the Japanese main fleet at Singapore sent a tremor of apprehension through Australia. At a briefing for reporters on 2 March 1944, Curtin tried to calm public disquiet by observing that a Japanese invasion was unlikely because of the lack of any transport ships among the enemy fleet. He correctly suggested that the Japanese were probably using the former British naval base as a 'funkhole', pulling back their damaged and defeated ships to Singapore rather than sending them to Japan where their presence would depress public morale. Australia could be confident, claimed Curtin, that 'there would now never be any danger to the eastern side of Australia'. Nevertheless, the more isolated coastline of Western Australia was at risk so long as the Japanese ships remained at Singapore, since the fleet of seven battleships and two aircraft carriers was 'much bigger than anything we have in the Indian Ocean or are likely to have for some time'.[1]

Although Britain's Eastern fleet had been reinforced, Admiral Somerville was forced to adopt the same 'cat and mouse' tactics he had used in 1942, ordering his ships out of their base at Trincomalee in Ceylon to seek shelter in the western reaches of the Indian Ocean. Any return of the ships to Trincomalee would have to be 'haphazard and occasional' so that the Japanese would be kept guessing as to their movements.[2] Meanwhile, Curtin asked Churchill for the Admiralty's opinion on the 'probability of Japanese incursions into the Indian Ocean', whether they were 'likely to attempt anything more than raids' and whether Britain had the 'capacity to repel such attacks'.[3] London seems to have anticipated the Australian nervousness. Curtin's querulous cable crossed with a steadying one from Churchill, sent at the instigation of Lord Cranborne, which dismissed fears that there was any serious danger to Western Australia. 'Our battleship squadron in Ceylon is well posted,' claimed Churchill, and 'our shore-based aircraft are strong'.[4] The British fleet was certainly well posted, far from the reach of the Japanese. As for shore-based aircraft in India and Ceylon, the absence of torpedo bombers made them unsuited for attacking an enemy fleet. Churchill was on firmer ground in claiming that Japan would not risk its fleet in a major naval offensive but would conserve its strength for the final stages of the war. All Australia had to fear, Churchill maintained, was 'the possibility of occasional offensive sorties'.[5]

Churchill's claims had the required effect. Curtin confided to journalists on 7 March that Churchill agreed the dominion 'has not much to fear from the Japanese concentration'. There still was a brief scare in Perth when reports came in of the Japanese fleet moving southward. 'We got everything in readiness for an attack,' said Curtin, 'but the Jap ships turned back.'[6] In fact, they had never left Singapore. The report had been a furphy. Moreover, Curtin's bravado concealed serious inadequacies in the defence of Western Australia that persisted more than two years after the attack on Pearl Harbor. As a British naval intelligence officer passing through Perth observed, 'Western Australia is pretty wide open.' The only immediate protection against a naval attack was from any American submarines that happened to be at their base at Fremantle, and from a squadron of Liberator bombers in far-off Darwin. Reinforcements of aircraft sent from eastern Australia to meet the expected Japanese attack were either totally inadequate or never arrived. The British naval officer noted that only 23 of the 86 aircraft sent from eastern Australia had arrived within two days, while no 'really offensive aircraft were sent at all'.[7] The reinforcement fiasco emphasised Britain's failure to protect even Australia's western coast, with Somerville able to provide only a vague and distant menace to the Japanese fleet while the American submarine commander at Fremantle vainly urged that at least part of the Eastern fleet be stationed at Fremantle.[8] Instead, the move of the Japanese fleet postponed yet again the arrival of British ships in Australian waters.[9]

The British had other worries, with Japanese troops in Burma mounting a major offensive in March 1944 against the defences around Imphal on the Indian border. Fortunately, this move was primarily to protect the Japanese position in Burma from an expected British offensive rather than to presage a move with their limited forces into India. In a series of desperate and prolonged battles over several months, the Japanese attack was blunted and then turned back into Burma, with British control of the air being a crucial factor in the outcome. So ended what one American historian hailed as the 'decisive battle of the war for Southeast Asia', even though most of South-East Asia would remain in Japanese hands until war's end.[10] Further south, Australian troops were completing their own hard-fought campaign for control of the Huon peninsula in New Guinea, while Chinese armies, far larger than the British or American forces being deployed against Japan, were battling for control of their homeland. For a time in early 1944 it seemed that the Chinese might collapse and allow the Japanese army to break through. But they held on, steadily bleeding the Japanese armies of their strength. Although not formidable in battle, the Chinese forces were numerically strong and had to be countered with stronger Japanese forces. More importantly, the extensive Chinese territory in Japanese hands had to be held and administered by troops that otherwise might have been used in Burma or sent to bolster the hard-pressed garrisons of the Pacific islands.

In the central Pacific, the US navy had grabbed the Gilbert and Marshall Islands from Japan, while the Japanese stronghold in the central Pacific, the island of Truk in the Carolinas group, was robbed of its naval and air strength in one devastating raid by an American carrier task force at the beginning of 1944. At the same time, Rabaul, Japan's stronghold in the south-west Pacific, was also neutralised by repeated Allied air attacks, although its 100 000-strong garrison was deemed too powerful to capture. Instead, and much against MacArthur's wish, it was bypassed by American troops landing in the Admiralty Islands to the north of Rabaul. The accelerating Allied effort was directed by military leaders confident of winning richer prizes as they hammered at the inner ring of Japan's defences.

As the Axis floundered, preparations were underway for the peace that would follow, although it was difficult to make conclusive plans when the postwar strength of the various powers was not known. It was also unclear whether there would be genuine international cooperation or a return to the prewar system of imperial autarky, by which the world was largely divided into closed-off systems of economic and political power.[11] As part of the Lend-Lease negotiations with Britain, the United States had extracted a much-disputed commitment from Churchill for lower tariffs after the war that would allow greater American access to the markets of Britain and its empire. This was enshrined in the Atlantic Charter that was concluded with Roosevelt at their Newfoundland meeting in August 1941.[12] Churchill had always favoured a policy of free trade, but he was acutely conscious of the political risks of forcing such a commitment on his national government composed of conservative imperialists such as Leo Amery. In order to concentrate his energies on the war, Churchill performed a precarious balancing act between the Americans, particularly the secretary of state, Cordell Hull, who demanded the abolition of imperial preferences, and some of his own supporters who refused to countenance such a prospect. By 1944, he was fast losing control as Washington intensified the pressure. A decision could not be delayed much longer.

When the issue came up for discussion at a ministerial meeting in February 1944, Amery sent a message from his sick bed blasting the Americans for their 'quasi religious free trade outlook' that was 'blended with an American economic Imperialism' that sought to shatter the British empire into 'separate fields for American exploitation'. Amery painted a picture of selfless dominions before the war loyally buying British manufactured goods. 'How anyone can imagine,' he intoned, 'that we can afford to drop that substantial bone for its shadow in the water I cannot conceive.'[13] His colleagues were not convinced. Britain's tough-talking home secretary, Herbert Morrison, expressed the brutal truth, that neither Britain nor the dominions could live merely on intra-imperial trade.[14] Moreover, as Cranborne correctly pointed out, the dominions would much prefer a general expansion in world trade than a return to the restrictive prewar system.[15] Bruce tried to press this point home with the imperial-minded Lord Croft, assuring him that Australia no longer favoured imperial preference and would not support the empire lobby in its efforts to have it preserved.[16]

Australia had not, however, abandoned its commitment to protectionist tariff policies *per se*, just the preference that these policies currently extended to British products. So there remained a considerable barrier to any agreement with the United States, with the Australians concerned that a general lowering of tariffs might devastate Australia's carefully nurtured secondary industries. As a way around this, the Australian government pushed for an international commitment to full employment and higher living standards. It was hoped that this would lead to sufficiently high consumption levels to guarantee ample markets for Australian surpluses of primary produce sold through orderly marketing schemes, while its growing secondary industries could find outlets in Asia.[17] The 1930s depression was still vivid in the minds of Labor leaders who sought to prevent the widely anticipated postwar recession and cement a political alliance between the industrial working class and various rural interests.

The second issue bedevilling Churchill was American anxiety about oil. Washington was pressing Britain to accommodate their postwar oil needs after reports that America might face an oil shortage. Congressmen urged Roosevelt to gain access to alternative supplies, particularly in the Middle East where Britain exercised a sphere of influence. When Washington called for a conference with Britain on the issue, Beaverbrook asked Churchill to 'pigeon hole' the American request. 'Oil,' wrote Beaverbrook, 'is the greatest single post-war asset remaining to us. We should refuse to divide our last asset with the Americans.'[18] In a paper prepared for Beaverbrook on the world oil reserve situation, it was suggested that instead of allowing the Americans into the Middle East, they could be provided with 'some of the less attractive areas' such as 'large areas in Australia and New Zealand and parts of Africa'.[19]

The third contentious issue was civil aviation, with all three issues combining in the minds of some leading British politicians into general opposition towards the United States. During a war cabinet meeting on 11 February 1944, Beaverbrook set out the choice that Britain faced, to be either 'a senior partner in the Empire or a junior partner in an association with the USA'.[20] It was the takeover battle of the century in which Great Britain Inc. was eventually to become the branch office of Wall Street. However, Beaverbrook and others were unwilling to give in without a struggle. While supporting the idea of collaboration with Washington, Beaverbrook nevertheless argued that Britain 'should aim, with an equal constancy, at maintaining and strengthening our own position as a world power'.[21]

Civil aviation was considered by many to be the key to postwar prosperity and security. Accordingly, British and American companies, backed by their governments, busily competed for routes across South America and Africa, while in Britain the aircraft companies surreptitiously designed new postwar civil aircraft under the cover of war work. The British ambassador in Washington, Lord Halifax, warned London in January 1944 that this intensifying Anglo–American competition was beginning to affect the wider relationship with Washington. He predicted that it would soon degenerate into a 'competitive struggle which will become increasingly naked'. Several weeks later, the war cabinet approved the development of a modern airfield at Heathrow for the use of military transport aircraft but also to provide 'an airfield which could be developed as an international civil airport for the capital of the Empire after the War'.[22] In the context of the stiffening Anglo–American competition over postwar aviation, Britain suddenly decided that a survey of P. G. Taylor's alternative air route across the Pacific could be justified by its plans for the war against Japan. Accordingly, officials in London dusted off Taylor's proposals of 1942 and suggested that he be part of the survey party. Taylor was ecstatic, proclaiming that it would fit into place 'the last section of a round the world route on which I have worked for years'.[23]

At the same time, Evatt was pressing for British naval forces in the Pacific, not so much to defeat the Japanese but as a counterweight to the Americans.[24]

The Australian navy also hoped for an enhanced role once the Royal Navy arrived. Until now, Blamey's troops had taken centre stage, recapturing New Guinea and saving Australia from possible invasion. But they would soon be left behind as MacArthur planned his return to the Philippines with an all-American cast. This gave the manpower-starved Australian navy its chance to have its moment of glory in the Pacific and to re-establish itself as the senior Australian service. However, it was hamstrung by having at its head a British admiral, Guy Royle, who had a limited grasp of political manoeuvring. Royle wanted an extra four to five thousand sailors to be enlisted to crew a mini-fleet of surplus ships that he hoped to secure from his colleagues in London. This fleet of modern ships would comprise an aircraft carrier, one or two cruisers and six destroyers. In his eagerness to achieve this proposal, Royle made the question a partisan football to be kicked around in the politically charged atmosphere of the advisory war council.[25]

Putting Curtin on the spot during a meeting of the council on 21 March was not the way for Royle to achieve his aims. When he suggested that Curtin take up the question of naval expansion during his stay in London, the prime minister adroitly sidestepped the trap that Royle had so clumsily laid and passed the question back to the chiefs of staff for resolution, leaving Royle and his colleagues to fight over the limited amount of manpower that had to be allocated between the three services. Following the meeting, Royle tried to rewrite the record of the discussion to suggest that Curtin had supported the navy's expansion. But he was firmly informed by Shedden's assistant that the battle would have to be fought among the chiefs of staff before Curtin would give it his approval. As a parting shot, Curtin apparently ordered Royle never again to abuse his access to the advisory war council.[26]

Juggling Australia's limited manpower was an almost impossible task, particularly when the army resisted Curtin's orders to release men from its ranks for food production. As Shedden warned Curtin in February 1944, manpower was inadequate to satisfy all claimants and the resulting political fallout 'will inevitably alienate some of [the government's] present support'. The government's targets for food production were not being met because people in lucrative industrial employment were reluctant to transfer back to rural industry, while the army and the munitions industry were mainly releasing unfit soldiers and workers who were just as unfit for the requirements of rural work. The unemployment lines were growing while angry farmers watched as their crops lay unharvested. According to Shedden the choice was clear: either the food targets must be reduced or the manpower found to fulfil them so as 'to stop this growing criticism'.[27]

In this atmosphere of mounting panic about manpower, Royle's proposal for an expanded Australian navy was received with dismay by defence planners. Not that the proposal was devoid of benefits, particularly if the ships could be obtained from Britain at little or no cost and if they included an aircraft carrier. Australia had never had an aircraft carrier, the value of which had been demonstrated during the Pacific war. Such ships clearly deserved to be a crucial part of any modern navy that had more than just defensive aspirations. Despite these benefits, Shedden was determined to prevent Royle steamrolling the proposal past Curtin, warning that it would only exacerbate the problem of food production and threaten Australia's capacity to send its army forward with MacArthur's advance. Moreover, argued Shedden, the possible arrival of British forces in the Pacific would make further demands on Australian food stocks. Most important, though, 'from the aspect of post-war policy, we cannot overlook the fact that the best service we can render to the future of Australia is to build up the R.A.A.F. to the maximum degree of our capacity'. This was an argument calculated to appeal to Curtin, who had long argued for the primacy of the air force over the navy, an argument that seemed to have been vindicated by the events following the Japanese attack on Pearl Harbor.[28]

Shedden's counselling worked. Although Royle fired one last shot over Curtin's bows, the prime minister refused to cede to the admiral's arguments. Curtin was angry that Churchill had not replied to his cable of October 1943 that had requested Britain's agreement to the retuning of Australia's war effort. Shedden triumphantly recorded that Curtin 'went so far as to say that if Mr Churchill did not choose to reply to his representations ... he certainly was not going to adopt such a humble attitude as to offer him gifts by manning additional ships'. Curtin was coming to the view that food, together with a limited military effort, would be Australia's best contribution to the Allied war effort.[29] During their forthcoming trip to London, Shedden and Blamey could ensure that Curtin did not deviate from this view.

Britain shared Australia's manpower problems. The demands of the forthcoming invasion of France had to be balanced with the demands of its civilian economy as it prepared to satisfy pent-up domestic demand and to capture postwar foreign markets for British goods. The British government agreed to a proposal from the powerful minister for labour, Ernest Bevin, to maintain control over the labour market and, following the defeat of Germany, to allocate men straight from the armed forces to designated factories.[30] However, if this scheme were to work, Britain had to limit its manpower obligations for the war against Japan. As the Americans pushed the Japanese back towards their home islands, the lifeline between the prospective British Pacific fleet and its supply bases lengthened. By March 1944, the 'fleet train' of ships considered necessary to supply the fleet had crept up from 134 to 158 ships, while the likely period between the end of the war against Germany and that against Japan was set at three years. The implications were daunting for a government gearing up to satisfy civilian needs and which soon would have to face its first election since 1935.[31] The chiefs of staff tried to allay the government's concern and limit the manpower demands by having Indian and dominion forces comprise a large part of the projected 'British presence' for the Pacific.[32]

For Churchill, the choices were simple. In allocating shipping, the first priority was to allow for 24 million tons of imports to be shipped into Britain during 1944 and 1945. The second priority was to allow any leftover shipping to be used for the fleet train. The third priority was the size of the naval fleet that could be used against Japan.[33] It was a strange way to fight a war, but Churchill hoped for a short fight, relying on the promised Russian entry into the war against Japan to bring it to a quick end, perhaps through a compromise peace. His colleagues agreed almost unanimously that Germany's defeat must bring better times immediately for the war-battered British civilians. Hugh Dalton, head of the board of trade, joined his ministerial colleagues during a war cabinet discussion on 13 April to 'stress the need to lift civilian standards and push export trade as soon as Germany is beaten'. Dalton observed that Churchill was 'always very responsive to this, though also very insistent that we must "do our utmost", whatever that might turn out to mean, to help the Americans to beat the Japs'. According to Churchill, once Russia joined the war against Japan, the Japanese 'might offer terms, short of unconditional surrender, which it might be well worth our while to examine'.[34]

While Churchill was planning a limited British effort against Japan, there was still no agreement, either in London or with Washington, about the form this effort should take. Churchill was doggedly committed to the proposed Sumatran operation, a plan that 'gravely concerned' Roosevelt, who wanted the British to secure and develop the links to China in upper Burma and establish Allied air control in the Pacific triangle between China, Formosa and Luzon.[35] While Churchill had the support of his war cabinet and the Foreign Office in seeking to recapture Singapore rather than play junior partner to the United States in the Pacific, his chiefs of staff threatened to resign en masse if Churchill insisted on the operation against their combined advice.[36]

The British army was fixated on the forthcoming invasion of France and quaked at the thought of fighting in Malaya with the limited resources allowed to it by the overriding priority that the European war still enjoyed. The navy wanted to prove its mettle in the annihilation of the Japanese fleet in the Pacific where it could play the leading British role and establish its claims to postwar seniority. Although Churchill refused to concede defeat, his cherished operation against Sumatra was impossible to mount without American logistical support in the form of landing ships. These Roosevelt refused to provide.[37] This refusal should have been the end of the matter, but Churchill was not ready to drop his pet project. Realising that the Americans were lukewarm about British naval forces operating in the Pacific, Churchill went behind the backs of his chiefs of staff and sent a cable to Roosevelt, inviting him to acknowledge that the British Pacific fleet would not be needed until the summer of 1945 at the earliest and that, in the interim, British forces would be better occupied pursuing an Indian Ocean strategy. Roosevelt readily complied.[38] The result was that planning, rather than military operations, continued, with Churchill hoping that time would provide him with the wherewithal to mount the Sumatran operation.

In the meantime, Churchill made a gesture to his chiefs of staff by ordering a mission to Australia to examine the logistical problems of basing the British effort there instead of in India. He was confident that the investigation would show that the costs of supplying forces at such a distance would finish the Pacific plan. Indeed, his shipping minister, Lord Leathers, had already advised him that the shortage of shipping would preclude the use of Australia as a base, while Curtin's oft-repeated complaints of a manpower shortage suggested that further problems would be encountered in pursuing the chiefs' preferred strategy. As Admiral Somerville reflected from his vantage point in Ceylon, 'the question of manpower is important since ... none is likely to be available in Australia and what there is is usually on strike'.[39]

On 11 March, Churchill cabled to Curtin seeking permission to dispatch his mission while making clear that it was to be 'on the strict understanding that we are engaging upon no commitments and reaching no firm decisions'.[40] The warning was well made, since Churchill had no intention of basing sizeable British forces in Australia. As he confided to Mountbatten on 18 March, he remained 'entirely opposed to shifting the British centre of gravity against Japan from the Indian Ocean to the Pacific, at any rate for the next eighteen months'. Although he had agreed to the mission going out to reconnoitre possible Australian bases and assess the problems of logistics, he assured Mountbatten that the dispatch of the mission 'in no way implies any decision to change the existing policy'.[41] In fact, the previous day he had pressed the chiefs of staff to adopt a variant of his Sumatran operation, suggesting that they now capture a small island off the tip of Sumatra. When they pointed out that the Japanese strength at Singapore would quickly defeat any such attempt, Churchill reluctantly retreated. Brooke was left to wonder in his diary 'whether I was Alice in Wonderland, or whether I was really fit for a lunatic asylum! I am honestly getting very doubtful about his balance of mind and it just gives me the cold shivers. I don't know where we are or where we are going as regards our strategy ...'[42] Not that the Australian government would have been disappointed if Churchill chose to base his forces elsewhere.

While British forces would have been helpful in 1942, the arrival of them so late in the war would now only soak up Australian manpower that would otherwise be directed into civilian industry and postwar reconstruction. Curtin and his chiefs of staff took fright at the prospect of the British mission, fearing also that this would compromise Australia's own plans to forge an independent military presence in the region. MacArthur too was worried that the injection of British forces into his region might compromise his supreme command of Allied forces. The Australian chiefs of staff advised that Britain already knew of Australia's potential and that anything else could be communicated by cable or through the British military mission already in Australia.[43]

Although Whitehall was taken aback by the negative Australian reaction, Churchill was relieved, instructing that the study now be made from material available in London. When the Admiralty deemed that this was insufficient, it eventually received permission to send a team to Australia under Admiral C. S. Daniel to study naval facilities, particularly in the north and west of Australia, which might be used by its Pacific fleet. Churchill had already prejudged the results, dismissing Daniel as 'a defeatist [who] certainly does not carry my confidence'.[44] Churchill tried to circumvent his chiefs of staff by encouraging Mountbatten both to continue with his operations in Burma and mount the Sumatran operation. Fortunately, Brooke managed to stop the cable from being sent, while complaining in his diary of feeling 'like a man chained to the chariot of a lunatic!! It is getting beyond my powers to control him.'[45] From Ceylon, Somerville could only wonder at the 'extraordinary cross currents at work in connection with the general strategical policy for the East' as he chafed at the further delay.[46]

At a meeting at Chequers on 8 April with officers of Britain's joint planning staff, together with representatives from Mountbatten's command, Churchill canvassed other options for the war against Japan while still expressing a strong preference for the Sumatran operation. If MacArthur resisted the idea of major British forces being based within his command, asked Churchill, why not slice off north-western Australia and base sufficient British forces there to be able to strike north at Timor, Borneo and the Celebes? Intelligence reports had already suggested that the Australian army would be able to contribute several divisions to such a 'British' force. Once in place, such forces would have the choice of tightening the stranglehold on Singapore and Malaya or striking northward with MacArthur towards Japan. Such an island-hopping strategy was also very economical in terms of troops, an important consideration in both London and Washington, where the prospect of fighting major land battles with the Japanese army was a daunting one. The fear of such battles spurred the development of the atomic bomb in America, while on a tropical island off the northern coast of Australia, Australian soldiers volunteered for a chemical warfare unit that was used by scientists, including the future Nobel Laureate Sir MacFarlane Burnett, in a British-inspired experiment to test the effects of mustard gas on unprotected troops in jungle conditions.[47]

The meeting at Chequers was another attempt by Churchill to go behind the back of his chiefs of staff and get the joint planning staff to line up beside him on Pacific strategy. But no decision could be made until Churchill and his chiefs reached agreement on the issue. With Britain's Pacific strategy still in a state of flux, Curtin left for Washington and London on 5 April 1944 to attend a conference of Commonwealth prime ministers. After having rejected several earlier invitations to visit either London or Washington, and politically strengthened by the recent federal election, Curtin was off to establish a new postwar pattern of cooperation between Australia and Britain and to win Allied agreement to Australia's changing war effort. Unlike Evatt, who had confronted his fear of flying, Curtin declined MacArthur's offer of a special aircraft and chose to travel to San Francisco in an Australian cruiser. When operational reasons prevented this, he went instead in a crowded and blacked-out American troopship on his first trip as prime minister outside of Australia.[48]

Curtin was farewelled by the British high commissioner, Sir Ronald Cross, and his wife, who went on board to wish Curtin and his wife *bon voyage*, taking them a bunch of flowers for their hot and stuffy cabin. They found Curtin shut away and 'very depressed'. Cross ascribed it to feelings of inadequacy at the prospect of dealing face to face with world leaders. Not even Cross's wife could cheer Curtin up, reported the high commissioner, so they quickly made their excuses and departed 'with all possible speed!'. Cross advised the Dominions Office that Curtin 'has probably not habitually thought much about the sort of things he will be called upon to discuss in

London, and he probably lacks the confidence that comes from knowledge and definite opinions'. As a result, it might be 'difficult to set him at his ease, the more so as he is sensitive and will be on the look-out for people trying to influence him by showing him great attention and flattery'. Cross claimed that Curtin was particularly apprehensive of Churchill and that he was 'anxious to justify himself and to stand well in Churchill's regard'.[49] There was an element of truth in this. Curtin certainly did want to rebuild the bridges between Canberra and London. However, he would find it beyond his power of persuasion.

NOTES

[1] Background briefing, 2 March 1944, MS 4675, Smith Papers, NLA.
[2] Somerville diary, 2 March 1944, ADD. MS. 52564, Cunningham Papers, BL.
[3] Cable, Curtin to Churchill, 4 March 1944, PREM 3/160/1, PRO.
[4] Minute, Cranborne to Churchill, 28 February 1944, and Cable, Churchill to Curtin, 3 March 1944, PREM 3/164/1, PRO.
[5] Cable, Churchill to Curtin, 3 March 1944, PREM 3/164/1, PRO; Cable, Mountbatten to Air Ministry, 25 February 1944, PREM 3/164/1, PRO.
[6] Background briefing, 7 March 1944, MS 4675, Smith Papers, NLA.
[7] Report by Captain Hillgarth, PREM 3/159/10, PRO.
[8] ibid; Somerville diary, 8 and 11 March 1944, ADD. MS. 52564, Cunningham Papers, BL.
[9] Churchill instructed that his favoured operation against Sumatra must be postponed because of the Japanese move, but that planning for it should continue. Minute, Churchill to Ismay, 7 March 1944, PREM 3/164/1, PRO.
[10] Liddell Hart, *History of the Second World War*, pp. 539–44; Spector, *Eagle against the Sun*, p. 361.
[11] Letter, Ismay to Casey, 14 March 1944, IV/Cas/2d, Ismay Papers, KC.
[12] For details of these discussions, see Reynolds, *The Creation of the Anglo–American Alliance*, and Gilbert, *Finest Hour*.
[13] Letter, Amery to Eden, 11 February 1944, Croft Papers, CRFT 1/2, CC.
[14] War Cabinet Conclusions/Confidential Annex, 11 February 1944, CAB 65/45, W.M. (44)18, PRO.
[15] Letter, Cranborne to Beaverbrook, 16 February 1944, BBK D/131, Beaverbrook Papers, HLRO.
[16] Talk with Lord Croft, 18 February 1944, CRS M100, 'February 1944', NAA.
[17] Cabinet submission by Evatt, 18 January 1944, CRS A2700/8/594, NAA.
[18] Letter, Beaverbrook to Churchill, 8 February 1944, BBK D/183, Beaverbrook Papers, HLRO.
[19] 'Synopsis of World Oil Reserve Situation', unsigned and undated paper, BBK D/189, Beaverbrook Papers, HLRO.
[20] War Cabinet Conclusions/Confidential Annex, 11 February 1944, CAB 65/45, W.M. (44)18, PRO.
[21] Memorandum by Beaverbrook, 21 February 1944, BBK D/421, Beaverbrook Papers, HLRO.
[22] Cable, Bruce to Curtin, 5 January 1944, enclosing a copy of Halifax's cable, CRS A5954, Box 345, NAA; Report by Attlee, 3 February 1944, CAB 66/46, W.P. (44)73, PRO.
[23] Letter, Taylor to Gowrie, 1 March 1944, MS 2852/4/22/28, Gowrie Papers, NLA; Letter, Taylor to J. G. Beohm, 27 March 1944, MS 2594/86, Taylor Papers, NLA.
[24] Report by Hillgarth, PREM 3/159/10, PRO; Note by Beamish, 29 February 1944, BEAM 3/5, Beamish Papers, CC.
[25] Report by Hillgarth, PREM 3/159/10, PRO.
[26] Advisory War Council Minutes, 21 March 1944, CRS A2682/7/1322, NAA; Gill, *Royal Australian Navy 1942–1945*, pp. 471–2; Message, Colonel Wilson to Royle, 22 March 1944, CRS A5954, Box 305, NAA; See also Advisory War Council Minute, 7 March 1944, CRS A5954, Box 510, NAA.

27 Memorandum by Shedden, 9 February 1944, CRS A5954, Box 468, NAA.

28 Memorandum by Shedden for Curtin, 23 March 1944, CRS A5954, Box 305, NAA.

29 Letter, Shedden to Wilson, 1 April 1944, CRS A5954, Box 305, NAA.

30 War Cabinet Conclusions, 17 February 1944, CAB 65/41, W.M. (44)22, PRO; Dalton diary, 15 December 1943, I/29/160, Dalton Papers, LSE.

31 Smith, *Task Force 57*, p. 112; Note by Lyttelton, 29 March 1944, CAB 66/48, W.P. (44)173, PRO.

32 Memorandum, Chiefs of Staff to Churchill, March 1944, PREM 3/160/7, PRO.

33 Minute, Churchill to Alexander and Cunningham, 9 April 1944, PREM 3/164/5, PRO; See also Minute, Churchill to Alexander and Cunningham, 10 March 1944, PREM 3/164/5, PRO.

34 Dalton diary, 13 April 1944, I/30/100, Dalton Papers, LSE.

35 Cable, Churchill to Mountbatten, 25 February 1944, and Cable, Roosevelt to Churchill, 25 February 1944, PREM 3/148/10, PRO; Alanbrooke diary, 24–25 February 1944, in Danchev and Todman (eds), *War Diaries*, pp. 524–5; Note by Churchill, 28 February 1944, PREM 3/260/12, PRO.

36 Bryant, *Triumph in the West*, pp. 161–71; Documents in PREM 3/160/1–8 and PREM 3/148/1–12, PRO; Minute, Churchill to Ismay, 15 April 1944, and Cable, Churchill to Roosevelt, 14 April 1944, PREM 3/260/12, PRO.

37 ibid.

38 Cable, Churchill to Roosevelt, 10 March 1944, Minutes, Colville to Private Office, 4 March 1944 and Ismay to Churchill, 6 March 1944, and Cable, Roosevelt to Churchill, 13 March 1944, PREM 3/160/8, PRO.

39 Note, Leathers to Churchill, 5 March 1944, PREM 3/160/7; Cable, Churchill to Dill, 10 March 1944, PREM 3/160/8; Note by Churchill, 7 March 1944, and Minute, Churchill to Leathers and Ismay, 14 March 1944, PREM 3/160/3, PRO; Somerville diary, 15 March 1944, ADD. MS. 52564, Cunningham Papers, BL.

40 Cable, Churchill to Curtin, 11 March 1944, PREM 3/160/1, PRO; See also Letter, Churchill to MacArthur, 12 March 1944, PREM 3/159/14, PRO.

41 Cable, Churchill to Mountbatten, 18 March 1944, PREM 3/160/1.

42 Alanbrooke diary, 17 March 1944, in Danchev and Todman (eds), *War Diaries*, p. 532.

43 Defence Committee Minute, 16 March 1944, CRS A2031/12/87/1944, NAA; Shedden's memoirs, Chap. 46, pp. 4–5, CRS A5954, Box 771, NAA.

44 Minute, Hollis to Churchill, 25 March 1944, and Minute, Churchill to Ismay, 27 March 1944, PREM 3/160/1, PRO; Somerville diary, 3 April 1944, ADD. MS. 52564, and Letter, Cunningham to Noble, 8 April 1944, ADD. MS. 52571, BL.

45 Alanbrooke diary, 23 March 1944, in Danchev and Todman (eds), *War Diaries*, p. 534.

46 Somerville diary, 26 March 1944, ADD. MS. 52564, Cunningham Papers, BL.

47 Minutes of a Staff Conference, 8 April 1944, PREM 3/160/8; Report by Hillgarth, PREM 3/159/10; Cable, Dill to Churchill, 30 March 1944, PREM 3/148/10, PRO; 'Summary of Work carried out by Australian Chemical Warfare Research and Experimental Section, November 1943–May 1944', CRS A5954, Box 362, NAA.

48 Shedden memoirs, Chap. 57, pp. 1–3, CRS A5954, Box 771, NAA.

49 Letter, Cross to Cranborne, 13 April 1944, Rc/4/24, Cross Papers, IWM.

FORTY-TWO

'America will scoop the World'

An exhausted and very relieved Australian prime minister walked cautiously down the gangway at San Francisco when the troopship *Lurline* berthed there on 19 April 1944. Curtin had spent the voyage pacing the deck at night, terrified that he might at any moment have to abandon ship. During the long torpid days, he was often shut away in his humid cabin with his ailing wife, while the returning American troops and a party of Australian war brides crowded the decks and scanned the horizon for some sign of the Californian coast. To Curtin's displeasure, the hard-drinking Blamey had brought cases of alcohol aboard the supposedly dry ship, with his partying often leaving him the worse for it. Once safely on American soil, Curtin opted to travel by train to Washington rather than risk his life in an aircraft.[1]

Australian officials in Washington were hoping that Curtin's visit would smooth American–Australian relations. Australia's first secretary in Washington, Alan Watt, cautioned that American officials were having 'to be handled with rather more care than usual', and warned Canberra against allowing the formerly warm relationship with Washington to cool too much since, 'if one looks twenty to fifty years ahead, Australia needs the support of the United States in the Pacific'. Watt worried that Curtin would not have time to restore the previous warmth and to raise Australia's standing in the discussions about postwar problems. Watt lamented that Australia would continue to find itself 'out in the cold as far as current world problems are concerned'.[2]

Curtin was simply not the man to pursue these questions. He had no one from the external affairs department in his entourage, no doubt partly for fear that they would report his moves to Evatt, but also from a lack of interest in these matters. Curtin had rejected Evatt's suggestions that the head of the external affairs department should accompany him to provide advice on foreign policy, arguing that the London meeting was not meant to be a policy conference but an exploratory meeting that would require follow-up conferences between the responsible ministers.[3] Apart from his personal secretary and press secretary, Curtin's principal adviser was the defence department head, Frederick Shedden, as well as the increasingly Anglophile General Blamey. His travelling companions reflected Curtin's limited overseas agenda, which was to gain Allied agreement to the partial demobilisation of Australian forces, to secure a place for Australia in the remaining operations against Japan, and to realign Australia firmly within the British imperial camp, albeit on a basis closer to partnership than the former subservience.

Curtin wanted to break down the wall of British hostility towards Australia that had built up during the war, and to ensure that the dominion's postwar destiny within the Commonwealth would not be compromised by its fleeting dalliance with America. Robert Menzies was back in charge of the United Australia Party and was determined to undermine the position that Curtin had developed by his war leadership. Menzies withdrew his MPs from the advisory war council, ending the spirit of cooperation that Curtin had extended to Menzies when the latter was prime minister, and generally mounted a more robust political attack on the government than either Fadden or Hughes had done. Curtin's long political experience made him conscious of Labor's possible vulnerability to charges of disloyalty to Britain. His 'looks to America' statement of December 1941, and his public disputes with Churchill in 1942, had left just such an opening for Menzies. Hence the presence among Curtin's party of his press secretary, Don Rodgers, who would ensure that there were many favourable press cables from London describing Curtin's supposedly warm relationship with Churchill and stressing his loyalty to Britain and its institutions.[4]

As far as the Washington visit was concerned, MacArthur had indicated to Curtin that there was nothing he wanted raised on his behalf. And Curtin had no wish to have serious discussions about matters that he first wanted to raise with the British government. So he restricted his meetings in the American capital to courtesy calls on various military and State Department officials. He did, though, fly to South Carolina for lunch with Roosevelt, who was recuperating from hypertension in the mansion of a friend. In a private meeting after the meal, Curtin tried to smooth over the rough patch in Australian–American relations caused by the Anzac agreement of January 1944. The agreement was designed to restrict American postwar influence in the Pacific to the northern hemisphere and to establish Australian and New Zealand influence in the southern hemisphere under the protective cover of the British. Just five days before Curtin met Roosevelt, the agreement had been described by the powerful Democrat senator for South Carolina, James Richards, as the 'unkindest, most disturbing cut of all' which 'in no way recognises or appreciates the dependence of Australia and New Zealand upon the U.S. Army, Navy, and Air Force'.[5]

Curtin had been alarmed by the damage the agreement had done to Australia's relationship with Washington and was more than willing to see it hang like a dead albatross around Evatt's political neck. So he was relieved when Roosevelt guessed that Curtin 'had had very little to do with the drafting, but that Evatt had done most of it and the others had merely agreed'. Curtin admitted that the agreement 'was made and carried in what may well prove to be an excess of enthusiasm' following a discussion in Canberra on 'the future of the white man in the Pacific' in which, Curtin claimed, fears had been expressed about a future Asiatic bloc of India and China turning against all white men. Roosevelt advised that 'it will be best to forget the whole incident'.[6]

The abstemious Curtin then spent several desultory days in Washington, blind to the charms of the capital in its springtime plumage and increasingly distracted by Blamey's hard drinking and womanising. At a meeting with the combined chiefs of staff, during which Blamey outlined Australia's military plans, the jaded general fell asleep as his Allied counterparts discussed the points he raised. Curtin was also beset by an illness that was variously described by newspapers as high blood pressure, sciatica or lumbago, but which his wife privately ascribed to his fear of the forthcoming flight across the Atlantic. His remaining appointments with American officials were cancelled while Curtin took to his bed in Blair House. When their flying boat eventually took off in the early hours of 28 April, Blamey dossed down in the plane's prime ministerial bunk while Curtin sat tight-lipped and stiffly upright, enduring the long flight across the dark and hostile ocean to Ireland and thence on to London.[7]

The British high commissioner, Sir Ronald Cross, had advised Whitehall that Curtin would be so keen to score a personal success that he may not be 'very insistent on anything if his insistence might result in his appearing publicly to have had a failure'. Cross warned the Dominions Office not to overwhelm Curtin with a whirl of social engagements as they usually did with dominion leaders. Curtin had 'simple tastes' and 'would not like being entertained in a social way and the simpler his surroundings, the more likely he is to enjoy himself'. Cross suggested that Churchill show Curtin 'personal attention' since the 'success he made of Dr. Evatt in 1942 had a transforming influence on Anglo–Australian relations'.[8]

Curtin was certainly keen to set aside the antagonism that had bedevilled wartime relations between London and Canberra. On landing, he was effusive in his praise for the people of Britain 'for having stood alone as the rampart of civilization and [for having] held the fort'. And he was careful to reject any idea of Australia moving away from Britain, declaring that he spoke for 'seven million Britishers' in the South Seas.[9] Menzies might have said it with more eloquence, but the sentiments would have been the same. And the practical measure that Curtin hoped to achieve during his time in London was one that Menzies might have approved. Curtin wanted Britain and the dominions to create a Commonwealth secretariat that could formalise the relationship between them and coordinate their foreign policies. He envisaged that the secretariat could be based in London and rotate through the various dominions. Curtin was ahead of his time in his vision of a Commonwealth in which Britain did not rule but merely participated like any other member. On this issue, Curtin was defeated before he began.

Neither the other members of the Commonwealth nor Britain shared Curtin's desire for closer integration of their foreign policies or the establishment of formal machinery to oversee it. Canada's position was well known and should have given Curtin pause before suggesting such a proposal. The British government decided to give Curtin time to raise the issue during the prime ministers' meeting, with Britain taking a back seat while Canada's prime minister, Mackenzie King, knocked the plan on the head. Such was the artful design of the trap set by the dominions secretary, Lord Cranborne, and laid out for the approval of the war cabinet some ten days before Curtin's aircraft lumbered into view.[10] In the event, Churchill did not even attend the meeting at which Curtin's plan was finished off by the Canadians. Curtin was upset by Churchill's absence, but it allowed Britain to escape the odium of quashing a proposal designed to strengthen the Commonwealth, and then permitted it to propose a compromise that would provide the form, but not the substance, of Curtin's proposal.[11]

Even Churchill realised that the days of whipping the empire into line were long past and that the prospects of reaching a joint agreement on anything were slender. Accordingly, Churchill had agreed with his war cabinet that the conference, beginning in the cabinet room of 10 Downing Street on 1 May, should be purely exploratory and that there should be no attempt to reach binding conclusions. To help ensure this, and to minimise dissension, the various high commissioners in London were excluded from the talks, other than the opening and closing sessions, during which they were included in the general photograph.[12] This would help soothe any ruffled feelings, while their absence from the conference table would prevent them pushing their prime ministers to resolve difficult issues. At least, that was the British plan. In the event, Curtin insisted on having Bruce, Blamey and Shedden seated with him 'to keep in mind questions that would be raised'.[13]

Britain was involved in discussions, mainly with Washington, of fairly intractable issues and did not want this conference to disturb them. More embarrassingly, there were a number of issues upon which the British cabinet had not been able to reach agreement, the prime example being postwar economic policy, with British ministers being at loggerheads over the direction that Britain should take in its talks with the United States. On this issue, Churchill proposed that he make only general statements at the conference about the desirability of fostering trade within the empire and set out in a non-committal way the state of the Anglo–American economic talks.[14] This would satisfy all sides: those who wanted a general boost to world trade and those who wanted to see an imperial trading bloc. The economic imperialists within the British government were left out in the cold. When Lord Croft sought Beaverbrook's help to distribute copies of the Empire Industries Association's bulletin to the four dominion prime ministers, Beaverbrook declined, warning that the 'perils of direct propaganda of this type are too great'.[15]

Another vexed question was the future world organisation. Churchill was adamant that peace and security would depend on the organisation being effectively controlled by three or four great powers (depending upon whether China was included), whereas Eden proposed ten to twelve nations for the council of such an organisation, with room for the dominions sitting in rotation.[16] With the British government so divided on this question, it had to avoid definitive discussions with the visiting prime ministers.

Curtin's political agenda was more immediate, but there were still pitfalls in his path to achieving Allied agreement to the reorientation of Australia's war effort. On 8 April, Australia's acting prime minister, Frank Forde, had announced that ninety thousand men would be released from the Australian army during the course of 1944. This was seized upon by the local and overseas press as an attempt by Australia to take a back seat in the Pacific war, reaping rewards as a food supplier and reducing the risks of fighting. In fact, Forde's announcement was old news and was designed for domestic consumption to cover the government's lamentable failure to discharge men and get them back onto the farms. MacArthur had agreed to the numbers in 1943, and most men were to be discharged for injury, illness or indiscipline. Only twenty thousand were to be specially discharged to cope with the needs of civil industry.[17]

Forde had issued the statement to assuage growing domestic concern about sluggish discharges into industry. Instead, he had blown up an international storm that threatened to buffet Curtin during his visit to the Allied capitals. Curtin immediately instructed Forde not to announce any change in the strength of the armed forces before first clearing it with him.[18] The damage was already done. Churchill was aghast at the idea of Australia directing men from the forces back onto the farms so as to profit from the war. Such calculations were considered permissible in British planning, but not where Australia was concerned.

Australia's intention was even worse than Churchill feared. So concerned was Forde about the needs of industry, particularly the lowly paid and otherwise unattractive dairying industry, that he teamed his press announcement with a secret suggestion to the army that farmers' requests for the release of particular troops be granted regardless of the troops' situation, thereby 'assisting in increasing production of butter for export to England'. In other words, troops would be taken from the front line to provide butter for Britain's bread. The army resisted this suggestion, maintaining that most of the troops requested for release were 'key personnel' in operational divisions of the AIF and awaiting orders from MacArthur to take the offensive against Japan.[19] So the manpower problem remained unresolved.

When Churchill read American press criticism of Forde's announcement, it confirmed all his own prejudices about the dominion. He instructed his chiefs of staff to report on the Australian war effort, which he personally felt to be 'a very poor show'. Churchill argued that five army divisions, rather than three, was the least that Australia should be maintaining outside the country, and he hoped his chiefs would back up this opinion with statistics that might be useful in his forthcoming talks with Curtin.[20] The chiefs of staff duly reported back on 1 May, but not in the terms expected by Churchill. Instead, they exonerated Australia. Considering the terrain and the tropical diseases with which they had to cope in New Guinea, the maintenance of two or three divisions throughout the campaign was 'a very remarkable achievement', concluded the chiefs. The Australian navy was similarly absolved, while the chiefs considered that the RAAF had been hampered by inadequate aircraft rather than by any failure of political or military will. In fact, the chiefs looked forward to integrating the Australian forces to allow for logistical support for the combined Commonwealth force.[21] It is doubtful whether these comments softened Churchill's entrenched prejudices.

The following day, Churchill asked his office to brief him on the subject of Australian manpower so that he would have ammunition for his discussion with Curtin.[22] He had planned weekend talks with Curtin at Chequers, where affairs of state could be determined round the fireplace with brandy and cigars. As an ex-alcoholic, this would have been very awkward for Curtin, and may explain his aversion to the social situations with which he was confronted in London. Apart from resisting liquid temptation, Curtin was also suspicious of being 'duchessed' by the British.

Despite the report of the chiefs of staff exonerating Australia for any perceived inadequacy in its contribution to the war, Churchill instructed Ismay on 4 May to have

a small body of competent officers forthwith begin to examine, in cold blood, what really is Australia's contribution. A separate, subsequent note might be written about New Zealand. They both say they are forced to maintain a great number of men under arms and are now compelled to withdraw them to grow everything we shall require in the Pacific etc. Let us have a look at it without the slightest desire to prove a case one way or the other.

Once again, Whitehall exonerated Australia in respect to its war effort, with Ismay pointing out that 'the degree of mobilisation for the war is greater in Australia than in the United States in both armed forces and munitions', although only if manpower employed in Allied food production were counted as part of the total mobilised manpower. Ismay tried to mollify Churchill, buttressing his favourable assessment with statistics and an assurance from Shedden that Australian troops would only be switched to agricultural production if Australia had to support greater American and British forces.[23]

Churchill was concerned that Australia's partial demobilisation might force Britain to play a much larger role in the Pacific than he intended. Churchill and his chiefs wanted the Australian troops to camouflage the relatively small British component in the contemplated British Commonwealth force. Similar motives lay behind Britain's wish that Australia man a British aircraft carrier and associated warships. That way some of the manpower burden of the Japanese war could be shifted from Britain to Australia. As well, the nucleus of a strong postwar Australian naval force would be formed that could patrol the Pacific at Britain's behest, protecting the most distant outposts of its once great empire.

Curtin was suspicious of the British moves, particularly concerning the offer of warships which he had been reluctant to accept in the absence of British approval for the reshaping of Australia's war effort. Accepting the ships would just add to Australia's manpower woes. In order to allay Australian concerns about British motives, Churchill assured the conference that British forces would begin to move to the Pacific as soon as ports could be secured in Europe by the forthcoming D-day landings. He reiterated his pledge that 'Britain had promised to do all she could against Japan and that that pledge would be carried out'. Contrary to the view of his chiefs of staff, he predicted that the war against Japan would not long outlast the war against Hitler, though this was a personal feeling for which Churchill 'had nothing in the way of facts to prove it by'.[24] In fact, Churchill knew of the secret and feverish development of the atomic bomb, and Stalin's secret undertaking to join the Allied effort against Japan as soon as Germany had surrendered.

On the day Curtin left Australia, Forde had called a conference of the chiefs of staff to discuss boosting the monthly manpower intake for the navy. Not surprisingly, there was stiff opposition, although the army was prepared to concede if an increase were needed to man additional ships. This would have given heart to Admiral Royle's campaign to have Australia accept British warships.[25] Despite explicit instructions from Curtin, Royle took his campaign back to the advisory war council on 20 April where he pressed the navy's manpower needs on the sympathetic conservative politicians, with Arthur Fadden and Percy Spender being two of the MPs who had remained on the council after Menzies had ordered the withdrawal of his UAP colleagues. Although Forde criticised Royle for stirring up the political waters, Forde later confided to a night-time press conference at Parliament House that Curtin was planning to 'seek the transfer of some cruisers or destroyers from the British fleet to Australia', when Curtin had not decided to do any such thing. One journalist observed that Forde was 'rather cautious in giving this information but intimated that they might be gift ships and would be given to Australia on the condition that we manned them'.[26]

Such a transfer was supported by the advisory war council at its meeting on 2 May, with Royle rounding off his campaign the following day with a statement to the war cabinet in favour of Australia accepting the ships. It would not only recoup the wartime losses of Australian ships, argued Royle, but also give a powerful show of Australian participation in the Pacific war, with 'ships steaming and fighting side by side with those of the British forces [providing] highly tangible evidence of our active participation in the war to the very end'.[27] Royle won converts on both sides of the political fence, with the government agreeing to increase the navy's intake at the expense of the army and air force.

Curtin was notified of Royle's attempted policy coup on 4 May in the midst of his discussions in London to reduce the commitments for Australian manpower. Although Curtin agreed to an increase in the naval intake to man various small ships being built in Australia, he was angry that Britain had not deigned to reply to a seven-month-old cable from Canberra requesting the return of three thousand Australian sailors serving with the Royal Navy. Curtin contrasted the tardy handling of this question in London with the 'urgency with which additional commitments have been pressed'.[28] Anxious to avoid further commitments if the Australian sailors were not going to be returned home, Curtin played a cat-and-mouse game with the Admiralty in which he adroitly sidestepped their attempts to corner him for discussions on the question of the 'gift' ships.

On 12 May, Churchill notified Curtin of Admiral Daniel's mission to Australia and of the need for his party to be reinforced with 'a few more sailors and soldiers'. He asked Curtin to meet the first lord of the Admiralty,

A. V. Alexander, and his naval chief, Admiral Cunningham, so that they might explain the need for extra men despite Curtin's reluctance to accept them. A week later, the Admiralty officials still had not met Curtin, who was soon to depart for Washington. Alexander begged Churchill to help collar the reluctant Australian since, he complained, Curtin 'does not seem anxious to come to the Admiralty!'.[29] Alexander neglected to inform Churchill that one of the matters they wanted to discuss with Curtin was the possible transfer of the British ships. This was part of the Admiralty's secret agenda inspired by Royle, who had informed London that Curtin would raise the question of his own accord and thereby allow the Admiralty to avoid the risk of appearing to pressure Australia into further commitments.

The Admiralty's plan nearly went awry during a meeting at Chequers on 21 May when Curtin raised the issue of the Australian sailors with the unprepared Churchill, asking him to allow the recall of the three thousand Australian sailors. These men would be almost sufficient to man the so-called 'gift' ships. Hiding his confusion, Churchill made a non-committal response to Curtin, while later demanding an explanation of it all from Alexander, who filled in the background to the issue and described Royle's part in it. The Australian newspaper boss Sir Keith Murdoch was also in London and had been briefed on the ships proposal. When Alexander confessed to Murdoch that Curtin had not yet raised the question of the ships, Murdoch offered to remind the prime minister about it. Murdoch's prompting, and the resulting realisation of Australian newspaper interest in the proposal, may well have been responsible for Curtin finally mentioning the matter to Churchill. Whatever the reason, Alexander was ecstatic that the matter was now on the table for discussion. As he informed Churchill, the offer to man the ships would not only 'show a welcome revival of Australian interest in the importance of a Navy but, if made and accepted, it would be a real contribution to our own manpower problem and ensure a satisfactory foundation for Australia's post-war fleet'. Alexander warned Churchill not to mention Royle's input and to pretend that the proposal was purely Australia's.[30] This Churchill did.

On 27 May, Churchill responded to Curtin's claim that Australia was being asked to find three or four thousand extra sailors to man the British ships. 'I think there must have been some misunderstanding on this,' wrote Churchill, 'since I am assured by [Admiral Cunningham] that no such proposal emanated from the Admiralty.' However, if Australia were willing to provide the men, Churchill was willing to provide an aircraft carrier and one or more cruisers.[31] Curtin's suspicions turned to anger when Murdoch inadvertently told him that Royle had been secretly conveying Australian moves to the Admiralty. The matter was finally decided for Curtin when Churchill declared that Australian sailors and airmen seconded to British forces would not be transferred home to ease the manpower shortage. Curtin was unlikely to aggravate the shortage by accepting the British ships. On 29 May, just before leaving London, Curtin cabled Forde recommending that a decision on manning the extra ships be delayed 'until all aspects of the war effort can be looked at together'.[32]

Curtin assumed that the British government's failure to reply to the cable of October 1943 about Australian manpower problems was due to rudeness. Certainly Churchill often ignored Australian needs and feelings, but this case had as much to do with Britain's failure to settle upon an acceptable Pacific strategy. Taking Churchill at his word, Curtin now believed that Britain's plans for the Pacific had been settled and that the Pacific fleet would arrive promptly, placing sudden and unbearable pressure on Australian manpower. During the prime ministers' meeting on 3 May, Curtin told Churchill bluntly that Australia would not be able to provide food and supplies for additional Allied forces without reducing the armed forces. Admiral Cunningham was taken aback by Curtin's apparent hostility, noting that he was 'rather rude and gave the impression that he did not want UK forces in Australia', with Cunningham concluding that Curtin and Blamey were 'in MacArthur's pocket'. When the meeting reconvened after lunch, Curtin dispelled this impression in Cunningham's mind when he made an 'excellent statement' claiming that Australia was 'anxious for UK forces but do not know how many they can support and are most anxious ... to keep forces in the field commensurate with the importance at the peace table of their views on the Pacific being taken into account'.[33]

With Australia's position clarified, it was possible to discuss the level of British forces likely to be based in Australia if Churchill approved the Pacific strategy. In a meeting with Blamey on 5 May, the British chiefs of staff set the maximum British force at six army divisions, 60 squadrons of aircraft, four battleships, five fleet carriers and associated escort ships.[34] Although these figures were useful for Australian planning purposes, they meant little until Britain's strategy for the Pacific war was determined. And it was clear that there was much more arguing to be done between Churchill and his military advisers before a Pacific strategy could be decided. When Churchill heard that the chiefs of staff had given Blamey their views on Pacific strategy, he rounded on them out of fear that they might win the strategic argument by default. Although Churchill admitted that Britain's indecision was 'not unfolding a creditable picture to history', he continued to oppose any strategy based upon southern Australia.[35]

Curtin seemed oblivious to the debate still raging within Whitehall. On the penultimate day of the conference, he and Mackenzie King hotly disputed whether Britain and the dominions had finalised plans for the war against Japan. King sarcastically recorded in his diary that

... I asked him to give me the outline of what they were. In doing that, he used the expression ... 'the British Government is to consider what it is going to do'. I took these words down in pencil and kept them so as to have that record. This was part of the argument that we were all agreed on plans.[36]

In fact, Whitehall still could not decide whether India or Australia would provide the base support for the British effort. Churchill and several of his ministers were pressing the Indian case, stressing the abundant and generally pliant Indian workforce, and the savings in shipping. Amery, who had favoured Australia, changed sides after hearing Curtin speak of the manpower difficulties in Australia. In a letter to Churchill, Amery asked whether 'anything could be made of Australia without so many off-sets as to more than countervail the advantages'.[37] Amery was writing to the converted.

Meanwhile, Churchill was alarmed that Mountbatten's Indian forces would be drawn into a jungle war in Burma that would preclude the bold amphibious strokes he envisaged along the Burmese coast and, later, against Sumatra.[38] He was determined to revive the Sumatran operation and recapture Britain's imperial territories in South-East Asia. Nothing could be done, however, until the great gulf was bridged between Britain's political and military leaders. General Ismay was determined to find some common ground between them since, as he confided to Mountbatten's chief of staff: 'It would be far better to agree to some plan, even though it may not be the best, and to push it forward unitedly and whole-heartedly, than to go on as we are doing at the moment.' The obvious solution was to opt for what Ismay termed a middle course: a combined British–Dominion effort based upon north-west Australia and striking northward towards Borneo, from where it could either link up with the American Pacific effort or turn southward to descend upon Singapore.[39] It was this compromise that the chiefs of staff finally adopted, with an 'Empire Force i.e. Australian Divisions and British Fleet to go for Amboina [Ambon in the Netherlands East Indies] late 1944 or early 1945'. They also conceded Curtin's point that, at least initially, such a force would operate under MacArthur's command.[40] However, Churchill remained far from willing to present a united front to the world as far as Pacific strategy was concerned.

One of the advantages of the middle course was that Britain could demobilise more of its forces once Germany was defeated rather than dispatch them against Japan. When the dominion prime ministers were told of Britain's demobilisation plans, Curtin immediately suspected that Britain wanted to shirk the all-out effort against Japan that Churchill had promised. Attlee assured him that military requirements would be paramount and that Britain's 'primary objective ... was to make the maximum contribution possible to the defeat of Japan'. Ernest Bevin chimed in, claiming that it was physically impossible to ship all of Britain's three million fighting men to the Far East, and it was that surplus that would be demobilised.[41] This was all nonsense. Military considerations in the Pacific were the last priority for British manpower. As the chiefs of staff revealed in proposing the compromise middle course, Britain expected the dominions to provide much of the manpower in what was now called the British empire effort against Japan.[42]

After three weeks in London, Curtin had still not achieved his objectives, partly because he avoided informal discussions with Churchill at which an agreement might have been reached. Curtin had dodged Churchill's initial invitation to visit Chequers, opting instead to accompany Shedden on a visit to the elderly Lord Hankey, telling Hankey that he had not gone to Chequers as he did not want 'to sit in an armchair and listen to one man!'. Although he later went to Chequers on three subsequent weekends, Curtin went to a cricket match at Lord's rather than join the other prime ministers when they accompanied Churchill on a weekend train journey to inspect preparations for the forthcoming D-day landings.[43] On his visit to Chequers on 21 May, Curtin was ostensibly invited to meet Churchill's daughters. To Curtin's consternation, 'he was instead ushered into a room where the Prime Minister had [Lord] Leathers, [Lord] Cherwell and [Major General] Hollis armed with a large note book'. Curtin peered through Churchill's cigar smoke for a sign of his daughters bearing an afternoon tea tray, but found himself dragooned into discussing the issue of British forces going to Australia. As he later told Bruce, 'he was taken completely by surprise but had to go in to bat'.[44] He did not score many runs.

As a result of this discussion, Curtin had to accept that Churchill would not release any of the Australians still fighting in Europe and the Middle East, or the Australian sailors manning six destroyers of Britain's Eastern fleet. Curtin's request for the transfer of some Australian squadrons serving in Britain was also refused. Churchill would only agree to send Australian service personnel home from Europe as soon as possible after the end of the war against Germany, and to release some of the Australian ground crew serving in the Middle East if they were replaced by equivalent reinforcements from Australia. Many of these airmen had been overseas for four years, twice the normal tour of duty, and were anxious to return home.[45] While Australia would welcome them back, their return would not provide any relief for the dominion's manpower problem if they had to be replaced with fresh reinforcements. It was not until a final meeting with Curtin at Chequers on 28 May, the day before his departure from London, that Churchill conceded that Australia could limit its war effort to the maintenance of six divisions for active operations, with three divisions being kept in the field at any one time; that the Australian navy could be kept at its present strength along with the new ships being constructed in Australia; and that the RAAF could be maintained at a strength of 53 squadrons. On top of this, Australian food exports to Britain would be kept at the 1944 level. In fact, Curtin was keen for Australia to send even more food to Britain so as to secure the dominion's share of the postwar British market.[46]

Despite Curtin's recalcitrance in London over the 'gift' ships, he remained keen to reintegrate the dominion into the imperial framework. In briefing Curtin, Australian defence chiefs had reaffirmed the principle of imperial defence, with each part of the empire 'to accept a primary responsibility for its own local defence and to co-operate fully with the other portions for the defence of the whole'. The role of the Australian navy would be, as before, 'to deter and delay invasion until the arrival of British Naval reinforcements enables us to assume the offensive'.[47] Such views accorded with Curtin's sentiments.

As Curtin reassured British MPs at a meeting of the Empire Parliamentary Association in the House of Commons, Australia remained a microcosm of Britain. 'We carry on out there,' he said,

as a British community in the South Seas, and we regard ourselves as the trustees for the British way of life in a part of the world where it is of the utmost significance to the British Commonwealth and to the British nation and to the British Empire — call it by any name that you will — that this land should have in the Antipodes a people and a territory corresponding in purpose and in outlook and in race to the Motherland itself.[48]

Despite this affirmation of imperial loyalty, and his support for imperial defence, the Australian government also had a newfound determination, forged out of bitter experience, not to be caught so completely defenceless in any future conflict. Increasing the population through immigration was one arm of this defence; developing an aircraft industry and a strong air force was another.

Australia's director-general of civil aviation, Daniel McVey, had preceded Curtin to London via the United States to clinch a proposal to build four-engine

British Lancaster bombers in Australia. In a meeting with Beaverbrook on 18 April, McVey had appealed to Beaverbrook's well-founded fears about the United States, claiming to have

seen in Washington a map of the Pacific as America hopes to see it after the War. All the Japanese mandated islands are shown annexed to the United States with American air lines flying to China, Malaya, the Philippines, the Dutch East Indies, Australia and New Zealand along entirely American owned island bases.

Beaverbrook realised that McVey's appeal was not disinterested, that the Australian 'naturally wants some of these islands for Australia'. However, he was impressed by McVey's graphic description of American aircraft factories preparing to produce the postwar generation of civil aircraft and by his warning that, unless Britain moved quickly, 'America will scoop the World'.[49] Although Beaverbrook was sympathetic to McVey's plea, he wanted to avoid discussing civil aviation at the Commonwealth conference, since a Commonwealth-approved proposal on civil aviation had already been submitted to the United States. When Curtin had demanded that civil aviation be placed on the agenda, London hoped that the discussion could be limited to Australia's proposal for the internationalisation of civil aviation, which could then be finished off.[50]

In fact, as McVey confided to Beaverbrook over lunch on 3 May, internationalisation was already finished as far as he was concerned. Only Evatt persisted with this ideal, which had been one of the pillars of the Anzac agreement in January, and which Evatt regarded as necessary to safeguard the postwar peace. What the dominion now wanted, according to McVey, was a scheme of 'Empire Co-operation in Air Transport' in which Britain and the dominions would form a joint imperial aviation company that would straddle the globe with a fast, prestige air service. Separate British and dominion airlines would then operate the slower trunk routes of the empire. Australian airlines would thus gain access to imperial airfields and become a major force across the Pacific and perhaps the Indian Ocean. Beaverbrook took up this suggestion, proposing it as the best way of gaining

Commonwealth cooperation in the air, although British officials tried to ensure that Britain had an effective veto power in the proposed joint company.[51] Britain also wanted to confront the American challenge over the supply of civil aircraft, and prevent Australia opting for American aircraft for its civil airlines. McVey agreed, suggesting to Curtin that the Australian services order British transport aircraft for use during the present conflict so as to 'permit the design and development of aircraft for post-war commercial purposes', although they would be 'delivered to the Services stripped of the internal furnishings and fittings required for post-war civil use'.[52] When the war was over, they could be quickly converted for civilian purposes.

With the Americans pressing Curtin to have discussions on civil aviation during his return stopover in Washington, Curtin wanted his fellow prime ministers to formulate a united approach on civil aviation so that the Americans could not pick them off one at a time as they had been attempting to do. Curtin and Beaverbrook agreed that a British air route across the Pacific needed to be settled and that landing rights at Honolulu should be sought in return for the already conceded American landing rights in Australia. As for alternative routes across the Pacific that might avoid an American stopover, Curtin agreed that they could be explored although he felt that such routes would not prove economic.[53] At MacArthur's prompting, Curtin had refused for the last two years to back P. G. Taylor's survey of an alternative trans-Pacific air route.

While Curtin was in London, Taylor was assuming command of a British-organised expedition to assess the viability of his route. At the last minute, objections from the American naval chief, Admiral King, prevented him from taking off. A furious Taylor returned to the fray, urging Britain to ignore the American objections and alleging that 'U.S. commercial airline people, who dominate both the Navy and Army air transport services, will, and have, put every obstacle in the way of this route, which they cannot control in the future because it does not go through any U.S. territory'. Taylor pointed to the damage to Australia and New Zealand if Britain submitted to this American 'bullying'. The two dominions, he claimed, were 'very ripe just now for strengthening ties with Britain' and the effect of his survey would 'give a warm feeling to a lot of British people in the S. W. Pacific'. Although Britain was wary of upsetting the Americans over such a peripheral issue, Whitehall had come to regard the route as necessary for Britain's effort in the Pacific war. It would also be useful in case Anglo–American talks on civil aviation broke down and there was a 'free-for-all'. With British support for his survey reaffirmed, Taylor returned to Washington at the end of June 1944 to try to overcome Admiral King's objections.[54]

As Beaverbrook had intended, there was little progress on postwar civil aviation at the London conference. On the eve of his departure to Canada with Curtin, McVey charged Beaverbrook with deliberately avoiding the issue so that no discussion could take place at the conference. Beaverbrook admitted to this but then mollified him by promising to adopt McVey's various proposals and ensure that he received the credit for their success.[55] In fact, Beaverbrook was hamstrung. Australian disappointment counted for little compared to the Canadian threat to strike out on their own using their strategic position as a stopover en route from Europe to America. There was also considerable opposition from the British air ministry, which wanted resources concentrated solely on winning the war. And there was Churchill, who deprecated the likely postwar importance of civil aviation and wished to accommodate the Americans on such contentious issues. With so little progress in London, Curtin declined the American invitation for talks on civil aviation, promising instead to examine the matter upon his return to Australia.[56]

Once the Commonwealth conference was done, and Curtin had left for Washington, Churchill was free to concentrate on the forthcoming D-day operation. With some of the remaining Commonwealth leaders in tow, Churchill went off in his train to view the last-minute preparations and, according to Brooke's account, made 'a thorough pest of himself' after his plan to view the operation from a cruiser was vetoed by the King.[57] Timed for 5 June, the operation was postponed by bad weather in the English Channel. Back in Downing Street, Churchill had his chiefs of staff to lunch and was 'in almost a hysterical state' as he waited to see if two years of careful planning would founder on the whim of the English weather.[58] He was banking upon a quick victory in Europe as the Allied armies converged on a cornered Germany. The date for the end of the European war was optimistically set at October 1944, after which it would be time to turn against the Japanese in the Pacific. Exactly how this would be done still remained to be decided.

NOTES

1   Shedden's Memoirs, Chap. 57, CRS A5954, Box 771, NAA; Horner, *High Command*, pp. 313–14, 507–8; Horner, *Defence Supremo*, pp. 192–3; Day, *John Curtin*, pp. 535–6.

2   Letter, Watt to Hood, 4 April 1944, MS 3788/1/1, Watt Papers, NLA; Letter, Watt to Hood, 29 February 1944, *DAFP*, Vol. 7, Doc. 59.

3   Letters, Evatt to Curtin, 24 March 1944 and Curtin to Evatt, 29 March 1944, *DAFP*, Vol. 7, Docs 94 and 101; Edwards, *Prime Ministers and Diplomats*, pp. 162–3.

4   Day, *John Curtin*, pp. 539–46; Horner, *High Command*, pp. 308–13.

5   *Daily Telegraph*, Sydney, 20 April 1944.

6   Thorne, *Allies of a Kind*, p. 486.

7   Horner, *High Command*, pp. 314, 507–8; Horner, *Defence Supremo*, p. 194; Day, *John Curtin*, pp. 538–9.

8   Critique of Curtin by Cross, 2 April 1944, enclosed in a letter to Cranborne, 13 April 1944, Rc/4/13, Cross Papers, IWM.

9   Day, *John Curtin*, pp. 539–40.

10 Memorandum by Cranborne, 18 April 1944, CAB 55/49, W.P. (44)210, PRO; See also Massey, *What's past is prologue*, p. 417.

11 Canada was the stumbling block not only for Curtin, but also for Churchill, who wanted to resurrect the prewar British empire so that Britain's postwar strength might more closely approximate that of the other great powers. Canada had its own ideas for the future of the Commonwealth, wishing to build upon its close relationships with both Britain and America to construct a quasi-independent place for itself at the head of the 'middle' powers. Granatstein, *Canada's War*, pp. 319–20.

12 War Cabinet Conclusions, 27 April 1944, CAB 65/42, W.M. (44)58, PRO.

13 Mackenzie King diary, 1 May 1944, in Horner, *Defence Supremo*, pp. 195–6.

14 ibid.

15 Letter, Beaverbrook to Croft, 2 May 1944, BBK D/131, Beaverbrook Papers, HLRO.

16 War Cabinet Conclusions, 27 April 1944, CAB 65/42, W.M. (44)58, PRO.

17 Advisory War Council Minutes, 20 April 1944, and Cable, Forde to Curtin, 20 April 1944, CRS A5954, Box 305, NAA.

18 Message, Forde to Fraser, 8 April 1944 and Cable, Curtin to Forde, 19 April 1944, CRS A5954, Box 305, NAA.

19 See documents in CRS A5954, Box 305, NAA.

20 Minute, Churchill to Ismay, 16 April 1944, PREM 3/63/8, PRO.

21 Note, Ismay to Churchill, 1 May 1944, PREM 3/63/8, PRO.

22 Minute, Colville to Jacob, 2 May 1944, PREM 3/63/8, PRO.

23 Minute, Churchill to Ismay, 4 May 1944, and Memorandum, Ismay to Churchill, 6 May 1944, PREM 3/63/8, PRO.

24 Pickersgill (ed.), *The Mackenzie King Record*, Vol. 1, p. 667.

25 Note by Shedden, 5 April 1944, CRS A5954, Box 305, NAA.

26 War Cabinet Minutes, 1 May 1944, CRS A2673/XIV, NAA; Press Conference, 28 April 1944, MS 4675, Smith Papers, NLA.

27 Advisory War Council Minutes, 2 May 1944, CRS A2682/7; Statement by Royle, 3 May 1944, CRS A5954, Box 305, NAA.

28 Cables, Forde to Curtin, 4 May 1944 and Curtin to Forde, 19 May 1944, CRS A5954, Box 305, NAA.

29 Letter, Churchill to Curtin, 12 May 1944; Minute, Alexander to Churchill, 19 May 1944, PREM 3/160/1, PRO.

30 Note, Alexander to Churchill, 23 May 1944, PREM 3/63/8, PRO.

31 Letter, Churchill to Curtin, 27 May 1944, PREM 3/160/2, PRO.

32 Cable, Curtin to Forde, 30 May 1944, CRS A5954, Box 305, NAA.

33 Shedden's Memoirs, Chap. 46, pp. 5–7, CRS A5954, Box 771, NAA; Summary of observations by Curtin, 3 May 1944, PREM 3/160/1; PMM (44)5th Meeting, Confidential Annex, PREM 3/160/2, PRO; Cunningham Diary, 3 May 1944, ADD. MS. 52577, Cunningham Papers, BL.

34 Cunningham Diary, 5 May 1944, ADD. MS. 52577, Cunningham Papers, BL.

35 Minutes, Churchill to Ismay, 5 and 14 May 1944, PREM 3/148/9 and 3/160/2, PRO.

36 Pickersgill (ed.), *The Mackenzie King Record*, Vol. 1, p. 685.

37 Letter, Amery to Churchill, 4 May 1944, PREM 3/160/1, PRO; See also Note, Cherwell to Churchill, 3 May 1944, and other documents in this file, PREM 3/160/3, PRO.

38 Minute, Churchill to Hollis, 7 May 1944; Staff Conference Minutes (extract), 8 May 1944, C.O.S.(44)148, PREM 3/148/9, PRO.

39 Letter, Ismay to Pownall, undated but most likely May 1944, Ismay IV/Pow/4/2a, Ismay Papers, KC.

40 Cunningham diary, 18 May 1944, ADD. MS. 52577, Cunningham Papers, BL.

41 Cable, Curtin to Forde, 19 May 1944, CRS A2679/16/1944, NAA.

42 Letter, Curtin to Churchill, 17 May 1944, PREM 3/63/8, PRO.

43 Horner, *Defence Supremo*, pp. 197, 204.

44 Talk with Curtin, 25 May 1944, CRS M100, 'May 1944', NAA.

45 Minutes of a Conference at Chequers, 21 May 1944, and Letter, Curtin to Churchill, 23 May 1944, PREM 3/63/8, PRO.

46 ibid; War Cabinet Conclusions, 16 and 18 May 1944, CAB 65/42, W.M. (44)64 and 65, PRO.

47 Defence Committee Minutes, 28 and 29 March 1944, CRS A2031/12/91/1944, NAA.

48 Address by Curtin, 17 May 1944, BEVN 6/21, Bevin Papers, CC.

49 Talk with McVey, 18 April 1944, BBK D/214, Beaverbrook Papers, HLRO.

50 Letters, Beaverbrook to Cranborne, 25 April 1944, and Cranborne to Beaverbrook, 26 April 1944, BBK D/254, Beaverbrook Papers, HLRO.

51 Message, Secretary, External Affairs to Director General, Civil Aviation, 15 May 1944, CRS A5954, Box 345, NAA; See also documents in BBK D/208, Beaverbrook Papers, HLRO; Letter, Drakeford to Curtin, 27 March 1944, *DAFP*, Vol. 7, Doc. 97.

52 Letter, Winant to Curtin, 4 May 1944, *DAFP*, Vol. 7, Doc. 130; Memorandum, McVey to Curtin, 15 May 1944, BBK D/214, Beaverbrook Papers, HLRO.

53 Cable, Curtin to Forde, 19 May 1944, CRS A5954, Box 345, NAA.

54 Report by Taylor, June 1944, and Letter, Taylor to Burghley, 18 June 1944, and other documents in this box, MS 2594/86, Taylor Papers, NLA.

55 Talk with McVey, 31 May 1944, CRS M104, NAA; For Beaverbrook's version of the conversation, see 'McVey on Commonwealth Airline', 31 May 1944, BBK D/214, Beaverbrook Papers, HLRO.

56 Talk with Beaverbrook, 2 June 1944, and Talk with Curtin, 25 May 1944, CRS M100, 'May 1944', NAA; Letter, Curtin to Hull, 5 June 1944, *DAFP*, Vol. 7, Doc. 185.

57 Alanbrooke diary, 4 June 1944, in Danchev and Todman (eds), *War Diaries*, p. 553.

58 Cunningham diary, 5 June 1944, ADD. MS. 52577, Cunningham Papers, BL.

FORTY-THREE

'we shall go on to the end'

The long-delayed invasion of France came on 6 June 1944, after an unseasonal storm in the English Channel had calmed sufficiently for the landing ships, crammed with troops, to set out from southern England on their historic mission. Across the darkened sky, swarms of aircraft dropped the first waves of parachute troops across the countryside of Normandy, while fighter aircraft fought off their German counterparts. As the sun rose on the settling sea, the massive Allied armada forged forward in a determined bid to breach Hitler's 'Atlantic wall'. From behind a deadly curtain of naval fire and aerial bombing, thousands of troops stumbled ashore among a jumble of amphibious tanks, jeeps and armoured cars. By day's end, some three thousand Allied troops, uncounted German defenders and hapless civilians lay contorted on the beaches and scattered among the trampled crops. The 'wall' had been breached and the armies were ashore.

Despite overwhelming Allied superiority in men and arms, particularly in the air, the invasion force was vulnerable during those first crucial hours and days until they had secured their supply line across the Channel and carved out a swathe of countryside to defend in depth against the expected German counterattack. By 8 June, the Allied armies had captured Bayeux with its celebrated tapestry of another historic invasion, and had secured a sufficient bridgehead to ensure that their preponderance of strength could be brought to bear against the German forces rushing to contain them. On the Italian front, American troops had entered Rome, which had been declared an open city by the retreating Germans. It seemed that German forces would soon be expelled from Italian soil altogether. In Russia, the front line writhed across several thousand kilometres from Finland south to the Crimea, with the debilitated but still formidable German armies retreating to the homeland from whence they had sprung with such vigour three years previously. It would now just be a matter of time before the Third Reich collapsed, but that would be of little consolation to the millions who were to die before the Allied victory was achieved.

From his distant Bavarian eyrie at Berchtesgaden, Hitler remembered the Armistice of 1918 and hoped that history might repeat itself, perhaps after his secret weapon, the flying bomb, rained terror on England. The people of London, who had endured so much, were now subject again to nightly attacks for which there was little warning and against which there was little defence. They would have to wait until the launching places could be captured. In the meantime, as Londoners huddled in their shelters, Allied scientists at Los Alamos, New Mexico, were working furiously on a secret weapon of their own. Atomic bombs would put Hitler's flying bombs in the shade, provided they worked and did not set off a chain reaction that would destroy the whole world as some worried scientists speculated. Australian uranium was one of the keys to this awesome secret, and Curtin had agreed in London to hand over this key to the British, promising to develop Australian supplies of uranium and reserve all the production for Britain's use.[1]

In the Pacific, the Japanese were still stoutly defending the contracting remnants of their short-lived empire. Between June and August 1944, the Mariana islands of Saipan, Tinian and Guam fell in quick and bloody succession to amphibious attacks by American marines pursuing the central Pacific strategy of Admiral King, while the Japanese fleet tried unsuccessfully to ward off the blows. With the capture of Guam on 8 August, the United States came within bomber range of Japan's cities, with their timber houses particularly vulnerable to the incendiary attacks that the Allies had been perfecting on the historic centres of German cities. Meanwhile, the island of Tinian became the base for B-29 bombers that would eventually unlock, Pandora-like, the power of the atom. Further south in New Guinea, the overwhelming superiority of MacArthur's forces saw them leapfrog effortlessly along its northern coastline in a series of quick operations that brought them control of that island by July, with the isolated pockets of Japanese defenders being left for later dispatch by Australian forces. The way was now clear for MacArthur to use New Guinea as a springboard to the Philippines, leaving behind the Australians to mop up after him.

The military successes helped to alleviate Australia's manpower problems, which were helped too by Curtin's efforts in London and Washington, with the combined chiefs of staff endorsing Churchill's grudging agreement for Australia to readjust its war effort. This was a victory of sorts for Curtin, and he announced it as such to his expectant cabinet upon his return to Canberra in early July.[2] He had also resisted the campaign for Australia to man British naval ships without having their sailors in Europe and elsewhere returned to them. More importantly, Curtin now knew that Australia would probably not have to support a huge Allied force in the Pacific after Germany's defeat. In a briefing to journalists on 3 July, Curtin dismissed as 'poppycock' the 'idea that millions of men might be based on Australia'. There was insufficient shipping, and the British were planning for a 'great contraction' of their armed forces once Germany was beaten. Boasting to reporters that he had 'got on handsomely with Mr Churchill', Curtin assured them nevertheless that the British would not welsh on their promises, that the 'British flag will fly' and that some British troops would be sent to Australia.[3]

Although Curtin had secured agreement in London and Washington to the changes Australia was planning in its war effort, there was still no agreement about what burdens would be placed upon Australia by the arrival of these British forces. Or even whether they would arrive at all, since American successes in the Pacific were threatening to make redundant the British 'middle' strategy that would strike at Borneo from north-western Australia. Blamey confidently expected to command these operations which would allow him to escape MacArthur's control and lead a Commonwealth force in a combined attack that might yet earn him his field marshal's baton. Although Curtin was as keen as Blamey to see some British forces in the Australian theatre, he wanted them to operate on MacArthur's terms. But the American general was planning to push on to the Philippines without Australian forces and opposed any Commonwealth force being established on his flank that might diminish the effect of this campaign. As a result, Curtin warned Churchill on 4 July that the proposed middle strategy was being overtaken by the speed of the American advance and that Britain should simply allocate its proposed Pacific fleet to MacArthur, arguing that it was 'the only effective means for placing the Union Jack in the Pacific alongside the Australian and American flags'. Curtin advised that MacArthur, once he had partially occupied the Philippines, was thinking of turning his attention to Borneo and the Netherlands East Indies, attacking from the north and thereby making redundant the planned British Commonwealth assault to be based on north-west Australia. Curtin did not say so, but such a contribution of British naval ships might also provide MacArthur with the maritime muscle to compete with his American naval colleagues in the race to Tokyo.[4]

Curtin's warning to Churchill reinforced the views of the American chiefs of staff who had visited London in the wake of the D-day operation. The Americans advised Whitehall that the British timetable for dispatching forces to the Pacific was increasingly out of phase with the progress of the Pacific war. They supported the middle strategy of their British counterparts, using Ambon as a launching pad to capture Borneo. Churchill's cabinet colleagues also had become convinced of this strategy. On 12 June, Eden advised Churchill that the Foreign Office supported the middle strategy as the one most likely to serve British interests. These were defined as the complete defeat of Japan; the re-establishment of British prestige, especially in British territories and China; and greater collaboration with the United States and the Soviet Union. Once in Borneo, British forces could join the attack against Japan itself, or descend upon Malaya as the Japanese had done in 1941. Whatever it did, Eden warned, Britain had to ensure that it could not subsequently be charged with 'having wilfully withheld our support from the United States operations now in progress in the Pacific in order to pursue objectives of our own having no relation to the main business in hand'. This was precisely what Churchill was guilty of, and what he intended to do again.[5]

Although the chiefs of staff had conceded that the Commonwealth effort might be under MacArthur's command rather than Mountbatten's, Churchill wanted the South East Asia Command (SEAC) extended to cover north-western Australia so that Britain could take charge of avenging the humiliating defeat at Singapore. As Churchill argued on 24 June, 'Rangoon and Singapore are great names in the British eastern world, and it will be an ill day for Britain if the War ends without our having made a stroke to regain these places'. If Australian and American forces agreed to pursue the middle strategy under British command, then he might support it. Then again, he might not. During a late-night meeting of his defence committee on 6 July, Churchill returned to his strategy of stalling for time rather than relinquish his Sumatra plan, or his 'island idiocy' as Cunningham called it.[6] Even though Attlee, Eden and Lyttelton now sided with the chiefs of staff, that only made Churchill 'madder than ever and he became ruder and ruder', as Brooke recorded in his diary. After making a difficult speech in the House of Commons on the subject of the flying bombs, Churchill was the worse for drink, being in 'a maudlin, bad tempered, drunken mood, ready to take offence at anything, suspicious of everybody, and in a highly vindictive mood against the Americans'. In such an atmosphere, nothing could be decided.[7]

The chiefs of staff were furious at Churchill's change of tack, but could take solace from having broken the solid political support that Churchill hitherto had enjoyed for his position. In these new circumstances, they welcomed Curtin's proposal as providing additional ammunition for their arguments, with the chiefs advising Churchill that Curtin's suggestion was 'in accord with our present view of the most effective initial contribution we could make' against Japan. It also presented Britain with the 'effective means of restoring Empire prestige in the Far East'. The only 'essential' change that the chiefs wanted to make to Curtin's plan was for the combined chiefs of staff to take control of MacArthur's command from the American chiefs of staff, so that Britain would have a 'proper share in the direction of operations to which we will be so largely contributing'.[8] However, neither MacArthur nor Curtin was prepared to agree to this.

Anxious to retain his position, MacArthur not only wanted to kill the middle strategy and prevent Blamey taking charge of it but also wanted to ensure that the Allied land effort in the Philippines was a purely American one, rather than a joint Australian–American effort as in New Guinea. Rather than forbidding Australian troops from taking part in the Philippines and risking his relationship with Curtin, MacArthur made an offer that he knew Blamey would not accept but which would maintain the fiction of his readiness to carry the Australians forward with him. MacArthur suggested that he use two Australian divisions, each linked to an American division and part of an American corps. Under this scheme, Australian commanders could only operate as commanders of separate divisions, with no place being available for Blamey, whom MacArthur was keen to remove as commander of Allied land forces. Instead of Blamey, MacArthur declared that he would be personally commanding the operation. At the same time he instructed that Blamey provide twelve Australian brigades for ongoing operations in New Guinea, rather than the seven brigades that Blamey had been planning to use. This dramatically reduced the possibility of Australians being available for the Philippines.[9]

The ongoing and increasingly heated disputes in London about Britain's Pacific strategy were conducted against the background of concerns about Britain's own manpower problems. There was no point in the chiefs of staff deciding on a grandiose strategy that could not be implemented for want of manpower. And the war cabinet was certainly keen to reduce the numbers in uniform as soon as the war against Germany would allow. Accordingly, the chiefs of staff were asked whether they could reduce their service levels to three million within one year of the defeat of Germany. That would be a reduction from an estimated 4 768 000 at the end of 1944, when the European war was confidently expected to be over. Such a massive reduction was impossible, argued the chiefs, pointing out that the war against Japan would need about one million men, Germany would have to be occupied and the Middle East secured for Britain. All in all, they claimed that 3 404 500 would be necessary, of whom perhaps one million would be Indian and colonial troops. They reminded Churchill of his repeated pledge to join in the war against Japan 'to the limit of our power' and warned, 'for reasons of our prestige in the Far East and in America, it would be inexpedient for us not to do so to a substantial extent'.[10]

As in Australia, the manpower figures were just not adding up, with the chancellor of the exchequer, Sir John Anderson, pointing out on 14 July that the war cabinet would have to cut the demand for manpower, starting with the services and the supply departments. In curtailing military commitments, Anderson advised that the greatest manpower savings could be made by reducing the British effort against Japan rather than by reducing the army of occupation in Europe.[11] That same day, the chiefs of staff met with Churchill in his underground bunker for what they hoped would provide 'a final solution' for the vexed Pacific strategy, only to find themselves faced with the same mixture of bluster, bombast and delay that they had experienced from Churchill for the past year.[12]

To the dismay of Brooke and his colleagues, Churchill once more brought the Sumatran operation back to life. Perhaps with Anderson's warnings about manpower in mind, Churchill expressed frustration at so many servicemen in India being tied up supporting operations in Burma, where the British counteroffensive was pushing back the exhausted Japanese. He also objected to contributing what he called 'driblets' to the Pacific as and when the Americans wanted. Britain had the men and it had an Eastern fleet that was growing in strength, but it lacked the landing ships to mount an operation across the Bay of Bengal to avenge what Churchill called the 'shameful disaster' of Singapore. With the strategic vacuum set to continue, Brooke called on Churchill to reject the advice of the chiefs if he must, 'but for heaven's sake let us have a decision!'. Instead, Churchill simply promised to decide within a week.[13] Then, when the week was up, he declared that he had to discuss it all with Mountbatten, who would have to be called back to London from his mountain retreat at Kandy in Ceylon, where life was reported to be so luxurious that junior officers were forced into debt to survive.[14] Summoning Mountbatten caused further delay despite the chiefs warning that facilities in Australia needed to be prepared immediately if the middle strategy were to succeed. Before Mountbatten had even arrived, Churchill shifted ground once more with a suggestion (or a threat) that if the

Sumatran operation was not mounted he would push for an attack against Rangoon rather than agree to the middle strategy.[15]

The concerns raised by Anderson about Britain's manpower problems had provided Churchill with powerful ammunition with which to defend his position on Pacific strategy. He fired off some of these rounds during a cabinet meeting on 26 July, attended by the chiefs of staff, describing the projected manpower levels for the war against Japan as 'ridiculous' and suggesting that Britain should ignore its previous pledges and simply ask Washington what support it required in the Pacific. Almost certainly, Britain would be called upon to contribute a minimum effort, since America was anxious that British forces be kept out of the Pacific. Or so Churchill surmised. Churchill's attack on service levels was supported by Lyttelton and Cherwell who, according to Cunningham, 'both wished to ration the Services for the Japanese war in the interests of (a) getting exports going, (b) raising the standard of living of the Civil population and (c) rebuilding the knocked down edifices and houses'. Cunningham was dismayed, particularly as his ships were set to play a leading role against Japan. He blasted ministers for trying to 'fight the war on a limited liability basis' and was relieved when Churchill suddenly called a truce, suggesting that he would write a paper setting out a solution to the problem. Again, decision making was placed on hold. Brooke was despairing, observing in his diary that Churchill 'cannot give decisions and fails to grip the Cabinet, just wanders on reminiscing! It is all heartbreaking.'[16]

Cunningham's relief also was short-lived. On 30 July, Churchill asked Cunningham what sort of Pacific fleet could be provided with just 400 000 men, instead of the 518 300 planned by the Admiralty. Although Cunningham was determined 'to bring him down to earth',[17] it was Cunningham who had to face political realities when Churchill then issued a directive on 3 August that cut manpower in the service and supply departments by 1 100 000. The navy was to be cut by 200 000, which Churchill justified by pointing to the 'over-powering [American] Naval force which will be available for the war against Japan'. The air force faced a similar cut, with Churchill dismissing the possibility of a large-scale British air effort against Japan. As for the army, it was planned to draw mainly on Indian manpower for the British contribution to the Pacific war. Of thirteen Indian divisions that were currently being used outside India, all but one would be retained for use against Japan.[18] Yet still there was no agreed strategy between Churchill and his chiefs of staff as to where these forces would be used.

Mountbatten finally arrived in London on 5 August for three days of intensive discussions with Churchill and the chiefs of staff about his operations in SEAC. After two days of talks, Brooke complained that their exhaustive meetings had settled 'absolutely nothing'. Although Mountbatten had convinced them that they should complete the capture of Burma by launching a seaborne assault on Rangoon, the chiefs believed that could be 'combined with a Pacific strategy of naval, air and Dominion forces operating from Australia'. Churchill, though, kept returning to his Sumatran operation and, complained Brooke, 'refuses to look at anything else'. Round and round the arguments went until well after midnight, and still there was no agreement. Brooke confided in his diary that he was at his 'wit's end and can't go on much longer!', while Cunningham simply described Churchill as 'a drag on the wheel of war'. The following day, exhausted and pressed for a decision by Churchill's imminent departure for Italy, the two sides finally reached a compromise. After Churchill and the chiefs each presented papers setting out their preferred options for the Far East, Ismay was directed to draft a joint paper drawing both documents together. Brooke quietly suggested that he use the material in the chiefs' paper, but embroider it with Churchill's phraseology. The ploy worked. They agreed to strike across the Bay of Bengal to attack Rangoon before the end of 1944. As General Pownall observed, both sides regarded the Rangoon operation as 'something different from the old arguments on which they had committed themselves so deeply'.[19] British forces would not become bogged down in northern Burma and Japanese forces would wither away in the Burmese wilderness. Churchill anticipated that the capture of Rangoon would release seven divisions for use elsewhere. From Rangoon, British forces could strike at the Malayan peninsula and Singapore.

Under the agreement, four Indian and two British divisions were to be moved from the European theatre as soon as they could be spared. As for the Pacific, Britain would offer its fleet in the 'main operations against the mainland of Japan or Formosa' in the confident expectation that the Americans would refuse it. Such a refusal, said Churchill, 'would be of enormous value as a bulwark against any accusation that we had not backed them up in the war against Japan'. As Cunningham caustically observed, Churchill 'wants to be able to have on record that the US refused the assistance of the British Fleet in the Pacific. He will be bitterly disappointed if they don't refuse!!!' Once the British offer was refused, the fleet would be offered instead as part of a 'British Empire Task Force under a British Commander, consisting of British, Australian and New Zealand land, sea and air forces, to operate under General MacArthur's supreme command'.[20] It was a confident show of activity after months of dithering. But it concealed many uncertainties. For one thing, the attack on Rangoon still relied for its success on the provision of American landing craft, on the war against Germany finishing according to plan, and on forces being made available from various sources 'including, if necessary, Australia'.[21] None of these things could be guaranteed.

Like Britain, Australia was rationalising its limited manpower. It needed rural workers to boost its production of primary produce so that it could recapture the country's traditional export markets as well as feed the Allied armies accumulating in the Pacific. To help find them, the government lifted health regulations that had restricted the use of prisoners of war in rural industries.[22] The government also faced continuing pressure from MacArthur, who refused to reduce his use of civilian labour,[23] and pressure from factory owners who wanted workers so they could capitalise on Australia's recent industrial development. The war cabinet's export committee warned that Australia would be left behind in the postwar export race when surplus capacity in Britain and America would capture local export markets that might otherwise have been won by Australia. The committee urged that Australia concentrate on those exports that would provide 'a sound trade foundation' while also being 'closely linked with the conduct of war and [the] rehabilitation of re-occupied areas'. So the development of export trade was added to the manpower equation, throwing out the calculations even further.[24] To make matters worse, the services resisted all attempts to cut back their numbers, with the defence committee declaring in August 1944 that the monthly intake of men into the services must increase rather than decrease. Curtin instructed instead that they aim to cut the army by thirty thousand and the air force by fifteen thousand by the end of June 1945. Only the navy was safe from cuts, although Royle was censured for his overactive pursuit of its interests.[25]

The Australian manpower problems raised serious questions as to whether the country could support substantial British forces. Not that Churchill was resigned to sending them there. Despite appearances, he remained committed to the operation against Sumatra, while his fleeting agreement with the chiefs of staff about Pacific strategy was overtaken by disputes about the course of operations in Europe where the Americans wanted to mount an invasion of southern France with forces from the Italian campaign. Churchill feared that any subtraction from the Allied strength in Italy would threaten the resounding victory that he hoped to achieve there, with the British commander in the Mediterranean, General Alexander, harbouring ambitious plans to force his way through the Alps to Austria and thereby pre-empt the Russians. Churchill shared these hopes. Rather than ruining Alexander's chances by mounting an attack in southern France, Churchill proposed instead that an attack be mounted on Brittany as a way of supporting the Allied forces that were steadily gaining the upper hand in Normandy. But he was overruled by the Americans, which left him 'raving' and 'absolutely unbalanced', according to Ismay. In this state of mind, he flew off to Italy on 10 August to see the situation for himself.[26]

The ongoing dispute over Pacific strategy was continuing to drive a wedge between Churchill and his chiefs. In Churchill's absence, Brooke rejoiced at the efficient running of the war that was possible when the British prime minister was away from the helm, with Brooke feeling that it had 'now reached the stage that for the good of the nation and for the good of his own reputation it would be a godsend if he could disappear out of public life'.[27] But it was not to be. Churchill was set on remaining till the end, and equally set on ensuring that Britain's effort in the Pacific would not be based on Australia. While Churchill was in Italy, Curtin sent a further reminder to London of the 'importance to the British Commonwealth of flying the Union Jack in the impending operations in the Pacific'. Curtin warned that the Americans wished to appear to win the war against Japan single-handed, and that the effect on Britain's empire would be grave if America was able to claim that it had 'fought a war on principle in the Far East and won it relatively unaided while the other Allies including ourselves did very little towards recovering our lost property'. Upon his return from Italy, Churchill assured Curtin that Britain would play its full part in the Pacific war, informing him of the British offer to Washington of a powerful Pacific fleet by mid-1945 to operate under American command in the assault on Japan. If the Americans declined to accept the British fleet in the main operations, Churchill proposed an empire task force for the south-west Pacific of British, Australian and New Zealand land, sea and air forces with a British commander but operating under MacArthur's supreme command.[28]

If Churchill thought Curtin would be mollified by this news, he was mistaken. In Curtin's view, arrangements were being made again for the south-west Pacific without consulting Australia. Although Curtin had pressed for British forces to participate in Pacific operations, he reminded Churchill that he could not countenance MacArthur's command being compromised by the arrival of independent Commonwealth forces under a British commander. MacArthur also advised Churchill that the British would only be welcome in a subservient position.[29] A rather puzzled Churchill asked his high commissioner, Sir Ronald Cross, who happened to be in London for consultations, if he could 'throw any light upon the trouble that appears to be stirring Mr. Curtin's mind'. Cross blamed MacArthur and Blamey for influencing Curtin, and Curtin's own propensity to be sensitive about 'anything that may touch Australian nationhood'. The three of them together were 'hypersensitive on command questions', advised Cross, and tended to 'smell a rat' without justification.[30] Cross had earlier reported to Churchill on a conversation with MacArthur in which the American had offered to use the British Pacific fleet as the 'spearhead of his attack upon the Philippines', claiming it as a 'great thing that an American General should sail into Manila under a British flag'.[31] No wonder Churchill had trouble disentangling these seemingly conflicting signals from Australia.

In replying to Curtin, Churchill presumed that the Australian government must have misunderstood the British proposal which, he assured both Curtin and MacArthur, was not designed to interfere with the existing command set-up in the south-west Pacific. Rather than taking Australian troops from MacArthur, it was intended to add a British naval force to MacArthur's command.[32] This was not strictly true, since Churchill had discussed removing Australian troops for the attack on Rangoon and subsequent operations. Moreover, the capture of Rangoon would release seven divisions from SEAC which Churchill planned to join with six British and Indian divisions from Europe and two Australian divisions to create a formidable force for use against Malaya and Singapore. In the face of the objections from Curtin and MacArthur, Churchill advised them that he was on his way to Quebec to discuss the Pacific strategy with Roosevelt and the American chiefs of staff. As for the lack of consultation with Australia, Churchill pointed out that it was the established and necessary practice for such plans to be drawn up without consulting every country involved in them. Anyway, as he reminded Curtin, 'when you were in England, we told you and General Blamey how our minds were working'.[33]

Although there were discussions with Curtin in London during May and June, there had been no firm Pacific strategy and consequently no agreement reached between Britain and Australia. There should have been some consultation once Churchill and the chiefs of staff had reached their compromise in August, but Churchill had never liked consulting with smaller powers, and particularly not with Australia. He refused to take Evatt's repeated hint that the appearance of consultation would satisfy the Australian government, and blithely continued to treat the dominion as Britain's fiefdom. Now, just as at Cairo, the future of Pacific strategy was about to be discussed in Quebec without any involvement or consultation with Australia. At least this time Australia had some forewarning of the conference and some sense of the British position. When the Australian press criticised the lack of representation at the Quebec conference, Curtin dispatched the head of Australia's military mission in Washington, General Lavarack. Although he would not be involved in the conference, the government could at least say that Lavarack was available for discussions with the participants.[34]

On 5 September, Churchill and the chiefs of staff went on board the *Queen Mary* for yet another voyage across the Atlantic to meet with the

Americans. This time, though, the Americans were clearly the dominant partner in the relationship, with their forces in Europe outnumbering those of Britain. Churchill was gloomy and ill-tempered throughout the humid voyage, suffering the effects of anti-malaria tablets combined with another bout of pneumonia. He also must have realised that his role was coming to an end. With Allied forces having rolled into Paris on 25 August and continuing to push the enemy back over the Belgian border, it seemed that Germany would soon be vanquished, although Churchill insisted that the European war might drag on into 1945. In a series of shipboard meetings, Churchill reneged once more on undertakings to boost the British effort against Japan, and ordered his chiefs not to discuss the option of basing British forces in the south-west Pacific. He also wanted a halt to any transfer of British and Indian troops from Italy to the Far East. With Churchill fixated on a mad plan to land at Trieste with a purely British force and then lunge through the Alps to capture Vienna, and being intent also on redressing the humiliation of Singapore, the operation against Rangoon was again in doubt. Churchill now insisted that British forces should not go on to clear northern Burma of the Japanese once they had secured its capital. As Brooke observed, this made the capture of Rangoon 'practically useless'. To cap it off, Churchill was also insisting on his Sumatran operation. With Churchill repudiating all that he had agreed with his chiefs of staff, it is not surprising that Brooke described that voyage as 'a ghastly time', complaining in his diary after one shipboard conference that Churchill 'talks absurdities and makes my blood boil to listen to his nonsense'.[35]

Churchill arrived at the Quebec conference confident that the Americans would refuse his offer of the British Pacific fleet for the final effort against the Japanese home islands. Instead, Admiral Leahy informally advised him on 12 September that the Americans would accept. The following day, during the first plenary session of the conference, Roosevelt responded to Churchill's grand gesture by saying, 'No sooner offered than accepted.' Cunningham was ecstatic, but his American counterpart, Admiral King, was livid. Although he grudgingly accepted the *fait accompli*, King made it clear that the British could not expect any logistical support from the US navy.[36] Churchill had gone into the conference conscious of the American criticism of Britain's effort against Japan and had armed himself with statistics to show that Britain was holding down many more Japanese than the Americans. The statistics omitted the Japanese bypassed and effectively neutralised by the American island-hopping strategy, such as the large garrison at Rabaul, and included on the British side those Japanese held down by Australian forces under American command.[37]

Despite his statistics, Churchill was annoyed to read press criticism of the British effort against Japan while he was meeting with Roosevelt. On 16 September, the Washington *Times-Herald* called for the United States to go it alone against Japan rather than allow Britain, France, Holland and Russia, which it dismissed as 'Johnny come-latelies', to contribute token forces at this late hour so they could demand an equal place at the peace table. If these countries were excluded, the United States could dictate the peace settlement and 'restore such of those pieces of empire as we decided upon to the British, Dutch, French and Portuguese on our own terms, and they will hold them henceforth by grace of our sufferance and generosity, and the world will know it'.[38] That same day, with the conference concluded, Churchill found himself interrogated on the issue by American journalists, with Churchill rejecting 'suggestions that the British wish to shirk their obligations in the Japanese war, and to throw the whole burden onto the United States'. Quite the opposite, he claimed. The problem was to get the Americans to allow the British into the Pacific, although the conference had sorted this out so that

Great Britain with her fleet and her air forces and, according to whatever plans are made, her military forces, all that can be carried by the shipping of the world to the scene of action will be represented in the main struggle against Japan. And we shall go on to the end.[39]

Churchill was now locked into a strategy that he had rejected for more than a year, with Brooke being relieved that Churchill, who he had described as 'a public menace', had finally adopted their 'sane strategy' and 'now accepts the naval contingent for the Pacific, a Dominion Task Force with MacArthur, etc'.[40] Churchill's chances of recapturing Malaya and Singapore now seemed unlikely. Not that Churchill had relinquished all hope in that regard.

Under the plans agreed at Quebec, Churchill intended to do a bit of everything: to contribute naval forces to the central Pacific effort against Japan; to partake in the long-range bombing of the Japanese mainland; to offer a naval task force and air units to serve with MacArthur; and to pursue his aim of recapturing British colonies. Despite this plethora of promises, he told his chiefs of staff that Singapore was still 'the supreme British objective in the whole of the Indian and Far Eastern theatres'.[41] The main British effort was therefore to be directed against Singapore. Of the 40 squadrons for use against Japan, Churchill intended that the majority should come from the dominions, with a large contingent from Canada. The naval task force that might be attached to MacArthur's command would not be an added dollop of British naval strength, but would be detached from the British Pacific fleet.[42]

Churchill was already backtracking on plans to transfer forces from Europe for the attack against Rangoon. He ordered the Indian divisions to remain in Italy until at least mid-December, and tank landing craft to be retained in the Mediterranean rather than proceed to Mountbatten's command. By the time Churchill had returned to London, the operation against Rangoon had slipped back to November 1945 to protect operations in Europe.[43] The British Pacific fleet was still due to arrive in the Pacific by early 1945, with Curtin being misled into believing that it would be based largely in Australia, when it was really intended to combine it with American naval forces in the central Pacific. When Churchill informed Curtin of the decisions reached at Quebec, Curtin promised 'complete co-operation' with British plans while warning that the extent of Australia's contribution would depend on another review of its manpower resources.[44] There was already pressure on Curtin to limit the Australian contribution.

A committee of the Australian war cabinet, chaired by the treasurer, Ben Chifley, claimed that the arrival of British forces would place Australia at an economic disadvantage. It recommended that the 'manpower allocations for indirect war and civilian purposes ... should not be curtailed in order to make provision for British Forces which may be based in Australia'. In particular, construction projects for the British forces 'should not be allowed to absorb men and materials which would otherwise be available for the housing programme'. The committee seems to have assumed that British troops as well as ships would arrive in Australia, whereas Churchill strongly opposed 'sending any British troops to join the Australians and New Zealanders under General MacArthur'.[45]

The decisions at Quebec foreshadowed a quickening of the war in the Pacific, although the British commitment remained lukewarm. As General Pownall cynically observed from his mountain vantage point in Kandy, the news from Quebec had transported Mountbatten to the 'seventh Heaven of delight', although Pownall sagely thought that Mountbatten should not 'get over-excited, or unduly pleased' until he was 'plumb certain of the resources'.[46] Australians could have done with some of Pownall's cynicism as they prepared to farewell the American forces and await the arrival of the British fleet, which they saw as an affirmation of Britain's blood ties with the dominion and a precursor of the empire's resurgence in the Pacific.

NOTES

[1] See *DAFP*, Vol. 7, Docs 154, 200–1, 210 and 284; See also Background briefing, 3 July 1944, MS 4675, Smith Papers, NLA.

[2] Cabinet Minutes, 4 July 1944, CRS 2703, Vol. II, NAA.

[3] Background briefing, 3 July 1944, MS 4675, Smith Papers, NLA.

[4] Cable, Curtin to Churchill, 4 July 1944, *DAFP*, Vol. 7, Doc. 212; Shedden's memoirs, Chap. 52, CRS A5954, Box 771, NAA; Horner, *High Command*, pp. 327–31.

[5] Note, Eden to Churchill, 12 June 1944, PREM 3/160/4, PRO.

[6] Cunningham diary, 11 and 14 June 1944, ADD. MS. 52577, Cunningham Papers, BL.

[7] Minute, Churchill to Ismay, 24 June 1944 and C.O.S. (44)225th Meeting (0), 6 July 1944, PREM 3/160/5, PRO; Alanbrooke diary, 6 July 1944, in Danchev and Todman (eds), *War Diaries*, pp. 566–7.

[8] Minute, Chiefs of Staff to Churchill, undated, PREM 3/160/5, PRO.

[9] Horner, *High Command*, pp. 335–7; Horner, *Defence Supremo*, pp. 207–12.

[10] Report by the Chiefs of Staff, 7 July 1944, CAB 66/52, W.P. (44)380, PRO.

[11] Memorandum by Anderson, 14 July 1944, CAB 66/52, W.P. (44)381, PRO.

[12] Alanbrooke diary, 14 July 1944, in Danchev and Todman (eds), *War Diaries*, p. 570; Cunningham diary, 14 July 1944, ADD. MS. 52577, Cunningham Papers, BL.

[13] Report by the Chiefs of Staff, 13 July 1944; Minutes of Staff Conference, 14 July 1944, PREM 3/160/5, PRO; Alanbrooke diary, 14 July 1944, in Danchev and Todman (eds), *War Diaries*, p. 570.

[14] Pownall diary, 20 July 1944, in Bond (ed.), *Chief of Staff*, Vol. 2, pp. 181–2; Letter, Ismay to Pownall, undated, IV/Pow/4/2a, Ismay Papers, KC; Letter, Cunningham to Layton, 19 July 1944, ADD. MS. 52571, Cunningham Papers, BL.

[15] Minute, Chiefs of Staff to Churchill, 20 July 1944, PREM 3/160/5; Minute, Churchill to Chiefs of Staff, 24 July 1944, PREM 3/148/9, PRO.

[16] Cunningham diary, 26 July 1944, ADD. MS. 52577, Cunningham Papers, BL; Alanbrooke diary, 26 July 1944, in Danchev and Todman (eds), *War Diaries*, pp. 574–5.

[17] ibid, 30 July 1944.

[18] Draft Directive by Churchill, 3 August 1944, CAB 66/53, W.P. (44)431; Memorandum by Chiefs of Staff, 18 August 1944, CAB 66/54, W.P. (44)452, PRO; Cunningham diary, 4 August 1944, ADD. MS. 52577, Cunningham Papers, BL.

19 Minutes of Staff Conference, 9 August 1944, PREM 3/149/7, PRO; Alanbrooke diary, 7–9 August 1944, in Danchev and Todman (eds), *War Diaries*, pp. 578–9; Cunningham diary, 7–9 August 1944, ADD. MS. 52577, Cunningham Papers, BL; Pownall diary, 29 August 1944, in Bond (ed.), *Chief of Staff*, Vol. 2, pp. 184–5.

20 Minutes of Staff Conference, 9 August 1944, PREM 3/149/7, PRO; Cunningham diary, 10 August 1944, ADD. MS. 52577, Cunningham Papers, BL; See also Somerville journal, 22 and 24 August 1944, SMVL 2/2, Somerville Papers, CC.

21 Cable, Chiefs of Staff to Joint Staff Mission, 12 August 1944, PREM 3/149/7, PRO.

22 War Cabinet Minute, 11 May 1944, CRS A5954, Box 305A, NAA.

23 Letter, MacArthur to Curtin, 12 July 1944, CRS A5954, Box 306, NAA.

24 Report by Senator R. V. Keane, 18 August 1944, CRS A2670/415/1944, NAA.

25 War Cabinet Minutes, 4 August 1944, CRS A2673/15/3691, NAA; See also Background briefing, 21 August 1944, MS 4675, Smith Papers, NLA.

26 This description of Churchill was reported by Ismay during a closed meeting of the Chiefs of Staff. Cunningham diary, 11 August 1944, ADD. MS. 52577, Cunningham Papers, BL; Gilbert, *Road to Victory*, p. 910.

27 Alanbrooke diary, 15 August 1944, in Danchev and Todman (eds), *War Diaries*, pp. 580–1.

28 Cable, Curtin to Churchill, 12 August 1944, and Cable 5, Churchill to Curtin, 23 August 1944, CAB 69/6, D.O. (44)13, PRO.

29 Note by General Lumsden, PREM 3/159/4; Cable, Curtin to Churchill, 3 September 1944, CAB 69/6, D.O. (44)13, PRO.

30 Note, Cross to Ismay, 4 September 1944, PREM 3/159/4, PRO.

31 Account of conversation between Cross and MacArthur on 16 August 1944, submitted to Churchill by Cross on 30 August 1944, Rc/4/19, Cross Papers, IWM.

32 Cable, Churchill to Lumsden, 4 September 1944, and Cable, Churchill to Curtin, 10 September 1944, CAB 69/6, D.O. (44)13, PRO.

33 ibid.

34 Cable, Curtin to Churchill, 14 September 1944, and Cable, Churchill to Curtin, 18 September 1944, CAB 69/6, D.O. (44)13, PRO; See also *Daily Telegraph*, Sydney, 18 September 1944.

35 Gilbert, *Road to Victory*, Chap. 50; Alanbrooke diary, 5–13 September 1944, in Danchev and Todman (eds), *War Diaries*, pp. 587–92; Cunningham diary, 8 September 1944, ADD. MS. 52577, Cunningham Papers, BL.

36 Cunningham's draft memoirs, p. 122, ADD. MS. 52581B, Cunningham Papers, BL; Alanbrooke diary, 14 September 1944, in Danchev and Todman (eds), *War Diaries*, pp. 592–3; Minute, Churchill to Ismay, 12 September 1944, PREM 3/160/6, PRO.

37 Draft statement by Churchill, 2 September 1944, PREM 3/149/11; Note, Ismay to Churchill, 10 September 1944, PREM 3/159/14, PRO.

38 *Times-Herald*, Washington, 16 September 1944.

39 Gilbert, *Road to Victory*, p. 967.

40 Alanbrooke diary, 10 and 12 September 1944, in Danchev and Todman (eds), *War Diaries*, pp. 590–1.

41 Minute, Churchill to Ismay, 12 September 1944, PREM 3/160/6, PRO.

42 ibid; Canadian Cabinet War Committee Minutes, 14 September 1944, PREM 3/329/6, PRO; See also Note by Hollis, 24 June 1944, CAB 69/6, D.O. (44)12, PRO.

43 Gilbert, *Road to Victory*, p. 980.

44 Cables, Churchill to Curtin, 18 September 1944 and Curtin to Churchill, 22 September 1944, and Minute, Alexander to Churchill, 26 September 1944, PREM 3/159/4, PRO; Shedden's memoirs, Chap. 52, CRS A5954, Box 771, NAA.

45 Report by Production Executive, 21 September 1944, CRS A2670/473/1944, NAA; Minute, Churchill to Ismay, 12 September 1944, PREM 3/160/6, PRO.

46 Pownall diary, 24 September 1944, in Bond (ed.), *Chief of Staff*, Vol. 2, p. 187.

FORTY-FOUR

'our powerful friends'

In late October 1944, more than seven hundred American warships, landing craft, troopships and supply vessels, supported by eight Australian naval ships, converged on the Philippines to bombard the meagre Japanese defences on the island of Leyte, before disgorging ashore more than 160 000 American troops. On 20 October, with their beachhead secured, General Douglas MacArthur stepped from a landing craft into the warm waters lapping at the island's beaches. As soldiers fanned out to protect MacArthur's historic moment, and newsreel cameras whirred to record it, the general declared to the people of the Philippines 'I have returned!' as he had famously promised to do upon his arrival in Australia in 1942. Now he was back, although many Filipinos would come to wish that he had passed on by and taken the battle to Japan instead of turning their islands into a battlefield. More than 100 000 of them would be killed in the fighting before it was done.[1] But for political reasons as much as anything, MacArthur was determined to redress the humiliation of his earlier defeat. The capture of the Philippines would also allow the Americans to control the offshore shipping routes and thereby cut Japan off from supplies of oil and other raw materials necessary for its war effort.

The attack on Leyte could not pass unchallenged by the Japanese navy, since the loss of the Philippines would soon leave its remaining warships hostage to the Americans. So the navy was sent out in a last-ditch attempt to stem the oncoming American tide, with fleets coming south from Japan and north from Singapore to draw the Americans into a decisive naval battle. Two new battleships, the largest in the world and supposedly unsinkable, were included among the powerful array of Japanese ships. Although they succeeded in catching the Americans partially off guard, they withdrew when the Japanese commander mistakenly believed that they in turn were about to be caught by the more powerful American forces rushing to crush them. In the separate naval engagements conducted during the landings, the Japanese lost three battleships, including one of their new ones, four aircraft carriers and nine cruisers whereas the American losses were comparatively light. The battle effectively removed the Japanese navy as a credible threat for the remainder of the war.[2]

Apart from the handful of Australian ships, the invasion of Leyte was an all-American operation, with the Australian army left behind in New Guinea, although MacArthur still held out the prospect of including two Australian divisions for the invasion of Luzon. As for the British navy, the ships of the Eastern fleet were still restricted to the Indian Ocean until arrangements could be made for their transfer to the Pacific. Their presence helped to cover the operations in Burma, beginning in mid-October with British and Indian forces under General Slim pushing off from Imphal in an offensive towards Mandalay. With the Allies enjoying numerical superiority on land and overwhelming superiority in the air, the bedraggled Japanese forces were forced into a fighting retreat. With Slim's forces being supplied by an efficient air cargo system using hundreds of American transport planes, the capture of distant Rangoon by land suddenly seemed possible. It all depended on the monsoon rains holding off and the Allied requirements in China, where the Japanese were mopping up large areas of territory, not robbing Slim of his all-important air support.

Nearly three years after Pearl Harbor, the British war against Japan was finally increasing in tempo, with the overstretched Japanese forces facing the inevitability of defeat in their recently occupied territories. Churchill was still intent, though, to minimise the British contribution in the Pacific and to use the Soviet Union to hasten the final defeat of Japan. Even the battles in Burma would have to make do without the expected support being sent from the Italian front. Churchill, Eden and Brooke had visited their forces in Italy on 8 October while on their way to meet with Stalin in Moscow, and had been impressed with the need to retain them there. With the American forces being unleashed on the Philippines and the British forces being let loose into Burma, Churchill was concerned during his meetings with Stalin to get confirmation of the Russian leader's determination to enter the war against Japan as soon as Germany had been defeated. This Stalin did during a conversation with Eden, promising to join the war against Japan two to three months after Germany's defeat. Churchill was absent from these discussions, having succumbed to a violent attack of diarrhoea, but later proclaimed Stalin's promise as 'the most important statement at the Conference'.[3] Russian entry into the Pacific war would ensure that a prolonged war against Japan would not be necessary.

With great battles being fought in the Philippines and Burma, and not an Australian soldier in sight, the Australian government came under political pressure to maintain an appearance of military activity. So began what the Australian journalist Peter Charlton has termed the 'unnecessary war', with Australian troops being ordered to take the offensive against Japanese garrisons cut off from sustenance by the swift strokes of the American advance. Like other island garrisons across the Pacific, these Japanese forces could have been safely contained until they surrendered with the eventual defeat of Japan. Instead, at a cost of more than one thousand Australian lives, and countless Japanese, a series of attacks would be launched from Bougainville to Borneo, from October 1944 until August 1945. Charlton largely blamed Australian generals, and mostly absolved Australian politicians, for organising these offensives.[4] He was certainly correct to depict the offensives as unnecessary, although absolving Australian political leaders of responsibility is questionable.

It is clear that Curtin felt that he was under political pressure to have his armies active. On 28 September 1944, he promised the advisory war council that he would discuss with MacArthur, during forthcoming talks in Canberra before the general's departure for the Philippines, 'the question of the acceptance, as an Allied responsibility, of operations for the neutralisation and ultimate liquidation of Japanese forces in rearward areas'.[5] At their meeting on 30 September, MacArthur advised Curtin that his island-hopping campaign had been 'exceedingly successful' in isolating Japanese forces 'and rendering them innocuous'. To have defeated them, said MacArthur, would have cost 'many thousands of lives' which 'would have represented so much waste'. When he was asked 'whether the policy of neutralising Japanese pockets contemplated an effort to liquidate them', he replied in the negative, indicating that his orders to Blamey 'would be confined to neutralisation'. Some comment was then apparently made, perhaps by Curtin, about the effect on the Australian troops of being confined just to garrison duties. This reflected the common view of Australian soldiers, from Gallipoli onwards, that they were ill suited to garrison duties and needed to be in the thick of the fighting. British commanders often obliged, throwing the Australians into the front line of any attack. MacArthur had some understanding of this and acknowledged that Australian commanders might find 'garrison duties irksome and might desire to undertake some active operations, but this would be a matter for direction by the Australian Authorities'.[6] He thereby absolved himself of any responsibility for what Australia might decide. Although, as the official war historian, Gavin Long, has pointed out, MacArthur's instruction to use twelve brigades to garrison the islands virtually ensured they would be drawn into active operations against the Japanese, whereas the seven brigades favoured by Blamey would have forced a more conservative containment policy on the Australians.[7]

It was not only to avoid ill-discipline among the troops that impelled Curtin and his colleagues to favour using them in wasteful operations against the Japanese. The government also wanted to maintain a substantial army in action so as to claim a seat at the Pacific peace conference that it wrongly expected would follow the Japanese surrender. There were also the problems of maintaining Australian morale and shoring up public support for restrictive war measures. It would be difficult to achieve these things without Australian forces being in action somewhere. As Shedden advised on 28 October, an active army would help to erode widespread public dissatisfaction with the war effort. The problem facing the government, warned Shedden, was to 'correct the threatened relaxation of the Nation's war effort, lest any drift should later have political repercussions'.[8] The implication seems clear: men were to kill and be killed to shore up the political position of the Labor Party.

It is not clear whether Curtin read Shedden's memorandum. He had spent nearly two weeks relaxing in Perth, leaving for Melbourne by train on 25 October. The burdens of war were weighing heavily on him, as he had indicated in a letter to an old friend the previous month, complaining that he 'was not trained to be a war lord. Yet fate pushed on to me at least the appearance of being one.' The stress of it all, combined with years of excessive drinking and smoking, had worn away at his heart. He fell ill during the train journey across the Nullarbor and was confined to his hotel for a few days in Melbourne before being rushed off to hospital where it was determined that Curtin had suffered a serious heart attack. He remained in hospital until the end of the year.[9]

Australia was also determined to recover by force of arms those territories it controlled before the war and to establish a claim on the destiny of those colonial territories that it coveted. Australia had emerged from the First World War with the prize of German New Guinea and now hoped for more, although not necessarily in terms of a formal empire. In mid-October, Evatt's unofficial ambassador and businessman at large, W. S. Robinson, reported on talks with the British dominions secretary, Lord Cranborne, the information minister, Brendan Bracken, and Lord Beaverbrook. Robinson assured Evatt that he had emphasised Australia's deep interest in the colonial question since 'our defence as well as our economic development very largely depends on our freedom of access and equality of economic opportunity in the New Hebrides, New Guinea, Timor, N.E.I. [Indonesia], Tonkin [Indo-China] etc'.[10]

As Robinson indicated, Australia was interested in creating an 'informal' sub-empire in the south seas, with access to the markets and American-built defence facilities of these European colonies. Evatt had considered taking over some of these strategically placed colonies, but had since abandoned the idea in the face of Anglo–American opposition and the problem of defending such acquisitions. Now he wanted a linked British and American defence shield behind which Australia could exercise power over its immediate neighbourhood. As Shedden argued, the events of the war 'should have convinced all Australians that their future will hinge on the maintenance of the goodwill of our powerful friends'.[11] The trade and customs minister, Senator Keane, expressed it more bluntly during a tour of North America when he argued that 'Great Britain and [the] United States will have to back Australia both during and after the war' since 'within a few hundred miles' of Australia's seven million whites were 'millions of coloured people'.[12] In stressing the need for the white race to stand together, Keane was repeating an argument used earlier by Curtin when appealing for American assistance in 1942.

Britain's attitude towards Australia and the Pacific remained equivocal. Rather than rebuilding its defence shield in the Pacific, Britain wanted to use Australian and other dominion forces to conceal the paucity of the British effort against Japan.[13] However, for a few months during late 1944, it seemed that Britain might assert its postwar interests in the Pacific more aggressively. It was an Australian aviator, P. G. Taylor, who prompted this when he finally convinced various officers within the air ministry to approve his plan to survey an alternative trans-Pacific air route, even without American permission.[14] As it happened, Admiral King reversed his previous opposition and agreed in early August 1944 to the survey flight being mounted, with the air ministry representative assuring him that the flight would be 'only a preliminary survey to ascertain whether or not it is possible to establish a reinforcing air route over the South Pacific'. Any subsequent development of the route would be subject to further discussion with Washington. According to this, the route was being developed to allow the transfer to the Pacific of British forces after the defeat of Germany. No mention was made of the postwar civil aviation aspect, although Taylor privately admitted that Britain's 'survival as a first rate nation in the air is the thing which is really at stake'.[15]

While Taylor was readying his flying boat for the epic survey, King withheld his final permission for the flight. Taylor railed against Britain's procrastination in the face of America's stalling tactics, observing angrily in a diary note that it was

now 8 months since Britain decided to do the survey flight. We are still standing by. The moon is waning. Pacific nights will be dark, the weather

*unknown. Diplomats and politicians and senior R.A.F. officers still quibble
about trifles and nothing effective is done ...*

According to a frustrated Taylor, there was a lesson in all this for Australia,
which 'must set out to establish herself as a self-contained nation' and 'not
count upon England at all for the future'. While Australia should do all it
could 'to hold and strengthen the British Empire', it must 'not again be left
in a state of weakness because of our belief in our strength coming from
outside Australia'.[16]

In London, worried air ministry officials consulted the Foreign Office
about whether the survey should proceed without King's permission.
Although the Foreign Office raised no objection to this course, King
suddenly announced that he had referred the matter to Roosevelt.[17] This
raised the stakes considerably. Now it would need Churchill's agreement for
the survey to go ahead without Roosevelt's sanction. Instead of this
becoming necessary, another reversal of policy saw American approval once
more being forthcoming. Taylor rushed back to Bermuda where his aircraft
and crew were waiting. On 27 September, with his engines at maximum
throttle, Taylor lifted his heavily laden aircraft from the water, turned off his
radio to block any last-minute messages and headed for Mexico on the first
leg of his trail-blazing flight. His first stop in the Pacific was Clipperton
Island, a huge submarine mountain, the peak of which rises only some
twenty metres above the Pacific. After an eventful six weeks surveying the
uninhabited French island for suitable landing sites, during which a
hurricane almost destroyed their anchored aircraft, Taylor completed his
flight across the Pacific to Sydney. He was confident that his successful
survey was being followed up by two British Dakota aircraft loaded with
engineering equipment to prepare an air base on Clipperton that might
challenge the supremacy of Hawaii as an aerial staging post.[18]

Instead, Taylor was met in Sydney by a signal from RAF Transport
Command, advising him that 'international considerations preclude any action
beyond [the] completion of [a] comprehensive survey of [the] route'. He was
told not to hold any talks 'of an official or unofficial nature' with American
representatives about the development of a permanent air route, nor was he

allowed to press Australia to develop the route for fear that it would 'embarrass ourselves and may jeopardise future high policy discussions'.[19] For four years Taylor had fought to prove the viability of this alternative route. Exhausted after his long flight, he now faced failure. Returning to Bermuda, this time via Hawaii, Taylor found the Dakotas grounded at Acapulco in Mexico.[20] Taylor's survey had sparked interest in Clipperton Island by both the French and the Mexicans, with the sovereignty of the isolated island having long been disputed between them. With Britain wanting it as a staging post on an all-British route around the world, the prospect loomed of a three-way tussle over an island in which Roosevelt had taken a close personal interest. Upon being advised that American security was threatened, and that the route would neutralise American control of Pacific air routes, Roosevelt insisted that Churchill abandon plans for the survey of Clipperton, citing as justification the 'Monroe Doctrine, air agreements now under discussion and American public opinion'.[21] Churchill immediately complied. He had been unaware of Taylor's plan, telling his chiefs of staff that it was 'astonishing [that] a step like this should be taken without Cabinet authority being sought'.[22]

The chiefs of staff were far from contrite, urging that a more detailed survey of Clipperton be completed and berating the Americans for being 'unreasonable in preventing our completing a survey of a route not passing through United States territory and designed to join two parts of the British Empire'. Moreover, argued the chiefs, the dominions had shown 'great interest' in the survey and would be disappointed if it were abandoned.[23] Churchill, however, was not prepared to defy Washington over such an issue, particularly when relations with America were already strained by British moves to restore the Greek monarchy by force of arms and when American support would be needed to reconstruct a devastated Europe and contain Russia's expanding influence. Anyway, the matter was settled when Roosevelt secretly dispatched an armed 'weather reporting party' to occupy Clipperton, telling Britain that it had been done 'as a matter of military urgency as a result of an increase in Japanese operations in the waters off the western sea frontier'. Britain was advised not to send any unauthorised parties to the island 'in order that there should be no possibility of incidents through mistaken identity'.[24]

On receipt of Roosevelt's peremptory message, Churchill advised the chiefs of staff and the air ministry that Britain 'really ought to lay off this'. When he learned that the French were sending a ship from Acapulco to Clipperton, Churchill urged Eden to warn the Americans.[25] Taylor vainly appealed to Churchill to press ahead despite the American occupation, suggesting that American commercial and military interests, without Roosevelt's knowledge, were seeking to seize the island from France and that Britain should join France in developing an air base there. Taylor was right in claiming that the Americans wanted to 'prevent us developing for war purposes what must later emerge as a peacetime asset to us', but he was wrong about Roosevelt being ignorant of the moves. Roosevelt had his own designs on Clipperton and was determined to exclude Britain, even suggesting that Mexico be given the island so America might then lease it from them.[26]

The Clipperton affair demonstrated the more subservient attitude that Churchill felt Britain must adopt towards the United States in matters of such distant concern. It should also have raised serious questions in Canberra about Britain's ability to assert its power on the other side of the world once the war was won. But the lesson seems to have been lost on the Australian government, which was still committed to reviving the prewar system of imperial defence. Hamstrung by its colonial past, and by the continued dependence on Britain and the United States which the events of the war seemed to confirm as inevitable, Australia watched from afar as its great power allies tussled over the isolated Pacific outcrop.

In civil aviation generally, Australia was similarly sidelined as the Allies competed for supremacy in the postwar skies. Australia was slow to replace its policy of internationalisation and was forced to follow London. When Washington called for a conference on civil aviation, Australia finally formulated a fresh policy, with the cabinet agreeing on 25 September 1944 to support the quick restoration of prewar Commonwealth services and the establishment of a new British service across the Pacific via Hawaii to Canada.[27] In London, the war cabinet continued to accelerate the design and production program for civil aircraft, taking care not to alert the Americans by developing the aircraft under the cover of 'transport types'. In November the British Overseas Airways Corporation (BOAC) was given the first of

25 converted Lancaster bombers to resume the route from London to Sydney in cooperation with Qantas. Meanwhile, Commonwealth delegates gathered in Montreal in October 1944 to discuss their approach to civil aviation prior to an international conference in Chicago which finally ended the push for internationalisation and established instead the basis for the postwar airline system by which nations retained the sovereignty of their skies and the ownership of their airlines and airports.[28]

While Britain's survey of the Clipperton route had been ostensibly to support the future British effort in the Pacific war, questions were being asked in Washington as to whether Britain should be permitted to play any part at all in that war.[29] This had been the inclination of Admiral King all along and now, with the heavy naval loss suffered by the Japanese during the battle for the Philippines, there seemed little purpose in sending any British naval ships to the Pacific. However, the devastating effect of the Japanese kamikaze planes made up for the relative lack of Japanese aircraft, their shortage of fuel and the inexperience of the Japanese pilots. The RAN cruiser, *Australia*, was the first ship to be deliberately targeted by a Japanese pilot off Leyte, with the aircraft crashing into the foremast and killing the captain and other officers on the bridge. The commodore of the Australian squadron, Captain John Collins, was badly injured, putting him out of immediate contention as the future naval chief, a position the government had marked out for him.[30] Once this desperate Japanese strategy was used more widely, it started to take a heavy toll on the hastily constructed American carriers with their wooden flight decks. Accordingly, the Americans were soon pleased to welcome the more heavily armoured British aircraft carriers to join the final thrust against Japan, where the kamikaze attacks were likely to be even more intense.

Despite Churchill's continuing reservations about the Pacific fleet, the Admiralty continued to plan for its dispatch. Although Australia was meant to provide its initial base facilities, Cunningham complained in October of 'a sort of passive resistance about the Australian Gov[ernmen]t's attitude'. This may have been because it was now intended to place the fleet under the command of the US naval chief in the Pacific, Admiral Chester Nimitz, based in Hawaii, rather than under MacArthur in the south-west Pacific. Curtin was usually sensitive to MacArthur's interests and views and, unbeknown to Cunningham, had been advised by MacArthur of the practical difficulties that Australia would face in having the British fleet based on eastern Australia, which MacArthur believed made little sense. Undeterred by the Australian attitude, the Admiralty decided in November that its Pacific fleet would arrive in Australia by the end of the following month.[31]

To appease the British sailors who would have to fight this distant and unpopular war, Churchill introduced measures to improve their amenities and instil in them the will to fight, with their beer ration being increased to a minimum of four pints per week. British women were to be encouraged to go to India to help at leave centres and so boost service morale, with Churchill urging the viceroy of India to 'do all that you can to encourage the British women now in India to play their full part'.[32] It was crucial that dissatisfaction be kept to a minimum, since Churchill had announced that a general election, the first one for ten years, would be held as soon as Germany was defeated. Churchill realised that his popularity would peak with the achievement of victory in Europe. Even if he lost the election, the Labour Party would have the unpopular task of fighting the war in the Pacific and maintaining relatively stringent wartime restrictions. This would probably ensure that it would be a one-term government and open the way for Churchill's triumphant return.[33]

Of course, all this was based on the increasingly outdated assumption that the Pacific war would continue for perhaps two or three years after the end of the war in Europe. After the American success at Leyte, and the stiffening of German resistance in Europe, the likely time difference between the two events was gradually shortened. And as the Japanese collapsed, so the competition intensified for the postwar control of Japanese-held territory. In appealing for more forces for his South East Asia Command, Mountbatten warned Beaverbrook in late October of worrying signs that the Americans might not let the British return to Singapore. He claimed that General Hurley, Roosevelt's representative in China, had threatened: 'If the British do not capture Singapore by themselves before the end of the war I doubt whether the Americans will let them have it back, in view of their record in the Far East.'[34] Despite Hurley's bluster, the Americans were committed to the restoration of the tattered British empire, although they were more equivocal about the return of French possessions.[35] Still, Britain suspected America's territorial ambitions, sometimes with good reason, and kept a proprietorial eye on its prewar territories.

At the same time as Mountbatten was warning of American moves regarding Singapore, the Foreign Office was concerned at possible American moves to exclude France from participation in the Pacific war and to claim French Indo-China as part of the American-controlled China theatre instead of the British-controlled South-East Asian theatre. Fearing that it would mean France being denied its colonies in Indo-China, Eden pointed out that any interference with French sovereignty 'would be passionately resented by France and would have incalculable results not only in the Far East but in Europe. It would also put in question the future of all other Far Eastern colonial possessions which had been overrun by Japan.' Eden saw it as part of a wider American conspiracy to restrict Britain to a minor role in the war against Japan. For this reason, and citing a cable from Curtin in support, Eden argued strongly that Britain 'should play a major role in the war against Japan and that our contribution should be not merely effective but spectacular'.[36] On 20 October, on their way back from Moscow, Eden and Churchill met with Mountbatten in Cairo to discuss future operations in his command, with a seaborne attack on Rangoon now postponed until November 1945. Despite this disappointment, Eden impressed upon Mountbatten the need to recapture at least Singapore and Rangoon before the Americans forced the Japanese to the peace table.[37] Their capture would secure Burma and Malaya for Britain's postwar empire.

While Australia was keen to see the return of the French to New Caledonia, it did not want a simple restoration of prewar colonial arrangements but the institution instead of a system of international trusteeship of these colonies which would have the effect of opening them up to Australian trade and influence. This had been one of the main objectives of the Anzac agreement in January 1944, with the discussions between Australia and New Zealand being renewed in late October 1944 when Australian and New Zealand ministers met in Wellington. The meeting between Australia's deputy prime minister, Frank Forde, Evatt, and New Zealand representatives called for a South Seas Regional Commission that would involve the Pacific peoples in their political and economic development. As in January, this meeting was largely intended to buttress dominion claims to a major voice in the peace settlement with Japan, and to reinforce their determination to restrict American postwar control to the northern Pacific. It also challenged European empires by calling for all colonies to be administered by the United Nations as trustees, with the regular international inspections and benevolent development that implied, rather than the prewar colonial system that had been marked by exploitation and subjugation.[38]

These discussions caused further anger on the part of the British government, with Cranborne urging his cabinet colleagues to 'make clear to [Australia and New Zealand] the deplorable results which are likely to ensue if regional discussions lead to public declarations of policy on matters of interest to other members of the Commonwealth without prior consultation'.[39] As if Britain was not continually doing this in relation to matters of vital interest to Australia. In this case, though, Cranborne thought the British government had reached an understanding with Curtin, when he was in London for the Commonwealth prime ministers' meeting in May, that any postwar system of colonial mandates should not include the colonies of the British empire. Adding to the British anger was the timing of the Wellington declaration, which occurred just as Britain was about to approach the United States on the issue of postwar colonial policy. Accordingly, the British government advised Australia that it would have to issue a public statement making clear its opposition to the colonial policy proposed by the dominions.[40]

The danger for Britain was if the dominions and the United States combined to exert pressure for the trusteeship model to be imposed on all the European colonies. With the Wellington declaration revealing a rift in the Commonwealth on this issue, Roosevelt made just such an overture during his first meeting with the new Australian minister in Washington, Frederic Eggleston, fresh from his former posting in China. Although Roosevelt made clear that he 'didn't like the wording' of the Australia–New Zealand Agreement, in so far as it related to America, he realised that there was room for agreement regarding colonies. Roosevelt claimed that Britain was coveting the Netherlands East Indies and that it should instead be offering independence to Malaya and Burma, in the same way that America was doing for the Philippines. Roosevelt 'thought the Americans and the Australians could work together on a liberal policy on these matters'.[41]

With Curtin still recuperating in hospital, Evatt could reassert Australia's commitment to the Anzac agreement. When Britain took umbrage at the Wellington declaration, Evatt denied that the dominions had changed their position since the prime ministers' meeting in London. Australia's position, he argued, had been established by the Anzac agreement in January and nothing since then had altered. Evatt was on weak ground since Curtin had cabled from London in May his 'agreement with the general principles enunciated by the Colonial Secretary'. Unfazed, Evatt simply denied such an agreement, arguing that the May meeting was 'merely a personal exchange of views'. He blamed elements within the Colonial Office for the British objections, believing that neither the Labour members of the war cabinet nor even Cranborne really supported these objections from 'the distant past'. Although Australia desired good relations with Britain, Evatt cautioned Bruce that 'we must not be asked to surrender principles to which we are committed. Still less should we be chided for our views by the Colonial Office.' In fact, Evatt confided that he was prepared to accept a British proposal for regional commissions, rather than an international commission, to oversee colonies.[42] For its part, Britain dismissed Evatt's retort as a minority view sent in the absence of Curtin and repeated its objection to the dominions holding discussions without consulting concerned members of the Commonwealth. Although it approved in principle the South Seas Regional Commission, it stipulated that its implementation would depend on agreement with the United States and on assurances that it would not interfere with Britain's colonies.[43]

Bruce counselled Evatt to adopt an attitude of 'sweet reasonableness' on the issue of trusteeship, adding that the dominions should have consulted London before issuing their declaration. In a private cable to Curtin, which found its way to Evatt, Bruce described Whitehall's dismay at the Wellington meeting and his embarrassment at Australia changing policy without consulting Britain. Bruce had repeatedly harassed Churchill over the issue of consultation, and now he stood accused of the same offence. He suggested that, before the declaration was endorsed, the clause relating to mandates be quietly dropped. When Evatt saw Bruce's latest attempt to dilute policies that he held dear, he managed to control his anger at the high commissioner and redirect it instead at the antediluvian officials of the Colonial Office, whom he regarded as the real villains.[44]

Evatt had been misled by idealistic pronouncements from the executive committee of the British Labour Party about the future of British colonies. Parliamentary Labour leaders such as Attlee and Bevan did not share these views nor, of course, did the Tories. Cranborne had received strong Conservative backing for his stand, with Lord Croft comparing international supervision of British colonies with outside 'supervision of Tasmania', maintaining that the British parliament would never 'consent to sharing its duties with people who have no concern whatever with the British Colonial Empire'.[45] Indeed, Britain moved quickly to pre-empt any move by Washington to 'put forward schemes which were unsatisfactory from our point of view, but [which] might attract support'. Rather than a system of international trusteeship, Britain proposed a system of regional commissions dominated by imperial powers. Continued British control of its colonies would be disguised by fine words about economic and social progress for native peoples. The reality was exposed during a war cabinet discussion of colonial policy when the chancellor of the exchequer, Sir John Anderson, warned his colleagues 'to ensure that such bodies [to promote colonial welfare] were not a means of putting pressure on us to spend money which we had not got'.[46] Despite this, Churchill was manoeuvred into signing an American-inspired declaration during the Yalta conference in early February 1945 which made British-mandated territories subject to trusteeship. Although he tried to ensure that the matter did not receive detailed discussion during the San Francisco conference in mid-1945, at which the United Nations Organisation was established, international supervision of colonial territories was now firmly on the agenda.[47]

While statesmen were sparring about colonial territories, MacArthur's campaign in the Philippines was proceeding at a cracking pace, with the Japanese defenders mostly retreating to the mountain ranges of the different islands where they put up a stout but futile defence. The Japanese were playing for time, but the strategy only increased the suffering for all involved. A similar situation prevailed in Burma where General Slim was meeting relatively little opposition to his offensive, with the weakened enemy mostly melting away in front of him. In practically all the territories they continued to hold, the Japanese were forced to rely on local food and other supplies to maintain themselves, since American submarines had sunk most of their merchant marine. As a result, malnutrition now competed with disease as the greatest cause of death for Japanese soldiers, while it was also rife among many of the subject peoples over whom they still reigned. On Bougainville, with Blamey's exhortation to 'exterminate these vermin' ringing in their ears,[48] Australian troops began the New Year with a strategically senseless offensive across daunting terrain and against a debilitated Japanese garrison. At least the end seemed finally to be in sight.

NOTES

[1] Dower, *War Without Mercy*, p. 296.

[2] Liddell Hart, *History of the Second World War*, pp. 649–59.

[3] Gilbert, *Road to Victory*, pp. 1020, 1038–9.

[4] Peter Charlton, *The Unnecessary War*, Melbourne, 1983.

[5] Advisory War Council Minutes, 28 September 1944, CRS A2682/8/1430, NAA.

[6] Note of Discussion between Curtin, MacArthur and Wilson, 30 September 1944, *DAFP*, Vol. 7, Doc. 305.

[7] Cited in Charlton, *The Unnecessary War*, pp. 19–20.

[8] Memorandum by Shedden, 28 October 1944, CRS A5954, Box 312, NAA.

[9] Day, *John Curtin*, pp. 552–5.

[10] Letter, Robinson to Evatt, 15 October 1944, 'Robinson, W. S., 1942–45(b)' folder, Evatt Collection, FUL.

[11] Memorandum by Shedden, 28 October 1944, CRS A5954, Box 312, NAA.

[12] *Province*, Vancouver, 3 January 1945.

[13] For instance, Churchill was looking to Indian troops to garrison British territories as they were recaptured from the Japanese. Minute, Churchill to Ismay, 25 May 1944, PREM 3/159/14, PRO.

[14] See, documents in MS 2594/86, Taylor Papers, NLA.

[15] Letter, Air Marshal Welsh to Admiral King, 7 August 1944, and Draft letter (not sent), Taylor to Welsh, MS 2594/86, Taylor Papers, NLA.

[16] Note by Taylor, MS 2594/46, Taylor Papers, NLA.

[17] Paper by Colyer, 3 September 1944, BBK D/208, Beaverbrook Papers, HLRO.

[18] Taylor, *The Sky Beyond*, p. 184.

[19] Message, RAF Dorval to Taylor, 1 November 1944, MS 2594/86, Taylor Papers, NLA.

[20] Taylor, *The Sky Beyond*, pp. 222–3.

[21] Thorne, *Allies of a Kind*, p. 666; Cable, Roosevelt to Churchill, 27 November 1944, BBK D/422, Beaverbrook Papers, HLRO.

[22] Minute, Churchill to Ismay, 28 November 1944, and Minute, Beaverbrook to Churchill, 4 December 1944, BBK D/422, Beaverbrook Papers, HLRO; Minute, Eden to Churchill, 4 December 1944, PREM 3/95, PRO.

[23] Report by Chiefs of Staff, 1 December 1944, PREM 3/95, PRO.

[24] Cable, Halifax to Foreign Office, 4 January 1945, PREM 3/95, PRO.

25 Minute, Churchill to Chiefs of Staff and Sinclair, 8 January 1945; Cable, Mexico to Foreign Office, 4 January 1945; Minute, Churchill to Eden, 6 January 1945, PREM 3/95, PRO; Cable, Churchill to Roosevelt, 10 January 1945, BBK D423, Beaverbrook Papers, HLRO.

26 Note by Taylor, undated, and Letter (draft), Taylor to Churchill, undated, MS 2594/86, Taylor Papers, NLA; Thorne, *Allies of a Kind*, p. 667.

27 Message, 25 August 1944, and other documents in this file, CRS A5954, Box 345; Cabinet Minutes, 25 September 1944, CRS A2703/II, NAA; Cable, Commonwealth Government to Fraser, 26 September 1944, *DAFP*, Vol. 7, Doc. 301.

28 War Cabinet Conclusions, 1 September 1944, CAB 65/43, W.M. (44)114 and War Cabinet Conclusions, 29 September 1944, CAB 65/47, W.M. (44)129, PRO; Cable, Cranborne to Commonwealth Government, 22 November 1944, CRS A5954, Box 343 and Cable, Drakeford to Forde, 9 November 1944, CRS A5954, Box 345, NAA.

29 Smith, *Task Force 57*, p. 71; Lord Halifax, *Fulness of Days*, p. 259.

30 Gill, *Royal Australian Navy 1942–1945*, pp. 511–13.

31 Cunningham diary, 5 and 24 October and 13 November 1944, ADD. MS. 52577, Cunningham Papers, BL; Note of Discussion between Curtin, MacArthur and Wilson, 30 September 1944, *DAFP*, Vol. 7, Doc. 305.

32 Directive by Churchill, and Directive to Viceroy by Churchill, 20 November 1944, CAB 66/58, W.P. (44)670 and 671, PRO.

33 See, J. M. Lee, *The Churchill Coalition*, London, 1980, pp. 174–5.

34 Letter, Mountbatten to Beaverbrook, 27 October 1944, BBK D/141, Beaverbrook Papers, HLRO.

35 As Adolf Berle, the former American assistant secretary of state, assured Beaverbrook, America 'wants the British Commonwealth a strong, solid, flourishing, prosperous, going concern, just as I should imagine England wants a strong, solid, and prosperous America — not merely for sentimental reasons but because both conditions are to the solid interest of both'. Letter, Berle to Beaverbrook, 30 December 1944, BBK D151, Beaverbrook Papers, HLRO. For the description of Hurley, see Letter, Henderson to Colville, 17 March 1945, PREM 3/159/12, PRO.

36 Memorandum by Eden, October 1944, PREM 3/180/7, PRO.

37 Letter, Mountbatten to Somerville, 14 November 1944, SMVL 9/2, Somerville Papers, CC.

38 Cable, Fraser to Commonwealth Government, 7 November 1944, *DAFP*, Vol. 7, Doc. 337.

39 Memorandum by Cranborne, 10 November 1944, CAB 66/57, W.P. (44)641, PRO.

40 War Cabinet Conclusions, 13 November 1944, CAB 65/44, W.M. (44)149, PRO; Cable, Cranborne to Commonwealth Government, 14 November 1944, *DAFP*, Vol. 7, Doc. 347.

41 Letter, Eggleston to Evatt, 21 November 1944, CRS A5954, Box 293, NAA.

42 See, *DAFP*, Vol. 7, Docs 349, 352–4; For Curtin's account of the May meeting on colonial policy, see CRS A2679/16/1944, NAA.

43 War Cabinet Conclusions, 24 November 1944, CAB 65/44, W.M. (44)155, PRO.

44 Cable, Bruce to Evatt, 27 November 1944, CRS M100, 'November 1944', NAA; Cable, Bruce to Curtin, 10 November 1944, *DAFP*, Vol. 7, Doc. 344; Louis, *Imperialism at Bay*, pp. 416–17.

45 Letter, Croft to Cranborne, 28 November 1944, CRFT 1/18, Croft Papers, CC.

46 War Cabinet Conclusions, 20 December 1944, CAB 65/44, W.M. (44)172, PRO.

47 Carlton, *Anthony Eden*, p. 251; Louis, *Imperialism at Bay*, Chaps 29–30; War Cabinet Conclusions, 19 March 1945, CAB 65/49, W.M. (45)33, PRO.

48 Dower, *War without Mercy*, p. 71.

FORTY-FIVE

'a luxury we cannot afford'

The optimism that had prevailed among Allied military leaders after the successful D-day landings and the apparent collapse of German defences in France had dissipated by the end of 1944. In mid-December, a daring German counteroffensive had pushed hundreds of Panzer tanks through the supposedly 'impassable' Ardennes and punched a hole through the thin cover of American forces that were meant to be holding that sector of the western front. Although the German offensive was soon brought to a shuddering halt, for want of petrol as much as anything else, it forced the Allies to revise their estimates of the likely end of the European war. Previously, there had been predictions of a German collapse by October 1944, while Eisenhower had wagered with Montgomery that it would be over by Christmas that year.[1] Now it was not even expected that Allied armies would be able to cross the Rhine before May 1945.

In the Pacific, General MacArthur had destroyed Japanese resistance on Leyte and in early January swooped onto the main Philippine island of Luzon. By the beginning of February, his troops had entered the suburbs of Manila where Japanese troops fought a fierce defensive battle, house by house, while others retreated to the mountainous interior. It took a month of desperate fighting in Manila before the defenders were subdued, by which time about 100 000 of the city's inhabitants had been killed. Meanwhile, American Superfortress bombers were raiding Japanese cities and would soon begin dropping the newly developed napalm that would engulf Tokyo and other vulnerable cities in devastating firestorms. There was worse to come. In Los Alamos, Allied physicists raced to perfect a means of detonating an atomic explosion. They expected to have eighteen plutonium bombs ready by August 1945.[2]

While thousands of Australian airmen continued to participate in the bombing of Germany, their compatriots in New Guinea, Bougainville and New Britain had taken over garrison duties from the American divisions which MacArthur had taken north to the Philippines. Not wanting to be left out of the action, and egged on by their government, the Australian commanders soon began offensives against the remaining pockets of half-starving Japanese troops. For several months, military censors enforced MacArthur's instruction to impose a news blackout on operations in the south-west Pacific, ostensibly to confuse the Japanese about Allied troop movements, but perhaps also to emphasise his achievements in the Philippines. As a result, the newspapers carried no stories of any action by Australian troops. Although they had been meant to join MacArthur in the second wave of attacks on the Philippines, the invasion of Luzon proceeded without a slouch hat in sight. By 10 January 1945, the *Canberra Times* cheekily implored 'anyone knowing the whereabouts of Australian soldiers in the South-West Pacific Area [to] please communicate at once with the Australian Government'.[3]

When the whereabouts of the troops became public, the Opposition loudly decried the use of first-class fighting forces in mopping-up operations of no strategic significance, while the press complained that the reports of the large-scale operations by American forces in the Philippines were pushing the lesser activities of the Australian forces off the front pages. With the Australian forces largely inactive, the British government asked in September 1944 for some of the troops to garrison British island colonies in the Pacific as they were recaptured from the Japanese. Although the Labor government was keen to restore the British empire's place in the Pacific, and boost Australia's place within it,[4] Curtin claimed that, while he was sympathetic to the British request, he was precluded from complying by the country's commitment to MacArthur, who had control of Australian troop dispositions. He would also have been conscious that the British request carried dangers of disputation with the Americans, since the request was motivated by concern in London that the Americans might claim the islands by right of conquest. Nevertheless, he soon after made an exception by allowing Australian troops to garrison Nauru, with its rich resources of phosphate on which Australian farmers relied to boost the fertility of their soil. The island was also just south of the equator, and therefore within the southern half of the Pacific from which the Australian government was determined to exclude the Americans.[5]

The Australian government's reluctance for its troops to garrison British colonies would have been predicated partly on the assumption that MacArthur would need the troops for his Philippines campaign. By early 1945, it was clear that the Australians would be excluded from any role in recapturing that American colony. With the government being anxious for its troops to be seen as taking a prominent part in the Pacific fighting, Shedden wrote to MacArthur on 15 February asking why Australian troops were not being used in the Philippines and claiming that 'Australian opinion considered it a point of honour' for their troops to be involved in such operations.[6] Indeed, the acting prime minister, Frank Forde, had told parliament in November 1944 that Australian army and air units would 'play a full part' in the Philippine operations.[7] But Blamey wanted to retain his divisions for use with the planned British Commonwealth force that he hoped to lead, while MacArthur used Blamey's opposition to justify the use of a purely American land force in the Philippines.[8]

When the Australian parliament reassembled in February 1945, Curtin found himself having to answer conservative charges regarding the activities of the Australian army. If they were not going forward with MacArthur to the Philippines, why could they not fight in Burma with the British? While Curtin agreed that Australia had 'a major political and national interest in the British Empire', he argued that it also had 'a major political issue nearer home, and that is to clear out the enemy who is still in occupation of territories for which this Government is politically responsible'. Defending their use in questionable offensives against Japanese garrisons that could have been contained until the end of the war with little effort or loss of life, Curtin pointed out that the Australian army remained under MacArthur's command, thereby wrongly implying that the offensives were being conducted on MacArthur's orders. Moreover, declared Curtin, the island campaign was 'not only commensurate with all the ambitions and the duty of this country, but is also clear evidence of the undoubted genuineness of Australia ... to fight where the fighting is hardest'.[9]

The uncertainty regarding the future role of the Australian troops might have been clarified by a meeting between Mountbatten and MacArthur. However, although Churchill was contemplating the use of two Australian divisions for the SEAC operations in Burma and Malaya, he steadfastly opposed Mountbatten visiting Australia to discuss such issues. Despite Mountbatten and MacArthur being supreme commanders in adjoining theatres, and although the British chiefs of staff had agreed in mid-1944 to a request from Mountbatten to visit Australia,[10] the two men would not meet for another year, and then only because MacArthur had shifted his headquarters from Australia to Manila. Part of the delay was due to the demands of planning for operations in Burma, but a large part was due to opposition from Churchill. When a visit to Australia seemed imminent in February 1945, the high commissioner, Sir Ronald Cross, suggested that Mountbatten use the opportunity to talk with the new governor-general, the Duke of Gloucester, as well as the Australian government and their chiefs of staff. Churchill reluctantly agreed to a brief visit provided that Mountbatten did not have any press interviews, fearing perhaps that the dashing commander might use such a public platform to bring pressure to bear for a greater British effort in the Pacific.[11]

Although both the British and American chiefs of staff agreed to the visit, Churchill abruptly withdrew his permission when it came back to him for final ratification on 7 March. Churchill now questioned 'the actual business [Mountbatten] has to transact with General MacArthur', maintaining that 'there can surely be no need for him to go to Australia'. Ismay pointed out the embarrassment of refusing the visit after having asked the Americans to approve it. As a way around Churchill's objections, he suggested that Canberra be cut from Mountbatten's itinerary and that the ban on press interviews be maintained. But Churchill was now adamant that the visit had to be cancelled.[12]

Churchill's objections to a meeting in Canberra between Mountbatten and Curtin reflected his continuing antipathy towards the dominion and its Labor government, as well as his ongoing desire to prevent the demands for Pacific operations detracting from the effort against Germany.[13] Churchill's hostility towards Australia was due not only to the many disputes he had had with Curtin and Evatt but also to the suspicion he harboured that Australia was profiting from the war at Britain's expense. In a paper prepared by Lord Keynes in April 1945 that compared the contributions of the various dominions, it was calculated that Australia had made a profit of £94 million in 1944, after deducting its payments to Britain from the payments made to Australia for war purchases and other services. While Canada was described as 'doing her full duty', Keynes claimed that Australia was 'scarcely doing a thing'.[14] Churchill also resented the limited extent of rationing in Australia compared with Britain, instructing officials to prepare a comparative study which found that Australia's traditional and continuing reliance on meat gave the appearance of relative luxury to its ration scale. Although Australians enjoyed a more palatable and varied wartime diet, the report concluded that the British and Australian diets were nutritionally similar.[15]

While Churchill could not help feeling resentful at what he wrongly felt to be a lacklustre Australian contribution to the war effort, the main British contribution to the Pacific war finally arrived in Australia in January 1945. Although the first echelons of the British Pacific fleet had arrived in Fremantle on 11 December 1944, the bulk of the fleet did not arrive until the following month after making diversionary attacks on Sumatra in a vain attempt to distract Japanese attention from the massive American invasion of Luzon. The warships were the first British forces to arrive in Australia apart from the token Spitfire squadrons, which had been partly manned by Australians anyway. Eventually the fleet would amount to about a third of

Britain's naval strength and comprise about one hundred ships of various types. Even then, it would be dwarfed by the contribution of the Americans, who managed to maintain four separate task forces in the Pacific, each of the same strength as the British fleet.[16]

The precise nature of Australia's support of the British fleet was finally decided on 7 December, just four days prior to the arrival of Fraser's flagship at Fremantle. It was agreed to contribute just over £22 million, made up of various resources from the building of barracks to the provision of canned meat and dental equipment. It was a considerable commitment in the face of a gaping deficiency of 85 000 in civilian manpower, with the government trying to make up the deficiency by switching civilian manpower from the support of the dwindling American forces to the arriving British forces.[17] Although Britain was reluctant to accept that Australia's contribution was limited by manpower shortages,[18] it was faced with similar problems itself. Just as Britain had accorded a low priority to the defence of the Pacific prior to the fall of Singapore, so it now accorded a low priority to the Pacific war in order to solve its pressing manpower and shipping shortages. With the defeat of Germany in sight, the British government accepted a plan by the labour minister, Ernest Bevin, on 2 December 1944 for the gradual re-allocation of manpower from military service to industry and reconstruction. Bevin was careful not to use the term 'demobilisation', although that is what he was planning, with the war against Japan to be fought by the call-up of eighteen-year-olds and those previously deferred from service.[19]

Bevin's plan, as well as the dispatch of the Pacific fleet, had been made on the assumption that victory in Europe was close. When the war dragged on through the winter of 1944–45, the strain on British shipping became intense, particularly as Britain was trying to prepare for postwar reconstruction as well as fight two wars and provide relief for the liberated countries of Europe. In these circumstances, it was with great relief that Keynes returned from talks in Washington at the beginning of February 1945 brandishing the news that the system of Lend-Lease would continue after Germany's defeat, during the so-called 'Stage 2' of the war, and that the United States would give Britain 'complete freedom to export (subject always to the needs of the war against Japan)'.[20]

The manpower and shipping shortages forced the Admiralty to confront the problems of basing its fleet in Australia while fighting a war up to ten thousand kilometres away. On 19 January, Cunningham wrote from the Admiralty warning Fraser of the 'great danger that we may dig ourselves too deeply in Australia' and urging that he base his fleet 'as far forward as possible'. To save on shipping, Cunningham suggested that the fleet's supplies from Britain should be shipped direct to the fleet's location in the Pacific, rather than to their base in Australia. This warning was reinforced three days later at a meeting of the chiefs of staff when the shipping minister attacked the size of the fleet train that was deemed necessary for the Pacific fleet. Cunningham conceded that 'the build up of the Pacific fleet both physical and logistical must be slowed up'. As one way of achieving this, he ordered that aircraft carriers destined for the Pacific be retained in the Indian Ocean until sufficient shipping was available to support them.[21] That same day, Lord Cherwell had advised Churchill to reject an Admiralty request for an increase in the fleet train, pointing to the 'great shortage of shipping and the consequent threatened fall in our imports and our stocks'. When it came before the war cabinet on 26 January, the Admiralty request was roundly condemned by ministers who questioned the need for so much shipping. A decision was deferred for two months while Cunningham re-examined the figures.[22]

With the Pacific commitment causing increasing concern in London, Churchill left for a conference with Roosevelt and Stalin in the Crimean city of Yalta. A few days before the meeting, Bruce had urged Curtin to remind Churchill of Australia's vital interest in the discussions, particularly those concerning the Pacific, and had deplored Britain's lack of consultation on the issues that were to be raised. It was 'clearly deplorable', declared Bruce, that Australia was again going to be 'faced with a series of faits accomplis'. Curtin was certainly concerned, but his poor health following his heart attack the previous year had sapped the fight out of him. He declined to adopt Bruce's suggestion of sending another cable of complaint to Churchill. Although he conceded to a visiting British official that there were matters of vital concern to Australia about to be discussed at Yalta, Curtin could only complain resignedly that 'apparently he was not to be consulted in advance', while remarking darkly that the 'time will come when someone sitting in this chair will say: "I won't put up with it."' Curtin was no longer the man to do it.[23]

On the eve of their departure from London, Churchill had informed Eden of his eagerness to have Russia enter the war against Japan as soon as possible after the defeat of Germany. This was despite the fact that Russia, through its likely capture of a warm water port on the Asian coastline, might become a Pacific power with possible negative implications for Australia's future security. His enthusiasm also contrasted with his strenuous opposition to Russia entering the war in 1941–42 when the security of Australia was at stake. More direct British interests were now involved in Churchill's calculations. As he informed Eden, 'the mere fact of a Russian declaration against Japan' could bring a quick end to the Pacific war that 'would undoubtedly save us many thousands of millions of pounds', assuring Eden at the same time that the chiefs of staff 'see no particular harm in the presence of Russia as a Pacific power'.[24] Such a quick end might also coincide with the British election campaign and tip the balance in Churchill's favour.

On their way to Yalta, British and American officials met on 1 February for preliminary talks in Malta during which the British discovered that the culmination of American plans for the Pacific war was timed for December that year, with an invasion of the Tokyo plain. As far as possible, the Americans wanted to avoid major land battles with the Japanese that could lead to heavy casualties and hamper the flow of the Allied advance. Like the British with their use of dominion and other forces, the Americans intended to use the reconstituted Philippine army and guerrilla forces to mop up the remaining Japanese in the Philippines.[25] That night, aboard the anchored cruiser *Orion*, Brooke told a satisfied Churchill of the American plans and the likely swift progress of their Pacific advance. The following day, when Churchill met with Roosevelt aboard the American cruiser *Quincy*, he proclaimed his eagerness to partake in the Pacific campaign and 'to go where a good opportunity would be presented of heavy fighting with the Japanese'. He singled out air warfare as 'the only way which the British had been able to discover of helping the main operations in the Pacific'. Unless he meant by this the provision of aircraft carriers, this was a curious comment given the lack of British air force units in the Pacific, other than the Spitfires in Australia. Twice Churchill offered British troops for deployment in China, only to be rejected by the US chiefs of staff.[26] As Churchill well knew, the Americans were not about to share with the British their special place at the right hand of Chiang Kai-shek. No matter. Churchill had achieved his aim: the record of the meeting would show that he had offered troops for the Pacific and the Americans had rejected them.[27]

At Yalta, Churchill pressed for Russia to join in issuing 'a Four-Power ultimatum calling upon Japan to surrender unconditionally, or else be subjected to the overwhelming weight of all the forces of the Four Powers'. Unlike the Anglo–American ultimatum to the Germans, this ultimatum was intended by Churchill to elicit a peace proposal from the Japanese short of an unconditional surrender. Churchill conceded that the Americans would have to decide the Allied response if such a Japanese proposal was received, although his own view was that 'some mitigation would be worthwhile if it led to the saving of a year or a year and a half in which so much blood and treasure would be poured out'. A frail Roosevelt agreed that the suggestion could be put to Stalin but thought the ultimatum was premature since the Japanese 'still seemed to think that they might get a satisfactory compromise'. More mass bombing of the Japanese home islands was necessary, said Roosevelt, before the Japanese would 'wake up to the true state of affairs'.[28]

Despite this discussion, most of the talking at Yalta was taken up with the fighting in Europe where Russian armies had made swift progress from the beginning of January, pushing the front line westward from Warsaw almost to within sight of Hitler's bunker in Berlin. While the Russian armies paused along the Oder River, gathering their strength for the decisive push at the German capital, Allied armies were shoving the demoralised Germans back across the Rhine. When the Pacific war was discussed, Churchill again supported Stalin's desire for the warm water port that the Russians had lost to the Japanese in 1905. In a secret agreement, Stalin promised to launch his Siberian army against the Japanese as soon as it could be organised after the defeat of Germany. This agreement was omitted from the official communiqué published at the conclusion of the conference on 9 February, with Churchill instructing also that there was 'no need whatever to inform the Dominions'.[29]

British strategy in the Pacific remained in a muddle. While the Admiralty was keen to be embroiled in the fighting, Churchill wanted to negotiate an end to the war before his Pacific fleet had a chance to show its mettle in operations alongside the Americans. Not that the Americans were keen to have the British alongside them, with Admiral King being particularly cool towards the British Pacific fleet and delaying a decision as to where it could operate. The Australians also were none too enthusiastic, restricting the amount of support they would provide for the fleet as they diverted resources to civilian pursuits and postwar reconstruction. Similarly, the British war cabinet was anxious about its manpower resources and steadily downgraded the priority of the Pacific war.

The British government had planned to switch 315 000 munition workers to civilian production during the first half of 1945. The prolongation of the war against Germany caused a cut in the number of munition workers available for civilian work, with the situation being exacerbated when the board of trade called for 375 000 additional workers in civilian industries to produce textiles, clothing, furniture, and house fittings, to begin the re-equipment of industry and to boost exports. While Churchill was away in Yalta, Sir John Anderson had warned the war cabinet of the 'grave difficulties' if these requirements were not met, calling for his colleagues to reconsider the whole manpower issue, 'including the strategic issues involved'.[30] The simple fact was that the greater the British effort in the Pacific, the fewer new houses could be built for returned service personnel, the less new clothes could be available for frustrated coupon-clutching customers and the less vigorous would be Britain's export drive to markets such as China, which had been starved of Western consumer goods. Not surprisingly, Cunningham reacted with dismay to the politicians' attempt to circumscribe the scope of his recently formed Pacific fleet. Fearing a hostile American action, he advised that it would be most unwise for Britain to restrict its operations against Japan just 'so as to release men for production of Civil goods to better the condition of the public'.[31] But there was an election in sight and Churchill had not been in the House of Commons for most of his adult life without learning the most basic of political lessons.

Once back in London, Churchill directed his war cabinet to give the civilian economy a 'considerable reinforcement', with the board of trade being allocated 275 000 additional workers for the first half of 1945. The manpower demands of the European war still retained the highest priority, but it was followed increasingly closely by the expansion of civil production. Although Churchill did not cut the level of forces allocated to the war against Japan, he did urge 'that there can be some delay in their build-up and equipment, including reserves'. Moreover, he instructed that older equipment, that otherwise might be scrapped, should be used against Japan rather than tie up manpower in the production of new equipment. Only equipment that was deemed essential was to be sent out to the Pacific, since the provision of equipment surplus to requirements was 'a luxury we cannot afford'.[32]

A fresh complication arose when new German submarines appeared in the Atlantic, threatening anew the British lifeline to the United States. It prompted the Admiralty to retain escort ships in European waters, which meant in turn that some of the aircraft carriers and battleships on their way to the Pacific had to be held back in the Indian Ocean until escort ships became available to protect them from Japanese submarines. Cunningham was so worried by the renewed German submarine offensive that he decided on 1 March to put the 'greatest effort into holding the U boats for the next 3 months', with everything being 'sacrificed to that object'.[33] In fact, the menace was not as dangerous as it seemed, but it came at the same time as German jet-powered aircraft appeared in the skies to challenge Allied air superiority and the longer range and more powerful V-2 rockets began a short-lived reign of terror on London. Even all together, they were little more than distractions on the road to Germany's imminent surrender.

While Britain's Pacific fleet faced further delays, the Americans remained coy about where it eventually might be deployed. America's Admiral Cooke, who had been at the Yalta conference in his new role as deputy director of naval operations, had gone on to Kandy to meet with Mountbatten, prompting him to request the use of the Pacific fleet for operations in the Indian Ocean. Mountbatten had experienced a succession of disappointments when promised reinforcements for his command had failed to materialise. With the latest manpower crisis in Britain likely to delay his operations against Burma and Malaya, he readily accepted Cooke's suggestion that the Pacific fleet be requested to return to take part in an attack on Phuket in Siam. As an exasperated Cunningham observed, Mountbatten was 'stupid enough' to cable this 'infuriating' suggestion to London, thereby 'allowing himself to be made a catspaw of to help the elements in the [US navy] who wish to prevent the [British] fleet operating in the Pacific'.[34] Cunningham and his fellow chiefs of staff were concerned that Churchill might fall for the American-inspired ploy and argued strongly against it while also pressing their American counterparts for a decision on the deployment of the fleet in the Pacific. But the Americans continued to temporise, with MacArthur wanting to retain it in his command for possible use against Borneo while Nimitz wanted to use it in the forthcoming invasion of Okinawa, the final stepping stone on the path to Japan.[35]

With the straight-talking Admiral Somerville having relinquished his command of the Eastern fleet to become the Admiralty representative in Washington, he was able to tackle King directly about the deployment of the British fleet and to press him for a quick decision.[36] In the meantime, Fraser, who had command of the British Pacific fleet, took his warships to the American-built facilities at Manus Island off the north coast of New Guinea, 'a dismal place' according to Fraser, where they waited in the tropical heat for news of their assignment. In early March, they returned to Sydney for two weeks, raising the morale of their sailors but straining the facilities of the harbour to the utmost. Still awaiting a decision, Fraser steamed his spruced-up ships back to Manus Island for more desultory battle practice. Finally, the fleet was assigned to Nimitz, with the ships being quickly deployed south-west of Okinawa to cover the upcoming American invasion, scheduled to be launched on Easter Sunday, 1 April 1945.[37] By this time, the Japanese fleet was all but destroyed, with the battleship strength of the combatants in the Pacific being 26 American and four British against six Japanese, while the strength in aircraft carriers was 25 American and six British against three Japanese. In terms of escort carriers, the Americans had 63 compared to just one Japanese.[38] Allied naval power was overwhelming.

With the Americans providing the preponderance of Allied forces in the Pacific, both Australia and Britain wanted only to exert the effort required to guarantee them a position of influence at the subsequent peace conference and to ensure the return of British colonies. To reduce the forces required to be sent from Britain, Churchill approved a plan to take the British aircrew from the Spitfire squadrons in Australia and attach them to Mountbatten's SEAC.[39] Meanwhile, the chiefs of staff pressed ahead with plans to establish a very long range (VLR) bombing force for use against Japan, with the chiefs appealing for Churchill's personal support to prevent it being 'elbowed out' by the Americans. To prevent the Americans using logistical problems as justification for delaying the deployment of the force, or even for excluding it altogether, the chiefs proposed to make it self-contained, with its own construction unit capable of creating an airfield on Luzon from where they wanted it to operate. It was hoped that the dominions, particularly Canada, would provide much of this force, with the chiefs asking Churchill to 'enlist Mr. Mackenzie King's interest and support'. When the Canadian prime minister's response was lukewarm, Churchill asked whether Britain could do without their assistance. Definitely not, replied the hard-pressed chiefs.[40] Australia was also reluctant to contribute to the VLR force, with Curtin making any contribution conditional on the return of Australian airmen from the European theatre. Instead of agreeing to that, Churchill reduced the planned size of the VLR force so that an additional Australian contribution was unnecessary, apart from two bomber squadrons and one transport squadron that would be based in Britain and available to support the proposed VLR force if required. In the event, the formation of the force would be pre-empted by the unexpectedly early Japanese surrender.[41]

The saga of the VLR force was another sign of Britain's reluctance to fulfil Churchill's earlier promises to send all its available strength against Japan once Germany was defeated. This reluctance was due in part to its waning power, but also to a changing view of the empire, with it being seen more as a liability than an asset. Even when Germany had been defeated, the burden of British commitments around the world, as it reoccupied its colonies and reasserted its power in areas such as the Middle East, was more than some ministers believed Britain was capable of bearing. This was particularly so when devastated British cities were competing for both labour and resources. In a report to the war cabinet on 20 March, Attlee called for the internationalisation of the Suez Canal and for the United States to help shoulder the defence burden in the Mediterranean. 'The time has gone,' Attlee argued, 'when Great Britain could afford to police the seas of the world for the benefit of others.' In Attlee's view, the empire had become an albatross around the neck of the struggling British taxpayer.[42] Rather than underpinning Britain's future prosperity, it was threatening to drain the country of its remaining wealth. This view affected the British government's attitude towards the Pacific war, since Britain's participation in that distant conflict was motivated largely by a desire to recapture its colonies.

As for the European war, it had seemed in the wake of the Ardennes offensive to be set to continue until the end of 1945 but now was expected to end by 31 May 1945. On 3 March, Churchill had visited his armies on the western front, where he had urinated on the concrete fortifications of the supposedly impregnable Siegfried Line that was built to keep the Allies out of Germany. With German defences collapsing, he returned three weeks later to do the same thing in the Rhine where a massive offensive by Montgomery had thrown his forces across that broad river and into the industrial heartland of the Ruhr.[43] While the quick march of the Allied armies into Germany might have been expected to free some of these forces for use against Japan, it seemed to have the opposite effect, particularly as the Pacific war was also expected to end sooner than had been anticipated. Two days after Attlee's report was submitted, the production minister, Oliver Lyttelton, urged Churchill to set a limit to the forces Britain planned to deploy against Japan. Lyttelton wanted to reduce the British forces to token proportions so that Britain could more quickly 'raise our standards in this country and regain our exports'. He suggested that Churchill remind the chiefs when planning their Pacific forces that the British contribution was only being done 'for potent political reasons', with the Americans already enjoying a 'dominating strength' against the Japanese and the war not expected to last more than twelve months after victory had been achieved in Europe.[44]

The ranking of British priorities was seen in the planned allocation of personnel shipping once Germany was defeated. On 24 March, Attlee set out what these priorities would be. Despite British agreement at Yalta that 'forces should be reoriented from the European theatre to the Pacific and Far East as a matter of highest priority', the top priority was shared between the demobilisation of British troops in Europe, the return of service personnel on leave after extended duty, the return of British Commonwealth prisoners of war, and shipping movements in support of approved Pacific operations. Second priority was given to moves for approved operations in SEAC and the return of dominion personnel for the war against Japan.[45] The prescription of Attlee and Lyttelton would ensure that little more than a token British effort would be mounted in the Pacific. To make certain of this, Churchill issued a directive on 14 April stipulating that it was of 'the utmost importance that releases from all three Services should begin not more than six weeks after the end of the German war' and that forces to be deployed against Japan 'should be related strictly to what can be brought into action in time to play a part with the assumed duration of the Japanese war'.[46]

With that settled, Churchill backed a plan to provide extra shipping to move 520 000 tons of animal foodstuffs from Argentina to Britain. The ships would bring an additional 75 000 tons of pork or bacon and 500 million eggs for the British breakfast table during 1946, with Churchill wanting the shipments to begin as soon as the European war ended. The plan was approved by the war cabinet despite objections that it would interfere with shipping movements for the war against Japan. As the historian Arthur Bryant later observed, the Pacific war 'had brought America into the fight and so ensured ultimate victory [but] had been for Britain only a consequential, though agonizing, incident in the long German war'.[47]

One of the worst moments during this 'agonizing incident' in the Pacific occurred on 1 April 1945 when more than one hundred thousand American troops stormed ashore on Okinawa, bringing them for the first time onto Japanese soil. During the three-month campaign that followed, the Americans blasted their way along the hundred-kilometre-long island, brandishing flamethrowers against the deeply dug defences while Japanese pilots hurtled their planes in desperation against the supporting warships offshore. The American attack provoked the Japanese navy to send out its giant battleship *Yamato*, which had survived the earlier naval battle in the Philippines, in a suicidal attempt to scatter the predominantly American fleet. It was sunk without ceremony but with great loss of life. Much to the relief of Admiral Cunningham in London, the British aircraft carrier *Indefatigable* was hit by the Japanese defenders during the invasion. While regretting the British casualties, he was 'glad that they have had some opposition'. As one of the British naval officers in the Pacific observed of his government's contribution to that war: 'It's well called the British "POLITICAL" Fleet.'[48] Meanwhile, in Tokyo the 'peace party' of Admiral Suzuki took power, although the new cabinet could see no easy or honourable way to end the war. There was little time left for negotiation.

NOTES

[1] Liddell Hart, *History of the Second World War*, pp. 593, 669.

[2] R. Rhodes, *The Making of the Atomic Bomb*, London, 1988, p. 560.

[3] Robertson, *Australia at War*, p. 174.

[4] In early October 1944, Curtin had expressed his disappointment to the acting British high commissioner in Canberra at the lack of any British naval component in the American attack on the Philippines. In this and other instances, Curtin was forever reminding London of the need to restore the prestige of the British empire in Asia and the Pacific. Cable, Acting High Commissioner to Dominions Office, 3 October 1944, PREM 3/164/6, PRO.

[5] Letter, Curtin to Hankinson, 7 September 1944, and Letter, Strahan to Hankinson, 14 September 1944, CRS A1608/S41/1/9 Pt 1, NAA.

[6] Letters, Shedden to MacArthur, 15 and 27 February 1945, CRS A5954, Box 75, NAA.

[7] Horner, *Defence Supremo*, p. 218.

[8] Discussion with General MacArthur, Tokyo, May 1946, CRS A5954, Box 3, NAA.

[9] Speech by Curtin, 22 February 1945, CRS A5954, Box 1605, NAA.

[10] Letters, Mountbatten to Murdoch, 26 June 1944, Murdoch to Mountbatten, 24 July 1944, and Mountbatten to Murdoch, 2 September 1944, MS 2823/44, Murdoch Papers, NLA.

[11] Minutes, Hollis to Churchill, 20 February and 6 March 1945, PREM 3/53/14, PRO.

[12] Minutes, Churchill to Ismay, 7 and 10 March 1945, and Ismay to Churchill, 9 March 1945, PREM 3/53/14, PRO.

[13] Cunningham diary, 13 December 1944, ADD. MS. 52577, Cunningham Papers, BL.

[14] Note by Anderson with memorandum by Keynes, 3 April 1945, CAB 66/65, W.P. (45)301, PRO.

[15] Submission by W. J. Scully, 30 January 1945, CRS A2700/14/1/794, NAA; See also Cable, Bruce to Forde, 25 May 1945, CRS M100, 'May 1945', NAA; Memorandum by Minister of Food, 11 June 1945, CAB 66/66, C.P. (45)29, PRO.

[16] Smith, *Task Force 57*, p. 108.

[17] Shedden's memoirs, Chap. 52, p. 8, CRS A5954, Box 771, Note by Shedden, 15 November 1944, CRS A5954, Box 309, and documents in CRS A5954, Box 306, NAA.

[18] Curtin had explained Australia's manpower problem during his visit to London in May 1944, but Bruce was still having to explain it to the Admiralty six months later. See Cable, Bruce to Curtin, 27 November 1944, CRS M100, 'November 1944', NAA.

[19] A. Bullock, *Ernest Bevin*, Oxford, 1985, p. 294.

[20] Report by Keynes and Sinclair, 2 February 1945, CAB 66/61, W.P. (45)77, PRO.

[21] Letter, Cunningham to Fraser, 19 January 1945, ADD. MS. 52572, Cunningham diary, 22 January 1945, ADD. MS. 52578, and Letter, Cunningham to Power, 23 January 1945, ADD. MS. 52562, Cunningham Papers, BL.

[22] Minute, Cherwell to Churchill, 22 January 1945, PREM 3/164/5; Minutes, Brooke to Churchill, 19 January 1945, and Churchill to Brooke, 21 January 1945, PREM 3/63/7, PRO; Cunningham diary, 26 January 1945, ADD. MS. 52578, Cunningham Papers, BL.

[23] Cable, Bruce to Curtin, 26 January 1945, CRS M100, 'January 1945', NAA; J. C. W. Reith, *Into the Wind*, London, 1949, p. 505.

[24] Gilbert, *Road to Victory*, p. 1162.

[25] CCS 184th Meeting, 1 February 1945, PREM 3/51/8, PRO.

[26] Minutes of First Plenary Session, 2 February 1945, PREM 3/51/4, PRO.

[27] See, Cunningham diary, 28 December 1944, ADD. MS. 52577, Cunningham Papers, BL; Note by Officer, 24 February 1945, MS 2629/1, Officer Papers, NLA; A. Shai, *Britain and China, 1941–47*, Oxford, 1984; Thorne, *Allies of a Kind*, Chap. 26.

[28] Minutes of Second Plenary Session, 9 February 1945, PREM 3/51/4, PRO.

[29] Gilbert, *Road to Victory*, p. 1207; Minute, Ismay to Churchill, 25 February 1945, PREM 3/51/10, PRO.

[30] Memorandum by Anderson, 12 February 1945, CAB 66/61, W.P. (45)87, PRO.

[31] Cunningham diary, 23 February 1945, ADD. MS. 52578, Cunningham Papers, BL.

[32] Directive by Churchill, 26 February 1945, CAB 66/62, W.P. (45)117, PRO.

[33] Cunningham diary, 1 March 1945, ADD. MS. 52578, Cunningham Papers, BL.

[34] For delays to Mountbatten's plans in February 1945, see PREM 3/149/3, PRO; Letters, Power to Cunningham, 1 March 1945 and Cunningham to Power, 13 March 1945, ADD. MS. 52562; Cunningham diary, 6 March 1945, ADD. MS. 52578, Cunningham Papers, BL; Mountbatten diary, 17 February 1945, in P. Ziegler (ed.), *Personal Diary of Admiral the Lord Louis Mountbatten 1943–1946*, London, 1988, p. 182.

[35] Cable, Chiefs of Staff to Joint Staff Mission, 7 March 1945, and Minute, Ismay to Churchill, 7 March 1945, PREM 3/149/3, PRO; Somerville journal, 28 February and 7 March 1945, SMVL 2/3, Somerville Papers, CC; Gill, *Royal Australian Navy 1942–1945*, pp. 616–7; Minute, Ismay to Churchill, 7 March 1945, PREM 3/164/6, PRO.

[36] Cable, Somerville to Cunningham, 9 March 1945, PREM 3/164/6, PRO.

[37] Letter, Fraser to Cunningham, 14 March 1945, ADD. MS. 52572, Cunningham Papers, BL.

[38] Advisory War Council Minutes, 7 March 1945, CRS A2682/8/988, NAA.

[39] Minute, Sinclair to Churchill, 27 February 1945, PREM 3/150/9, PRO; Cable, Cranborne to Commonwealth Government, 20 April 1945, CRS A5954, Box 231, NAA.

[40] Memorandum, Chiefs of Staff to Churchill, 19 March 1945, and other documents in PREM 3/142/5, PRO; See also Cunningham diary, 19 March 1945, ADD. MS. 52578, Cunningham Papers, BL.

[41] Cable, Curtin to Churchill, 23 March 1945, and Cable, Churchill to Curtin, 20 April 1945, PREM 3/63/8, PRO.

[42] Report by Attlee, 20 March 1945, CAB 66/63, W.P. (45)197, PRO.

[43] Alanbrooke diary, 3 and 26 March 1945, in Danchev and Todman (eds), *War Diaries*, pp. 667–8, 677–8.

[44] Minute, Lyttelton to Churchill, 22 March 1945, and other documents in PREM 3/159/14, PRO.

[45] Memorandum by Attlee, 24 March 1945, CAB 66/63, W.P. (45)192, PRO.

[46] Directive by Churchill, 14 April 1945, CAB 66/64, W.P. (45)250, PRO.

[47] Note by Churchill, 16 April 1945, CAB 66/65, W.P. (45)252, PRO; Bryant, *Triumph in the West*, p. 460.

[48] Cunningham diary, 3 April 1945, ADD. MS. 52578, Cunningham Papers, BL; Edwards diary, 21 April 1945, REDW 1/7, Edwards Papers, CC.

FORTY-SIX

'the most frightful man in the world'

The American invasion of Okinawa in April 1945 revealed the terrible price that would have to be paid during the invasion of the Japanese main islands. About 12 000 American troops and other personnel were killed in the fighting for Okinawa, while 150 000 Japanese perished. Estimated casualties for the invasion of the Japanese island of Kyushu were in the order of 250 000 American dead and wounded. And that was just the first of the Japanese islands that the Allies would have to conquer. MacArthur, who was appointed to command army forces throughout most of the Pacific and ordered to plan the conquest of Japan proper, confided to a visiting British intelligence officer that the 'chances of the Japs packing up was 50/50' but he wanted 'to kill some more first'. That meant more of his own troops would also be killed. According to MacArthur, his 'troops had not yet met the Japanese Army properly, and that when they did they were going to take heavy casualties'.[1]

From the island of Guam, American bombers continued their deadly flights over Japanese cities. In one late-night raid on Tokyo on 9 March, more than fifty square kilometres of buildings were destroyed by the combination of napalm and high explosives; at least eighty thousand people were killed and perhaps as many as two hundred thousand in the resulting firestorm. Three hundred thousand houses, built of paper and wood, were consumed in the fires. 'We knew we were going to kill a lot of women and kids when we burned [a] town,' wrote the American air force commander, Curtis LeMay, but it 'had to be done'.[2] Similar justifications for horrendous war crimes would be rejected out of hand by the victorious Allies during trials at Nuremberg and Tokyo.

One of the most notorious bombing raids against Germany occurred on 13 February 1945 when the largely untouched city of Dresden was subjected to area bombing with incendiaries. The attack had no strategic significance and was intended simply to spread death and terror among the civilian population, many of whom were refugees who had fled to Dresden in the face of the oncoming Russians or from other towns and cities destroyed by bombing. Although he later tried to escape responsibility for it, the merciless attack was launched on Churchill's command, partly to impress the Russians who were close to capturing the city. Before they took off, the bomber crews were told that the attack was 'to show the Russians when they arrive what Bomber Command can do'. The incendiaries set off a firestorm that laid waste the city and incinerated as many as one hundred thousand men, women and children. The name of the city became a byword for infamy in a war where the mass killing of civilians had become the airmen's lot. Germany was too punch-drunk to notice the destruction of Dresden, although public opinion in Allied countries shrank from the horror of it all once the details leaked out.[3] It had all been so unnecessary, since Allied armies were close to achieving victory on land. By mid-April, Vienna had been occupied by the Russians while the British and Americans had crossed the Rhine and were streaming across Germany almost unopposed. Hitler's instructions to torch the countryside in front of the Allied armies was ignored by his demoralised and defeated subordinates.

After three years of desultory activity in Burma, the British and Indian forces of General Slim were rolling remorselessly towards Rangoon from the north, hoping to get there before the onset of the monsoon bogged their advance. Although they wanted to enter the city as triumphant vanquishers, they were pre-empted at the last moment by a combined amphibious and airborne operation on 1 May that took control of the undefended city before linking up with the advance elements of Slim's army. Burma became a killing field where thousands of straggling Japanese soldiers perished, many from starvation. Across in Bougainville, Australian troops took no prisoners as they continued the offensive strategy that Blamey justified as being necessary to restore Australia's image in the eyes of the native peoples.[4] Meanwhile, the key to Japan's surrender was being fashioned in New Mexico, with the question of using the new weapon falling to the newly elected vice president, Harry Truman, who took over as president after Roosevelt succumbed to a massive stroke on 12 April. News of the atomic bomb had been kept from Truman till then, but he was now informed in guarded terms of this 'explosive great enough to destroy the whole world' which might give Washington the power to 'dictate our own terms at the end of the war'.[5]

Curtin, whose own hold on life was ebbing, paid tribute to the dead president, telling parliament that the president's passing had 'lessened to some degree ... mankind's hopes of a better day'. Ever since his return to Canberra in January, Curtin had lacked the strength to provide the vigorous leadership that the nation required for the coming transition to peace. But he stubbornly held on to power, believing that Labor MPs were akin to 'standard bearers in a holy war [who] must go on to the end and not yield while life is left to us'. Even when the press raised questions about his health and predicted his resignation, the increasingly testy Curtin, who had given up his heavy smoking, refused to admit to his condition.[6] It caused a state of partial paralysis in Canberra, with decisions being constantly delayed by having to be referred to a prime minister who had lost the resolution to lead. The frustrated and distraught Chifley, who had served as Curtin's closest adviser and confidant, described that time as 'the worst six months' of his life.[7] And it only got worse when Curtin was taken off to hospital in late April with congestion of the lungs.

Among the issues waiting to be addressed were the shape of the United Nations Organisation, the future of colonial territories and the peace settlement in the Pacific. Evatt had already convinced the war cabinet in January to limit Australia's contribution to the Allied control commission to govern postwar Germany to just ten officers. As he pointed out, the Australian government had not been consulted on the organisation of the commission or on the treatment of Germany, and the Australians would only serve as part of the British contingent.[8] As for the United Nations, Australia was in a relatively strong position in the discussions with London, since Britain was keen to have the support of its dominions in the many matters that would have to be thrashed out during the establishment of the organisation. Consultation was suddenly *de rigueur* in Whitehall, with Cranborne urging his ministerial colleagues to have the 'closest liaison' with the dominions. He accepted a South African suggestion for a meeting of Commonwealth representatives prior to the international conference and warned his colleagues to be prepared to modify British policy as a result of the Commonwealth discussions.[9]

The Commonwealth talks took place in London at the beginning of April, with the delegates being confronted with two main problems. One concerned the voting procedure in the proposed security council of the United Nations, which Britain wanted to restrict just to the 'Great Powers', whereas the dominions wanted it opened to representatives of all the powers. The second matter concerned the future of colonial territories and the power of the United Nations to interfere in their administration, with Britain keen to prevent such interference with its colonial administration. Australia's view on these issues was put by Evatt and Frank Forde, Curtin's loyal but ineffectual deputy. Curtin had not clarified which of the two was meant to be leading the delegation, with Evatt and Forde still bickering about it when they landed in London at the beginning of April. Instead of asking Curtin for direction, they effectively appealed to Bruce to adjudicate on the issue, with Bruce recording how Evatt apologised for his 'discourteous' behaviour during his previous visit and now claimed that he 'had found all my telegrams useful; entirely agreed with my point of view and especially appreciated my frankness with regard to the Colonial question'. Forde arrived next at the high commissioner's office to complain that Evatt was trying to usurp his position as the ranking minister of the delegation. Although having little respect for Evatt's character, Bruce acknowledged his ability compared to Forde, who he dismissed as 'a decent little man without any very great capacity'. Accordingly, he advised Forde 'very strongly not to attempt, in order to maintain his position as leader, to take on jobs that Evatt was more fitted to do'.[10]

The British government was dragged into the dispute when Evatt raised the matter with Cranborne, with the dominions secretary telling Evatt diplomatically that Forde's position as deputy prime minister meant that he had to be treated as the delegation leader until Curtin instructed otherwise. Knowing that Curtin would not support him, Evatt again appealed to Bruce for his backing, pledging 'all the support and assistance of himself and the Australian Government' in any campaign Bruce might be contemplating to secure a post in the United Nations.[11] Although Bruce had certainly been considering such a move when his high commissionership came to an end, he realised that Evatt could not be relied upon to support him in any campaign to get it. Anyway, he would hardly go against the wishes of Curtin, who was responsible for his prolonged tenure in London. So the issue of seniority continued to dog the discussions in London and would prove even more divisive during the subsequent conference in San Francisco. Nevertheless, it did not prevent Evatt from ensuring that the London meeting would produce a meaningful discussion of the differences that existed between the dominions, with Evatt clarifying in his own mind the way in which he wanted the United Nations to develop. According to Paul Hasluck, who was part of Evatt's team in London, the British government was left in no doubt that it would face at San Francisco 'a very determined, able and non-compliant Australian delegate'.[12]

During the London discussions, Evatt pursued some of the issues that he considered to be vital to Australia's future as an independent 'middle' power rather than as a subservient member of the British empire. He was determined to break the great power monopoly over international decision making that had so frustrated him during the war and which he regarded as a future threat to peace. He succeeded in diluting the proposed veto power of the great powers which, under the draft plan, would prevent any changes to the United Nations charter that did not have their unanimous approval. Such a provision could cripple the organisation's ability to act and would certainly diminish the influence of smaller countries.[13] But the most heated discussions in London concerned the issue of international trusteeship for colonies, with Evatt being determined to have such a system enshrined as part of the role of the United Nations.

The British government had wanted discussion of colonial policy to be excluded from the agenda of the San Francisco conference, anticipating the hostility of the smaller powers. When that proved impossible, it sought to restrict discussion to those territories held under mandate from the defunct League of Nations, whose sovereignty now needed to be regularised under the aegis of the United Nations. On the eve of the London meeting on 4 April, there was a wide-ranging discussion of the issue within the British war cabinet, with the view of the Colonial Office prevailing. The war cabinet agreed that the United Nations should take over the prewar system of colonial mandates but the mandate system should not be extended to include other colonial territories although they 'might voluntarily be placed under trusteeship'. And such voluntary placement of territories into trusteeship could only be done by the imperial power rather than at the request of the colonial people. In other words, India could not be placed under United Nations trusteeship at the request of the Indians, only at the behest of the British. To further protect the British hold over India, the war cabinet decided to oppose any move by Australia to have the United Nations charter guarantee the political independence of its members.[14]

With its colonial secretary sick with mumps, and Eden staying away from the meeting, it was left to the permanent secretary of the Foreign Office, Sir Alexander Cadogan, to put much of the British case to the dominion representatives. As Cadogan wrote in his diary, he was 'left to face the music, which was unharmoniously played by [New Zealand prime minister Peter] Fraser and Evatt', who both rejected the British position. Cadogan haughtily confided to his diary that he could not decide 'whether Evatt and Fraser are more stupid than offensive'. The historian W. Roger Louis claimed that Evatt 'plunged into the sea of the trusteeship controversy like a hungry shark', devouring the self-interested arguments of Whitehall with a sharp legal and historical mind that established the basis for his later stand at San Francisco. Doubtless, it was sweet revenge for Evatt after Curtin had given his imprimatur to British colonial policy during his visit to London in 1944 without consulting with his Australian colleagues.[15]

Evatt's stand on trusteeship was motivated by the usual political mix of idealism and pragmatism. On the one hand, he wanted to advance the position of native peoples through the establishment of a system of international inspection, while also hastening the eventual dissolution of European empires. At the same time, he was conscious that Australia's regional interests and ambitions would be advanced by breaking down the old imperial barriers to trade and investment. Moreover, if the European powers' grip on their colonies could be loosened, their status as great powers would be less secure and Australia's standing as a middle power made that much stronger.[16] In pushing his views on trusteeship, Evatt seems to have been partly influenced by position papers developed within the British Labour Party during 1944, one of which had called for a system of colonial trusteeship along the lines that Evatt later supported at San Francisco. Since the Labour Party was expected to form Britain's postwar government, Evatt would have felt that he was part of a wider consensus on this and other issues. In fact, Labour leader Clem Attlee would later describe the proponents of trusteeship as people 'whose views were based on admirable sentiments but great lack of practical knowledge of actual conditions'.[17]

Britain was determined to retrieve its own colonies and saw the return of colonies to the other European powers as being essential to ensuring that it could achieve this in the face of possible American opposition. Accordingly, the chiefs of staff acknowledged in April 1945 that the early return of French and Dutch forces to the Far East was 'both militarily and politically advantageous'.[18] To ease the way of the French, Britain opposed the entry of Chinese forces into French Indo-China for fear that it would 'encourage false ideas of expansion and martial glory'. Instead, Japanese-occupied Indo-China was kept firmly within Mountbatten's command so that it could be handed back at the end of the war to the French. This would, in turn, help legitimise the British return to Malaya and Hong Kong while also having positive ramifications in Europe where, as the Foreign Office reminded Churchill, 'France is our nearest neighbour and we have a vital interest in her restoration as a strong and friendly power'.[19]

Churchill needed little reminding about that, or about the restoration of Britain's own colonies, which he was adamant must be returned. He rejected

pressure from Roosevelt to agree to independence for India and he insisted
on the return of Hong Kong to British control. When Roosevelt's
representative in China, General Hurley, visited London on 11 April,
Churchill brushed aside his 'civil banalities' and told him bluntly about
Hong Kong that 'never would we yield an inch of the territory that was
under the British Flag'.[20] His trenchant comments came in the wake of a war
cabinet meeting that had discussed the ways in which Britain might
circumvent the pressure from the Australian and New Zealand delegates at
the London conference in favour of voluntary trusteeship, by which imperial
powers would agree to place their colonies under international supervision.
Australia argued for this so that it could ensure colonies such as Portuguese
Timor were adequately defended and avoid a repetition of 1942. It would
also 'improve the conditions of backward peoples and aid them along the
road to self-government'. However, Britain would have none of it, with
Cranborne arguing that 'there can be no question of our agreeing to place
any of our Colonial territories other than those at present administered
under mandate under any form of trusteeship'.[21]

Nevertheless, to appease the dominion delegates at the London meeting,
Cranborne convinced his colleagues not to block the concept of voluntary
trusteeship, while making it clear that Britain would not be volunteering any
of its own colonies. As Churchill observed, they could leave it to the French
and Dutch, who could be counted upon to oppose this attempt to interfere
in the running of their colonies. It would not be that easy. When the British
attitude was relayed to the dominion delegates, Evatt declared that it would
be 'better for the United Kingdom Government not to accept the principle of
trusteeship at all than to accept and refuse to apply it to their own
territories'.[22] The stage was set for a confrontation at San Francisco.

The conference at San Francisco opened two weeks later, with Evatt
leading the fight for colonial trusteeship. On the opposite side was
Cranborne, who led the British team and who hoped to have the discussions
dispensed with in a month, despite objections from Evatt who, according to
a cynical Cranborne, was 'violently opposed to any limitations ... because it
will curtail his opportunities of shining on the World Stage'.[23] As it
happened, the conference lasted two months, during which time Evatt

orchestrated a frenzied campaign to promote trusteeship, to the great frustration of the British delegation. After a month of dealing with Evatt at San Francisco, Cadogan bitterly described him 'as the most frightful man in the world [who] makes long and tiresome speeches on every conceivable subject, always advocating the wrong thing and generally with a view to being inconvenient and offensive to us, and boosting himself'. Cadogan claimed that 'everyone by now hates Evatt so much that his stock has gone down a bit and he matters less'.[24] Certainly the British and Americans resented Evatt's tactics enormously, but the resentment was largely a sign of his success, with Britain and the United States being forced to compromise much more than they wished on the issue of trusteeship. In the wake of Roosevelt's death, Washington had moderated its objections to colonialism, while also being keener to retain a string of captured Pacific islands for strategic purposes after the war. The US Congress was reluctant to relinquish island territories over which so much American blood had been spilled. So Britain and the United States formed an unlikely alliance against the rest of the Commonwealth. As Cranborne confided to a colleague, the American 'house has in fact come to have so much glass in its constructions that they cannot afford to throw stones at others'.[25]

The eventual compromise created a new category of colony that combined security with trusteeship and left the United States with its newly won bases across the Pacific. Churchill was happy to concede US control over islands whose sovereignty Britain and America had fiercely contested prior to the war. It suited Britain for the United States to continue as a fellow imperial power and be less able to adopt the moral high ground on colonies, as Roosevelt had been doing during the war with his promise to give independence to the Philippines. The American bases across the Pacific would also help to protect the adjacent British colonies.[26] The system would see Britain concede partial sovereignty over its territories, with the trusteeship council of the United Nations being able to inspect colonies and report on whether the controlling powers were fulfilling their international obligations. The council would also provide a forum to which the native peoples could appeal against injustices by the imperial power. Although this was a diluted version of Evatt's proposal, it marked a watershed in the history of decolonisation, acknowledging the changes that had taken place during the war and preparing for the gradual extinction of western empires, at least in the formal sense.

The conference at San Francisco was conducted against the background of Germany's collapse. On 25 April, the day the conference opened, Russian forces completed their encircling of Berlin. Five days later, Hitler was dead by his own hand. As his body burned in the rubble, German soldiers continued their useless defence of the shattered capital, fighting street by street as their generals sought to surrender. On 2 May, the guns of the German army fell silent on the Italian front. With American and British armies streaming across western Germany in a triumphant and largely unopposed procession towards Berlin, the remaining German armies quickly followed suit. The torture of the continent was finally brought to an end at midnight on 8 May.

In the Pacific, the embattled Japanese garrisons in the caves and tunnels of their island fortresses put up an equally futile but more stubborn resistance. Although MacArthur wanted to kill more Japanese before accepting their surrender, and was planning a massive invasion of the plain around Tokyo, the planners and the politicians in Washington were counting the likely cost in American dead of such a hard-fought campaign. There was also an increasing American desire to transform a defeated Japan into a bulwark against Russian expansion. Like Britain off the coast of Europe, it was hoped that Japan could act as a virtual American aircraft carrier off the coast of Asia. Britain too was keen to see a quick end to the Pacific war, so that it could set about unimpeded on the rehabilitation of its bomb-damaged cities and the restoration of its factories to civilian purposes. With the likely end of the Pacific war being brought forward, Churchill was adamant that Britain's contribution to the war must be as limited as possible. When his chiefs of staff asked at the beginning of May for shipping to transport the requirements of the VLR bomber force to the Pacific, Churchill resisted their pressure and berated their grandiose plans for the far-off war. This was 'the real evil we have to face', thundered Churchill, predicting that the world would be 'strangled in its development by demands for the war on Japan which have absolutely no relation to the number of warships or troops or aircraft which can be engaged there'.[27]

When the chiefs of staff persisted, Churchill relented and referred the question to his minister for war transport, Lord Leathers. Churchill reminded Leathers of Britain's pledge to participate in the bombing of Japan 'to the utmost limit which the bases will allow' and suggested that the end of the European war should now provide 'sufficient easement to enable us to implement our undertaking to bomb Japan'. Leathers grudgingly conceded that it might be possible to provide cargo shipping for the VLR force while still increasing imports into Britain during the first half of 1946.[28] Of course, the VLR force was a long way short of Churchill's pledge to transfer to the Pacific all the force that Britain could muster. It was a pledge that was repeated by his high commissioner in Canberra, Sir Ronald Cross, in a broadcast to mark the end of the European war. Cross told his Australian wireless audience that Britain had 'heavy scores to settle with the Japanese', with its participation in the Pacific war having 'priority over all other interests' and claiming that Britain would 'employ every man, every gun, ship and aeroplane that can be used in this business'.[29] In fact, its participation in the Pacific remained well below the demands of demobilisation and reconstruction in the list of Britain's priorities.

When the Admiralty asked for an increase in the fleet train to allow its Pacific fleet to operate away from Sydney for longer periods, thereby avoiding American criticism and maintaining 'Imperial prestige', Lord Cherwell counselled Churchill to oppose it for fear of worsening the shortfall in imports. The British people were already 'short of coal and clothing', argued Cherwell, and 'cannot be asked to face further cuts in food, building materials, etc' even if that meant restricting the operations of the fleet.[30] The matter was brought before the cabinet on 5 June, with the all-party war cabinet having ceased to operate with the end of the European war and the calling of a general election. Churchill and his Conservative colleagues were firmly in charge and mindful of the coming election, with Churchill now declaring that 'full consideration must be given to the United Kingdom import programme and the demands of the civil population in this country'.[31]

With the government restricting its resources, Japan collapsing faster than anticipated and Britain's aims being divided between the Indian and Pacific

Oceans, Whitehall remained undecided about the main thrust of the limited British effort. After the surprising defeat of the Japanese in Burma, one option was to concentrate on Mountbatten's command, with his planners reassessing their timetable after the sudden fall of Rangoon and Mountbatten pressing for the use of the Pacific fleet to support his operations.[32] A second option was to recapture Borneo and the Netherlands East Indies, while the third option was to join the American onslaught against the Japanese home islands. All these options could be pursued simultaneously, but it would dissipate the British effort and give an impression of British weakness everywhere. One option had to prevail if Britain was to achieve the desired political effect.

The army chief, Field Marshal Brooke, wanted to concentrate on Malaya using mainly Australian and Indian troops, while both the Admiralty and the air force wanted to fight with the Americans against Japan itself. As Admiral Cunningham argued, Britain would have difficulty taking a 'prominent part in the Eastern settlements if we have devoted ourselves solely to mopping up operations'. While the Americans were opposed to the British mounting any operations in SEAC that might detract from the main effort against Japan, they agreed on 12 May that an invasion of Malaya, preparatory to an attack on Singapore, could be mounted so long as it did not prejudice operations in the Pacific. With American approval, the chiefs brought forward the Malayan operation to mid-August, hoping to recapture Singapore before the Japanese surrender.[33]

Although Britain was relying on the use of dominion and Indian forces to fulfil its aims in the Far East, Eden was offered an additional option by the Americans, with General Marshall advising that German prisoners were volunteering to help fight the Japanese. Marshall tentatively suggested that the Germans could clear various passed-over Pacific islands, 'letting them and the Japanese kill each other there'. Eden assured Marshall that he was 'not shocked by the proposal'. Indeed, the war cabinet had already considered a proposal to use sixty thousand German prisoners for labour purposes in the war against Japan.[34] Anything would be considered to help alleviate the manpower problem and hasten the return by Britain to peacetime pursuits. And nothing would be allowed to force Britain into making a larger contribution to the Pacific war than was absolutely necessary. It was presumably for this reason that Churchill continued with his trenchant opposition to any early meeting between Mountbatten and MacArthur, particularly if it was to be held in the glare of press publicity in Australia.

The meeting had been on Mountbatten's agenda for a year, but Churchill had always managed to prevent it occurring. Cross was apparently unaware that the visit was off and advised London in April that Canberra should not be omitted from Mountbatten's itinerary, for fear of giving the impression that Australia was not being consulted about military operations in their region, particularly as they envisaged using Australian forces. The Duke of Gloucester mounted similar arguments through Buckingham Palace in June 1945, urging that Mountbatten should have talks with Curtin, the advisory war council and the Australian press.[35] Although there were no longer any operational reasons preventing Mountbatten's absence from his headquarters at Kandy, Churchill still insisted that any meeting with MacArthur be as brief as possible and that it not be held in Australia. This might have prevented it occurring yet again had Ismay not seized upon Churchill's conditional approval and pointed out that MacArthur's headquarters had shifted recently to the Philippines. Ismay also revealed that Mountbatten wanted to visit London as well, for consultations after the defeat of Germany. His presence would remind British voters of the distant battles that still had to be fought against Japan and the further privation that still had to be faced. This was the last thing that Churchill wanted in the flush of European victory and in the midst of an election campaign. Attuned to Churchill's concerns, Ismay suggested that Mountbatten be allowed to visit MacArthur in the Philippines in late June provided that he did 'not go on to Australia, or give Press conferences anywhere' and that he be kept out of Britain until after the election. 'Yes, exactly,' Churchill scribbled.[36]

A further factor restraining the use of British forces against Japan was the increasing concern, particularly by Churchill, at the possible power vacuum created by any hasty withdrawal of Allied forces from Europe. With Russian armies spread across eastern Europe, and Anglo–American armies melting away, Churchill feared that Stalin might try to assert his dominance over western Europe as well.[37] Although Churchill was sanguine about Russian expansion in the Pacific, its expansion in Europe was another matter. The planners were instructed to assess how Britain could resist militarily any undue demands put by the Russians in Germany, while Churchill appealed to President Truman on 12 May to retain American troops in Europe until they had reached an understanding with Stalin on the status of Yugoslavia, Austria and Poland. Warning of another bloodbath if these issues were not settled before the withdrawal of the Anglo–American armies, Churchill conjured up the spectre of an 'iron curtain' being drawn across the Russian front.[38] It was an image that he had borrowed from the Nazi propagandist Joseph Goebbels and which Churchill would later use publicly to great effect.[39]

Churchill's war strategy had relied upon the Russians shouldering the main burden of the fighting. After they had suffered tens of millions of casualties doing so, the Russians now wanted their share of the spoils. Churchill should not have been as surprised as he claimed to be at seeing the 'Russian bear sprawled over Europe'. With the European war over for less than a week, an appalled Brooke was concerned that Churchill was 'already longing for another war! Even if it entailed fighting Russia!' Churchill asked Brooke to examine how they might be able to force the Russian army back to Russia prior to the demobilisation of the British and American armies. Brooke rightly judged the whole idea 'fantastic and the chances of success quite impossible'. Britain would just have to accept that 'from now onwards Russia is all powerful in Europe'. That was something that Churchill was not prepared to accept. After fighting the European war to a finish at the cost of about thirty million dead, Churchill seemed to suggest that it had all been for nothing, telling his cabinet on 11 June that 'never in his life had he been more worried by the European situation'. He warned that the Russians 'had a 2 to 1 land superiority over our forces' and 'any time that it took their fancy they could march across the rest of Europe and drive us back into our island'.[40]

As a result of Churchill's concern, Truman agreed to their early meeting with Stalin at Potsdam in July to settle the outstanding problems of Europe. Meanwhile, the withdrawal went on as planned, with American personnel in Europe being scheduled to be reduced from 3 270 000 in June 1945 to

1 530 000 by December 1945. They were not all going home, with 1 200 000 being transferred to the Pacific. Churchill advised his colleagues that he would warn Truman that 'if his armies go too soon, they will probably have to come back pretty quick'.[41] While anxious to retain American forces in Europe even though Germany had been defeated, Churchill supported moves to withdraw British troops from SEAC prior to victory being achieved against Japan. On 8 June, the war minister, Sir James Grigg, told the House of Commons that long-serving personnel in Mountbatten's command would be repatriated four months earlier than previously planned. This politically popular decision caused havoc to Mountbatten's plans to invade Malaya. Describing it as 'quite disgraceful' and an 'electioneering dodge', Cunningham claimed that it 'looks to have wrecked all our plans for offensives down the Malay peninsula and the taking of Singapore'. And it served little political purpose. Although the men were released from their formations, there was insufficient shipping to return them to Britain. 'Surely it is very silly', declared Churchill furiously, that after 'having faced all the grave military disadvantages of releasing these men, of which I approve, to dawdle them about in India'. Dismayed that there were no compensating political advantages, Churchill told Leathers tersely, 'I rely on you to fix this.'[42]

Brooke, who was already hard pressed to muster sufficient forces for the Far East, was horrified that political considerations were dominating their planning for the Pacific. 'Heaven help democracies if they must have elections in wars!' he wrote in his diary. With military planners confronting all sorts of practical difficulties in deciding on the British land contribution to the Pacific war, the chiefs finally suggested to Churchill on 28 June that Britain offer the Americans 'a small land force of some three to five divisions to participate in the main attack against Japan'.[43] But they faced opposition from the chancellor of the exchequer, who called for a reduction in the planned military effort so as to allow 'civil industries and services ... to receive the additional manpower they require in order to enable them to make a reasonable start in 1945 with the most urgent tasks of civil reconstruction'. It was a popular view, with the Conservative MP Sir Harold Nicolson confiding in his diary that the Pacific war 'arouses no interest at all, but only a nauseated distaste'.[44]

Australia also wanted to make only sufficient effort against Japan to ensure a seat at the expected postwar peace conference, while at the same time being careful not to demobilise so hastily as to arouse American criticism. On 9 February 1945, Shedden had warned Curtin that such criticism could be forthcoming from Washington but still urged him to elicit from MacArthur 'his operational plans as they affect the Australian Forces, with a view to determining the stage at which appropriate reductions can be made'. Curtin accepted this advice, refusing to release more manpower immediately for civilian industry and reminding parliament on 28 April that Australia was well placed compared with countries ravaged by war. Nevertheless, he did promise to release some manpower by the end of June.[45] When that time came close, Evatt and Forde protested from San Francisco, warning that an announcement 'might have an adverse effect on various Conference proposals and also on the part we shall be able to play in the final Pacific settlement'. But the domestic pressures were too intense. On 28 June, the war cabinet under the acting prime minister, Ben Chifley, announced the release of 50 000 men for civilian industry while also deciding against any more construction work for the British Pacific fleet so that it would not detract from the government's house building program.[46]

As with Britain, the direction of Australia's symbolic effort remained unclear. MacArthur had promised to use Australian troops for the invasion of the main Japanese island of Honshu, planned for early 1946. In the interim, he kept them occupied with the capture of Borneo, an enterprise of little strategic significance now that the Americans controlled Okinawa and had effectively cut the maritime connection between Japan and its forces in South-East Asia. The ostensible reason was to capture the oilfields of Borneo and to provide a port for the British Pacific fleet, although the Admiralty was loath for its ships to be based in a port so distant from Japan. Cunningham dismissed it all as another American attempt 'to keep the B.P.F. away to the South'. Although the British army was keen to take over from MacArthur in SWPA, Cunningham rightly reasoned that his military counterparts wanted control of SWPA primarily to let them transfer Australian divisions to SEAC 'and keep their own at home'.[47] But it never came to that. The war in the Pacific was proceeding to an American timetable, rather than a British one.

Even had they taken control of SWPA, the British would have faced opposition to the transfer of Australian divisions to SEAC. Despite pressure from London, on 28 May the Australian government reaffirmed its commitment to push on with MacArthur in the final drive against Japan while allowing Mountbatten just a token Australian force to take part in the recapture of Singapore where so many Australians remained imprisoned. MacArthur described Canberra's commitment to continue on towards Tokyo as a 'wise political move on [the] part of [a] Pacific power such as Australia'. Not only was the Australian army meant to go forward with MacArthur, but the Australian naval squadron remained attached to the American Seventh Fleet and the air force, apart from three squadrons proposed for Britain's VLR force, remained with MacArthur.[48] As for the ongoing operations against Japanese garrisons in Bougainville and elsewhere, they were to be scaled back to economise on manpower, limit casualties and allow for further releases from the army. On 6 June, the advisory war council approved a report by Blamey under which only those operations likely to incur 'relatively light casualties' would be undertaken.[49]

As a further move to limit its manpower commitments, the government again deferred a decision on whether to accept the offer of British warships that the Admiralty had tried to press upon Curtin a year before. The British now wanted Australia to pay for the 'gift' ships in order to help offset the cost of basing its Pacific fleet there. But Australia refused to pay for ships that were not really necessary, given the age of its existing ships and the overwhelming American naval presence in the Pacific. Interestingly, one of the Australian objections to the British warships was based on the aircraft carrier having to operate for logistical reasons as part of the British Pacific fleet rather than alongside the existing Australian naval squadron that was operating with the American fleet. The Australians probably realised that the Admiralty wanted the ships to fight under a British flag, which would thereby overstate the relatively small British contribution to the Pacific war.[50]

Australia's own contribution to the war had shrunk considerably since MacArthur's invasion of the Philippines, with repeated promises by MacArthur to use the Australians in the Philippine operations coming to nothing. With some of the front-line troops not having been in action for two years, both Blamey and the government were keen to see them used somewhere. MacArthur suggested that Blamey was at fault for making it difficult for him to use the Australians as single divisions. He also blamed a lack of shipping for his inability to move the Australian troops forward from their training bases in northern Australia. It was not until April 1945 that the Australians were eventually sent into battle by MacArthur in a series of operations designed to capture strategic points along the east coast of Borneo to provide the basis for an invasion of Java in July. MacArthur planned to use two Australian divisions to mount the latter invasion, but was thwarted by Blamey, who withheld one of the divisions. Admiral King then stepped in and proposed that the Australians capture instead the oilfields of Brunei, which had a port that could be used as a base by the British Pacific fleet. As a result, MacArthur had to defer the invasion of Java, thereby saving the lives of the many Australians who would probably have been killed in what would have been a risky operation that was no longer of any consequence to the defeat of Japan.[51]

The Borneo operations still went ahead. On 1 May, Australian troops stormed ashore on the island of Tarakan and captured its airfield, but were unable to have it ready in time to support the operations around Brunei where the 9th Division landed on 10 June. With the capture of Brunei Bay, the British Pacific fleet had its port in Borneo although, as the Admiralty had made clear prior to the operations being launched, it had no wish for a port so far from the main operations against Japan. And its warships never used it. More was to come, with an operation on 1 July launching Australia's 7th Division against Balikpapan on Borneo's south-east coast despite Blamey and his colleagues agreeing that it had no real object. When Chifley questioned MacArthur about it, the American general insisted that the operation proceed, warning that he would appeal to London and Washington if Australia attempted to withhold its division. Although Curtin was consulted in hospital, he was in no condition to repeat his defiance of Churchill over Burma. The war cabinet also complied. As a result, hundreds of Australian troops were killed effecting the capture of Borneo, and all for no purpose. Not that anyone much noticed at the time. MacArthur's attention was elsewhere after having been ordered by the US chiefs of staff on 3 April to prepare his forces for an invasion of Japan. The attention of the Australian government was also distracted, with Curtin in hospital from late April and Evatt and Forde away in London, and later in San Francisco.[52]

The British government had the most to gain from the operations in Borneo, even if its fleet never used its waters as a base. The recapture of the British and Dutch colonies on the island conformed with London's aim to ensure the restoration of the European colonies in South-East Asia to the control of their former empires. It was better that the Australians capture Borneo than the Americans, or that it remain uncaptured and be left to a subsequent peace conference to sort out. Not that the British were watching the events closely. Churchill was preoccupied with the election campaign, traversing Britain in a vain attempt to retain his leadership of the country when the people finally cast their long-delayed ballots on 5 July. The final tally was not counted until three weeks after, so that the votes of the service personnel around the world could be included. In the interim, Churchill retreated to the south of France for a brief painting holiday before flying to Berlin on 15 July for a meeting with Truman and Stalin to settle the organisation of postwar Europe. In case Churchill lost the election, Labour leader Clem Attlee went along as an observer. While the three leaders met near the German city of Potsdam, an American bomber group was practising in the Pacific for the pinpoint delivery of a new weapon that would change the face of the world.

NOTES

[1] Letter, Penney to Sinclair, 2 May 1945, PENNEY 5/1, Penney Papers, KC.
[2] Cited in Rhodes, *The Making of the Atomic Bomb*, p. 649; Hoyt, *Japan's War*, pp. 383–7.
[3] Hastings, *Bomber Command*, pp. 341–5.
[4] Appreciation by Blamey, 18 May 1945, CRS A2670/209/1945, NAA.
[5] Rhodes, *The Making of the Atomic Bomb*, p. 618.
[6] Day, *John Curtin*, pp. 567–8.
[7] Ross, *John Curtin*, p. 378.
[8] Memorandum by Evatt, 8 January 1945, CRS A2670/23/1945, NAA.
[9] War Cabinet Conclusions, 11 January 1945, CAB 65/49, W.M. (45)4; Memorandum by Cranborne, 16 February 1945, CAB 66/62, W.P. (45)99, PRO.
[10] Talks with Evatt and Forde, 2 April 1945, CRS M100, 'April 1945', NAA.
[11] Talks with Sir Eric Machtig and Evatt, 3 April 1945, CRS M100, 'April 1945', NAA.
[12] Paul Hasluck, *Diplomatic Witness*, Melbourne, 1980, p. 173.
[13] Speech by Evatt, 9 April 1945, BEVN 6/29, Bevin Papers, CC.
[14] War Cabinet Conclusions, 3 April 1945, CAB 65/50, W.M. (45)38, PRO.

15 Cadogan diary, 4–13 April 1945, ACAD 1/15, Cadogan Papers, CC; Louis, *Imperialism at Bay*, p. 505.

16 C. Hartley Grattan, 'The Southwest Pacific since the First World War', in W. S. Livingston and W. R. Louis (eds), *Australia, New Zealand, and the Pacific Islands since the First World War*, Austin, 1979, p. 215.

17 Draft policy document discussed on 5 April 1944, BEVN 2/12, Bevin Papers, CC; Clement Attlee, *As it happened*, London, 1954, p. 156.

18 Cable, Chiefs of Staff to Joint Staff Mission, 21 April 1945, PREM 3/180/7, PRO; See also Minute, Eden to Churchill, 2 June 1945, PREM 3/221/7, PRO.

19 Note by the Foreign Office, 28 March 1945, PREM 3/159/12, PRO.

20 Note by Churchill, 11 April 1945, PREM 3/159/12, PRO.

21 Memorandum by Cranborne, 10 April 1945, CAB 66/64, W.P. (45)228, PRO.

22 War Cabinet Conclusions, 12 April 1945, CAB 65/50, W.M. (45)42, PRO; Louis, *Imperialism at Bay*, p. 510.

23 Letter, Cranborne to Emrys-Evans, 29 April 1945, ADD. MS. 58263, Emrys-Evans Papers, BL.

24 Cadogan diary, 23 May 1945, in Dilks (ed.), *The Diaries of Sir Alexander Cadogan*, p. 745.

25 Letter, Cranborne to Emrys-Evans, 29 May 1945, ADD. MS. 58263, Emrys-Evans Papers, BL.

26 Louis, *Imperialism at Bay*, Chap. 33; War Cabinet Conclusions, 14 May 1945, CAB 65/50, W.M. (45)61, PRO.

27 Minute, Ismay to Churchill, 2 May 1945, and Minute, Churchill to Ismay, 3 May 1945, PREM 3/142/7, PRO.

28 Minute, Churchill to Leathers, 10 May 1945, and Minute, Leathers to Churchill, 16 May 1945, PREM 3/142/7, PRO.

29 Talk by Cross, 8 May 1945, RC/2/47, Cross Papers, IWM.

30 Memorandum by Alexander, 23 May 1945, CAB 66/65, W.P. (45)323; Note by Cherwell, 31 May 1945, PREM 3/164/5, PRO.

31 Cabinet Conclusions, 5 June 1945, CAB 65/53, C.M. (45)5, PRO.

32 Mountbatten's attempts to retrieve ships from the British Pacific fleet angered officials at the Admiralty; Somerville agreed with Cunningham that Britain's name 'would certainly stink if we took ships away from the B.P.F. for mopping up in S.E.A.C.'. Letter, Somerville to Cunningham, 15 May 1945, ADD. MS. 52563, Cunningham Papers, BL; Letter, Cunningham to Somerville, 9 May 1945, SMVL 9/3, Somerville Papers, CC; Cable, Mountbatten to Chiefs of Staff, 4 May 1945, PREM 3/149/10, PRO.

33 Cunningham diary, 11 May 1945, ADD. MS. 52578, Cunningham Papers, BL; Cables, Joint Staff Mission to Chiefs of Staff, 6 and 30 April and 12 May 1945, and Chiefs of Staff to Mountbatten, 16 May 1945, PREM 3/149/11, 3/149/10 and 3/160/8, PRO.

34 Cable, Eden to Churchill, 14 May 1945, PREM 3/484 and Memorandum by Grigg, 10 May 1945, CAB 66/65, W.P. (45)292, PRO.

35 Letter, Cross to Cranborne, 23 April 1945, and Minute, Ismay to Churchill, 2 June 1945, PREM 3/53/14, PRO.

36 Minute by Churchill, 1 June 1945 and Minutes, Peck to Ismay, Ismay to Peck and Ismay to Churchill, 2 June 1945, PREM 3/53/14, PRO.

37 Cable, Churchill to Eden, 11 May 1945, PREM 3/484, PRO.

38 Cables, Churchill to Truman, 12 May 1945, PREM 3/484, PRO.

39 Hugh Thomas, *Armed Truce*, London, 1986, Chap. 23.

40 Alanbrooke diary, 13 and 24 May and 11 June 1945, in Danchev and Todman (eds), *War Diaries*, pp. 690, 693, 697.

41 Cable, Wilson to Chiefs of Staff, 16 May 1945, and Minute, Churchill to Ismay, 9 June 1945, PREM 3/484, PRO.

42 Cunningham diary, 9 June 1945, ADD. MS. 52578, BL; See also Alanbrooke diary, 11, 19 and 20 June 1945, in Danchev and Todman (eds.), *War Diaries*, pp. 697–9; Minute, Churchill to Ismay, 16 June 1945, PREM 3/149/10, PRO.

43 Alanbrooke diary, 20, 21 and 28 June 1945, in Danchev and Todman (eds.), *War Diaries*, pp. 698–700; Cunningham diary, 28 June 1945, ADD. MS. 52578, BL.

44 Memorandum by Anderson, 29 June 1945, CAB 66/67, C.P. (45)53, PRO; Letter, Nicolson to his son, 27 May 1945, in Sir H. Nicolson, *Diaries and Letters*, Vol. 2, p. 466.

45 Paper by Shedden, 9 February 1945, CRS A5954, Box 309; Speech by Curtin, 28 February 1945, CRS A5954, Box 1605, NAA.

[46] Cable, Forde and Evatt to Chifley, 5 June 1945, 'United Nations — Cables' folder, Evatt Papers, FUL; War Cabinet Minutes, 28 June 1945, CRS A2673/XVI/4291 and 4292, NAA.

[47] Cunningham diary, 16, 19 and 26 April 1945, ADD. MS. 52578, Cunningham Papers, BL; See also Cable, Chiefs of Staff to Joint Staff Mission, 12 April 1945, and Cable, Wilson to Chiefs of Staff, 13 April 1945, PREM 3/159/7, PRO.

[48] Cable, Gairdner to Churchill, 12 May 1945, PREM 3/159/7, PRO; War Cabinet Minutes, 28 May 1945, CRS A2673/XVI/4216, NAA.

[49] Advisory War Council Minutes, 6 June 1945, CRS A2682/8/1550, NAA.

[50] Memorandum by Chifley, 31 May 1945, CRS A2679/24/1945, and War Cabinet Minutes, CRS A2673/XVI/4241, NAA; War Cabinet Conclusions, 20 April 1945, CAB 65/50, W.M. (45)48, PRO.

[51] Horner, *High Command*, Chaps 16 and 17.

[52] ibid., pp. 405–6.

FORTY-SEVEN

'enduring the unendurable'

The destruction of Japanese cities by fire-bombing, the sinking of the imperial navy and the American conquest of the Philippines and Okinawa forced the Japanese to confront the certainty of their defeat. But surrendering was made difficult for the Japanese by the Allied insistence that it be unconditional, with the possible implications that had for the position of the emperor. However, Hirohito had inspected first hand the devastation of Tokyo and was aware that the war could not be won. Accordingly, at a sombre conference of his military and political leaders on 22 June 1945, he finally instructed them to find a way out of the bloody morass into which he had led the nation. With the Soviet Union still neutral in the Pacific war, the Japanese government turned towards Stalin in the hope that he might intercede with Churchill and Truman to produce a peace short of the unconditional surrender demanded by the Allies. But Moscow had its own long-held ambitions in the Pacific and was busily preparing to launch its forces against the Japanese so that it could seize a swathe of disputed territory from Tokyo. Soviet power, already cementing its hold on eastern Europe, was about to project into the Pacific.

Churchill arrived in Potsdam, just west of the ruins of Berlin, on 15 July. Along with his military advisers also came Clem Attlee, with Churchill hoping that Attlee's presence, as they awaited the result of the general election, would provide a show of national unity and thereby strengthen his hand with the Russians. The various delegations took up residence in a series of villas overlooking a lake in which Brooke that night tried unsuccessfully to catch pike. Over the following days, they drove into Berlin to view the devastation that they had visited upon their vanquished enemy, touring the Reichstag and the remains of Hitler's bunker where the scorch marks of his cremation could still be seen on an outside wall. The destruction of the city was nothing compared with what the Americans had in store for the Japanese, with the American secretary for war, Henry Stimson, handing Churchill a brief note during the first plenary session of the conference which announced enigmatically: 'Babies satisfactorily born.' As Stimson explained over lunch, the 'babies' referred to the atomic bomb that had been tested for the first time just 24 hours before in the desert of New Mexico. The dramatic explosion was deliberately timed to coincide with the Potsdam talks.[1]

The American battleship *Indianapolis*, with its deadly cargo securely stowed, was already on its way to a rendezvous with history at Hiroshima. The American physicist Robert Oppenheimer, who had supervised the New Mexico test, recalled the awestruck scientists as they watched the cauldron of fire boil into the night sky and the terrible implications of their handiwork hit home:

A few people laughed, a few people cried. Most people were silent. I remembered the line from the Hindu scripture, the Bhagavad-Gita: Vishnu is trying to persuade the Prince that he should do his duty and to impress him he takes on his multi-armed form and says, 'Now I am become Death, the destroyer of worlds.'[2]

The bomb was Churchill's saviour, promising a speedy finish to the Pacific war and perhaps holding off the threat that Churchill now discerned from the Russian armies in Europe. It would also help to alleviate Britain's seemingly intractable manpower problems.

Prior to going to Potsdam, Churchill had urged a near doubling of the target figure of 135 000 women to be demobilised by December 1945.[3] He also wanted to bring German prisoners of war to Britain to help with the reconstruction of its bombed-out cities, and to delay the repatriation of Italian prisoners in Britain despite the Italians now being notionally on the Allied side.[4] But he faced opposition from the chancellor of the exchequer, Sir John Anderson, who wanted the release of servicewomen to be slowed down while 300 000 more men were released instead. As he argued, there could be no guarantee that the demobilised servicewomen would go into the factories where more workers were desperately needed. Even with the release of all these additional men, advised Anderson, there would not be 'any appreciable improvement in civilian standards' nor would there be much progress towards 'the restoration of our export trade'. These objectives could best be achieved, claimed Anderson, if further cutbacks were made in Britain's planned effort against Japan. He asked Churchill to keep this 'prominently in mind' at Potsdam.[5]

Cutting back on the limited British commitment to the Pacific was not an easy matter. In the case of the VLR bomber force, Britain had progressively reduced its plans for this force to just twenty squadrons, many of them to be drawn from the dominions. The deployment of the first ten squadrons had been accepted in principle by the Americans in early June, with the remaining ten to be accepted when conditions permitted.[6] It was difficult to find makeshift airfields on which to base these squadrons, with hundreds of bombers already crowding the hastily constructed bases surrounding Japan like crows around a carcass. There was little space for the British planes, should they ever arrive, and few Japanese cities left that were worth bombing. When the air ministry suggested cutting back the VLR force to just ten squadrons as a way of reducing the pressure on British manpower, Churchill immediately agreed. However, the new air minister, Harold Macmillan, reminded the British cabinet that the United States had already accepted Britain's offer to send twenty squadrons, which was already much less than they had previously been planning. It would be 'very inadvisable', argued Macmillan, 'to go back on this decision in view of our relations with the Americans'.[7]

Although Churchill had been excited by news of the successful atomic bomb test, he could not be certain that it would be sufficient by itself to force the Japanese to surrender. Indeed, the US chiefs of staff were still pressing ahead with plans for an invasion of Kyushu followed by an invasion of the Tokyo plain on Honshu, with all the massive expenditure of lives and resources that those operations would entail. One of Churchill's aims at Potsdam was to avoid this by convincing the Americans to soften their demand for the unconditional surrender of Japan, even though he had insisted on its imposition on Germany at the cost of needless casualties and months of futile fighting. The Australian government had strong views about this and on the need to hold Hirohito accountable, but it was never consulted.

Just prior to Potsdam, and before the atomic bomb test, the British government had suggested to the Americans that the constitutional powers of Emperor Hirohito could be left intact after the Japanese surrender to ease the problem of controlling the Japanese population. Britain feared that Japan would require a 'total and protracted military occupation, combined with the assumption of all the functions of Government', which would result in a 'strain on both manpower and physical resources'.[8] Just as it wanted to limit its contribution to the Pacific war, so it wanted to limit any commitment to a postwar occupation force. Australia was informed by the British government that these suggestions were being made to the Americans, but it was not asked to contribute to the discussions. Cabling from London, an angry Bruce told Canberra on 18 July that it was unforgivable that Britain, Russia and the United States should decide the Japanese surrender terms when Russia had not even declared war and the British had played such a lukewarm role in the Pacific. Bruce told Chifley that he had already protested at 'the way in which we have been treated' and suggested that Chifley do likewise before the surrender terms had been finally decided.[9]

Chifley had been prime minister for less than a week, after having been elected on 12 July to replace Curtin, who had died on 5 July. For six weeks, Curtin's condition had worsened after being admitted to hospital on 29 April with congestion of the lungs. Although he was allowed back to the

Lodge, he was never well enough to leave his bed. He told those concerned colleagues who came to call that, in the event of his death, Chifley was his preferred successor. Evatt might have mounted a challenge to Chifley, but he was on board ship on his way back from San Francisco, with the ship in a state of radio silence as protection against enemy submarines. Despite the keenness of Evatt's ambition, it is unlikely that his presence in Canberra would have made much difference to the final result that saw Chifley receive 45 votes in the ballot of Labor MPs, compared with fifteen or sixteen for Curtin's deputy, the hapless Frank Forde. According to the rules, the absent Evatt's name was submitted but only attracted one or perhaps two votes. With the dour but competent Chifley in charge, the government in Canberra could finally be given new life and direction.

Meanwhile, Churchill found to his surprise that the Americans proved remarkably receptive to his suggestion for a soft peace. On 17 July, the American naval chief, Admiral Leahy, told Churchill to provide the American delegation with a memorandum setting out the British case, thereby ensuring that the responsibility for any softening of the terms would fall on Churchill's ageing shoulders. When Churchill then heard from Stalin later that afternoon of the Japanese peace overtures, he warily declared that Britain would help the Americans in the Pacific 'to the full'. Presumably anxious that the conference record not portray him as grasping the Japanese olive branch too eagerly, Churchill confided to Stalin that it was the Americans who were starting to question the sense of demanding unconditional surrender if it entailed the sacrifice of perhaps another million Allied lives to achieve it. And when he alerted Truman to the peace offer the following day, Churchill was careful not to press the Americans to accept it, while at the same time emphasising to Truman the 'tremendous cost in American life and, to a smaller extent, in British life' that would ensue from enforcing it. Churchill was relieved to see that Truman was clearly aware of the 'terrible responsibilities that rested upon him in regard to the unlimited effusion of American blood'. In fact, American interception of Japanese diplomatic cables had already alerted Truman about the Japanese offer.[10]

While Brooke was off fishing unsuccessfully in a far-off river that had been fished out by German SS soldiers using hand grenades, Churchill was given more detailed results by the Americans of the atomic bomb test. He later recalled his relief at the news that a full-scale invasion of Japan might no longer be necessary. Churchill claimed that such an invasion would have meant the 'loss of a million American lives and half that number of British — or more if we could get them there: for we were resolved to share the agony'. He did not explain how Britain could suffer half a million dead when the latest plans only committed perhaps 100 000 Commonwealth troops to the invasion, many of them from the dominions. Instead of this 'nightmare picture' of slaughter, Churchill envisaged the whole war ending in 'one or two violent shocks'. By dropping the atomic bomb on their cities, argued Churchill, the Allies were doing the Japanese a favour since it would give them 'an excuse which would save their honour and release them from their obligation of being killed to the last fighting man'.[11]

Churchill also expected that the bombs would avoid the need to have the Russians enter the Pacific war. The Americans too had become keen to delay and possibly avoid Russian involvement in the Pacific for fear that it would use such involvement to convert a defeated Japan into a communist satellite, as it seemed determined to do to the countries of eastern Europe. In contrast, the United States wanted to use Japan as a bulwark against Russian expansion in the Pacific.[12] Churchill also welcomed the bomb as providing an economical means to hold the Russians in check in Europe, with Britain now being able to 'just blot out Moscow' if Russia resisted. When he returned from his fishing trip on 23 July, Brooke found that Churchill was 'completely carried away' with these prospects, with Brooke trying in vain to 'crush his over-optimism'.[13] Churchill wanted to tell Stalin of the bomb in order to make the Russians 'a little more humble'. In fact, Stalin already knew of the bomb from his spy network. And the Russians were determined to join the war against the prostrate Japan, as Stalin had promised to do as soon as Germany was defeated. Stalin made that clear at a banquet in Churchill's villa on 23 July. With an RAF band providing the music, and amid the many speeches and toasts, the Russian dictator declared that he looked forward to Russia joining Britain and America in the struggle against Japan and, according to Cunningham, 'toasted our next meeting in Seoul or Tokyo'.[14] The Allies were advised that the Russians would be ready to enter the war on 15 August, while the Americans rushed to have their bombs ready before that date so that they might force a Japanese surrender before the Russians could declare war.[15] As the development of the atomic bomb had been a joint Anglo–American project, the British had to give their formal approval for its use against Japan, which Churchill had already done on 4 July.

Although its contribution to the Pacific war was relatively small, the British government wanted to take a full part in determining its strategic direction. The British chiefs of staff tried to make this argument at Potsdam, but with little success. While the Americans would allow the British to participate in the invasion of Japan, they would not concede any of its strategic control. If the British were not happy with that, they could withhold their forces. But the invasion would still go ahead according to plans worked out by the Americans. As Cunningham acknowledged in his diary, because 'of the disparity in the size of the forces to be employed this is I think reasonable. [Admiral] King tried to be rude about it but nobody paid any attention to him.'[16]

On 24 July, the three Allied leaders met to discuss a joint declaration directed at Tokyo in response to the Japanese peace feelers and with the prospect of the early use of the atomic bomb. Despite Churchill and Truman earlier agreeing that some softening in the Allied terms could be considered, their joint declaration with Stalin called for Japan's unconditional surrender under threat of 'prompt and utter destruction'. Publicly issued two days later, it was promptly rejected by Japan for not preserving the position of Hirohito. Had the Allies modified their demand, the Japanese might well have accepted and thereby removed the opportunity for the Americans to use the atomic bomb. A demonstration of the bomb's explosive power was needed to ascertain its effect on people and buildings, and also to overawe Stalin while ensuring, as Truman believed, that Japan would 'fold up before Russia comes in'.[17] As such, the decision to use the bomb was largely a political one. It was not referred to the combined chiefs of staff, something that Cunningham thought to be 'a great pity' since they might have advised that 'neither the atom bomb nor the invasion were necessary to induce Japan to surrender'.[18] Eisenhower shared this opinion, pointing out to Stimson that 'the Japanese were ready to surrender and it wasn't necessary to hit them with that awful thing'. Moreover, he 'hated to see our country be the first to use such a weapon'.[19] Whatever quibbles might have been expressed, they were ignored. Stimson had spent $2 billion developing the bomb and was anxious for the US Congress to see the results of this expenditure.

By the time that the Potsdam declaration was issued on 26 July, Churchill had returned to London and was out of office. Attlee's Labour Party had won a crushing victory in the election and was returned with a majority of 146 seats. A disappointed Churchill immediately resigned on hearing the news, making a radio broadcast to the British people in which he regretted that he had 'not been permitted to finish the work against Japan' while claiming that 'all plans and preparations have been made, and the results may come much quicker than we have hitherto been entitled to expect'.[20] Meanwhile, Attlee returned to Potsdam on 28 July with the new British foreign secretary, Ernest Bevin, to conclude the talks with Stalin and Truman.

Australia's Labor government welcomed the election of its counterpart in London, believing that Australia's voice would be heard more sympathetically by the new government. And the first issue that it raised was a protest over the Potsdam declaration. Evatt had been assured during the London conference in April that Australia, as a principal combatant in the Pacific and a country with a vital interest in Japan's future status, would be consulted before peace terms were imposed on Tokyo. In the wake of the Potsdam conference, Evatt now observed to Bruce that there was a 'grave danger of our being gradually excluded from all important discussions preliminary to and involving [the] making of peace settlements in Europe and armistice settlement with Japan'. Evatt naively believed that the new Labour government would 'better appreciate [the] great importance of [the] matter to Australia'.[21]

Evatt's response to Potsdam was hardly calculated to endear him to the incoming British government, with Evatt making a bitter and public denunciation of the way in which Australia had been treated by its great power allies. He revealed that the declaration had been made without consultation with Australia, and that the government had learned of its terms by way of the press. Evatt was particularly affronted by China being a signatory to the declaration while Australia was not. According to Evatt, 'Australia's interest and concern are no less significant than those of China', an assertion that implied a fair degree of ignorance about the suffering incurred by the Chinese at the hands of Japan and the war effort that China had mounted. Evatt was not prepared to have Japan receive milder treatment than Germany, 'having regard to the outrageous cruelties and barbarities systematically practised under the Imperialist regime'. With Australian newspapers reporting allegations of various Japanese war crimes against Australian personnel, this was a sensitive political issue. Evatt also feared that Australia would be imperilled again if Japan was not adequately subdued by the Allies. He criticised those, presumably in Whitehall, who had failed to learn from the 'many early disasters of the Japanese war' and who 'do not realise that the post-war security of the peoples of Australia and New Zealand and of India too are ... directly dependent upon the terms of the peace settlement with Japan'.[22]

In an angry cable to Bevin on 28 July, Evatt denounced the Potsdam declaration as the 'last straw', with the ultimatum to Japan having been made 'without any reference to Australia which for more than two years bore the brunt of the Pacific struggle from the British point of view'.[23] Evatt also sent an appeal to the leading Labourite, Harold Laski, complaining that Australia was being given less consideration than after the First World War and asking Laski to use his influence with Attlee and Bevin on Australia's behalf. He sent similar messages to the prime ministers of New Zealand, Canada and South Africa, hoping that the other dominions would be similarly outraged.[24] But they weren't. The South African prime minister, Jan Smuts, told Evatt that he should not try to sit alongside the great powers. The best he could hope for was to have Australian views considered by Britain. After all, argued Smuts, Australia and the other dominions were only 'minor belligerents and it is awkward for us to claim more than this as Dominions under the British wing'.[25]

Sensing a fresh storm in Anglo–Australian relations, Bruce went to see Bevin on 3 August following the foreign secretary's return from Potsdam. Although Bruce had helped to inspire this new storm, he was now more concerned with smoothing it over, assuring Bevin that he 'had merely come to ascertain if there was any method of handling the matter without friction'. He found that Bevin was 'quite outspoken' about Evatt's insistence on inclusion into great power discussions, with Bevin flatly refusing to concede Evatt's demand. Bevin told Bruce that he would reply to Evatt in a tone that would be 'quite sympathetic towards Australia's desire for consultation, but will be quite frank on the subject of Evatt's specific proposals'. So Evatt's hopes of having Australia punch above its weight, as Billy Hughes had done at Versailles in 1919, were dashed. He would have to be content with his achievements at San Francisco. Nevertheless, Bruce assured Evatt that his talks with Bevin had been 'a refreshing experience' which promised much more consultation than under the 'old regime'.[26]

Australia's demand for a prominent place at any Pacific peace conference rested upon the extent of its contribution to that war. It was a contribution that had become relatively minor over the previous two years as MacArthur increasingly left Australian forces on the sidelines of his operations. To its frustration, Australia found that Britain was also going to deny Australia its chance to take a leading part in the final defeat of Japan. Whitehall was operating according to the timetable established at Potsdam, which envisaged that hostilities against Japan might not finally cease until November 1946. Although it was planning to create a Commonwealth land force for use in the Pacific, the Australian government realised that victory would probably come sooner than the British expected and the Commonwealth force would be too late to play an effective role in securing that victory. Accordingly, although Australia had called for Britain to increase its presence in the Pacific war for the sake of imperial prestige, Australia was now unwilling to contribute its divisions to the tardy Commonwealth force. Matters were not helped by the British election, which disrupted planning for the force.[27] It was only on 4 July, the day before the election, that Churchill finally approved the concept of a British land force participating in the invasion of Japan. And he approved it without reading the relevant paper prepared by Brooke, who had to explain it all for Churchill on a map, with Brooke being left wondering how much the exhausted Churchill 'really understood'.[28]

With the plan approved by Churchill, Bruce advised Canberra that it envisaged a Commonwealth force of five divisions assembling in India before going into action during the invasion of the Tokyo plain in March 1946. It was hoped that some of the land force and most of the tactical air force of fifteen squadrons would be provided by Australia and New Zealand.[29] It was too little, too late. As the timing indicated, the British were planning to contribute to the second Allied invasion wave rather than the first wave against Kyushu, which the Americans had scheduled for November 1945. Even without knowledge of the atomic bomb, it was clear that the war could well be over before the end of 1945 once Russia joined the fray. Although Australia was committed to the Commonwealth, it was determined to have its flag flying among the Allied troops that first stepped ashore in Japan. As Billy Hughes pointed out during a meeting of the advisory war council on 19 July, the 'primary consideration was actual participation in the main offensive against Japan'. Although Hughes would have preferred Australia to participate within the context of a Commonwealth force rather than an American one, if such a force 'could not be organised in time to take part in the main offensive, then Australia herself should not fail to participate in these operations'.[30]

Britain's late and relatively minor contribution to the Pacific war reinforced in some Australian minds the lessons of 1942 and effectively caused a second 'looks to America' episode as the Chifley government opted to go forward with MacArthur so as 'to strengthen future Australian–American relations which are of paramount importance from the aspect of security in the post-war period'. As for the Commonwealth force, Australia would only contribute a token force to a British assault on Malaya in order to avenge the defeat of Singapore.[31] And it would not allow these British forces to be based in Australia, due to the extra burden it would impose on Australia's manpower. Moreover, if the control of SWPA was shifted from MacArthur to Mountbatten, Chifley made clear that the British government would have to guarantee Australia the same level of control it had enjoyed over strategic decisions under MacArthur and control of its own forces.[32] The war cabinet had already refused a British request to invade two Japanese-occupied islands in the Solomons, despite concern from London that 'the natives would suffer severely from loss of food supplies and enemy violence' while Britain's 'inability to protect them would be gravely detrimental to British prestige and create a serious local political situation'. The war cabinet agreed with Blamey's assessment of the operation as being 'strategically unsound', despite previous operations being mounted by Blamey for similar reasons.[33]

Australia was also loath to support the British Pacific fleet if it meant cutting back on its housing program or other reconstruction projects, with Admiral Cunningham complaining on 5 July that Australia was seeking to play 'less and less part in the war'. Six days later, the war cabinet confirmed its decision to release 64 000 men from the services 'to provide for housing and other high priority needs of the civil economy', irrespective of the demands for the Pacific fleet. When Chifley explained the Australian position to Admiral Fraser, the admiral was left with the impression that it was all due to political factors. Which was partly true, although Fraser was unable to understand that Australia might have good reasons for not wanting any longer to play the part of the dutiful colony. During his meeting with the gravel-voiced Chifley, the New Zealand prime minister, Peter Fraser, asserted that the Pacific fleet had been sent at Australia's request and on the understanding that it would be adequately supported.[34] Chifley was quick to rebut this view. Certainly, Australian requests for a British fleet had been made repeatedly in 1941 and 1942, but the warships had never been sent when they were needed for Australia's protection. Now they were simply a burden rather than a salvation.

Britain's tardiness in organising a land force for the invasion of Japan was partly due to a misconception about the likely timetable for such an invasion, but also due to London's overriding desire to recapture Singapore. And one reason for wanting to capture Singapore was to allow Britain to base its fleet there and remove the need for Australian logistical support. While Mountbatten was rushing to organise Singapore's capture prior to any general Japanese surrender, he was slowed down by the fear that it might involve a prolonged siege of the island. Only after capturing Singapore would Britain countenance sending troops against the Japanese home islands. As Cunningham observed in a letter to Admiral Fraser, there were 'nearly a million first line troops in Honshu backed up by some seven million

Home Guard: it seems to me that, physically, it will take a long time to kill all these'.[35]

At the Potsdam conference, the Americans had reduced Britain's offer of five Commonwealth divisions down to three, while also stipulating that the force was to be integrated into the American army and use American equipment and logistical support. It would also be kept in reserve rather than going ashore in the first wave. As commander of the invasion force, MacArthur also stipulated that no Indian divisions be included because of 'linguistic and administrative complications'. These were humiliating conditions for Britain to accept, but its contribution to the Pacific had been token from the start. Now the Americans would ensure that its effect would be lost beneath the weight of American armour. At sea, the British Pacific fleet was deliberately excluded from the naval operations that destroyed the remnants of the Japanese fleet at the end of July, with America's Admiral Halsey being determined to 'forestall a possible post-war claim by Britain that she had delivered even a part of the final blow that demolished the Japanese Fleet'.[36]

Instead of getting part of the command in MacArthur's operations in the north Pacific, Britain was relegated to the south-west Pacific where it would assume control of part of MacArthur's old command, taking the region west of the Celebes and Java, while Australia took the eastern part and the Philippines was hived off into MacArthur's new command. But the transfer of control would be deferred until Mountbatten was able to exercise effective command of the Straits of Malacca, which would have to await his capture of Singapore. Under its new Labour government, Britain accepted its reduced status in the Pacific with apparent equanimity. As Bevin advised the defence committee on 8 August, Britain's 'original offer of up to 5 divisions was made very largely with a political object, i.e. to remove any idea in the United States and the Far East that we were not pulling our weight in the Far Eastern war and to re-establish our position in the eyes of the Far Eastern peoples'. MacArthur's conditions on the use of the force meant that these aims would probably not be achieved, with the Commonwealth force becoming 'an unadvertised component of the American machine'. During the defence committee discussion, Brooke indicated that the three

Commonwealth divisions would comprise one British and one Australian division, while the remaining division would be made up of one Canadian and two New Zealand brigades. It would take more than six months before the force would be available for action in Japan after first training in the United States with American equipment. To counter the negative public perceptions that this would create, Bevin urged that the British propaganda machine should stress the force's individuality, while the government tried again to have it used in the decisive assault on Honshu.[37] But such an assault was already in doubt after the successful dropping two days earlier of the atomic bomb on Hiroshima.

News of the bomb caused a sensation, but it did not bring an immediate Japanese surrender. So the British government continued to discuss and plan for operations that could not be mounted until the following year. While the defence committee wrestled with its plans for the Pacific, the second atomic bomb had already been loaded into an American B-29 bomber parked on the runway of Tinian Island in the Marianas. It was destined to be dropped on the city of Kokura, set on the northern tip of Kyushu. If that city was obscured by cloud, Nagasaki was the alternative target. On 9 August, with Russian armies finally launching a wide-scale attack against Japanese forces in Manchuria, the American bomber crew searched unsuccessfully for a break in the hazy conditions over Kokura before heaving their aircraft around to head home by way of Nagasaki. The weather over Nagasaki was also unsuitable until, at the last moment, a small gap in the clouds allowed the bombardier to set his sight on a stadium several kilometres from the specified dropping point. Exploding at about five hundred metres above the city in a blinding burst of light and heat, about 70 000 inhabitants of the harbourside city were killed, some quickly and some agonisingly slowly over the following days. As the world waited for the Japanese reaction, a third atomic bomb was prepared for delivery, possibly on Tokyo itself, while further massed incendiary raids on other Japanese cities continued the conventional killing.

In the wake of Nagasaki's destruction, the Japanese government agreed the following day to submit to the terms of the Potsdam declaration except in so far as it affected the prerogatives of the emperor. The message caused confusion in London as to its meaning and how the Allies should react. As Cunningham confided in his diary, the Allies now had to decide whether the message 'constitutes unconditional surrender'. He recalled how Churchill had shown the chiefs of staff the draft Potsdam declaration and been told by all his chiefs that 'something about the emperor should be included. Now instead of having a formula of our own we have this Japanese formula which no one can really understand.'[38] The British cabinet covered their confusion by passing the responsibility to the Americans, telling Washington that 'if they were of opinion that the clause affecting the Emperor was acceptable, we should agree'.[39]

Australia was not consulted, which was probably a good thing since Evatt was determined that Japanese militarism be ripped out by the roots, telling London that Hirohito should be removed and 'held responsible for Japan's acts of aggression and war crimes'. According to Evatt, the emperor should be forced to descend from his celestial throne to sign the surrender document and then be thrown into prison to await trial as a war criminal.[40] This would have lengthened the war considerably. When Evatt learned of the Japanese offer, he reiterated Australia's view that 'the present Imperial-Militarist system be not only discredited but completely broken'. The Japanese people could only be made to 'appreciate their defeat', argued Evatt, by the 'visible dethronement of the system'. Without it, Evatt predicted that a later generation would face a 'recrudescence of aggression in the Pacific'. He opposed the idea of saving 'the face of the emperor', and insisted that Britain should support Australia in pressing for Hirohito to be put on trial. He asked that no reply be made to the Japanese until Australia had read the Japanese offer and commented upon it. Evatt copied his cable to Washington, Chungking and Moscow, once again emphasising the dominion's right to propound a different foreign policy to that of Britain.[41]

Despite Australia's principled and legalistic stand, the United States and Britain had to deal with a Japanese nation that still had considerable forces arrayed across Asia and the Pacific, from Rabaul to Singapore and from Canton to Siam, along with many more in Japan itself. From experience, the Allies feared that the piecemeal defeat of these forces would incur horrendous casualties among the Allied armies, whereas the peaceful surrender of these far-flung forces could probably be achieved by a simple order of the emperor. By not calling Hirohito to account for his crimes, the Allies might save the many lives that would otherwise be lost in forcing the surrender. His preservation would also assist in the orderly and economical administration of postwar Japan. So the Americans were deliberately obtuse about Hirohito's future in their reply to the Japanese offer, insisting only that he sign the surrender document and that he be subject to the authority of the Allied supreme commander. These terms satisfied the American electorate while leaving the Japanese a straw of honour to grasp.

Despite hostile comments from Australia and China, the British did not heed the objections from Evatt. As Churchill had made clear at Potsdam, the British government was prepared to demand even less of Hirohito than the Americans and it now suggested to Washington that the emperor should not have to sign the surrender but only be made to issue a command to his forces to end hostilities. Britain argued that this would 'secure the immediate surrender of the Japanese in all outlying areas and thereby save American, British and Allied lives'.[42] Washington concurred in this, announcing that the United States, Britain, Russia and China had agreed to the surrender terms. Hirohito's position was secured. 'So now it's up to the Japs,' wrote the Foreign Office head, Sir Alexander Cadogan, on 11 August. A frustrated Evatt instructed Bruce that same day to 'spare no effort to see that on this occasion definite action is not taken without our prior knowledge or consent'. But Britain was almost as hamstrung as Australia over this, with the Americans asserting their dominance in the Pacific to determine the Allied position. As Cadogan observed after a British cabinet meeting on 14 August, Washington was 'going ahead on surrender terms etc., without showing much disposition to consult us. We must accept this, and if Dominions complain we can say that we, too, were not consulted.'[43] Armed with atomic bombs, and with its forces sprawled across the Pacific, the United States was not about to brook any interference as it brought the war to a close.

The end came on 15 August with a masterful understatement by Hirohito that crackled over Japanese wireless sets, announcing that 'the war situation has developed not necessarily to Japan's advantage'. Citing the American use of 'a new and most cruel bomb' as his reason, the diminutive emperor called on his subjects to 'pave the way for a grand peace for all generations to come by enduring the unendurable and suffering what is insufferable'.[44] At last, the conflict was over, although the agony would continue for many of its victims. Prisoners of war still had to be freed, returned to their homes and nursed back to health, and about two hundred thousand citizens of Hiroshima and Nagasaki faced a lingering death from radiation sickness. The Pacific war had ended in the devastation and defeat of Japan, but it also had given strength to the independence forces across Asia that, over the succeeding decades, would throw off the shackles of European imperialism.

NOTES

[1] Martin Gilbert, *Never Despair*, London, 1988, p. 62; Alanbrooke diary, 15–19 July 1945, in Danchev and Todman (eds), *War Diaries*, pp. 705–7.

[2] Cited in Rhodes, *The Making of the Atomic Bomb*, p. 676.

[3] Note by Churchill, 3 July 1945, CAB 66/67, C.P. (45)61, PRO.

[4] Gilbert, *Never Despair*, p. 60.

[5] Memorandum by Anderson, 11 July 1945, CAB 66/67, C.P. (45)72, PRO.

[6] Minute, Ismay to Churchill, 5 June 1945, PREM 3/142/7, PRO.

[7] Memorandum by Macmillan, 11 July 1945, CAB 66/67, C.P. (45)75, PRO; For documents on Canada's reluctance to contribute to the VLR force, see PREM 3/142/5, PRO.

[8] Cable, Dominions Office to Chifley, 17 July 1945, CRS A5954, Box 453, NAA.

[9] Cable, Bruce to Chifley, 18 July 1945, CRS M100, 'July 1945', NAA.

[10] Cunningham diary, 16 July 1945, ADD. MS. 52578, Cunningham Papers, BL; Gilbert, *Never Despair*, pp. 63–4, 68–9.

[11] Churchill, *The Second World War*, Vol. 6, pp. 552–3.

[12] See Talk with M. E. Dening, 18 June 1945, CRS M100, 'June 1945', NAA; Letter, Penney to Sinclair, 2 May 1945, 5/1, Penney Papers, KC.

[13] Alanbrooke diary, 23 July 1945, in Danchev and Todman (eds), *War Diaries*, p. 709.

[14] Cunningham diary, 20 and 23 July 1945, ADD. MS. 52578, Cunningham Papers, BL.

[15] Cited in Rhodes, *The Making of the Atomic Bomb*, p. 689.

[16] Cunningham diary, 18 and 23 July 1945, ADD. MS. 52578, Cunningham Papers, BL; See also Alanbrooke diary, 17 and 18 July 1945, in Danchev and Todman (eds), *War Diaries*, pp. 706–7.

[17] Rhodes, *The Making of the Atomic Bomb*, pp. 688, 692.

[18] Cunningham's draft memoirs, p. 136, ADD. MS. 52581B, Cunningham Papers, BL.

[19] Cited in Rhodes, *The Making of the Atomic Bomb*, p. 688.

[20] Gilbert, *Never Despair*, p. 109.

[21] Cable, Evatt to Bruce, 27 July 1945, CRS M100, 'July 1945', NAA.

[22] Cable, Evatt to Bruce, 30 July 1945, CRS M100, 'July 1945', NAA.

[23] Cable, Evatt to Bevin, 28 July 1945, *DAFP*, Vol. 8, Doc. 146.

[24] Cables, Evatt to Laski, 1 August 1945, and Evatt to Fraser, King and Smuts, 4 August 1945, *DAFP*, Vol. 8, Docs 148, 154, 155.

[25] Cable, Smuts to Evatt, 9 August 1945, *DAFP*, Vol. 8, Doc. 169.

[26] Talk with Ernest Bevin, 3 August 1945, CRS M100, 'August 1945', NAA; Cable, Bruce to Evatt, 4 August 1945, *DAFP*, Vol. 8, Doc. 157.

27 Letter, Rourke to Shedden, 26 June 1945, CRS A5954, Box 1615, NAA.

28 Alanbrooke diary, 4 July 1945, in Danchev and Todman (eds), *War Diaries*, p. 702.

29 Cable, Bruce to Forde, 6 July 1945, CRS M100, 'July 1945', NAA.

30 Advisory War Council Minutes, 19 July 1945, CRS A2682/8/1583, NAA.

31 Advisory War Council Agendum, CRS A2679/35/1945, NAA.

32 Cable (draft), Chifley to Dominions Office, CRS A2679/35/1945, NAA.

33 Memorandum by Fraser, 13 June 1945, CRS A2670/259/1945, NAA.

34 Letters, Cunningham to Fraser, 5 July 1945, and Fraser to Cunningham, 17 July 1945, ADD. MS. 52572, Cunningham Papers, BL; War Cabinet Minutes, 11 July 1945, CRS A2673/XVI/4328, and Cable, Chifley to Bruce, 17 July 1945, CRS M100, 'July 1945', NAA.

35 Cable, Mountbatten to Chiefs of Staff, 10 July 1945, PREM 3/149/9, PRO; Letter, Cunningham to Fraser, 5 July 1945, ADD. MS. 52572, BL.

36 Memorandum by Chiefs of Staff, 7 August 1945, CAB 69/7, D.O. (45)2, PRO; Gill, *Royal Australian Navy*, Vol. 2, p. 665.

37 Memorandum by Bevin, 8 August 1945, CAB 69/7, D.O. (45)3, PRO; Defence Committee Minutes, 8 August 1945, CAB 69/7, D.O. (45)2, PRO.

38 Cunningham diary, 10 August 1945, ADD. MS. 52578, Cunningham Papers, BL.

39 Alanbrooke diary, 10 August 1945, in Danchev and Todman (eds), *War Diaries*, pp. 716-7.

40 Cable, External Affairs to Australian Legation, Washington, 10 August 1945, CRS A3300/290, NAA.

41 Cables, Commonwealth Government to Dominions Secretary, 11 and 12 August 1945, CRS A5954, Box 453, NAA.

42 Cables, Dominions Secretary to Commonwealth Government, 11 August 1945, CRS A5954, Box 453; Cable, Evatt to Bruce, 10 August 1945, CRS M100, 'August 1945', NAA.

43 Cadogan diary, 11 and 14 August 1945, in Dilks (ed.), *The Diaries of Sir Alexander Cadogan*, p. 781; Cable, External Affairs to Bruce, 11 August 1945, CRS M100, 'August 1945'; Cable, Dominions Secretary to Commonwealth Government, 11 August 1945, CRS A5954, Box 453, NAA.

44 Rhodes, *The Making of the Atomic Bomb*, pp. 745-6.

CONCLUSION

'the war has been fought in vain'

On 2 September 1945, an armada of Allied warships rode at anchor in Tokyo Bay, where it had been planned to launch the decisive invasion of Japan. Instead of that calamitous event, General MacArthur presided over a solemn and peaceful ceremony on the afterdeck of the battleship USS *Missouri*. After all the blood-letting and the misery, the Japanese foreign minister, dressed in top hat and tails, was ready to sign the instrument of surrender. Witnessed by lines of sailors from the *Missouri*, as well as Allied officers from all the services, Admiral Fraser signed on behalf of Britain while General Blamey did the honours for Australia. Chifley had insisted on Blamey signing separately on behalf of Australia in order to emphasise the dominion's stature as a principal combatant in the Pacific war and to buttress its demand for a place at any subsequent peace conference. Notably absent from the shipboard ceremony was Emperor Hirohito, who had been absolved by Britain from the humiliation of attending.

In the wake of the Tokyo event, similar surrender ceremonies took place across the western Pacific, although the Japanese command structure was mostly left intact to ease the burden on the Allies of reimposing control on the colonial peoples. To help ensure the cooperation of local Japanese commanders, the producers of British propaganda broadcasts were instructed to 'avoid recriminations and questions of war guilt', to 'ignore reports of possible after-effects of the atomic bomb' and to 'keep off the Japanese treatment of Prisoners of War'.[1] For Japanese garrisons in places like Singapore, there was little sense of them having been defeated in the field of battle. As Mountbatten's political adviser observed, from the psychological viewpoint 'the war has been fought in vain'. British weakness in the Far East, together with the suddenness of the surrender, forced them to allow the Japanese to 'follow their own concept of the surrender' and to 'look on the whole process as a handover rather than a surrender'.[2]

The sudden end to the Pacific war had caught Britain unprepared. It had assumed that its troops would be able to recapture Singapore before Japan's surrender, and thereby avenge its ignoble loss in 1942 and rebuild British prestige in the minds of its imperial subjects. Instead, Mountbatten's planned invasion of Malaya became an unopposed landing while British parachutists dropped peacefully among the startled inhabitants of Singapore. Australia had offered to provide a parachute battalion for Singapore but, because of the shortage of shipping and the rushed schedule, had to be content with sending 120 troops by air as soon as an airfield became available.[3] The situation in Hong Kong was more complicated. With the Chinese keen to have their territory back, it became a contest between the British and Chinese as to whose forces would arrive first to take the surrender of the Japanese garrison. The situation was complicated further by Hong Kong coming within the supreme command of General MacArthur, with the Americans being more than a little ambivalent about Hong Kong being returned to Britain. Indeed, shortly before his death, Roosevelt had become obsessed with the idea of wresting the island from Churchill's grasp, while Churchill had been equally adamant that he would never let it go.[4]

The British had been planning to recapture Hong Kong in a joint operation with the Americans, but the end of hostilities forced them to adopt what Brooke described as 'emergency arrangements'. On 10 August, as the general Japanese surrender was being negotiated, Brooke urged the British cabinet to dispatch its Pacific fleet there before the Chinese could assert their own claim to sovereignty over the island. With the closest Commonwealth troops being the Australians in Borneo and on the island of Morotai, Attlee appealed to Chifley for a brigade of troops to follow up the fleet and disarm the Japanese garrison, while the fleet went on to 'show the British flag in the main Chinese ports'. The British also sent a token force to take control from the Japanese in French Indo-China, prior to the arrival of French forces. However, rather than disarming the Japanese, the British used them to maintain order and suppress a bid for independence by Vietnamese rebels.[5]

With Australia having committed itself to the postwar Commonwealth, the British request for troops to disarm the Japanese in Hong Kong should have been straightforward. Instead, it placed the dominion in somewhat of a quandary. Although Shedden and the Australian chiefs of staff supported the notion of sending both a naval and military contingent to Hong Kong, Shedden also pointed out that it would necessarily impede Australia's demobilisation program; Evatt also warned that it would be resented by the Chinese, who might be inspired to retaliate by criticising the White Australia policy. After having been a leading force in the anti-colonial movement at San Francisco, Evatt could hardly support the return of the British colonisers to Hong Kong. He was presumably hoping that the argument about the possible criticism of the White Australia policy by the Chinese might win his colleagues over to his point of view. In the end, the government compromised by refusing the use of its troops but agreeing to the short-term loan of some Australian minesweepers, which were rushed across from the Philippines to clear the way for the British fleet.[6]

With warships from the Pacific fleet leaving for Hong Kong from their base at Manus Island on 20 August, Cunningham was relieved that the 'Hong Kong muddle appears to be clearing up', with the British government being 'quite determined to take possession'. Although determined to do just that, the British were prevented by MacArthur from accepting the surrender of the Japanese garrison until MacArthur had taken the formal surrender of the Japanese government in Tokyo. Although MacArthur told a British intelligence officer that he was 'very angry' over the high-handed and pre-emptive British action in rushing their warships into Hong Kong, he accepted the *fait accompli* and instructed that, when it came time for the

Japanese in Hong Kong to surrender, they should do so to the British rather than to the Chinese.[7]

For all the criticisms from the British Labour Party concerning the evils of colonialism, and Attlee's concerns about the costs of empire, it seemed that his government was determined to resurrect the old empire despite the postwar financial strictures. Indeed, it was the financial stringency that made Britain eager to regain Hong Kong and Singapore, thereby allowing its fleet to be transferred to those ports and not have to be supported from more distant and expensive Australian ports. Cunningham told his commanders that it was 'essential that we reduce our expenditure in the East' since the 'country's financial position is just frightful'. Although Attlee tentatively questioned the need for restoring Britain's naval bases at Singapore and Hong Kong, the Admiralty justified it by alluding to the value such work would have in 'restarting British trade to China and the East Indies'. Bevin threw his considerable political weight behind it, convincing the defence committee on 7 September to base the Pacific fleet at Hong Kong where its presence could provide a 'beneficial and steadying influence on various treaty undertakings involving ourselves, the Russians and the Chinese'. It was even planned to have a spare infantry brigade in the Far East 'for use at Shanghai or elsewhere if required'.[8]

As it had indicated over Hong Kong, the Australian government was no longer so prepared to give unquestioning support to Britain's empire. Australia had its own interests to consider and it no longer shrank from asserting them. Although much of its forces were scattered across the Pacific and South-East Asia, retrieving the colonies of Britain, France, Portugal and the Netherlands, the Australian government was determined to make a sizeable commitment of its forces to MacArthur for the occupation of Japan. In fact, the government doubled the forces recommended by its chiefs of staff for this purpose, proposing to contribute two cruisers, two destroyers, two brigades of troops and three squadrons of Mustang fighter planes. And Australia was careful to declare that its contribution was being made in its role as a 'principal Pacific Power which has for so long borne the heat and burden of the struggle against Japan'. To emphasise this point, it wanted its forces to be independent and commanded by an Australian officer who would be responsible to MacArthur rather than to the commander of the proposed British Commonwealth force which Whitehall was planning. Australia refused to make its forces part of the Commonwealth force, which London wanted to be commanded by a British officer with an Australian officer as its army commander.[9]

The Australian insistence on having its own occupation force was inspired partly by its resentment at being repeatedly ignored by Washington and London when decisions were being made concerning the Pacific war. Chifley certainly expressed resentment on 17 August when announcing plans for the occupation force, complaining publicly about the lack of recognition given to Australia by the Allies when formulating the surrender terms for Japan.[10] The spat over the position of Hirohito was merely the latest in a long line of similar disputes, with the British government harbouring its own feelings of deep-seated resentment towards the Australians. The attempt to have its own occupation force just seemed to confirm the British suspicion that Australians were intent on being unhelpful to the wider imperial purpose. Bruce warned Chifley that British ministers were 'hot and bothered' by the public criticism, with Bruce appealing for Chifley not to destroy the supposedly 'favourable atmosphere' that had been created in the wake of Churchill's demise. For his part, Attlee agreed not to respond publicly to Chifley's criticism and asked that Chifley 'ensure that a similar restraint from public controversy is exercised in Australia'.[11]

The issue could have been resolved when the Australian chiefs of staff advised the government that its unilateral decision to double the size of the occupation force, and thereby allow it to operate independently of the Commonwealth force, was not feasible. With the demands of demobilisation, and the need to occupy and disarm territories across the south-west Pacific, the services could not also supply the manpower needed for an independent force in Japan that would necessitate separate base installations, repair facilities and other logistical requirements.[12] Equally anxious to resolve the issue and end this 'deplorable example of lack of unity', Britain made a compromise suggestion of its own. Eager to use the Australian force to increase the impact of its own contribution, Britain offered to let an Australian commander lead the whole Commonwealth force, rather than just the military contingent as previously contemplated. This was not as great a concession as it seemed. As Attlee assured his worried ministers, the proposed command structure would leave the British chiefs of staff with ultimate control over the Australian officer.[13]

To the intense annoyance of the British, Chifley persisted with his push for an independent Australian force, pointing out to Attlee that Britain's proposed Commonwealth force would not include Canadian or South African forces and that the British naval forces would not be under the control of the Commonwealth force commander. As such, it would hardly be a Commonwealth force at all. Moreover, Australia's participation in it would deny the dominion 'a role appropriate to our status and the contribution which we have made to the victory in the Pacific'. Chifley was confident that MacArthur would provide them with such a role if they went independently and served under his command.[14] Whitehall was taken aback by Chifley's intransigence, with Cunningham describing it as a 'rude reply' to Britain's attempted compromise. The issue might have escalated further had Evatt not been in London to smooth things over. The often-testy minister had been sent there by Chifley to take part in the ongoing discussions related to the United Nations. While there, he would act as Australia's resident minister and temporarily take over Bruce's duties, with Chifley having declined an offer by Bruce to stay on as high commissioner.[15]

Evatt's main interest was in shaping the United Nations, for which he needed British support to be successful. With the dispute over the occupation force posing a possible impediment to cooperation over the United Nations, Evatt told British ministers that he would try to 'persuade the Australian Government to reverse their decision and take a more favourable view of the suggested composite British Commonwealth force'.[16] In the face of Evatt's pressure, and the practical concerns of its own chiefs of staff, the government agreed to back down in the hope that 'it might be possible to use the occasion to demonstrate Australian leadership in Pacific affairs and the Pacific settlement'. Chifley would allow Australian participation in the Commonwealth force on condition that its commander and the majority of the headquarters staff were Australian and that the commander would report directly to MacArthur and be responsible largely to the Australian chiefs of staff. This would implicitly recognise Australia as the Commonwealth country with the primary interest in the Pacific while also providing 'an opportunity for experience in the joint higher direction of British Commonwealth Forces in the Pacific'. The practical considerations behind the backdown were seen in Chifley reducing Australia's initial military force from two brigades to one. Chifley's cable caused relief in London, where the now Lord Alanbrooke proclaimed: 'Thank heaven, for if they had been allowed to refuse our last offer of an Australian Command and a Combined Chief of Staff organisation ... it would have been the end of all Imperial co-operation.'[17] It would also have required a larger British contribution had the Australian forces not swung round behind the Commonwealth banner.

The issue over the occupation force revealed once again that Australia could be prevailed upon to dance to the British tune, albeit in its own way. It also showed that Australia's ambitions had outrun its capacity to achieve them. The plans that Evatt had earlier entertained for an extensive sub-empire in the south-west Pacific had faded, with Australia now supporting the return of the European powers to the control of their former colonies. Australia also looked forward to the revival of the old system of imperial defence which had proved so incapable of safeguarding Australia's security in 1942. In his last major speech to parliament in February 1945, Curtin had sketched out his limited vision of Australia's postwar defence and foreign policy. According to Curtin, the dominion's foreign policy 'must always be in harmony with that of the British Commonwealth as a whole', with Canberra's role being to 'give advice, to state its view, now and again to criticise, and to make suggestions which, in its view, would strengthen the family relationship'. Independence was not a realistic option, argued Curtin, since Australia's 'articulation in the world would be more impressive as a member of a family than it could ever be if we made it as a separate and distinct entity'.[18] It was rather reminiscent of a statement made six years earlier by Menzies, in which the conservative leader had declared that Australia maintains its 'independent existence primarily because we belong to a family of nations'.[19] Neither leader was prepared to confront the daunting implications of Australia's wartime experience.

During the 1920s and 1930s, the dominion had enmeshed itself into the system of imperial defence, with any doubts being quelled by the repeated assurances of Britain's ability and willingness to rush to Australia's protection should the need ever arise. The Singapore naval base was proffered as a sign of Britain's sincerity. In return, Australia organised its defence forces so that they could respond quickly to Britain's needs in Europe while leaving Australia's local defence relatively neglected. There had been several voices in the 1930s, Curtin being prominent among them, who had pointed to the inherent contradiction in imperial defence and the danger of Australia being left undefended in the event of another European war. But they had been largely ignored by conservative governments that were unwilling to concede the position of peril into which they had led the nation.

While the policy had had the advantage of allowing Australia to skimp on defence, and to concentrate instead on developing the continent that its people had barely begun to occupy, the bankruptcy of the system was revealed at Singapore in 1942. Australia suddenly faced the prospect of invasion and had alarmingly few means of warding it off. Its calls for the much-promised assistance from London went largely unrequited. Britain's attention was elsewhere. Fortunately for Australia, the attention of the Japanese was also elsewhere. Their forces were occupied in China and securing their easily won territories in South-East Asia. Although conscious of the potential threat posed by Australia as a base for a future American counterattack, the Japanese were deterred by distance from attempting an occupation of the continent and were confident that it could be isolated from American reinforcement.

Britain's expulsion from the Far East in 1942, and its agreement with the United States to concentrate on fighting Germany first and later to send largely token forces against Japan in 1945, was the culmination of circumstances stretching back for nearly a century. Its early entry into the industrial age compared with its competitors had given it the opportunity to acquire an extensive empire that would be beyond its long-term capacity to defend. The Boer War and the First World War had revealed the extent to which Britain had overextended itself and had brought new competitors to the fore. Although it was clear that Britain's accidental empire would have to be reduced to a size more suited to its capacity to defend, it was able to defer the painful adjustment with policies based on a mixture of bluff and bluster. The system of imperial defence was just one of those policies, allowing Britain to draw on the growing strength of the dominions to compensate for its own waning strength relative to the rising powers of Germany, Russia, Japan and the United States.

Under the system of imperial defence, Britain persuaded Australia to make the defence of the wider empire its first priority, elevating it above the defence of the Australian continent and causing it to commit forces in 1939 to the defence of British interests in the Middle East, just as it had done in 1914. But the gradual contraction of Britain's ability to defend all its imperial possessions and protect all its worldwide interests forced it to choose between competing priorities. Despite the imperial rhetoric of the interwar years, the Far East was relegated to a distant fourth place behind the defence of Britain and the north Atlantic, the defence of British interests in the Mediterranean and the Middle East, and the defence of India.

This harsh reality was realised by some Australians in 1942, when the promised British fleet never appeared. Perhaps most Australians, though, preferred to believe that Britain still had the will, but simply lacked the means, to fulfil its historic defence promises to Australia. This was not the case. Certainly Britain had a limited capacity to respond to Australia's plight in 1942, but only because it was choosing to concentrate its resources overwhelmingly on the struggle against Italy and Germany. Britain had decided where its primary interests resided and had acted accordingly. British fighter aircraft that could have been used to secure Singapore and the south-west Pacific were sent to places like Turkey in the vain hope that they would be used against the Germans. The naval fleet that was supposedly intended for Singapore was squandered in the Mediterranean. And the tanks and troops that could have defended Malaya were lost in the seesaw battles of the Middle East, many of which had a dubious strategic purpose.

The events of the war caused Australia to confront the reality of its situation in the Pacific, far from its great power protector. Although earlier governments had made tentative attempts to assert distinctive Australian interests, it was only during the war that Australia developed the capacity to formulate a foreign policy of its own. With the appointment of representatives across the world, and the creation of a diplomatic service, Australia was able to draw on sources of information and advice that were largely independent of the British Foreign Office. Curtin's 'looks to America' statement in December 1941 was a symbolic sign of change in Canberra's outlook, although there was no simple switch of Australian allegiance from London to Washington. That would occur piecemeal and over a much longer time frame. For Curtin, the close relationship with the United States was a temporary expedient to meet the emergency that the country faced. Which is how the Americans regarded the wartime relationship with Australia. The proximity of Australia to the short-lived Japanese empire was the reason why the United States decided that Australia had to be secured.

At the end of the war, the Australian government of Ben Chifley largely sought to reconstruct the imperial framework, albeit with Australia playing a more assertive role. Dependent for defence advice on officials like Sir Frederick Shedden, who had been rewarded with a knighthood by Curtin, the government believed that the British connection could still provide for Australia's future security, so long as it was supported by a strong United Nations Organisation and reinforced by a greater presence of the United States in the Pacific. In largely rushing back to old certainties, Australia abandoned the attempts that were foreshadowed in the Anzac agreement of 1944 to create a sub-empire in the south-west Pacific. With both Britain and the United States refusing to recognise the claims of Australia and New Zealand to regional pre-eminence, Australia seemed to have little choice.

The war had seen Australia take several steps along the road towards independence. It had finally ratified the Statute of Westminster, it had declared war against Japan independently of Britain, and it had begun the creation of a professional diplomatic service. Australian governments had resisted several attempts by Britain to deploy Australian troops on operations that seemed to have little chance of success. Even Menzies managed to stamp his foot at Churchill over the Tobruk garrison. Later, Curtin's defiance of Churchill and Roosevelt over the dispatch of Australian troops to Burma provided a potent example of what could be achieved when a prime minister had a clear-eyed appreciation of Australia's interests. At other times, though, even Curtin could be prevailed upon to do the bidding of the great powers, such as when he allowed Australians to garrison Ceylon, when he retreated from the Anzac agreement, when he appointed the Duke of Gloucester or when, shortly before his death, he approved the assault on Borneo.

For Australia to enjoy more than a semblance of independence will require more than the constitutional changes that a future republic might bring. Independence has to be exercised. And that requires the ability and strength to formulate policies based on a clear appreciation of Australian interests and being able, when necessary, to withstand pressure from great power allies that seek to impose their views. For too long, Australia has largely looked at the world through British and then American eyes. What has been good for London or Washington has not necessarily been good for Australia. That should have been starkly clear after the experience of 1942. There were lessons for Australia in the war. It is not too late to learn them.

NOTES

[1] Cables, Dominions Secretary to Commonwealth Government, 23 and 30 August 1945, CRS A5954, Box 437, NAA; Letter, Dening to Sterndale-Bennett, 31 August 1945, 5/18, Penney Papers, KC.

[2] Paper by Penney, 23 August 1945, and Letter, Mountbatten to MacArthur, 16 August 1945, 5/11 and 13, Penney Papers, KC.

[3] Defence Committee Minute, 23 August 1945, CRS A5954, Box 453, NAA.

[4] Halifax, *Fulness of days*, pp. 249–50; Note by Churchill, 11 April 1945, PREM 3/159/12, PRO.

[5] Cabinet Conclusions, 10 August 1945, CAB 128/1, C.M. (45)20, PRO; Alanbrooke diary, 10 August 1945, in Danchev and Todman (eds), *War Diaries*, pp. 716–7; Cable, Attlee to Chifley, 11 August 1945, CRS A5954, Box 453, NAA; Memorandum by Chiefs of Staff, 13 August 1945, CAB 69/7, D.O. (45)5, PRO; Memoir of Allied Disarmament Mission in Saigon 1945, Cheshire Papers, CC.

[6] Message, Shedden to Chifley, 12 August 1945; Paper by Shedden, 17 August 1945; See also Cable, Rourke to Shedden, 12 August 1945, CRS A5954, Box 453; War Cabinet Minute, 17 August 1945, CRS A2670/379/1945, NAA.

[7] Cunningham diary, 15–17, 22–23 August 1945, ADD. MS. 52578 and Letter, Cunningham to Fraser, 20 August 1945, ADD. MS. 52572, Cunningham Papers, BL; Gill, *Royal Australian Navy*, Vol. 2, p. 683; Cable, Dominions Secretary to Commonwealth Government, 18 August and 3 September 1945, CRS A5954, Box 453, NAA; Defence Committee Minutes, 31 August 1945, CAB 69/7, D.O. (45)4, PRO; Paper by Penney after visit to MacArthur, 23 August 1945, 5/13, Penney Papers, KC.

[8] Note by Hollis, 4 September 1945, CAB 69/7, D.O. (45)10; Defence Committee Minutes, 7 and 14 September 1945, CAB 69/7, D.O. (45)5 and 6, PRO; Cunningham diary, 20 August, 7, 14, 17, 21 and 22 September, 5 October 1945, ADD. MS. 52578, and Letter, Cunningham to Power, 17 September 1945, ADD. MS. 52562, BL.

[9] War Cabinet Minute, 17 August 1945, CRS A2670/379/1945, NAA; Defence Committee Minutes, 13 August 1945, CAB 69/7, D.O. (45)3, PRO; See also Note by Quealy, 14 August 1945, and 'Surrender Terms for Japan', unsigned note for Shedden, 14 August 1945, CRS A5954, Box 453, NAA.

[10] Press statement by Chifley, 17 August 1945, and Cable, Dominions Secretary to Commonwealth Government, 20 August 1945, CRS A5954, Box 453, NAA.

[11] Cable, Bruce to Chifley, and Cable (draft), Attlee to Chifley, 25 August 1945, CRS M100, 'August 1945', NAA.

[12] Defence Committee Minute, 22 August 1945, CRS A5954, Box 453, NAA.

[13] Note by Hollis, 30 August 1945, CAB 69/7, D.O. (45)9 and Defence Committee Minutes, 31 August 1945, CAB 69/7, D.O. (45)4, PRO; Alanbrooke diary, 30 August 1945, in Danchev and Todman (eds), *War Diaries*, p. 721.

[14] Cable, Chifley to Attlee, 10 September 1945, *DAFP*, Vol. 8, Doc. 240.

[15] Cunningham diary, 14 September 1945, ADD. MS. 52578, Cunningham Papers, BL; Cable, Chifley to Bruce, 28 August 1945, *DAFP*, Vol. 8, Doc. 223.

[16] Defence Committee Minutes, 14 September 1945, CAB 69/7, D.O. (45)6, PRO.

[17] Cables, Evatt to Chifley and Beasley, 14 September 1945, and Chifley to Attlee, 21 September 1945, *DAFP*, Docs 246 and 256; War Cabinet Minutes, 19 September 1945, CRS A2673/XVI/4400, NAA; Alanbrooke diary, 27 September 1945, in Bryant, *Triumph in the West*, p. 490; See also Letter, Rourke to Shedden, 10 September 1945, CRS A5954, Box 1615, NAA.

[18] Speech by Curtin, 28 February 1945, CRS A5954, Box 1605, NAA.

[19] *Herald*, Melbourne, 17 October 1939.

SELECT BIBLIOGRAPHY

MANUSCRIPTS

British Library, London
Admiral Sir A. B. Cunningham, Papers
P. Emrys-Evans, Papers
Oliver Harvey, Papers
Admiral Sir James Somerville, Papers

Cambridge University Library
Viscount Templewood, Papers
W. Mackenzie King, Diary (microfiche)

Churchill College Archives, Cambridge
A. V. Alexander, Papers
Earl Attlee, Papers
Rear Admiral T. P. H. Beamish, Papers
Ernest Bevin, Papers
Sir Alexander Cadogan, Papers
Lord Caldecote, Papers
Lord Chandos, Papers
Sir Walter Crocker, Memoirs
Lord Croft, Papers

Admiral Sir A. B. Cunningham, Papers
Admiral Sir William Davis, Papers
Admiral Sir Reginald Drax, Papers
Admiral Sir Ralph Edwards, Diaries and Papers
Air Marshal Sir Thomas W. Elmhirst, Memoirs and Papers
Captain Godfrey French, Memoirs
Admiral J. H. Godfrey, Papers
Captain Russell Grenfell, Papers
Sir Percy James Grigg, Papers
Lord Halifax, Papers (microfilm)
Lord Hankey, Papers
Sir H. M. Knatchbull-Hugesson, Diaries and Correspondence
Sir Eric Phipps, Papers
Cecil Roberts, Papers
Sir Horace Seymour, Papers
General Sir Edward Spears, Papers
Lord Swinton, Papers
Gerald Wilkinson, Diary
Admiral Sir Algernon Willis, Papers

Diplomatic Record Office, Tokyo
A.6.6.0.1–1–6, Domestic Affairs (Australia)

Flinders University Library, Adelaide
Dr H. V. Evatt, Papers

House of Lords Record Office, London
Lord Beaverbrook, Papers
David Lloyd George, Papers
Lord Wakehurst, Papers

Imperial War Museum, London
Admiral Sir John Crace, Papers
Sir Ronald Cross, Papers (microfilm)
Vice Admiral J. W. Durnford, Papers
John Hughes, Papers
Admiral Sir Edward Parry, Papers

India Office Library, London
Sir Reginald Dorman-Smith, Papers

John Curtin Prime Ministerial Library, Perth
Address by Curtin to the Empire Parliamentary Association,
    17 May 1944
Broadcast by Curtin, 7 May 1944
General Douglas MacArthur's Official Correspondence,
    1942–44, Microfilm reel 414
General Douglas MacArthur, Commander-in-Chief Correspondence,
    1942–44, Microfilm reel 414
Improvements in the Machinery for Empire Cooperation
    desired by the Australian Government: Memorandum by Curtin,
    15 May 1944
Papers relating to Curtin from the Roosevelt Library
Prime Minister's Visit to England: Itinerary and Engagements
Transcripts of Interviews: John Buckley, Hazel Craig,
    Rev. Hector Harrison, Adele Hodges, Frederick McLaughlin,
    Malcolm Mackay, Alan and Jean Salisbury
Volumes of newspaper cuttings, Elsie Macleod Collection

King's College, London
Lord Alanbrooke, Papers
Air Chief Marshal Sir Robert Brooke-Popham, Papers
Lord Ismay, Papers
Captain Liddell Hart, Papers
Major-General W. R. C. Penney, Papers

London School of Economics
Hugh Dalton, Papers

National Archives of Australia, Canberra
CRS CP 156/1, General Correspondence of the Rt Hon. John Curtin,
    October 1941–December 1944
CRS CP 290/7, Cables from the Prime Minister of Great Britain and the
    Secretary of State for Dominion Affairs 1939–1943

CRS CP 290/8, Cables to and from Sir Earle Page during his visit to London 1941 (25 September–29 December)

CRS CP 290/9, Cables to and from Rt Hon. Robert Menzies and party during his visit to London, 21 January–26 May 1941

CRS CP 290/16, Papers relating to Wartime Policy 1940–45

CRS M100, S. M. Bruce, Monthly War Files

CRS M103, S. M. Bruce, Supplementary War Files

CRS M104, S. M. Bruce, Folders of Annual Correspondence

CRS M113, S. M. Bruce, Travel and Appointment Diaries

AA 1970/559, S. M. Bruce, Miscellaneous Papers, 1939–45

CRS A461, Prime Minister's Department, Correspondence Files, Multiple Number Series (Third System), 1934–50

CRS A664, Department of Defence, Correspondence Files, multiple number series, 1935–1958

CRS A705, Department of Air, Correspondence Files, multiple number series, 1922–1960

CRS A1608, Prime Minister's Department, Correspondence Files, Secret and Confidential War Series (Fourth System), 1939–45

CRS A816, Department of Defence, Correspondence Files, multiple number series, 1935–1958

CRS A1068, Department of External Affairs, Correspondence Files, multiple number series

CRS A2031, Defence Committee Minutes 1939–45

CRS A2670, War Cabinet Agenda, 1939–46

CRS A2673, War Cabinet Minutes, 1939–46

CRS A2676, War Cabinet Minutes without Agenda Files, 1939–46

CRS A2679, Advisory War Council Agenda, 1940–45

CRS A2682, Advisory War Council Minutes, 1940–45

CRS A2697, Cabinet Secretariat, Menzies and Fadden Ministries, minutes and submissions, 1939–41

CRS A2700, Cabinet Secretariat, Curtin, Forde and Chifley Ministries, Cabinet Agenda 1941–49

CRS A2703, Cabinet Secretariat, Curtin, Forde and Chifley Ministries, Cabinet Minutes 1941–49

CRS A2908, Australian High Commission, UK, Correspondence Files,
    1920–1968
CRS A3300, Australian Legation to USA, Correspondence Files, 1939–48
CRS A5954, Sir Frederick Shedden, Papers
CRS M1415, Folders of Miscellaneous Correspondence of
    Rt Hon. J. A. Curtin, 1941–45
CRS M1416, Folders of Correspondence on 'Special Subjects' of
    Rt Hon. J. A. Curtin, 1941–45

National Archives of Australia, Melbourne
R. G. Casey, Papers

National Library of Australia, Canberra
Lord Casey, Diary
L. F. Crisp, Papers
J. J. Dedman, Papers
Sir Frederick Eggleston, Papers
Frank Forde, Transcript of Interview
Lord Gowrie, Papers
Henry B. S. Gullett, Papers
Rev. Hector Harrison, Papers
R. V. Keane, Papers
Sir John Latham, Papers
J. A. Lyons, Papers
Norman Makin, Papers
E. A. Mann, Papers
Sir Robert Menzies, Papers
Sir Keith Murdoch, Papers
Sir Keith Officer, Papers
Sir Earle Page, Papers
Don Rodgers, Papers and Transcript of Interview
Lloyd Ross, Papers
F. T. Smith, Transcripts of Curtin's press conferences
Sir Percy Spender, Papers
P. G. Taylor, Papers

E. G. Theodore, Papers
Eddie Ward, Papers
Sir Alan Watt, Papers

National Maritime Museum, Greenwich
Lord Chatfield, Papers
Admiral Kelly, Papers
Admiral Sir William Tennant, Papers

Public Record Office, London
CAB 65, War Cabinet Conclusions and Confidential Annexes
CAB 66, War Cabinet Memoranda
CAB 69, War Cabinet Defence Committee (Operations), Minutes and
    Memoranda
PREM 1, 3, 4, 7 and 10, Prime Minister's Papers

Reading University Library
Waldorf Astor, Papers
Nancy Astor, Papers

Scottish Record Office, Edinburgh
Lord Lothian, Papers

University of Melbourne Archives
W. S. Robinson, Papers

REFERENCE WORKS
Graeme Davison, John Hirst and Stuart Macintyre (eds), *Oxford
    Companion to Australian History*, Oxford University Press,
    Melbourne, 1998
Geoffrey Serle, *Australian Dictionary of Biography*, Melbourne University
    Press, Melbourne, 1966–(2002)

DOCUMENTS, MEMOIRS, DIARIES, CONTEMPORARY BOOKS
L. S. Amery, *The Forward View*, Bles, London, 1935
Clement Attlee, *As It Happened*, Viking Press, New York, 1954
Australian Institute of International Affairs, *Australia and the Pacific*,
    Princeton, 1944

Earl of Avon, *The Eden Memoirs: The Reckoning*, Cassell, London, 1965

Stuart Ball (ed.), *Parliament and Politics in the Age of Churchill and Attlee: The Headlam Diaries 1935–1951*, Cambridge University Press, Cambridge, 1999

J. Barnes and D. Nicholson (eds), *The Leo Amery Diaries 1929–1945: The Empire at Bay*, Hutchinson, London, 1988

David Black (ed.), *In His Own Words: John Curtin's Speeches and Writings*, Paradigm Books, Perth, 1995

Brian Bond (ed.), *Chief of Staff: The diaries of Lieutenant-General Sir Henry Pownall*, Archon Books, London, 1974

A. A. Calwell, *Be Just and Fear Not*, Lloyd O'Neil, Melbourne, 1972

Richard Casey, *Double or Quit: Some Views on Australian Development and Relations*, Cheshire, Melbourne, 1949

——*Personal Experience 1939–46*, Constable, London, 1962

Winston Churchill, *The Second World War*, Vols 1–6, Cassell, London, 1948–54

John Colville, *The Churchillians*, Weidenfeld & Nicolson, London, 1981

——*Footprints in Time*, Collins, London, 1976

——*The Fringes of Power: Downing Street Diaries 1939–1955*, Hodder & Stoughton, London, 1985

H. C. Coombs, *Trial Balance*, Macmillan, Melbourne, 1981

A. D. Cooper, *Old Men Forget*, Hart-Davis, London, 1953

Frank Crowley (ed.), *Modern Australia in Documents*, Vol. 2, Wren, Melbourne, 1973

Alex Danchev and Daniel Todman (eds), *War Diaries 1939–1945: Field Marshal Lord Alanbrooke*, Weidenfeld & Nicolson, London, 2001

David Dilks (ed.), *The Diaries of Sir Alexander Cadogan O.M. 1938–1945*, Cassell, London, 1971

P. G. Edwards (ed.), *Australia Through American Eyes 1935–1945*, University of Queensland Press, Brisbane, 1979

Arthur Fadden, *They Called Me Artie: The Memoirs of Sir Arthur Fadden*, Jacaranda Press, Brisbane, 1969

J. F. C. Fuller, *Empire Unity and Defence*, Arrowsmith, Bristol, 1934

Lord Halifax, *Fulness of Days*, Collins, London, 1957

W. Averell Harriman and E. Abel, *Special Envoy to Churchill and Stalin 1941–1946*, Hutchinson, London, 1975

Paul Hasluck, *Diplomatic Witness*, Melbourne University Press, Melbourne, 1980

Cordell Hull, *The Memoirs of Cordell Hull*, Vol. 1, Macmillan, New York, 1948

Robert Rhodes James (ed.), *Chips: The Diaries of Henry Channon*, Weidenfeld & Nicolson, London, 1967

——*Winston S. Churchill: His Complete Speeches 1897–1963*, Vol. 6, Chelsea House, New York, 1974

Warren Kimball (ed.), *Churchill and Roosevelt: The Complete Correspondence*, 3 Vols, Collins, London, 1984

Cecil King, *With Malice Toward None: A War Diary*, Sidgwick & Jackson, London, 1970

Clem Lloyd and Richard Hall (eds), *Backroom Briefings: John Curtin's War*, National Library of Australia, Canberra, 1997

Douglas MacArthur, *Reminiscences*, Crest, New York, 1965

N. Mansergh (ed.), *Documents and Speeches on British Commonwealth Affairs 1931–1952*, Vol. 1, Oxford University Press, London, 1953

A. W. Martin and Patsy Hardy (eds), *Dark and hurrying days: Menzies' 1941 diary*, National Library of Australia, Canberra, 1993

Vincent Massey, *What's Past is Prologue*, Macmillan, Toronto, 1963

Neville Meaney (ed.), *Australia and the World: A Documentary History from the 1870s to the 1970s*, Longman Cheshire, Melbourne, 1985

R. G. Menzies, *Afternoon Light*, Cassell, Melbourne, 1967

——*The Measure of the Years*, Cassell, Melbourne, 1970

——'To the People of Britain at War' from the Prime Minister of Australia: Speeches by the Right Honourable Robert Gordon Menzies delivered in Great Britain in 1941*, Longmans Green and Co., London, 1941

——*Speech is of Time: Selected Speeches and Writings*, Cassell, London, 1958

Lord Moran, *Winston Churchill: The Struggle for Survival 1940–1965*, Constable, London, 1966

D. R. Murray (ed.), *Documents on Canadian External Relations*, Vols. 7–8, Department of External Affairs, Ottawa, 1974 and 1976

R. G. Neale et al (eds), *Documents on Australian Foreign Policy 1937–49*, Vols 1–8, AGPS Press, Canberra, 1975–89

Sir Harold Nicolson, *Diaries and Letters*, Vol. 2, Collins, London, 1967

Earle Page, *Truant Surgeon*, Angus & Robertson, Sydney, 1963

Joan Penglase and David Horner (eds), *When the War Came to Australia: Memories of the Second World War*, Allen & Unwin, Sydney, 1992

J. W. Pickersgill (ed.), *The Mackenzie King Record*, 2 Vols, University of Toronto Press, Toronto, 1960 and 1968

John Robertson and John McCarthy (eds), *Australian War Strategy 1939–1945*, University of Queensland Press, Brisbane, 1985

Clement Semmler (ed.), *The War Diaries of Kenneth Slessor*, University of Queensland Press, Brisbane, 1985

R. Sherwood, *The White House Papers of Harry L. Hopkins*, Vol. 1, Eyre and Spottiswoode, London, 1948

J. Van der Poel (ed.), *Selections from the Smuts Papers*, Vol. 6, Cambridge University Press, Cambridge, 1973

Rev. J. W. C. Wand, *Has Britain Let Us Down?*, Oxford University Press, Melbourne, 1942

Patrick Weller (ed.), *Caucus Minutes 1901–1949*, Melbourne University Press, Melbourne, 1975

Sumner Welles, *The Time for Decision*, Hamish Hamilton, London, 1944

Philip Ziegler (ed.), *Personal Diary of Admiral the Lord Louis Mountbatten 1943–1946*, Collins, London, 1988

OTHER BOOKS

Paul Addison, *The Road to 1945*, Cape, London, 1975

E. M. Andrews, *Isolationism and Appeasement in Australia: Reactions to the European Crises, 1935–1939*, Australian National University Press, Canberra, 1970

Elisabeth Barker, *Churchill and Eden at War*, Macmillan, London, 1978

Correlli Barnett, *The Audit of War*, Macmillan, London, 1986

Paul Bartrop, *Australia and the Holocaust, 1933–45*, Australian Scholarly Publishing, Melbourne, 1994

Joan Beaumont (ed.), *Australia's War 1914–18*, Allen & Unwin, Sydney, 1995

Roger Bell, *Unequal Allies: Australian–American Relations and the Pacific War*, Melbourne University Press, Melbourne, 1977

Geoffrey Bolton, *Oxford History of Australia*, Vol. 5, Oxford University Press, Melbourne, 1990

Brian Bond, *British Military Policy Between the Two World Wars*, Clarendon Press, Oxford, 1980

Judith Brett, *Robert Menzies' Forgotten People*, Macmillan, Sydney, 1992

Carl Bridge (ed.), *Munich to Vietnam: Australia's Relations with Britain and the United States Since the 1930s*, Melbourne University Press, Melbourne, 1991

Ken Buckley et al, *Doc Evatt*, Longman Cheshire, Melbourne, 1994

Paul Burns, *The Brisbane Line Controversy: Political Opportunism versus National Security, 1942–45*, Allen & Unwin, Sydney, 1998

S. J. Butlin, *War Economy 1939–1942*, Australian War Memorial, Canberra, 1955

S. J. Butlin and C. B. Schedvin, *War Economy 1942–1945*, Australian War Memorial, Canberra, 1977

Raymond Callahan, *Churchill: Retreat from Empire*, Costello, Tunbridge Wells, 1984

David Carlton, *Anthony Eden*, Allen Lane, London, 1981

Peter Charlton, *The unnecessary war*, Macmillan, Melbourne, 1983

L. F. Crisp, *Ben Chifley*, Longmans, Melbourne, 1961

Peter Crockett, *Evatt: A Life*, Oxford University Press, Melbourne, 1993

David Day (ed.), *Brave New World: Dr H. V. Evatt and Australian Foreign Policy*, University of Queensland Press, Brisbane, 1996

David Day, *Chifley*, HarperCollins, Sydney, 2001

——*Claiming a Continent*, Revised Edition, HarperCollins, Sydney, 2001

——*The Great Betrayal: Britain, Australia and the Onset of the Pacific War, 1939–42*, Angus & Robertson, Sydney, 1988

——*John Curtin: A Life*, HarperCollins, Sydney, 1999

——*Menzies and Churchill at War*, Angus & Robertson, Sydney, 1986

——*Reluctant Nation: Australia and the Allied Defeat of Japan, 1942–45*, Oxford University Press, Melbourne, 1992

David Dilks (ed.), *Retreat from Power*, Vol. 2, Macmillan, London, 1981

John Dower, *War without mercy*, Faber, London, 1986

Ian Drummond, *British Economic Policy and the Empire 1919–1939*, Allen & Unwin, London, 1972

Cecil Edwards, *Bruce of Melbourne: Man of Two Worlds*, Heinemann, London, 1965

P. G. Edwards, *Prime Ministers and Diplomats: The Making of Australian Foreign Policy, 1901–1949*, Oxford University Press, Melbourne, 1983

R. A. Esthus, *From Enmity to Alliance: US–Australian Relations, 1931–41*, University of Washington Press, Seattle, 1964

Ross Fitzgerald, *'Red Ted': The Life of E. G. Theodore*, University of Queensland Press, Brisbane, 1994

Martin Gilbert, *Finest Hour: Winston S. Churchill 1939–1941*, Heinemann, London, 1983

——*Road to Victory: Winston S. Churchill 1941–1945*, Heinemann, London, 1986

G. H. Gill, *Royal Australian Navy 1939–1945*, 2 Vols, Australian War Memorial, Canberra, 1957 and 1958

D. Gillison, *Royal Australian Air Force 1939–1942*, Australian War Memorial, Canberra, 1962

J. L. Granatstein, *Canada's War: The Politics of the Mackenzie King Government, 1939–1945*, Oxford University Press, Toronto, 1975

Russell Grenfell, *Main Fleet to Singapore*, Faber & Faber, London, 1951

Paul Haggie, *Britannia at Bay: the defence of the British Empire against Japan, 1931–1941*, Clarendon Press, Oxford, 1981

Ian Hamill, *The Strategic Illusion*, Singapore University Press, Singapore, 1981

W. K. Hancock, *Smuts: The Fields of Force, 1919–50*, Vol. 2, Cambridge University Press, Cambridge, 1968

——*Survey of British Commonwealth Affairs: Problems of Economic Policy 1918–1939*, Oxford University Press, London, 1940

Paul Hasluck, *The Government and the People 1939–45*, 2 Vols, Australian War Memorial, Canberra, 1952 and 1970

Cameron Hazlehurst (ed.), *Australian Conservatism*, Australian National University Press, Canberra, 1979

Cameron Hazlehurst, *Menzies Observed*, Allen & Unwin, Sydney, 1979

F.H. Hinsley, *British Intelligence in the Second World War*, Vol. 1, HMSO, London, 1979

R. F. Holland, *Britain and the Commonwealth Alliance 1918–1939*, Macmillan, London, 1981

David Horner (ed.), *The Commanders: Australian Military Leadership in the Twentieth Century*, Allen & Unwin, Sydney, 1984

——*The Battles that Shaped Australia*, Allen & Unwin, Sydney, 1982

David Horner, *Crisis of Command: Australian Generalship and the Japanese Threat, 1941–1943*, Australian National University Press, Canberra, 1978

——*Defence Supremo: Sir Frederick Shedden and the Making of Australian Defence Policy*, Allen & Unwin, Sydney, 2000

——*High Command: Australia and Allied Strategy 1939–1945*, Allen & Unwin, Sydney, 1982

——*Inside the War Cabinet: Directing Australia's War Effort, 1939–45*, Allen & Unwin, Sydney, 1996

Michael Howard, *The Continental Commitment*, Temple Smith, London, 1972

W. J. Hudson (ed.), *Towards a Foreign Policy, 1914–1941*, Cassell, Melbourne, 1967

W. J. Hudson, *Casey*, Oxford University Press, Melbourne, 1986

W. J. Hudson and M. P. Sharp, *Australian independence: colony to reluctant kingdom*, Melbourne University Press, Melbourne, 1988

A. Iriya, *The origins of the Second World War in Asia and the Pacific*, Longman, London, 1987

David Irving, *Churchill's war: the struggle for power*, Veritas, Bullsbrook, Western Australia, 1987

Robert Rhodes James, *Churchill: A Study in Failure 1900–1939*, Weidenfeld & Nicolson, London, 1970

——*Anthony Eden*, Weidenfeld & Nicolson, London, 1986

Roy Jenkins, *Winston Churchill*, Macmillan, London, 2001

Mark Johnston, *Fighting the Enemy: Australian soldiers and their adversaries in World War II*, Cambridge University Press, Melbourne, 2000

Warren Kimball, *Forged in War: Churchill, Roosevelt and the Second World War*, HarperCollins, London, 1997

J. M. Lee, *The Churchill coalition 1940–1945*, Batsford, London, 1980

G. Long, *Greece, Crete and Syria*, Australian War Memorial, Canberra, 1953

W. R. Louis, *British Strategy in the Far East, 1919–1939*, Clarendon Press, Oxford, 1971

——*Imperialism at Bay: The United States and the Decolonization of the British Empire, 1941–1945*, Clarendon Press, Oxford, 1977

Peter Lowe, *Britain in the Far East: A Survey from 1819 to the Present*, Longman, London, 1981

——*Great Britain and the Origins of the Pacific War*, Clarendon Press, Oxford, 1977

John Lukacs, *Five Days in London: May 1940*, Scribe Publications, Melbourne, 1999

John McCarthy, *Australia and Imperial Defence 1918–39: A Study in Air and Sea Power*, University of Queensland Press, Brisbane, 1976

——*A last call of empire: Australian aircrew, Britain and the Empire Air Training Scheme*, Australian War Memorial, Canberra, 1988

Stuart Macintyre, *Oxford History of Australia*, Vol. 4, Oxford University Press, Melbourne, 1986

M. McKernan and M. Browne (eds), *Australia: Two centuries of war and peace*, Australian War Memorial, Canberra, 1988

A. F. Madden and W. H. Morris-Jones (eds), *Australia and Britain: Studies in a Changing Relationship*, Cass and Co., London, 1980

N. Mansergh, *The Commonwealth Experience*, Vol. 2, 2nd edition, Macmillan, London, 1982

——*Survey of British Commonwealth Affairs: Problems of Wartime Co-operation and Post-War Change, 1939–52*, Oxford University Press, London, 1958

A. J. Marder, *Old Friends, New Enemies: The Royal Navy and the Imperial Japanese Navy: Strategic Illusions, 1936–1941*, Clarendon Press, Oxford, 1981

A. W. Martin, *Robert Menzies: A Life*, 2 Vols, Melbourne University Press, Melbourne, 1993 and 1999

James Neidpath, *The Singapore Naval Base and the Defence of Britain's Eastern Empire, 1919–1941*, Clarendon Press, Oxford, 1981

George Odgers, *Air War against Japan 1943–1945*, Australian War Memorial, Canberra, 1957

Ritchie Ovendale, *Appeasement and the English Speaking World*, University of Wales Press, Cardiff, 1975

Henry Pelling, *Winston Churchill*, Macmillan, London, 1974

F. W. Perry, *The Commonwealth armies*, Manchester University Press, Manchester, 1988

Ben Pimlott, *Hugh Dalton*, Cape, London, 1985

Trevor Reese, *Australia, New Zealand and the United States*, Oxford University Press, London, 1969

David Reynolds, *Britannia Overruled: British Policy and World Power in the Twentieth Century*, Longman, London, 1991

——*The Creation of the Anglo–American Alliance 1937–41: A Study in Competitive Co-operation*, Europa Publications, London, 1981

John Robertson, *Australia at War 1939–1945*, Heinemann, Melbourne, 1981

Stephen Roskill, *Hankey, Man of Secrets*, Vol. 3, Collins, London, 1974

——*Churchill and the Admirals*, Collins, London, 1977

——*The War at Sea, 1939–1945*, 2 Vols, HMSO, London, 1954 and 1956

Lloyd Ross, *John Curtin*, Sun Books, Melbourne, 1977

Michael Schaller, *Douglas MacArthur: The Far Eastern General*, Oxford University Press, New York, 1989

Aron Shai, *Britain and China, 1941–47*, Macmillan, London, 1984

Peter Smith, *Task Force 57: The British Pacific fleet, 1944–1945*, Kimber, London, 1969

Gavin Souter, *Acts of Parliament: A narrative history of Australia's Federal Legislature*, Melbourne University Press, Melbourne, 1988

Andrew Spaull, *John Dedman: A Most Unexpected Labor Man*, Hyland Press, Melbourne, 1998

Ronald Spector, *Eagle against the sun: the American war with Japan*, Penguin, London, 1987

Alfred Stirling, *Lord Bruce*, Hawthorn Press, Melbourne, 1974

A. J. P. Taylor et al, *Churchill: Four Faces and the Man*, Penguin, London, 1969

A. J. P. Taylor, *Beaverbrook*, Hamish Hamilton, London, 1972

Kylie Tennant, *Evatt: politics and justice*, Angus & Robertson, Sydney, 1970

Christopher Thorne, *Allies of a Kind: The United States, Britain and the War Against Japan, 1941–1945*, Hamish Hamilton, London, 1978

——*The Issue of War: States, Societies and the Far Eastern Conflict of 1941–1945*, Hamish Hamilton, London, 1985

Alan Watt, *The Evolution of Australian Foreign Policy 1938–1965*, Cambridge University Press, Cambridge, 1967

P. N. Wrinch, *The Military Strategy of Winston Churchill*, Department of Government, Boston University, Boston, 1961

Kenneth Young, *Churchill and Beaverbrook*, Eyre and Spottiswoode, London, 1966

Philip Ziegler, *Mountbatten*, Collins, London, 1985

JOURNAL ARTICLES

E. M. Andrews, 'The Australian Government and Appeasement', *Australian Journal of Politics and History*, April 1967

David Day, 'Anzacs on the run: the view from Whitehall, 1941–2', *Journal of Imperial and Commonwealth History*, May 1986

——'H. V. Evatt and the "Beat Hitler First" strategy: scheming politician or an innocent abroad?', *Historical Studies*, October 1987

——'P. G. Taylor and the alternative Pacific air route, 1939–45', *Australian Journal of Politics and History*, 32, 1 (1986)

——'Promise and performance: Britain's Pacific pledge, 1943–45', *War and Society*, September 1986

——'An undiplomatic incident: S. M. Bruce and the moves to curb Churchill, February 1942', *Journal of Australian Studies*, November 1986

Vin D'Cruz, 'Menzies' Foreign Policy, 1939–41', *Australian Quarterly*, September 1967

J. J. Dedman, 'The return of the A.I.F. from the Middle East', *Australian Outlook*, August 1967

——'The Brisbane Line', *Australian Outlook*, August 1968

P. G. Edwards, 'Labor's Vice-Regal Appointments: The Case of John Curtin and the Duke of Gloucester', *Labour History*, November 1992

——'R. G. Menzies's Appeals to the United States, May-June, 1940', *Australian Outlook*, April 1974

——'S. M. Bruce, R. G. Menzies and Australia's War Aims and Peace Aims, 1939–40', *Historical Studies*, April 1976

Ian Hamill, 'An Expeditionary Force Mentality?: The Despatch of Australian Troops to the Middle East, 1939–1940', *Australian Outlook*, August 1977

Peter Love, 'Curtin, MacArthur and conscription, 1942–43', *Historical Studies*, October 1977

John McCarthy, 'Australia and Imperial Defence: Co-operation and Conflict, 1918–1939', *Australian Journal of Politics and History*, December 1974

——'Australia: a view from Whitehall 1939–45', *Australian Outlook*, December 1974

Neville Meaney, 'Australia's foreign policy: history and myth', *Australian Outlook*, August 1969

John Robertson, 'Australian war policy 1939–1945', *Historical Studies*, October 1977

——'Australia and the "Beat Hitler First" strategy, 1941–42: a problem in wartime consultation', *Journal of Imperial and Commonwealth History*, May 1983

R. Tamchina, 'In Search of Common Causes: The Imperial Conference of 1937', *Journal of Imperial and Commonwealth History*, Vol. 1, 1972–73

PUBLISHED AND UNPUBLISHED LECTURES

Kim E. Beazley, *John Curtin: An Atypical Labor Leader*, Australian National University Press, Canberra, 1972

H. C. Coombs, *John Curtin — A Consensus Prime Minister?*, Australian National University Press, Canberra, 1984

Lloyd Ross, *John Curtin for Labor and for Australia*, Australian National University Press, Canberra, 1971

UNPUBLISHED PAPERS

Lynette Finch, 'Revealing Unsuspected Powers of Leadership: Analysing the Myth of John Curtin', unpublished paper, 1999

THESES

W. J. Hemmings, 'Australia and Britain's Far Eastern Defence Policy, 1937–42', BLit thesis, Oxford, 1972

A. Pooley, 'Fears Real and Imagined: Australia and the Threat from Japan, August–November 1939', BA(Hons) thesis, La Trobe University, 2002

B. Primrose, 'Australian Naval Policy 1919–1942: A Case Study in Empire Relations', PhD thesis, ANU, 1974

D. F. Woodward, 'Australian Diplomacy in the Second World War — Relations with Britain and the US 1939–41 under the Menzies and Fadden Governments', BA(Hons) thesis, Flinders University, 1973

P. Wright, 'Great Britain, Australia and the Pacific Crisis, 1939–1941', MA thesis, Manchester University, 1974

INDEX